EC and UK Competition Law

EC and UK Competition Law: Commentary, Cases and Materials offers a clear, concise and comprehensive account of the competition rules of the EC and the UK. These rules have witnessed a phenomenal increase in significance over the years. In the case of EC competition rules, these have become an important source of consultation, increasingly serving as a model followed by many countries when adopting or developing competition rules within their domestic legal systems. This book is therefore of international interest. It offers a single up-to-date source of all the important cases, legislation and guidelines clearly annotated and presented in a highly accessible way. With a detailed commentary and case studies (with model answers), this book will eliminate the need for students to consult multiple sources. Key developments in both EC and UK competition law are covered, as well as the most recent EC and UK judgments and decisions.

MAHER M. DABBAH is a lecturer at Queen Mary, University of London. He previously taught at King's College London. He specialises in competition law, and has published widely on competition law and policy. His publications include articles in journals, essays in books, edited volumes and monographs. His most recent book is *The Internationalization of Antitrust Policy* (Cambridge University Press). He is a regular speaker at competition law conferences and acts as a consultant to a variety of governmental and non-governmental organisations and firms in the Middle East, Europe and the USA. His work involves training judges, lawyers, economists and government officials and advisors; advising on competition law projects; drafting legislation, agreements and guidelines; and conducting negotiation. Currently he is pioneering several projects looking into possible reform of the competition laws of several countries. He was called to the Bar in England and Wales and was awarded a Harmsworth Major Scholarship.

EC and UK Competition Law

Commentary, Cases and Materials

MAHER M. DABBAH

School of Law, Queen Mary, University of London and
barrister of the Middle Temple

CAMBRIDGE
UNIVERSITY PRESS

CAMBRIDGE UNIVERSITY PRESS
Cambridge, New York, Melbourne, Madrid, Cape Town, Singapore, São Paulo

Cambridge University Press
The Edinburgh Building, Cambridge CB2 2RU, UK

Published in the United States of America by Cambridge University Press, New York

www.cambridge.org
Information on this title: www.cambridge.org/9780521849975

First published 2004
Reprinted 2006

Printed in the United Kingdom at the University Press, Cambridge

A catalogue record for this book is available from the British Library

ISBN-13 978-0-521-84997-5 hardback
ISBN-10 0-521-84997-7 hardback
ISBN-13 978-0-521-60468-0 paperback
ISBN-10 0-521-60468-0 paperback

To my great and wonderful parents

Contents

Contents

Preface

The competition rules of the EC and the UK have witnessed a phenomenal increase in significance over the years. The rules are bound together by a special relationship. Apart from the 'blood-tie' connecting them, they have developed in such a way that makes it absolutely vital for competition lawyers (a term I employ in a loose sense here to refer also to students), at least in the UK, to familiarise themselves with both. Indeed, the various developments which have taken place over the years, such as the enactment of the modernisation Regulation, Regulation 1/2003, have made this all the more important; thus it is quite difficult to study, specialise and focus on one set of rules without considering the other. The present book is intended to give proper recognition to this important fact.

While no book on this topic can claim to be comprehensive, it is hoped that this book will fill a gap in the market by providing detailed commentary with a broad selection of relevant extracts from cases, current EC and UK competition law provisions and official guidelines published by the relevant competition authorities. I have inserted no extracts from literature, whether books or articles published in legal journals. Some chapters however include a list of further reading which the reader may find useful to consult. The book includes case studies with model answers in order to give it an extra practical flavour. There are also diagrams and a flowchart which have been included to explain difficult concepts and ideas.

In preparing this book, I have received much appreciated help and support. I would like to thank my research assistants (and former students), Bruce McGinn and Christopher Lipka. Bruce was involved from an early stage and demonstrated a very sound understanding of competition law and an incredible ability to meet the very tight deadlines I often imposed. Christopher became involved later on and showed a strong and important dedication to the project.

In addition, I would like to express my warm gratitude to Dr Yoram Danziger, Dr Tamar Gidron, Professor Meir Heth, Professor Geraint Thomas and my many colleagues and friends in the world of competition law for their very generous encouragement and support. I am greatly indebted to two true friends and allies, Mr Christopher Brown and Mr Manish Das, who offered very helpful comments on the chapters. I also would like to thank the very friendly and able staff at Cambridge University Press. In particular, I would like to express my appreciation to Mrs Kim Hughes who offered me extremely valuable help and support. It has been my absolute pleasure to work with her.

Finally, my greatest debt goes to my parents, to whom I dedicate this book. Nothing I have achieved could have been possible without them.

I have aimed to state the law as it stood on 1 July 2004.

Guidance to reader

1. I have inserted no footnotes in the commentary. Footnotes in the book are those appearing originally in the extracted materials and every effort has been made to keep the original numbering, although not all footnotes have been reproduced.

2. The commentary contains no case citation. This was done in order to make the text easier to read. Cases appear by name in the commentary. The table of cases at the beginning of the book includes full citation and case name. Some cases are a bit unusual in the sense that they are widely known by a different name: for example the case of *A. Ahlström Osakeyhtio v. Commission* which in some places in the commentary appears as 'Woodpulp'. The table of cases has been arranged in such a way that if the reader looks 'Woodpulp' up, he or she will be referred to *A. Ahlström Osakeyhtio v. Commission* with the full citation.

3. Numbers and words appearing in square brackets in extracts and quotes reflect the renumbering of the EC Treaty and other changes and revision.

4. The book does not include chapters on either State Aid or the international aspect of Competition Law and policy. This should not (I hope!) be seen as a shortcoming given that (a) as far as students are concerned, the vast majority of courses on EC and UK competition law taught at different institutions do not include these topics in their syllabus, and (b) for other readers, including competition law practitioners and academics, handling work related to these topics does not really involve reading one or two chapters in a textbook devoted to the competition rules of the EC and the UK. Furthermore, in light of the phenomenal increase in their significance in recent years, these topics merit separate examination, especially since they have developed into 'autonomous' areas within the field of competition law. Squeezing them into two chapters of a book with a particular focus does not do them justice and is not quite beneficial. There is now an abundance of literature on the topics which the reader would be best advised to consult.

5. Certain EC cases have no European Court Reports (ECR) or Official Journal (OJ) citation, with only a Common Market Law Reports (CMLR) citation. One or two cases have no citation at all. This is because these were not available at the time the book went into production.

6. When the book went into production, the Office of Fair Trading (OFT) was still revising a number of its Competition Act 1998 guidelines. The extracted

materials from these include the latest version(s) as published by the OFT. I do not anticipate that any final changes which the OFT will make to these documents will affect the extracts in the book; however the reader may find it useful to consult the OFT's website for the most recent drafts of its guidelines: this is always good practice. The guidelines I am referring to are OFT400, OFT401, OFT402, OFT403, OFT404, OFT407, OFT414, OFT415, OFT418, OFT419 and OFT423, although not all of these are extracted in the book whether in full or in part.

European materials

Commission Notices and Guidelines

UK materials

Statutory instruments

Guidelines

OFT GUIDELINES

UK Competition Commission Guidelines

Table of cases

EC cases (including Commission Decisions, and CFI and ECJ) Judgments

UK cases

US cases

Abbreviations

ALJ	Antitrust Law Journal
Bus. L. I.	Business Law International
CA	Court of Appeal
CAT	Competition Appeal Tribunal
CC	Competition Commission
CDO	Competition Disqualification Order
CDU	Competition Disqualification Undertaking
CFI	European Court of First Instance
CompAR	Competition Appeal Reports
Comp. L. I.	Competition Law Insight
CMLR	Common Market Law Reports
CMLRev	Common Market Law Review
DG COMP	Directorate of the European Commission responsible for competition policy
DTI	Department of Trade and Industry
ECJ	European Court of Justice
ECLR	European Competition Law Review
ECMR	European Community Merger Regulation
ECN	European Competition Network
ECR	European Court Reports
EEA	European Economic Area
EIPR	European Intellectual Property Review
ELRev	European Law Review
FCLI	Fordham Corporate Law Institute
GCR	Global Competition Review
HC	High Court
HHI	Herfindahl-Hirschman Index
NCAs	National Competition Authorities
OFT	Office of Fair Trading
OJ	Official Journal of the European Communities
SLC	Substantial lessening of competition

1
Introduction

The field of competition law has seen remarkable changes and developments over the past two decades, the extent of which can be rivalled by few other areas of law. Perhaps the most significant development has been an impressive geographical expansion and proliferation worldwide. At the end of the 1980s, there were only about ten systems of competition law. Today, around 100 jurisdictions with a variety of economic systems and in differing states of development have established systems of competition law. Roughly a dozen further countries are currently in the final stages of turning competition bills into law. Moreover, the competition law debate – meaning the debate on whether to introduce a system of competition law – features high on the agenda of many governments around the world and is already in the committee stage of others.

Doubtless the impressive increase in the attractiveness and geographical scope of competition law heralds a growing belief that market systems deliver a better outcome than that yielded by state control, planning and national monopoly management. This belief has resulted from one of the most important developments of the twentieth century, namely the shift in many parts of the world towards liberalisation and the privatisation of domestic economies. With this shift, countries have come to realise that competition can act as a force to enhance innovation and economic growth as well as supporting the social development of countries and their citizens.

Market forces and competition have become widely recognised as appropriate means of managing national economies. Some economists argue that competition is an absolutely vital component of a successful market economy. Competition acts responsively to set prices at levels the market will bear, largely without intervention, in a manner impossible through central control. Monopoly, these theorists argue, is wasteful, leads to poor quality of products and services, stifles innovation and may encourage restriction in output, all of which is likely to harm consumers.

However, given these advantages and the supposedly 'maintenance-free' self-righting virtues of competition, it seems odd that we should need powerful laws to sustain, foster and protect free competition. Perhaps the biggest irony to stem from the 'Cold War' ideological battleground (and the resounding 'victory' of capitalism over communism) is that, although robust and generally reliable at producing sustainable growth and relative stability, the free market, like any other system, is prone to manipulation and corruption at the hands of greedy individuals. Moreover, although competition is encouraged and fostered throughout the market (to take a recent UK example, competition in directory enquiry services), governments are also discovering that free competition cannot, without more, manage all aspects of national economies satisfactorily. Certain markets are arguably more conducive to state control, as might be gleaned from the state of UK rail services and debate on re-nationalisation. Sometimes, no matter how well competitive structures are protected, countervailing interests thwart any notion of a totally free market. Many markets require regulation and active intervention in the interest of public policy, such as water services, newspapers and even legal services. A recurring theme throughout this book, therefore, is the non-competition interests that inform certain competition law systems and, accordingly, areas from which the application of competition law is excluded or restricted.

1 A reflection on terminology

Competition law is a jargon-heavy interdisciplinary area; hence it is desirable at this early stage of the book to give an overview of some basic concepts and ideas. Three important concepts merit special consideration. These are 'competition,' 'competition law' and 'competition policy'.

(A) Competition

I The concept of competition

A discussion of competition law ought always to begin with an examination of the concept of competition, its underlying theories and its economic basis. This is not mere academic indulgence but important for a number of reasons, most importantly because there is in fact no formal or official definition of competition (not forgetting of course the argument against the desirability of competition in the marketplace altogether). Indeed, a brief survey of the numerous definitions, whether given by academics or appearing in the statutory provisions that operate in different countries, can serve to demonstrate this.

Perhaps the most neutral, non-controversial approach is to view competition as a process of rivalry between actors in the marketplace. Businesses, of course, have but one aim: to market their products and services to customers in order to make a profit. Thus, competition is the process by which firms strive to win customers. A certain degree of emphasis must be placed on the term 'process' because competition is an on-going fundamental part of the market economy. Hence, we are not talking about a one-off or short-term event. The process should never end. Competition is the flywheel of the free economy, the expression of its spirit, and both the cause and the result of its successful operation. It is evolutionary in substance, dynamic in form and it adapts to suit time and circumstance.

Putting this philosophical aspect aside for the moment, it should not be forgotten that competition is concerned with the marketplace and for this reason, it is essential to come to grips with certain fundamental economic concepts when evaluating various competition policy debates. To begin with, economists look at markets in terms of supply and demand structures, each pulling in opposite directions to strike a balance in the value to be attributed to a scarce resource. This dynamic plays out in the process of competition such that, when there is demand for a resource, it is desirable to supply it on the market. A supplier sees an opportunity to profit, which means a prospect of a yield on investment of capital (and effort) exceeding what the individual or firm might expect from investing in any other activity. But it is important to realise that price is constrained on the supply side not only by actual competitors in the market (who are inspired to supply that resource more efficiently or on more favourable terms) but also by the threat of potential competitors who might make an investment and move into the market if the price levels are high (or 'supra-competitive'). An oft-forgotten aspect of this process is the act of leaving the market when prices drop below competitive levels, thereby remedying the supply surplus. (This is explained in more depth under *Allocative efficiency* and *Productive efficiency* at pp. 6–7 below). A similar and corresponding dynamic occurs on the demand side of the market.

Most 'problems' with the process of competition (described below under 'Competition law') stem from bottlenecks and distortions in supply and demand, for instance, because potential competitors are restrained from entering the market, resulting in the power to charge supra-competitive prices by virtue of a dearth of competitors. The European Commission has published extensive theoretical analysis on competition policy, particularly in relation to the exception to the prohibition on anti-competitive agreements (Article 81(3) EC), as extracted in chapter 4.

Thus it can be seen that economic analysis is fundamental to the formulation of competition policy and application of competition law. Indeed, the economic philosophy of competition has become its dominant intellectual discourse. Competition law and policy have developed in such a way that any study that fails to appreciate the role competition plays within the market economy is neither justifiable nor indeed possible. For this reason, before addressing questions such as 'what is competition law?' and 'what are its aims?', it is vital to come to grips with the nature of the process of competition and its operation.

II The models of competition

There are several models that economists use to understand and analyse competition theoretically, each serving different purposes.

(a) Perfect competition

The theory of perfect competition emerged as the result of a traditional economic approach to competition which presupposes rational actors producing and supplying goods and services in the most efficient manner possible under conditions of perfect competition. This entails a very large number of competitors all equal in size, producing or marketing homogeneous products and incurring no costs in entering or exiting the market. Moreover, it also assumes perfect information on the demand side of the market such that all customers know the price charged by any supplier. Accordingly, suppliers are only price-takers with no power to influence the demand structure on the market.

It can be shown analytically that perfect competition results in the most efficient allocation of economic resources such as to maximize the net benefit a customer derives from each purchase ('consumer surplus') and allocate products to customers who value them most according to individual demand and willingness to pay. This is known as allocative efficiency (discussed further below at pp. 6–7 below). Furthermore, this model demonstrates that competition enhances productive efficiency: constrained by competition, each producer has an incentive to supply more efficiently in order to increase returns, a tendency which acts over the long term to force all producers towards the most efficient means of production.

It is apparent from a survey of the world of competition law that this model remains influential on competitive policy. However, its usefulness and applicability is limited both by its problematic assumptions and a degree of ambiguity about its goals. To be fair, it must be emphasised that it is only a model. Obviously, there are very few, if any, markets where the abovementioned assumptions hold true (although it can be argued that much market intervention, e.g. information requirements on consumer goods, are aimed at enhancing the 'perfection' of competitive conditions). Products are rarely perfectly homogenous and consumer loyalties tend to allow 'brand name' producers to charge higher prices without a corresponding loss in business. Moreover, producers may not be entirely rational, for example prioritising market esteem over maximum profitability.

Furthermore, even the most prominent proponents of perfect competition theory admit that competition law is sometimes concerned with other costs of production such as environmental or cultural costs ('externalities') something not accounted for by perfect competition. Indeed, many competition law regimes can be said to be concerned with non-economic goals. Consumer welfare and economic efficiency are not the only goals of society, which might also include, for example imposing responsibility on producers for occupational safety or preventing environmental contamination. Furthermore, given that market structures and behaviour are invariably extremely complex – with infinite variation in business models, ongoing technological advances, etc. – it is almost impossible to draft rules suitable for achieving economic efficiency and consumer welfare of all situations.

Markets are disorganised in substance and often haphazard in structure. Therefore, they are very far from approximating perfect competition having evolved and adapted over time to what they are at any given time. Accordingly, other models have emerged with which to analyse competition.

(b) Dynamic competition

Dynamic competition involves the idea of achieving an optimal degree of innovation in the market as well as the diffusion of technological advances over time. The emphasis of this approach is on the aim of overall economic efficiency and it has come to be known as the 'total welfare approach'. Dynamic competition regards competition as a continuing process, based on market innovation. Thus, firms that achieve competitive advantages as a result of market oligopolies or positions of market dominance should be allowed to exploit these advantages. In this sense proponents of the theory are not too concerned about market power and an unbalanced market structure or at least much less so than proponents of perfect competition.

(c) Workable competition

The reality of the marketplace is actually quite different from any theoretical world. Indeed, given that the discipline of economics is often subject to pragmatic concerns to limit intervention in the marketplace to situations of market failure, economists are forced to adapt theory as a rigid system to more of a structural 'goal' of maintaining conditions conducive to competition. The interesting aspect of workable competition is that it is an idea and not strictly a theory, operating like a norm and adapting to prevailing market conditions and structure. Thus, shifts in the behaviour of firms, the political aims of the competition authorities and even issues such as the effects of globalisation are all relevant policy considerations. In reality, this notion of competition is sensible, pragmatic and logical: so long as competition 'works' there is no need to intervene in the marketplace. Intervention by competition authorities is reserved for situations of market failure.

(B) Competition law

It is doubtful whether it is possible to define 'competition law' comprehensively and uncontroversially. Despite the best efforts of literature on the topic this may be because the aims and objectives of competition law are as fluid and changing as competition itself. Perhaps the least controversial definition is that competition law is concerned with applying legal rules and standards to address

[5]

market imperfections and to preserve, promote and sometimes restore market conditions conducive to competition. In other words it is law used to protect competition.

In some jurisdictions, it is called 'competition' (or 'antitrust') law. In a second category of jurisdictions, it is called 'restrictive business practices' law. In a third category, it is called the 'law against unfair competition'. This list is not exhaustive and other names can be identified. An important question is whether these are actually the same thing. As is widely known, competition law and antitrust law (to take the example of the EC and the USA) are the same, though of course differences pertain in the substantive provisions and enforcement. However, it is doubtful whether the same thing can be said about a restrictive business practices law, which tends to be more concerned with how powerful firms use their market strength.

One further interesting point to bear in mind about competition law is that unlike most other areas of law it tends to have extraterritorial effects, particularly in its aim of protecting a market structure conducive to competition. This probably results more from globalising trends in business than from competition law itself. For example, a transaction between two US firms such as a merger could have anti-competitive effects on the supply of goods and services in the EC and be prohibited by one competition authority but cleared elsewhere. This aspect is addressed further in relation to mergers in chapters 10, 11 and 13, although it can potentially arise under other competition law provisions.

As alluded to above, the process of competition can produce various desirable (and undesirable) economic and non-economic outcomes, and competition law can fruitfully be considered in terms of its underlying aims.

I Economic goals

The first category can be identified as economic goals. These concern issues such as efficiency and the maximisation of consumer welfare. There is no doubt that one of the principal objectives of competition law is to achieve economic efficiency in the market. Understanding this point requires a consideration of two important sub-concepts mentioned above: 'allocative efficiency' and 'productive efficiency'.

(a) Allocative efficiency

This form of efficiency is concerned with the demand side of the market. It occurs where consumers always obtain a product or service they desire at the price they are willing to pay. Accordingly resources are always allocated to the highest value uses. Moreover, prices are constrained on the supply side to the 'marginal cost' of production (the cost of each additional unit of production including sufficient returns to justify the producer's capital investment but no more). This pertains because competing producers always have an incentive to produce one more unit of production so long as the price of each unit (the 'marginal revenue') exceeds marginal cost (i.e. demand exceeds supply). In such a 'seller's market', the producer faces both actual competitors (who undercut one another to attract customers) and potential competitors (who might enter the market attracted by a prospect of 'supra-competitive prices', i.e. prices above marginal cost). Thus the price tends always to converge with marginal cost. Moreover, there is no incentive for any producer to limit output because he or she alone cannot influence overall supply when other rational actors will simply move in to meet demand. Hence, the producer will continue to produce as long as price is equal to the prevailing marginal cost.

It is believed that allocative efficiency is in the interest of consumers resulting in lower prices, better product quality and ultimately more choice.

(b) Productive efficiency

Productive efficiency is considered on the production side of the market. It pertains where a producer manufactures products and services at the lowest possible cost. So long as no single producer can increase price beyond marginal cost – because doing so might lead some of its customers to look for a cheaper source of supply or attract potential competitors to enter the market – each producer has an incentive to supply more efficiently in order to increase marginal revenue, a tendency which acts over the long term to force all producers towards the most efficient means of production. Economic theory suggests that this increases the overall wealth of society because it minimises unnecessary resources to be expended on production.

As noted above, these efficiencies are theoretical and predicated on perfect competition (see pp. 4–5 above). Therefore, one should be somewhat sceptical about the true outcome in practice.

II Social goals

This category addresses issues of consumer protection outside the technical economic efficiencies explained above. The concern here is with protecting and safeguarding the consumer (or perhaps even certain supplier groups such as employees) from the exercise of market power and broader socio-economic power held by large firms. It might also aim to protect the opportunities and interests of small and medium-size firms, democratic values and principles and the public interest. Put differently, the concern is to ensure some degree of market fairness and equity. It is clear that this is an expression of wholly non-economic 'democratic' principles of justice and equality of bargaining power.

III Other goals

A third category of goals concerns broader political aims, such as those relating to the processes of integration in economic unions and free trade areas.

The justification for identifying this as a separate category is grounded in the judicial recognition of these aims and also on the fact that any description of competition law and policy, including their development, derives ultimately from practical experience. The EC provides a good illustration of this, where the goal of building a single market has formed a central *raison d'être* in the development and application of the various competition law provisions in the EC Treaty. (See e.g. Article 2 EC, discussed below at p. 10).

This point is central to any discussion of competition law and policy, namely that one should be careful of categorical generalisations about the goals of competition law. Practical application in different jurisdictions throughout the world demonstrates that competition law can apply to many situations besides the above-mentioned categories of economic and social goals. These situations sometimes relate to specific sectors in the national economy and sometimes even broader sectors extending across national boundaries, such as the EC.

(C) Competition policy

The final concept to mention here is 'competition policy', which is ultimately an expression of prevailing politics. Competition policy is quite a broad term, and like the concepts of competition and competition law, it has been given different interpretations in different jurisdictions and in different contexts. Essentially, competition policy deals with the scope of public authorities' intervention beyond certain market imperfections, such as market failures. Market failure, in this sense, relates to circumstances in which private forces within the market fail either to sustain desirable activities or to act as a check on undesirable activities carried out by firms. A point that follows directly from this is that individual countries formulate different public policy on competition. Accordingly, public authorities, *a fortiori* competition authorities, enjoy considerable discretion in the practical implementation of these policies. Moreover, it is certainly arguable that a country's efforts to enact a competition law regime can also be termed competition policy.

2 The competition rules of the EC and the UK

The purpose behind this part of the chapter is to introduce the reader to the EC and UK systems of competition law and the operation of these systems. This is necessarily only an overview: the remainder of the book examines these systems in detail.

(A) EC law

EC competition law was created for a unique set of circumstances and has become a robust and well-established system of competition law. EC competition law is enforced in a special context, namely a wider system designed to eliminate barriers between countries and enhance the creation of a single market. The Treaty of Rome, signed in 1957, creates fundamental freedoms – free movement of goods, free movement of capital, free movement of labour and freedom of establishment and services – created principally through the abolition of all barriers erected by the Member States. The draughtsmen of the Treaty realised at the time that these freedoms could not be secured if such barriers were simply replaced by restraints imposed by and resulting from the behaviour of private firms, because either type of restraint could jeopardise this goal. Consequently, competition law provisions incorporated in the Treaty have taken an important role that can be considered usefully alongside EC law relating to those fundamental freedoms.

Another aspect of EC competition law that follows directly from the previous one is that its self-proclaimed political goals have meant a departure from the 'traditional' approach. Unlike systems of competition law in other jurisdictions, including the UK, EC competition law was not adopted predominantly to enhance efficiency and ensure consumer welfare or protect social interests. EC competition law takes a 'European' regulatory approach and reflects cultures and values particular to the European continent. Further, it should be borne in mind that the EC Treaty created a new legal order in the realm of international law, within which Member States of the EC have limited their sovereign rights in several fields, including the field of competition law and policy.

I The competition law chapter of the EC Treaty

The fundamental competition rules of the EC can be found in Chapter 1 of Part III of the Treaty. The Chapter consists of nine Articles, Articles 81–89 EC. There are also important competition law instruments outside the Chapter, mainly in the form of Regulations. Among these are Regulation 1/2003, the Modernisation Regulation (on the implementation of the rules on competition laid down in Articles 81 and 82), Regulation 2790/99 (on the application of 81(3) to categories of vertical agreements), Regulation 2658/2000 (on the application of Article 81(3) to categories of specialisation agreements), Regulation 2659/2000 (on the application of Article 81(3) to categories of research and development agreements), Regulation 139/2004 (the 'Merger Regulation') and Regulation 772/2004 (on the application of Article 81(3) to categories of technology transfer agreements).

Two Treaty provisions – Articles 81 and 82 – deserve special mention as they will be examined in great detail in later chapters. Article 81(1) prohibits agreements, decisions by associations of undertakings and concerted practices which restrict or distort competition and which may affect trade between Member States. By virtue of Article 81(2), an agreement etc. caught by paragraph (1) is declared void. However, the prohibition may be declared inapplicable in the case of agreements etc. which satisfy the efficiency and public benefit requirements of Article 81(3). The second provision, Article 82, prohibits any abuse by one or more undertakings of a dominant position in the common market or a substantial part of it which may affect trade between Member States. One piece of secondary legislation should also be mentioned here, namely the Merger Regulation, which applies to mergers with 'Community dimension'.

II Contextualising the competition rules of the EC

EC competition rules, notwithstanding their apparent clarity, should not be read in isolation but rather in conjunction with several other important Articles of the EC Treaty. These are Articles 2, 3(g), 4, 5, 10 and 12. Article 2 is a very important provision setting out the objectives of the EC:

The Community shall have as its task, by establishing a common market and an economic and monetary union and by implementing common policies or activities referred to in Articles 3 and 4, to promote throughout the Community a harmonious, balanced and sustainable development of economic activities, a high level of employment and of social protection, equality between men and women, sustainable and non-inflationary growth, a high degree of competitiveness and convergence of economic performance, a high level of protection and improvement of the quality of the environment, the raising of the standard of living and quality of life, and economic and social cohesion and solidarity among Member States.

These objectives are followed by Article 3, which sets out the principal activities of the Community. Of particular relevance is paragraph (g) of that provision, which states that the activities of the Community include establishing 'a system ensuring that competition in the internal market is not distorted'.

Article 4 in turn provides in paragraph (1) that:

For the purposes set out in Article 2, the activities of the Member States and the Community shall include, as provided in this Treaty and in accordance with the timetable set out therein, the adoption of an economic policy which is based on the close coordination of Member States' economic policies, on the internal market and on the definition of common objectives, and conducted in accordance with the principle of an open market economy with free competition.

Article 5 contains the subsidiarity principle, which can be understood as the principle that deals with the division of competence between the Community institutions and the Member States:

The Community shall act within the limits of the powers conferred upon it by this Treaty and of the objectives assigned to it therein.

In areas which do not fall within its exclusive competence, the Community shall take action, in accordance with the principle of subsidiarity, only if and insofar as the objectives of the proposed action cannot be sufficiently achieved by the Member

States and can therefore, by reason of the scale or effects of the proposed action, be better achieved by the Community.

Any action by the Community shall not go beyond what is necessary to achieve the objectives of this Treaty.

Article 10 is an important provision on the obligations placed on Member States (including their domestic courts) under the EC Treaty:

Member States shall take all appropriate measures, whether general or particular, to ensure fulfilment of the obligations arising out of this Treaty or resulting from action taken by the institutions of the Community. They shall facilitate the achievement of the Community's tasks.

They shall abstain from any measure which could jeopardise the attainment of the objectives of this Treaty.

Finally, there is the anti-discrimination principle contained in Article 12:

Within the scope of application of this Treaty, and without prejudice to any special provisions contained therein, any discrimination on grounds of nationality shall be prohibited.

These provisions are important to bear in mind because they set the context in which the competition rules are applied and explain the goals they are attempting to achieve.

III Institutional framework

Article 7 of the EC Treaty provides that the tasks entrusted to the Community, including interpretation, application and enforcement of EC law, shall be carried out by separate autonomous institutions. Three principal institutions, namely the European Commission (Commission), the European Court of First Instance (CFI) and the European Court of Justice (ECJ), are concerned with the interpretation and enforcement of competition law, and they have consequently defined its parameters and goals. Although they have at times provoked controversy surrounding its application, it has been argued that because their decisions filter down as binding precedent and inform the judiciary and law-makers in the Member States they gain a legitimacy and degree of acceptance national governments cannot ignore. Accordingly, these institutions have also been highly influential on disparate Member State competition regimes and in creating a 'competition culture' in the EC.

(a) European Commission

The use of law to protect competition in the EC meant addressing anti-competitive behaviour and practices of private firms beyond the boundaries of individual Member States. For this reason it was essential for a supra-national body to be empowered to take action at Community level. The decision was made at an early stage to put the European Commission at the centre of EC competition law and policy. It seems this was decided because there was little confidence that Member State judges and administrators, business firms and their lawyers would be able to apply the EC competition rules either correctly or even in good faith. Another reason was that the Commission already had experienced legal and economic experts, which made it more suitable and qualified than Member State authorities and courts to decide competition cases with legal, economic and political significance. It should also be noted that the decision of the six founding Member States to hand over responsibilities to the Commission should be set against the background of economic growth experienced by the EC at an early stage of its life, which corresponded exactly to the aim of the Treaty as expressed in Article 2 EC.

This accords with the Commission's own view on the matter. It has emphasised repeatedly that competition policy was not widely known throughout the EC. According to the Commission, centralised enforcement was the only appropriate system to ensure the proper functioning of the single market at a time when interpretation, particularly of policy aspects such as Article 81(3) (the efficiency and public benefit exemption), remained uncertain. The Commission was able to establish uniform application of the competition rules throughout the Member States. It could also promote market integration by preventing the erection of private barriers and by creating a body of rules acceptable to all the Member States and the business community.

The process of institutional centralisation was initiated by Regulation 17/62, which specifically defined the role of the Commission in EC competition policy. Regulation 17/62 has now been replaced by Regulation 1/2003, which makes important steps toward decentralisation in the enforcement of the competition rules of the EC (described further in chapter 14). Very notably, the Regulation abolished the system of notification of agreements to the Commission and enhanced the role that domestic competition authorities and courts play in the application of Articles 81 and 82, giving them the power to apply Article 81(3).

The institutional structure of the Commission is very complex. Two important points should be made on that structure. First, the Commission is divided into departments. Competition law and policy is dealt with by DG COMP (the Competition Directorate-General). Secondly, within DG COMP are various sectoral units which deal with both mergers and anti-competitive behaviour. Until recently, the Commission had a specialised 'Merger Task Force' which dealt exclusively with mergers. That has now largely been disbanded. Those who wish to learn about the Commission's institutional structure in detail are advised to consult the relevant sources on this, including the Commission's website, to be found at http://europa.eu.int/comm/.

(b) European Court of First Instance

The CFI was established in 1989 and marked the creation of a specialist court, created to deal among other things with application of competition rules. One of the functions of the CFI is to conduct judicial review of the Commission's decisions, known as the Article 230 procedure. The judgments of the CFI are, in turn, subject to appeal to the ECJ. There have been many such appeals over the years.

(c) European Court of Justice

The ECJ sits atop the judicial pyramid in the EC. It is an intellectual leader in EC law in general and in EC competition law in particular, resulting partly from the ECJ's own conception of its role in curing the so-called 'Eurosclerosis' which afflicted the Community during the first two decades of its existence and partly from the Court's teleological vision of the Treaty and the centrality of competition law. As noted above, the trickle-down effect into domestic legal rulings has enhanced the power of the Treaty over Member States policy.

The ECJ has developed EC competition law mainly by advancing the concepts and ideals it created over the first two decades following 1957. A major cornerstone has been the ECJ's unique interpretive method, namely teleological reasoning. The ECJ considered EC competition law within a specific context: a means of ensuring single market integration. It viewed centralised authority vested in the Commission as indispensable to this goal. Accordingly, it was willing to interpret EC competition law such as to enhance the powers of the Commission *vis-à-vis* the Member States and their domestic competition authorities and courts. In this way, the ECJ gave the Commission leeway and discretion to advance particular policy developments of competition law. By allowing the expansion of the prerogatives of the Commission, the ECJ strengthened EC competition law.

(d) Domestic courts

It is important to mention that Articles 81 and 82 are directly applicable in their entirety. This means that they become part of the legal system of the Member States without requiring any action by the Member States. They are also directly effective, meaning that they may be invoked by individuals, whether claimants or defendants in proceedings before domestic courts. In this way, domestic courts have a very important role to play in applying EC competition rules. This role has been enhanced considerably over the years, especially in light of the Commission's modernisation programme (see chapter 14).

It is worth pointing out another important provision in the EC Treaty, namely Article 234 EC, which gives the domestic courts of Member States the chance to enter into a dialogue with the ECJ on EC law. This provision has been very useful in the context of EC competition law, not only in starting and developing such a dialogue but also in engaging domestic courts in the application of EC competition rules thereby fostering a 'competition culture'. Article 234 allows a domestic court or tribunal to refer specific questions to the ECJ on matters of EC law arising in the course of proceedings. The ECJ then provides a preliminary ruling laying down, in the abstract, the principles of EC competition law to be applied to the case in question but aims to avoid ruling on questions of fact, which falls within the jurisdiction of the domestic courts.

(B) UK law

I General

The UK system of competition law has witnessed fascinating changes over the years. There is now an abundance of literature describing developments over the past fifty years; hence, no attempt will be made here to provide an exhaustive account of historical developments. Suffice it to say that the previous system was largely ineffective, difficult to understand and incredibly confusing to handle. The competition authorities lacked sufficient powers and resources to enforce the law effectively and the regime was deeply politically influenced. Anti-competitive business practices flourished and went undetected and unpunished.

A long chain of developments, including changes of Prime Minister and Government, triggered a heated debate on reform to the competition rules of the UK. Indeed, it was widely accepted that a radical reform was necessary, but the question remained as to how this could best be achieved, in particular whether the law and enforcement system should reflect the EC regime. Many important steps were taken during the 1990s, enriching and shaping the debate, but it was not until the end of the 1990s that concrete steps were taken.

It began with the enactment of the Competition Act 1998 (CA1998), which repealed previous legislation, such as the Restrictive Practices Court Act 1976, the Restrictive Trade Practices Act 1976, the Resale Prices Act 1976, the Restrictive Trade Practices Act 1977 and certain provisions of the Competition Act 1980. This was a major development and the new legislation received a very warm welcome. CA1998 made the UK system of competition law more effective, especially through new powers conferred upon the Office of Fair Trading (OFT) to fight harmful anti-competitive practices such as cartels and abuses of market dominance. CA1998 introduced two important pillars, the Chapter I and the Chapter II prohibitions, modelled on Articles 81 and 82 respectively.

However, it was quite clear that the CA1998 left unfinished business, and a drive for further reform featured prominently in the current Government's ambition to build a 'world-class' system of competition law in the UK. This led to the publication of many interesting and highly significant reports and papers and eventually a draft Bill that later became the Enterprise Act 2002 (EA2002).

Whilst not featuring any further modelling on the competition rules of the EC and dealing extensively with insolvency law, the Act made some very significant changes to the UK competition law enforcement regime, including creating a new cartel offence (see chapter 7). EA2002 also contains key provisions particularly to do with mergers, designed to replace the competition provisions of the old Fair Trading Act 1973. It is submitted that the adoption of the CA1998 and the EA2002 lay the framework for a world-class system of competition law.

II The institutional structure

The CA1998 and the EA2002 confer enforcement and other powers on to a variety of bodies and individuals. These include the Office of Fair Trading (OFT), the Competition Commission (CC), the Competition Appeal Tribunal (CAT), sectoral regulators (such as the Gas and Electricity Markets Authority 'Ofgem', the Director General of Water Services 'Ofwat' and the Office of Communications 'Ofcom'), the civil and criminal courts, the Secretary of State for Trade and Industry, the Secretary of State for Constitutional Affairs and the Serious Fraud Office. Of these bodies and individuals, the OFT, the CC and the CAT are important to note, given their central role in the application and enforcement of UK competition rules.

(a) Office of Fair Trading

The OFT is an independent body responsible for 'making markets work well for consumers', largely through assessment of business practices and competitive structures in various markets and by advising businesses on the application of competition and consumer protection law. The EA2002 created a new corporate board structure within the OFT which consists of a Chairman and executive and non-executive directors appointed by the Secretary of State for Trade and Industry; the old post of Director General of Fair Trading (DGFT) has been abolished. With regard to competition law, besides its responsibility for applying the provisions of the CA1998 and keeping abreast of merger activity under EA2002, the OFT has the power to disqualify company directors, and it works to coordinate enforcement activity with other regulators and its international counterparts.

(b) Competition Commission

Where the OFT finds competitive conditions detrimental to consumers, it may make a referral to the CC, an independent public body which was established by the CA1998 (in relation to mergers the OFT has a *duty* to refer certain mergers – see chapter 11). The CC is charged with conducting inquiries into mergers, markets and regulated industries. The CC applies a competition-based test in order to answer competition questions and to make and implement decisions on appropriate remedies. Although it may also receive referrals from the Secretary of State for Trade and Industry or sectoral regulators, the CC has no power to undertake inquiries of its own initiative.

(c) Competition Appeal Tribunal

Where the decisions of the OFT (or other regulators) are disputed, affected parties have recourse to the CAT, a specialist judicial body with cross-disciplinary expertise in law, economics, business and accountancy, established under the EA2002 to hear and decide appeals and other applications or claims involving competition or economic regulatory issues. The CAT, which replaced the old Competition Commission appeal tribunals (CCAT) set up under the CA1998, can also review decisions made by the Secretary of State, the OFT and the CC in respect of mergers or market investigation references under the EA2002. Cases are heard before a panel of three members with relevant expertise. There is a further appeal from the decisions of the CAT on points of law or size of financial penalty to the Court of Appeal or Court of Session in Scotland or Court of Appeal of Northern Ireland in Northern Ireland.

Further reading

Amato *Antitrust and the Bounds of Power* (Hart Publishing, 1997)
Bellamy and Child (ed. P. Roth) *European Community Law of Competition* (Sweet & Maxwell, 5th edn, 2001)
Faull and Nikpay *The EC Law of Competition* (OUP, 1999)
Gerber *Law and Competition in Twentieth Century Europe* (OUP, 1998)
Rodger and MacCulloch (eds.) *The UK Competition Act* (Hart Publishing, 2000)

2
Economic analysis and market definition

1 Introduction

The discussion in chapter 1 indicated how economics and economic analysis – particularly patterns of supply and demand – play an important role in the area of competition law and policy. Competition law is principally concerned with situations where problems may arise as a result of firms having market power. Obviously, when dealing with situations of market power, two important questions arise: first how to measure market power, and second how to go about appraising situations of market power under competition law. Before one can approach the first of these questions, it is essential to define the relevant market, because market power does not exist in the abstract but only in relation to a relevant market.

This chapter is concerned with economic analysis and the important issue of market definition under EC and UK competition law. This topic has seen some remarkable developments, as well as an increase in significance, over the years. This is hardly surprising in light of the central role that market definition plays in assessing economic strength.

Before commencing this discussion, it is important – especially for the aspiring competition lawyer – to understand that although it is essential to have an understanding of how market definition works, it is almost always carried out in practice by expert economists. Indeed, it is such a complex and difficult exercise that, until a ruling is made on the point by the authorities, experienced practitioners are always careful to make reservations about advice they give, due to possible uncertainty in the area. For the sake of legal certainty, however, as explained below, EC and UK competition authorities, like their counterparts in several other jurisdictions, have offered very helpful guidance about how to go about defining the relevant market. Accordingly, the issue of market definition should be seen in the manner of a conceptual tool for understanding the aims of competition law and the practical workings of the market.

2 EC law

Defining the relevant market has always been important in the application of the various competition law provisions of the EC Treaty. It is particularly important when dealing with three questions: whether an agreement has an appreciable 'effect' on competition under Article 81(1); whether a firm or group of firms holds a dominant position for the purposes of Article 82; and whether a concentration is compatible with the Common Market under the Merger Regulation.

The importance of the Commission defining the relevant market and providing reasons for a particular market definition was established in the early case law of the ECJ. A notable judgment here is *Continental Can*.

Continental Can v. Commission [1973] ECR 215

US-based Continental Can used Schmalbach-Lubeca-Werke AG ('SLW') in Europe to supply light metal containers and lids for glass containers for foodstuffs packaging. Continental used another company, Europemballage Corporation, to purchase a majority share and take over control of a competing company ('TDV'). Although the EC did not at that time have a regime for controlling mergers, the Commission held that structural measures such as acquisitions could constitute abuse of a dominant position contrary to Article 82, by altering the supply and demand structure in the relevant market. The ECJ was asked to consider the validity of this interpretation of the Treaty.

The ECJ held that Article 82 could be applied in this way. However, as the extract below explains, the application for annulment of the Commission's decision succeeded because the Commission had not defined the relevant market sufficiently to demonstrate the existence of a dominant position.

ECJ

32 ... the definition of the relevant market is of essential significance, for the possibilities of competition can only be judged in relation to those characteristics of the products in question by virtue of which those products are particularly apt to satisfy an inelastic need and are only to a limited extent interchangeable with other products.

33 In this context recitals Nos 5 to 7 of the second part of the Decision deal in turn with a 'market for light containers for canned meat products', a 'market for light containers for canned seafood', and a 'market for metal closures for the food packing industry, other than crown corks,' all allegedly dominated by SLW and in which the disputed merger threatens to eliminate competition. The Decision does not, however, give any details of how these three markets differ from each other, and must therefore be considered separately. Similarly, nothing is said about how these three markets differ from the general market for light metal containers, namely the market for metal containers for fruit and vegetables, condensed milk, olive oil, fruit juices and chemico-technical products. In order to be regarded as constituting a distinct market, the products in question must be individualized, not only by the mere fact that they are used for packing certain products, but by particular characteristics of production which make them specifically suitable for this purpose.

Consequently, a dominant position on the market for light metal containers for meat and fish cannot be decisive, as long as it has not been proved that competitors from other sectors of the market for light metal containers are not in a position to enter this market, by a simple adaptation, with sufficient strength to create a serious counterweight.

34   Besides, there are in the Decision itself indications which make one doubt whether the three markets are to be considered separately from other markets for light metal containers, indications which rather lead one to conclude that they are parts of a larger market. In the first part of the statement of reasons, where, under letter J, it deals with the main competitors of SLW in Germany and of TDV in Benelux, the Decision mentions a German undertaking which holds a higher share of production of light metal containers for fruit and vegetables than SLW, and another one which supplies 38 to 40 per cent of the German demand for crown corks: this seems to confirm that the production of metal cans for meat and fish cannot be considered separately from the production of metal cans for other purposes and that, when considering the production of metal closures, crown corks must not be left out. Furthermore, the Decision, when examining the possibilities of competition by substitutes, does not – in No 16 of its second part – confine itself to the three relevant 'markets', but deals with the market for light metal containers for other purposes as well; in this connection it states that these containers could be replaced by containers made of other material to a limited extent only. The fact that the Commission could not maintain this allegation in view of the facts put forward by the applicants in the course of the proceedings, proves in itself how necessary it is sufficiently to define the market concerned in order that the relative strength of the undertakings in such a market might be considered.

35   Since there are in the Decision no data on the particular characteristics of metal containers for meat and fish and metal closures (other than crown corks) designed for the food packing industry, whereby these goods constitute separate markets which could be dominated by the manufacturer holding the highest share of this market, it is for this reason characterized by an uncertainty which has an effect on the other statements from which the Decision infers the absence of real or potential competition in the market in question.

36   Besides, as far as potential competition from large consumers capable of manufacturing their own cans is concerned, the Decision alleges in No 18 that such competition is out of the question due to the heavy capital investments involved and the technical lead of the Continental group in this field, whereas in the last paragraph in J No 3 it is stated that in the Belgian market the Marie Thumas Cannery through its subsidiary Eurocan makes metal containers for its own use and for sale to other consumers. This contradiction is a further indication of the Commission's uncertainty with regard to the definition of the market or markets concerned. In letter (E) of No 30 of the statement of reasons in the Decision, it is stated that 'except for Marie Thumas/Eurocan, manufacturers of their own cans do not make

more than they themselves need and are not suppliers of empty metal contain-ers', while, on the contrary, under K No 2, second paragraph, it says that certain German firms who manufacture their own had begun to market their surplus output of metal containers. It can be concluded from all this that some undertakings which have begun to manufacture their own containers were able to overcome the tech-nological difficulties, yet the Decision does not contain any criteria for evaluating the power of competition of these undertakings. These considerations show further contradictions which, likewise, affect the validity of the Decision contested.

The judgment of the ECJ was a major defeat to the Commission on the facts of the case. In the years that followed, the Commission became much more sophisticated in its approach to market definition for a variety of reasons. One reason was that it gained a vast amount of experience particularly following the introduction of a specific mechanism for dealing with mergers in 1989, which led to the Commission having to consider the issue of market definition in hundreds of cases a year.

In 1997 the Commission took the positive step of introducing a Notice dealing with the issue of market definition. Widely known as the *Notice on Market Definition*, it provides extremely valuable guidance on the principles of market definition and offers an insight into how the Commission defines the relevant market for the purposes of EC competition law.

Commission Notice on the definition of relevant market for the purposes of Community competition law OJ (1997) C 372/5

I. INTRODUCTION

1   The purpose of this notice is to provide guidance as to how the Commission applies the concept of relevant product and geographic market in its ongoing enforcement of Community competition law, in particular the application of [Regulation 1/2003 and Regulation 139/2004], their equivalents in other sectoral applications such as transport, coal and steel and agriculture, and the relevant provisions of the EEA Agreement.[1] Throughout this notice, references to Articles [81] and [82] of the Treaty and to merger control are to be understood as referring to the equivalent provisions in the EEA Agreement and the ECSC Treaty.

2   Market definition is a tool to identify and define the boundaries of competition between firms. It serves to establish the framework within which competition policy is applied by the Commission. The main purpose of market definition is to identify

---

1 The focus of assessment in State aid cases is the aid recipient and the industry/sector concerned rather than identification of competitive constraints faced by the aid recipient. When consideration of market power and therefore of the relevant market are raised in any particular case, elements of the approach outlined here might serve as a basis for the assessment of State aid cases.

in a systematic way the competitive constraints that the undertakings involved[2] face. The objective of defining a market in both its product and geographic dimension is to identify those actual competitors of the undertakings involved that are capable of constraining those undertakings' behaviour and of preventing them from behaving independently of effective competitive pressure. It is from this perspective that the market definition makes it possible *inter alia* to calculate market shares that would convey meaningful information regarding market power for the purposes of assessing dominance or for the purposes of applying Article [81].

3　It follows from point 2 that the concept of 'relevant market' is different from other definitions of market often used in other contexts. For instance, companies often use the term 'market' to refer to the area where it sells its products or to refer broadly to the industry or sector where it belongs.

4　The definition of the relevant market in both its product and its geographic dimensions often has a decisive influence on the assessment of a competition case. By rendering public the procedures which the Commission follows when considering market definition and by indicating the criteria and evidence on which it relies to reach a decision, the Commission expects to increase the transparency of its policy and decision-making in the area of competition policy.

5　Increased transparency will also result in companies and their advisers being able to better anticipate the possibility that the Commission may raise competition concerns in an individual case. Companies could, therefore, take such a possibility into account in their own internal decision-making when contemplating, for instance, acquisitions, the creation of joint ventures, or the establishment of certain agreements. It is also intended that companies should be in a better position to understand what sort of information the Commission considers relevant for the purposes of market definition.

6　The Commission's interpretation of 'relevant market' is without prejudice to the interpretation which may be given by the Court of Justice or the Court of First Instance of the European Communities.

II. DEFINITION OF RELEVANT MARKET

Definition of relevant product market and relevant geographic market

7　The Regulations based on Article [81] and [82] of the Treaty ... as well as in section 6 of Form CO with respect to [the Merger] Regulation ... on the control of concentrations having a Community dimension have laid down the following definitions, 'Relevant product markets' are defined as follows:

2　For the purposes of this notice, the undertakings involved will be, in the case of a concentration, the parties to the concentration; in investigations within the meaning of Article [82] of the Treaty, the undertaking being investigated or the complainants; for investigations within the meaning of Article [81], the parties to the Agreement.

'A relevant product market comprises all those products and/or services which are regarded as interchangeable or substitutable by the consumer, by reason of the products' characteristics, their prices and their intended use'.

8   'Relevant geographic markets' are defined as follows:
'The relevant geographic market comprises the area in which the undertakings concerned are involved in the supply and demand of products or services, in which the conditions of competition are sufficiently homogeneous and which can be distinguished from neighbouring areas because the conditions of competition are appreciably different in those areas'.

9   The relevant market within which to assess a given competition issue is therefore established by the combination of the product and geographic markets. The Commission interprets the definitions in paragraphs 7 and 8 (which reflect the case-law of the Court of Justice and the Court of First Instance as well as its own decision-making practice) according to the orientations defined in this notice.

Concept of relevant market and objectives of Community competition policy

10   The concept of relevant market is closely related to the objectives pursued under Community competition policy. For example, under the Community's merger control, the objective in controlling structural changes in the supply of a product/service is to prevent the creation or reinforcement of a dominant position as a result of which effective competition would be significantly impeded in a substantial part of the common market. Under the Community's competition rules, a dominant position is such that a firm or group of firms would be in a position to behave to an appreciable extent independently of its competitors, customers and ultimately of its consumers.[3] Such a position would usually arise when a firm or group of firms accounted for a large share of the supply in any given market, provided that other factors analysed in the assessment (such as entry barriers, customers' capacity to react, etc.) point in the same direction.

11   The same approach is followed by the Commission in its application of Article [82] of the Treaty to firms that enjoy a single or collective dominant position. Within the meaning of Regulation [1/2003], the Commission has the power to investigate and bring to an end abuses of such a dominant position, which must also be defined by reference to the relevant market. Markets may also need to be defined in the application of Article [81] of the Treaty, in particular, in determining whether an appreciable restriction of competition exists or in establishing if the condition pursuant to Article [81(3)(b)] for an exemption from the application of Article [81(1)] is met.

---

3 Definition given by the Court of Justice in its judgment of 13 February 1979 in Case 85/76, *Hoffmann-La Roche* [1979] ECR 461, and confirmed in subsequent judgments.

12   The criteria for defining the relevant market are applied generally for the analysis of certain types of behaviour in the market and for the analysis of structural changes in the supply of products. This methodology, though, might lead to different results depending on the nature of the competition issue being examined. For instance, the scope of the geographic market might be different when analysing a concentration, where the analysis is essentially prospective, from an analysis of past behaviour. The different time horizon considered in each case might lead to the result that different geographic markets are defined for the same products depending on whether the Commission is examining a change in the structure of supply, such as a concentration or a cooperative joint venture, or examining issues relating to certain past behaviour.

Basic principles for market definition

Competitive constraints

13   Firms are subject to three main sources of competitive constraints: demand substitutability, supply substitutability and potential competition. From an economic point of view, for the definition of the relevant market, demand substitution constitutes the most immediate and effective disciplinary force on the suppliers of a given product, in particular in relation to their pricing decisions. A firm or a group of firms cannot have a significant impact on the prevailing conditions of sale, such as prices, if its customers are in a position to switch easily to available substitute products or to suppliers located elsewhere. Basically, the exercise of market definition consists in identifying the effective alternative sources of supply for the customers of the undertakings involved, in terms both of products/services and of geographic location of suppliers.

14   The competitive constraints arising from supply side substitutability other than those described in paragraphs 20 to 23 and from potential competition are in general less immediate and in any case require an analysis of additional factors. As a result such constraints are taken into account at the assessment stage of competition analysis.

Demand substitution

15   The assessment of demand substitution entails a determination of the range of products which are viewed as substitutes by the consumer. One way of making this determination can be viewed as a speculative experiment, postulating a hypothetical small, lasting change in relative prices and evaluating the likely reactions of customers to that increase. The exercise of market definition focuses on prices for operational and practical purposes, and more precisely on demand substitution arising from small, permanent changes in relative prices. This concept can provide clear indications as to the evidence that is relevant in defining markets.

16   Conceptually, this approach means that, starting from the type of products that the undertakings involved sell and the area in which they sell them, additional products and areas will be included in, or excluded from, the market definition

[23]

depending on whether competition from these other products and areas affect or restrain sufficiently the pricing of the parties' products in the short term.

17   The question to be answered is whether the parties' customers would switch to readily available substitutes or to suppliers located elsewhere in response to a hypothetical small (in the range 5% to 10%) but permanent relative price increase in the products and areas being considered. If substitution were enough to make the price increase unprofitable because of the resulting loss of sales, additional substitutes and areas are included in the relevant market. This would be done until the set of products and geographical areas is such that small, permanent increases in relative prices would be profitable. The equivalent analysis is applicable in cases concerning the concentration of buying power, where the starting point would then be the supplier and the price test serves to identify the alternative distribution channels or outlets for the supplier's products. In the application of these principles, careful account should be taken of certain particular situations as described within paragraphs 56 and 58.

18   A practical example of this test can be provided by its application to a merger of, for instance, soft-drink bottlers. An issue to examine in such a case would be to decide whether different flavours of soft drinks belong to the same market. In practice, the question to address would be whether consumers of flavour A would switch to other flavours when confronted with a permanent price increase of 5% to 10% for flavour A. If a sufficient number of consumers would switch to, say, flavour B, to such an extent that the price increase for flavour A would not be profitable owing to the resulting loss of sales, then the market would comprise at least flavours A and B. The process would have to be extended in addition to other available flavours until a set of products is identified for which a price rise would not induce a sufficient substitution in demand.

19   Generally, and in particular for the analysis of merger cases, the price to take into account will be the prevailing market price. This may not be the case where the prevailing price has been determined in the absence of sufficient competition. In particular for the investigation of abuses of dominant positions, the fact that the prevailing price might already have been substantially increased will be taken into account.

Supply substitution

20   Supply-side substitutability may also be taken into account when defining markets in those situations in which its effects are equivalent to those of demand substitution in terms of effectiveness and immediacy. This means that suppliers are able to switch production to the relevant products and market them in the short term[4] without incurring significant additional costs or risks in response to small and permanent changes in relative prices. When these conditions are met, the additional production

---

4 That is such a period that does not entail a significant adjustment of existing tangible and intangible assets (see paragraph 23).

that is put on the market will have a disciplinary effect on the competitive behaviour of the companies involved. Such an impact in terms of effectiveness and immediacy is equivalent to the demand substitution effect.

21   These situations typically arise when companies market a wide range of qualities or grades of one product; even if, for a given final customer or group of consumers, the different qualities are not substitutable, the different qualities will be grouped into one product market, provided that most of the suppliers are able to offer and sell the various qualities immediately and without the significant increases in costs described above. In such cases, the relevant product market will encompass all products that are substitutable in demand and supply, and the current sales of those products will be aggregated so as to give the total value or volume of the market. The same reasoning may lead to group different geographic areas.

22   A practical example of the approach to supply-side substitutability when defining product markets is to be found in the case of paper. Paper is usually supplied in a range of different qualities, from standard writing paper to high quality papers to be used, for instance, to publish art books. From a demand point of view, different qualities of paper cannot be used for any given use, i.e. an art book or a high quality publication cannot be based on lower quality papers. However, paper plants are prepared to manufacture the different qualities, and production can be adjusted with negligible costs and in a short time-frame. In the absence of particular difficulties in distribution, paper manufacturers are able therefore, to compete for orders of the various qualities, in particular if orders are placed with sufficient lead time to allow for modification of production plans. Under such circumstances, the Commission would not define a separate market for each quality of paper and its respective use. The various qualities of paper are included in the relevant market, and their sales added up to estimate total market value and volume.

23   When supply-side substitutability would entail the need to adjust significantly existing tangible and intangible assets, additional investments, strategic decisions or time delays, it will not be considered at the stage of market definition. Examples where supply-side substitution did not induce the Commission to enlarge the market are offered in the area of consumer products, in particular for branded beverages. Although bottling plants may in principle bottle different beverages, there are costs and lead times involved (in terms of advertising, product testing and distribution) before the products can actually be sold. In these cases, the effects of supply-side substitutability and other forms of potential competition would then be examined at a later stage.

Potential competition

24   The third source of competitive constraint, potential competition, is not taken into account when defining markets, since the conditions under which potential competition will actually represent an effective competitive constraint depend on the analysis of specific factors and circumstances related to the conditions of entry. If required,

[25]

this analysis is only carried out at a subsequent stage, in general once the position of the companies involved in the relevant market has already been ascertained, and when such position gives rise to concerns from a competition point of view.

III. EVIDENCE RELIED ON TO DEFINE RELEVANT MARKETS

The process of defining the relevant market in practice

Product dimension

25   There is a range of evidence permitting an assessment of the extent to which substitution would take place. In individual cases, certain types of evidence will be determinant, depending very much on the characteristics and specificity of the industry and products or services that are being examined. The same type of evidence may be of no importance in other cases. In most cases, a decision will have to be based on the consideration of a number of criteria and different items of evidence. The Commission follows an open approach to empirical evidence, aimed at making an effective use of all available information which may be relevant in individual cases. The Commission does not follow a rigid hierarchy of different sources of information or types of evidence.

26   The process of defining relevant markets may be summarized as follows: on the basis of the preliminary information available or information submitted by the undertakings involved, the Commission will usually be in a position to broadly establish the possible relevant markets within which, for instance, a concentration or a restriction of competition has to be assessed. In general, and for all practical purposes when handling individual cases, the question will usually be to decide on a few alternative possible relevant markets. For instance, with respect to the product market, the issue will often be to establish whether product A and product B belong or do not belong to the same product market. It is often the case that the inclusion of product B would be enough to remove any competition concerns.

27   In such situations it is not necessary to consider whether the market includes additional products, or to reach a definitive conclusion on the precise product market. If under the conceivable alternative market definitions the operation in question does not raise competition concerns, the question of market definition will be left open, reducing thereby the burden on companies to supply information.

Geographic dimension

28   The Commission's approach to geographic market definition might be summarized as follows: it will take a preliminary view of the scope of the geographic market on the basis of broad indications as to the distribution of market shares between the parties and their competitors, as well as a preliminary analysis of pricing and price differences at national and Community or EEA level. This initial view is used basically as a working hypothesis to focus the Commission's enquiries for the purposes of arriving at a precise geographic market definition.

29   The reasons behind any particular configuration of prices and market shares need to be explored. Companies might enjoy high market shares in their domestic markets just because of the weight of the past, and conversely, a homogeneous presence of companies throughout the EEA might be consistent with national or regional geographic markets. The initial working hypothesis will therefore be checked against an analysis of demand characteristics (importance of national or local preferences, current patterns of purchases of customers, product differentiation/brands, other) in order to establish whether companies in different areas do indeed constitute a real alternative source of supply for consumers. The theoretical experiment is again based on substitution arising from changes in relative prices, and the question to answer is again whether the customers of the parties would switch their orders to companies located elsewhere in the short term and at a negligible cost.

30   If necessary, a further check on supply factors will be carried out to ensure that those companies located in differing areas do not face impediments in developing their sales on competitive terms throughout the whole geographic market. This analysis will include an examination of requirements for a local presence in order to sell in that area the conditions of access to distribution channels, costs associated with setting up a distribution network, and the presence or absence of regulatory barriers arising from public procurement, price regulations, quotas and tariffs limiting trade or production, technical standards, monopolies, freedom of establishment, requirements for administrative authorizations, packaging regulations, etc. In short, the Commission will identify possible obstacles and barriers isolating companies located in a given area from the competitive pressure of companies located outside that area, so as to determine the precise degree of market interpenetration at national, European or global level.

31   The actual pattern and evolution of trade flows offers useful supplementary indications as to the economic importance of each demand or supply factor mentioned above, and the extent to which they may or may not constitute actual barriers creating different geographic markets. The analysis of trade flows will generally address the question of transport costs and the extent to which these may hinder trade between different areas, having regard to plant location, costs of production and relative price levels.

Market integration in the Community

32   Finally, the Commission also takes into account the continuing process of market integration, in particular in the Community, when defining geographic markets, especially in the area of concentrations and structural joint ventures. The measures adopted and implemented in the internal market programme to remove barriers to trade and further integrate the Community markets cannot be ignored when assessing the effects on competition of a concentration or a structural joint venture. A situation where national markets have been artificially isolated from each other because of the existence of legislative barriers that have now been removed will

[27]

generally lead to a cautious assessment of past evidence regarding prices, market shares or trade patterns. A process of market integration that would, in the short term, lead to wider geographic markets may therefore be taken into consideration when defining the geographic market for the purposes of assessing concentrations and joint ventures.

The process of gathering evidence

33   When a precise market definition is deemed necessary, the Commission will often contact the main customers and the main companies in the industry to enquire into their views about the boundaries of product and geographic markets and to obtain the necessary factual evidence to reach a conclusion. The Commission might also contact the relevant professional associations, and companies active in upstream markets, so as to be able to define, in so far as necessary, separate product and geographic markets, for different levels of production or distribution of the products/services in question. It might also request additional information from the undertakings involved.

34   Where appropriate, the Commission will address written requests for information to the market players mentioned above. These requests will usually include questions relating to the perceptions of companies about reactions to hypothetical price increases and their views of the boundaries of the relevant market. They will also ask for provision of the factual information the Commission deems necessary to reach a conclusion on the extent of the relevant market. The Commission might also discuss with marketing directors or other officers of those companies to gain a better understanding on how negotiations between suppliers and customers take place and better understand issues relating to the definition of the relevant market. Where appropriate, they might also carry out visits or inspections to the premises of the parties, their customers and/or their competitors, in order to better understand how products are manufactured and sold.

35   The type of evidence relevant to reach a conclusion as to the product market can be categorized as follows:

Evidence to define markets – product dimension

36   An analysis of the product characteristics and its intended use allows the Commission, as a first step, to limit the field of investigation of possible substitutes. However, product characteristics and intended use are insufficient to show whether two products are demand substitutes. Functional interchangeability or similarity in characteristics may not, in themselves, provide sufficient criteria, because the responsiveness of customers to relative price changes may be determined by other considerations as well. For example, there may be different competitive constraints in the original equipment market for car components and in spare parts, thereby leading to a separate delineation of two relevant markets. Conversely, differences in

product characteristics are not in themselves sufficient to exclude demand substitutability, since this will depend to a large extent on how customers value different characteristics.

37   The type of evidence the Commission considers relevant to assess whether two products are demand substitutes can be categorized as follows:

38   *Evidence of substitution in the recent past.*   In certain cases, it is possible to analyse evidence relating to recent past events or shocks in the market that offer actual examples of substitution between two products. When available, this sort of information will normally be fundamental for market definition. If there have been changes in relative prices in the past (all else being equal), the reactions in terms of quantities demanded will be determinant in establishing substitutability. Launches of new products in the past can also offer useful information, when it is possible to precisely analyse which products have lost sales to the new product.

39   There are a number of quantitative tests that have specifically been designed for the purpose of delineating markets. These tests consist of various econometric and statistical approaches estimates of elasticities and cross-price elasticities[5] for the demand of a product, tests based on similarity of price movements over time, the analysis of causality between price series and similarity of price levels and/or their convergence. The Commission takes into account the available quantitative evidence capable of withstanding rigorous scrutiny for the purposes of establishing patterns of substitution in the past.

40   *Views of customers and competitors.*   The Commission often contacts the main customers and competitors of the companies involved in its enquiries, to gather their views on the boundaries of the product market as well as most of the factual information it requires to reach a conclusion on the scope of the market. Reasoned answers of customers and competitors as to what would happen if relative prices for the candidate products were to increase in the candidate geographic area by a small amount (for instance of 5% to 10%) are taken into account when they are sufficiently backed by factual evidence.

41   *Consumer preferences.*   In the case of consumer goods, it may be difficult for the Commission to gather the direct views of end consumers about substitute products. Marketing studies that companies have commissioned in the past and that are used by companies in their own decision-making as to pricing of their products and/or marketing actions may provide useful information for the Commission's delineation of the relevant market. Consumer surveys on usage patterns and attitudes, data from consumer's purchasing patterns, the views expressed by retailers and more generally, market research studies submitted by the parties and their competitors are taken into account to establish whether an economically significant proportion of consumers

5 Own-price elasticity of demand for product X is a measure of the responsiveness of demand for X to percentage change in its own price. Cross-price elasticity between products C and Y is the responsiveness of demand for product X to percentage change in the price of product Y.

consider two products as substitutable, also taking into account the importance of brands for the products in question. The methodology followed in consumer surveys carried out ad hoc by the undertakings involved or their competitors for the purposes of a merger procedure or a procedure pursuant to [Regulation 1/2003] will usually be scrutinized with utmost care. Unlike pre-existing studies, they have not been prepared in the normal course of business for the adoption of business decisions.

42   *Barriers and costs associated with switching demand to potential substitutes.* There are a number of barriers and costs that might prevent the Commission from considering two prima facie demand substitutes as belonging to one single product market. It is not possible to provide an exhaustive list of all the possible barriers to substitution and of switching costs. These barriers or obstacles might have a wide range of origins, and in its decisions, the Commission has been confronted with regulatory barriers or other forms of State intervention, constraints arising in downstream markets, need to incur specific capital investment or loss in current output in order to switch to alternative inputs, the location of customers, specific investment in production process, learning and human capital investment, retooling costs or other investments, uncertainty about quality and reputation of unknown suppliers, and others.

43   *Different categories of customers and price discrimination.* The extent of the product market might be narrowed in the presence of distinct groups of customers. A distinct group of customers for the relevant product may constitute a narrower, distinct market when such a group could be subject to price discrimination. This will usually be the case when two conditions are met: (a) it is possible to identify clearly which group an individual customer belongs to at the moment of selling the relevant products to him, and (b) trade among customers or arbitrage by third parties should not be feasible.

Evidence for defining markets – geographic dimension

44   The type of evidence the Commission considers relevant to reach a conclusion as to the geographic market can be categorized as follows:

45   *Past evidence of diversion of orders to other areas.* In certain cases, evidence on changes in prices between different areas and consequent reactions by customers might be available. Generally, the same quantitative tests used for product market definition might as well be used in geographic market definition, bearing in mind that international comparisons of prices might be more complex due to a number of factors such as exchange rate movements, taxation and product differentiation.

46   *Basic demand characteristics.* The nature of demand for the relevant product may in itself determine the scope of the geographical market. Factors such as national preferences or preferences for national brands, language, culture and life style, and the need for a local presence have a strong potential to limit the geographic scope of competition.

47   *Views of customers and competitors.*   Where appropriate, the Commission will contact the main customers and competitors of the parties in its enquiries, to gather their views on the boundaries of the geographic market as well as most of the factual information it requires to reach a conclusion on the scope of the market when they are sufficiently backed by factual evidence.

48   *Current geographic pattern of purchases.*   An examination of the customers' current geographic pattern of purchases provides useful evidence as to the possible scope of the geographic market. When customers purchase from companies located anywhere in the Community or the EEA on similar terms, or they procure their supplies through effective tendering procedures in which companies from anywhere in the Community or the EEA submit bids, usually the geographic market will be considered to be Community-wide.

49   *Trade flows/pattern of shipments.*   When the number of customers is so large that it is not possible to obtain through them a clear picture of geographic purchasing patterns, information on trade flows might be used alternatively, provided that the trade statistics are available with a sufficient degree of detail for the relevant products. Trade flows, and above all, the rationale behind trade flows provide useful insights and information for the purpose of establishing the scope of the geographic market but are not in themselves conclusive.

50   *Barriers and switching costs associated to divert orders to companies located in other areas.*   The absence of trans-border purchases or trade flows, for instance, does not necessarily mean that the market is at most national in scope. Still, barriers isolating the national market have to identified before it is concluded that the relevant geographic market in such a case is national. Perhaps the clearest obstacle for a customer to divert its orders to other areas is the impact of transport costs and transport restrictions arising from legislation or from the nature of the relevant products. The impact of transport costs will usually limit the scope of the geographic market for bulky, low-value products, bearing in mind that a transport disadvantage might also be compensated by a comparative advantage in other costs (labour costs or raw materials). Access to distribution in a given area, regulatory barriers still existing in certain sectors, quotas and custom tariffs might also constitute barriers isolating a geographic area from the competitive pressure of companies located outside that area. Significant switching costs in procuring supplies from companies located in other countries constitute additional sources of such barriers.

51   On the basis of the evidence gathered, the Commission will then define a geographic market that could range from a local dimension to a global one, and there are examples of both local and global markets in past decisions of the Commission.

52   The paragraphs above describe the different factors which might be relevant to define markets. This does not imply that in each individual case it will be necessary to obtain evidence and assess each of these factors. Often in practice the evidence

provided by a subset of these factors will be sufficient to reach a conclusion, as shown in the past decisional practice of the Commission.

IV. CALCULATION OF MARKET SHARE

53   The definition of the relevant market in both its product and geographic dimensions allows the identification of the suppliers and the customers/consumers active on that market. On that basis, a total market size and market shares for each supplier can be calculated on the basis of their sales of the relevant products in the relevant area. In practice, the total market size and market shares are often available from market sources, i.e. companies' estimates, studies commissioned from industry consultants and/or trade associations. When this is not the case, or when available estimates are not reliable, the Commission will usually ask each supplier in the relevant market to provide its own sales in order to calculate total market size and market shares.

54   If sales are usually the reference to calculate market shares, there are nevertheless other indications that, depending on the specific products or industry in question, can offer useful information such as, in particular, capacity, the number of players in bidding markets, units of fleet as in aerospace, or the reserves held in the case of sectors such as mining.

55   As a rule of thumb, both volume sales and value sales provide useful information. In cases of differentiated products, sales in value and their associated market share will usually be considered to better reflect the relative position and strength of each supplier.

V. ADDITIONAL CONSIDERATIONS

56   There are certain areas where the application of the principles above has to be under-taken with care. This is the case when considering primary and secondary markets, in particular, when the behaviour of undertakings at a point in time has to be anal-ysed pursuant to Article [82]. The method of defining markets in these cases is the same, i.e. assessing the responses of customers based on their purchasing decisions to relative price changes, but taking into account as well, constraints on substitution imposed by conditions in the connected markets. A narrow definition of market for secondary products, for instance, spare parts, may result when compatibility with the primary product is important. Problems of finding compatible secondary products together with the existence of high prices and a long lifetime of the primary prod-ucts may render relative price increases of secondary products profitable. A different market definition may result if significant substitution between secondary products is possible or if the characteristics of the primary products make quick and direct consumer responses to relative price increases of the secondary products feasible.

57   In certain cases, the existence of chains of substitution might lead to the definition of a relevant market where products or areas at the extreme of the market are not directly substitutable. An example might be provided by the geographic dimension

of a product with significant transport costs. In such cases, deliveries from a given plant are limited to a certain area around each plant by the impact of transport costs. In principle, such an area could constitute the relevant geographic market. However, if the distribution of plants is such that there are considerable overlaps between the areas around different plants, it is possible that the pricing of those products will be constrained by a chain substitution effect, and lead to the definition of a broader geographic market. The same reasoning may apply if product B is a demand substitute for products A and C. Even if products A and C are not direct demand substitutes, they might be found to be in the same relevant product market since their respective pricing might be constrained by substitution to B.

58   From a practical perspective, the concept of chains of substitution has to be cor-roborated by actual evidence, for instance related to price interdependence at the extremes of the chains of substitution, in order to lead to an extension of the relevant market in an individual case. Price levels at the extremes of the chains would have to be of the same magnitude as well.

3 UK law

Defining the relevant market is also important when considering the application of UK competition rules in a variety of situations. For example, the application of the Chapter I and Chapter II prohibitions under the Competition Act 1998 require a definition of the relevant market; and so do the application of the provisions of the Enterprise Act 2002 in relation to mergers and market inves-tigations.

In line with the approach followed by the European Commission in seeking to provide guidance on how the issue of market definition should be handled, the OFT has published a useful document (*Market Definition* (OFT403)) which explains how it defines the relevant market. The *Guideline* was revised by the OFT in July 2004 in light of Regulation 1/2003, the Modernisation Regulation (see chapter 14). Among other things, the *Guideline* shows that the OFT takes the same view as the European Commission, namely that the issue of market definition is a conceptual framework to use as a tool to determine the market power and potential market power firms possess.

OFT403

The purpose of market definition

2.1   Market definition is not an end in itself but a key step in identifying the competitive constraints acting on a supplier of a given product or service. Market definition provides a framework for competition analysis. For example, market shares can be calculated only after the market has been defined and, when considering the potential for new entry, it is necessary to identify the market that might be entered. Market definition is usually the first step in the assessment of market power.

2.2   Therefore, market definition is important in the process of establishing whether or not particular agreements or conduct fall within the scope of the competition rules:
- Article 81 and section 2(1) of the Act (the Chapter I prohibition) apply only to agreements which have as their object or effect an 'appreciable' prevention, restriction or distortion of competition. The appreciability test usually requires definition of a relevant market and demonstration that the agreement would have an appreciable effect on competition within that market,[7] and
- Article 82 and section 18(1) of the Act (the Chapter II prohibition) apply only to dominant undertakings. The OFT would not consider an undertaking to be dominant unless that undertaking had substantial market power. Market definition is usually the first step in assessing whether an undertaking has substantial market power.

2.3   In addition to its value in providing a framework for competition analysis, an appropriately defined relevant market may provide information that allows an investigation to be closed at an early stage. For analysis under Article 81 and/or the Chapter I prohibition, where an agreement involves undertakings whose combined share of the relevant market is low, the agreement is unlikely to raise competition concerns unless it contains price fixing, market sharing or bid rigging restrictions.[9] Market definition is also important when assessing whether an undertaking's market share is below market share thresholds set out in certain block exemptions.

2.4   For analysis under Article 82 and/or the Chapter II prohibition, undertakings with low market shares will usually not possess market power individually. Therefore, an investigation of an individual undertaking whose market share is low can normally be closed at an early stage.[10]

The hypothetical monopolist test

2.5   The process of defining a market typically begins by establishing the closest substitutes to the product[11] (or group of products) that is the focus of the investigation. These substitute products are the most immediate competitive constraints on the behaviour of the undertaking supplying the product in question. In order to establish

---

7   An exception is where agreements have as their object the prevention, restriction or distortion of competition. In these cases, market definition is not necessarily a pre-requisite for finding an infringement: see Case T-62/98 *Volkswagen AG v Commission* [2000] ECR II-2707 at paragraphs 230 to 232. The relevant market would, however, need to be defined in order to determine the 'relevant turnover' of undertakings for the purpose of assessing the amount of any penalties (see the OFT's *Guidance as to the appropriate amount of a penalty* (OFT423)).

...

9   See the competition law guideline *Article 81 and the Chapter I prohibition* (OFT401).

10 See the competition law guidelines *Article 82 and the Chapter II prohibition* (OFT402) and *Assessment of market power* (OFT415).

11 The focus of the investigation may be a product or a serive. The term 'product' is used for convenience and should be interpreted throughout this guideline to mean good, service or property right.

which products are 'close enough' substitutes to be in the relevant market, a conceptual framework known as the hypothetical monopolist test (the test) is usually employed.

2.6 Before describing the test in detail, it should be emphasised that defining a market in strict accordance with the test's assumptions is rarely possible. Even if the test described below could be conducted precisely, the relevant market is, in practice, no more than an appropriate frame of reference for analysis of the competitive effects. Nevertheless, the conceptual framework of the hypothetical monopolist test is important as it provides a structure within which evidence on market definition can be gathered and analysed.

2.7 In essence the test seeks to establish the smallest product group (and geographical area) such that a hypothetical monopolist controlling that product group (in that area) could profitably sustain 'supra competitive' prices, i.e. prices that are at least a small but significant amount above competitive levels. That product group (and area) is usually the relevant market.

2.8 If, for example, a hypothetical monopolist over a candidate product group could not profitably sustain supra competitive prices, then the candidate product group would be too narrow to be a relevant market. If, on the other hand, a hypothetical monopolist over a subset of a candidate product group could profitably sustain supra competitive prices, then the relevant market would usually be narrower than the candidate product group.

2.9 The steps in applying this approach are as follows. We start by considering a hypothetical monopolist of the focal product (i.e. the product under investigation[12]) which operates in a focal area (i.e. an area under investigation in which the focal product is sold). We assume the hypothetical monopolist supplies no other products and sells in no other areas.

2.10 We then ask whether it would be profitable for the hypothetical monopolist to sustain the price of the focal product a small but significant amount (e.g. 5 to 10 ten per cent[13]) above competitive levels.[14] If the answer to this question is 'yes', the test is complete. The product and area under the hypothetical monopolist's control is (usually) the relevant market.

12 Where there is more than one product under investigation, the test will usually be applied separately for each of the products.
13 The OFT will normally consider a price 5 to 10 per cent above competitive levels to be 'small but significant'. However, this is only as an indicative range. If a price sustained 5 to 10 per cent above competitive levels would not be profitable but a higher price would be, a hypothetical monopolist could profitably sustain prices significantly above competitive levels and so the test is complete.
14 When carrying out the test, we assume that the hypothetical monopolist is not subject to economic regulation that would affect its pricing behaviour and that the prices of products outside of the hypothetical monopolist's control are held constant at their competitive levels. However, while not considered as part of the test, the issues of regulation and the pricing strategies of competitors would be considered as part of the overall competitive assessment.

2.11   If the answer to this question is 'no', this is typically because a sufficiently large number of customers would switch some of their purchases to other substitute products (or areas).[15] In this case, we assume further that the hypothetical monopolist controls both the focal product and its closest substitute.[16] We then repeat the process, but this time in relation to the larger set of products (or areas) under the hypothetical monopolist's control.

2.12   As before, we ask whether it would be profitable to sustain prices 5 to 10 per cent above competitive levels. If so, the test is complete. The relevant market is (usually) the focal product and its closest substitute. If not, we assume the hypothetical monopolist also controls the second closest substitute to the focal product and repeat the process once more. We continue expanding the product group in this way (i.e. by adding in the next best substitute) until we have found a group of products (or areas) for which it is profitable for the hypothetical monopolist to sustain prices 5 to 10 per cent above competitive levels.[17]

2.13   When the test is complete for the first time, the relevant market has usually been defined. However, occasionally it will be appropriate to define the relevant market to be wider than the narrowest product group (or area) that passes the test (see, for example, the discussion of supply side substitution in Parts 3 and 4).

Practical issues

2.14   In practice, defining a market requires balancing various types of evidence and the exercise of judgement. However, it is not an end in itself. Where there is strong evidence that the relevant market is one of a few plausible market definitions, and the competitive assessment is shown to be largely unaltered by which one of these market definitions is adopted, it may not be necessary to define the market uniquely.

---

15 Sometimes the pricing strategy would not be profitable because of responses by other suppliers – this is known as supply side substitution and is discussed in Parts 3 and 4.

16 The best substitute to the focal product could be another product sold in the same area or the focal product sold in a different area.

17 Although the test discussed here refers to a hypothetical monopolist, it should be noted that an undertaking with less than 100 per cent of a relevant market may nevertheless have market power. For example, suppose the market has been defined such that a hypothetical monopolist would profitably sustain prices at, say, 10 per cent above competitive levels. First, since market power is a matter of degree, this leaves sufficient room for an undertaking with less than 100 per cent of the market to exercise market power by sustaining prices above competitive levels, even if that undertaking would not increase prices by as much as a hypothetical monopolist. Second, an undertaking with less than 100 per cent market share may have the ability to weaken any competition that it faces and thereby consolidate its market power even further. Third, undertakings in the market may dampen competition by co-ordinating their behaviour. In the extreme, if they colluded perfectly, a group of undertakings could behave as if they were a hypothetical monopolist. These issues should be considered as part of the assessment of market power. See the competition law guideline *Assessment of market power* (OFT415).

2.15   A market definition should normally contain two dimensions: a product and geo-graphic area.[18] It is often practical to define the relevant product market first and only then to define the relevant geographic market.

...

THE PRODUCT MARKET

The demand side

3.1   This part discusses some of the practical issues that need to be addressed when defining the relevant product market.

3.2   As described above in Part 2, the market definition process usually starts by looking at a relatively narrow potential definition. This would normally be one (or more) of the products which two parties to an agreement both produce, or one (or more) of the products which are the subject of a complaint about conduct, i.e. the focal product (or focal group of products). Previous experience and common sense will normally indicate the narrowest potential market definition, which will be taken as the starting point for the analysis.

3.3   As set out in Part 2, the next question is whether a hypothetical monopolist of the focal product could profitably sustain prices a small but significant amount above competitive levels. The price increase must be large enough that a response from customers is reasonably likely, but not so large that the price rise would inevitably lead to a substantial shift in demand, and so lead to markets being defined so widely that market shares convey no meaningful information on market power. The OFT will normally consider a price 5 to 10 per cent above competitive levels to be 'small but significant'.[19]

3.4   Following the price rise, customers may switch some of their purchases from the focal product to other substitute products (demand side substitution). It is not nec-essary for all customers, or even the majority, to switch. The important factor is whether the volume of purchases likely to be switched is large enough to prevent a hypothetical monopolist profitably sustaining prices 5 to 10 per cent above com-petitive levels.[20]

3.5   Substitute products do not have to be identical to be included in the same market. For example, in its report on *Matches and Disposable Lighters*, the then Monopolies and

---

18 Time is a third dimension that sometimes applies, see Part 5.

19 See Part 5 for a discussion of whether the current price is a reasonable proxy for the competitive price.

20 The customers most likely to switch are sometimes called 'marginal' customers. Where a relatively high proportion of marginal customers purchase a product, a sustained 5 to 10 per cent price rise above competitive levels is less likely to be profitable.
    . . .

Mergers Commission included matches and disposable lighters in the same market because customers viewed them as close substitutes. Similarly, the products' prices do not have to be identical. For example, if two products perform the same purpose, but one is of a higher price and quality, they might be included in the same market. The question is whether the price of one sufficiently constrains the price of the other. Although one is of a lower quality, customers might still switch to this product if the price of the more expensive product rose such that they no longer felt that the higher quality justified the price differential.

3.6   The important issue is whether the undertaking could sustain prices sufficiently above competitive levels. Customers may take time to respond to a sustained rise in the price of the focal product. As a rough rule of thumb, if substitution would take longer than one year, the products to which customers eventually switched would not be included in the same market as the focal product. Products to which customers would switch within a year without incurring significant switching costs[22] are more likely to be included in the relevant market. However, the relevant time period in which to assess switching behaviour may be significantly shorter than one year, for example in industries where transactions are made very frequently. A case by case analysis of switching is therefore appropriate.

3.7   Evidence on substitution from a number of different sources may be considered. Although the information used will vary from case to case and will be considered in the round[23] the following evidence and issues are often likely to be important:

- Evidence from the undertakings active in the market and their commercial strategies may be useful. For example, company documents may indicate which products the undertakings under investigation believe to be the closest substitute to their own products. Company documents such as internal communications, public statements, studies on consumer preferences or business plans may provide other useful evidence.[24]
- Customers and competitors will often be interviewed. In particular, customers can sometimes be asked directly how they would react to a hypothetical price rise, although because of the hypothetical nature of the question, answers may need to be treated with a degree of caution. Survey evidence might also provide information on customer preferences that would help to assess substitutability: for example, evidence on how customers rank particular products, whether and to what extent brand loyalty exists, and which characteristics of products are the most important to their decision to purchase.

---

22 From a customer's point of view, switching costs can be defined as the real or perceived costs that are incurred when changing supplier but which are not incurred by remaining with the current supplier.

23 *Aberdeen Journals Limited v. Office of Fair Trading* [2003] CAT 11 (*Aberdeen Journals (No. 2)*) at [128].

24 *Aberdeen Journals (No. 2)*, at [175] *et seq.*

- A significant factor in determining whether substitution takes place is whether customers would incur costs in substituting products. High switching costs relative to the value of the product will make substitution less likely.
- Evidence on product characteristics may provide useful information where customer substitution patterns are likely to be influenced significantly by those characteristics. Where the objective characteristics of products are very similar and their intended uses the same this would be good evidence that the products are close substitutes. However, the following caveats should be noted. First, even where products apparently have very similar characteristics and intended use, switching costs and brand loyalty may affect how substitutable they are in practice. Second, just because products display similar physical characteristics, this does not necessarily mean that customers would view them to be close substitutes. For example, peak customers may not view rail travel during off peak times to be a close substitute for rail travel at peak times.[25] Third, products with very different physical characteristics may be close substitutes if, from a customer's point of view, they have a very similar use.
- Patterns in price changes can be informative. For example, two products showing the same pattern of price changes, for reasons not connected to costs or general price inflation, would be consistent with (although not proof of) these two products being close substitutes. Customer reactions to price changes in the past may also be relevant. Evidence that a relatively large proportion of customers had switched to a rival product in response to a relatively small price rise in the focal product would provide evidence that these two goods are close substitutes.[27] Equally price divergence over time, without significant levels of substitution, would be consistent with the two products being in separate markets.
- Evidence on own or cross price elasticities of demand may also be examined if it is available. The own price elasticity of demand measures the rate at which demand for a product (e.g. the focal product) changes when its price goes up or down. The cross price elasticity of demand measures the rate at which demand for a product (e.g. a rival product) changes when the price of another product (e.g. the focal product) goes up or down.
- In some cases 'critical loss' analysis may be relevant. One definition of critical loss is the minimum percentage loss in volume of sales required to make a 5 (or 10) per cent price increase on a product unprofitable. The critical percentage tends to be lower when an undertaking has a high mark up over unit costs (since each sale lost entails a relatively large loss in profit). However, the fact that an undertaking can set a high mark up might also demonstrate that its current customer base is not particularly price sensitive. These potentially opposing effects might need to

25 See Part 5 for a discussion of how time may affect market definition.
· · ·

27 Although switching behaviour may be distorted if current prices are significantly different from competitive prices. See Part 5 for a discussion of market definition when prices are not competitive.

be balanced and assessed in conjunction with other evidence (e.g. estimates of elasticities of demand).

• Evidence on the price:concentration relationship may also be informative. Price:concentration studies examine how the price of a product in a distinct area varies according to the number (or share of supply) of other products sold in the same area. These studies are useful where data are available for several distinct areas with varying degrees of concentration. For example, if observations of prices in several geographic areas suggest that when two products are sold in the same area prices are significantly lower than when they are not, this might suggest that the two products are close substitutes (provided that it is possible to distinguish this from the effect of other factors which might explain the price differences).

Price discrimination

3.8   The test described in Part 2 assumes that the hypothetical monopolist charges all customers the same price for the focal product. However, in some cases the hypothetical monopolist may be able to charge some customers a higher price than others, where the price difference is not related to higher costs of serving those customers. This is called 'price discrimination'. Price discrimination requires that customers cannot arbitrage.[28] The undertaking could be able to discriminate between customers due to a variety of reasons, for example:

• some customers may face such high switching costs that they might be 'locked in' to purchasing a particular product (e.g. a customer might use a product as an input to its production process and switching to a rival product might entail costs of quality assuring that product as well as adjusting its production process)

• customer demand may differ according to time, e.g. demand for transport services at peak times is much less price sensitive than off peak demand for the same service, and

• customer demand for an input may differ according to the purpose for which it is used (for example, if different manufacturers transform the same input into different end products, they may have different derived demands for that input).[29]

3.9   Where a hypothetical monopolist would (or would be likely to) price discriminate significantly between groups of customers, each of these groups may form a separate market. If so, a relevant market might be defined as sales of the relevant product in the relevant geographic area to a particular customer group. For example, a hypothetical monopolist of a train service might be able to price discriminate between peak and

---

28 For example, customers purchasing at low prices must not be able to sell on sufficient quantities to customers paying higher prices to undermine price discrimination. Price discrimination by a dominant undertaking is considered in the competition law guideline *Assessment of conduct* (OFT414).

29 Derived demand describes the situation where the input purchaser's demand for the input is derived from the demand for the final product that the input is used to make.

off peak customers. In this case, peak travel and off peak travel might be in separate markets.[30]

Chains of substitution

3.10 Sometimes a focal product will be part of a long and unbroken chain of substitutes. For example, consider 5 products, labelled A to E, which are differentiated by their perceived quality.[31] Assume that the closer two products are in the alphabet, the more substitutable they are from the point of view of customers. Thus consumers whose favourite product is C consider B and D to be very good substitutes for C but consider A and E to be poorer substitutes for C. Even though all products in the chain are substitutes, this does not mean that the whole chain is the relevant market. For example, it may be that a hypothetical monopolist of three products next to each other in the chain could profitably sustain prices 5 to 10 per cent above competitive levels.[32] In short, the hypothetical monopolist test is a way of determining what range of products in the chain constitutes the relevant product market.

The supply side

3.11 This section addresses how the supply side of the market might be relevant to market definition.

3.12 If prices rise, undertakings that do not currently supply a product might be able to supply it at short notice and without incurring substantial sunk costs.[33] This may prevent a hypothetical monopolist profitably sustaining prices 5 to 10 per cent above competitive levels. This form of substitution is carried out by suppliers and hence is known as supply side substitution.

3.13 An example is the supply of paper for use in publishing.[34] Paper is produced in various different grades dependent on the coating used. From a customer's point of view, the different types of paper may not be viewed as substitutes, but because they are produced using the same plant and raw materials, it may be relatively easy for manufacturers to switch production between different grades. A hypothetical monopolist in one grade of paper might not profitably sustain supra competitive

---

30 However, from a supply side perspective peak and off peak travel may be in the same market. Supply side substitution is discussed below.
31 E.g. speed of spin cycle for washing machines, or sharpness of picture definition for digital cameras.
32 It is worth noting that market definition may differ according to the focal product. In the example given, products A, B and C may form the relevant market when product B is the focal product, while products B, C and D may form the relevant market when product C is the focal product.
33 In this context, a sunk cost is a cost incurred on entering a market that is not recoverable on exiting that market. These could, for example, include investments in product placement, distribution, and production technology.
34 The European Commission, in the course of a merger investigation, defined the market for the supply of paper for use in publishing based on supply side substitution in *Torras/Sarrio* Case IV/M166 OJ [1992] C58/00, [1992] 4 CMLR 341.

[41]

prices because manufacturers currently producing other grades would rapidly start supplying that grade.

3.14 Analysing supply side substitution raises similar issues to the analysis of barriers to entry (discussed further in the competition law guideline *Assessment of market power* (OFT415)). Supply side substitution can be thought of as a special case of entry – entry that occurs quickly (e.g. less than one year), effectively (e.g. on a scale large enough to affect prices), and without the need for substantial sunk investments. Supply side substitution addresses the questions of whether, to what extent, and how quickly, undertakings would start supplying a market in response to a hypothetical monopolist attempting to sustain supra competitive prices.

3.15 When assessing the scope for supply side substitution, the evidence from some or all of the following sources may be relevant:
- potential suppliers might be asked whether substitution was technically possible, about the costs of switching production between products, and the time it would take to switch production. The key question is whether it would be profitable to switch production given a small (e.g. 5 to 10 per cent) price increase above competitive levels
- potential suppliers might be asked whether they had spare capacity or were free or willing to switch production. Undertakings may be prevented from switching production because all their existing capacity was tied up, e.g. they may be committed to long term contracts. There might also be difficulties obtaining necessary inputs or finding distribution outlets. Undertakings may be unwilling to switch production from an existing product to a new one, if producing the former product is more profitable than the latter
- although potential suppliers may be able to supply the market, there may be reasons why customers would not use their products, so the views of customers might be sought, and
- more generally customers may also be able to supply wider information about potential suppliers. Customers that are businesses (not consumers) might take actions to encourage potential suppliers to enter.

3.16 There are two ways to account for supply side substitution when defining markets and calculating market shares. First, it might be appropriate to define a market based on the similarity of the conditions of supply. For example, adopting a market definition such as the 'supply of paper for use in publishing' might avoid the need to define and analyse many separate markets for individual grades of paper, for which the competitive assessment was qualitatively similar. If so, market shares would be based on overall capacity to provide paper for use in publishing.

3.17 Second, it might be appropriate to take each existing demand side market, assume prices in that market are sustained 5 to 10 per cent above competitive levels and consider what share of that market would likely be taken by new products produced by potential alternative suppliers in response to that price rise. This share can then be attributed to potential alternative suppliers when calculating market shares.

3.18   The OFT will not factor supply side substitution into market definition unless it is reasonably likely to take place, and already has an impact by constraining the supplier of the product or group of products in question. What matters ultimately is that all competitive constraints from the supply side are properly taken into account in the analysis of market power. Whether a potential competitive constraint is labelled 'supply side substitution' (and so part of market definition) or 'potential entry' (and so not within the market) should not matter for the overall competitive assessment. If there is any serious doubt about whether or not to account for possible supply side substitution when defining the market and calculating market shares, the market will be defined only on the basis of demand side substitutability, and the supply side constraint in question will be considered when analysing potential entry.[35]

THE GEOGRAPHIC MARKET

4.1   Geographic markets are defined using the same process as that used to define product markets. The geographic market may be national (i.e. the United Kingdom), smaller than the United Kingdom (e.g. local or regional), wider than the United Kingdom (e.g. part of Europe including the United Kingdom), or even worldwide. This part outlines some practical issues which are particularly relevant to geographic market definition:
   • demand side issues
   • supply side issues, and
   • imports

The demand side

4.2   As with the product market, the objective is to identify substitutes which are sufficiently close that they would prevent a hypothetical monopolist of the focal product in one area from profitably sustaining prices 5 to 10 per cent above competitive levels. The process starts by looking at a relatively narrow area – the focal area. This might be the area supplied by the parties to an agreement or the subject of a complaint about conduct or, if that area were relatively wide, past experience might suggest a narrower area that is more appropriate. The hypothetical monopolist test is applied to this area, and repeated over wider geographic areas as appropriate until the hypothetical monopolist would find it profitable to sustain prices 5 to 10 per

---

35 Some competition authorities prefer to define markets solely on the demand side, leaving supply side issues to the analysis of new entry. Both approaches are valid and should produce the same conclusions on the question of market power, provided that supply side issues are examined at some point.

cent above competitive levels in the area(s) in question (see Part 2 for further details of the hypothetical monopolist test).

4.3   The principles applied in defining the geographic market are the same as those for the product market. For example, the analysis of price discrimination and chains of substitution would proceed in the same way as set out in Part 3 above. The evidence used to define geographic markets on the demand side will usually be similar to the information used to define the product market (see paragraph 3.7). In addition to that evidence, the value of a product in relation to costs of search and transport is often an important factor in defining geographic markets. The higher the relative value, the more likely customers are to travel further in search of cheaper supplies. The mobility of customers may also be a relevant factor.

4.4   For consumer products, geographic markets may often be quite narrow, e.g. where sufficient numbers of consumers are unlikely to switch to products sold in neighbouring towns or regions, let alone countries. For wholesaling or manufacturing markets, customers may be in a better position to switch between suppliers in different regions, providing transport costs are not too high.

The supply side

4.5   This entails looking at the potential for undertakings in other (e.g. neighbouring) territories to supply the focal area. When defining the geographic market, supply side substitution is analysed using the same conceptual approach set out for the product market. Therefore, the main evidence will usually mirror the information gathered on product market definition (see paragraph 3.15). Where the price of a product is low relative to its transport costs, this might indicate a relatively narrow geographic market.

Imports

4.6   When considering whether the geographic market should be defined more widely than a national market, data on imports may be informative. Significant imports of the product may indicate that the market is wider than a national market. However, the presence of imports in a territory will not always mean that the market is international, for a number of reasons. First, imports may come only from international operations of domestic suppliers, in which case they may not act as an independent constraint on domestic firms. Second, in order to import on a larger scale, international suppliers may require substantial investments in establishing distribution networks or branding their products in the destination country. Third, there may be quotas which limit the volume of imports into the destination country. These factors may mean that suppliers of the relevant product located outside the national market would not provide a sufficient constraint on domestic suppliers to be included in the same relevant geographic market.

4.7   Conversely, a lack of imports does not necessarily mean that the market cannot be international. The potential for imports may still be an important source of substitution should prices rise. For example, when the European Commission looked at a merger between bus manufacturers in Germany, it found that although imports were low at the time, there were no significant barriers to imports from the rest of the Community should prices in Germany rise.[36]

OTHER ISSUES

Temporal markets

5.1   A third possible dimension to market definition is time. Examples of how the timing of production and purchasing can affect markets include:
- peak and off peak services. This can be a factor in transport services or utilities such as electricity supply
- seasonal variations, such as summer versus winter months, and
- innovation/inter-generational products. Customers may defer expenditure on present products because they believe innovation will soon produce better products or because they own an earlier version of the product, which they consider to be a close substitute for the current generation.

5.2   A time dimension might be appropriate where:
- it is not possible for customers to substitute between time periods. For example, peak customers might not view peak and off peak train tickets as substitutes, and
- suppliers cannot substitute between time periods. For example, capacity to produce fruit may vary between time periods and it may not be possible to store fruit from one period to another.

5.3   To some extent, the time dimension is simply an extension of the product dimension: i.e. the product can be defined as the supply of train services at a certain time of day.

The competitive price versus the current price

5.4   Throughout this guideline, the hypothetical monopolist test has been couched in terms of a hypothetical monopolist profitably sustaining prices above competitive levels. However, where an undertaking has market power, it may operate in a market where the current price is substantially different from the competitive price.

5.5   For example, an undertaking with market power may well have already raised prices above competitive levels to its profit maximising level. If so, the undertaking would not profitably sustain prices above current levels. If it tried to sustain higher prices, consumers would switch to purchasing other products. However, it would be wrong to argue that these products prevented the undertaking from exercising market power

36 *Mercedes-Benz/Kassbohrer* Case IV/M477 OJ [1995] L211/1, [1995] 4 CMLR 573.

[45]

and so it would usually be inappropriate to include them in the relevant market. This problem is sometimes known as the cellophane fallacy after a US case involving cellophane products.[37]

5.6   The possibility that market conditions are distorted by the presence of market power (or other factors) will be accounted for when all the evidence on market definition is weighed in the round. For example, where prices are likely to differ substantially from their competitive levels, caution must be exercised when dealing with the evidence on switching patterns as such evidence may not be a reliable guide to what would occur in normal competitive conditions.[38]

Previous cases

5.7   In many cases a market may have already been investigated and defined by the OFT or by another competition authority. Sometimes, earlier definitions can be informative when considering the appropriate product or area to use when commencing the hypothetical monopolist test. However, although previous cases can provide useful information, the market definition used may not always be the appropriate one for future cases. First, competitive conditions may change over time. In particular, innovation may make substitution between products easier, or more difficult, and therefore change the market definition. Therefore, the relevant market concerned must be identified according to the particular facts of the case in hand.[39]

5.8   Second, a previous product market definition that concerned an area outside the United Kingdom, would not necessarily apply to an area in the United Kingdom if the purchasing behaviour of customers differed significantly between those two areas.

5.9   Third, behaviour by an undertaking with market power can affect market definition. For example, suppose an earlier investigation had defined a market to be relatively wide because of the scope for both demand side and supply side substitution. A dominant undertaking in that market might raise customer switching costs or foreclose some possibilities for supply side substitution. If so, this might affect the appropriate definition of the relevant market.

Differentiated products

5.10   When markets contain differentiated products (i.e. products that are differentiated by features such as brand, location or quality) there may not be a clear cut off point delineating the boundary of the market. This can mean that there is no clear distinction between products that are 'in' the market and those that lie outside it.

---

37 *US v El Du Pont de Nemours & Co* [1956] 351 US 377.
38 Evidence on market definition may be distorted if prices are sustained below competitive levels, as, for example, may occur in an investigation of predatory pricing. See *Aberdeen Journals (No. 2)* at [262].
39 *Aberdeen Journals Limited v Director General of Fair Trading* [2002] CAT 4 at [139].

Therefore, even if two products do not lie within the same market for the purposes of one investigation, this does not rule out the possibility that they will be in the same relevant market in another.[40]

Markets with portfolios of products

5.11   In some cases the relevant product market may consist of 'bundles' of what are otherwise distinct products. For example, if a relevant product market was 'one stop grocery shopping', the market may include bundles of groceries that normally make up a weekly shop. Whether this is appropriate depends on the investigation. For example, if the investigation concerned the supply of a particular grocery item to a retailer, it would usually be appropriate to consider that item as a distinct product as opposed to bundled together with other products. The perspective of customers will be important in assessing the appropriate frame of reference.

MARKET DEFINITION FOR AFTER MARKETS

6.1   An after market is a market for a secondary product, that is, a product which is purchased only as a result of buying a primary product. For example, a customer would purchase a printer cartridge (a secondary product) only for use with a printer (the primary product). Another example is replacement heads for razors (the secondary product) and razors (the primary product). The primary product and the secondary product are 'complementary'.[41]

6.2   Three possible ways of approaching market definition in after markets are often put forward:
   • a 'system' market: a unified market for the primary product and the secondary product (e.g. a market for all razors *and* replacement heads)
   • multiple markets: a market for primary products and separate markets for the secondary product(s) associated with each primary product (e.g. one market for all razors, individual markets for each type of replacement head), and
   • dual markets: a market for the primary product and a separate market for the secondary product (e.g. one market for all razors, a separate market for all replacement heads).

40   For example, recall the discussion of chains of substitution at paragraph 3.10 where products A to E were all substitutes for each other (to varying degrees) and where a hypothetical monopolist of three products next to each other in the chain could profitably sustain supra competitive prices. In this case, if the focal product is B alone, it is possible to define products A, B and C to be the relevant market. However, when investigating the conduct of an undertaking that supplies both products B and E, the appropriate frame of reference for the competitive assessment may include products A to E. (Of course, the analysis of competitive effects would account for the fact that customers do not view all products to be equally good substitutes.)

41   Products A and B are complementary products if the demand for product B goes up when the price of product A goes down by a relatively small amount, other things being equal.

6.3   The appropriate definition depends on the facts of the case. A system market is likely to be appropriate where customers engage in 'whole life costing' (see paragraphs 6.5 to 6.6 below), or where effective primary market competition ensures that the overall system price is not excessive, or where reputation effects mean that setting a supra competitive price for the secondary product would significantly harm a supplier's profits on future sales of its primary product.

6.4   Where none of the conditions set out in paragraph 6.3 apply, a multiple markets or a dual markets definition may be appropriate. The former is likely where, having purchased a primary product, customers are locked in to using only a restricted number of secondary products that are compatible with the primary product. A dual markets definition is appropriate where secondary products are compatible with all primary products (and perceived to be so by customers).

Whole life costing

6.5   Whole life costing occurs where customers correctly anticipate the cost of future necessary purchases of the secondary market product when buying the primary product. For example, if a razor (with a 'life' of five replacement heads) costs £10, and each replacement head costs £2, the whole life cost of the razor would be £20. This depends on customers being able to form reasonable expectations on future prices of the secondary product when purchasing the primary product.

6.6   Whole life costing means that customers view the purchase of the primary and secondary product as a 'system', or a unified 'deal'. Whole life costing may mean that a 'system market' definition is appropriate where:
   • it is relatively easy to obtain and comprehend information on the secondary market product, and relatively easy to predict how much of the secondary market product is likely to be required over the life time of the primary product, so that customers are *able* to whole life cost
   • the price of (or likely expenditure on) the secondary product is a relatively high proportion of the primary product's price, so that customers are *likely* to whole life cost, and
   • *sufficient* customers are able and likely to whole life cost so that it would be unprofitable for a supplier to set a supra competitive system price due to the number of customers that would adapt their purchasing behaviour in the primary market (within a reasonable period of time).[42]

Primary market competition

6.7   If suppliers produce both primary products and secondary products, and if, once the primary product is purchased, the same supplier's secondary product must also be purchased (as other suppliers' products would not be compatible), customers can

42 This requires that enough, but not necessarily all, customers whole life cost and that it is not possible to price discriminate between those who do and those who do not.

be said to be 'locked in' once they have made their choice in the primary market. Therefore, customers might appear vulnerable to being charged supra competitive prices in the after market. In this sense, there is arguably a separate market for each secondary product.

6.8   However, the fact that customers may be locked in to particular after market purchases does not necessarily mean that, overall, a supplier can profitably sustain a system price above competitive levels. If there is effective competition in the primary market, undertakings would not earn excessive profits overall as any profits extracted in the after market would be 'competed away' in the primary market, resulting in lower priced primary products.[43] In this situation, a 'system' market definition is usually appropriate.

6.9   In short, where customers are locked in to purchasing a particular secondary product once they have purchased a primary product, competition problems are possible although they are more likely to arise where an undertaking has market power in the primary market.[44]

Reputation

6.10   A supplier might not wish to increase prices of its secondary product for existing customers if that would earn it a reputation for exploitation and significantly reduce its ability to attract new or repeat customers to its primary product. Reputation is more likely to be important where suppliers have the prospect of relatively large numbers of new or repeat customers and where undertakings cannot price discriminate between new or repeat customers and other customers.

4 Comments

Clearly, there are many similarities between the Commission's *Notice* and the OFT's *Guideline*. There are several points which should be made in relation to the principles covered in these key documents.

(A) General observations

It is obvious that market definition is a step that must be taken in order to be able to make a particular assessment: for example, to establish the existence of a dominant position under Article 82 and the Chapter II prohibition. Therefore, it is described as a means and not an end. It is helpful and, in many respects, vital. For example it allows authorities to do the following:

---

43 This would occur even if customers do not whole life cost.
44 It should be noted that even if the overall system price is not excessive, the relative prices of the primary and secondary goods are not necessarily optimal.

- define the boundaries of competition in a particular market, including identifying in a systematic way whether competitive constraints on the behaviour of firms exist;
- calculate the market shares of the operators in the market; and
- establish a framework for applying the various competition rules.

(B) Basic principles of market definition

There are three dimensions to market definition: relevant product market, relevant geographical market and (rarely) relevant temporal market.

I Relevant product market

The legal test for defining the relevant market is that of interchangeability, i.e. whether products X, Y and Z are interchangeable or substitutable. This test was formulated by the ECJ in *Continental Can* (see paragraph 32 of the judgment).

Interchangeability in the vast majority of cases is considered from the demand side of the market, meaning from the customer's perspective; though in some cases the supply side of the market will be considered as well. This normally happens in cases where an assessment of the demand side of the market provides insufficient or inconclusive information on how the relevant product market should be defined. In paragraph 22 of the *Notice on Market Definition* the Commission gives as an example the production of paper. Looking at the supply side of the market entails identifying firms who are able to switch to producing an additional product, (such as metal enclosures surplus to in-house requirements in *Continental Can*) as a response to an increase in the price of such products. (See paragraph 36 of that judgment for the ECJ's assessment). Substitution at the supply level should only be taken into account when the switch in production will happen within a period short enough that does not imply a significant adjustment of existing assets (like machinery) of the firm.

Several factors can be relied upon when measuring interchangeability. These include physical characteristics, intended use and price. Consideration of 'physical characteristics' involves looking at things like the shape and perhaps size of the product under consideration (usually the product which the firm under investigation makes) and comparing it with other products. 'Intended use' involves an enquiry into the particular use the customer intends for the product under consideration and whether another product could satisfy that intended use. 'Price' is a factor considered under EC and UK competition law, as in other jurisdictions such as the USA, using the so-called SSNIP test (Small but Significant Non-transitory Increase in Price). In the decisional practice of the EC and UK competition authorities, this test plays a major role when defining the relevant product market and takes the form of the following question: If there is a small (which is quantified for guidance purposes as 5–10 per cent) non-transitory (meaning permanent) increase in the price of product X (the product under consideration) will customers purchasing X switch to purchasing product Y? An affirmative answer would mean that X and Y are in the same relevant product market.

It is important to note that while in practice the relevant product market is defined in a large number of cases using the hypothetical SSNIP test, there are situations where price is not the only factor taken into account when examining interchangeability. Under EC competition law, for example, while the Commission places heavy emphasis in its *Notice* on price, the ECJ has continued to emphasise the significance of other factors, such as physical characteristics and intended use. In the UK, the OFT has stated that it will not necessarily rely on the SSNIP test in every single case, for example, in those cases where it may be difficult to quantify the 5–10 per cent increase in price.

II Relevant geographic market

The relevant geographic market is defined as a geographical area in which the firms under examination are involved in the supply and demand matrix of the relevant product and services (determined following a definition of the relevant product market). The conditions of competition in this area must be sufficiently homogeneous, and it will be regarded as distinct from neighbouring geographical areas because the conditions of competition prevalent in those areas are appreciably different.

As in the case of the relevant product market, the SSNIP test may be used when defining the relevant geographic market, but with a slight difference. In this context the question posed above will be rephrased as follows: would the customers of firm A switch to readily available substitutes or firms located in other geographical areas in response to a small but significant (5–10 per cent) permanent increase in the price of the product offered by firm A. An answer in the affirmative would lead to these other areas being included in the relevant geographical market.

As one might appreciate, however, the SSNIP test may not be conclusive in this context; therefore looking at additional factors may be helpful and indeed vital. These factors include past evidence of diversion of orders from one geographical area to other geographical areas and the customers' current geographic pattern of purchases; trade flows; the nature of demand for the relevant product; national preferences or preferences for national brands; culture and lifestyle; and language. Furthermore, factors such as barriers and switching costs for firms located in other areas may also be taken into account. An important factor which is perhaps the clearest hurdle for customers and firms to divert their orders and supplies to other areas is the impact of transport costs and transport restrictions which may follow from the existence of specific national laws or the nature of the relevant products. Moreover, there is no doubt that the size, fragility and weight of products, and the physical geographic characteristics of some countries can have a serious impact on transport costs and hence the scope of the geographic market. This factor is compounded where the product has a relatively low price and must be transported in great volumes. On the other hand, the existence or absence of different kinds of regulatory barriers is also relevant when defining the relevant geographical market.

A note of caution should be inserted here, however, namely that there is no scope for applying a single standard in all situations. Defining the relevant geographical market varies according to the relevant geographical location. This is a point of particular significance in the context of comparing EC and UK competition law. In the EC, for example, as a result of the fact that it is a community of independent countries, the exercise would be far more complex than the case in the UK, which is a single country and where, unlike the EC situation, issues of single market objective and market integration, cultural/linguistic differences, regulatory barriers or national preferences are not relevant.

III Relevant temporal market

A third dimension to market definition may be relevant in some cases. This dimension is referred to as the relevant temporal market and which is defined with reference to time. Examples of the relevant temporal market can be found in part 5 of the OFT *Guideline* and include inter-generational products, peak and off-peak services and products or services the supply, consumption or receipt of which depends on seasonal variations (e.g. ice cream or Christmas decorations).

(C) Sources of information when defining the relevant market

Numerous sources could prove valuable for a competition authority when seeking to define the relevant market. The parties involved may be required to provide a definition of the relevant market. For example, under Regulation 139/2004 (see chapter 10), the Commission asks and expects the firms concerned to define the relevant market and to provide very detailed additional information to allow it to examine the definition given by the parties. In addition, market studies conducted by independent bodies, such as consumer associations and consultancy practices, and the views of customers and competitors of the parties may be taken into account by a competition authority. When a competition authority carrieds an investigation it will request information from both customers and competitors. Such requests are frequently extremely detailed, so as to assist the authority in defining both product and geographic markets.

On the basis of all of this information, and that which may come from other sources, a competition authority can be expected to be in a position to establish the relevant markets concerned or, at least, the few possible relevant markets. In fact, in view of the constraints on resources, many competition authorities define the relevant markets only when strictly necessary. In the area of EC merger control, for instance, if none of the conceivable alternative market definitions for the operation in question gives rise to competition concerns, the Commission normally does not reach a conclusive finding on the issue of market definition and leaves the question open (for an example, see the Commission's decision in *Schibsted/Telia/Telenor*, extracted at pp. 497–506 below).

Further reading

Baker and Wu 'Applying the market definition guidelines of the European Commission' (1998) 19 ECLR 273
Bishop and Walker *The Economics of EC Competition Law* (Sweet & Maxwell, 2002)

3
Collusion between undertakings: the prohibition

1 Introduction

A basic but fundamental concern of competition law is the prevention of collusion between firms which has harmful effects on competition and often leads to the detriment of consumers. For this reason, systems of competition law have specific provisions and mechanisms for dealing with situations where firms tend to collude. The task of a competition authority or court is to determine whether a particular situation infringes such provisions and subsequently to decide how to deal with it.

Both the EC and UK systems of competition law include specific provisions against collusion between undertakings. These are found in Article 81 EC and in the Chapter I prohibition of the Competition Act 1998 (CA1998) respectively.

The aim of this chapter is to provide a general overview of the elements of these two provisions. Their application in specific situations, for example in relation to vertical agreements and horizontal agreements, is covered in later chapters of the book.

2 EC law

(A) Introduction to Article 81

Article 81 EC is an extremely important provision of the competition law chapter of the EC Treaty. The Article declares:

1   The following shall be prohibited as incompatible with the common market: all agreements between undertakings, decisions by association of undertakings and concerted practices which may affect trade between Member States and which have as their object or effect the prevention, restriction or distortion of competition within the common market, and in particular those which:
  a) directly or indirectly fix purchase or selling prices or any other trading conditions;
  b) limit or control production, markets, technical development or investment;
  c) share markets or sources of supply;
  d) apply dissimilar conditions to equivalent transactions with other trading parties, thereby placing them at a competitive disadvantage;
  e) make the conclusion of contracts subject to acceptance by other trading parties of supplementary obligations which, by their nature or according to commercial usage, have no connection with the subject of such contracts.

2   Any agreements or decisions prohibited pursuant to this Article shall be automatically void.

3   The provisions of paragraph 1 may, however, be declared inapplicable in the cases of:
   – any agreement or category of agreement between undertakings;
   – any decision or category of decisions by associations of undertakings;
   – any concerted practice or category of concerted practices;
   which contributes to improving the production or distribution of goods or to promoting technical or economic progress, while allowing consumers a fair share of the resulting benefit, and which does not:
   a) impose on the undertakings concerned restrictions which are not indispensable to the attainment of these objectives;
   b) afford such undertakings the possibility of eliminating competition in respect of a substantial part of the products in question.

The structure of Article 81 was outlined briefly in chapter 1. There are three individual paragraphs: 81(1) contains the prohibition, 81(2) declares that an agreement, decision by association of undertakings or concerted practice infringing paragraph (1) is void, and 81(3) affords an exemption where the specific criteria set out in that paragraph are met.

The aim of Article 81 is to preclude restrictive (commonly referred to as anti-competitive) agreements and other forms of collusion between independent firms whether in horizontal relationships (operating at the same level of the market, for example, two manufacturers of competing products) or, vertical relationships (operating at different levels of the market, for example, a supplier and a distributor).

Of course, whether an agreement is caught by Article 81(1) depends on policy objectives being pursued under the provision. An important point to note, as should be apparent from chapter 1, is that, like EC competition law in general, Article 81 is used to achieve objectives that go beyond the maximisation of consumer welfare in an economic technical sense. Special reference should be made here to the single market objective, which is of primary importance under EC competition rules.

The following discussion will consider the first paragraph of Article 81; the second and third paragraphs of the Article will be dealt with in the following chapter.

(B) Elements of Article 81(1)

Finding a breach of Article 81(1) requires showing:
• the existence of *undertakings*
• *collusion* between those undertakings: agreement, decision or concerted practice

- the collusion has as its *object or effect* the prevention, restriction or distortion of competition
- an *effect on trade* between Member States
- the effect on both competition and trade (notes 3 and 4) is not *de minimis* (meaning the effect is *appreciable*)

These ingredients will be considered in turn:

I Existence of undertakings

(a) What is an undertaking?

The definition of an undertaking (a concept that appears elsewhere in the competition law chapter of the EC, including Article 82 and Regulation 139/2004) does not come from the EC Treaty but from the case law of the ECJ. Numerous cases have dealt with this concept and demonstrate that it is defined very widely. In *Höfner and Elser v. Macrotron* the ECJ observed at paragraph 21, that there is one key characteristic: 'the concept of an undertaking encompasses every entity engaged in an economic activity, regardless of the legal status of the entity and the way in which it is financed'.

This important statement has recently been complemented by the ECJ's judgment in the case of *Wouters* (facts set out below at p. 69) in which the ECJ decided that Members of the Bar of Amsterdam are undertakings for the purposes of Article 81(1) (a finding that, according to the ECJ, is not affected by the fact that the practice of the profession is regulated and that the services offered by members of the Bar are complex and technical in nature). In establishing that members of the Bar carry on an economic activity, the ECJ referred in paragraph 48 to the fact that:

48   Members of the Bar offer, for a fee, services in the form of legal assistance consisting in the drafting of opinions, contracts and other documents and representation of clients in legal proceedings. In addition, they bear the financial risks attaching to the performance of those activities since, if there should be an imbalance between expenditure and receipts, they must bear the deficit themselves.

This finding should be considered alongside paragraphs 50–64 of this judgment in which the ECJ dealt with the question of whether the Bar of the Netherlands was an 'association of undertakings', a concept which is dealt with below. The basic point to note about the concept of an undertaking that emerges from *Höfner* and *Wouters*, however, is that the nature of the entity engaged in an economic activity, its legal status and the way in which it is financed are irrelevant.

(b) Examples of undertakings

The following are examples of bodies that have been regarded as undertakings for the purposes of Article 81: natural persons, such as artists or inventors

(*Remia BV v. Commission*), a pension fund (*Albany International BV v. Stitching*), sporting bodies, such as The International Federation of Football Association (*Distribution of Package Tours During the 1990 World Cup*), customs agents (*Commission v. Italy* (1998)) and public bodies or corporations, such as the Federal Employment Office in Germany (*Höfner*); in relation to the last example, it is worth noting that a body will not be caught where and to the extent it is exercising public law powers (*Corinne Bodson v. Pompes Funèbres*). Recently, the ECJ held in *AOK Bundesverband and others v. Ichthyol-Gesellschaft Cordes, Hermani & Co and others* that the sickness funds in the German statutory health insurance scheme were not undertakings since their activities are not economic in nature. The ECJ also held that groups representing those bodies, such as the fund associations, were not 'associations of undertakings' for the purposes of Article 81(1).

(c) The 'single economic unit' situation

There are many situations in the business world where undertakings may be 'linked' in such a way as to form what is known as a 'single economic entity'. An obvious example is a parent and its subsidiary. Whether Article 81(1) applies to an agreement between undertakings that form a single economic entity has been considered by the Commission, the CFI and the ECJ on several occasions; many of the ECJ's judgments are helpful on this issue. They include *Corinne Bodson, Centrafarm v. Sterling, ICI v. Commission, Béguelin Imports v. GL Imports Export* and *Viho v. Commission*. Under this line of case law it is clear that Article 81(1) does not apply in the case of a parent-subsidiary situation where the subsidiary lacks real freedom to determine its own course of conduct on the market. In *Viho* the ECJ gave a very clear and detailed analysis of this issue. In the case, Parker Pen Ltd sold stationery products through local subsidiaries on terms specific to the local market and refused to deal on other terms with Viho Europe BV, a Dutch office equipment wholesaler and would-be distributor. Viho applied to the Commission for a declaration that Parker's business structure constituted 'agreements between undertakings' in breach of Article 81(1). The ECJ said the following:

15   It should be noted, first of all, that it is established that Parker holds 100% of the shares of its subsidiaries in Germany, Belgium, Spain, France and the Netherlands and that the sales and marketing activities of its subsidiaries are directed by an area team appointed by the parent company and which controls, in particular, sales targets, gross margins, sales costs, cash flow and stocks. The area team also lays down the range of products to be sold, monitors advertising and issues directives concerning prices and discounts.

16   Parker and its subsidiaries thus form a single economic unit within which the subsidiaries do not enjoy real autonomy in determining their course of action in the

market, but carry out the instructions issued to them by the parent company controlling them.

17   In those circumstances, the fact that Parker's policy of referral, which consists essentially in dividing various national markets between its subsidiaries, might produce effects outside the ambit of the Parker group which are capable of affecting the competitive position of third parties cannot make Article [81(1)] applicable, even when it is read in conjunction with Article 2 and Article 3 (c) and (g) of the Treaty. On the other hand, such unilateral conduct could fall under Article [82] of the Treaty if the conditions for its application, as laid down in that article, were fulfilled.

18   The Court of First Instance was therefore fully entitled to base its decision solely on the existence of a single economic unit in order to rule out the application of Article [81(1)] to the Parker group.

It is important to note that the single economic unit situation is different from that of the 'succession', where, for example, A (infringing competition rules) and B (not infringing competition rules), two independent autonomous firms may later become one as a result of B taking over A. Such a situation demands careful consideration, especially because the Commission may want to impose penalties in relation to the infringement committed by A. For further discussion of this issue see *Compagnie Royale v. Commission* and *All Weather Sports Benelux BV v. Commission*.

II Forms of collusion

This section considers the forms of collusion which may be caught under Article 81(1): Agreements, decisions and concerted practices. By way of a general comment on these three terms one should note that they are interpreted very widely.

(a) Agreement

What amounts to an agreement for the purposes of Article 81(1) has been a contentious issue in the case law. However, one thing is abundantly clear: an agreement does not have to be in writing. Oral, informal and gentlemen's agreements all fall within the scope of the Article. All that seems to be required for there to be an agreement under Article 81(1) is some form of consensus between two or more undertakings – also referred to as a 'meeting between minds' or a 'concurrence of wills' (see the recent judgment of the CFI in *Volkswagen AG v. Commission* (2003)). Clearly, an agreement can be bilateral or multi-lateral. The judgment of the CFI in *Bayer v. Commission* (with which the ECJ agreed on appeal (*Commission v. Bayer*)) is a useful examination of the meaning of agreement.

Commission v. Bayer AG [2004] 4 CMLR 13

Bayer AG, the parent in a major European pharmaceutical group, was a manufacturer and supplier of Adalat, the price of which was fixed by health authorities
in France and Spain at a level about 40% less than the UK price. Wholesalers
in Europe, exploiting the price difference, began parallel-importing to the UK.
In response, Bayer's subsidiaries imposed a policy of refusing to supply French
and Spanish wholesalers beyond certain levels. The Commission viewed this
as a tacit agreement between Bayer and the wholesalers contrary to Article
[81(1)]. Bayer who contested the Commission decision before the CFI argued
that the Decision penalises unilateral conduct outside the scope of the Article and claimed that the Commission had given the concept of an agreement
a meaning beyond the precedents in the case-law on Article 81(1). The CFI
annulled the Commission Decision. An appeal was made to the ECJ.

CFI

66   The case-law shows that, where a decision on the part of a manufacturer constitutes
      unilateral conduct of the undertaking, that decision escapes the prohibition in Article
      [81(1)] of the Treaty ...

67   It is also clear from the case-law in that in order for there to be an agreement within
      the meaning of Article [81(1)] of the Treaty it is sufficient that the undertakings in
      question should have expressed their joint intention to conduct themselves on the
      market in a specific way ...

68   As regards the form in which that common intention is expressed, it is sufficient for
      a stipulation to be the expression of the parties' intention to behave on the market
      in accordance with its terms ...

69   It follows that the concept of an agreement within the meaning of Article [81(1)]
      of the Treaty, as interpreted by the case-law, centres around the existence of a
      concurrence of wills between at least two parties, the form in which it is manifested
      being unimportant so long as it constitutes the faithful expression of the parties'
      intention.

70   In certain circumstances, measures adopted or imposed in an apparently unilateral
      manner by a manufacturer in the context of his continuing relations with his dis-
      tributors have been regarded as constituting an agreement within the meaning of
      Article [81(1)] of the Treaty ...

71   That case-law shows that a distinction should be drawn between cases in which
      an undertaking has adopted a genuinely unilateral measure, and thus without the
      express or implied participation of another undertaking, and those in which the
      unilateral character of the measure is merely apparent. Whilst the former do not
      fall within Article [81(1)] of the Treaty, the latter must be regarded as revealing an
      agreement between undertakings and may therefore fall within the scope of that

article. That is the case, in particular, with practices and measures in restraint of competition which, though apparently adopted unilaterally by the manufacturer in the context of its contractual relations with its dealers, nevertheless receive at least the tacit acquiescence of those dealers.

72   It is also clear from that case-law that the Commission cannot hold that apparently unilateral conduct on the part of a manufacturer, adopted in the context of the contractual relations which he maintains with his dealers, in reality forms the basis of an agreement between undertakings within the meaning of Article [81(1)] of the Treaty if it does not establish the existence of an acquiescence by the other partners, express or implied, in the attitude adopted by the manufacturer ...

The judgment of the CFI in *Bayer v. Commission* is a highly interesting one which must be regarded as correct in law. On the facts of the case, the CFI's criticism of the Commission seems justified. Particularly noteworthy is paragraph 69 in which the CFI states that the concept of an agreement centres upon the existence of a concurrence of wills between at least two undertakings.

This judgment is significant on different levels. At one level, it is arguable that this is a judgment about the promotion of the single market objective and the fact that it has not (yet) been achieved in the pharmaceutical market. At a conceptual level, the CFI makes an important point about whether unilateral behaviour on the part of undertakings can be caught by Article 81(1) or falls within the remit of Article 82. The distinction which the CFI makes in this case is between genuine and merely apparent unilateral behaviour: clearly the CFI puts the latter within the scope of the concept of agreements caught by Article 81(1) while the former is outside. Conceptually, this seems to be correct and it is also helpful that this analysis is in fact consistent with several other judgments (referred to by the CFI in its judgment) in which this issue was also considered. See *Ford v. Commission, AEG Telefunken v. Commission, Sandoz v. Commission, Tipp-ex GmbH v. Commission, Volkswagen AG v. Commission* (2000) (upheld on appeal by the ECJ in *Volkswagen AG v. Commission* (2003)).

However, the Commission's appeal against the ruling of the CFI was set within the context of the promotion of the single market objective. The Commission argued that the CFI ruling moved the goalposts of what the Commission must establish in order to prove an agreement for the purposes of Article 81(1) existed and called into question its policy of fighting trading restrictions aiming to hinder parallel import. On the Commission's side Sweden intervened in support of parallel imports. Bayer argued that the Commission was improperly equating the role of Article 28 (Member State measures preventing free movement of goods) with an infringement of Article 81(1), thereby attempting to harmonise the price of pharmaceutical products without any adjustment in the Member State laws. The proper route, rather, was under Article 28, attacking the laws that led to price differences. The ECJ heard argument on the following pleas made by the appellants as to the required characteristics of an agreement.

A system for monitoring and penalties for non-compliance

80   In examining the alleged intention of Bayer to impose an export ban, the Court of First Instance held, on the one hand, that the Commission has not proved to the requisite legal standard either that Bayer France and Bayer Spain imposed an export ban on their respective wholesalers, or that Bayer established a systematic monitoring of the actual final destination of the packets of Adalat supplied after the adoption of its new supply policy ... or that it made supplies of this product conditional on compliance with the alleged export ban (paragraph 109 of the judgment under appeal).

81   Moreover, in its further examination as to whether, as alleged, the wholesalers intended to adhere to Bayer's policy, the Court recalled, referring to what it had just held, that the Commission has not sufficiently established in law that Bayer adopted a systematic policy of monitoring the final destination of the packets of Adalat supplied, that it applied a policy of threats and penalties against wholesalers who had exported them, that, therefore, Bayer France and Bayer Spain imposed an export ban on their respective wholesalers, or, finally, that supplies were made conditional on compliance with the alleged export ban (paragraph 119 of the judgment under appeal).

82   It is clear from that judgment that, in holding that there was no system of subsequent monitoring and penalties established by Bayer, the Court's intention was, first, to reply to the factual argument raised by the Commission that Bayer had imposed an export ban on the wholesalers which was put in place by identifying the exporting wholesalers and applying successive reductions in the volumes of medicinal products delivered to them if it became apparent that they were exporting all or part of those products.

83   Secondly, the Court of First Instance did not in any event consider that the absence of a system of subsequent monitoring and penalties in itself implied the absence of an agreement prohibited by Article [81(1)] of the Treaty. On the other hand, such an absence was regarded as one of the relevant factors in the analysis concerning Bayer's alleged intention to impose an export ban and, therefore, the existence of an agreement in this case. In that regard, although the existence of an agreement does not necessarily follow from the fact that there is a system of subsequent monitoring and penalties, the establishment of such a system may nevertheless constitute an indicator of the existence of an agreement.

84   Concerning the complaints of alleged misinterpretation of the judgments in *Sandoz* and *Ford*, on the ground that, in those judgments, the Court of Justice did not examine whether there was a system of subsequent monitoring and penalties before holding that there was an agreement prohibited by Article [81(1)] of the Treaty, it should be reiterated that verification of the existence of such a system is not necessary in all cases for an agreement contrary to that provision to be considered to have been concluded.

85   In *Sandoz*, the manufacturer had sent invoices to its suppliers carrying the express words export prohibited, which had been tacitly accepted by the suppliers... The Court could therefore hold that there was an agreement prohibited by Article [81(1)], without being required to seek proof of that in the existence of a system of subsequent monitoring.

86   In *Ford*, the Court of Justice assimilated to an agreement the decision of a motor manufacturer not to supply right-hand drive vehicles to German dealers in order to remove the possibility of them exporting those cars to the United Kingdom market. It is sufficient to note, in the context of the present plea, that, in this case, there was a simple refusal to sell and not a sale allegedly subject to certain conditions imposed on distributors and that, therefore, a system of subsequent monitoring would in any event have been superfluous.

87   As for the arguments of the Commission, the Kingdom of Sweden and EAEPC [European Association of Euro Pharmaceutical Companies], to the effect that a system of subsequent controls was required by the system preventing supply established by Bayer, it should be noted that those arguments tend to underline the unilateral character of the latter's actions as regards the restriction of parallel imports.

88   The mere fact that the unilateral policy of quotas implemented by Bayer, combined with the national requirements on the wholesalers to offer a full product range, produces the same effect as an export ban does not mean either that the manufacturer imposed such a ban or that there was an agreement prohibited by Article [81(1)] of the Treaty.

89   Therefore, in holding that the Commission had not established to the requisite legal standard the existence of a system of subsequent monitoring and penalties on wholesalers, the Court of First Instance has not erred in law. The Court must therefore dismiss the plea by BAI and the Commission arguing that such a system of subsequent controls and penalties on wholesalers is not a precondition for the existence of an agreement within the meaning of Article [81(1)] of the Treaty.

...

Need for the manufacturer to require a particular line of conduct from the wholesalers or to seek to obtain their adherence to its policy

96   It does not appear from the judgment under appeal that the Court of First Instance took the view that an agreement within the meaning of Article [81(1)] of the Treaty could not exist unless one business partner demands a particular line of conduct from the other.

97   On the contrary, in paragraph 69 of the judgment under appeal, the Court of First Instance set out from the principle that the concept of an agreement within the meaning of Article [81(1)] of the Treaty centres around the existence of a concurrence of wills between at least two parties, the form in which it is manifested being

unimportant so long as it constitutes the faithful expression of the parties' intention. The Court further recalled, in paragraph 67 of the same judgment, that for there to be an agreement within the meaning of Article [81(1)] of the Treaty it is sufficient that the undertakings in question should have expressed their common intention to conduct themselves on the market in a specific way.

98   Since, however, the question arising in this case is whether a measure adopted or imposed apparently unilaterally by a manufacturer in the context of the continuous relations which it maintains with its wholesalers constitutes an agreement within the meaning of Article [81(1)] of the Treaty, the Court of First Instance examined the Commission's arguments, as set out in recital 155 of the contested decision, to the effect that Bayer infringed that article by imposing an export ban as part of the ... continuous commercial relations [of Bayer France and Bayer Spain] with their customers, and that the wholesalers' subsequent conduct reflected an implicit acquiescence in that ban (paragraph 74 of the judgment under appeal).

99   Concerning the argument that the Court of First Instance wrongly considered it necessary to prove an express export ban on the part of Bayer, it is clear from the Court's analysis concerning the system for monitoring the distribution of the consignments of Adalat delivered (see paragraphs 44 to 48 of this judgment) that it did not in any way require proof of an express ban.

100   Concerning the appellants' arguments that the Court of First Instance should have acknowledged that the manifestation of Bayer's intention to restrict parallel imports could constitute the basis of an agreement prohibited by Article [81(1)] of the Treaty, it is true that the existence of an agreement within the meaning of that provision can be deduced from the conduct of the parties concerned.

101   However, such an agreement cannot be based on what is only the expression of a unilateral policy of one of the contracting parties, which can be put into effect without the assistance of others. To hold that an agreement prohibited by Article [81(1)] of the Treaty may be established simply on the basis of the expression of a unilateral policy aimed at preventing parallel imports would have the effect of confusing the scope of that provision with that of Article [82] of the Treaty.

102   For an agreement within the meaning of Article [81(1)] of the Treaty to be capable of being regarded as having been concluded by tacit acceptance, it is necessary that the manifestation of the wish of one of the contracting parties to achieve an anti-competitive goal constitute an invitation to the other party, whether express or implied, to fulfil that goal jointly, and that applies all the more where, as in this case, such an agreement is not at first sight in the interests of the other party, namely the wholesalers.

103   Therefore, the Court of First Instance was right to examine whether Bayer's conduct supported the conclusion that the latter had required of the wholesalers, as a condition of their future contractual relations, that they should comply with its new commercial policy.

104   Concerning the judgment in *Sandoz*, relied upon by the appellants, it is undisputed that, in that case, the manufacturer had sought the cooperation of wholesalers in order to eliminate or reduce parallel imports, their cooperation being necessary, in the circumstances of that case, in order to attain that objective. In such a context, the insertion by the manufacturer of the words export prohibited on invoices amounted to a demand for a particular line of conduct on the part of the wholesalers. That is not the case here.

105   The appellants have also relied on the judgments in *AEG* and *Ford*, arguing that, in those judgments, in the context of apparently unilateral measures adopted by the manufacturer in relation to its distributors, the Court held that there was an agreement within the meaning of Article [81(1)] of the Treaty without enquiring as to the existence of a demand on the part of that manufacturer.

106   However, the need to demonstrate the conclusion of an agreement within the meaning of Article [81(1)] of the Treaty did not arise in those cases. The question there was whether the measures adopted by the manufacturers formed part of the selective distribution agreements previously concluded between the manufacturers and their distributors and, therefore, whether those measures had to be taken into account in order to assess the compatibility of those agreements with the competition rules.

107   In *AEG*, the manufacturer had, in applying a selective distribution agreement which had previously been adjudged compatible with Article [81(1)] of the Treaty, begun to refuse to approve distributors who met the qualitative criteria of that agreement, and did so in order to maintain a high level of prices or to exclude certain modern channels of distribution. It was thus a question of establishing whether the Commission could base its investigation on the conduct adopted by the manufacturer when applying a selective distribution agreement in order to determine whether that agreement, as applied in a particular case, was contrary to Article [81(1)] of the Treaty.

108   In *Ford*, the Court stated in paragraph 12 of its judgment that [t]he applicants and the Commission all agree that the main issue in this case is whether the Commission was entitled to refuse an exemption under Article [81(3)] of the Treaty for Ford AG's main dealer agreement by reason of the fact that that undertaking had discontinued supplies of right-hand-drive cars to its German distributors.

109   Therefore, the existence of an agreement capable of infringing Article [81(1)] of the Treaty having already been established, the Court was able to confine itself in those cases to examining the question whether measures subsequently adopted by the manufacturer formed part of the agreement in question and whether they ought, therefore, to be taken into account when examining the compatibility of that agreement with Article [81(1)]. Such a question does not therefore correspond to that raised in this case, which is whether the very existence of an anti-competitive agreement has been established. The appellants cannot therefore rely on *AEG* and

Ford in support of their argument that an agreement prohibited by Article [81(1)] of the Treaty has come into existence.

110   As for the arguments of the Kingdom of Sweden and EAEPC, who argue that a demand arises from the combined effect of Bayer's quota policy and the obligation which wholesalers are under to maintain national stocks, without there being any need for an express demand that exports be limited, it is sufficient to note that such an argument merely serves to demonstrate the unilateral nature of Bayer's commercial policy, which could be carried out without the cooperation of the wholesalers. As it has already been established that the judgments in *AEG* and *Ford* do not apply to this case, the interveners cannot rely on them in support of their arguments either. Therefore, the mere fact that there is a hindrance to parallel imports is not sufficient to demonstrate the existence of an agreement prohibited by Article [81(1)] of the Treaty.

111   In the light of the above, the argument based on the need for the manufacturer to require a particular line of conduct from the wholesalers must be rejected.

. . .

The true intention of the wholesalers as a factor in establishing the 'meeting of minds'

118   On the substance, it should be recalled that the Court of First Instance set out from the general principle that in order for there to be an agreement within the meaning of Article [81(1)] of the Treaty it is sufficient that the undertakings in question should have expressed their joint intention to conduct themselves on the market in a specific way (paragraph 67 of the judgment under appeal). Having concluded, when examining the alleged intention of Bayer to impose an export ban, that the latter had not imposed such a ban, the Court of First Instance proceeded to make an analysis of the wholesalers' conduct in order to determine whether there was nevertheless an agreement prohibited by Article [81(1)] of the Treaty.

119   In that context, it first rejected the argument that an agreement was established by reason of a tacit acceptance by the wholesalers of the alleged export ban, since, as it had just held, the Commission had not sufficiently established in law either that Bayer had imposed such a ban or that the supply of medicinal products was conditional on compliance with that alleged ban (see paragraphs 119 and 122 of the judgment under appeal).

120   In those circumstances, the Court of First Instance went on to examine whether having regard to the actual conduct of the wholesalers following the adoption by the applicant of its new policy of restricting supplies, the Commission could legitimately conclude that they acquiesced in that policy (paragraph 124 of the judgment under appeal).

121   The Court of First Instance thus sought to determine whether, in the absence of an export ban, the wholesalers nevertheless shared the intention of Bayer to prevent parallel imports. In the context of that analysis, the Court of First Instance did not make any error of law by referring to the genuine wishes of the wholesalers to continue ordering medicinal products for export and for the needs of the national market.

122   In any event, as the Advocate General points out in point 108 of his Opinion, the plea concerning the absence of a meeting of minds presupposes that there was a declared intention on the part of the wholesalers to join in with the intention of Bayer to prevent parallel imports. However, as has been pointed out in paragraphs 52 and 53 of this judgment, the Court of First Instance held that the documents supplied by the Commission do not establish that the wholesalers wished to give Bayer the impression that, in response to its declared wish, they were proposing to reduce their orders to a given level.

123   The wholesalers' strategy was, on the contrary, by distributing orders for export amongst the various branches, to make Bayer believe that the needs of the national markets had grown. Far from establishing the existence of a meeting of minds, that strategy merely constituted an attempt by the wholesalers to turn to their advantage the application of Bayer's unilateral policy, the implementation of which did not depend on their cooperation.

124   It follows that the Court must dismiss as unfounded the plea that the Court of First Instance was wrong to find a lack of concordance between the wishes of Bayer and the wishes of the wholesalers concerning Bayer's policy seeking to reduce parallel imports.

. . .

The need for subsequent acquiescence with measures forming part of business relations under existing general agreements as acceptance

141   . . . The mere concomitant existence of an agreement which is in itself neutral and a measure restricting competition that has been imposed unilaterally does not amount to an agreement prohibited by [Article 81(1)]. Thus, the mere fact that a measure adopted by a manufacturer, which has the object or effect of restricting competition, falls within the context of continuous business relations between the manufacturer and its wholesalers is not sufficient for a finding that such an agreement exists.

142   The case of *Sandoz* concerned an export ban imposed by a manufacturer in the context of continuous business relations with wholesalers. The Court of Justice held that there was an agreement prohibited by Article [81(1)] of the Treaty. However, as the Court of First Instance points out in paragraphs 161 and 162 of the judgment under appeal, that conclusion was based upon the existence of an export ban imposed by the manufacturer which had been tacitly accepted by the wholesalers. In that

regard, at paragraph 11 of the *Sandoz* judgment, the Court of Justice held that [t]he repeated orders of the products and the successive payments without protest by the customer of the prices indicated on the invoices, bearing the words export prohibited, constituted a tacit acquiescence on the part of the latter in the clauses stipulated in the invoice and the type of commercial relations underlying the business relations between Sandoz PF and its clientele. The existence of a prohibited agreement in that case therefore rested not on the simple fact that the wholesalers continued to obtain supplies from a manufacturer which had shown its intention to prevent exports, but on the fact that an export ban had been imposed by the manufacturer and tacitly accepted by the wholesalers. Therefore, the appellants cannot usefully rely on the *Sandoz* judgment in support of their plea that the Court of First Instance erred in law by requiring acquiescence of the wholesalers in the measures imposed by the manufacturer.

The ECJ makes several important points that should be emphasised. First, the existence of measures hindering parallel import is not *per se* evidence of any agreement (paragraph 110). Second, it can sometimes be relevant to look at the other party's true intention to determine whether a measure is actually unilateral (paragraph 121), but in this case the policy did not require any co-operation by the wholesalers. Third, continuing to engage in business relations under non-offending agreements while being subject to the imposition of uni-lateral behaviour is not necessarily evidence of an agreement to accept the latter (paragraph 141).

Finally, the difference between the application of Article 81 and Article 82 is the existence of an agreement, the latter is concerned with unilateral conduct and only applies to undertakings with a dominant market position (see chapter 9). As the ECJ stated:

70   The attempt to use Article [81(1)] of the Treaty to penalise an undertaking not in a dominant position which decides to refuse deliveries to wholesalers, in order to prevent them from making parallel exports, clearly disregards the necessary conditions for applying Article [81] and the general system of the Treaty. Under that system, measures adopted by a Member State which prevent parallel exports are indeed prohibited by Article [28] of the Treaty, but unilateral measures taken by private undertakings are subject to restrictions, by virtue of the principles of that Treaty, only if the undertaking in question occupies a dominant position on the market, within the meaning of Article [82] of the Treaty, which is not the case here.

(b) Single overall agreement

In some situations, the degree, nature of involvement and participation of firms in an agreement varies from time to time, with the result that one firm could be said to have participated in some of the meetings but was not always involved in the operation of the agreement. In other words, this is a situation comprising several sub-agreements. Of course, one option open to the Commission when examining such agreements is to establish the existence of each individual agreement. However, this increases the burden on the Commission enormously. For this reason, the Commission has turned to a 'single overall agreement' concept, which has also been upheld by the Community Courts. This means that in some cases where detailed arrangements or different sub-agreements exist, the Commission's approach will be to bind these together and conclude that a single overall agreement existed without looking at the sub-agreements individually. This approach has been applied and upheld in a number of cases: see Commission's decisions in *Polypropylene* and *PVC* and judgment of CFI in *Tréfileurope v. Commission*.

(c) Decision by associations of undertakings

Article 81(1) also prohibits decisions taken by an association of undertakings. This serves to preclude the possibility of firms colluding with one another in ways other than by agreement, especially where trade associations are concerned. In fact, trade associations have sometimes been used as vehicles by firms to drive down the road to collusion. Whether a decision has been made by an association of undertakings in this case is interpreted very widely and can include rules or regulation made by an association of undertakings such as those contained in its constitution (*National Sulphuric Acid Association*), the code or regulations under which its members operate (*Visa International – Multilateral Interchange Fee*) and even non-binding recommendations by the association (*VDS v. Commission*).

Whether there is an association of undertakings is an important preliminary question, and on which the judgment of *Wouters* provides helpful guidance (considered above in the context of the term undertaking, and further below at pp. 234–240), in which the ECJ found that a professional organisation that enjoys regulatory powers, such as the Bar of the Netherlands, constitutes an association of undertakings and is within the scope of application of Article 81.

Wouters v. Nederlandse Orde van Advocaten [2002] ECR I-1577

The applicants sought to challenge a Dutch prohibition on partnerships between lawyers and accountants ('Regulation 1993'). The measure was designed to safeguard independence of legal advisors and professional ethics. An Article 234 referral was made to the ECJ asking, *inter alia*, whether a professional regulatory association could be an 'association of undertakings' for the purpose of Article 81. That being so, the ECJ considered whether such a prohibition could have an adverse effect on competition affecting trade between Member States and what criteria would be relevant in such a determination.

ECJ

58   When it adopts a regulation such as the 1993 Regulation, a professional body such as the Bar of the Netherlands is neither fulfilling a social function based on the principle of solidarity, unlike certain social security bodies (*Poucet and Pistre* ...), nor exercising powers which are typically those of a public authority (*Sat Fluggesellschaft* ...). It acts as the regulatory body of a profession, the practice of which constitutes an economic activity.

59   In that respect, the fact that Article 26 of the Advocatenwet also entrusts the General Council with the task of protecting the rights and interests of members of the Bar cannot *a priori* exclude that professional organisation from the scope of application of Article [81] of the Treaty, even where it performs its role of regulating the practice of the profession of the Bar ...

60   Next, other indications support the conclusion that a professional organisation with regulatory powers, such as the Bar of the Netherlands, cannot escape the application of Article [81] of the Treaty.

61   First, it is clear from the Advocatenwet that the governing bodies of the Bar are composed exclusively of members of the Bar elected solely by members of the profession. The national authorities may not intervene in the appointment of the members of the Supervisory Boards, College of Delegates or the General Council ...

62   Second, when it adopts measures such as the 1993 Regulation, the Bar of the Netherlands is not required to do so by reference to specified public-interest criteria. Article 28 of the Advocatenwet, which authorises it to adopt regulations, does no more than require that they should be in the interest of the 'proper practice of the profession' ...

63   Lastly, having regard to its influence on the conduct of the members of the Bar of the Netherlands on the market in legal services, as a result of its prohibition of certain multi-disciplinary partnerships, the 1993 Regulation does not fall outside the sphere of economic activity.

Having found that the Bar of the Netherlands was an association of undertakings, the ECJ then added at paragraph 66 of its judgment that it is immaterial that the constitution of the Bar of the Netherlands was regulated by public law. Furthermore, the legal framework within which decisions by an association of undertakings are taken and how Member States classify such a framework in their domestic laws are not relevant when considering the application of Article 81(1). With regard to Regulation 1993, the ECJ stated in paragraph 64 that the Regulation constitutes an expression of intent of the delegates of the members of the Bar to act in a particular manner in carrying on their economic activity.

(d) Concerted practice

It would be wrong to think it is easy for a competition authority to establish the existence of an anti-competitive agreement between firms. The fact is that firms engaging in anti-competitive behaviour have developed, especially in recent years, extremely sophisticated means of hiding or destroying evidence relating to their behaviour and operating in secret. This makes the task of a competition authority to prove an infringement of the competition rules hugely difficult, if not sometimes impossible. For this reason, the EC system of competition law – like scores of other systems around the world – includes a 'safety net', which is found in the concept of a concerted practice.

Conceptually, a concerted practice is not easy to define with certainty, and its application to the facts of a given case is inherently difficult because it depends on circumstantial evidence. A situation in which the application of the concept is particularly difficult is the parallel behaviour/oligopolistic interdependence situation (considered in chapter 7).

The two most important cases to consider in understanding the meaning of a concerted practice are *ICI v. Commission ('Dyestuffs')* (for facts see pp. 269–276 below) and the *Sugar Cartel* case. In *ICI*, the ECJ stated as follows:

64   Article [81] draws a distinction between the concept of 'concerted practices' and that of 'agreements between undertakings' or of 'Decisions by associations of undertakings'; the object is to bring within the prohibition of that Article a form of coordination between undertakings which, without having reached the stage where an agreement properly so-called has been concluded, knowingly substitutes practical cooperation between them for the risks of competition.

65   By its very nature, then, a concerted practice does not have all the elements of a contract but may *inter alia* arise out of coordination which becomes apparent from the behaviour of the participants.

A 'concerted practice' is therefore a form of coordination between undertakings where parties have not reached the stage of an actual agreement, but knowingly coordinate their actions and cooperate instead of competing with one another. This may lead to abnormal competitive conditions on a given market. According to the ECJ, such practical cooperation amounts to a 'concerted practice', particularly if it enables the firms concerned to 'consolidate established positions to the detriment of effective freedom of movement of the products in the common market and of the freedom of consumers to choose their suppliers' (paragraph 68). In practice ascertaining whether a concerted practice exists is sometimes a very difficult task. on occasion activities which may seem innocent to a business person may in fact be concerted practices. For example, if one firm accepts complaints from another to the effect that competition from the former is damaging to the latter, then this conduct may amount to a concerted practice. However, where a firm aligns its price to the highest price charged by a competitor, this is not necessarily evidence of a concerted practice but may be explained by an attempt to obtain the maximum profit (see chapter 7).

In the second case, *Sugar Cartel*, the ECJ repeated its definition of concerted practices from *Dyestuffs*, adding that establishing a concerted practice can only be properly evaluated if the facts relied on (by the Commission) are considered as a *whole* after taking into account the characteristics of the market in question. In the case, the applicant sugar suppliers sought to challenge a Commission Decision alleging breaches of Articles 81 and 82 by measures protecting the sugar market of Italy, the Netherlands and parts of Germany. The market was unusual in that there was a quota system of production, affecting competition on the supply side. However, lack of barriers between Member States, flexibility in dealer prices, evidence of negotiations, and non-price factors left a residual field of competition. The evidence showed that deliveries were consistently channelled to designated consignees rather than end customers, a policy implemented by both Belgian and Dutch producers. The ECJ said as follows on the concept of concerted practice:

173   The criteria of coordination and cooperation laid down by the case-law of the court, which in no way require the working out of an actual plan, must be understood in the light of the concept inherent in the provisions of the Treaty relating to competition that each economic operator must determine independently the policy which he intends to adopt on the common market including the choice of the persons and undertakings to which he makes offers or sells.

174   Although it is correct to say that this requirement of independence does not deprive economic operators of the right to adapt themselves intelligently to the existing and anticipated conduct of their competitors, it does however strictly preclude any direct or indirect contact between such operators, the object or effect whereof is either to influence the conduct on the market of an actual or potential competitor or to disclose to such a competitor the course of conduct which they themselves have decided to adopt or contemplate adopting on the market.

In paragraph 191, the ECJ went on to set out what has become a classically broad definition of a concerted practice: the applicants infringed the prohibition, 'because they knowingly substituted for the risks of competition practical cooperation between them, which culminated in a situation which did not correspond to the normal conditions of the market'.

Dyestuffs and *Sugar Cartel* make clear that a concerted practice is different from an agreement and that the working out of an actual plan is not necessary. Furthermore, for a concerted practice to be caught by Article 81(1) the Commission does not need to show that it has anti-competitive effects on the market (See *Hüls AG v. Commission*). Obviously, this makes the task of the

Commission much easier when seeking to declare that a particular behaviour is a concerted practice or significant evidence of it.

(e) Comment on classification of agreement and concerted practice

An apposite question to ask under Article 81(1) is whether in any given situation the Commission could adopt a joint classification of an agreement/concerted practice in order to establish an infringement. This question has been raised on several occasions, in particular by firms who were keen to undermine the Commission's finding that their behaviour amounted to a breach of Article 81(1). The Community Courts have aided the Commission quite considerably in this respect by holding that joint classification was permissible where an alleged breach of Article 81(1) includes elements of both an agreement and a concerted practice. This means that the Commission does not have to prove both an agreement and a concerted practice throughout the duration of the breach (see *Commission v. Anic*).

III Preventing, restricting or distorting competition: the object or effect requirement

For an agreement to be caught by Article 81(1) it must have as its object or effect a 'restriction of competition'. There are examples in the Article itself of the kinds of agreements that may be caught under the provision: price-fixing, market-sharing agreements etc. However, it is important to note that this list is not exhaustive and other examples have emerged under the case law.

There are several key points to note. The first is that 'object' or 'effect' are alternatives and not cumulative. This point was made by the ECJ in *Société Technique Minière v. Maschinenbau Ulm* ('STM').

This means that where an agreement clearly has the object of restricting competition (such as one set out in the examples in Article 81(1)(a)–(e)), one does not need to go further and prove its effect. For example, in *Consten and Grundig v. Commission* (discussed further in chapter 5) the agreement in question had a clause granting a distributor absolute territorial protection, which was held to have the 'object' of restricting competition. However, when the ECJ does not believe that the agreement in question aims to restrict competition, it must therefore go on to consider its effect. A good example (besides *STM*) is *Javico v. Yves St Laurent*.

Javico International and Javico AG v. Yves Saint Laurent Parfums SA ('YSLP') [1998] ECR I-1983

The dispute in this case, which led to an Article 234 reference, concerned a contract under which Javico International agreed to sell YSLP's luxury cosmetic products in the Ukraine, Russia and Slovenia (non-Member States) and undertook not to re-import them back into the EC. The ECJ considered the applicability of Article 81(1) to this situation.

ECJ

12   In order to determine whether agreements such as those concluded by YSLP with Javico fall within the prohibition laid down by that provision it is necessary to consider whether the purpose or effect of the ban on supplies which they entail is to restrict to an appreciable extent competition within the common market and whether the ban may affect trade between Member States.

13   As far as agreements intended to apply within the Community are concerned, the Court has already held that an agreement intended to deprive a reseller of his commercial freedom to choose his customers by requiring him to sell only to customers established in the contractual territory is restrictive of competition within the meaning of Article [81(1)] of the Treaty ...

14   Similarly, the Court has held that an agreement which requires a reseller not to resell contractual products outside the contractual territory has as its object the exclusion of parallel imports within the Community and consequently restriction of competition in the common market... Such provisions, in contracts for the distribution of products within the Community, therefore constitute by their very nature a restriction of competition ...

...

19   In the case of agreements of this kind, stipulations of the type mentioned in the question must be construed not as being intended to exclude parallel imports and marketing of the contractual product within the Community but as being designed to enable the producer to penetrate a market outside the Community by supplying a sufficient quantity of contractual products to that market. That interpretation is supported by the fact that, in the agreements at issue, the prohibition of selling outside the contractual territory also covers all other non-member countries.

20   It follows that an agreement in which the reseller gives to the producer an undertaking that he will sell the contractual products on a market outside the Community cannot be regarded as having the object of appreciably restricting competition within the common market or as being capable of affecting, as such, trade between Member States.

21   Consequently, the agreements at issue, in that they prohibit the reseller Javico from selling the contractual product outside the contractual territory assigned to it, do not constitute agreements which, by their very nature, are prohibited by Article [81(1)] of the Treaty. Similarly, the provisions of the agreements in question, in that they prohibit direct sales within the Community and re-exports of the contractual product to the Community, cannot be contrary, by their very nature, to Article [81(1)] of the Treaty.

22 Although the contested provisions of those agreements do not, by their very nature, have as their object the prevention, restriction or distortion of competition within the common market within the meaning of Article [81(1)], it is, however, for the national court to determine whether they have that effect. Appraisal of the effects of those agreements necessarily implies taking account of their economic and legal context . . . and, in particular, of the fact that YSLP has established in the Community a selective distribution system enjoying an exemption.

23 In that regard, it is first necessary to determine whether the structure of the Community market in the relevant products is oligopolistic, allowing only limited competition within the Community network for the distribution of those products.

24 It must then be established whether there is an appreciable difference between the prices of the contractual products charged in the Community and those charged outside the Community. Such a difference is not, however, liable to affect competition if it is eroded by the level of customs duties and transport costs resulting from the export of the product to a non-member country followed by its re-import into the Community.

25 If that examination were to disclose that the contested provisions of the agreements concerned had the effect of undermining competition within the meaning of Article [81(1)] of the Treaty, it would also be necessary to determine whether, having regard to YSLP's position on the Community market and the extent of its production and its sales in the Member States, the contested provisions designed to prevent direct sales of the contractual products in the Community and re-exports of them to the Community entail any risk of an appreciable effect on the pattern of trade between the Member States such as to undermine attainment of the objectives of the common market.

26 In that regard, intra-Community trade cannot be appreciably affected if the products intended for markets outside the Community account for only a very small percentage of the total market for those products in the territory of the common market.

27 It is for the national court, on the basis of all the information available to it, to determine whether the conditions are in fact fulfilled for the agreements at issue to be caught by the prohibition laid down in Article [81(1)] of the Treaty.

Having made these points, the ECJ summarised what have become known as the 'Javico Criteria' in paragraph 28 of the judgment:

28 Accordingly, the answer to the first question must be that Article [81(1)] of the Treaty precludes a supplier established in a Member State of the Community from imposing on a distributor established in another Member State to which the supplier entrusts the distribution of his products in a territory outside the Community a prohibition of making any sales in any territory other than the contractual territory, including

the territory of the Community, either by direct marketing or by re-exportation from the contractual territory, if that prohibition has the effect of preventing, restricting or distorting competition within the Community and is liable to affect the pattern of trade between Member States. This might be the case where the Community market in the products in question is characterised by an oligopolistic structure or by an appreciable difference between the prices charged for the contractual product within the Community and those charged outside the Community and where, in view of the position occupied by the supplier of the products at issue and the extent of the supplier's production and sales in the Member States, the prohibition entails a risk that it might have an appreciable effect on the pattern of trade between Member States such as to undermine attainment of the objectives of the common market.

Establishing the effect of an agreement is a much harder task than determining its object, given the depth of economic analysis required to establish the relevant market and alleged anti-competitive effects. In *Brasserie de Haecht v. Wilkin*, the ECJ stated that considering the effect of an agreement under Article 81(1) requires having regard to the economic and legal context of the agreement in order to evaluate the context in which such effect occurs. Chapter 5 which deals with vertical agreements considers the issue of effect in more detail.

In April 2004, the Commission published, as part of the Commission's Modernisation Package, a Notice entitled *Guidelines on the application of Article 81(3)*. Although the subject matter of the *Notice* is largely irrelevant to the present discussion (but is discussed further in the next chapter), paragraphs 21–27 deal with the requirement of object or effect under Article 81(1) and for this reason it would be helpful to include them here.

Guidelines on the application of Article 81(3)

21 Restrictions of competition *by object* are those that by their very nature have the potential of restricting competition. These are restrictions which in light of the objectives pursued by the Community competition rules have such a high potential of negative effects on competition that it is unnecessary for the purposes of applying Article 81(1) to demonstrate any actual effects on the market. This presumption is based on the serious nature of the restriction and on experience showing that restrictions of competition by object are likely to produce negative effects on the market and to jeopardise the objectives pursued by the Community competition rules. Restrictions by object such as price fixing and market sharing reduce output and raise prices, leading to a misallocation of resources, because goods and services demanded by customers are not produced. They also lead to a reduction in consumer welfare, because consumers have to pay higher prices for the goods and services in question.

22 The assessment of whether or not an agreement has as its object the restriction of competition is based on a number of factors. These factors include, in particular, the

content of the agreement and the objective aims pursued by it. It may also be necessary to consider the context in which it is (to be) applied and the actual conduct and behaviour of the parties on the market.[27] In other words, an examination of the facts underlying the agreement and the specific circumstances in which it operates may be required before it can be concluded whether a particular restriction constitutes a restriction of competition by object. The way in which an agreement is actually implemented may reveal a restriction by object even where the formal agreement does not contain an express provision to that effect. Evidence of subjective intent on the part of the parties to restrict competition is a relevant factor but not a necessary condition.

23   Non-exhaustive guidance on what constitutes restrictions by object can be found in Commission block exemption regulations, guidelines and notices. Restrictions that are blacklisted in block exemptions or identified as hardcore restrictions in guidelines and notices are generally considered by the Commission to constitute restrictions by object. In the case of horizontal agreements restrictions of competition by object include price fixing, output limitation and sharing of markets and customers.[28] As regards vertical agreements the category of restrictions by object includes, in particular, fixed and minimum resale price maintenance and restrictions providing absolute territorial protection, including restrictions on passive sales.[29]

24   If an agreement is not restrictive of competition by object it must be examined whether it has restrictive effects on competition. Account must be taken of both actual and potential effects.[30] In other words the agreement must have likely anti-competitive effects. In the case of restrictions of competition by effect there is no presumption of anti-competitive effects. For an agreement to be restrictive by effect it must affect actual or potential competition to such an extent that on the relevant market negative effects on prices, output, innovation or the variety or quality of goods and services can be expected with a reasonable degree of probability.[31] Such negative effects must be appreciable. The prohibition rule of Article 81(1) does

---

27 See Joined Cases 29/83 and 30/83, *CRAM and Rheinzink*, [1984] ECR 1679, paragraph 26, and Joined Cases 96/82 and others, *ANSEAU-NAVEWA*, [1983] ECR 3369, paragraphs 23–25.

28 See the Guidelines on horizontal cooperation agreements, paragraph 25, and Article 5 of Commission Regulation 2658/2000 on the application of Article 81(3) of the Treaty to categories of specialisation agreements, OJ 2000 L 304, p. 3.

29 See Article 4 Commission Regulation 2790/1999 on the application of Article 81(3) of the Treaty to categories of vertical agreements and concerted practices, OJ 1999 L 336, p. 21, and the *Guidelines on Vertical Restraints* ..., paragraph 46 *et seq.* See also Case 279/87, *Tipp-Ex*, [1990] ECR I- 261, and Case T-62/98, *Volkswagen v Commission*, [2000] ECR II-2707, paragraph 178.

30 See paragraph 77 of the judgment in *John Deere* ...

31 It is not sufficient in itself that the agreement restricts the freedom of action of one or more of the parties, see paragraphs 76 and 77 of the judgment in *Métropole television (M6)* ... This is in line with the fact that the object of Article 81 is to protect competition on the market for the benefit of consumers.

not apply when the identified anti-competitive effects are insignificant.[32] This test reflects the economic approach which the Commission is applying. The prohibition of Article 81(1) only applies where on the basis of proper market analysis it can be concluded that the agreement has likely anti-competitive effects on the market.[33] It is insufficient for such a finding that the market shares of the parties exceed the thresholds set out in the Commission's *de minimis* notice. Agreements falling within safe harbours of block exemption regulations may be caught by Article 81(1) but this is not necessarily so. Moreover, the fact that due to the market shares of the parties, an agreement falls outside the safe harbour of a block exemption is in itself an insufficient basis for finding that the agreement is caught by Article 81(1) or that it does not fulfil the conditions of Article 81(3). Individual assessment of the likely effects produced by the agreement is required.

25   Negative effects on competition within the relevant market are likely to occur when the parties individually or jointly have or obtain some degree of market power and the agreement contributes to the creation, maintenance or strengthening of that market power or allows the parties to exploit such market power. Market power is the ability to maintain prices above competitive levels for a significant period of time or to maintain output in terms of product quantities, product quality and variety or innovation below competitive levels for a significant period of time. In markets with high fixed costs undertakings must price significantly above their marginal costs of production in order to ensure a competitive return on their investment. The fact that undertakings price above their marginal costs is therefore not in itself a sign that competition in the market is not functioning well and that undertakings have market power that allows them to price above the competitive level. It is when competitive constraints are insufficient to maintain prices and output at competitive levels that undertakings have market power within the meaning of Article 81(1).

26   The creation, maintenance or strengthening of market power can result from a restriction of competition between the parties to the agreement. It can also result from a restriction of competition between any one of the parties and third parties, e.g. because the agreement leads to foreclosure of competitors or because it raises competitors' costs, limiting their capacity to compete effectively with the contracting parties. Market power is a question of degree. The degree of market power normally required for the finding of an infringement under Article 81(1) in the case of agreements that are restrictive of competition by effect is less than the degree of market power required for a finding of dominance under Article 82.

---

32 See e.g. Case 5/69, *Völk*, [1969] ECR 295, paragraph 7. Guidance on the issue of appreciability can be found in the *Commission Notice on agreements of minor importance* which do not appreciably restrict competition under Article 81(1) of the Treaty, OJ 2001 C, 368, p. 13. The notice defines appreciability in a negative way. Agreements, which fall outside the scope of the *de minimis* notice, do not necessarily have appreciable restrictive effects. An individual assessment is required.

33 See in this respect Joined Cases T-374/94 and others, *European Night Services*, [1998] ECR II-3141.

27   For the purposes of analysing the restrictive effects of an agreement it is normally necessary to define the relevant market. It is normally also necessary to examine and assess, *inter alia*, the nature of the products, the market position of the parties, the market position of competitors, the market position of buyers, the existence of potential competitors and the level of entry barriers. In some cases, however, it may be possible to show anti-competitive effects directly by analysing the conduct of the parties to the agreement on the market. It may for example be possible to ascertain that an agreement has led to price increases. The guidelines on horizontal cooperation agreements and on vertical restraints set out a detailed framework for analysing the competitive impact of various types of horizontal and vertical agreements under Article 81(1).

Particularly useful to note in the *Notice* is the discussion of market power (starting at paragraph 25), which could have arisen or may arise as a result of the agreement between the parties. In addition, it is worth mentioning paragraph 18 of the *Notice* in which the Commission sets out two important questions: (1) Does the agreement restrict actual or potential competition? (2) Would actual or potential competition exist without the alleged restrictions? As the Commission explains, the second question looks at the *objective necessity* of the restriction in a given agreement. According to the Commission, these questions provide a useful framework for assessing whether an agreement is restrictive of competition.

IV May affect trade between Member States

An agreement which may affect trade between Member States is within the scope of Article 81(1). Essentially, this requirement defines the boundary between the application of EC competition law and domestic competition rules of the Member States. Thus, Article 81(1) will not apply where this jurisdictional requirement is not satisfied. This requirement has been widely construed, and even agreements entered into by firms from one and the same Member State can be caught (*Vereeniging van Cementhandelaren (VCH) v. Commission*).

Since Article 81 entered into force, the Commission has always relied on the case law of the ECJ when assessing whether the requirement of effect on trade between Member States is satisfied. Numerous cases have dealt with this issue, including the test used to determine its application. A key case to mention in this regard is *STM* where the ECJ stated that:

> For this requirement to be fulfilled it must be possible to foresee with a sufficient degree of probability on the basis of a set of objective factors of law or of fact that the agreement in question may have an influence, direct or indirect, actual or potential, on the pattern of trade between Member States.

The previously cited Commission Modernisation Package includes a Notice entitled the *Guidelines on effect on trade between Member States* in which it explains the meaning of the requirement, the test to be used and how the Commission believes it ought to be handled. The *Notice* is based on the case law of the Community Courts but is without prejudice to further judicial interpretation. Students, in particular, are strongly encouraged to read the Notice.

Guidelines on the effect on trade OJ (2004) C 101/81

2.2 *The concept of 'trade between Member States'*

19   The concept of 'trade' is not limited to traditional exchanges of goods and services across borders.[10] It is a wider concept, covering all cross-border economic activity including establishment.[11] This interpretation is consistent with the fundamental objective of the Treaty to promote free movement of goods, services, persons and capital.

20   According to settled case law the concept of 'trade' also encompasses cases where agreements or practices affect the competitive structure of the market. Agreements and practices that affect the competitive structure inside the Community by eliminating or threatening to eliminate a competitor operating within the Community may be subject to the Community competition rules.[12] When an undertaking is or risks being eliminated the competitive structure within the Community is affected and so are the economic activities in which the undertaking is engaged.

21   The requirement that there must be an effect on trade between Member States. implies that there must be an impact on cross-border economic activity involving at least two Member States. It is not required that the agreement or practice affect trade between the whole of one Member State and the whole of another Member State. Articles 81 and 82 may be applicable also in cases involving part of a Member State, provided that the effect on trade is appreciable.[13]

22   The application of the effect on trade criterion is independent of the definition of relevant geographic markets. Trade between Member States may be affected also in cases where the relevant market is national or sub-national.

---

10 Throughout these guidelines the term 'products' covers both goods and services.
11 See Case 172/80, *Züchner*, [1981] ECR p. 2021, paragraph 18. See e.g. Case C-309/99, *Wouters*, [2002] ECR I-1577, paragraph 95, Case C-475/99, *Ambulanz Glöckner*, [2001] ECR I-8089, paragraph 49, Joined Cases C-215/96 and 216/96, *Bagnasco*, [1999] ECR I-135, paragraph 51, Case C-55/96, *Job Centre*, [1997] ECR I-7119, paragraph 37, and Case C-41/90, *Höfner and Elser*, [1991] ECR I-1979, paragraph 33.
12 See e.g. Joined Cases T-24/93 and others, *Compagnie maritime belge*, [1996] ECR II-1201, paragraph 203, and paragraph 23 of the judgment in *Commercial Solvents* cited.
13 See e.g. Joined Cases T-213/95 and T-18/96, *SCK and FNK*, [1997] ECR II-1739.
     . . .

2.3. The notion 'may affect'

23   The function of the notion 'may affect' is to define the nature of the required impact on trade between Member States. According to the standard test developed by the Court of Justice, the notion 'may affect' implies that it must be possible to foresee with a sufficient degree of probability on the basis of a set of objective factors of law or fact that the agreement or practice may have an influence, direct or indirect, actual or potential, on the pattern of trade between Member States.[15] [16] As mentioned in paragraph 20 above the Court of Justice has in addition developed a test based on whether or not the agreement or practice affects the competitive structure. In cases where the agreement or practice is liable to affect the competitive structure inside the Community, Community law jurisdiction is established.

24   The 'pattern of trade'-test developed by the Court of Justice contains the following main elements, which are dealt with in the following sections:
(a) 'A sufficient degree of probability on the basis of a set of objective factors of law or fact',
(b) An influence on the 'pattern of trade between Member States',
(c) 'A direct or indirect, actual or potential influence' on the pattern of trade.

2.3.1. A sufficient degree of probability on the basis of a set of objective factors of law or fact

25   The assessment of effect on trade is based on objective factors. Subjective intent on the part of the undertakings concerned is not required. If, however, there is evidence that undertakings have intended to affect trade between Member States, for example because they have sought to hinder exports to or imports from other Member States, this is a relevant factor to be taken into account.

26   The words 'may affect' and the reference by the Court of Justice to 'a sufficient degree of probability' imply that, in order for Community law jurisdiction to be established, it is not required that the agreement or practice will actually have or

---

15 See e.g. the judgment in Züchner cited in footnote 11 and Case 319/82, *Kerpen & Kerpen*, [1983] ECR 4173, Joined Cases 240/82 and others, *Stichting Sigarettenindustrie*, [1985] ECR p. 3831, paragraph 48, and Joined Cases T-25/95 and others, *Cimenteries CBR*, [2000] ECR II-491, paragraph 3930.

16 In some judgments mainly relating to vertical agreements the Court of Justice has added wording to the effect that the agreement was capable of hindering the attainment of the objectives of a single market between Member States, see e.g. Case T-62/98, *Volkswagen*, [2000] ECR II-2707, paragraph 179, and paragraph 47 of the *Bagnasco* judgment . . . , and Case 56/65, *Société Technique Minière*, [1966] ECR 337. The impact of an agreement on the single market objective is thus a factor which can be taken into account.

has had an effect on trade between Member States. It is sufficient that the agreement or practice is 'capable' of having such an effect.[17]

27   There is no obligation or need to calculate the actual volume of trade between Member States affected by the agreement or practice. For example, in the case of agreements prohibiting exports to other Member States there is no need to estimate what would have been the level of parallel trade between the Member States concerned, in the absence of the agreement. This interpretation is consistent with the jurisdictional nature of the effect on trade criterion. Community law jurisdiction extends to categories of agreements and practices that are capable of having cross-border effects, irrespective of whether a particular agreement or practice actually has such effects.

28   The assessment under the effect on trade criterion depends on a number of factors that individually may not be decisive.[18] The relevant factors include the nature of the agreement and practice, the nature of the products covered by the agreement or practice and the position and importance of the undertakings concerned.[19]

29   The nature of the agreement and practice provides an indication from a qualitative point of view of the ability of the agreement or practice to affect trade between Member States. Some agreements and practices are by their very nature capable of affecting trade between Member States, whereas others require more detailed analysis in this respect. Cross-border cartels are an example of the former, whereas joint ventures confined to the territory of a single Member State are an example of the latter. This aspect is further examined in section 3 below, which deals with various categories of agreements and practices.

30   The nature of the products covered by the agreements or practices also provides an indication of whether trade between Member States is capable of being affected. When by their nature products are easily traded across borders or are important for undertakings that want to enter or expand their activities in other Member States, Community jurisdiction is more readily established than in cases where due to their nature there is limited demand for products offered by suppliers from other Member States or where the products are of limited interest from the point of view of cross-border establishment or the expansion of the economic activity carried out from such place of establishment.[20] Establishment includes the setting-up by undertakings in one Member State of agencies, branches or subsidiaries in another Member State.

17 See e.g. Case T-228/97, *Irish Sugar*, [1999] ECR II-2969, paragraph 170, and Case 19/77, *Miller*, [1978] ECR 131, paragraph 15.

18 See e.g. Case C-250/92, *Gøttrup-Klim.* [1994] ECR II-5641, paragraph 54.

19 See e.g. Case C-306/96, *Javico*, [1998] ECR I-1983, paragraph 17, and paragraph 18 of the judgment in *Béguelin*.

20 Compare in this respect the judgments in *Bagnasco* and *Wouters* cited in footnote 11.

31   The market position of the undertakings concerned and their sales volumes are indicative from a quantitative point of view of the ability of the agreement or practice concerned to affect trade between Member States ...

32   In addition to the factors already mentioned, it is necessary to take account of the legal and factual environment in which the agreement or practice operates. The relevant economic and legal context provides insight into the potential for an effect on trade between Member States. If there are absolute barriers to cross-border trade between Member States, which are external to the agreement or practice, trade is only capable of being affected if those barriers are likely to disappear in the foreseeable future. In cases where the barriers are not absolute but merely render cross-border activities more difficult, it is of the utmost importance to ensure that agreements and practices do not further hinder such activities. Agreements and practices that do so are capable of affecting trade between Member States.

2.3.2. An influence on the 'pattern of trade between Member States'

33   For Articles 81 and 82 to be applicable there must be an influence on the 'pattern of trade between Member States.'

34   The term 'pattern of trade' is neutral. It is not a condition that trade be restricted or reduced.[21] Patterns of trade can also be affected when an agreement or practice causes an increase in trade. Indeed, Community law jurisdiction is established if trade between Member States is likely to develop differently with the agreement or practice compared to the way in which it would probably have developed in the absence of the agreement or practice.[22]

35   This interpretation reflects the fact that the effect on trade criterion is a jurisdictional one, which serves to distinguish those agreements and practices which are capable of having cross-border effects, so as to warrant an examination under the Community competition rules, from those agreements and practices which do not.

2.3.3. A 'direct or indirect, actual or potential influence' on the pattern of trade

36   The influence of agreements and practices on patterns of trade between Member States can be 'direct or indirect, actual or potential.'

37   Direct effects on trade between Member States normally occur in relation to the products covered by an agreement or practice. When, for example, producers of a

---

21 See e.g. Case T-141/89, *Tréfileurope*, [1995] ECR II-791, Case T-29/92, *Vereniging van Samenwerkende Prijsregelende Organisaties in de Bouwnijverheid (SPO)*, [1995] ECR II-289, as far as exports were concerned, and Commission Decision in *Volkswagen (II)*, OJ 2001 L 264, p. 14.

22 See in this respect Case 71/74, *Frubo*, [1975] ECR 563, paragraph 38, Joined Cases 209/78 and others, *Van Landewyck*, [1980] ECR 3125, paragraph 172, Case T-61/89, *Dansk Pelsdyravler Forening*, [1992] ECR II-1931, paragraph 143, and Case T-65/89, *BPB Industries and British Gypsum*, [1993] ECR II-389, paragraph 135.

particular product in different Member States agree to share markets, direct effects are produced on trade between Member States on the market for the products in question. Another example of direct effects being produced is when a supplier limits distributor rebates to products sold within the Member State in which the distributors are established. Such practices increase the relative price of products destined for exports, rendering export sales less attractive and less competitive.

38   Indirect effects often occur in relation to products that are related to those covered by an agreement or practice. Indirect effects may, for example, occur where an agreement or practice has an impact on cross-border economic activities of undertakings that use or otherwise rely on the products covered by the agreement or practice.[23] Such effects can, for instance, arise where the agreement or practice relates to an intermediate product, which is not traded, but which is used in the supply of a final product, which is traded. The Court of Justice has held that trade between Member States was capable of being affected in the case of an agreement involving the fixing of prices of spirits used in the production of cognac.[24] Whereas the raw material was not exported, the final product – cognac – was exported. In such cases Community competition law is thus applicable, if trade in the final product is capable of being appreciably affected.

39   Indirect effects on trade between Member States may also occur in relation to the products covered by the agreement or practice. For instance, agreements whereby a manufacturer limits warranties to products sold by distributors within their Member State of establishment create disincentives for consumers from other Member States to buy the products because they would not be able to invoke the warranty.[25] Export by official distributors and parallel traders is made more difficult because in the eyes of consumers the products are less attractive without the manufacturer's warranty.[26]

40   Actual effects on trade between Member States are those that are produced by the agreement or practice once it is implemented. An agreement between a supplier and a distributor within the same Member State, for instance one that prohibits exports to other Member States, is likely to produce actual effects on trade between Member States. Without the agreement the distributor would have been free to engage in export sales. It should be recalled, however, that it is not required that actual effects are demonstrated. It is sufficient that the agreement or practice be capable of having such effects.

41   Potential effects are those that may occur in the future with a sufficient degree of probability. In other words, foreseeable market developments must be taken into

---

23 See in this respect Case T-86/95, *Compagnie Générale Maritime and others*, [2002] ECR II-1011, paragraph 148, and paragraph 202 of the judgment in *Compagnie maritime belge* cited in footnote 12.

24 See Case 123/83, *BNIC v. Clair*, [1985] ECR 391, paragraph 29.

25 See Commission Decision in *Zanussi*, OJ L 322, 16.11.1978, p. 36, paragraph 11.

26 See in this respect Case 31/85, *ETA Fabrique d'Ebauches*, [1985] ECR 3933, paragraph 11.

account.[27] Even if trade is not capable of being affected at the time the agreement is concluded or the practice is implemented, Articles 81 and 82 remain applicable if the factors which led to that conclusion are likely to change in the foreseeable future. In this respect it is relevant to consider the impact of liberalisation measures adopted by the Community or by the Member State in question and other foreseeable measures aiming at eliminating legal barriers to trade.

42   Moreover, even if at a given point in time market conditions are unfavourable to cross-border trade, for example because prices are similar in the Member States in question, trade may still be capable of being affected if the situation may change as a result of changing market conditions.[28] What matters is the ability of the agreement or practice to affect trade between Member States and not whether at any given point in time it actually does so.

43   The inclusion of indirect or potential effects in the analysis of effects on trade between Member States does not mean that the analysis can be based on remote or hypothetical effects. The likelihood of a particular agreement to produce indirect or potential effects must be explained by the authority or party claiming that trade between Member States is capable of being appreciably affected. Hypothetical or speculative effects are not sufficient for establishing Community law jurisdiction. For instance, an agreement that raises the price of a product which is not tradable reduces the disposable income of consumers. As consumers have less money to spend they may purchase fewer products imported from other Member States. However, the link between such income effects and trade between Member States is generally in itself too remote to establish Community law jurisdiction.

V The *de minimis* doctrine

The final requirement that must be shown in order to establish an infringement of Article 81(1) is that the effect on competition and trade should be appreciable (i.e. not *de minimis*). The requirement of appreciability, widely known as the *de minimis* doctrine, is not part of the wording of Article 81(1) but was incorporated by the ECJ.

This section will consider the application of the doctrine first in relation to the prevention, restriction or distortion of competition and second with respect to the effect on trade between Member States.

(a) Preventing, restricting or distorting of competition: de minimis

For many years, the application of the *de minimis* doctrine in relation to the competition element of Article 81(1) was handled on the basis of the case law of the ECJ and the first case in which the doctrine was introduced: *Völk v*

---

27 See Joined Cases C-241/91 P and C-242/91 P, *RTE (Magill)*, [1995] ECR I-743, paragraph 70, and Case 107/82, *AEG*, [1983] ECR 3151, paragraph 60.
28 See paragraph 60 of the *AEG* judgment cited in the previous footnote.

Vervaecke. However, following many years of experience and being driven to provide clarity as to the operation of the prohibition in Article 81(1) and its application, the Commission introduced a Notice in 1996 (which became known as the '*de minimis* Notice'), which applied in relation to both the competition and trade elements in Article 81(1).

That Notice has been replaced by a more recent one, also known as the '*de minimis* Notice', introduced in 2001. Unlike its predecessor, the 2001 Notice applies only to the 'competition' element in the Article, but like its predecessor and other Commission Notices it lacks the binding force of the law.

Commission Notice on agreements of minor importance which do not appreciably restrict competition under Article 81(1) of the Treaty establishing the European Community (*de minimis*) OJ (2001) C 368/11

(I)

1   Article 81(1) prohibits agreements between undertakings which may affect trade between Member States and which have as their object or effect the prevention, restriction or distortion of competition within the common market. The Court of Justice of the European Communities has clarified that this provision is not applicable where the impact of the agreement on intra-Community trade or on competition is not appreciable.

2   In this notice the Commission quantifies, with the help of market share thresholds, what is not an appreciable restriction of competition under Article 81 of the EC Treaty. This negative definition of appreciability does not imply that agreements between undertakings which exceed the thresholds set out in this notice appreciably restrict competition. Such agreements may still have only a negligible effect on competition and may therefore not be prohibited by Article 81(1).[2]

3   Agreements may in addition not fall under Article 81(1) because they are not capable of appreciably affecting trade between Member States. This notice does not deal with this issue. It does not quantify what does not constitute an appreciable effect on trade. It is however acknowledged that agreements between small and medium-sized undertakings, as defined in the Annex to Commission Recom-

. . .

2 See, for instance, the judgment of the Court of Justice in Joined Cases C-215/96 and C-216/96 *Bagnasco (Carlos) v Banca Popolare di Novara and Casa di Risparmio di Genova e Imperia* (1999) ECR I-135, points 34–35. This notice is also without prejudice to the principles for assessment under Article 81(1) as expressed in the Commission notice 'Guidelines on the applicability of Article 81 of the EC Treaty to horizontal cooperation agreements', OJ C 3, 6.1.2001, in particular points 17–31 inclusive, and in the Commission notice 'Guidelines on vertical restraints', OJ C 291, 13.10.2000, in particular points 5–20 inclusive.

mendation 96/280/EC,[3] are rarely capable of appreciably affecting trade between Member States. Small and medium-sized undertakings are currently defined in that recommendation as undertakings which have fewer than 250 employees and have either an annual turnover not exceeding EUR 40 million or an annual balance-sheet total not exceeding EUR 27 million.

4   In cases covered by this notice the Commission will not institute proceedings either upon application or on its own initiative. Where undertakings assume in good faith that an agreement is covered by this notice, the Commission will not impose fines. Although not binding on them, this notice also intends to give guidance to the courts and authorities of the Member States in their application of Article 81.

5   This notice also applies to decisions by associations of undertakings and to concerted practices.

6   This notice is without prejudice to any interpretation of Article 81 which may be given by the Court of Justice or the Court of First Instance of the European Communities.

(II)

7   The Commission holds the view that agreements between undertakings which affect trade between Member States do not appreciably restrict competition within the meaning of Article 81(1):
   (a) if the aggregate market share held by the parties to the agreement does not exceed 10% on any of the relevant markets affected by the agreement, where the agreement is made between undertakings which are actual or potential competitors on any of these markets (agreements between competitors);[4] or
   (b) if the market share held by each of the parties to the agreement does not exceed 15% on any of the relevant markets affected by the agreement, where the agreement is made between undertakings which are not actual or potential competitors on any of these markets (agreements between non-competitors).

3 [OJ 1996 L 107, p. 4. With effect from 1.1.2005 this recommendation will be replaced by Commission Recommendation 2003/361/EC concerning the definition of micro, small and medium-sized enterprises, OJ 2003 L 124, p. 36.]

4 On what are actual or potential competitors, see the Commission notice *Guidelines on the applicability of Article 81 of the EC Treaty to horizontal cooperation agreements*, OJ C 3, 6.1.2001, paragraph 9. A firm is treated as an actual competitor if it is either active on the same relevant market or if, in the absence of the agreement, it is able to switch production to the relevant products and market them in the short term without incurring significant additional costs or risks in response to a small and permanent increase in relative prices (immediate supply-side substitutability). A firm is treated as a potential competitor if there is evidence that, absent the agreement, this firm could and would be likely to undertake the necessary additional investments or other necessary switching costs so that it could enter the relevant market in response to a small and permanent increase in relative prices.

In cases where it is difficult to classify the agreement as either an agreement between competitors or an agreement between non-competitors the 10% threshold is applicable.

8   Where in a relevant market competition is restricted by the cumulative effect of agreements for the sale of goods or services entered into by different suppliers or distributors (cumulative foreclosure effect of parallel networks of agreements having similar effects on the market), the market share thresholds under point 7 are reduced to 5%, both for agreements between competitors and for agreements between non-competitors. Individual suppliers or distributors with a market share not exceeding 5% are in general not considered to contribute significantly to a cumulative foreclosure effect.[5] A cumulative foreclosure effect is unlikely to exist if less than 30% of the relevant market is covered by parallel (networks of) agreements having similar effects.

9   The Commission also holds the view that agreements are not restrictive of competition if the market shares do not exceed the thresholds of respectively 10%, 15% and 5% set out in point 7 and 8 during two successive calendar years by more than 2 percentage points.

10   In order to calculate the market share, it is necessary to determine the relevant market. This consists of the relevant product market and the relevant geographic market. When defining the relevant market, reference should be had to the Notice on the definition of the relevant market for the purposes of Community competition law.[6] The market shares are to be calculated on the basis of sales value data or, where appropriate, purchase value data. If value data are not available, estimates based on other reliable market information, including volume data, may be used.

11   Points 7, 8 and 9 do not apply to agreements containing any of the following hardcore restrictions:
     (1) as regards agreements between competitors as defined in point 7, restrictions which, directly or indirectly, in isolation or in combination with other factors under the control of the parties, have as their object:[7]
         (a) the fixing of prices when selling the products to third parties;
         (b) the limitation of output or sales;
         (c) the allocation of markets or customers;

5 See also the Commission Notice *Guidelines on vertical restraints* OJ C 291, 13.10.2000, in particular paragraphs 73, 142, 143 and 189. While in the guidelines on vertical restraints in relation to certain restrictions reference is made not only to the total but also to the tied market share of a particular supplier or buyer, in this notice all market share thresholds refer to total market shares.
6 OJ C 372, 9.12.1997, p. 5.
7 Without prejudice to situations of joint production with or without joint distribution as defined in Article 5, paragraph 2, of Commission Regulation (EC) No 2658/2000 and Article 5, paragraph 2, of Commission Regulation (EC) No 2659/2000, OJ L 304, 5.12.2000, pp. 3 and 7 respectively.

(2) as regards agreements between non-competitors as defined in point 7, restrictions which, directly or indirectly, in isolation or in combination with other factors under the control of the parties, have as their object:

    (a) the restriction of the buyer's ability to determine its sale price, without prejudice to the possibility of the supplier imposing a maximum sale price or recommending a sale price, provided that they do not amount to a fixed or minimum sale price as a result of pressure from, or incentives offered by, any of the parties;

    (b) the restriction of the territory into which, or of the customers to whom, the buyer may sell the contract goods or services, except the following restrictions which are not hardcore:

        – the restriction of active sales into the exclusive territory or to an exclusive customer group reserved to the supplier or allocated by the supplier to another buyer, where such a restriction does not limit sales by the customers of the buyer,

        – the restriction of sales to end users by a buyer operating at the wholesale level of trade,

        – the restriction of sales to unauthorised distributors by the members of a selective distribution system, and

        – the restriction of the buyer's ability to sell components, supplied for the purposes of incorporation, to customers who would use them to manufacture the same type of goods as those produced by the supplier;

    (c) the restriction of active or passive sales to end users by members of a selective distribution system operating at the retail level of trade, without prejudice to the possibility of prohibiting a member of the system from operating out of an unauthorised place of establishment;

    (d) the restriction of cross-supplies between distributors within a selective distribution system, including between distributors operating at different levels of trade;

    (e) the restriction agreed between a supplier of components and a buyer who incorporates those components, which limits the supplier's ability to sell the components as spare parts to end users or to repairers or other service providers not entrusted by the buyer with the repair or servicing of its goods;

(3) as regards agreements between competitors as defined in point 7, where the competitors operate, for the purposes of the agreement, at a different level of the production or distribution chain, any of the hardcore restrictions listed in paragraph (1) and (2) above.

12   (1) For the purposes of this notice, the terms 'undertaking', 'party to the agreement', 'distributor', 'supplier' and 'buyer' shall include their respective connected undertakings.

    (2) 'Connected undertakings' are:

    (a) undertakings in which a party to the agreement, directly or indirectly:

        – has the power to exercise more than half the voting rights, or

   – has the power to appoint more than half the members of the supervisory board, board of management or bodies legally representing the undertaking, or

   – has the right to manage the undertaking's affairs;

(b) undertakings which directly or indirectly have, over a party to the agreement, the rights or powers listed in (a);

(c) undertakings in which an undertaking referred to in (b) has, directly or indirectly, the rights or powers listed in (a);

(d) undertakings in which a party to the agreement together with one or more of the undertakings referred to in (a), (b) or (c), or in which two or more of the latter undertakings, jointly have the rights or powers listed in (a);

(e) undertakings in which the rights or the powers listed in (a) are jointly held by:

   – parties to the agreement or their respective connected undertakings referred to in (a) to (d), or

   – one or more of the parties to the agreement or one or more of their connected undertakings referred to in (a) to (d) and one or more third parties.

(3) For the purposes of paragraph 2(e), the market share held by these jointly held undertakings shall be apportioned equally to each undertaking having the rights or the powers listed in paragraph 2(a).

(b) Effect on trade: de minimis

Following the introduction of the 2001 *de minimis Notice*, the application of the *de minimis* doctrine in relation to the requirement of effect on trade between Member States continued to be handled on the basis of the case law of the Community Courts; several judgments have played a role here (see *Compagnie Générale v. Commission*, and *Erauw-Jacquery v. La Hesbignonne Société Cooperative*).

As mentioned above, however, the Commission has recently published a detailed Notice which contains a new section dealing with the application of the doctrine in relation to effect on trade. This is a highly interesting and positive step by the Commission especially since, like the 2001 *de minimis* Notice, the *Notice* shows the increasing prominence the Commission has given to an economics-based approach to the application of Article 81(1), following many years of heavy reliance on a formalistic approach.

Guidelines on the effect on trade OJ (2004) C 101/81

(i) General principle

44   The effect on trade criterion incorporates a quantitative element, limiting Community law jurisdiction to agreements and practices that are capable of having effects of a certain magnitude. Agreements and practices fall outside the scope of application

of Articles 81 and 82 when they affect the market only insignificantly having regard to the weak position of the undertakings concerned on the market for the products in question.[29] Appreciability can be appraised in particular by reference to the position and the importance of the relevant undertakings on the market for the products concerned.[30]

45   The assessment of appreciability depends on the circumstances of each individual case, in particular the nature of the agreement and practice, the nature of the products covered and the market position of the undertakings concerned. When by its very nature the agreement or practice is capable of affecting trade between Member States, the appreciability threshold is lower than in the case of agreements and practices that are not by their very nature capable of affecting trade between Member States. The stronger the market position of the undertakings concerned, the more likely it is that an agreement or practice capable of affecting trade between Member States can be held to do so appreciably.[31]

46   In a number of cases concerning imports and exports the Court of Justice has considered that the appreciability requirement was fulfilled when the sales of the undertakings concerned accounted for about 5% of the market.[32] Market share alone, however, has not always been considered the decisive factor. In particular, it is necessary also to take account of the turnover of the undertakings in the products concerned.[33]

47   Appreciability can thus be measured both in absolute terms (turnover) and in relative terms, comparing the position of the undertaking(s) concerned to that of other players on the market (market share). This focus on the position and importance of the undertakings concerned is consistent with the concept 'may affect', which implies that the assessment is based on the ability of the agreement or practice to affect trade between Member States rather than on the impact on actual flows of goods and services across borders. The market position of the undertakings concerned and their turnover in the products concerned are indicative of the ability of an agreement or practice to affect trade between Member States. These two elements are reflected in the presumptions set out in paragraphs 52 and 53 below.

29 See Case 5/69, *Völk*, [1969] ECR 295, paragraph 7.
30 See e.g. paragraph 17 of the judgment in *Javico* . . . , and paragraph 138 of the judgment in *BPB Industries and British Gypsum* . . .
31 See paragraph 138 of the judgment in *BPB Industries and British Gypsum* . . .
32 See e.g. paragraphs 9 and 10 of the *Miller* judgment, and paragraph 58 of the *AEG* judgment.
33 See Joined Cases 100/80 and others, *Musique Diffusion Française*, [1983] ECR p. 1825, paragraph 86. In that case the products in question accounted for just above 3% of sales on the national markets concerned. The Court held that the agreements, which hindered parallel trade, were capable of appreciably affecting trade between Member States due to the high turnover of the parties and the relative market position of the products, compared to those of products produced by competing suppliers.

48   The application of the appreciability test does not necessarily require that relevant markets be defined and market shares calculated.[34] The sales of an undertaking in absolute terms may be sufficient to support a finding that the impact on trade is appreciable. This is particularly so in the case of agreements and practices that by their very nature are liable to affect trade between Member States, for example because they concern imports or exports or because they cover several Member States. The fact that in such circumstances turnover in the products covered by the agreement may be sufficient for a finding of an appreciable effect on trade between Member States is reflected in the positive presumption set out in paragraph 53 below.

49   Agreements and practices must always be considered in the economic and legal context in which they occur. In the case of vertical agreements it may be necessary to have regard to any cumulative effects of parallel networks of similar agreements.[35] Even if a single agreement or network of agreements is not capable of appreciably affecting trade between Member States, the effect of parallel networks of agreements, taken as a whole, may be capable of doing so. For that to be the case, however, it is necessary that the individual agreement or network of agreements makes a significant contribution to the overall effect on trade.[36]

2.4.2. Quantification of appreciability

50   It is not possible to establish general quantitative rules covering all categories of agreements indicating when trade between Member States is capable of being appreciably affected. It is possible, however, to indicate when trade is normally not capable of being appreciably affected. Firstly, in its notice on agreements of minor importance which do not appreciably restrict competition in the meaning of Article 81(1) of the Treaty (the *de minimis* rule)[37] the Commission has stated that agreements between small and medium-sized undertakings (SMEs) as defined in the Annex to Commission Recommendation 96/280/EC[38] are normally not capable of affecting trade between Member States. The reason for this presumption is the fact that the activities of SMEs are normally local or at most regional in nature. However, SMEs may be subject to Community law jurisdiction in particular where they engage in cross-border economic activity. Secondly, the Commission considers it appropriate to set out general principles indicating when trade is normally not capable of being appreciably affected, i.e. a standard defining the absence of an

---

34 See in this respect paragraphs 179 and 231 of the *Volkswagen* judgment ..., and Case T-213/00, *CMA CGM and others*, [2003] ECR I-, paragraphs 219 and 220.

35 See e.g. Case T-7/93, *Langnese-Iglo*, [1995] ECR II-1533, paragraph 120.

36 See paragraphs 140 and 141 of the judgment in *Vereniging van Groothandelaren in Bloemkwekerijprodukten* ...

37 Commission *Notice on agreements of minor importance which do not appreciably restrict competition under Article 81(1) of the Treaty*, OJ 2001 C 368, p. 13, paragraph 3.

38 OJ 1996 L 107, p. 4. With effect from 1.1.2005 this recommendation will be replaced by Commission Recommendation 2003/361/EC concerning the definition of micro, small and medium-sized enterprises, OJ 2003 L 124, p. 36.

appreciable effect on trade between Member States (the NAAT-rule). When applying Article 81, the Commission will consider this standard as a negative rebuttable presumption applying to all agreements within the meaning of Article 81(1) irrespective of the nature of the restrictions contained in the agreement, including restrictions that have been identified as hardcore restrictions in Commission block exemption regulations and guidelines. In cases where this presumption applies the Commission will normally not institute proceedings either upon application or on its own initiative. Where the undertakings assume in good faith that an agreement is covered by this negative presumption, the Commission will not impose fines.

51   Without prejudice to paragraph 53 below, this negative definition of appreciability does not imply that agreements, which do not fall within the criteria set out below, are automatically capable of appreciably affecting trade between Member States. A case by case analysis is necessary.

52   The Commission holds the view that in principle agreements are not capable of appreciably affecting trade between Member States when the following cumulative conditions are met:

(a) The aggregate market share of the parties on any relevant market within the Community affected by the agreement does not exceed 5%, and

(b) In the case of horizontal agreements, the aggregate annual Community turnover of the undertakings concerned[39] in the products covered by the agreement does not exceed 40 million Euro. In the case of agreements concerning the joint buying of products the relevant turnover shall be the parties' combined purchases of the products covered by the agreement.

In the case of vertical agreements, the aggregate annual Community turnover of the supplier in the products covered by the agreement does not exceed 40 million Euro. In the case of licence agreements the relevant turnover shall be the aggregate turnover of the licensees in the products incorporating the licensed technology and the licensor's own turnover in such products. In cases involving agreements concluded between a buyer and several suppliers the relevant turnover shall be the buyer's combined purchases of the products covered by the agreements.

The Commission will apply the same presumption where during two successive calendar years the above turnover threshold is not exceeded by more than 10% and the above market threshold is not exceeded by more than 2 percentage points. In cases where the agreement concerns an emerging not yet existing market and where as a consequence the parties neither generate relevant turnover nor accumulate any relevant market share, the Commission will not apply this presumption. In such cases appreciability may have to be assessed on the basis of the position of the parties on related product markets or their strength in technologies relating to the agreement.

39 The term 'undertakings concerned' shall include connected undertakings as defined in paragraph 12.2 of the Commission's *Notice on agreements of minor importance which do not appreciably restrict competition under Article 81(1) of the Treaty establishing the European Community*, (OJ 2001 C 368, 22.12.2001, p. 13).

53   The Commission will also hold the view that where an agreement by its very nature is capable of affecting trade between Member States, for example, because it concerns imports and exports or covers several Member States, there is a rebuttable positive presumption that such effects on trade are appreciable when the turnover of the parties in the products covered by the agreement calculated as indicated in paragraphs 52 and 54 exceeds 40 million Euro. In the case of agreements that by their very nature are capable of affecting trade between Member States it can also often be presumed that such effects are appreciable when the market share of the parties exceeds the 5% threshold set out in the previous paragraph. However, this presumption does not apply where the agreement covers only part of a Member State (see paragraph 90 below).

54   With regard to the threshold of 40 million Euro (cf. paragraph 52 above), the turnover is calculated on the basis of total Community sales excluding tax during the previous financial year by the undertakings concerned, of the products covered by the agreement (the contract products). Sales between entities that form part of the same undertaking are excluded.[40]

55   In order to apply the market share threshold, it is necessary to determine the relevant market.[41] This consists of the relevant product market and the relevant geographic market. The market shares are to be calculated on the basis of sales value data or, where appropriate, purchase value data. If value data are not available, estimates based on other reliable market information, including volume data, may be used.

56   In the case of networks of agreements entered into by the same supplier with different distributors, sales made through the entire network are taken into account.

57   Contracts that form part of the same overall business arrangement constitute a single agreement for the purposes of the NAAT-rule. Undertakings cannot bring themselves inside these thresholds by dividing up an agreement that forms a whole from an economic perspective.

Paragraph 58 of the *Notice* provides that the Commission will apply the negative presumption (referred to in these paragraphs) to all agreements, including those that by their nature are capable of producing an effect on trade as well as to agreements that involve trade within firms located outside the EC. Paragraph 59 then goes on to say that outside the scope of the negative presumption, the Commission will take into account qualitative elements such as those relating to the nature of the agreement or the product in question. In paragraphs 61–72, 77–92 and 100–109, the Commission provides additional guidance by considering various common types of agreements, such as agreements involving import and exports with firms based in third countries and horizontal and

40 See the previous footnote.
41 When defining the relevant market, reference should be made to the *Notice on the definition of the relevant market for the purposes of Community competition law* (OJ C 372, 9.12.1997, p. 5.)

vertical agreements covering part or whole of a Member State as well as several Member States.

(C) Concluding remarks

It should be clear from the above that the requirements of Article 81(1) are interpreted widely. The increasing reliance by the Commission on an economics-based approach, especially when considering 'effect on competition and trade', is a very welcome development in the application of the provision. Particularly helpful has been the Commission's practice of publishing guidance, which will be valuable not only to business firms and their legal advisors but also to national courts and national competition authorities in Member States. This is especially relevant in light of the Commission's Modernisation programme which makes Article 81 directly applicable in its entirety (which is now in operation in twenty-five Member States). It is also invaluable for Member States who have modelled their competition provisions on Article 81. One such Member State is the UK.

3 UK law

(A) General

There is benefit in looking at the application of the prohibition on collusion between firms under Article 81 before dealing with this issue under UK competition law because the relevant provision in UK law, the Chapter I prohibition of the CA1998 (set out below), is modelled on Article 81. As a result of the attitude of the UK favouring alignment with the EC competition rules insofar as possible, it is considerably easier to understand the position under UK law. This attitude can be seen from, among other things, the recent changes which the UK Government made to the CA1998 and the revision of the various publications under the Act carried out by the OFT (see in particular chapters 4, 5 and 14) in light of EC Regulation 1/2003, the Modernisation Regulation. A very important provision in achieving consistency between UK and EC law is section 60 CA1998 as amended by the Enterprise Act 2002, which provides the following:

S. 60 Principles to be applied in determining questions

(1) The purposes of this section is to ensure that so far as is possible (having regard to any relevant differences between the provisions concerned), questions arising under this Part in relation to competition within the United Kingdom are dealt with in a manner which is consistent with the treatment of corresponding questions arising in Community law in relation to competition within the Community.

[95]

(2) At any time when the court determines a question arising under this Part, it must act (so far as is compatible with the provisions of this Part and whether or not it would otherwise be required to do so) with a view to securing that there is no inconsistency between –

    (a) the principles applied, and decision reached, by the court in determining that question; and

    (b) the principles laid down by the Treaty and the European Court, and any relevant decision of that Court, as applicable at that time in determining any corresponding question arising in Community law.

(3) The court must, in addition, have regard to any relevant decision or statement of the Commission.

(4) Subsections (2) and (3) also apply to –

    (a) the OFT; and

    (b) any person acting on behalf of the OFT, in connection with any matter arising under this Part.

(5) In subsections (2) and (3), "court" means any court or tribunal.

(6) In subsections (2) (b) and (3), "decision" includes a decision as to –

    (a) the interpretation of any provision of Community law;

    (b) the civil liability of an undertaking for harm caused by its infringement of Community law.

The OFT has explained the relevance of section 60, which applies to the OFT, CC and domestic courts, in the following way:

OFT Guideline The Major Provisions (OFT400)

4.13   When applying the Chapter I and Chapter II prohibitions, the United Kingdom authorities are under a dual obligation. First, they must ensure that there is no inconsistency with either the principles laid down by the EC Treaty and the European Court or any relevant decision of the European Court. Secondly, the United Kingdom authorities must have regard to any relevant decision or statement of the European Commission. In the OFT's view this is limited to decisions or statements which have the authority of the European Commission as a whole, such as, for example, decisions on individual cases under Articles 81 and 82. It would also include European Commission Notices and clear statements which the European Commission has published about its policy approach in the Annual Report on Competition Policy.

4.14   The obligation to ensure consistency applies only to the extent that this is possible, having regard to any relevant differences between the provisions concerned. This means that there will be certain areas where the Community principles will not be relevant. For example the EC single market objectives designed to establish a European common market would not be relevant to the domestic prohibition system.

(B) The Chapter I prohibition

The Chapter I prohibition is contained in section 2 of the CA1998.

S. 2 Agreements etc. preventing, restricting or distorting competition

(1) Subject to section 3, agreements between undertakings, decisions by associations of undertakings or concerted practices which –

(a) may affect trade within the United Kingdom, and

(b) have as their object or effect the prevention, restriction or distortion of competition within the United Kingdom,

are prohibited unless they are exempt in accordance with the provisions of this Part.

(2) Subsection (1) applies, in particular, to agreements, decisions or practices which –

(a) directly or indirectly fix purchase or selling prices or any other trading conditions;

(b) limit or control production, markets, technical development or investment;

(c) share markets or sources of supply;

(d) apply dissimilar conditions to equivalent transactions with other trading parties, thereby placing them at a competitive disadvantage;

(e) make the conclusion of contracts subject to acceptance by the other parties of supplementary obligations which, by their nature or according to commercial usage, have no connection with the subject of such contracts.

(3) Subsection (1) applies only if the agreement, decision or practice is, or is intended to be, implemented in the United Kingdom.

(4) Any agreement or decision which is prohibited by subsection (1) is void.

(5) A provision of this Part which is expressed to apply to, or in relation to, an agreement is to be read as applying equally to, or in relation to, a decision by an association of undertakings or a concerted practice (but with any necessary modifications).

(6) Subsection (5) does not apply where the context otherwise requires.

(7) In this section "the United Kingdom" means, in relation to an agreement which operates or is intended to operate only in a part of the United Kingdom, that part.

(8) The prohibition imposed by subsection (1) is referred to in this Act as "the Chapter I prohibition".

It is clear from section 2(8) that the term 'Chapter I prohibition' comes from the section itself. Section 2(1) and (4) are based on Article 81(1) and (2) and extensive similarities should be apparent in the language of these provisions, though differences do exist. For example, the reference to 'effect on trade between Member States' which appears in Article 81(1), does not appear in the

[97]

section; other differences of expression can be noted by reading the two provisions alongside one another.

Similarities also exist between the two provisions in relation to the meaning that has been given to the terms 'undertaking', 'agreement', 'decision by association of undertakings', 'concerted practice' and 'object or effect of prevention, restriction or distortion of competition'. In other words, these terms have been interpreted consistently with their interpretation by the Community Courts under Article 81(1). More crucially, they have also been interpreted widely. These terms will be considered in turn, with the focus being given to the case law under the CA1998 and, where relevant, to statements made by the OFT.

I Undertaking

It should be noted that while the CA1998 sometimes uses the term 'person' instead, section 59 stipulates that 'person' should be taken to include 'undertaking'. The OFT has defined the concept in its *Guideline OFT400* (paragraph 2.6) as one which 'covers any natural or legal person engaged in an economic activity, regardless of its legal status and the way in which it is financed.[7] It includes companies, firms, businesses, partnerships, individuals operating as sole traders, agricultural co-operatives, associations of undertakings (e.g. trade associations), non profit-making organisations and (in some circumstances) public entities that offer goods or services on a given market'. According to the paragraph, the key consideration in assessing whether an entity is an undertaking for the purposes of the Chapter I prohibition is whether it is engaged in an economic activity.

The CCAT (the predecessor of the CAT) has said the following on the concept, although in the case it did not need to deal with whether the General Insurance Standards Council (GISC) was an undertaking for the purposes of its decision.

Institute of Independent Insurance Brokers v. Director General of Fair Trading [2001] CompAR 62

GISC sought to impose a self-regulatory system on the entire general insurance industry. Its rules required all insurer members to deal only with intermediaries who were also GISC members (Rule F42). Independent intermediaries would therefore be forced to join GISC. IIB and its members considered that such compulsion threatened to eradicate the possibility for independent brokers to differentiate themselves on the market from tied agents and direct insurance sales operations and suppressed the possibility of alternative regulatory bodies (such as the IIB and ABTA). The DGFT's decision that the GISC rules did not prevent, restrict or distort competition was challenged by the IIB and ABTA.

---

7 See Case C-41/90 *Höfner and Elser v Macrotron* [1991] ECR I-1979, [1993] 4 CMLR 306 and Case T-319/99 *Fenin v Commission*, judgment of [2003] 4.3.2003.

The CCAT held that Rule F42 is an appreciable restriction of competition as it affects the dealings of the vast majority of insurers and intermediaries in the UK general insurance market. The CCAT also noted that the effect of the GISC rules taken together was to restrict the possibilities for alternative forms of regulation, which might also appreciably affect competition.

CCAT

252 ... [T]he concept of undertaking encompasses every entity engaged in an economic activity regardless of the legal status of the entity and the way it is financed. The basic test is whether the entity in question is engaged in an activity which consists in offering goods and services on a given market and which could, at least in principle, be carried out by a private actor in order to make a profit. By contrast, while public bodies carrying on economic activities may be regarded as undertakings, 'activities in the exercise of official authority' are sheltered from the application of the competition rules. The test is whether the activity in question is to be analysed as 'the exercise of public powers' or as 'economic activities': Case 118/85 *Commission v Italy* [1987] ECR 2599 paragraph 7. One test for whether the activity in question constitutes the exercise of public powers, or of official authority, is whether the activity in question 'is connected by its nature, its aim and the rules to which it is subject with the exercise of powers which are typically those of a public authority' (See paragraph 76 of the opinion of the Advocate Genreal Jacobs in *Ambulanz Glöckner*, citing Case 364/92 *Eurocontrol* [1994] ECR I-43, paragraph 30).

253 To illustrate the difference between the exercise of 'public powers' or 'official authority' on the one hand and 'economic activity' on the other hand, in *Ambulanz Glöckner* itself Advocate General Jacobs concluded that the provision of ambulance services, including emergency services, was an 'economic activity' and thus within the rules on competition, since those were not services that must necessarily be carried out by public entities (paragraph 68 of his opinion). On the other hand, the grant or refusal by a public authority under statute of an authorisation to provide ambulance services fell outside the rules on competition, since it was 'a typical administrative decision taken in the exercise of prerogatives conferred by law which are usually reserved for public authorities' (paragraph 76). Other illustrative examples of the exercise of public authority falling outside Arts 81 and 82 of the Treaty include the arrangements for international air traffic control made by the European Organisation for the Safety of Air Navigation, an international organisation set up and run by 14 Contracting States in pursuance of an international Convention (see *Eurocontrol*, cited above), the fixing by public authorities under statute of tariffs for the use of German waterways (Case C-153/93 *Germany v Delta Schiffahrts* [1994] ECR I-2517); and anti-pollution surveillance carried out by virtue of a public authorisation which was held to be 'a task in the public interest which forms part of the essential functions of the State as regards protection of the environment in sensitive areas' and thus 'connected by its nature, its aim and the rules to which it is subject

with the exercise of powers … which are typically those of a public authority … '
(Case 343/95 *Cali & Figli v SEPG* [1997] ECR I-1547, at paragraphs 22 to 23)

The CCAT then turned to consider whether the GISC was an undertaking.

254   … GISC is a private company that has been set up by the industry itself without any
statutory basis. It exists solely by contract. GISC is not accountable to Parliament,
nor to Ministers, nor indeed to anyone other than those in the industry who belong
to GISC. As far as the constitution of GISC is concerned, GISC is run by a Board
of Directors most of whom are, or have been, active in the industry. At present only
two out of the Board of some 16 members are 'public interest' directors recruited,
so we are told, through head-hunters and not appointed by a public authority. It is
true that it is currently proposed that there should be five 'public interest directors',
but that still leaves the 'outside' directors in a substantial minority *vis-à-vis* the ten
'industry' directors (see paragraphs 53 to 55 above). There is no independent chairman (without industry connections). It is also proposed that in future the directors
will be elected by the Members of GISC, who will become shareholders in the
company, six directors being elected by intermediaries and four directors elected
by insurers. This change is proposed, notably, in order that 'the Board would be
directly accountable to regulated businesses' and in order to give 'the regulated
businesses a greater say in the running of the company'. There is to be weighted
voting, on the basis that 'a large business in the industry should, in principle, have
a greater number of votes than a small business'. A number of these changes are
proposed on the basis of the principles of the Combined Code, which is a publicly
available document dealing with the principles of corporate governance relevant to
listed public companies in the United Kingdom (See paragraphs 55 to 58 above).

255   On this basis GISC appears to us to have the features normally to be found in a
private sector organisation or company accountable to its members, rather than a
publicly constituted body exercising 'public powers'. We note also that, in the cases
cited to us where the exercise of official or public authority was held to fall outside
the competition rules, the activity in question had been exercised on some statutory
basis of one kind or another. In the present case, GISC lacks any such statutory
foundation.

…

257   Lastly, while it is true that the assumption of regulatory powers in respect of general
insurance could properly be an activity of the State, for example under the FSMA,
the setting up of a framework for promoting professional standards and consumer
protection in general insurance is not an activity which, by reason of its intrinsic
nature, can necessarily only be carried out by public authorities, as the case law
appears to require. Self evidently GISC, the IIB and ABTA are all private sector
bodies who have sought to establish self-regulatory or quality assurance schemes
of one kind or another in the industries in which they operate. While we do not

doubt the good intentions of those concerned, it seems to us clear that each of those bodies is acting not solely in the public interest but also in the commercial interests of their members in promoting the various schemes in question. In the case of GISC, emphasis has been placed on developing the GISC brand, creating what GISC sees as a 'level playing field', and avoiding the threat of statutory intervention. Although GISC itself is not run for profit, the particular structure set up under the GISC Rules would hardly have been adopted if the industry did not see real commercial advantages in proceeding in the way it has.

The OFT has also followed a similar line to that of the Commission and the Community Courts with regard to the application of the Chapter I prohibition in the 'single economic entity' situation, as it explains in paragraph 2.7 of its *Guideline OFT401*.

With regard to the question of whether a public sector body is considered to be an undertaking for the purposes of the Chapter I prohibition, it has been answered by the CAT (of Northern Ireland) in a highly interesting manner in its judgment in *BetterCare*.

BetterCare Group v. Director General of Fair Trading [2002] CAT 7

The applicant, a private care home operator, appealed against a decision of the Director General that the North & West Belfast Health and Social Services Board was not subject to the CA1998. North & West purchased care services from Bettercare as part of its duty to provide residential care. Bettercare argued that North & West was an undertaking, but the Director General considered that the public nature of its functions precluded it from being an 'undertaking' for the purposes of the Act.

The Competition Appeals Tribunal (of Northern Ireland) allowed the appeal and remitted the matter to the Director General, ruling that North & West was subject to the Act. The 'undertaking' was creating a demand met by private homes on a contractual basis and was therefore active in the market for the supply of residential and nursing care, both as a user of services and by providing direct care itself, an activity going beyond regulatory or administrative operations.

CAT

191   Taking first North & West's activity of 'contracting out' to independent providers, it seems to us that, as regards 'contracting out', North & West may properly be described as engaging in commercial transactions in services. In effect, the essence of many, if not most, 'economic' activities is the making of commercial contracts. North & West appears to be engaged, on a regular basis, in entering into commercial contracts affecting some 30 homes managed by independent providers in North & West's operational area.

192   The independent providers in question are providing services for which North &
       West has a demand. That demand results from the fact that North & West has decided
       to fulfil its functions on the basis of commercial transactions. We have no doubt that
       the contracts between North & West and the independent providers may properly
       be described as 'commercial transactions', since no private sector operator would
       enter into a contract with North & West which was not a commercial transaction.
       In making such contracts, it seems to us that North & West is necessarily engaged
       in transactions of an economic character and thus in an 'economic activity' for the
       purposes of the application of the competition rules.

193   It does not seem to us to matter that in this particular case North & West is the
       acquirer, rather than the offeror, of the services in question.

. . .

195   Moreover, we have no doubt that North & West is active as a player in a market or
       markets.

196   The first market in which North & West is active, as a contracting out purchaser, is
       the market for the supply of residential and nursing care services in Northern Ireland.
       It is apparent that over recent years the public authorities in Northern Ireland and
       elsewhere in the United Kingdom have progressively withdrawn from, or limited, the
       extent to which they are able or willing to provide residential or nursing care in their
       own statutory homes. Instead, those authorities have entered the market themselves
       to buy the beds they need from independent providers, presumably in pursuit of the
       objectives of giving greater choice to consumers and stimulating competition among
       providers (paragraph 158 above). In North & West's area some 80 per cent of the
       demand for residential and nursing care is now met by independent providers. This
       trend has apparently expanded the commercial market for the supply of residential
       and nursing care services, and/or has created a specific sub-sector of that market,
       namely the supply of residential and nursing care services by independent providers
       to HSS trusts and similar bodies. The fact that that market or sub-market has been
       created or expanded by the decision of the public authorities to rely on independent
       providers, does not alter the fact that there is such a market, and that North & West
       is an active player in that market.

197   The nature of the market may be illustrated by the admittedly sketchy information
       which we have about the United Kingdom contained in exhibit CC4 to Mr Caldwell's
       witness statement: see paragraphs 155 *et seq* above. That document refers to 'The
       Care Industry – Market size and trends'. In document CC4 'The Care Industry' is
       divided into three sectors, the private (for profit) operators, the voluntary (not for
       profit) organisations, and the statutory homes provided principally by NHS trusts
       and local authorities. The total market is said to be worth some $9 billion. The
       figures in document CC4 again illustrate the progressive withdrawal of the public
       sector from direct supply in both absolute and percentage terms. The percentage of
       residents in statutory homes now accounts for only 16.9 per cent of the whole, as

against 46.5 per cent in 1988. In absolute terms the number of residents in statutory homes (88,900), is now not much higher than the number of residents in voluntary (not for profit) homes (73,100), and very substantially less than those in the private (for profit) sector (363,900): see paragraphs 156 to 157 above.

198   However, as we understand it, a very substantial proportion of the residents in the private (for profit) sector are provided with beds on the basis of commercial transactions entered into between private homes, on the one hand, and NHS trusts and local authorities, on the other, whereby the latter purchase beds in private homes. From the point of view of the private homes, these are, as we have said, plainly business transactions. Equally, from the point of view of the NHS trusts and local authorities, one would expect those bodies to enter into such transactions on as 'business-like' basis as possible, seeking to secure the best terms they can.

199   It seems to us that the supply of residential care or nursing services by what appear to be some thousands of independent providers to NHS trusts and local authorities all over the United Kingdom is in a real sense 'big business'. That business is apparently worth several billion pounds a year. In those circumstances, transactions in the market for the supply of nursing and residential care services between independent providers on the one hand, and NHS or HSS trusts, or local authorities, on the other, seem to us as a matter of common sense to constitute 'economic activity' or be 'directed at' (to use the phrase from *Film Purchases by German Television Stations*) 'economic activity', irrespective of whether that activity is by sellers or purchasers. Indeed, it would be surprising if the Act did not cover such a large sector of economic activity.

200   There is, in addition, a second way in which North & West is active in a market, in that North & West itself runs eight residential homes, of which five are for elderly persons. North & West is thus itself part of 'the offer' in the market for residential care services in Northern Ireland. We stress, once again, that we have not gone into the facts of this case, in particular as to exactly how residents are 'allocated' as among the different homes available. It does appear, however, from the general rationale of the policy of contracting out (paragraph 158 above), and from such documents as the Care Homes Directory, cited above, and clause 8.3 of the contract with Bettercare, that residents have a choice of home, and can choose between a private, voluntary or statutory home. While competition between the various homes may perhaps be imperfect in practice, because of the special features of this particular market, we can see no reason to exclude in principle the possibility that all three kinds of home in Northern Ireland are in fact competing for the custom of the potential resident, whether that potential resident is 'self funded' or not, at least as regards the services and facilities offered and probably, at least to some extent, on price. The advertisements placed by North & West itself and other HSS Trusts in the Care Homes Directory seem to confirm that these bodies actively seek residents: see paragraphs 143 and 147 above. Again, this direct participation

by North & West in the market for residential care services seems to us to be, in principle, an economic activity.

201   Thirdly, it must be borne in mind that North & West does not supply its services gratuitously. Whether in respect of its purchasing activities, or in respect of its own residential homes, North & West seeks to recover as much as possible of the cost for the services it provides from the resident in question. It may not, in most cases, be able to recover the full cost, but it is undoubtedly remunerated for the activities that it carries on. That seems to us, again, to be 'economic' activity.

At first glance, it seems that the CAT's judgment does not sit comfortably with that of the CFI in *FENIN v. Commission*, where the CFI stated that a public sector body will not be considered to be an undertaking under Article 81(1) if it is involved in the acquisition of goods or services in order to provide a social service. However, a closer look at the factual situation of these cases reveals significant differences, which could explain the different conclusions reached.

II Collusion between undertakings

(a) Agreement

The OFT has said the following on the concept of 'agreement' in paragraph 2.8 of its *Guideline OFT401*: 'Agreement has a wide meaning and covers agreements whether legally enforceable or not, written or oral; it includes so-called *gentlemen's agreements*. There does not have to be a physical meeting of the parties for an agreement to be reached: an exchange of letters or telephone calls may suffice if a consensus is arrived at as to the action each party will, or will not, take.'

Obviously this definition follows that given to the concept under Article 81(1). Furthermore, it is important to note that, like the approach of the Commission and the Community Courts under Article 81(1), the OFT has also relied on the concept of a 'single overall agreement' under the Chapter I prohibition (see decision of the OFT in *Hasbro UK Ltd, Argos Ltd and Littlewoods Ltd*, 2 December 2003 which is currently on appeal before the CAT).

(b) Decision by association of undertakings

The concept of an 'association of undertakings' has also been given a wide definition. It is important to note that it is irrelevant whether a body is involved in commercial activities of its own: it can still be considered an association of undertakings. With regard to what amounts to a decision, as with Article 81(1), the following have been considered to be decisions for the purposes of the Chapter I prohibition: the rules of an association, its code and the recommendations it produces (see decision of the OFT in *Film Distributors' Association*, Decision 6 February 2002). The OFT states the following in *Guideline OFT401*.

2.10   ... Trade associations are the most common form of associations of undertakings, but the provisions are not limited to any particular type of association. A decision by a trade association may include, for example, the constitution or rules of an association of undertakings or its recommendations or other activities.[9] In the day to day conduct of the business of an association, resolutions of the management committee or of the full membership in general meeting, binding decisions of the management or executive committee of the association, or rulings of its chief executive, the effect of which are to limit the commercial freedom of action of the members in some respect, may all be 'decisions' of the association. The key consideration is whether the effect of the decision, whatever form it takes, is to limit the freedom of action of the members in some commercial matter. A trade association's co-ordination of its members' conduct in accordance with its constitution may also be a decision even if its recommendations are not binding on its members, and may not have been fully complied with. It will be a question of fact in each case whether an association of undertakings is itself a party to an agreement.

(c) Concerted practice

The definition which was given by the ECJ in the case of *Dyestuffs* of the concept of concerted practice has been adopted under the Chapter I prohibition in the Guidelines published under the CA1998 as well as the decisional practice of the OFT (see *Hasbro UK Ltd, Argos Ltd and Littlewoods Ltd*, above p. 104). The OFT has stated the following in its Guideline on *Article 81 and the Chapter 1 prohibition (OFT401)*:

2.12   ... [A] concerted practice may exist where there is informal co-operation without any formal agreement or decision.

2.13   In considering if a concerted practice exists, the OFT will follow relevant Community precedents established under Article 81. Two main elements will need to be established:
   • the existence of positive contacts between the parties, and
   • that the contact has the object or effect of changing the market behaviour of the undertakings in a way which may not be dictated by market forces.

2.14   The following are examples of factors which the OFT may consider in establishing if a concerted practice exists:
   • whether the parties knowingly enter into practical co-operation
   • whether behaviour in the market is influenced as a result of direct or indirect contact between undertakings
   • whether parallel behaviour is a result of contact between undertakings leading to conditions of competition which do not correspond to normal conditions of the market
   • the structure of the relevant market and the nature of the product involved

9 See National Sulphuric Acid Association Ltd, Re OJ L260, 3.10.80, p. 24; [1980] 3 CMLR 429.

• the number of undertakings in the market and, where there are only a few undertakings, whether they have similar cost structures and outputs.

III Prevention, restriction or distortion of competition: the object or effect requirement

As with Article 81(1), the requirements of 'object' or 'effect' under section 2 CA1998 are alternatives. According to the OFT, any agreement 'might be said to restrict competition to some degree, in that it restricts the freedom of action of the parties. That does not, however, necessarily mean that the agreement has or will have an appreciable effect on competition, and the OFT does not adopt such a narrow approach. The OFT will assess the effect of an agreement on competition within the common market and/or within the United Kingdom or a part of it by examining an agreement it in its economic context' (paragraph 2.22 of *Guideline OFT401*).

This statement highlights the OFT's policy, in keeping with section 60 CA1998, of applying the test in the same broad manner as that set out by the ECJ in cases such as *STM* (see above at p. 73 above). Examples of agreements said to have as their object a restriction of competition involve price fixing or market sharing agreements. The CCAT stated in *Institute of Independent Insurance Brokers v. Director General of Fair Trading* (see p. 98 above) that such agreements by their nature restrict competition and so it is not necessary to examine whether they in fact have an effect of restricting competition. The CCAT, referring to the judgment of the ECJ in *STM*, further explained in paragraph 170 of its ruling that when considering the effect of an agreement it is necessary to take the following factors into account: the economic context in which the firms operate, the products or services covered by the agreement, the structure of the market concerned and the actual conditions in which the agreement operates.

IV Effect on trade in the UK

The OFT has dealt with how the term 'United Kingdom' should be understood in *Guideline OFT401*; obviously the definition is based on what appears in the CA1998 itself. It has stated that in practice it will focus on the effect on competition, meaning that it is very unlikely that an agreement which restricts competition in the UK does not also affect trade in the UK (see paragraph 2.21).

V The *de minimis* doctrine

As in the case under Article 81(1), the doctrine of appreciability (*de minimis*) is also incorporated in the application of the Chapter I prohibition. An important difference between the two provisions which must be noted in this regard, however, is that the doctrine under the latter does not apply in relation to the requirement of 'effect on trade in the UK': it applies in relation to the 'prevention, restriction or distortion of competition' heading only.

The OFT explains the doctrine and its application in *Guideline OFT401*. In view of the fact that the OFT can now directly apply both Article 81 and the Chapter I prohibition, the original test (contained in the old version of the *Guideline* which set the bar of appreciability at 25 per cent market share threshold) has been modified to reflect the one set out by the European Commission in its *de minimis* Notice. The revised version of the *Guideline* states that agreements will fall within the Chapter I prohibition and/or Article 81 if their object or effect is to appreciably prevent, restrict or distort competition within the common market or the United Kingdom, depending on which provision is relied upon (paragraph 2.23 of the *Guideline*). In paragraph 2.24 of the *Guideline*, the OFT repeats what the European Commission set out in its *de minimis Notice*, with regard to market share thresholds. That is to say, agreements between undertakings do not appreciably restrict competition if the aggregate market share of the parties in any of the relevant markets does not exceed 10 per cent (in the case of competing undertakings) or 15 per cent (in the case of non-competing undertakings). Similarly, as in the *de minimis* Notice both of these thresholds are reduced to 5 per cent if competition on the relevant market is restricted by the cumulative foreclosure effect of parallel networks of agreements that have similar effects on the market.

Paragraph 2.25 of the *Guideline* provides non-exhaustive examples of anti-competitive agreements, which might appreciably restrict competition (by object or effect) and fall within the Chapter I prohibition and Article 81 EC. Some of these examples are based on the identical lists of examples appearing in Article 81(1)(a)–(e) and section 2(2)(a)–(e) CA1998. The examples mentioned in the *Guideline* include agreements aiming at: price fixing, market sharing, collusive tendering, control of production, information sharing, joint purchasing or selling, exchange of (non-)price information, restricting advertising, setting technical or design standards and fixing trading conditions.

Paragraphs 2.26–2.27 of the *Guideline* also heavily rely on and refer to the European Commission's *de minimis* Notice, stating that the OFT will have regard to the European Commission's approach (paragraph 2.26 of the *Guideline*). Furthermore, if the OFT considers that undertakings have relied on the *de minimis* Notice in good faith, it will not impose a financial penalty for an infringement of Article 81 and/or the Chapter I prohibition (paragraph 2.27 of the *Guideline*). If however, the market shares do indeed exceed the thresholds as set out in paragraph 2.24, the OFT may still find, taking into account other facts such as entry conditions, that the agreement does not have an appreciable effect on competition (paragraph 2.28 of the *Guideline*). Paragraph 2.29 of the *Guideline* also clarifies the point that the market share thresholds discussed in paragraph 2.24 apply to undertakings and their groups. That is to say, each party to an agreement will include any other undertakings that it controls or is controlled by and also any undertakings that those controlling/controlled undertakings may control. This potentially casts the net as wide as possible to push the market share of the parties to an agreement over the threshold figures.

[107]

As the position under UK is very similar to that under EC law, the reader is referred to the European Commission's *de minimis* Notice (see pp. 86–90 above).

(C) Concluding remarks

It is clear that the interpretation and application of section 2 CA1998 have been developed in harmony with Article 81(1). This should be particularly helpful to business firms and their legal advisors when considering the possible application of the two provisions, and it is also a sensible policy approach by UK authorities given the Commission's modernisation programme and its direct impact on UK competition law. Indeed, the OFT's revision of its various guidelines under the CA1998 is a positive step, which will foster greater consistency on the part of the OFT when applying Article 81(1) and/or the Chapter I prohibition.

Further reading

Garzaniti and Scassellati-Sforzoloni 'Liability of successor undertakings for infringements of EC competition law committed prior to corporate reorganisations' (1995) 16 ECLR 348

Jakobsen and Broberg 'The concept of agreement in Article 81(1) EC: on the manufacturer's right to prevent parallel trade within the European Community' (2002) 23 ECLR 127

Johsua 'Attitudes to anti-trust enforcement in the EU and US: dodging the traffic wardens, or respecting the law?' (1995) FCLI 85

Wils 'The undertaking as subject of EC competition law and the imputation of infringements to natural or legal persons' (2000) 25 ELRev 99

4

Collusion between undertakings: exemptions and exclusions

1 Introduction

The previous chapter dealt with the wide scope of Article 81(1) and the Chapter I prohibition, including some of the policy objectives that they are used to promote. In light of the enormous breadth of commercial agreements and practices that could be caught by these provisions and consequently suffer the draconian consequences of being rendered void, it is sensible to provide for exemptions to enable agreements and practices which promote innovation, investment, consumer welfare and other activities which may be beneficial to competition. Moreover, some kinds of agreements and situations are outside the scope of the prohibition by virtue of an exclusion.

This chapter deals with exemptions and exclusions from the Article 81(1) and the Chapter I prohibition.

2 EC law

(A) Exemption

The exemption provision under Article 81 features in its third paragraph and provides the following:

The provisions of paragraph 1 may, however, be declared inapplicable in the case of:
– any agreement or category of agreement between undertakings;
– any decision or category of decisions by associations of undertakings;
– any concerted practice or category of concerted practices;
which contributes to improving the production or distribution of goods or to promoting technical or economic progress, while allowing consumers a fair share of the resulting benefit, and which does not:
(a) impose on the undertakings concerned restrictions which are not indispensable to the attainment of these objectives;
(b) afford such undertakings the possibility of eliminating competition in respect of a substantial part of the products in question.

I General

Given the sweeping inclusivity of Article 81(1), it is absolutely crucial to ask whether an agreement, a decision or a concerted practice caught by that

Article might be exempted. For this reason, Article 81(3) is extremely important in practice and acts as a shield for firms in dispute with the Commission. It is worth remembering that the CFI has confirmed that potentially *any* infringing agreement etc. can be exempted. However, anyone involved in dealings with the Commission will quickly come to appreciate that, unlike Article 81(1), Article 81(3) has been interpreted very restrictively. Furthermore, given that an application of the paragraph requires a complex and detailed evaluation involving both economic criteria and public policy considerations, the general attitude of Community Courts has been to regard the Commission as the most suitable body to conduct such an analysis and therefore defer to its view (see *Consten and Grundig v. Commission, Remia BV v. Commission*). As a result the Commission has come to enjoy wide discretion under Article 81(3). Yet, to be fair, it would be incorrect to say that this discretion has gone unchecked by the Community's Courts as there are several important cases where the Commission's discretion has been subject to close scrutiny (see *Publishers' Association v. Commission, Métropole Télévision SA v. Commission* and *European Night Services v. Commission*). In *European Night Services*, the CFI annulled the Commission decision, emphasising both the obligation on the Commission to set out the facts in individual cases and also the considerations that have had decisive importance in the context of its decisions. The CFI stated that while the Commission is not required to discuss the issues of law and fact and all the considerations which led it to adopt its decision, it is required under the EC Treaty to make clear to the CFI and the firms concerned the circumstances under which it has applied the competition rules of the EC, including Article 81(3). Thus, when a Commission decision applying EC competition law lacks important analytical data vital to the application of EC competition law provisions, the Commission is not entitled to remedy such defect by adducing this data for the first time before the CFI.

Over the years, the Commission has accumulated a wealth of experience on the application of Article 81(3). In April 2004, the Commission published a Notice as part of the Modernisation Package: *Guidelines on the application of Article 81(3)*. This is a welcome document because it clarifies the criteria and establishes an analytical framework for the application of Article 81(3). Article 81(3) is not an easy provision to apply in practice and its aims have remained to some extent unclear. In light of the fact that national competition authorities and national courts now have the power to apply Article 81(3), the Commission has felt the particular need to develop a methodology for the application of this provision within an analytical framework.

II The exemption criteria

Article 81(3) contains two positive and two negative criteria, all of which must be satisfied. The burden is on the parties to show compliance (*VBVB and VBBB v. Commission*). However, these criteria are exhaustive, and so do not depend on any other criteria; when they are met the exemption applies. The Commission has stated that objectives pursued by other provisions of the EC Treaty can be taken into account when dealing with the application of Article 81(3) to the extent that they can be subsumed by these criteria:

(a) contributing to improving the production or distribution of goods or to promoting technical or economic progress; and

(b) allowing consumers a fair share of the resulting benefit; and

(c) not imposing on the undertakings concerned restrictions which are not indispensable to the attainment of these objectives; and

(d) not affording such undertakings the possibility of eliminating competition in respect of a substantial part of the products in question.

These criteria have been considered by the Community Courts and the Commission on numerous occasions in the case law, and recently the Commission shed considerable light on them in its *81(3)* Notice.

(a) Contributing to improving the production or distribution of goods or to promoting technical or economic progress

Although 81(3) refers to goods, but it applies by analogy to services. The ECJ has said that the first criterion, which defines the kind of benefits that can be taken into account, must be understood in accordance with the spirit of Article 81. In *Consten and Grundig* (for facts see p. 166 below), the ECJ stated that when considering 'improvement':

[T]his improvement cannot be identified with all the advantages which the parties to the agreement obtain from it in their production or distribution activities. These advantages are generally indisputable and show the agreement as in all respects indispensable to an improvement as understood in this sense. This subjective method, which makes the content of the concept of 'improvement' depend upon the special features of the contractual relationships in question, is not consistent with the aims of Article [81] . . . This improvement must in particular show appreciable objective advantages of such a character as to compensate for the disadvantages which they cause in the field of competition.

A detailed explanation of this criterion can be found in the Commission Notice.

Guidelines on the application of Article 81(3) OJ (2004) C 101/97

49   It follows from the case law of the Court of Justice that only objective benefits can be taken into account.[67] This means that efficiencies are not assessed from the subjective point of view of the parties.[68] Cost savings that arise from the mere

---

67 See e.g. the judgement in *Consten and Grundig* . . .
68 See in this respect Commission Decision in *Van den Bergh Foods* (OJ 1998 L 246, p. 1).

exercise of market power by the parties cannot be taken into account. For instance, when companies agree to fix prices or share markets they reduce output and thereby production costs. Reduced competition may also lead to lower sales and marketing expenditures. Such cost reductions are a direct consequence of a reduction in output and value. The cost reductions in question do not produce any pro-competitive effects on the market. In particular, they do not lead to the creation of value through an integration of assets and activities. They merely allow the undertakings concerned to increase their profits and are therefore irrelevant from the point of view of Article 81(3).

50   The purpose of the first condition of Article 81(3) is to define the types of efficiency gains that can be taken into account and be subject to the further tests of the second and third conditions of Article 81(3). The aim of the analysis is to ascertain what are the objective benefits created by the agreement and what is the economic importance of such efficiencies. Given that for Article 81(3) to apply the pro-competitive effects flowing from the agreement must outweigh its anti-competitive effects, it is necessary to verify what is the link between the agreement and the claimed efficiencies and what is the value of these efficiencies.

51   All efficiency claims must therefore be substantiated so that the following can be verified:
(a) The *nature* of the claimed efficiencies;
(b) The *link* between the agreement and the efficiencies;
(c) The *likelihood* and *magnitude* of each claimed efficiency; and
(d) *How* and *when* each claimed efficiency would be achieved.

52   Letter (a) allows the decision-maker to verify whether the claimed efficiencies are objective in nature, *cf.* paragraph 49 above.

53   Letter (b) allows the decision-maker to verify whether there is a sufficient causal link between the restrictive agreement and the claimed efficiencies. This condition normally requires that the efficiencies result from the economic activity that forms the object of the agreement. Such activities may, for example, take the form of distribution, licensing of technology, joint production or joint research and development. To the extent, however, that an agreement has wider efficiency enhancing effects within the relevant market, for example because it leads to a reduction in industry wide costs, these additional benefits are also taken into account.

54   The causal link between the agreement and the claimed efficiencies must normally also be direct.[69] Claims based on indirect effects are as a general rule too uncertain and too remote to be taken into account. A direct causal link exists for instance where a technology transfer agreement allows the licensees to produce new or improved products or a distribution agreement allows products to be distributed at lower cost or valuable services to be produced. An example of indirect effect would be a case

69 See in this respect Commission Decision in *Glaxo Wellcome* (OJ 2001 L 302, p. 1).

where it is claimed that a restrictive agreement allows the undertakings concerned to increase their profits, enabling them to invest more in research and development to the ultimate benefit of consumers. While there may be a link between profitability and research and development, this link is generally not sufficiently direct to be taken into account in the context of Article 81(3).

55   Letters (c) and (d) allow the decision-maker to verify the value of the claimed efficiencies, which in the context of the third condition of Article 81(3) must be balanced against the anti-competitive effects of the agreement, see paragraph 101 below. Given that Article 81(1) only applies in cases where the agreement has likely negative effects on competition and consumers (in the case of hardcore restrictions such effects are presumed) efficiency claims must be substantiated so that they can be verified. Unsubstantiated claims are rejected.

56   In the case of claimed cost efficiencies the undertakings invoking the benefit of Article 81(3) must as accurately as reasonably possible calculate or estimate the value of the efficiencies and describe in detail how the amount has been computed. They must also describe the method(s) by which the efficiencies have been or will be achieved. The data submitted must be verifiable so that there can be a sufficient degree of certainty that the efficiencies have materialised or are likely to materialise.

57   In the case of claimed efficiencies in the form of new or improved products and other non-cost based efficiencies, the undertakings claiming the benefit of Article 81(3) must describe and explain in detail what is the nature of the efficiencies and how and why they constitute an objective economic benefit.

58   In cases where the agreement has yet to be fully implemented the parties must substantiate any projections as to the date from which the efficiencies will become operational so as to have a significant positive impact in the market.

Efficiencies normally stem an integration of economic activities allowing firms to combine assets or entrust certain activities to one another enabling them to achieve together what would take more risk, effort and expense alone. Within businesses, there is an ongoing choice at each stage of the production process – research, production, wholesale, retail etc. – whether an activity is best done in-house or by outsourcing. In the following paragraphs the Commission explains the different types of efficiencies, marking the distinction between cost efficiencies and qualitative efficiencies.

Guidelines on the application of Article 81(3) OJ (2004) C 101/97

Cost efficiencies

64   Cost efficiencies flowing from agreements between undertakings can originate from a number of different sources. One very important source of cost savings is the

development of new production technologies and methods. In general, it is when technological leaps are made that the greatest potential for cost savings is achieved. For instance, the introduction of the assembly line led to a very substantial reduction in the cost of producing motor vehicles.

65   Another very important source of efficiency is synergies resulting from an integration of existing assets. When the parties to an agreement combine their respective assets they may be able to attain a cost/output configuration that would not otherwise be possible. The combination of two existing technologies that have complementary strengths may reduce production costs or lead to the production of a higher quality product. For instance, it may be that the production assets of firm A generate a high output per hour but require a relatively high input of raw materials per unit of output, whereas the production assets of firm B generate lower output per hour but require a relatively lower input of raw materials per unit of output. Synergies are created if by establishing a production joint venture combining the production assets of A and B the parties can attain a high(er) level of output per hour with a low(er) input of raw materials per unit of output. Similarly, if one undertaking has optimised one part of the value chain and another undertaking has optimised another part of the value chain, the combination of their operations may lead to lower costs. Firm A may for instance have a highly automated production facility resulting in low production costs per unit whereas B has developed an efficient order processing system. The system allows production to be tailored to customer demand, ensuring timely delivery and reducing warehousing and obsolescence costs. By combining their assets A and B may be able to obtain cost reductions.

66   Cost efficiencies may also result from economies of scale, i.e. declining cost per unit of output as output increases. To give an example: investment in equipment and other assets often has to be made in indivisible blocks. If an undertaking cannot fully utilise a block, its average costs will be higher than if it could do so. For instance, the cost of operating a truck is virtually the same regardless of whether it is almost empty, half-full or full. Agreements whereby undertakings combine their logistics operations may allow them to increase the load factors and reduce the number of vehicles employed. Larger scale may also allow for better division of labour leading to lower unit costs. Firms may achieve economies of scale in respect of all parts of the value chain, including research and development, production, distribution and marketing. Learning economies constitute a related type of efficiency. As experience is gained in using a particular production process or in performing particular tasks, productivity may increase because the process is made to run more efficiently or because the task is performed more quickly.

67   Economies of scope are another source of cost efficiency, which occur when firms achieve cost savings by producing different products on the basis of the same input. Such efficiencies may arise from the fact that it is possible to use the same components and the same facilities and personnel to produce a variety of products.

Similarly, economies of scope may arise in distribution when several types of goods are distributed in the same vehicles. For instance, a producer of frozen pizzas and a producer of frozen vegetables may obtain economies of scope by jointly distributing their products. Both groups of products must be distributed in refrigerated vehicles and it is likely that there are significant overlaps in terms of customers. By combining their operations the two producers may obtain lower distribution costs per distributed unit.

68   Efficiencies in the form of cost reductions can also follow from agreements that allow for better planning of production, reducing the need to hold expensive inventory and allowing for better capacity utilisation. Efficiencies of this nature may for example stem from the use of 'just in time'. purchasing, i.e. an obligation on a supplier of components to continuously supply the buyer according to its needs thereby avoiding the need for the buyer to maintain a significant stock of components which risks becoming obsolete. Cost savings may also result from agreements that allow the parties to rationalise production across their facilities.

Qualitative efficiencies

69   Agreements between undertakings may generate various efficiencies of a qualitative nature which are relevant to the application of Article 81(3). In a number of cases the main efficiency enhancing potential of the agreement is not cost reduction; it is quality improvements and other efficiencies of a qualitative nature. Depending on the individual case such efficiencies may therefore be of equal or greater importance than cost efficiencies.

70   Technical and technological advances form an essential and dynamic part of the economy, generating significant benefits in the form of new or improved goods and services. By cooperating undertakings may be able to create efficiencies that would not have been possible without the restrictive agreement or would have been possible only with substantial delay or at higher cost. Such efficiencies constitute an important source of economic benefits covered by the first condition of Article 81(3). Agreements capable of producing efficiencies of this nature include, in particular, research and development agreements. An example would be A and B creating a joint venture for the development and, if successful, joint production of a cell-based tyre. The puncture of one cell does not affect other cells, which means that there is no risk of collapse of the tyre in the event of a puncture. The tyre is thus safer than traditional tyres. It also means that there is no immediate need to change the tyre and thus to carry a spare. Both types of efficiencies constitute objective benefits within the meaning of the first condition of Article 81(3).

71   In the same way that the combination of complementary assets can give rise to cost savings, combinations of assets may also create synergies that create efficiencies of a qualitative nature. The combination of production assets may for instance lead to the production of higher quality products or products with novel features. This may for instance be the case for licence agreements, and agreements providing for

joint production of new or improved goods or services. Licence agreements may, in particular, ensure more rapid dissemination of new technology in the Community and enable the licensee(s) to make available new products or to employ new production techniques that lead to quality improvements. Joint production agreements may, in particular, allow new or improved products or services to be introduced on the market more quickly or at lower cost.[70] In the telecommunications sector, for example, cooperation agreements have been held to create efficiencies by making available more quickly new global services.[71] In the banking sector cooperation agreements that made available improved facilities for making cross-border payments have also been held to create efficiencies falling within the scope of the first condition of Article 81(3).[72]

72   Distribution agreements may also give rise to qualitative efficiencies. Specialised distributors, for example, may be able to provide services that are better tailored to customer needs or to provide quicker delivery or better quality assurance throughout the distribution chain.[73]

(b) Allowing consumers a fair share of the resulting benefit

Paragraphs 85–92 of the *Notice* deal with the interpretation and application of the second criterion as follows.

Guidelines on the application of Article 81(3) OJ (2004) C 101/97

85   The concept of *'fair share'* implies that the pass-on of benefits must at least compensate consumers for any actual or likely negative impact caused to them by the restriction of competition found under Article 81(1). In line with the overall objective of Article 81 to prevent anti-competitive agreements, the net effect of the agreement must at least be neutral from the point of view of those consumers directly or likely affected by the agreement.[80] If such consumers are worse off following the agreement, the second condition of Article 81(3) is not fulfilled. The positive effects of an agreement must be balanced against and compensate for its

---

70 See e.g. Commission Decision in *GEAE/P&W* (OJ 2000 L 58, p. 16); in *British Interactive Broadcasting/Open* (OJ 1999 L 312, p. 1); and in *Asahi/Saint Gobain* (OJ 1994 L 354, p. 87).
71 See e.g. Commission Decision in *Atlas* (OJ 1996 L 239, p. 23), and in *Phoenix/Global One* (OJ 1996 L 239, p. 57).
72 See e.g. Commission Decision in *Uniform Eurocheques* (OJ 1985 L 35, p. 43).
73 See e.g. Commission Decision in *Cégétel + 4* (OJ 1999 L 88, p. 26).
80 See in this respect the judgement in *Consten and Grundig*, where the Court of Justice held that the improvements within the meaning of the first condition of Article 81(3) must show appreciable objective advantages of such character as to compensate for the disadvantages which they cause in the field of competition.

negative effects on consumers.[81] When that is the case consumers are not harmed by the agreement. Moreover, society as a whole benefits where the efficiencies lead either to fewer resources being used to produce the output consumed or to the production of more valuable products and thus to a more efficient allocation of resources.

86   It is not required that consumers receive a share of each and every efficiency gain identified under the first condition. It suffices that sufficient benefits are passed on to compensate for the negative effects of the restrictive agreement. In that case consumers obtain a fair share of the overall benefits.[82] If a restrictive agreement is likely to lead to higher prices, consumers must be fully compensated through increased quality or other benefits. If not, the second condition of Article 81(3) is not fulfilled.

87   The decisive factor is the overall impact on consumers of the products within the relevant market and not the impact on individual members of this group of consumers.[83] In some cases a certain period of time may be required before the efficiencies materialise. Until such time the agreement may have only negative effects. The fact that pass-on to the consumer occurs with a certain time lag does not in itself exclude the application of Article 81(3). However, the greater the time lag, the greater must be the efficiencies to compensate also for the loss to consumers during the period preceding the pass-on.

88   In making this assessment it must be taken into account that the value of a gain for consumers in the future is not the same as a present gain for consumers. The value of saving 100 Euro today is greater than the value of saving the same amount a year later. A gain for consumers in the future therefore does not fully compensate for a present loss to consumers of equal nominal size. In order to allow for an appropriate comparison of a present loss to consumers with a future gain to consumers, the value of future gains must be discounted. The discount rate applied must reflect the rate of inflation, if any, and lost interest as an indication of the lower value of future gains.

89   In other cases the agreement may enable the parties to obtain the efficiencies earlier than would otherwise be possible. In such circumstances it is necessary to take account of the likely negative impact on consumers within the relevant market once this lead-time has lapsed. If through the restrictive agreement the parties obtain a strong position on the market, they may be able to charge a significantly higher price than would otherwise have been the case. For the second condition of Article 81(3) to be satisfied the benefit to consumers of having earlier access to the products must

---

81 It is recalled that positive and negative effects on consumers are in principle balanced within each relevant market (*cf.* paragraph 43 above).
82 See in this respect paragraph 48 of the *Metro (I)* judgment . . .
83 See paragraph 163 of the judgement in *Shaw* . . .

be equally significant. This may for instance be the case where an agreement allows two tyre manufacturers to bring to market three years earlier a new substantially safer tyre but at the same time, by increasing their market power, allows them to raise prices by 5%. In such a case it is likely that having early access to a substantially improved product outweighs the price increase.

90   The second condition of Article 81(3) incorporates a sliding scale. The greater the restriction of competition found under Article 81(1) the greater must be the efficiencies and the pass-on to consumers. This sliding scale approach implies that if the restrictive effects of an agreement are relatively limited and the efficiencies are substantial it is likely that a fair share of the cost savings will be passed on to consumers. In such cases it is therefore normally not necessary to engage in a detailed analysis of the second condition of Article 81(3), provided that the three other conditions for the application of this provision are fulfilled.

91   If, on the other hand, the restrictive effects of the agreement are substantial and the cost savings are relatively insignificant, it is very unlikely that the second condition of Article 81(3) will be fulfilled. The impact of the restriction of competition depends on the intensity of the restriction and the degree of competition that remains following the agreement.

92   If the agreement has both substantial anti-competitive effects and substantial pro-competitive effects a careful analysis is required. In the application of the balancing test in such cases it must be taken into account that competition is an important long-term driver of efficiency and innovation. Undertakings that are not subject to effective competitive constraints – such as for instance dominant firms – have less incentive to maintain or build on the efficiencies. The more substantial the impact of the agreement on competition, the more likely it is that consumers will suffer in the long run.

It is interesting to note that, although the ECJ has emphasised the need for *objective* benefits sufficient to compensate for anti-competitive effects, this assessment will inevitably require some degree of subjectivity about what can constitute a consumer benefit and how to quantify such benefits. There may also be a tendency for non-competition considerations to become part of the equation. Now that national competition authorities and courts have been empowered to apply Article 81(3) under Regulation 1/2003, it will be crucial to take measures to avoid divergence of application. Paragraphs 95–104 of the *Notice* establish an analytical framework for assessing 'consumer pass-on' of efficiency gains in relation to cost efficiencies and other efficiencies. The Commission acknowledges that in many situations it is hard to calculate consumer pass-on (see paragraph 103). Hence, according to the Commission, firms are only required to support their claims by providing, where reasonable, estimates and other data in a given case.

Guidelines on the application of Article 81(3) OJ (2004) C 101/97

Pass-on and balancing of cost efficiencies

95 When markets, as is normally the case, are not perfectly competitive, undertakings are able to influence the market price to a greater or lesser extent by altering their output.[85] They may also be able to price discriminate amongst customers.

96 Cost efficiencies may in some circumstances lead to increased output and lower prices for the affected consumers. If due to cost efficiencies the undertakings in question can increase profits by expanding output, consumer pass-on may occur. In assessing the extent to which cost efficiencies are likely to be passed on to consumers and the outcome of the balancing test contained in Article 81(3) the following factors are in particular taken into account:
(a) The characteristics and structure of the market,
(b) The nature and magnitude of the efficiency gains,
(c) The elasticity of demand, and
(d) The magnitude of the restriction of competition.
All factors must normally be considered. Since Article 81(3) only applies in cases where competition on the market is being appreciably restricted ... there can be no presumption that residual competition will ensure that consumers receive a fair share of the benefits. However, the degree of competition remaining on the market and the nature of this competition influences the likelihood of pass-on.

97 The greater the degree of residual competition the more likely it is that individual undertakings will try to increase their sales by passing on cost efficiencies. If undertakings compete mainly on price and are not subject to significant capacity constraints, pass-on may occur relatively quickly. If competition is mainly on capacity and capacity adaptations occur with a certain time lag, pass-on will be slower. Pass-on is also likely to be slower when the market structure is conducive to tacit collusion.[86] If competitors are likely to retaliate against an increase in output by one or more parties to the agreement, the incentive to increase output may be tempered, unless the competitive advantage conferred by the efficiencies is such that the undertakings concerned have an incentive to break away from the common policy adopted on the market by the members of the oligopoly. In other words, the efficiencies generated by the agreement may turn the undertakings concerned into so-called 'mavericks'.[87]

---

85 In perfectly competitive markets individual undertakings are price takers. They sell their products at the market price, which is determined by overall supply and demand. The output of the individual undertaking is so small that any individual undertaking's change in output does not affect the market price.

86 Undertakings collude tacitly when in an oligopolistic market they are able to coordinate their action on the market without resorting to an explicit cartel agreement.

87 This term refers to undertakings that constrain the pricing behaviour of other undertakings in the market who might otherwise have tacitly colluded.

98   The nature of the efficiency gains also plays an important role. According to economic theory undertakings maximise their profits by selling units of output until marginal revenue equals marginal cost. Marginal revenue is the change in total revenue resulting from selling an additional unit of output and marginal cost is the change in total cost resulting from producing that additional unit of output. It follows from this principle that as a general rule output and pricing decisions of a profit maximising undertaking are not determined by its fixed costs (i.e. costs that do not vary with the rate of production) but by its variable costs (i.e. costs that vary with the rate of production). After fixed costs are incurred and capacity is set, pricing and output decisions are determined by variable cost and demand conditions. Take for instance a situation in which two companies each produce two products on two production lines operating only at half their capacities. A specialisation agreement may allow the two undertakings to specialise in producing one of the two products and scrap their second production line for the other product. At the same time the specialisation may allow the companies to reduce variable input and stocking costs. Only the latter savings will have a direct effect on the pricing and output decisions of the undertakings, as they will influence the marginal costs of production. The scrapping by each undertaking of one of their production lines will not reduce their variable costs and will not have an impact on their production costs. It follows that undertakings may have a direct incentive to pass on to consumers in the form of higher output and lower prices efficiencies that reduce marginal costs, whereas they have no such direct incentive with regard to efficiencies that reduce fixed costs. Consumers are therefore more likely to receive a fair share of the cost efficiencies in the case of reductions in variable costs than they are in the case of reductions in fixed costs.

99   The fact that undertakings may have an incentive to pass on certain types of cost efficiencies does not imply that the pass-on rate will necessarily be 100%. The actual pass-on rate depends on the extent to which consumers respond to changes in price, i.e. the elasticity of demand. The greater the increase in demand caused by a decrease in price, the greater the pass-on rate. This follows from the fact that the greater the additional sales caused by a price reduction due to an increase in output the more likely it is that these sales will offset the loss of revenue caused by the lower price resulting from the increase in output. In the absence of price discrimination the lowering of prices affects all units sold by the undertaking, in which case marginal revenue is less than the price obtained for the marginal product. If the undertakings concerned are able to charge different prices to different customers, i.e. price discriminate, pass-on will normally only benefit price sensitive consumers.[88]

100   It must also be taken into account that efficiency gains often do not affect the whole cost structure of the undertakings concerned. In such event the impact on the price

---

88 The restrictive agreement may even allow the undertaking in question to charge a higher price to customers with a low elasticity of demand.

to consumers is reduced. If for example an agreement allows the parties to reduce production costs by 6%, but production costs only make up one third of the costs on the basis of which prices are determined, the impact on the product price is 2%, assuming that the full amount is passed-on.

101   Finally, and very importantly, it is necessary to balance the two opposing forces resulting from the restriction of competition and the cost efficiencies. On the one hand, any increase in market power caused by the restrictive agreement gives the undertakings concerned the ability and incentive to raise price. On the other hand, the types of cost efficiencies that are taken into account may give the undertakings concerned an incentive to reduce price, see paragraph 98 above. The effects of these two opposing forces must be balanced against each other. It is recalled in this regard that the consumer pass-on condition incorporates a sliding scale. When the agreement causes a substantial reduction in the competitive constraint facing the parties, extraordinarily large cost efficiencies are normally required for sufficient pass-on to occur.

Pass-on and balancing of other types of efficiencies

102   Consumer pass-on can also take the form of qualitative efficiencies such as new and improved products, creating sufficient value for consumers to compensate for the anti-competitive effects of the agreement, including a price increase.

103   Any such assessment necessarily requires value judgment. It is difficult to assign precise values to dynamic efficiencies of this nature. However, the fundamental objective of the assessment remains the same, namely to ascertain the overall impact of the agreement on the consumers within the relevant market. Undertakings claiming the benefit of Article 81(3) must substantiate that consumers obtain countervailing benefits (see in this respect paragraphs 57 and 86 above).

104   The availability of new and improved products constitutes an important source of consumer welfare. As long as the increase in value stemming from such improvements exceeds any harm from a maintenance or an increase in price caused by the restrictive agreement, consumers are better off than without the agreement and the consumer pass-on requirement of Article 81(3) is normally fulfilled. In cases where the likely effect of the agreement is to increase prices for consumers within the relevant market it must be carefully assessed whether the claimed efficiencies create real value for consumers in that market so as to compensate for the adverse effects of the restriction of competition.

(c)   Not imposing on the undertakings concerned restrictions which are not indispensable to the attainment of these objectives

The third criterion in Article 81(3) implies that a two-fold test must be satisfied. First the agreement in question must be necessary for the attainment of the efficiencies. Second, the individual restrictions of competition which the agreement gives rise to must also be reasonably necessary in order to achieve the efficiencies. The following paragraphs of the *Notice* deal with this criterion.

Guidelines on the application of Article 81(3) OJ (2004) C 101/97

74   In the context of the third condition of Article 81(3) the decisive factor is whether or not the restrictive agreement and individual restrictions make it possible to perform the activity in question more efficiently than would likely have been the case in the absence of the agreement or the restriction concerned. The question is not whether in the absence of the restriction the agreement would not have been concluded, but whether more efficiencies are produced with the agreement or restriction than in the absence of the agreement or restriction.[74]

75   The first test contained in the third condition of Article 81(3) requires that the efficiencies be specific to the agreement in question in the sense that there are no other economically practicable and less restrictive means of achieving the efficiencies. In making this latter assessment the market conditions and business realities facing the parties to the agreement must be taken into account. Undertakings invoking the benefit of Article 81(3) are not required to consider hypothetical or theoretical alternatives. The Commission will not second guess the business judgment of the parties. It will only intervene where it is reasonably clear that there are realistic and attainable alternatives. The parties must only explain and demonstrate why such seemingly realistic and significantly less restrictive alternatives to the agreement would be significantly less efficient.

76   It is particularly relevant to examine whether, having due regard to the circumstances of the individual case, the parties could have achieved the efficiencies by means of another less restrictive type of agreement and, if so, when they would likely be able to obtain the efficiencies. It may also be necessary to examine whether the parties could have achieved the efficiencies on their own. For instance, where the claimed efficiencies take the form of cost reductions resulting from economies of scale or scope the undertakings concerned must explain and substantiate why the same efficiencies would not be likely to be attained through internal growth and price competition. In making this assessment it is relevant to consider, *inter alia*, what is the minimum efficient scale on the market concerned. The minimum efficient scale is the level of output required to minimise average cost and exhaust economies of scale.[75] The larger the minimum efficient scale compared to the current size of either of the parties to the agreement, the more likely it is that the efficiencies will be deemed to be specific to the agreement. In the case of agreements that produce substantial synergies through the combination of complementary assets

---

74   As to the former question, which may be relevant in the context of Article 81(1), see paragraph 18 above.

75   Scale economies are normally exhausted at a certain point. Thereafter average costs will stabilise and eventually rise due to, for example, capacity constraints and bottlenecks.

and capabilities the very nature of the efficiencies give rise to a presumption that the agreement is necessary to attain them.

77   These principles can be illustrated by the following hypothetical example: A and B combine within a joint venture their respective production technologies to achieve higher output and lower raw material consumption. The joint venture is granted an exclusive licence to their respective production technologies. The parties transfer their existing production facilities to the joint venture. They also transfer key staff in order to ensure that existing learning economies can be exploited and further developed. It is estimated that these economies will reduce production costs by a further 5%. The output of the joint venture is sold independently by A and B. In this case the indispensability condition necessitates an assessment of whether or not the benefits could be substantially achieved by means of a licence agreement, which would be likely to be less restrictive because A and B would continue to produce independently. In the circumstances described this is unlikely to be the case since under a licence agreement the parties would not be able to benefit in the same seamless and continued way from their respective experience in operating the two technologies, resulting in significant learning economies.

78   Once it is found that the agreement in question is necessary in order to produce the efficiencies, the indispensability of each restriction of competition flowing from the agreement must be assessed. In this context it must be assessed whether individual restrictions are reasonably necessary in order to produce the efficiencies. The parties to the agreement must substantiate their claim with regard to both the nature of the restriction and its intensity.

79   A restriction is indispensable if its absence would eliminate or significantly reduce the efficiencies that follow from the agreement or make it significantly less likely that they will materialise. The assessment of alternative solutions must take into account the actual and potential improvement in the field of competition by the elimination of a particular restriction or the application of a less restrictive alternative. The more restrictive the restraint the stricter the test under the third condition.[76] Restrictions that are blacklisted in block exemption regulations or identified as hardcore restrictions in Commission guidelines and notices are unlikely to be considered indispensable.

80   The assessment of indispensability is made within the actual context in which the agreement operates and must in particular take account of the structure of the market, the economic risks related to the agreement, and the incentives facing the parties. The more uncertain the success of the product covered by the agreement, the more a restriction may be required to ensure that the efficiencies will materialise. Restrictions may also be indispensable in order to align the incentives of the parties and ensure that they concentrate their efforts on the implementation of the agreement. A restriction may for instance be necessary in order to avoid hold-up problems once a

76 See in this respect paragraphs 392 to 395 of the judgment in *Compagnie Générale Maritime* . . .

substantial sunk investment has been made by one of the parties. Once for instance a supplier has made a substantial relationship-specific investment with a view to supplying a customer with an input, the supplier is locked into the customer. In order to avoid that *ex post* the customer exploits this dependence to obtain more favourable terms, it may be necessary to impose an obligation not to purchase the component from third parties or to purchase minimum quantities of the component from the supplier.[77]

81   In some cases a restriction may be indispensable only for a certain period of time, in which case the exception of Article 81(3) only applies during that period. In making this assessment it is necessary to take due account of the period of time required for the parties to achieve the efficiencies justifying the application of the exception rule.[78] In cases where the benefits cannot be achieved without considerable investment, account must, in particular, be taken of the period of time required to ensure an adequate return on such investment . . .

(d) Not affording such undertakings the possibility of eliminating competition in respect of a substantial part of the products in question

The final criterion in 81(3) is concerned with the concept of 'elimination of competition'. In simple terms, if an agreement leads to elimination of competition then it cannot benefit from an exemption under Article 81(3). There are detailed paragraphs in the *Notice* which explain the criterion including the concept and how its application should be handled in practice.

Guidelines on the application of Article 81(3) OJ (2004) C 101/97

105   . . . Ultimately the protection of rivalry and the competitive process is given priority over potentially pro-competitive efficiency gains which could result from restrictive agreements. The last condition of Article 81(3) recognises the fact that rivalry between undertakings is an essential driver of economic efficiency, including dynamic efficiencies in the shape of innovation. In other words, the ultimate aim of Article 81 is to protect the competitive process. When competition is eliminated the competitive process is brought to an end and short-term efficiency gains are outweighed by longer-term losses stemming *inter alia* from expenditures incurred by the incumbent to maintain its position (rent seeking), misallocation of resources, reduced innovation and higher prices.

106   The concept in Article 81(3) of elimination of competition in respect of a substantial part of the products concerned is an autonomous Community law concept specific

---

77 See for more detail paragraph 116 of the *Guidelines on Vertical Restraints* . . .

78 See Joined Cases T-374/94 and others, *European Night Services*, [1998] ECR II-3141, paragraph 230.

to Article 81(3).[89] However, in the application of this concept it is necessary to take account of the relationship between Article 81 and Article 82. According to settled case law the application of Article 81(3) cannot prevent the application of Article 82 of the Treaty.[90] Moreover, since Articles 81 and 82 both pursue the aim of maintaining effective competition on the market, consistency requires that Article 81(3) be interpreted as precluding any application of this provision to restrictive agreements that constitute an abuse of a dominant position.[91] [92] However, not all restrictive agreements concluded by a dominant undertaking constitute an abuse of a dominant position. This is for instance the case where a dominant undertaking is party to a non-full function joint venture,[93] which is found to be restrictive of competition but at the same time involves a substantial integration of assets.

107   Whether competition is being eliminated within the meaning of the last condition of Article 81(3) depends on the degree of competition existing prior to the agreement and on the impact of the restrictive agreement on competition, i.e. the reduction in competition that the agreement brings about. The more competition is already weakened in the market concerned, the slighter the further reduction required for competition to be eliminated within the meaning of Article 81(3). Moreover, the greater the reduction of competition caused by the agreement, the greater the likelihood that competition in respect of a substantial part of the products concerned risks being eliminated.

108   The application of the last condition of Article 81(3) requires a realistic analysis of the various sources of competition in the market, the level of competitive constraint that they impose on the parties to the agreement and the impact of the agreement on this competitive constraint. Both actual and potential competition must be considered.

89 See Joined Cases T-191/98, T-212/98 and T-214/98, *Atlantic Container Line (TACA)*, [2003] ECR II-, paragraph 939, and Case T-395/94, *Atlantic Container Line*, [2002] ECR II-875, paragraph 330.
90 See Joined Cases C-395/96 P and C-396/96 P, *Compagnie maritime belge*, [2000] ECR I-1365, paragraph 130. Similarly, the application of Article 81(3) does not prevent the application of the Treaty rules on the free movement of goods, services, persons and capital. These provisions are in certain circumstances applicable to agreements, decisions and concerted practices within the meaning of Article 81(1), see to that effect Case C-309/99, *Wouters*, [2002] ECR I-1577, paragraph 120.
91 See in this respect Case T-51/89, *Tetra Pak (I)*, [1990] ECR II-309, and Joined Cases T-191/98, T-212/98 and T-214/98, *Atlantic Container Line (TACA)*, [2003] ECR II-, paragraph 1456.
92 This is how paragraph 135 of the *Guidelines on vertical restraints* and paragraphs 36, 71, 105, 134 and 155 of the *Guidelines on horizontal cooperation agreements . . .* should be understood when they state that in principle restrictive agreements concluded by dominant undertakings cannot be exempted.
93 Full function joint ventures, i.e. joint ventures that perform on a lasting basis all the functions of an autonomous economic entity, are covered by Council Regulation 139/2004 on the control of concentrations between undertakings (OJ 2004 L 24, p. 1).

109   While market shares are relevant, the magnitude of remaining sources of actual competition cannot be assessed exclusively on the basis of market share. More extensive qualitative and quantitative analysis is normally called for. The capacity of actual competitors to compete and their incentive to do so must be examined. If, for example, competitors face capacity constraints or have relatively higher costs of production their competitive response will necessarily be limited.

110   In the assessment of the impact of the agreement on competition it is also relevant to examine its influence on the various parameters of competition. The last condition for exception under Article 81(3) is not fulfilled, if the agreement eliminates competition in one of its most important expressions. This is particularly the case when an agreement eliminates price competition[94] or competition in respect of innovation and development of new products.

111   The actual market conduct of the parties can provide insight into the impact of the agreement. If following the conclusion of the agreement the parties have implemented and maintained substantial price increases or engaged in other conduct indicative of the existence of a considerable degree of market power, it is an indication that the parties are not subject to any real competitive pressure and that competition has been eliminated with regard to a substantial part of the products concerned.

112   Past competitive interaction may also provide an indication of the impact of the agreement on future competitive interaction. An undertaking may be able to eliminate competition within the meaning of Article 81(3) by concluding an agreement with a competitor that in the past has been a 'maverick'.[95] Such an agreement may change the competitive incentives and capabilities of the competitor and thereby remove an important source of competition in the market.

113   In cases involving differentiated products, i.e. products that differ in the eyes of consumers, the impact of the agreement may depend on the competitive relationship between the products sold by the parties to the agreement. When undertakings offer differentiated products the competitive constraint that individual products impose on each other differs according to the degree of substitutability between them. It must therefore be considered what is the degree of substitutability between the products offered by the parties, i.e. what is the competitive constraint that they impose on each other. The more the products of the parties to the agreement are close substitutes the greater the likely restrictive effect of the agreement. In other words, the more substitutable the products the greater the likely change brought about by the agreement in terms of restriction of competition on the market and the more likely it is that competition in respect of a substantial part of the products concerned risks being eliminated.

114   While sources of actual competition are usually the most important, as they are most easily verified, sources of potential competition must also be taken into account.

94 See paragraph 21 of the judgment in *Metro (I)*.
95 See paragraph 97 above.

The assessment of potential competition requires an analysis of barriers to entry facing undertakings that are not already competing within the relevant market. Any assertions by the parties that there are low barriers to market entry must be supported by information identifying the sources of potential competition and the parties must also substantiate why these sources constitute a real competitive pressure on the parties.

115 In the assessment of entry barriers and the real possibility for new entry on a significant scale, it is relevant to examine, *inter alia*, the following:

(i) The regulatory framework with a view to determining its impact on new entry.

(ii) The cost of entry including sunk costs. Sunk costs are those that cannot be recovered if the entrant subsequently exits the market. The higher the sunk costs the higher the commercial risk for potential entrants.

(iii) The minimum efficient scale within the industry, i.e. the rate of output where average costs are minimised. If the minimum efficient scale is large compared to the size of the market, efficient entry is likely to be more costly and risky.

(iv) The competitive strengths of potential entrants. Effective entry is particularly likely where potential entrants have access to at least as cost efficient technologies as the incumbents or other competitive advantages that allow them to compete effectively. When potential entrants are on the same or an inferior technological trajectory compared to the incumbents and possess no other significant competitive advantage entry is more risky and less effective.

(v) The position of buyers and their ability to bring onto the market new sources of competition. It is irrelevant that certain strong buyers may be able to extract more favourable conditions from the parties to the agreement than their weaker competitors.[96] The presence of strong buyers can only serve to counter a *prima facie* finding of elimination of competition if it is likely that the buyers in question will pave the way for effective new entry.

(vi) The likely response of incumbents to attempted new entry. Incumbents may for example through past conduct have acquired a reputation of aggressive behaviour, having an impact on future entry.

(vii) The economic outlook for the industry may be an indicator of its longer-term attractiveness. Industries that are stagnating or in decline are less attractive candidates for entry than industries characterised by growth.

(viii) Past entry on a significant scale or the absence thereof.

III Types of exemption

There are two types of exemption under Article 81(3): individual and block. The former is individual in the sense that it is granted to an individual agreement. Before Regulation 1/2003 came into force, this would have required prior notification by the parties of the agreement to the Commission. However, since 1

---

96 See in this respect Case T-228/97, *Irish Sugar*, [1999] ECR II-2969, paragraph 101.

May 2004, notification of agreements to the Commission is no longer possible: this mechanism has been abolished (see chapter 14).

Block exemptions on the other hand are conferred by way of a market or transaction-specific regulation, which applies to categories of agreements that satisfy specified criteria. Four key block exemptions will be dealt with in later chapters of the book. These were adopted in relation to vertical agreements (see chapter 5), transfer of technology (see chapter 6) and horizontal specialisation and research and development agreements (see chapter 8).

The block exemption mechanism has great practical value. Among other things, such Regulations have clarified the Commission's approach to the application of Article 81(3) to certain categories of agreements and enhanced legal certainty while relieving firms from the expense of notifying their agreements to the Commission for an individual exemption and waiting with uncertainty as to what the Commission's announcement will be.

In the past, block exemption Regulations adopted under Article 81(3) have tended to be highly formalistic. However the vast majority have been replaced by more 'modern' Regulations, which adopt an economics-based approach. Notable examples of such methodology can be found in Regulation 2790/99, the vertical agreements block exemption Regulation.

(B) Exclusion

Several sectors are excluded, either wholly or in part, from the scope of EC competition rules. These include highly sensitive sectors covering areas ranging from agriculture to nuclear energy and military equipment. Certain provisions of the EC Treaty provide special rules for such sectors.

3 UK law

(A) Exemption

The exemption from the Chapter I prohibition under the CA1998 is contained in more complex and detailed provisions than Article 81(3). However, the fundamental ideas and the criteria for exemption as well as some of the types of exemption under the Chapter are based on Article 81(3), the relevant Community case law and the decisional practice of the Commission.

I The exemption criteria

The criteria for exemption are set out in section 9 CA1998; for an exemption to be granted, two positive and two negative criteria must be met. Given that section 9 is based on Article 81(3) and that there is a duty of consistency, the commentary, cases and materials in the previous part are relevant when dealing with the application of the section. Like Article 81(3), the criteria in section 9 are exhaustive.

S. 9 The criteria for individual and block exemptions

This section applies to any agreement which –

(a) contributes to –

    (i) improving production or distribution, or

    (ii) promoting technical or economic progress,

    while allowing consumers a fair share of the resulting benefit; but

(b) does not–

    (i) impose on the undertakings concerned restrictions which are not indispensable to the attainment of those objectives; or

    (ii) afford the undertakings concerned the possibility of eliminating competition in respect of a substantial part of the products in question.

The wording of the section is identical to that of Article 81(3). The only difference is that the phrase 'of goods' which appears in the first criterion under Article 81(3) is absent from section 9 CA1998. This has no significance in practice and the OFT has made it clear that this section applies to goods and services. As we saw above the European Commission has stated that Article 81(3) also applies to both.

The OFT states in its *Guideline on Article 81 and the Chapter I prohibition* (OFT401) that it will have regard to the European Commission Notice on Article 81(3) when applying the Article or section 9 CA1998.

II Types of exemption

The following types of exemption exist under CA1998:

(a) Individual exemption

In line with the European Commission's decision to abolish notification as part of its Modernisation programme, the UK Government too decided to abolish the notification system under the CA1998 by removing sections 4–5, 7, 12–16 and 20–24 of the Act. Individual exemptions which were granted by the OFT prior to 1 May 2004 will be valid until their expiry, after which they will not be renewed; although the OFT retains the power to cancel such exemptions.

(b) Block exemption

A mechanism for adopting block exemptions is also available under the CA1998. However, unlike the EC system of competition law this mechanism has been used infrequently. The relevant sections that deal with block exemptions under the CA1998 are sections 6 and 8. A third provision, section 7 of the Act, which used to exist and which contained the 'opposition' procedure has been repealed.

[129]

(c) Parallel exemption

The concept of parallel exemptions under the CA1998 is not related to Article 81(3); nor was it based on the latter. No such exemption exists under EC competition law. Nonetheless, the concept applies in situations closely connected to Article 81(3). The exemption applies to an agreement, on which the European Commission has made a finding of inapplicability of competition rules under Article 10 of Regulation 1/2003 (meaning a finding that Article 81 does not apply to the agreement either because the requirements of 81(1) are not fulfilled or because the criteria in 81(3) are met) or one which is covered by an EC block exemption regulation or would be covered if the agreement had an effect on trade between Member States. Paragraph 5.13 of *OFT401* states that where an agreement has no effect on trade between Member States but it would be covered by an EC block exemption regulation if it had such an effect and therefore benefit from a parallel exemption the OFT may nevertheless impose conditions on the parallel exemption or cancel the exemption if the agreement has effects within the UK, or a part of it, which are incompatible with section 9 CA1998.

A specific (and detailed) section (s. 10) features in the CA1998 which deals with parallel exemption.

(d) Other agreements exemption

Section 11 CA1998 deals with an additional situation in which an exemption may be granted. This is referred to as the 'other agreements' exemption, which has an extremely narrow scope and has not assumed any significance in practice. The section refers to situations where a ruling is made by virtue of Article 84 EC on the question of whether or not agreements of a particular kind are caught by Article 81. It states that when such a ruling is made, it does not prevent such agreements from being subject to the Chapter 1 prohibition. Subsection 2 provides, however, that 'the Secretary of State may by regulations make such provision as he considers appropriate for the purpose of granting an exemption from the Chapter 1 prohibition, in prescribed circumstances in respect of such agreements'.

(B) Exclusion

Under the CA1998 a wide range of agreements and situations are excluded from the scope of the Chapter 1 prohibition. This means that the prohibition does not apply in relation to these. The excluded agreements and situations appear mainly in Schedules 1–3. The table below contains details of various exclusions. It is worth noting that the Secretary of State has the power to add to, amend or cancel these exclusions in certain circumstances.

Table 4.1	
Situation/agreement excluded	*Source*
An agreement relating to land	Section 50 CA1998 and The Competition Act 1998 (Land Agreements Exclusion and Revocation) Order 2004
An agreement to the extent to which it would result in merger within the meaning of the provisions of the Enterprise Act 2002 (see chapter 11)	Schedule 1 CA1998, Part I
An agreement which could result in a concentration (merger) with Community dimension (see chapter 10)	Schedule 1 CA1998, Part II
An agreement subject to competition scrutiny under the Broadcasting Act 1990, the Financial Services and Markets Act 2000 or the Communications Act 2003	Schedule 2 CA1998
An agreement required in order to comply with, and to the extent that it is, a planning obligation	Schedule 3 CA1998, section 1
An agreement to the extent to which relates to any of the rules or guidance produced by a European Economic Area regulated market which is for the constitution of that market	Schedule 3 CA1998, section 3
An undertaking entrusted with the operation of services of general economic interest or having the character of a revenue-producing monopoly in so far as the prohibition would obstruct the performance, in law or in fact, of the particular tasks assigned to that undertaking	Schedule 3 CA1998, section 4
An agreement to the extent to which it is made to comply with a legal requirement	Schedule 3 CA1998, section 5
An agreement necessary to avoid conflict with international obligations of the UK and which is subject to an order by the Secretary of State	Schedule 3 CA1998, section 6
An agreement necessary for compelling reasons of public policy and which is subject to an order by the Secretary of State	Schedule 3 CA1998, section 7
An agreement relating to farmers' association, or to production of or trade in 'agricultural products' as defined in the EC Treaty and in EC Regulation 26/62	Schedule 3 CA1998, section 9

[131]

5
Vertical agreements

1 Introduction

Entering into a vertical agreement is one of the obvious options available to firms wishing to sell their products and services in the downstream market, the other options include 'vertical integration'. Before dealing with vertical agreements, however, it is useful to briefly consider the vertical integration option first. A firm wishing to vertically integrate in a particular market may do so in one of three different ways: the firm may deal with a subsidiary company, which in turn sells to customers and consumers; it may directly sell its products in its retail outlets or through the Internet. The availability of such options to a firm considering vertical integration does not however mean that achieving this goal is an undertaking free from difficulties. Indeed, there are many factors which may discourage a firm from choosing to vertically integrate. For example, the cost of vertical integration may be extremely high for the firm concerned. Also it may lack the appropriate knowledge and expertise in relation to handling the sale of its products; furthermore it may not be familiar with the market concerned, its conditions and the habits of customers and consumers. In this case, the decision of the firm concerned may be tilted towards entering into a vertical agreement. Vertical agreements give rise to interesting competition law questions and they have received special treatment in many systems of competition law.

This chapter deals with the application of EC and UK competition law to vertical agreements, an area of the law which – in the case of both the EC and the UK – has seen a radical change of approach over the years; in particular since the end of the 1990s: in the case of the EC with the adoption of EC Regulation 2790/99 and the publication of the Commission's *Guidelines on vertical restraints* (2000) and more recently in March 2004 in the case of the UK, with the decision of the Government to repeal the exclusion for vertical restraints from the scope of the Chapter I prohibition of the Competition Act 1998 (CA1998). Part 2 of the chapter will deal with the treatment of vertical agreements under EC competition law; their treatment under UK competition law is dealt with in part 3.

2 EC law

(A) Regulation 2790/99

Under EC competition law, restraints featuring in vertical agreements are considered to be less harmful than those contained within horizontal agreements. The Commission's approach to vertical agreements under Regulation 2790/99 is economic-based, as opposed to the formalistic approach adopted by its predecessors. Indeed, the change in the Commission's thinking and approach did not start emerging until around the mid-1990s. In 1997 the Commission published the *Green Paper on Vertical Restraints* and with that the Commission declared the debate open on whether reform was necessary in this area. The views presented in the Green Paper were quite radical and seem to have strengthened the opinion that the Commission's concern when assessing the pro and anti-competitive effects of vertical agreements should be with the structure of the market and their impact on the market rather than their legal form. In the end the debate settled in favour of adopting a new block exemption Regulation, Regulation 2790/99, which came to replace various block exemption Regulations which existed previously.

Regulation 2790/99 OJ 1999 L 336/21

THE COMMISSION OF THE EUROPEAN COMMUNITIES,
Having regard to the Treaty establishing the European Community,
Having regard to Council Regulation No 19/65/EEC of 2 March 1965 on the application of Article [81(3)] of the Treaty to certain categories of agreements and concerted practices, as last amended by Regulation (EC) No 1215/1999, and in particular Article 1 thereof,
Having published a draft of this Regulation,
Having consulted the Advisory Committee on Restrictive Practices and Dominant Positions,

Whereas:

(1)   Regulation No 19/65/EEC empowers the Commission to apply Article 81(3) of the Treaty (formerly Article 85(3)) by regulation to certain categories of vertical agreements and corresponding concerted practices falling within Article 81(1).

(2)   Experience acquired to date makes it possible to define a category of vertical agreements which can be regarded as normally satisfying the conditions laid down in Article 81(3).

(3)   This category includes vertical agreements for the purchase or sale of goods or services where these agreements are concluded between non-competing undertakings, between certain competitors or by certain associations of retailers of goods; it also includes vertical agreements containing ancillary provisions on the assignment

or use of intellectual property rights; for the purposes of this Regulation, the term 'vertical agreements' includes the corresponding concerted practices.

(4) For the application of Article 81(3) by regulation, it is not necessary to define those vertical agreements which are capable of falling within Article 81(1); in the individual assessment of agreements under Article 81(1), account has to be taken of several factors, and in particular the market structure on the supply and purchase side.

(5) The benefit of the block exemption should be limited to vertical agreements for which it can be assumed with sufficient certainty that they satisfy the conditions of Article 81(3).

(6) Vertical agreements of the category defined in this Regulation can improve economic efficiency within a chain of production or distribution by facilitating better coordination between the participating undertakings; in particular, they can lead to a reduction in the transaction and distribution costs of the parties and to an optimisation of their sales and investment levels.

(7) The likelihood that such efficiency-enhancing effects will outweigh any anti-competitive effects due to restrictions contained in vertical agreements depends on the degree of market power of the undertakings concerned and, therefore, on the extent to which those undertakings face competition from other suppliers of goods or services regarded by the buyer as interchangeable or substitutable for one another, by reason of the products' characteristics, their prices and their intended use.

(8) It can be presumed that, where the share of the relevant market accounted for by the supplier does not exceed 30%, vertical agreements which do not contain certain types of severely anti-competitive restraints generally lead to an improvement in production or distribution and allow consumers a fair share of the resulting benefits; in the case of vertical agreements containing exclusive supply obligations, it is the market share of the buyer which is relevant in determining the overall effects of such vertical agreements on the market.

(9) Above the market share threshold of 30%, there can be no presumption that vertical agreements falling within the scope of Article 81(1) will usually give rise to objective advantages of such a character and size as to compensate for the disadvantages which they create for competition.

(10) This Regulation should not exempt vertical agreements containing restrictions which are not indispensable to the attainment of the positive effects mentioned above; in particular, vertical agreements containing certain types of severely anti-competitive restraints such as minimum and fixed resale-prices, as well as certain types of territorial protection, should be excluded from the benefit of the block exemption established by this Regulation irrespective of the market share of the undertakings concerned.

(11) In order to ensure access to or to prevent collusion on the relevant market, certain conditions are to be attached to the block exemption; to this end, the exemption of non-compete obligations should be limited to obligations which do not exceed a definite duration; for the same reasons, any direct or indirect obligation causing the members of a selective distribution system not to sell the brands of particular competing suppliers should be excluded from the benefit of this Regulation.

(12) The market-share limitation, the non-exemption of certain vertical agreements and the conditions provided for in this Regulation normally ensure that the agreements to which the block exemption applies do not enable the participating undertakings to eliminate competition in respect of a substantial part of the products in question.

(13) In particular cases in which the agreements falling under this Regulation neverthe-less have effects incompatible with Article 81(3), the Commission may withdraw the benefit of the block exemption; this may occur in particular where the buyer has significant market power in the relevant market in which it resells the goods or provides the services or where parallel networks of vertical agreements have similar effects which significantly restrict access to a relevant market or competi-tion therein; such cumulative effects may for example arise in the case of selective distribution or non-compete obligations.

(14) Regulation No 19/65/EEC empowers the competent authorities of Member States to withdraw the benefit of the block exemption in respect of vertical agreements having effects incompatible with the conditions laid down in Article 81(3), where such effects are felt in their respective territory, or in a part thereof, and where such territory has the characteristics of a distinct geographic market; Member States should ensure that the exercise of this power of withdrawal does not prejudice the uniform application throughout the common market of the Community competition rules or the full effect of the measures adopted in implementation of those rules.

(15) In order to strengthen supervision of parallel networks of vertical agreements which have similar restrictive effects and which cover more than 50% of a given market, the Commission may declare this Regulation inapplicable to vertical agreements containing specific restraints relating to the market concerned, thereby restoring the full application of Article 81 to such agreements.

(16) This Regulation is without prejudice to the application of Article 82.

(17) In accordance with the principle of the primacy of Community law, no measure taken pursuant to national laws on competition should prejudice the uniform application throughout the common market of the Community competition rules or the full effect of any measures adopted in implementation of those rules, including this Regulation,

HAS ADOPTED THIS REGULATION:

Article 1

For the purposes of this Regulation:

(a) 'competing undertakings' means actual or potential suppliers in the same product market; the product market includes goods or services which are regarded by the buyer as interchangeable with or substitutable for the contract goods or services, by reason of the products' characteristics, their prices and their intended use;

(b) 'non-compete obligation' means any direct or indirect obligation causing the buyer not to manufacture, purchase, sell or resell goods or services which compete with the contract goods or services, or any direct or indirect obligation on the buyer to purchase from the supplier or from another undertaking designated by the supplier more than 80% of the buyer's total purchases of the contract goods or services and their substitutes on the relevant market, calculated on the basis of the value of its purchases in the preceding calendar year;

(c) 'exclusive supply obligation' means any direct or indirect obligation causing the supplier to sell the goods or services specified in the agreement only to one buyer inside the Community for the purposes of a specific use or for resale;

(d) 'selective distribution system' means a distribution system where the supplier undertakes to sell the contract goods or services, either directly or indirectly, only to distributors selected on the basis of specified criteria and where these distributors undertake not to sell such goods or services to unauthorised distributors;

(e) 'intellectual property rights' includes industrial property rights, copyright and neighbouring rights;

(f) 'know-how' means a package of non-patented practical information, resulting from experience and testing by the supplier, which is secret, substantial and identified: in this context, 'secret' means that the know-how, as a body or in the precise configuration and assembly of its components, is not generally known or easily accessible; 'substantial' means that the know-how includes information which is indispensable to the buyer for the use, sale or resale of the contract goods or services; 'identified' means that the know-how must be described in a sufficiently comprehensive manner so as to make it possible to verify that it fulfils the criteria of secrecy and substantiality;

(g) 'buyer' includes an undertaking which, under an agreement falling within Article 81(1) of the Treaty, sells goods or services on behalf of another undertaking.

Article 2

1 Pursuant to Article 81(3) of the Treaty and subject to the provisions of this Regulation, it is hereby declared that Article 81(1) shall not apply to agreements or concerted practices entered into between two or more undertakings each of which operates, for the purposes of the agreement, at a different level of the production

or distribution chain, and relating to the conditions under which the parties may purchase, sell or resell certain goods or services ('vertical agreements').

This exemption shall apply to the extent that such agreements contain restrictions of competition falling within the scope of Article 81(1) ('vertical restraints').

2   The exemption provided for in paragraph 1 shall apply to vertical agreements entered into between an association of undertakings and its members, or between such an association and its suppliers, only if all its members are retailers of goods and if no individual member of the association, together with its connected undertakings, has a total annual turnover exceeding EUR 50 million; vertical agreements entered into by such associations shall be covered by this Regulation without prejudice to the application of Article 81 to horizontal agreements concluded between the members of the association or decisions adopted by the association.

3   The exemption provided for in paragraph 1 shall apply to vertical agreements containing provisions which relate to the assignment to the buyer or use by the buyer of intellectual property rights, provided that those provisions do not constitute the primary object of such agreements and are directly related to the use, sale or re-sale of goods or services by the buyer or its customers. The exemption applies on condition that, in relation to the contract goods or services, those provisions do not contain restrictions of competition having the same object or effect as vertical restraints which are not exempted under this Regulation.

4   The exemption provided for in paragraph 1 shall not apply to vertical agreements entered into between competing undertakings; however, it shall apply where competing undertakings enter into a non-reciprocal vertical agreement and:
    (a) the buyer has a total annual turnover not exceeding EUR 100 million, or
    (b) the supplier is a manufacturer and a distributor of goods, while the buyer is a distributor not manufacturing goods competing with the contract goods, or
    (c) the supplier is a provider of services at several levels of trade, while the buyer does not provide competing services at the level of trade where it purchases the contract services.

5   This Regulation shall not apply to vertical agreements the subject matter of which falls within the scope of any other block exemption regulation.

Article 3

1   Subject to paragraph 2 of this Article, the exemption provided for in Article 2 shall apply on condition that the market share held by the supplier does not exceed 30% of the relevant market on which it sells the contract goods or services.

2   In the case of vertical agreements containing exclusive supply obligations, the exemption provided for in Article 2 shall apply on condition that the market share

held by the buyer does not exceed 30% of the relevant market on which it purchases the contract goods or services.

Article 4

The exemption provided for in Article 2 shall not apply to vertical agreements which, directly or indirectly, in isolation or in combination with other factors under the control of the parties, have as their object:
(a) the restriction of the buyer's ability to determine its sale price, without prejudice to the possibility of the supplier's imposing a maximum sale price or recommending a sale price, provided that they do not amount to a fixed or minimum sale price as a result of pressure from, or incentives offered by, any of the parties;
(b) the restriction of the territory into which, or of the customers to whom, the buyer may sell the contract goods or services, except:
   – the restriction of active sales into the exclusive territory or to an exclusive customer group reserved to the supplier or allocated by the supplier to another buyer, where such a restriction does not limit sales by the customers of the buyer,
   – the restriction of sales to end users by a buyer operating at the wholesale level of trade,
   – the restriction of sales to unauthorised distributors by the members of a selective distribution system, and
   – the restriction of the buyer's ability to sell components, supplied for the purposes of incorporation, to customers who would use them to manufacture the same type of goods as those produced by the supplier;
(c) the restriction of active or passive sales to end users by members of a selective distribution system operating at the retail level of trade, without prejudice to the possibility of prohibiting a member of the system from operating out of an unauthorised place of establishment;
(d) the restriction of cross-supplies between distributors within a selective distribution system, including between distributors operating at different level of trade;
(e) the restriction agreed between a supplier of components and a buyer who incorporates those components, which limits the supplier to selling the components as spare parts to end-users or to repairers or other service providers not entrusted by the buyer with the repair or servicing of its goods.

Article 5

The exemption provided for in Article 2 shall not apply to any of the following obligations contained in vertical agreements:

[139]

(a) any direct or indirect non-compete obligation, the duration of which is indefinite or exceeds five years. A non-compete obligation which is tacitly renewable beyond a period of five years is to be deemed to have been concluded for an indefinite duration. However, the time limitation of five years shall not apply where the contract goods or services are sold by the buyer from premises and land owned by the supplier or leased by the supplier from third parties not connected with the buyer, provided that the duration of the non-compete obligation does not exceed the period of occupancy of the premises and land by the buyer;

(b) any direct or indirect obligation causing the buyer, after termination of the agreement, not to manufacture, purchase, sell or resell goods or services, unless such obligation:
  - relates to goods or services which compete with the contract goods or services, and
  - is limited to the premises and land from which the buyer has operated during the contract period, and
  - is indispensable to protect know-how transferred by the supplier to the buyer,
  and provided that the duration of such non-compete obligation is limited to a period of one year after termination of the agreement; this obligation is without prejudice to the possibility of imposing a restriction which is unlimited in time on the use and disclosure of know-how which has not entered the public domain;

(c) any direct or indirect obligation causing the members of a selective distribution system not to sell the brands of particular competing suppliers.

Article 6

The Commission may withdraw the benefit of this Regulation, pursuant to Article 7(1) of Regulation No 19/65/EEC, where it finds in any particular case that vertical agreements to which this Regulation applies nevertheless have effects which are incompatible with the conditions laid down in Article 81(3) of the Treaty, and in particular where access to the relevant market or competition therein is significantly restricted by the cumulative effect of parallel networks of similar vertical restraints implemented by competing suppliers or buyers.

Article 7

Where in any particular case vertical agreements to which the exemption provided for in Article 2 applies have effects incompatible with the conditions laid down in Article 81(3) of the Treaty in the territory of a Member State, or in a part thereof, which has all the characteristics of a distinct geographic market, the competent authority of that Member State may withdraw the benefit of application of this Regulation in respect of that territory, under the same conditions as provided in Article 6.

Article 8

1 Pursuant to Article 1 a of Regulation No 19/65/EEC, the Commission may by regulation declare that, where parallel networks of similar vertical restraints cover more than 50% of a relevant market, this Regulation shall not apply to vertical agreements containing specific restraints relating to that market.

2 A regulation pursuant to paragraph 1 shall not become applicable earlier than six months following its adoption.

Article 9

1 The market share of 30% provided for in Article 3(1) shall be calculated on the basis of the market sales value of the contract goods or services and other goods or services sold by the supplier, which are regarded as interchangeable or substitutable by the buyer, by reason of the products' characteristics, their prices and their intended use; if market sales value data are not available, estimates based on other reliable market information, including market sales volumes, may be used to establish the market share of the undertaking concerned. For the purposes of Article 3(2), it is either the market purchase value or estimates thereof which shall be used to calculate the market share.

2 For the purposes of applying the market share, threshold provided for in Article 3 the following rules shall apply:
   (a) the market share shall be calculated on the basis of data relating to the preceding calendar year;
   (b) the market share shall include any goods or services supplied to integrated distributors for the purposes of sale;
   (c) if the market share is initially not more than 30% but subsequently rises above that level without exceeding 35%, the exemption provided for in Article 2 shall continue to apply for a period of two consecutive calendar years following the year in which the 30% market share threshold was first exceeded;
   (d) if the market share is initially not more than 30% but subsequently rises above 35%, the exemption provided for in Article 2 shall continue to apply for one calendar year following the year in which the level of 35% was first exceeded;
   (e) the benefit of points (c) and (d) may not be combined so as to exceed a period of two calendar years.

Article 10

1 For the purpose of calculating total annual turnover within the meaning of Article 2(2) and (4), the turnover achieved during the previous financial year by the relevant party to the vertical agreement and the turnover achieved by its connected undertakings in respect of all goods and services, excluding all taxes and other duties, shall be added together. For this purpose, no account shall be taken of dealings between

the party to the vertical agreement and its connected undertakings or between its connected undertakings.

2   The exemption provided for in Article 2 shall remain applicable where, for any period of two consecutive financial years, the total annual turnover threshold is exceeded by no more than 10%.

Article 11

1   For the purposes of this Regulation, the terms 'undertaking', 'supplier' and 'buyer' shall include their respective connected undertakings.

2   'Connected undertakings' are:
(a) undertakings in which a party to the agreement, directly or indirectly:
  – has the power to exercise more than half the voting rights, or
  – has the power to appoint more than half the members of the supervisory board, board of management or bodies legally representing the undertaking, or
  – has the right to manage the undertaking's affairs;
(b) undertakings which directly or indirectly have, over a party to the agreement, the rights or powers listed in (a);
(c) undertakings in which an undertaking referred to in (b) has, directly or indirectly, the rights or powers listed in (a);
(d) undertakings in which a party to the agreement together with one or more of the undertakings referred to in (a), (b) or (c), or in which two or more of the latter undertakings, jointly have the rights or powers listed in (a);
(e) undertakings in which the rights or the powers listed in (a) are jointly held by:
  – parties to the agreement or their respective connected undertakings referred to in (a) to (d), or
  – one or more of the parties to the agreement or one or more of their connected undertakings referred to in (a) to (d) and one or more third parties.

3   For the purposes of Article 3, the market share held by the undertakings referred to in paragraph 2(e) of this Article shall be apportioned equally to each undertaking having the rights or the powers listed in paragraph 2(a).

Article 12

1   The exemptions provided for in Commission Regulations (EEC) No 1983/8, (EEC) No 1984/83 and (EEC) No 4087/88 shall continue to apply until 31 May 2000.

2   The prohibition laid down in Article 81(1) of the EC Treaty shall not apply during the period from 1 June 2000 to 31 December 2001 in respect of agreements already in force on 31 May 2000 which do not satisfy the conditions for exemption provided for in this Regulation but which satisfy the conditions for exemption provided for in Regulations (EEC) No 1983/83, (EEC) No 1984/83 or (EEC) No 4087/88.

Article 13

This Regulation shall enter into force on 1 January 2000.
It shall apply from 1 June 2000, except for Article 12(1) which shall apply from 1 January 2000.
This Regulation shall expire on 31 May 2010.

(B) The application of the Regulation

The Commission has explained important points related to the substance and application of the Regulation in its *Guidelines*.

I The safe harbour of the Regulation

Paragraph 21 of the *Guidelines* explains the application criteria for the Regulation contained in Article 3 of the Regulation. The presumption of legality under the Regulation which applies to vertical agreements depends on the market share of the supplier or buyer. Generally, it is the market share of the supplier which determines the applicability of the Regulation, unless the vertical agreement contains an exclusive supply obligation within the meaning of Article 1(c) in which case the market share of the buyer determines the applicability of the exemption. In either case however the market share must not exceed the threshold of 30 per cent as set out in Article 3 if the exemption is to apply.

II The scope of the Regulation

There are several important issues to be noted in relation to the scope of the Regulation.

(a) The definition of vertical agreements

Article 2(1) of the Regulation defines the term vertical agreements. The Commission states in the *Guidelines* that there are three elements in the definition.

Guidelines on Vertical Restraints OJ (2000) C 291/1

(24)   . . .

- the agreement or concerted practice is between two or more undertakings. Vertical agreements with final consumers not operating as an undertaking are not covered; More generally, agreements with final consumers do not fall under Article 81(1), as that article applies only to agreements between undertakings, decisions by associations of undertakings and concerted practices. This is without prejudice to the possible application of Article 82 of the Treaty;
- the agreement or concerted practice is between undertakings each operating, for the purposes of the agreement, at a different level of the production or distribution chain. This means for instance that one undertaking produces a raw material which

[143]

the other undertaking uses as an input, or that the first is a manufacturer, the second a wholesaler and the third a retailer. This does not preclude an undertaking from being active at more than one level of the production or distribution chain;

– the agreements or concerted practices relate to the conditions under which the parties to the agreement, the supplier and the buyer, 'may purchase, sell or re-sell certain goods or services'. This reflects the purpose of the Block Exemption Regulation to cover purchase and distribution agreements. These are agreements which concern the conditions for the purchase, sale or resale of the goods or services supplied by the supplier and/or which concern the conditions for the sale by the buyer of the goods or services which incorporate these goods or services. For the application of the Block Exemption Regulation both the goods or services supplied by the supplier and the resulting goods or services are considered to be contract goods or services. Vertical agreements relating to all final and intermediate goods and services are covered. The only exception is the automobile sector, as long as this sector remains covered by a specific block exemption such as that granted by Commission Regulation (EC) No 1475/95.[1] The goods or services provided by the supplier may be resold by the buyer or may be used as an input by the buyer to produce his own goods or services.

(b) Vertical agreements between competitors

Guidelines on Vertical Restraints OJ (2000) C 291/1

(26)   Article 2(4) of the Block Exemption Regulation explicitly excludes from its application 'vertical agreements entered into between competing undertakings'. . . However, the vertical aspects of such agreements need to be assessed under these Guidelines. Article 1(a) of the Block Exemption Regulation defines competing undertakings as 'actual or potential suppliers in the same product market', irrespective of whether or not they are competitors on the same geographic market. Competing undertakings are undertakings that are actual or potential suppliers of the contract goods or services or goods or services that are substitutes for the contract goods or services. A potential supplier is an undertaking that does not actually produce a competing product but could and would be likely to do so in the absence of the agreement in response to a small and permanent increase in relative prices. This means that the undertaking would be able and likely to undertake the necessary additional investments and supply the market within 1 year. This assessment has to be based on realistic grounds; the mere theoretical possibility of entering a market is not sufficient.[3]

---

1 OJ L 145, 29.6.1995, p. 25.
3 See Commission Notice on the definition of the relevant market for the purposes of Community competition law, OJ C 372, 9.12.1997, p. 5, at paras. 20–24, the Commission's Thirteenth Report on Competition Policy, point 55, and Commission Decision 90/410/EEC in Case No IV/32.009 – *Elopak/Metal BoxOdin*, OJ L 209, 8.8.1990, p. 15.

(27)   There are three exceptions to the general exclusion of vertical agreements between competitors, all three being set out in Article 2(4) and relating to non-
reciprocal agreements. Non-reciprocal means, for instance, that while one manufacturer becomes the distributor of the products of another manufacturer, the latter
does not become the distributor of the products of the first manufacturer. Non-
reciprocal agreements between competitors are covered by the Block Exemption
Regulation where (1) the buyer has a turnover not exceeding EUR 100 million,
or (2) the supplier is a manufacturer and distributor of goods, while the buyer
is only a distributor and not also a manufacturer of competing goods, or (3) the
supplier is a provider of services operating at several levels of trade, while the
buyer does not provide competing services at the level of trade where it purchases
the contract services. The second exception covers situations of dual distribution,
i.e. the manufacturer of particular goods also acts as distributor of the goods in
competition with independent distributors of his goods. A distributor who provides specifications to a manufacturer to produce particular goods under the distributor's brand name is not to be considered a manufacturer of such own-brand
goods. The third exception covers similar situations of dual distribution, but in this
case for services, when the supplier is also a provider of services at the level of
the buyer.

(c) Vertical agreements containing provisions on intellectual property rights (IPRs)

By virtue of Article 2(3), the Regulation also applies to vertical agreements
containing certain clauses relating to the assignment of IPRs to or use of IPRs
by the buyer. All other vertical agreements containing IPR clauses are excluded.
The Regulation applies to vertical agreements containing IPR clauses when the
conditions set out in Article 2(3) are satisfied.

(d) The relationship between the Regulation and other block exemption Regulations

According to Article 2(5), the Regulation does not apply to vertical agreements
falling within the scope of any other block exemption Regulation, which means
that situations where an agreement is covered by block exemption Regulations,
such as Regulation 772/2004 on the transfer of technology (see chapter 6).

III Hardcore restrictions under the Regulation

Article 4 contains a list of 'hardcore' restrictions, the inclusion of which in a
vertical agreement disapplies the exemption provided by the Regulation. This
means that the benefit of the block exemption is lost for the entire agreement if
there is one or more 'hardcore' restriction (see paragraph 66 of the *Guidelines*).
To use the language of the Guidelines: there is no severability in relation to
hardcore restrictions. However, severability is possible where the conditions set
out in Article 5 (see pp. 149–151 below) are satisfied. The *Guidelines* provide
a helpful explanation of the restrictions in Article 4 in the following paragraphs.

Guidelines on Vertical Restraints OJ (2000) C 291/1

Article 4(a)

(47)   The hardcore restriction set out in Article 4(a) of the Block Exemption Regulation concerns resale price maintenance (RPM), that is agreements or concerted practices having as their direct or indirect object the establishment of a fixed or minimum resale price or a fixed or minimum price level to be observed by the buyer. In the case of contractual provisions or concerted practices that directly establish the resale price, the restriction is clear cut. However, RPM can also be achieved through indirect means. Examples of the latter are an agreement fixing the distribution margin, fixing the maximum level of discount the distributor can grant from a prescribed price level, making the grant of rebates or reimbursement of promotional costs by the supplier subject to the observance of a given price level, linking the prescribed resale price to the resale prices of competitors, threats, intimidation, warnings, penalties, delay or suspension of deliveries or contract terminations in relation to observance of a given price level. Direct or indirect means of achieving price fixing can be made more effective when combined with measures to identify price-cutting distributors, such as the implementation of a price monitoring system, or the obligation on retailers to report other members of the distribution network who deviate from the standard price level. Similarly, direct or indirect price fixing can be made more effective when combined with measures which may reduce the buyer's incentive to lower the resale price, such as the supplier printing a recommended resale price on the product or the supplier obliging the buyer to apply a most-favoured-customer clause. The same indirect means and the same 'supportive' measures can be used to make maximum or recommended prices work as RPM. However, the provision of a list of recommended prices or maximum prices by the supplier to the buyer is not considered in itself as leading to RPM.

. . .

Article 4(b)

(49)   The hardcore restriction set out in Article 4(b) of the Block Exemption Regulation concerns agreements or concerted practices that have as their direct or indirect object the restriction of sales by the buyer, in as far as those restrictions relate to the territory into which or the customers to whom the buyer may sell the contract goods or services. That hardcore restriction relates to market partitioning by territory or by customer. That may be the result of direct obligations, such as the obligation not to sell to certain customers or to customers in certain territories or the obligation to refer orders from these customers to other distributors. It may also result from indirect measures aimed at inducing the distributor not to sell to such customers, such as refusal or reduction of bonuses or discounts, refusal to supply, reduction of supplied volumes or limitation of supplied volumes to the demand within the allocated territory or customer group, threat of contract termination or profit pass-over obligations. It may further result from the supplier not providing a Community-wide

guarantee service, whereby all distributors are obliged to provide the guarantee service and are reimbursed for this service by the supplier, even in relation to products sold by other distributors into their territory. These practices are even more likely to be viewed as a restriction of the buyer's sales when used in conjunction with the implementation by the supplier of a monitoring system aimed at verifying the effective destination of the supplied goods, e.g. the use of differentiated labels or serial numbers. However, a prohibition imposed on all distributors to sell to certain end users is not classified as a hardcore restriction if there is an objective justification related to the product, such as a general ban on selling dangerous substances to certain customers for reasons of safety or health. It implies that also the supplier himself does not sell to these customers. Nor are obligations on the reseller relating to the display of the supplier's brand name classified as hardcore.

Exceptions in Article 4(b)

(50)   There are four exceptions to the hardcore restriction in Article 4(b) of the Block Exemption Regulation. The first exception allows a supplier to restrict active sales by his direct buyers to a territory or a customer group which has been allocated exclusively to another buyer or which the supplier has reserved to itself. A territory or customer group is exclusively allocated when the supplier agrees to sell his product only to one distributor for distribution in a particular territory or to a particular customer group and the exclusive distributor is protected against active selling into his territory or to his customer group by the supplier and all the other buyers of the supplier inside the Community. The supplier is allowed to combine the allocation of an exclusive territory and an exclusive customer group by for instance appointing an exclusive distributor for a particular customer group in a certain territory. This protection of exclusively allocated territories or customer groups must, however, permit passive sales to such territories or customer groups. For the application of Article 4(b) of the Block Exemption Regulation, the Commission interprets 'active' and 'passive' sales as follows:

– 'Active' sales mean actively approaching individual customers inside another distributor's exclusive territory or exclusive customer group by for instance direct mail or visits; or actively approaching a specific customer group or customers in a specific territory allocated exclusively to another distributor through advertisement in media or other promotions specifically targeted at that customer group or targeted at customers in that territory; or establishing a warehouse or distribution outlet in another distributor's exclusive territory.

– 'Passive' sales mean responding to unsolicited requests from individual customers including delivery of goods or services to such customers. General advertising or promotion in media or on the Internet that reaches customers in other distributors' exclusive territories or customer groups but which is a reasonable way to reach customers outside those territories or customer groups, for instance to reach customers in nonexclusive territories or in one's own territory, are passive sales.

[147]

(51)   Every distributor must be free to use the Internet to advertise or to sell products. A restriction on the use of the Internet by distributors could only be compatible with the Block Exemption Regulation to the extent that promotion on the Internet or sales over the Internet would lead to active selling into other distributors' exclusive territories or customer groups. In general, the use of the Internet is not considered a form of active sales into such territories or customer groups, since it is a reasonable way to reach every customer. The fact that it may have effects outside one's own territory or customer group results from the technology, i.e. the easy access from everywhere. If a customer visits the web site of a distributor and contacts the distributor and if such contact leads to a sale, including delivery, then that is considered passive selling. The language used on the web site or in the communication plays normally no role in that respect. Insofar as a web site is not specifically targeted at customers primarily inside the territory or customer group exclusively allocated to another distributor, for instance with the use of banners or links in pages of providers specifically available to these exclusively allocated customers, the website is not considered a form of active selling. However, unsolicited e-mails sent to individual customers or specific customer groups are considered active selling. The same considerations apply to selling by catalogue. Notwithstanding what has been said before, the supplier may require quality standards for the use of the Internet site to resell his goods, just as the supplier may require quality standards for a shop or for advertising and promotion in general. The latter may be relevant in particular for selective distribution. An outright ban on Internet or catalogue selling is only possible if there is an objective justification. In any case, the supplier cannot reserve to itself sales and/or advertising over the Internet.

(52)   There are three other exceptions to the second hardcore restriction set out in Article 4(b) of the Block Exemption Regulation. All three exceptions allow for the restriction of both active and passive sales. Thus, it is permissible to restrict a wholesaler from selling to end users, to restrict an appointed distributor in a selective distribution system from selling, at any level of trade, to unauthorised distributors in markets where such a system is operated, and to restrict a buyer of components supplied for incorporation from reselling them to competitors of the supplier. The term 'component' includes any intermediate goods and the term 'incorporation' refers to the use of any input to produce goods.

(53)   The hardcore restriction set out in Article 4(c) of the Block Exemption Regulation concerns the restriction of active or passive sales to end users, whether professional end users or final consumers, by members of a selective distribution network. This means that dealers in a selective distribution system, as defined in Article 1(d) of the Block Exemption Regulation, cannot be restricted in the users or purchasing agents acting on behalf of these users to whom they may sell. For instance, also in a selective distribution system the dealer should be free to advertise and sell with the help of the Internet. Selective distribution may be combined with exclusive distribution provided that active and passive selling is not restricted anywhere. The

supplier may therefore commit itself to supplying only one dealer or a limited number of dealers in a given territory.

Article 4(c)

(54)   In addition, in the case of selective distribution, restrictions can be imposed on the dealer's ability to determine the location of his business premises. Selected dealers may be prevented from running their business from different premises or from opening a new outlet in a different location. If the dealer's outlet is mobile ('shop on wheels'), an area may be defined outside which the mobile outlet cannot be operated.

Article 4(d)

(55)   The hardcore restriction set out in Article 4(d) of the Block Exemption Regulation concerns the restriction of cross-supplies between appointed distributors within a selective distribution system. This means that an agreement or concerted practice may not have as its direct or indirect object to prevent or restrict the active or passive selling of the contract products between the selected distributors. Selected distributors must remain free to purchase the contract products from other appointed distributors within the network, operating either at the same or at a different level of trade. This means that selective distribution cannot be combined with vertical restraints aimed at forcing distributors to purchase the contract products exclusively from a given source, for instance exclusive purchasing. It also means that within a selective distribution network no restrictions can be imposed on appointed wholesalers as regards their sales of the product to appointed retailers.

Article 4(e)

(56)   The hardcore restriction set out in Article 4(e) of the Block Exemption Regulation concerns agreements that prevent or restrict end-users, independent repairers and service providers from obtaining spare parts directly from the manufacturer of these spare parts. An agreement between a manufacturer of spare parts and a buyer who incorporates these parts into his own products (original equipment manufacturer (OEM)), may not, either directly or indirectly, prevent or restrict sales by the manufacturer of these spare parts to end users, independent repairers or service providers. Indirect restrictions may arise in particular when the supplier of the spare parts is restricted in supplying technical information and special equipment which are necessary for the use of spare parts by users, independent repairers or service providers. However, the agreement may place restrictions on the supply of the spare parts to the repairers or service providers entrusted by the original equipment manufacturer with the repair or servicing of his own goods. In other words, the original equipment manufacturer may require his own repair and service network to buy the spare parts from it.

IV Exclusions under Article 5

Article 5 provides for exclusions of certain clauses from the coverage of the Regulation. As noted above however, in such a case the Regulation continues to apply to the remainder of the agreement in question if it is possible to sever the infringing clauses. The *Guidelines* deal with the exclusions under Article 5 in paragraphs 58–61.

Guidelines on Vertical Restraints OJ (2000) C 291/1

(58)   The first exclusion is provided in Article 5(a) of the Block Exemption Regulation and concerns non-compete obligations. Non-compete obligations are obligations that require the buyer to purchase from the supplier or from another undertaking designated by the supplier more than 80% of the buyer's total purchases during the previous year of the contract goods and services and their substitutes (see the definition in Article 1(b) of the Block Exemption Regulation), thereby preventing the buyer from purchasing competing goods or services or limiting such purchases to less than 20% of total purchases. Where for the year preceding the conclusion of the contract no relevant purchasing data for the buyer are available, the buyer's best estimate of his annual total requirements may be used. Such non-compete obligations are not covered by the Block Exemption Regulation when their duration is indefinite or exceeds five years. Non-compete obligations that are tacitly renewable beyond a period of five years are also not covered by the Block Exemption Regulation. However, non-compete obligations are covered when their duration is limited to five years or less, or when renewal beyond five years requires explicit consent of both parties and no obstacles exist that hinder the buyer from effectively terminating the non-compete obligation at the end of the five year period. If for instance the agreement provides for a five-year non-compete obligation and the supplier provides a loan to the buyer, the repayment of that loan should not hinder the buyer from effectively terminating the non-compete obligation at the end of the five-year period; the repayment needs to be structured in equal or decreasing instalments and should not increase over time. This is without prejudice to the possibility, in the case for instance of a new distribution outlet, to delay repayment for the first one or two years until sales have reached a certain level. The buyer must have the possibility to repay the remaining debt where there is still an outstanding debt at the end of the non-compete obligation. Similarly, when the supplier provides the buyer with equipment which is not relationship-specific, the buyer should have the possibility to take over the equipment at its market asset value at the end of the non-compete obligation.

(59)   The five-year duration limit does not apply when the goods or services are resold by the buyer 'from premises and land owned by the supplier or leased by the supplier from third parties not connected with the buyer.' In such cases the non-compete obligation may be of the same duration as the period of occupancy of the point of

sale by the buyer (Article 5(a) of the Block Exemption Regulation). The reason for this exception is that it is normally unreasonable to expect a supplier to allow competing products to be sold from premises and land owned by the supplier without his permission. Artificial ownership constructions intended to avoid the five-year limit cannot benefit from this exception.

(60)   The second exclusion from the block exemption is provided for in Article 5(b) of the Block Exemption Regulation and concerns post term non-compete obligations. Such obligations are normally not covered by the Block Exemption Regulation, unless the obligation is indispensable to protect know-how transferred by the supplier to the buyer, is limited to the point of sale from which the buyer has operated during the contract period, and is limited to a maximum period of one year. According to the definition in Article 1(f) of the Block Exemption Regulation the know-how needs to be 'substantial', meaning 'that the know-how includes information which is indispensable to the buyer for the use, sale or resale of the contract goods or services'.

(61)   The third exclusion from the block exemption is provided for in Article 5(c) of the Block Exemption Regulation and concerns the sale of competing goods in a selective distribution system. The Block Exemption Regulation covers the combination of selective distribution with a non-compete obligation, obliging the dealers not to resell competing brands in general. However, if the supplier prevents his appointed dealers, either directly or indirectly, from buying products for resale from specific competing suppliers, such an obligation cannot enjoy the benefit of the Block Exemption Regulation. The objective of the exclusion of this obligation is to avoid a situation whereby a number of suppliers using the same selective distribution outlets prevent one specific competitor or certain specific competitors from using these outlets to distribute their products (foreclosure of a competing supplier which would be a form of collective boycott).[1]

V Withdrawal of the Regulation

Articles 6 and 7 respectively provide that the Commission and competent national competition authorities may withdraw the benefit of the Regulation in certain situations. The *Guidelines* deal with this issue in paragraphs 71–79. A withdrawal by the Commission for example means that Article 81(1) will apply and the Commission will bear the burden of establishing an infringement and that Article 81(3) does not apply.

VI Disapplication of the Regulation

Article 8 gives the Commission the power to declare the Regulation inapplicable to vertical agreements in any given market where parallel networks of similar

---

1 An example of indirect measures having such exclusionary effects can be found in Commission Decision 92/428/EEC in Case No IV/33.542 – *Parfum Givenchy* (OJ L 236, 19.8.1992, p. 11).

vertical restraints cover more than 50 per cent of that market (this has been considered by the ECJ in the case of *Delimitis v. Henninger Bräu:* see pp. 162–165 below). In this case the benefit of the Regulation will be removed and the full application of Article 81(1) and (3) will be restored. The existence of Article 8 means that the Commission will have a choice between Articles 6 and 8 which the Commission will make taking into account, among other things, the number of competing undertakings contributing to the cumulative effect on the market. The power under Article 8 is explained in detail in paragraphs 80–87 of the *Guidelines*.

(C) The pro- and anti-competitive effects of vertical restraints

Having considered the application and scope of the Regulation, it would be helpful to shed some light on the Commission's views in relation to the pro- and anti-competitive effects of vertical restraints.

Vertical restraints are considered on the whole to be pro-competitive; though it is also possible for them to generate certain anti-competitive effects. Paragraph 103 of the *Guidelines* shows that the Commission believes that such effects include:

- foreclosure of other suppliers or other buyers by raising barriers to entry;
- reduction of inter-brand competition between the firms operating on a market, including facilitation of both explicit and tacit collusion amongst suppliers or buyers;
- reduction of intra-brand competition between distributors of the same brand;
- the creation of obstacles to market integration, including, above all, limitations on the freedom of consumers to purchase goods or services in any Member State they may choose.

With regard to the pro-competitive or positive effects of vertical restraints, which in certain situations are likely to be efficiency enhancing and lead to the development of new markets, paragraph 116 of the *Guidelines* provides:

Guidelines on Vertical Restraints OJ (2000) C 291/1

(116)   The following reasons may justify the application of certain vertical restraints:

(1)   To 'solve a "free-rider" problem'. One distributor may free-ride on the promotion efforts of another distributor. This type of problem is most common at the wholesale and retail level. Exclusive distribution or similar restrictions may be helpful in avoiding such free-riding. Free-riding can also occur between suppliers, for instance where one invests in promotion at the buyer's premises, in general at the retail level, that may also attract customers for its competitors. Non-compete type restraints can help to overcome this situation of free-riding.

For there to be a problem, there needs to be a real free-rider issue. Free-riding between buyers can only occur on pre-sales services and not on after-sales services. The product will usually need to be relatively new or technically complex as the customer may otherwise very well know what he or she wants, based on past purchases. And the product must be of a reasonably high value as it is otherwise not attractive for a customer to go to one shop for information and to another to buy. Lastly, it must not be practical for the supplier to impose on all buyers, by contract, effective service requirements concerning presales services.

Free-riding between suppliers is also restricted to specific situations, namely in cases where the promotion takes place at the buyer's premises and is generic, not brand specific.

(2)   To 'open up or enter new markets'. Where a manufacturer wants to enter a new geographic market, for instance by exporting to another country for the first time, this may involve special 'first time investments' by the distributor to establish the brand in the market. In order to persuade a local distributor to make these investments it may be necessary to provide territorial protection to the distributor so that he can recoup these investments by temporarily charging a higher price. Distributors based in other markets should then be restrained for a limited period from selling in the new market. This is a special case of the free-rider problem described under point (1).

(3)   The 'certification free-rider issue'. In some sectors, certain retailers have a reputation for stocking only 'quality' products. In such a case, selling through these retailers may be vital for the introduction of a new product. If the manufacturer cannot initially limit his sales to the premium stores, he runs the risk of being de-listed and the product introduction may fail. This means that there may be a reason for allowing for a limited duration a restriction such as exclusive distribution or selective distribution. It must be enough to guarantee introduction of the new product but not so long as to hinder large-scale dissemination. Such benefits are more likely with 'experience' goods or complex goods that represent a relatively large purchase for the final consumer.

(4)   The so-called 'hold-up problem'. Sometimes there are client-specific investments to be made by either the supplier or the buyer, such as in special equipment or training. For instance, a component manufacturer that has to build new machines and tools in order to satisfy a particular requirement of one of his customers. The investor may not commit the necessary investments before particular supply arrangements are fixed.

However, as in the other free-riding examples, there are a number of conditions that have to be met before the risk of under-investment is real or significant. Firstly, the investment must be relationship-specific. An investment made by the supplier is considered to be relationship-specific when, after termination of the contract, it cannot be used by the supplier to supply other customers and can only be sold at a significant loss. An investment made by the buyer is considered to be relationship-specific when, after termination of the contract, it cannot be used by the buyer to purchase and/or use products supplied by other suppliers and can only be sold at a significant loss. An investment is thus relationship-specific because for instance it can only be used to produce a brand-specific component or to store a particular

[153]

brand and thus cannot be used profitably to produce or resell alternatives. Secondly, it must be a long-term investment that is not recouped in the short run. And thirdly, the investment must be asymmetric; i.e. one party to the contract invests more than the other party. When these conditions are met, there is usually a good reason to have a vertical restraint for the duration it takes to depreciate the investment. The appropriate vertical restraint will be of the non-compete type or quantity-forcing type when the investment is made by the supplier and of the exclusive distribution, exclusive customer - allocation or exclusive supply type when the investment is made by the buyer.

(5)   The 'specific hold-up problem that may arise in the case of transfer of substantial know-how'. The know-how, once provided, cannot be taken back and the provider of the know-how may not want it to be used for or by his competitors. In as far as the know-how was not readily available to the buyer, is substantial and indispensable for the operation of the agreement, such a transfer may justify a non-compete type of restriction. This would normally fall outside Article 81(1).

(6)   'Economies of scale in distribution'. In order to have scale economies exploited and thereby see a lower retail price for his product, the manufacturer may want to concentrate the resale of his products on a limited number of distributors. For this he could use exclusive distribution, quantity forcing in the form of a minimum purchasing requirement, selective distribution containing such a requirement or exclusive purchasing.

(7)   'Capital market imperfections'. The usual providers of capital (banks, equity markets) may provide capital sub-optimally when they have imperfect information on the quality of the borrower or there is an inadequate basis to secure the loan. The buyer or supplier may have better information and be able, through an exclusive relationship, to obtain extra security for his investment. Where the supplier provides the loan to the buyer this may lead to non-compete or quantity forcing on the buyer. Where the buyer provides the loan to the supplier this may be the reason for having exclusive supply or quantity forcing on the supplier.

(8)   'Uniformity and quality standardisation'. A vertical restraint may help to increase sales by creating a brand image and thereby increasing the attractiveness of a product to the final consumer by imposing a certain measure of uniformity and quality standardisation on the distributors. This can for instance be found in selective distribution and franchising.

(D) The Commission's methodology of analysis

The Commission explains methodology of analysis when assessing vertical restraints in paragraph 120 of the Guidelines. This involves, in general, four steps:
• First, the firms involved need to define the relevant market in order to establish the market share of the supplier or the buyer, depending on the vertical restraint involved.

- If the relevant market share does not exceed the 30 per cent threshold, the vertical agreement is covered by the Regulation, subject to the hardcore restrictions and conditions set out in the other provisions of the Regulation.
- If the relevant market share is above the 30 per cent threshold, it is necessary to assess whether the vertical agreement falls within Article 81(1).
- If the vertical agreement falls within Article 81(1), it is necessary to examine whether it fulfils the conditions for exemption under Article 81(3).

There are several important points to note about the Commission's methodology and approach. First, there is a very clear and important emphasis placed on market shares. Second, the Commission adopts a pragmatic approach. Third, a vertical agreement which falls within the scope of the Regulation is not necessarily caught by Article 81(1). Fourth, the Commission may withdraw the benefit of the Regulation in a case even when the market share threshold is not exceeded.

Finally, there is one important issue which arises under the last two of the four steps in the methodology of analysis, namely the situation where the 30 per cent threshold is exceeded. In this case the Commission will consider the application of Articles 81(1) and 81(3).

I Article 81(1)

The Commission provides, in paragraphs 121–133 of the *Guidelines*, a helpful account of its assessment of Article 81(1) in cases where the market share threshold of 30 per cent is exceeded. It explains that in such cases a full competition analysis will be made taking into account a number of factors, which are important to establish whether a vertical agreement is within the scope of the prohibition. These factors include the market position of the supplier and competitors, the market position of the buyer, barriers to entry, the maturity of the market and the nature of the product. In paragraph 133 the Commission states that other factors may have to be considered in the assessment of particular vertical restraints. One factor worth mentioning is the cumulative effect resulting from the existence of similar agreements on the market.

II Article 81(3)

The Commission deals with the application of Article 81(3) in paragraphs 134–136 of the *Guidelines*. These paragraphs are not extracted here given that the application of Article 81(3) was dealt with quite extensively in the previous chapter, to which the reader is referred.

(E) The different categories of vertical restraints

The Commission believes that vertical restraints can be divided into four different categories: single branding, limited distribution, resale price maintenance and market partitioning. The present section provides an overview of

[155]

the meaning and scope of each of these groups – as given in the *Guidelines* – before the next section deals with their assessment by the Commission.

I Single branding

Guidelines on Vertical Restraints OJ (2000) C 291/1

(106)   Under the heading of 'single branding' come those agreements which have as their main element that the buyer is induced to concentrate his orders for a particular type of product with one supplier. This component can be found amongst others in non-compete and quantity-forcing on the buyer, where an obligation or incentive scheme agreed between the supplier and the buyer makes the latter purchase his requirements for a particular product and its substitutes only, or mainly, from one supplier. The same component can be found in tying, where the obligation or incentive scheme relates to a product that the buyer is required to purchase as a condition of purchasing another distinct product. The first product is referred to as the 'tied' product and the second is referred to as the 'tying' product.

II Limited distribution

Guidelines on Vertical Restraints OJ (2000) C 291/1

(109)   Under the heading of 'limited distribution' come those agreements which have as their main element that the manufacturer sells to only one or a limited number of buyers. This may be to restrict the number of buyers for a particular territory or group of customers, or to select a particular kind of buyers. This component can be found amongst others in:
  – exclusive distribution and exclusive customer allocation, where the supplier limits his sales to only one buyer for a certain territory or class of customers;
  – supply and quantity-forcing on the supplier, where an obligation or incentive scheme agreed between the supplier and the buyer makes the former sell only or mainly to one buyer;
  – selective distribution, where the conditions imposed on or agreed with the selected dealers usually limit their number;
  – after-market sales restrictions which limit the component supplier's sales possibilities.

III Resale price maintenance

Guidelines on Vertical Restraints OJ (2000) C 291/1

(111)   Under the heading of 'resale price maintenance' (RPM) come those agreements whose main element is that the buyer is obliged or induced to resell not below

a certain price, at a certain price or not above a certain price. This group comprises minimum, fixed, maximum and recommended resale prices. Maximum and recommended resale prices, which are not hardcore restrictions, may still lead to a restriction of competition by effect.

IV Market partitioning

Guidelines on Vertical Restraints OJ (2000) C 291/1

(113)   Under the heading of 'market partitioning' come agreements whose main element is that the buyer is restricted in where he either sources or resells a particular product. This component can be found in exclusive purchasing, where an obligation or incentive scheme agreed between the supplier and the buyer makes the latter purchase his requirements for a particular product, for instance beer of brand X, exclusively from the designated supplier, but leaving the buyer free to buy and sell competing products, for instance competing brands of beer. It also includes territorial resale restrictions, the allocation of an area of primary responsibility, restrictions on the location of a distributor and customer resale restrictions.

(F) Assessment of the categories

I Single branding

The meaning of single branding is discussed in paragraph 106 of the *Guidelines* (extracted above). The following paragraphs of the *Guidelines* deal with the treatment by the Commission of this category of vertical restraints.

Guidelines on Vertical Restraints OJ (2000) C 291/1

(138)   A non-compete arrangement is based on an obligation or incentive scheme which makes the buyer purchase practically all his requirements on a particular market from only one supplier. It does not mean that the buyer can only buy directly from the supplier, but that the buyer will not buy and resell or incorporate competing goods or services. The possible competition risks are foreclosure of the market to competing suppliers and potential suppliers, facilitation of collusion between suppliers in case of cumulative use and, where the buyer is a retailer selling to final consumers, a loss of in-store inter-brand competition. All three restrictive effects have a direct impact on inter-brand competition.

(139)   Single branding is exempted by the Block Exemption Regulation when the supplier's market share does not exceed 30% and subject to a limitation in time of five years for the non-compete obligation. Above the market share threshold or beyond the time limit of five years, the following guidance is provided for the assessment of individual cases.

(140) The 'market position of the supplier' is of main importance to assess possible anti-competitive effects of non-compete obligations. In general, this type of obligation is imposed by the supplier and the supplier has similar agreements with other buyers.

(141) It is not only the market position of the supplier that is of importance but also the extent to and the duration for which he applies a non-compete obligation. The higher his tied market share, i.e. the part of his market share sold under a single branding obligation, the more significant foreclosure is likely to be. Similarly, the longer the duration of the non-compete obligations, the more significant foreclosure is likely to be. Non-compete obligations shorter than one year entered into by non-dominant companies are in general not considered to give rise to appreciable anti-competitive effects or net negative effects. Non-compete obligations between one and five years entered into by non-dominant companies usually require a proper balancing of pro- and anti-competitive effects, while non-compete obligations exceeding five years are for most types of investments not considered necessary to achieve the claimed efficiencies or the efficiencies are not sufficient to outweigh their foreclosure effect. Dominant companies may not impose non-compete obligations on their buyers unless they can objectively justify such commercial practice within the context of Article 82.

(142) In assessing the supplier's market power, the 'market position of his competitors' is important. As long as the competitors are sufficiently numerous and strong, no appreciable anti-competitive effects can be expected. It is only likely that competing suppliers will be foreclosed if they are significantly smaller than the supplier applying the non-compete obligation. Foreclosure of competitors is not very likely where they have similar market positions and can offer similarly attractive products. In such a case foreclosure may however occur for potential entrants when a number of major suppliers enter into non-compete contracts with a significant number of buyers on the relevant market (cumulative effect situation). This is also a situation where non-compete agreements may facilitate collusion between competing suppliers. If individually these suppliers are covered by the Block Exemption Regulation, a withdrawal of the block exemption may be necessary to deal with such a negative cumulative effect. A tied market share of less than 5% is not considered in general to contribute significantly to a cumulative foreclosure effect.

(143) In cases where the market share of the largest supplier is below 30% and the market share of the five largest suppliers (concentration rate (CR) 5) is below 50%, there is unlikely to be a single or a cumulative anti-competitive effect situation. If a potential entrant cannot penetrate the market profitably, this is likely to be due to factors other than non-compete obligations, such as consumer preferences. A competition problem is unlikely to arise when, for instance, 50 companies, of which none has an important market share, compete fiercely on a particular market.

(144) 'Entry barriers' are important to establish whether there is real foreclosure. Wherever it is relatively easy for competing suppliers to create new buyers or find alternative buyers for the product, foreclosure is unlikely to be a real problem.

However, there are often entry barriers, both at the manufacturing and at the distribution level.

(145) 'Countervailing power' is relevant, as powerful buyers will not easily allow themselves to be cut off from the supply of competing goods or services. Foreclosure which is not based on efficiency and which has harmful effects on ultimate consumers is therefore mainly a risk in the case of dispersed buyers. However, where non-compete agreements are concluded with major buyers this may have a strong foreclosure effect.

(146) Lastly, 'the level of trade' is relevant for foreclosure. Foreclosure is less likely in case of an intermediate product. When the supplier of an intermediate product is not dominant, the competing suppliers still have a substantial part of demand that is 'free'. Below the level of dominance a serious foreclosure effect may however arise for actual or potential competitors where there is a cumulative effect. A serious cumulative effect is unlikely to arise as long as less than 50% of the market is tied. When the supplier is dominant, any obligation to buy the products only or mainly from the dominant supplier may easily lead to significant foreclosure effects on the market. The stronger his dominance, the higher the risk of foreclosure of other competitors.

(147) Where the agreement concerns supply of a final product at the wholesale level, the question whether a competition problem is likely to arise below the level of dominance depends in large part on the type of wholesaling and the entry barriers at the wholesale level. There is no real risk of foreclosure if competing manufacturers can easily establish their own wholesaling operation. Whether entry barriers are low depends in part on the type of wholesaling, i.e. whether or not wholesalers can operate efficiently with only the product concerned by the agreement (for example ice cream) or whether it is more efficient to trade in a whole range of products (for example frozen foodstuffs). In the latter case, it is not efficient for a manufacturer selling only one product to set up his own wholesaling operation. In that case anti-competitive effects may arise below the level of dominance. In addition, cumulative effect problems may arise if several suppliers tie most of the available wholesalers.

(148) For final products, foreclosure is in general more likely to occur at the retail level, given the significant entry barriers for most manufacturers to start retail outlets just for their own products. In addition, it is at the retail level that non-compete agreements may lead to reduced in-store inter-brand competition. It is for these reasons that for final products at the retail level, significant anti-competitive effects may start to arise, taking into account all other relevant factors, if a non-dominant supplier ties 30% or more of the relevant market. For a dominant company, even a modest tied market share may already lead to significant anti-competitive effects. The stronger its dominance, the higher the risk of foreclosure of other competitors.

(149) At the retail level a cumulative foreclosure effect may also arise. When all companies have market shares below 30% a cumulative foreclosure effect is unlikely if the

total tied market share is less than 40% and withdrawal of the block exemption is therefore unlikely. This figure may be higher when other factors like the number of competitors, entry barriers etc. are taken into account. When not all companies have market shares below the threshold of the Block Exemption Regulation but none is dominant, a cumulative foreclosure effect is unlikely if the total tied market share is below 30%.

(150) Where the buyer operates from premises and land owned by the supplier or leased by the supplier from a third party not connected with the buyer, the possibility of imposing effective remedies for a possible foreclosure effect will be limited. In that case intervention by the Commission below the level of dominance is unlikely.

(151) In certain sectors the selling of more than one brand from a single site may be difficult, in which case a foreclosure problem can better be remedied by limiting the effective duration of contracts.

(152) A so-called 'English clause', requiring the buyer to report any better offer and allowing him only to accept such an offer when the supplier does not match it, can be expected to have the same effect as a non-compete obligation, especially when the buyer has to reveal who makes the better offer. In addition, by increasing the transparency of the market it may facilitate collusion between the suppliers. An English clause may also work as quantity-forcing. Quantity-forcing on the buyer is a weaker form of non-compete, where incentives or obligations agreed between the supplier and the buyer make the latter concentrate his purchases to a large extent with one supplier. Quantity-forcing may for example take the form of minimum purchase requirements or non-linear pricing, such as quantity rebate schemes, loyalty rebate schemes or a two-part tariff (fixed fee plus a price per unit). Quantity-forcing on the buyer will have similar but weaker foreclosure effects than a non-compete obligation. The assessment of all these different forms will depend on their effect on the market. In addition, Article 82 specifically prevents dominant companies from applying English clauses or fidelity rebate schemes.

(153) Where appreciable anti-competitive effects are established, the question of a possible exemption under Article 81(3) arises as long as the supplier is not dominant. For non-compete obligations, the efficiencies described in paragraph 116, points 1 (free riding between suppliers), 4, 5 (hold-up problems) and 7 (capital market imperfections) may be particularly relevant.

(154) In the case of an efficiency as described in paragraph 116, points 1, 4 and 7, quantity forcing on the buyer could possibly be a less restrictive alternative. A non-compete obligation may be the only viable way to achieve an efficiency as described in paragraph 116, point 5 (hold-up problem related to the transfer of know-how).

(155) In the case of a relationship-specific investment made by the supplier (see efficiency 4 in paragraph 116), a non-compete or quantity forcing agreement for the period of depreciation of the investment will in general fulfil the conditions of Article 81(3). In the case of high relationship-specific investments, a non-compete obligation

exceeding five years may be justified. A relationship-specific investment could, for instance, be the installation or adaptation of equipment by the supplier when this equipment can be used afterwards only to produce components for a particular buyer. General or market-specific investments in (extra) capacity are normally not relationship-specific investments. However, where a supplier creates new capacity specifically linked to the operations of a particular buyer, for instance a company producing metal cans which creates new capacity to produce cans on the premises of or next to the canning facility of a food producer, this new capacity may only be economically viable when producing for this particular customer, in which case the investment would be considered to be relationship-specific.

(156)   Where the supplier provides the buyer with a loan or provides the buyer with equipment which is not relationship-specific, this in itself is normally not sufficient to justify the exemption of a foreclosure effect on the market. The instances of capital market imperfection, whereby it is more efficient for the supplier of a product than for a bank to provide a loan, will be limited (see efficiency 7 in paragraph 116). Even if the supplier of the product were to be the more efficient provider of capital, a loan could only justify a non-compete obligation if the buyer is not prevented from terminating the non-compete obligation and repaying the outstanding part of the loan at any point in time and without payment of any penalty. This means that the repayment of the loan should be structured in equal or decreasing instalments and should not increase over time and that the buyer should have the possibility to take over the equipment provided by the supplier at its market asset value. This is without prejudice to the possibility, in case for example of a new point of distribution, to delay repayment for the first one or two years until sales have reached a certain level.

(157)   The transfer of substantial know-how (efficiency 5 in paragraph 116) usually justifies a non-compete obligation for the whole duration of the supply agreement, as for example in the context of franchising.

(158)   Below the level of dominance the combination of non-compete with exclusive distribution may also justify the non-compete obligation lasting the full length of the agreement. In the latter case, the non-compete obligation is likely to improve the distribution efforts of the exclusive distributor in his territory (see paragraphs 161 to 177).

When discussing single branding it is important to consider the case of *Delimitis*, which clearly demonstrates the importance of undertaking an economic analysis when considering the effect of such agreement. Note however that the judgment refers to Regulation 1984/83. This is the block exemption Regulation which dealt with exclusive purchasing and has been replaced by Regulation 2790/99.

[161]

Stergios Delimitis v Henninger Bräu AG **[1991] ECR I-935**

This Article 234 reference arose out of a 'tied pub' agreement, similar to many others on the market, between a publican (Delimitis) and a brewery (Henninger Bräu), under which the former was required to purchase a minimum quantity of a range of products from the latter but was nonetheless allowed to purchase additional products from undertakings in other Member States. The ECJ was called upon to consider, among other things, the compatibility of such an agreement with Article 81 and the relevance of a 'cumulative effect' of many similar agreements.

ECJ

10   Under the terms of beer supply agreements, the supplier generally affords the reseller certain economic and financial benefits, such as the grant of loans on favourable terms, the letting of premises for the operation of a public house and the provision of technical installations, furniture and other equipment necessary for its operation. In consideration for those benefits, the reseller normally undertakes, for a predetermined period, to obtain supplies of the products covered by the contract only from the supplier. That exclusive purchasing obligation is generally backed by a prohibition on selling competing products in the public house let by the supplier.

11   Such contracts entail for the supplier the advantage of guaranteed outlets, since, as a result of his exclusive purchasing obligation and the prohibition on competition, the reseller concentrates his sales efforts on the distribution of the contract goods. The supply agreements, moreover, lead to cooperation with the reseller, allowing the supplier to plan his sales over the duration of the agreement and to organize production and distribution effectively.

12   Beer supply agreements also have advantages for the reseller, inasmuch as they enable him to gain access under favourable conditions and with the guarantee of supplies to the beer distribution market. The reseller's and supplier's shared interest in promoting sales of the contract goods likewise secures for the reseller the benefit of the supplier's assistance in guaranteeing product quality and customer service.

13   If such agreements do not have the object of restricting competition within the meaning of Article [81(1)], it is nevertheless necessary to ascertain whether they have the effect of preventing, restricting or distorting competition.

14   In its judgment in Case 23/67 *Brasserie De Haecht v Wilkin* [1967] ECR 407, the Court held that the effects of such an agreement had to be assessed in the context in which they occur and where they might combine with others to have a cumulative effect on competition. It also follows from that judgment that the cumulative effect of several similar agreements constitutes one factor amongst others in ascertaining whether, by way of a possible alteration of competition, trade between Member States is capable of being affected.

[162]

15   Consequently, in the present case it is necessary to analyse the effects of a beer supply agreement, taken together with other contracts of the same type, on the opportunities of national competitors or those from other Member States, to gain access to the market for beer consumption or to increase their market share and, accordingly, the effects on the range of products offered to consumers.

16   In making that analysis, the relevant market must first be determined. The relevant market is primarily defined on the basis of the nature of the economic activity in question, in this case the sale of beer. Beer is sold through both retail channels and premises for the sale and consumption of drinks. From the consumer's point of view, the latter sector, comprising in particular public houses and restaurants, may be distinguished from the retail sector on the grounds that the sale of beer in public houses does not solely consist of the purchase of a product but is also linked with the provision of services, and that beer consumption in public houses is not essentially dependent on economic considerations. The specific nature of the public house trade is borne out by the fact that the breweries organize specific distribution systems for this sector which require special installations, and that the prices charged in that sector are generally higher than retail prices.

17   It follows that in the present case the reference market is that for the distribution of beer in premises for the sale and consumption of drinks. That finding is not affected by the fact that there is a certain overlap between the two distribution networks, namely inasmuch as retail sales allow new competitors to make their brands known and to use their reputation in order to gain access to the market constituted by premises for the sale and consumption of drinks.

18   Secondly, the relevant market is delimited from a geographical point of view. It should be noted that most beer supply agreements are still entered into at a national level. It follows that, in applying the Community competition rules, account is to be taken of the national market for beer distribution in premises for the sale and consumption of drinks.

19   In order to assess whether the existence of several beer supply agreements impedes access to the market as so defined, it is further necessary to examine the nature and extent of those agreements in their totality, comprising all similar contracts tying a large number of points of sale to several national producers (judgment in Case 43/69 *Bilger v Jehle* [1970] ECR 127). The effect of those networks of contracts on access to the market depends specifically on the number of outlets thus tied to national producers in relation to the number of public houses which are not so tied, the duration of the commitments entered into, the quantities of beer to which those commitments relate, and on the proportion between those quantities and the quantities sold by free distributors.

20   The existence of a bundle of similar contracts, even if it has a considerable effect on the opportunities for gaining access to the market, is not, however, sufficient in itself to support a finding that the relevant market is inaccessible, inasmuch as

[163]

it is only one factor, amongst others, pertaining to the economic and legal context in which an agreement must be appraised (Case 23/67 *Brasserie De Haecht*, cited above). The other factors to be taken into account are, in the first instance, those also relating to opportunities for access.

21   In that connection it is necessary to examine whether there are real concrete possibilities for a new competitor to penetrate the bundle of contracts by acquiring a brewery already established on the market together with its network of sales outlets, or to circumvent the bundle of contracts by opening new public houses. For that purpose it is necessary to have regard to the legal rules and agreements on the acquisition of companies and the establishment of outlets, and to the minimum number of outlets necessary for the economic operation of a distribution system. The presence of beer wholesalers not tied to producers who are active on the market is also a factor capable of facilitating a new producer's access to that market since he can make use of those wholesalers' sales networks to distribute his own beer.

22   Secondly, account must be taken of the conditions under which competitive forces operate on the relevant market. In that connection it is necessary to know not only the number and the size of producers present on the market, but also the degree of saturation of that market and customer fidelity to existing brands, for it is generally more difficult to penetrate a saturated market in which customers are loyal to a small number of large producers than a market in full expansion in which a large number of small producers are operating without any strong brand names. The trend in beer sales in the retail trade provides useful information on the development of demand and thus an indication of the degree of saturation of the beer market as a whole. The analysis of that trend is, moreover, of interest in evaluating brand loyalty. A steady increase in sales of beer under new brand names may confer on the owners of those brand names a reputation which they may turn to account in gaining access to the public-house market.

23   If an examination of all similar contracts entered into on the relevant market and the other factors relevant to the economic and legal context in which the contract must be examined shows that those agreements do not have the cumulative effect of denying access to that market to new national and foreign competitors, the individual agreements comprising the bundle of agreements cannot be held to restrict competition within the meaning of Article [81(1)] of the Treaty. They do not, therefore, fall under the prohibition laid down in that provision.

24   If, on the other hand, such examination reveals that it is difficult to gain access to the relevant market, it is necessary to assess the extent to which the agreements entered into by the brewery in question contribute to the cumulative effect produced in that respect by the totality of the similar contracts found on that market. Under the Community rules on competition, responsibility for such an effect of closing off the market must be attributed to the breweries which make an appreciable contribution thereto. Beer supply agreements entered into by breweries whose contribution to the

cumulative effect is insignificant do not therefore fall under the prohibition under Article [81(1)].

25   In order to assess the extent of the contribution of the beer supply agreements entered into by a brewery to the cumulative sealing-off effect mentioned above, the market position of the contracting parties must be taken into consideration. That position is not determined solely by the market share held by the brewery and any group to which it may belong, but also by the number of outlets tied to it or to its group, in relation to the total number of premises for the sale and consumption of drinks found in the relevant market.

26   The contribution of the individual contracts entered into by a brewery to the sealing-off of that market also depends on their duration. If the duration is manifestly excessive in relation to the average duration of beer supply agreements generally entered into on the relevant market, the individual contract falls under the prohibition under Article [81(1)]. A brewery with a relatively small market share which ties its sales outlets for many years may make as significant a contribution to a sealing-off of the market as a brewery in a relatively strong market position which regularly releases sales outlets at shorter intervals.

27   The reply to be given to the first three questions is therefore that a beer supply agreement is prohibited by Article [81(1)] of the [EC] Treaty, if two cumulative conditions are met. The first is that, having regard to the economic and legal context of the agreement at issue, it is difficult for competitors who could enter the market or increase their market share to gain access to the national market for the distribution of beer in premises for the sale and consumption of drinks. The fact that, in that market, the agreement in issue is one of a number of similar agreements having a cumulative effect on competition constitutes only one factor amongst others in assessing whether access to that market is indeed difficult. The second condition is that the agreement in question must make a significant contribution to the sealing-off effect brought about by the totality of those agreements in their economic and legal context. The extent of the contribution made by the individual agreement depends on the position of the contracting parties in the relevant market and on the duration of the agreement.

II Limited distribution

As we saw above, within this category, the producer sells to one or a limited number of distributors. Several examples of limited distribution may be identified.

(a) Exclusive distribution

In an exclusive distribution agreement the supplier agrees to sell his products only to one distributor for resale in a particular territory. At the same time the distributor is usually prevented from actively selling into other exclusively allocated territories. When considering the application of Article 81(1) to exclusive distribution agreements, it is essential to refer to *Consten and Grundig v. Commission* which was mentioned briefly in chapter 3. The case is vital because the ECJ confirmed that Article 81(1) does apply to vertical agreements and found that such agreements might erect barriers along national boundaries in the EC thus frustrating the single market objective (paragraphs 15–19). The judgment is extremely helpful in terms of offering an insight into the general application of Article 81 in situations where a distributor is granted absolute territorial protection under a vertical agreement.

Etablissements Consten S.a.R.L. and Grundig-Verkaufs-GmbH v. Commission of the European Economic Community [1966] ECR 299

Grundig, a German electronics manufacturer, appointed Consten, a French marketing company, as its sole sales and service representative for France, the Saar and Corsica. Like Grundig's distributors in other countries, Consten undertook not to supply products or services outside its territory. For the purposes of sales and marketing in the area, Consten was granted exclusive rights to use a trade mark (GINT) owned by Grundig. UNEF, who was selling Grundig's products in France at lower prices and whom Consten was suing for unfair competition and breach of trade mark, applied to the Commission for a declaration that the agreement between Consten and Grundig breached Article 81. Consten and Grundig later appealed the Commission's decision to the ECJ.

ECJ

The complaints relating to the concept of 'agreements ... which may affect trade between Member States'

25   The applicants and the German government maintain that the Commission has relied on a mistaken interpretation of the concept of an agreement which may affect trade between Member States and has not shown that such trade would have been greater without the agreement in dispute.

26   The defendant replies that this requirement in Article [81(1)] is fulfilled once trade between Member States develops, as a result of the agreement, differently from the way in which it would have done without the restriction resulting from the agreement, and once the influence of the agreement on market conditions reaches a certain degree. Such is the case here, according to the defendant, particularly in view of the impediments resulting within the common market from the disputed agreement as regards the exporting and importing of Grundig products to and from France.

27   The concept of an agreement 'which may affect trade between Member States' is intended to define, in the law governing cartels, the boundary between the areas respectively covered by Community law and national law. It is only to the extent to which the agreement may affect trade between Member States that the deterioration in competition caused by the agreement falls under the prohibition of Community law contained in Article [81] otherwise it escapes the prohibition.

28   In this connexion, what is particularly important is whether the agreement is capable of constituting a threat, either direct or indirect, actual or potential, to freedom of trade between Member States in a manner which might harm the attainment of the objectives of a single market between states. Thus the fact that an agreement encourages an increase, even a large one, in the volume of trade between states is not sufficient to exclude the possibility that the agreement may 'affect' such trade in the above mentioned manner. In the present case, the contract between Grundig and Consten, on the one hand by preventing undertakings other than Consten from importing Grundig products into France, and on the other hand by prohibiting Consten from re-exporting those products to other countries of the common market, indisputably affects trade between Member States. These limitations on the freedom of trade, as well as those which might ensue for third parties from the registration in France by Consten of the GINT trademark, which Grundig places on all its products, are enough to satisfy the requirement in question.

. . .

The complaints concerning the criterion of restriction on competition

30   The applicants and the German government maintain that since the Commission restricted its examination solely to Grundig products the Decision was based upon a false concept of competition and of the rules on prohibition contained in Article [81(1)], since this concept applies particularly to competition between similar products of different makes; the Commission, before declaring Article [81(1)] to be applicable, should, by basing itself upon the 'rule of reason', have considered the economic effects of the disputed contrast upon competition between the different makes. There is a presumption that vertical sole distributorship agreements are not harmful to competition and in the present case there is nothing to invalidate that presumption. On the contrary, the contract in question has increased the competition between similar products of different makes.

31   The principle of freedom of competition concerns the various stages and manifestations of competition. Although competition between producers is generally more noticeable than that between distributors of products of the same make, it does not thereby follow that an agreement tending to restrict the latter kind of competition should escape the prohibition of Article [81(1)] merely because it might increase the former.

32   Besides, for the purpose of applying Article [81(1)], there is no need to take account of the concrete effects of an agreement once it appears that it has as its object the prevention, restriction or distortion of competition.

33   Therefore the absence in the contested Decision of any analysis of the effects of the agreement on competition between similar products of different makes does not, of itself, constitute a defect in the Decision.

34   It thus remains to consider whether the contested Decision was right in founding the prohibition of the disputed agreement under Article [81(1)] on the restriction on competition created by Grundig products alone. The infringement which was found to exist by the contested Decision results from the absolute territorial protection created the said contract in favour of Consten on the basis of French law. The applicants thus wished to eliminate any possibility of competition at the wholesale level in Grundig products in the territory specified in the contrast essentially by two methods.

35   First, Grundig undertook not to deliver even indirectly to third parties products intended for the area covered by the contract. The restrictive nature of that undertaking is obvious if it is considered in the light of the prohibition on exporting which was imposed not only on Consten but also on all the other sole concessionnaires of Grundig, as well as the German wholesalers. Secondly, the registration in France by Consten of the GINT trade mark, which Grundig affixes to all its products, is intended to increase the protection inherent in the disputed agreement, against the risk of parallel imports into France of Grundig products, by adding the protection deriving from the law on industrial property rights. Thus no third party could import Grundig products from other Member States of the Community for resale in France without running serious risks.

36   The defendant properly took into account the whole distribution system thus set up by Grundig. In order to arrive at a true representation of the contractual position the contract must be placed in the economic and legal context in the light of which it was concluded by the parties. Such a procedure is not to be regarded as an unwarrantable interference in legal transactions or circumstances which were not the subject of the proceedings before the Commission.

37   The situation as ascertained above results in the isolation of the French market and makes it possible to charge for the products in question prices which are sheltered from all effective competition. In addition, the more producers succeed in their efforts to render their own makes of product individually distinct in the eyes of the consumer, the more the effectiveness of competition between producers tends to diminish. Because of the considerable impact of distribution costs on the aggregate cost price, it seems important that competition between dealers should also be stimulated. The efforts of the dealer are stimulated by competition between distributors of products of the same make. Since the agreement thus aims at isolating the French market for Grundig products and maintaining artificially, for products

of a very well-known brand, separate national markets within the Community, it is therefore such as to distort competition in the common market.

38 It was therefore proper for the contested Decision to hold that the agreement constitutes an infringement of Article [81(1)]. No further considerations, whether of economic data (price differences between France and Germany, representative character of the type of appliance considered, level of overheads borne by Consten) or of the corrections of the criteria upon which the Commission relied in its comparisons between the situations of the French and German markets, and no possible favourable effects of the agreement in other respects, can in any way lead, in the face of the abovementioned restrictions, to a different solution under Article [81(1)].

. . .

The submissions concerning the finding of an infringement in respect of the agreement on the GINT trade mark

44 The applicants complain that the Commission infringed Articles [30], [295] and [307] of the [EC] Treaty and furthermore exceeded the limits of its powers by declaring that the agreement on the registration in France of the GINT trade mark served to ensure absolute territorial protection in favour of Consten and by excluding thereby, in Article 3 of the operative part of the contested Decision, any possibility of Consten's asserting its rights under national trade mark law, in order to oppose parallel imports.

45 The applicants maintain more particularly that the criticized effect on competition is due not to the agreement but to the registration of the trade mark in accordance with French law, which gives rise to an original inherent right of the holder of the trade mark from which the absolute territorial protection derives under national law.

46 Consten's right under the contract to the exclusive use in France of the GINT trade mark, which may be used in a similar manner in other countries, is intended to make it possible to keep under surveillance and to place an obstacle in the way of parallel imports. Thus, the agreement by which Grundig, as the holder of the trade mark by virtue of an international registration, authorized Consten to register it in France in its own name tends to restrict competition.

47 Although Consten is, by virtue of the registration of the GINT trade mark, regarded under French law as the original holder of the rights relating to that trade mark, the fact nevertheless remains that it was by virtue of an agreement with Grundig that it was able to effect the registration.

48 That agreement therefore is one which may be caught by the prohibition in Article [81(1)]. The prohibition would be ineffective if Consten could continue to use the trade mark to achieve the same object as that pursued by the agreement which has been held to be unlawful.

[169]

49   Articles [30], [295] and [307] of the Treaty relied upon by the applicants do not exclude any influence whatever of Community law on the exercise of national industrial property rights.

50   Article [30], which limits the scope of the rules on the liberalization of trade contained in title I, chapter 2, of the Treaty, cannot limit the field of application of Article [81]. Article [295] confines itself to stating that the 'Treaty shall in no way prejudice the rules in Member States governing the system of property ownership'. The injunction contained in Article 3 of the operative part of the contested Decision to refrain from using rights under national trade mark law in order to set an obstacle in the way of parallel imports does not affect the grant of those rights but only limits their exercise to the extent necessary to give effect to the prohibition under Article [81(1)]. The power of the Commission to issue such an injunction for which provision is made in Article 3 of Regulation No 17/62 of the Council is in harmony with the nature of the Community rules on competition which have immediate effect and are directly binding on individuals.

51   Such a body of rules, by reason of its nature described above and its function, does not allow the improper use of rights under any national trade mark law in order to frustrate the Community's law on cartels.

52   Article [307] which has the aim of protecting the rights of third countries is not applicable in the present instance.

53   The abovementioned submissions are therefore unfounded.

. . .

The complaints concerning the application of Article [81(3)]

58   The applicants, supported on several points by the German government, allege *inter alia* that all the conditions for application of the exemption, the existence of which is denied in the contested Decision, are met in the present case. The defendant starts from the premise that it is for the undertakings concerned to prove that the conditions required for exemption are satisfied.

59   The undertakings are entitled to an appropriate examination by the Commission of their requests for Article [81(3)] to be applied. For this purpose the Commission may not confine itself to requiring from undertakings proof of the fulfilment of the requirements for the grant of the exemption but must, as a matter of good administration, play its part, using the means available to it, in ascertaining the relevant facts and circumstances.

60   Furthermore, the exercise of the Commission's powers necessarily implies complex evaluations on economic matters. A judicial review of these evaluations must take account of their nature by confining itself to an examination of the relevance of the facts and of the legal consequences which the Commission deduces therefrom.

This review must in the first place be carried out in respect of the reasons given for the Decisions which must set out the facts and considerations on which the said evaluations are based.

61   The contested Decision states that the principal reason for the refusal of exemption lies in the fact that the requirement contained in Article [81(3)(a)] is not satisfied.

62   The German government complains that the said Decision does not answer the question whether certain factors, especially the advance orders and the guarantee and after-sales services, the favourable effects of which were recognized by the Commission, could be maintained intact in the absence of absolute territorial protection.

63   The contested Decision admits only by way of assumption that the sole distributorship contract in question contributes to an improvement in production and distribution. Then the contested Decision examines the question 'whether an improvement in the distribution of goods by virtue of the sole distribution agreement could no longer be achieved if parallel imports were admitted'. After examining the arguments concerning advance orders, the observation of the markets and the guarantee and after-sales services, the Decision concluded that 'no other reason which militates in favour of the necessity for absolute territorial protection has been put forward or hinted at'.

64   The question whether there is an improvement in the production of distribution of the goods in question, which is required for the grant of exemption, is to be answered in accordance with the spirit of Article [81]. First, this improvement cannot be identified with all the advantages which the parties to the agreement obtain from it in their production or distribution activities. These advantages are generally indisputable and show the agreement as in all respects indispensable to an improvement as understood in this sense. This subjective method, which makes the content of the concept of 'improvement' depend upon the special features of the contractual relationships in question, is not consistent with the aims of Article [81]. Furthermore, the very fact that the Treaty provides that the restriction of competition must be 'indispensable' to the improvement in question clearly indicates the importance which the latter must have. This improvement must in particular show appreciable objective advantages of such a character as to compensate for the disadvantages which they cause in the field of competition.

65   The argument of the German government, based on the premise that all those features of the agreement which favour the improvement as conceived by the parties to the agreement must be maintained intact, presupposes that the question whether all these features are not only favourable but also indispensable to the improvement of the production or distribution of the goods in question has already been settled affirmatively. Because of this the argument not only tends to weaken the requirement of indispensability but also among other consequences to confuse solicitude for the

specific interests of the parties with the objective improvements contemplated by the Treaty.

66   In its evaluation of the relative importance of the various factors submitted for its consideration, the Commission on the other hand had to judge their effectiveness by reference to an objectively ascertainable improvement in the production and distribution of the goods, and to decide whether the resulting benefit would suffice to support the conclusion that the consequent restrictions upon competition were indispensable. The argument based on the necessity to maintain intact all arrangements of the parties in so far as they are capable of contributing to the improvement sought cannot be reconciled with the view propounded in the last sentence. Therefore, the complaint of the federal government, based on faulty premises, is not such as can invalidate the Commission's assessment.

67   The applicants maintain that the admission of parallel imports would mean that the sole representative would no longer be in a position to engage in advance planning.

68   A certain degree of uncertainty is inherent in all forecasts of future sales possibilities. Such forecasting must in fact be based on a series of variable and uncertain factors. The admission of parallel imports may indeed involve increased risks for the concessionnaire who gives firm orders in advance for the quantities of goods which he considers he will be able to sell. However, such a risk is inherent in all commercial activity and thus cannot justify special protection on this point.

69   The applicants complain that the Commission did not consider on the basis of concrete facts whether it is possible to provide guarantee and after-sales services without absolute territorial protection. They emphasize in particular the importance for the reputation of the Grundig name of the proper provision of these services for all the Grundig machines put on the market. The freeing of parallel imports would compel Consten to refuse these services for machines imported by its competitors who did not themselves carry out these services satisfactorily. Such a refusal would also be contrary to the interests of consumers.

70   As regards the free guarantee service, the Decision states that a purchaser can normally enforce his right to such a guarantee only against his supplier and subject to conditions agreed with him. The applicant parties do not seriously dispute that statement.

71   The fears concerning the damage which might result for the reputation of Grundig products from an inadequate service do not, in the circumstances, appear justified.

72   In fact, UNEF, the main competitor of Consten, although it began selling Grundig products in France later than Consten and while having had to bear not inconsiderable risks, nevertheless supplies a free guarantee and after-sales services against remuneration upon conditions which, taken as a whole, do not seem to have harmed the reputation of the Grundig name. Moreover, nothing prevents the applicants from informing consumers, through adequate publicity, of the nature of the services and

any other advantages which may be offered by the official distribution network for Grundig products. It is thus not correct that the publicity carried out by Consten must benefit parallel importers to the same extent.

73 Consequently, the complaints raised by the applicants are unfounded.

74 The applicants complain that the Commission did not consider whether absolute territorial protection was still indispensable to enable the risk costs borne by Consten in launching the Grundig products on the French market to be amortized.

75 The defendant objects that before the adoption of the contested Decision it had at no time become aware of any market introduction costs which had not been amortized.

76 This statement by the defendant has not been disputed. The Commission cannot be expected of its own motion to make inquiries on this point. Further, the argument of the applicants amounts in substance to saying that the concessionnaire would not have accepted the agreed conditions without absolute territorial protection. However, that fact has no connexion with the improvements in distribution referred to in Article [81(3)].

77 Consequently this complaint cannot be upheld.

78 The applicant Grundig maintains, further, that without absolute territorial protection the sole distributor would not be inclined to bear the costs necessary for market observation since the result of his efforts might benefit parallel importers.

79 The defendant objects that such market observation, which in particular allows the application to the products intended for export to France of technical improvements desired by the French consumer, can be of benefit only to Consten.

80 In fact, Consten, in its capacity as sole concessionnaire which is not threatened by the contested Decision, would be the only one to receive the machines equipped with the features adapted especially to the French market.

81 Consequently this complaint is unfounded.

82 The complaints made against that part of the Decision which relates to the existence in the present case of the requirements of Article [81(3)(a)], considered separately and as a whole, do not appear to be well founded. Since all the requirements necessary for granting the exemption provided for in Article [81(3)] must be fulfilled, there is therefore no need to examine the submissions relating to the other requirements for exemption.

In agreeing with the Commission that once the object of an agreement has been found to be anti-competitive there is no need to consider the effect of the agreement, the ECJ has rejected the opinion of Advocate General Roemer who was highly critical of the Commission. According to the Advocate General, it was wrong that Article 81(1) should be applied on the basis of purely theoretical considerations in situations which upon close examination show no appreciable effect on competition. Thus, in the opinion of the Advocate General, one should look at the market *in concreto*.

The approach of the ECJ in *Consten and Grundig* should be compared with its approach in *Societe Technique Miniere v. Maschinenbau Ulm GmbH* (STM), a case decided shortly after *Consten and Grundig*. *STM* concerned an Article 234 reference on the application of Article 81(1) to an agreement containing an 'exclusive right of sale' which did not prohibit re-exportation, did not prevent parallel imports, did not restrict sale of competing products, nor grant absolute territorial protection to the distributor. The lack of absolute territorial protection in the *STM* case marks the main difference between it and *Consten and Grundig*. In *STM*, the ECJ, in addition to confirming that the 'automatically void' provision in Article 81(2) only applies to those offending clauses of the agreement affected by the prohibition in Article 81(1), or to the whole agreement if those clauses are not severable from the agreement itself, found that there was no object restrictive of competition, meaning that the effect of the agreement had to be considered. An important paragraph to note in the judgment is paragraph 26, which contains the factors the ECJ said should be considered when looking at the effect of the agreement.

26   The competition in question must be understood within the actual context in which it would occur in the absence of the agreement in dispute. In particular it may be doubted whether there is an interference with competition if the said agreement seems really necessary for the penetration of a new area by an undertaking. Therefore, in order to decide whether an agreement containing a clause 'granting an exclusive right of sale' is to be considered as prohibited by reason of its object or of its effect, it is appropriate to take into account in particular the nature and quantity, limited or otherwise, of the products covered by the agreement, the position and importance of the grantor and the concessionnaire on the market for the products concerned, the isolated nature of the disputed agreement or, alternatively, its position in a series of agreements, the severity of the clauses intended to protect the exclusive dealership or, alternatively, the opportunities allowed for other commercial competitors in the same products by way of parallel re-exportation and importation.

The Commission discusses exclusive distribution in paragraphs 161–174 of the *Guidelines*.

Guidelines on Vertical Restraints OJ (2000) C 291/1

(161)   ... The possible competition risks [of exclusive distribution] are mainly reduced intra-brand competition and market partitioning, which may in particular facilitate price discrimination. When most or all of the suppliers apply exclusive distribution this may facilitate collusion, both at the suppliers' and distributors' level.

(162)   Exclusive distribution is exempted by the Block Exemption Regulation when the supplier's market share does not exceed 30%, even if combined with other non-hardcore vertical restraints, such as a non-compete obligation limited to five years, quantity forcing or exclusive purchasing. A combination of exclusive distribution and selective distribution is only exempted by the Block Exemption Regulation if active selling in other territories is not restricted. Above the 30% market share threshold, the following guidance is provided for the assessment of exclusive distribution in individual cases.

(163)   The market position of the supplier and his competitors is of major importance, as the loss of intra-brand competition can only be problematic if inter-brand competition is limited. The stronger the 'position of the supplier', the more serious is the loss of intra-brand competition. Above the 30% market share threshold there may be a risk of a significant reduction of intra-brand competition. In order to be exemptable, the loss of intra-brand competition needs to be balanced with real efficiencies.

(164)   The 'position of the competitors' can have a dual significance. Strong competitors will generally mean that the reduction in intra-brand competition is outweighed by sufficient inter-brand competition. However, if the number of competitors becomes rather small and their market position is rather similar in terms of market share, capacity and distribution network, there is a risk of collusion. The loss of intra-brand competition can increase this risk, especially when several suppliers operate similar distribution systems. Multiple exclusive dealerships, i.e. when different suppliers appoint the same exclusive distributor in a given territory, may further increase the risk of collusion. If a dealer is granted the exclusive right to distribute two or more important competing products in the same territory, inter-brand competition is likely to be substantially restricted for those brands. The higher the cumulative market share of the brands distributed by the multiple dealer, the higher the risk of collusion and the more inter-brand competition will be reduced. Such cumulative effect situations may be a reason to withdraw the benefit of the Block Exemption Regulation when the market shares of the suppliers are below the threshold of the Block Exemption Regulation.

(165)   'Entry barriers' that may hinder suppliers from creating new distributors or finding alternative distributors are less important in assessing the possible anti-competitive effects of exclusive distribution. Foreclosure of other suppliers does not arise as long as exclusive distribution is not combined with single branding.

(166)   Foreclosure of other distributors is not a problem if the supplier which operates the exclusive distribution system appoints a high number of exclusive distributors in the same market and these exclusive distributors are not restricted in selling to other non-appointed distributors. Foreclosure of other distributors may however become a problem where there is 'buying power' and market power downstream, in particular in the case of very large territories where the exclusive distributor becomes the exclusive buyer for a whole market. An example would be a super-market chain which becomes the only distributor of a leading brand on a national

[175]

food retail market. The foreclosure of other distributors may be aggravated in the case of multiple exclusive dealership. Such a case, covered by the Block Exemption Regulation when the market share of each supplier is below 30%, may give reason for withdrawal of the block exemption.

(167)   'Buying power' may also increase the risk of collusion on the buyers' side when the exclusive distribution arrangements are imposed by important buyers, possibly located in different territories, on one or several suppliers.

(168)   'Maturity of the market' is important, as loss of intra-brand competition and price discrimination may be a serious problem in a mature market but may be less relevant in a market with growing demand, changing technologies and changing market positions.

(169)   'The level of trade' is important as the possible negative effects may differ between the wholesale and retail level. Exclusive distribution is mainly applied in the distribution of final goods and services. A loss of intra-brand competition is especially likely at the retail level if coupled with large territories, since final consumers may be confronted with little possibility of choosing between a high price/high service and a low price/low service distributor for an important brand.

(170)   A manufacturer which chooses a wholesaler to be its exclusive distributor will normally do so for a larger territory, such as a whole Member State. As long as the wholesaler can sell the products without limitation to downstream retailers there are not likely to be appreciable anti-competitive effects if the manufacturer is not dominant. A possible loss of intra-brand competition at the wholesale level may be easily outweighed by efficiencies obtained in logistics, promotion etc, especially when the manufacturer is based in a different country. Foreclosure of other wholesalers within that territory is not likely as a supplier with a market share above 30% usually has enough bargaining power not to choose a less efficient wholesaler. The possible risks for inter-brand competition of multiple exclusive dealerships are however higher at the wholesale than at the retail level.

(171)   The combination of exclusive distribution with single branding may add the problem of foreclosure of the market to other suppliers, especially in case of a dense network of exclusive distributors with small territories or in case of a cumulative effect. This may necessitate application of the principles set out above on single branding. However, when the combination does not lead to significant foreclosure, the combination of exclusive distribution and single branding may be pro-competitive by increasing the incentive for the exclusive distributor to focus his efforts on the particular brand. Therefore, in the absence of such a foreclosure effect, the combination of exclusive distribution with non-compete is exemptable for the whole duration of the agreement, particularly at the wholesale level.

(172)   The combination of exclusive distribution with exclusive purchasing increases the possible competition risks of reduced intra-brand competition and market partitioning which may in particular facilitate price discrimination. Exclusive distribution

already limits arbitrage by customers, as it limits the number of distributors and usually also restricts the distributors in their freedom of active selling. Exclusive purchasing, requiring the exclusive distributors to buy their supplies for the particular brand directly from the manufacturer, eliminates in addition possible arbitrage by the exclusive distributors, who are prevented from buying from other distributors in the system. This enhances the possibilities for the supplier to limit intra-brand competition while applying dissimilar conditions of sale. The combination of exclusive distribution and exclusive purchasing is therefore unlikely to be exempted for suppliers with a market share above 30% unless there are very clear and substantial efficiencies leading to lower prices to all final consumers. Lack of such efficiencies may also lead to withdrawal of the block exemption where the market share of the supplier is below 30%.

(173)   The 'nature of the product' is not very relevant to assessing the possible anti-competitive effects of exclusive distribution. It is, however, relevant when the issue of possible efficiencies is discussed, that is after an appreciable anti-competitive effect is established.

(174)   Exclusive distribution may lead to efficiencies, especially where investments by the distributors are required to protect or build up the brand image. In general, the case for efficiencies is strongest for new products, for complex products, for products whose qualities are difficult to judge before consumption (so-called experience products) or of which the qualities are difficult to judge even after consumption (so-called credence products). In addition, exclusive distribution may lead to savings in logistic costs due to economies of scale in transport and distribution.

(b) Selective distribution

Selective distribution is a special type of distribution. This arrangement did not benefit from any block exemption prior to Regulation 2790/99. During that time, complete reliance had to be placed on the decisional practice of the Commission and the case law of the ECJ; in particular on the case of *Metro v. Commission*. The adoption of Regulation 2790/99 has brought the principles of the ECJ's judgment and the Commission's decision in the block exemption regime. However, this important development has not meant that the principles developed in relation to selective distribution prior to the Regulation would no longer be of value. On the contrary, they are still very important to consider and the case of *Metro* is still highly relevant, especially when assessing whether or not a selective distribution system is caught by Article 81(1) in the first place.

Metro SB-Großmarkte GmbH & Co. KG v Commission
[1977] ECR 1875

Metro, a German 'cash and carry' wholesaler, applied to contest a Commission Decision regarding a third party, SABA, which had a selective distribution system for consumer electronics. SABA refused to admit Metro as a distributor because Metro's sales method did not meet certain marketing criteria. In response to a complaint by Metro, subject to certain amendments, the Commission approved SABA's terms and criteria. In an appeal action, one of the questions the ECJ was asked to consider concerned whether the terms of the selective distribution system fell foul of Article 81(1).

ECJ

B – the application of Article [81(3)]

23   In this connexion the applicant's complaints are based in substance on four points, namely:

(a) the obligation imposed upon SABA distributors, both wholesalers and retailers, to ensure that resellers to whom they supply SABA equipment are appointed distributors and to carry out a certain number of checks in this connexion;

(b) the prohibition imposed upon SABA wholesalers in the Federal Republic of Germany on supplies to so-called 'institutional' consumers;

(c) the obligation on such wholesalers when supplying so-called 'trade' consumers to ensure that they apply the equipment purchased only for such purposes as will promote the efficiency of the business, to the exclusion of all private use;

(d) the obligation imposed upon wholesalers to participate in the development of the SABA network by agreeing with SABA on six-monthly supply estimates.

The applicant maintains that those factors constitute restrictions on competition in respect of which the Commission has granted the exemption referred to in Article [81(3)] although such restrictions are not indispensable to the attainment in the present case of the objectives of that provision and, furthermore, they jeopardize the existence of other distribution channels, such as the self-service wholesale trade, based on a different competitive policy.

. . .

25   It must be considered whether all the elements contested by the applicant have been correctly classified by the Commission with regard to the applicability or otherwise of the prohibition under Article [81(1)] and, if they fall within the terms of that prohibition, whether the Commission's exemption of them pursuant to Article [81(3)] constitutes a proper application of that provision.

(1) the obligation imposed upon SABA distributors to supply for resale only to appointed wholesalers or retailers

26   The applicant claims that the obligation imposed upon wholesalers to check personally before delivering supplies to a reseller whether the latter has in fact been appointed a SABA dealer, in particular by recording in a register and strictly checking the numbers of all SABA Articles supplied, together with the date of sale and

the name of the purchaser, exceeds what is necessary to maintain a selective network and constitutes an obligation which is incompatible with the structure of the self-service wholesale trade.

27   To be effective, any marketing system based on the selection of outlets necessarily entails the obligation upon wholesalers forming part of the network to supply only appointed resellers and, accordingly, the right of the relevant producer to check that that obligation is fulfilled. Provided that the obligations undertaken in connexion with such safeguards do not exceed the objective in view they do not in themselves constitute a restriction on competition but are the corollary of the principal obligation and contribute to its fulfilment.

The Commission considered that the obligations imposed in this connexion under the agreement do not exceed what is necessary for an adequate control and constitute a normal duty for a wholesaler since, in the case of consumer durables, the identification of the retailers supplied and of the goods delivered constitutes a normal requirement in running a wholesale business.

Accordingly, since such obligations concerning verification do not exceed what is necessary for the attainment of their objective and in so far as they are designed to ensure respect for the conditions of appointment regarding the criteria as to technical qualifications, they fall outside the scope of Article [81(1)] Whereas, in so far as they guarantee the fulfilment of more stringent obligations, they will fall within the terms of the prohibition contained in Article [81(1)], unless they together with the principal obligation to which they are related are exempted where appropriate pursuant to Article [81(3)]. Whether the above-mentioned obligations are in accordance with the Treaty therefore depends upon the appraisal which must be made of the other elements which the applicant has criticized.

(2) the prohibition on direct supplies to institutional consumers

28   Whilst the Commission required SABA to refrain from imposing upon wholesalers the prohibition on supplies to trade consumers it permitted that undertaking to maintain the prohibition on supplies to private customers, including large-scale 'institutional' consumers such as schools, hospitals, military establishments, administrations and other customers of the same nature.

The Commission considers that, apart from the fact that this limitation on the activity of wholesalers is in accordance with the requirements of German legislation, it does not constitute a restriction on competition within the meaning of Article [81(1)] of the Treaty because it corresponds to the separation of the functions of wholesaler and retailer and because if such a separation did not obtain the former would enjoy an unjustified competitive advantage over the latter which, since it would not correspond to benefits supplied, would not be protected under Article [81].

29   It is established that various Member States have enacted legislation entailing obligations and charges, in particular in the field of social security and taxation, which

differ as between the retail and wholesale trades, so that competition would be distorted if wholesalers, whose costs are in general proportionally lighter precisely because of the marketing stage at which they operate, competed with retailers at the retail stage, in particular on supplies to private customers.

The Commission did not infringe Article [81(1)] in considering that this separation of functions is in principle in accordance with the requirement that competition shall not be distorted. Furthermore, the applicant does not dispute this view and indeed states that the organization of its marketing system is such as to respect that distinction, whilst maintaining that the provision of direct supplies to large-scale, so-called 'institutional', consumers constitutes one of the functions of a wholesaler.

In this connexion it relies upon the wording of Article 2(2) of the Council Directive of 25 February 1964 concerning the attainment of freedom of establishment and freedom to provide services in respect of activities in wholesale trade, according to which: 'for the purpose of this Directive,' 'wholesale trade activities' 'means activities pursued by any natural person, or company or firm, who habitually and by way of trade buys goods in his own name and on his own account and resells such goods to other wholesale or retail traders, or to processors, or to professional, trade or large-scale users.'

30   That Directive provides a definition of the function of wholesalers for the purposes of the application of the rules of the Treaty concerning freedom of establishment and freedom to provide services but it is not to be considered that its purpose is to solve the problems of competition referred to in Article [81].

Whilst it is indeed the case with numerous products, such as foodstuffs, that certain private customers, such as institutions, purchase in large quantities, their institutional nature does not imply that they have the status of large-scale customers for products of every kind.

When the Commission considered that with regard to the products manufactured by SABA it was unnecessary to distinguish between the different kinds of consumers other than trade or professional consumers the Commission did not exceed its power of appraisal in this sphere.

This finding is given added weight by the fact that it is for the applicant in any event to prove that in the market for electronic equipment for leisure purposes it is or has been approached by institutional private customers, other than trade or professional consumers, with a view to large-scale deliveries, but that it has failed to produce any evidence thereof in support of its statements on this point.

(3) the obligation imposed upon wholesalers when they supply trade consumers to ensure that the SABA equipment purchased will be used for trade or professional purposes

31   Paragraph 15 of the contested Decision reads: 'under the distribution agreement for SABA wholesalers (clause 2(2)), SABA wholesalers in the Federal Republic are

also obliged to refrain from supplying SABA products to consumers in the Federal Republic, including West Berlin, except where the consumer
– can prove he is engaged in trade;
– uses the SABA products only for such commercial purposes as will promote the efficiency of the business; and
– signs a declaration drawn up by SABA designed to ensure that he does in fact so use the products and setting out the commercial purpose in such manner as can be objectively verified and prohibiting any other use or resale.'

32   It is clear from those considerations that in the course of the administrative stage of the dispute the Commission recognized, in accordance with Metro's argument, that the prohibition on sales by SABA wholesalers to retailers who do not deal in electronic equipment for the leisure market but who wish to buy SABA equipment in order to use it for trade or professional purposes in their business was not in accordance with Article [81(1)] and did not qualify for exemption pursuant to Article [81(3)].

This elimination of an improper restriction on competition must, however, be reconciled with compliance with the prohibition on the delivery by wholesalers of supplies for customers' private requirements.

Accordingly, the producer may properly check on the fulfilment of this obligation, which is necessary for the maintenance of the structure of his two-stage marketing system, as he would otherwise be unable to require appointed retailers to provide the services necessary to the efficient functioning of a selective distribution system.

The applicant makes the statement, without however adducing any convincing evidence therefore, that the obligations concerning checks which are required in this connexion under the cooperation agreements are incompatible with the requirements of the self-service wholesale trade and thus contribute to the elimination of that form of competition.

33   According to the information supplied by the applicant itself the self-service wholesale trade is in essence based upon the fact that access to the sales area is reserved exclusively to holders of a personal purchaser's card which makes it possible not only to establish the name of the customer but also to check whether the holder is a natural or legal person running a commercial, small craft or industrial undertaking.

Furthermore, in order to conform with German legislation, at any rate in the 'non-food' department, a check is made before the goods are removed in order to ascertain whether they have been bought for resale or for trade or commercial use in the purchaser's undertaking and not for his private requirements.

The check required under the cooperation agreement has substantially the same scope, except that that agreement obliges the wholesaler to require the purchaser to sign a declaration to the effect that the purchase was made for trade or professional purposes.

In those circumstances it does not appear that that extra requirement is unreasonable or that it constitutes a serious obstacle which is incompatible with the very nature of the self-service wholesale trade, when regard is had to the opportunities for abuse afforded merely by the extension of the opportunities of sale for purposes other than resale.

This finding is strengthened by the fact that the obligation imposed does not require a personal check to the effect that purchasers fulfil the obligations which they undertake.

(4) the obligation upon wholesalers to participate in the development of the SABA distribution network by signing cooperation agreements

34   According to paragraph 9 of the Decision appointment as a SABA wholesaler in the Federal Republic of Germany or West Berlin is subject to the following conditions: 'SABA has informed the Commission that in principle it is willing to supply any wholesaler in the Federal Republic of Germany or West Berlin who:

(a) keeps a specialized shop, i.e. one where over 50% of the turnover relates to the sale of radio, television, tape-recording or other electrical equipment, or has set up a department specializing in the wholesale of radio, television and tape-recording equipment with a turnover comparable to that of a wholesaler specializing in electronic equipment for leisure purposes;

(b) participates in the creation and consolidation of the SABA sales network;

(c) participates in the SABA service system and has in particular a qualified staff to give proper advice and supply technical service to customers;

(d) signs the SABA cooperation agreement;

(e) signs the SABA agreements and complies with the provisions of the distribution agreement relevant for their area'

35   The applicant maintains that the obligations mentioned at points (a) (relating to a specialized shop or department), (b) (consolidation of the SABA network) and (d) (cooperation agreements) constitute restrictions on competition which are prohibited pursuant to Article [81(1)] and that the Commission was not empowered to grant an exemption pursuant to Article [81(3)] since the conditions for such an exemption were not fulfilled.

The obligation at point (a) to set up a special department with a turnover comparable to that of a specialist wholesaler

. . .

37   The obligation upon non-specialist wholesalers to open a special department for electronic equipment for the domestic leisure market is designed to guarantee the sale of the products concerned under appropriate conditions and accordingly does not constitute a restriction on competition within the meaning of Article [81(1)].

On the other hand, the requirement to achieve a turnover comparable to that of a specialist wholesaler exceeds the strict requirements of the qualitative criteria inherent in a selective distribution system and it must accordingly be appraised in the light of Article [81(3)].

38   Nevertheless, that obligation is linked in the present case to the obligation, repeated in the cooperation agreements, to achieve an adequate turnover, so that it must be considered in conjunction with the said agreements.

The obligations mentioned at points (b) (to participate in the consolidation of the sales network) and (d) (to sign cooperation agreements)

39   The obligations mentioned at point (b), namely to participate in the creation and consolidation of the sales network, and at point (d), namely to sign cooperation agreements under which the wholesaler undertakes to achieve a turnover which SABA considers to be adequate and which involve six-monthly supply contracts and obligations relating to stocks, exceed both the normal obligations involved in running a wholesale business and the requirements of a selective distribution system based on qualitative criteria.

      Those obligations bind appointed distributors closely to SABA and may entail the exclusion of undertakings which, although they fulfil the qualitative conditions for appointment, cannot or will not undertake such obligations, which thus indirectly bring about a limitation in the number and establishment of outlets.

      Accordingly, they can be exempted from the prohibition contained in Article [81(1)] only if the conditions contained in Article [81(3)] are fulfilled.

40   However, the Commission maintains (paragraph 28 of the Decision) that the obligation upon wholesalers to participate 'in the creation of a distribution network' does not constitute a restriction on competition coming within the ambit of Article [81(1)].

      That appraisal does not take proper cognizance of the scope of that provision, since the function of a wholesaler is not to promote the products of a particular manufacturer but rather to provide for the retail trade supplies obtained on the basis of competition between manufacturers, so that obligations entered into by a wholesaler which limit his freedom in this respect constitute restrictions on competition.

      Nevertheless, that erroneous appraisal does not vitiate the contested Decision because it appears that the obligation to participate in the creation of the SABA distribution network is in fact connected with the obligations listed in the cooperation agreement which the Commission considered to constitute a restriction on competition permissible only under Article [81(3)].

      It is accordingly necessary to consider whether those conditions have been fulfilled

. . .

43   With regard to the first condition set out [in Article 81(3)], the conclusion of supply contracts for six months taking account of the probable growth of the market should

[183]

make it possible to ensure both a certain stability in the supply of the relevant products, which should allow the requirements of persons obtaining supplies from the wholesaler to be more fully satisfied, and, since such supply contracts are of relatively short duration, a certain flexibility, enabling production to be adapted to the changing requirements of the market.

Thus a more regular distribution is ensured, to the benefit both of the producer, who takes his share of the planned expansion of the market in the relevant product, of the wholesaler, whose supplies are secured, and, finally, of the undertakings which obtain supplies from the wholesaler, in that the variety of available products is increased.

Another improvement in distribution is provided under the clause in the cooperation agreement obliging SABA to compensate wholesalers for service performed under guarantee and to supply spare parts necessary for repairs under guarantee.

Furthermore, the establishment of supply forecasts for a reasonable period constitutes a stabilizing factor with regard to the provision of employment which, since it improves the general conditions of production, especially when market conditions are unfavourable, comes within the framework of the objectives to which reference may be had pursuant to Article [81(3)].

44   Secondly, it must be considered whether the restrictions imposed on wholesalers under the cooperation agreement are indispensable to the attainment of the objectives in view.

45   If there were no undertakings covering a period of a given duration the relationship between the producer and appointed wholesalers could only take the form of occasional contact which would not make it possible to achieve the stability necessary to enable specialist wholesalers and producers to undertake the other obligations which guarantee improved supplies.

In considering that the cooperation agreement, by restricting the period covered by the supply contract to six months, remained within the limits of what is necessary the Commission clearly did not exceed the margin of discretion which it possesses in this sphere.

46   According to Article [81(3)] agreements restricting competition must, in order to qualify for exemption, not only improve the distribution of goods but also allow consumers a fair share of the resulting benefit.

47   According to the contested Decision the conditions of supply for wholesalers under the cooperation agreement are such as to provide direct benefit for consumers in that they ensure continued supplies and the provision of a wider range of goods by retailers for private customers.

Furthermore, the lively competition existing on the market in electronic equipment for leisure purposes exercises sufficient pressure to induce SABA and the wholesalers to pass on to consumers the benefits arising from the rationalization of production and the distribution system based on the cooperation agreement.

48   In the circumstances of the present case regular supplies represent a sufficient advantage to consumers for them to be considered to constitute a fair share of the benefit resulting from the improvement brought about by the restriction on competition permitted by the Commission.

Even if it is doubtful whether the requirement in this connexion of Article [81(3)] can be said to be satisfied by the assumption that the pressure of competition will be sufficient to induce SABA and the wholesalers to pass on to consumers a part of the benefit derived from the rationalization of the distribution network, the grant of exemption may, however, in the present case be considered as sufficiently justified by the advantage which consumers obtain from an improvement in supplies.

49   Finally, it must be considered whether the obligations contained in the cooperation agreement do not afford the undertakings concerned the possibility of eliminating competition in respect of a substantial part of the products in question.

50   It is clear from the foregoing considerations that the conditions laid down by SABA for appointment as a wholesaler may largely be fulfilled without inconvenience by self-service wholesale undertakings.

Nevertheless, although the supply estimates which wholesalers are obliged to sign under the cooperation agreements in all probability constitute an element foreign to the methods appropriate to that distribution channel, it does not appear that, in weighing up, in the context of the electronic leisure equipment sector, the relative importance of the need for cooperation agreements, giving sufficient coherence to SABA's marketing network, especially with regard to specialist wholesalers, on the one hand, and the surmountable difficulties which that involves for self-service wholesale traders, on the other, and deciding in favour of the former, the Commission exceeded its discretionary power in this sphere.

The outcome could be different if, in particular as the result of an increase in selective distribution networks of a nature similar to SABA's, self-service wholesale traders were in fact eliminated as distributors on the market in electronic equipment for leisure purposes.

Nevertheless, it is clear from the foregoing considerations that this was not so when the contested Decision was adopted.

Accordingly, that Decision is not manifestly based on a mistaken appraisal of the economic factors conditioning competition in the sector in question.

Guidelines on Vertical Restraints OJ (2000) C 291/1

(184)   Selective distribution agreements, like exclusive distribution agreements, restrict on the one hand the number of authorised distributors and on the other the possibilities of resale. The difference with exclusive distribution is that the restriction of the number of dealers does not depend on the number of territories but on selection criteria linked in the first place to the nature of the product. Another difference with exclusive distribution is that the restriction on resale is not a restriction on active selling to a territory but a restriction on any sales to non-authorised distributors,

leaving only appointed dealers and final customers as possible buyers. Selective distribution is almost always used to distribute branded final products.

(185)   The possible competition risks are a reduction in intra-brand competition and, especially in case of cumulative effect, foreclosure of certain type(s) of distributors and facilitation of collusion between suppliers or buyers. To assess the possible anti-competitive effects of selective distribution under Article 81(1), a distinction needs to be made between purely qualitative selective distribution and quantitative selective distribution. Purely qualitative selective distribution selects dealers only on the basis of objective criteria required by the nature of the product such as training of sales personnel, the service provided at the point of sale, a certain range of the products being sold etc.[1] The application of such criteria does not put a direct limit on the number of dealers. Purely qualitative selective distribution is in general considered to fall outside Article 81(1) for lack of anti-competitive effects, provided that three conditions are satisfied. First, the nature of the product in question must necessitate a selective distribution system, in the sense that such a system must constitute a legitimate requirement, having regard to the nature of the product concerned, to preserve its quality and ensure its proper use. Secondly, resellers must be chosen on the basis of objective criteria of a qualitative nature which are laid down uniformly for all potential resellers and are not applied in a discriminatory manner. Thirdly, the criteria laid down must not go beyond what is necessary.[2] Quantitative selective distribution adds further criteria for selection that more directly limit the potential number of dealers by, for instance, requiring minimum or maximum sales, by fixing the number of dealers, etc.

(186)   Qualitative and quantitative selective distribution is exempted by the Block Exemption Regulation up to 30% market share, even if combined with other non-hardcore vertical restraints, such as non-compete or exclusive distribution, provided active selling by the authorised distributors to each other and to end users is not restricted. The Block Exemption Regulation exempts selective distribution regardless of the nature of the product concerned. However, where the nature of the product does not require selective distribution, such a distribution system does not generally bring about sufficient efficiency enhancing effects to counterbalance a significant reduction in intra-brand competition. If appreciable anti-competitive effects occur, the benefit of the Block Exemption Regulation is likely to be withdrawn. In addition, the following guidance is provided for the assessment of selective distribution in individual cases which are not covered by the Block Exemption Regulation or in the case of cumulative effects resulting from parallel networks of selective distribution.

1 See for example judgment of the Court of First Instance in Case T-88/92 *Groupement d'achat Edouard Leclerc v Commission* [1996] ECR II-1961.
2 See judgments of the Court of Justice in Case 31/80 *L'Oréal v PVBA* [1980] ECR 3775, paragraphs 15 and 16; Case 26/76 *Metro I* [1977] ECR 1875, paragraphs 20 and 21; Case 107/82 *AEG* [1983] ECR 3151, paragraph 35; and of the Court of First Instance in Case T-19/91 *Vichy v Commission* [1992] ECR II415, paragraph 65.

(187)   The market position of the supplier and his competitors is of central importance
         in assessing possible anti-competitive effects, as the loss of intra-brand competi-
         tion can only be problematic if inter-brand competition is limited. The stronger
         the position of the supplier, the more problematic is the loss of intrabrand com-
         petition. Another important factor is the number of selective distribution networks
         present in the same market. Where selective distribution is applied by only one
         supplier in the market which is not a dominant undertaking, quantitative selective
         distribution does not normally create net negative effects provided that the con-
         tract goods, having regard to their nature, require the use of a selective distribution
         system and on condition that the selection criteria applied are necessary to ensure
         efficient distribution of the goods in question. The reality, however, seems to be
         that selective distribution is often applied by a number of the suppliers in a given
         market.

(188)   The position of competitors can have a dual significance and plays in particular a
         role in case of a cumulative effect. Strong competitors will mean in general that
         the reduction in intra-brand competition is easily outweighed by sufficient inter-
         brand competition. However, when a majority of the main suppliers apply selective
         distribution there will be a significant loss of intra-brand competition and possible
         foreclosure of certain types of distributors as well as an increased risk of collusion
         between those major suppliers. The risk of foreclosure of more efficient distributors
         has always been greater with selective distribution than with exclusive distribution,
         given the restriction on sales to non-authorised dealers in selective distribution.
         This is designed to give selective distribution systems a closed character, making
         it impossible for non-authorised dealers to obtain supplies. This makes selective
         distribution particularly well suited to avoid pressure by price discounters on the
         margins of the manufacturer, as well as on the margins of the authorised dealers.

(189)   Where the Block Exemption Regulation applies to individual networks of selective
         distribution, withdrawal of the block exemption or disapplication of the Block Ex-
         emption Regulation may be considered in case of cumulative effects. However, a
         cumulative effect problem is unlikely to arise when the share of the market covered
         by selective distribution is below 50%. Also, no problem is likely to arise where
         the market coverage ratio exceeds 50%, but the aggregate market share of the five
         largest suppliers (CR5) is below 50%. Where both the CR5 and the share of the
         market covered by selective distribution exceed 50%, the assessment may vary de-
         pending on whether or not all five largest suppliers apply selective distribution.
         The stronger the position of the competitors not applying selective distribution, the
         less likely the foreclosure of other distributors. If all five largest suppliers apply
         selective distribution, competition concerns may in particular arise with respect to
         those agreements that apply quantitative selection criteria by directly limiting the
         number of authorised dealers. The conditions of Article 81(3) are in general un-
         likely to be fulfilled if the selective distribution systems at issue prevent access to
         the market by new distributors capable of adequately selling the products in ques-
         tion, especially price discounters, thereby limiting distribution to the advantage of

certain existing channels and to the detriment of final consumers. More indirect forms of quantitative selective distribution, resulting for instance from the combination of purely qualitative selection criteria with the requirement imposed on the dealers to achieve a minimum amount of annual purchases, are less likely to produce net negative effects, if such an amount does not represent a significant proportion of the dealer's total turnover achieved with the type of products in question and it does not go beyond what is necessary for the supplier to recoup his relationship-specific investment and/or realise economies of scale in distribution. As regards individual contributions, a supplier with a market share of less than 5% is in general not considered to contribute significantly to a cumulative effect.

(190) 'Entry barriers' are mainly of interest in the case of foreclosure of the market to non-authorised dealers. In general entry barriers will be considerable as selective distribution is usually applied by manufacturers of branded products. It will in general take time and considerable investment for excluded retailers to launch their own brands or obtain competitive supplies elsewhere.

(191) 'Buying power' may increase the risk of collusion between dealers and thus appreciably change the analysis of possible anti-competitive effects of selective distribution. Foreclosure of the market to more efficient retailers may especially result where a strong dealer organisation imposes selection criteria on the supplier aimed at limiting distribution to the advantage of its members.

(192) Article 5(c) of the Block Exemption Regulation provides that the supplier may not impose an obligation causing the authorised dealers, either directly or indirectly, not to sell the brands of particular competing suppliers. This condition aims specifically at avoiding horizontal collusion to exclude particular brands through the creation of a selective club of brands by the leading suppliers. This kind of obligation is unlikely to be exemptable when the CR5 is equal to or above 50%, unless none of the suppliers imposing such an obligation belongs to the five largest suppliers in the market.

(193) Foreclosure of other suppliers is normally not a problem as long as other suppliers can use the same distributors, i.e. as long as the selective distribution system is not combined with single branding. In the case of a dense network of authorised distributors or in the case of a cumulative effect, the combination of selective distribution and a non-compete obligation may pose a risk of foreclosure to other suppliers. In that case the principles set out above on single branding apply. Where selective distribution is not combined with a non-compete obligation, foreclosure of the market to competing suppliers may still be a problem when the leading suppliers apply not only purely qualitative selection criteria, but impose on their dealers certain additional obligations such as the obligation to reserve a minimum shelf-space for their products or to ensure that the sales of their products by the dealer achieve a

minimum percentage of the dealer's total turnover. Such a problem is unlikely to arise if the share of the market covered by selective distribution is below 50% or, where this coverage ratio is exceeded, if the market share of the five largest suppliers is below 50%.

(194) Maturity of the market is important, as loss of intra-brand competition and possible foreclosure of suppliers or dealers may be a serious problem in a mature market but is less relevant in a market with growing demand, changing technologies and changing market positions.

(195) Selective distribution may be efficient when it leads to savings in logistical costs due to economies of scale in transport and this may happen irrespective of the nature of the product (efficiency 6 in paragraph 116). However, this is usually only a marginal efficiency in selective distribution systems. To help solve a free-rider problem between the distributors (efficiency 1 in paragraph 116) or to help create a brand image (efficiency 8 in paragraph 116), the nature of the product is very relevant. In general the case is strongest for new products, for complex products, for products of which the qualities are difficult to judge before consumption (so-called experience products) or of which the qualities are difficult to judge even after consumption (so-called credence products). The combination of selective and exclusive distribution is likely to infringe Article 81 if it is applied by a supplier whose market share exceeds 30% or in case of cumulative effects, even though active sales between the territories remain free. Such a combination may exceptionally fulfil the conditions of Article 81(3) if it is indispensable to protect substantial and relationship-specific investments made by the authorised dealers (efficiency 4 in paragraph 116).

(196) To ensure that the least anti-competitive restraint is chosen, it is relevant to see whether the same efficiencies can be obtained at a comparable cost by for instance service requirements alone.

(c) Exclusive supply

Exclusive supply limits the number of buyers to whom a supplier sells its products. A definition of the term is contained in Article 1(c) of the Regulation. The paragraph refers to the situation where there is only *one buyer* inside the Community to which the supplier sells. In relation to intermediate goods or services, it means that there is only *one buyer* inside the Community or that there is only *one buyer* inside the Community for the purposes of a specific use. In exclusive supply situations, it is the market share of the buyer which must not exceed the 30 per cent threshold set out in the Regulation if the exclusive supply situation is to benefit from an exemption (provided of course that the other relevant conditions of the Regulation are satisfied). Where that threshold is exceeded, it would be helpful to consult paragraphs 204–212 of the *Guidelines*.

Guidelines on Vertical Restraints OJ (2000) C 291/1

(204)   The main competition risk of exclusive supply is foreclosure of other buyers. The market share of the buyer on the upstream purchase market is obviously important for assessing the ability of the buyer to 'impose' exclusive supply which forecloses other buyers from access to supplies. The importance of the buyer on the downstream market is however the factor which determines whether a competition problem may arise. If the buyer has no market power downstream, then no appreciable negative effects for consumers can be expected. Negative effects can however be expected when the market share of the buyer on the downstream supply market as well as the upstream purchase market exceeds 30%. Where the market share of the buyer on the upstream market does not exceed 30%, significant foreclosure effects may still result, especially when the market share of the buyer on his downstream market exceeds 30%. In such cases withdrawal of the block exemption may be required. Where a company is dominant on the downstream market, any obligation to supply the products only or mainly to the dominant buyer may easily have significant anti-competitive effects.

(205)   It is not only the market position of the buyer on the upstream and downstream market that is important but also the extent to and the duration for which he applies an exclusive supply obligation. The higher the tied supply share, and the longer the duration of the exclusive supply, the more significant the foreclosure is likely to be. Exclusive supply agreements shorter than five years entered into by non-dominant companies usually require a balancing of pro- and anti-competitive effects, while agreements lasting longer than five years are for most types of investments not considered necessary to achieve the claimed efficiencies or the efficiencies are not sufficient to outweigh the foreclosure effect of such long-term exclusive supply agreements.

(206)   The market position of the competing buyers on the upstream market is important as it is only likely that competing buyers will be foreclosed for anti-competitive rea-sons, i.e. to increase their costs, if they are significantly smaller than the foreclosing buyer.

         Foreclosure of competing buyers is not very likely where these competitors have similar buying power and can offer the suppliers similar sales possibilities. In such a case, foreclosure could only occur for potential entrants, who may not be able to secure supplies when a number of major buyers all enter into exclusive supply contracts with the majority of suppliers on the market. Such a cumulative effect may lead to withdrawal of the benefit of the Block Exemption Regulation.

(207)   Entry barriers at the supplier level are relevant to establishing whether there is real foreclosure. In as far as it is efficient for competing buyers to provide the goods or services themselves via upstream vertical integration, foreclosure is unlikely to be a real problem. However, often there are significant entry barriers.

(208)   Countervailing power of suppliers is relevant, as important suppliers will not easily allow themselves to be cut off from alternative buyers. Foreclosure is therefore mainly a risk in the case of weak suppliers and strong buyers. In the case of strong suppliers the exclusive supply may be found in combination with non-compete. The combination with non-compete brings in the rules developed for single branding. Where there are relationship-specific investments involved on both sides (hold-up problem) the combination of exclusive supply and non-compete i.e. reciprocal exclusivity in industrial supply agreements is usually justified below the level of dominance.

(209)   Lastly, the level of trade and the nature of the product are relevant for foreclosure. Foreclosure is less likely in the case of an intermediate product or where the product is homogeneous. Firstly, a foreclosed manufacturer that uses a certain input usually has more flexibility to respond to the demand of his customers than the wholesaler/retailer has in responding to the demand of the final consumer for whom brands may play an important role. Secondly, the loss of a possible source of supply matters less for the foreclosed buyers in the case of homogeneous products than in the case of a heterogeneous product with different grades and qualities.

(210)   For homogeneous intermediate products, anti-competitive effects are likely to be exemptable below the level of dominance. For final branded products or differentiated intermediate products where there are entry barriers, exclusive supply may have appreciable anti-competitive effects where the competing buyers are relatively small compared to the foreclosing buyer, even if the latter is not dominant on the downstream market.

(211)   Where appreciable anti-competitive effects are established, an exemption under Article 81(3) is possible as long as the company is not dominant. Efficiencies can be expected in the case of a hold-up problem (paragraph 116, points 4 and 5), and this is more likely for intermediate products than for final products. Other efficiencies are less likely. Possible economies of scale in distribution (paragraph 116, point 6) do not seem likely to justify exclusive supply.

(212)   In the case of a hold-up problem and even more so in the case of scale economies in distribution, quantity forcing on the supplier, such as minimum supply requirements, could well be a less restrictive alternative.

(d) Exclusive customer allocation

As we saw above, exclusive customer allocation belongs to the limited distribution group. The Commission provides in the *Guidelines* an explanation of this type of vertical restraint and guidance on how the application of the Regulation should be handled in these cases.

[191]

Guidelines on Vertical Restraints OJ (2000) C 291/1

(178)   In an exclusive customer allocation agreement, the supplier agrees to sell his products only to one distributor for resale to a particular class of customers. At the same time, the distributor is usually limited in his active selling to other exclusively allocated classes of customers. The possible competition risks are mainly reduced intra-brand competition and market partitioning, which may in particular facilitate price discrimination. When most or all of the suppliers apply exclusive customer allocation, this may facilitate collusion, both at the suppliers' and the distributors' level.

(179)   Exclusive customer allocation is exempted by the Block Exemption Regulation when the supplier's market share does not exceed the 30% market share threshold, even if combined with other non-hardcore vertical restraints such as non-compete, quantity-forcing or exclusive purchasing. A combination of exclusive customer allocation and selective distribution is normally hardcore, as active selling to end users by the appointed distributors is usually not left free. Above the 30% market share threshold, the guidance provided in paragraphs 161 to 177 applies *mutatis mutandis* to the assessment of exclusive customer allocation, subject to the following specific remarks.

(180)   The allocation of customers normally makes arbitrage by the customers more difficult. In addition, as each appointed distributor has his own class of customers, non-appointed distributors not falling within such a class may find it difficult to obtain the product. This will reduce possible arbitrage by non-appointed distributors. Therefore, above the 30% market share threshold of the Block Exemption Regulation exclusive customer allocation is unlikely to be exemptable unless there are clear and substantial efficiency effects.

(181)   Exclusive customer allocation is mainly applied to intermediate products and at the wholesale level when it concerns final products, where customer groups with different specific requirements concerning the product can be distinguished.

(182)   Exclusive customer allocation may lead to efficiencies, especially when the distributors are required to make investments in for instance specific equipment, skills or know-how to adapt to the requirements of their class of customers. The depreciation period of these investments indicates the justified duration of an exclusive customer allocation system. In general the case is strongest for new or complex products and for products requiring adaptation to the needs of the individual customer. Identifiable differentiated needs are more likely for intermediate products, that is products sold to different types of professional buyers. Allocation of final consumers is unlikely to lead to any efficiencies and is therefore unlikely to be exempted.

[192]

III Resale price maintenance

Resale price maintenance may involve, among other things, requiring the buyer not to sell below or above a particular price or to sell at a particular price. Paragraphs 226–228 of the *Guidelines* contain some helpful guidance on the possible competition problems which may arise in cases of some resale price maintenance and also on how they should be assessed under the Regulation.

Guidelines on Vertical Restraints OJ (2000) C 291/1

(226)   The possible competition risk of maximum and recommended prices is firstly that the maximum or recommended price will work as a focal point for the resellers and might be followed by most or all of them. A second competition risk is that maximum or recommended prices may facilitate collusion between suppliers.

(227)   The most important factor for assessing possible anti-competitive effects of maximum or recommended resale prices is the market position of the supplier. The stronger the market position of the supplier, the higher the risk that a maximum resale price or a recommended resale price leads to a more or less uniform application of that price level by the resellers, because they may use it as a focal point. They may find it difficult to deviate from what they perceive to be the preferred resale price proposed by such an important supplier on the market. Under such circumstances the practice of imposing a maximum resale price or recommending a resale price may infringe Article 81(1) if it leads to a uniform price level.

(228)   The second most important factor for assessing possible anti-competitive effects of the practice of maximum and recommended prices is the market position of competitors. Especially in a narrow oligopoly, the practice of using or publishing maximum or recommended prices may facilitate collusion between the suppliers by exchanging information on the preferred price level and by reducing the likelihood of lower resale prices. The practice of imposing a maximum resale price or recommending resale prices leading to such effects may also infringe Article 81(1).

IV Market partitioning

Paragraph 113 of the *Guidelines* (extracted above at p. 157) provides an explanation of the market partitioning category. Paragraph 114 provides details of the main negative effect on competition of the category which include a reduction of intra-brand competition that may help the supplier to divide the market and thus hinder market integration as well as facilitate price discrimination. Moreover, collusion (either at the level of distributor or supplier) may be facilitated when most or all competing suppliers limit the sourcing or resale possibilities of their buyers.

V Other types of vertical restraints

The examples of vertical restraints mentioned above are not exhaustive. Other examples can be found, and two additional example which are specifically mentioned in the *Guidelines* are 'franchising' and 'tying'.

(a) Franchising

An early case in which the ECJ considered franchise agreements was *Pronuptia de paris v. Schillaglis*. Mrs Schillgalis ('the franchisee') sold bridal wear under franchising agreements with Pronuptia de Paris GmbH and its French parent company ('the franchisor') whereby the franchisee received an exclusive right to use the Pronuptia trade mark in Hamburg, Oldenburg and Hanover, and to advertise in those areas, subject to the franchisor's approval of the advertising. The franchisee was to pay licence fees of 10 per cent of her turnover. The franchisor brought proceedings in Germany to recover the licence fees, to which the franchisee replied that the agreements were void under Article 81(1). A referral was made to the ECJ under Article 234 on the impact of Article 81(1) on franchise agreements.

The ECJ held that clauses in a franchise agreement resulting in partitioning of markets between franchisor and franchisees or among franchisees amount to a restriction of competition. However, such agreements do not aim to restrict or distort competition in so far as they intend to protect the franchisor's know-how or the goodwill of the franchise network. Accordingly the individual agreement must be considered to ascertain its effect on competition. Furthermore, there is a risk of concerted practices with respect to the application of any recommended prices.

In the *Guidelines*, the Commission deals with franchising in paragraphs 199–200.

Guidelines on Vertical Restraints OJ (2000) C 291/1

(199) (Franchise agreements contain licences of intellectual property rights relating in particular to trade marks or signs and know-how for the use and distribution of goods or services. In addition to the licence of IPRs, the franchisor usually provides the franchisee during the life of the agreement with commercial or technical assistance. The licence and the assistance are integral components of the business method being franchised. The franchisor is in general paid a franchise fee by the franchisee for the use of the particular business method. Franchising may enable the franchisor to establish, with limited investments, a uniform network for the distribution of his products. In addition to the provision of the business method, franchise agreements usually contain a combination of different vertical restraints concerning the products being distributed, in particular selective distribution and/or non-compete and/or exclusive distribution or weaker forms thereof.)

(200)   The coverage by the Block Exemption Regulation of the licensing of IPRs contained in franchise agreements is dealt with in paragraphs 23 to 45. As for the vertical restraints on the purchase, sale and resale of goods and services within a franchising arrangement, such as selective distribution, non-compete or exclusive distribution, the Block Exemption Regulation applies up to the 30% market share threshold for the franchisor or the supplier designated by the franchisor.[1] The guidance provided earlier in respect of these types of restraints applies also to franchising, subject to the following specific remarks:

1) In line with general rule 8 (see paragraph 119), the more important the transfer of know-how, the more easily the vertical restraints fulfil the conditions for exemption.

2) A non-compete obligation on the goods or services purchased by the franchisee falls outside Article 81(1) when the obligation is necessary to maintain the common identity and reputation of the franchised network. In such cases, the duration of the non-compete obligation is also irrelevant under Article 81(1), as long as it does not exceed the duration of the franchise agreement itself.

(b) Tying

Tying involves a situation where the supplier makes the sale of one product conditional upon the purchase of another product. The situation is considered further in chapter 9, in the context of abuse of dominance. In the *Guidelines*, there are several paragraphs which deal with tying (paragraphs 215–224). These paragraphs explain, among other things, the negative effects of tying (the main one being foreclosure on the market of the tied product). The paragraphs also deal with the circumstances under which tying is exempted under the Regulation: when the market share of the supplier on both the tied product and tying product markets does not exceed the 30% threshold set out in Article 3 of the Regulation. Where that threshold is exceeded, the Commission will assess the situation on a case-by-case basis taking into account, among other things, the market position of the supplier and its competitors and countervailing buyer power.

3 UK law

The treatment of vertical agreements under UK competition law has differed from that under EC competition law for several reasons. A major concern for the European Commission when dealing with vertical agreements has been the single market objective. This goal has no direct relevance when applying the domestic competition rules of the UK. Furthermore, the fact that UK competition law, in particular the CA1998, is concerned with dealing with serious breaches

---

1   See also paragraphs *AEG* [1983] ECR 3151, paragraph 35; and of the Court of First Instance in Case T-19/91 *Vichy v. Commission* [1992] ECR II-415, paragraph 65. See also paragraphs 89 to 95, in particular paragraph 95.

of competition law such as cartels and abuses of dominance, a policy decision was made when adopting the Act to exclude vertical agreements from the scope of the Chapter I prohibition. This was effected by an exclusion order which was made under section 50 of the CA1998. The exclusion did not however, mean that vertical agreements were outside UK competition law altogether: they may be caught by the Chapter II prohibition of the CA1998 and also by the market investigation provisions of the Enterprise Act 2002 (see chapter 12). For example, a market investigation reference may be made where vertical agreements on a particular market have the effect of preventing the entry of new competitors, without there being established collusion between the firms concerned.

In light of the EC modernisation programme (which as was noted in previous chapters led to the adoption of Regulation 1/2003, the Modernisation Regulation) the UK Government proposed in July 2001 to repeal the exclusion for vertical agreements from the Chapter I prohibition ('the verticals exclusion'). A consultation period followed that proposal which included hearing the views of interested parties, in particular those of firms active in the newspaper and magazine sectors. Two important consultation documents dealing with the subject-matter of the proposal were published by the Department of Trade and Industry in April and June 2003. At the end of the consultation period the Government announced on 1 March 2004 its decision to repeal the exclusion. Recognising the existence of legitimate business concern about its decision, the Government has made provision for a transitional period of one year, which started on 1 May 2004 (when Regulation 1/2003 entered into force). This means that the verticals exclusion has been repealed with effect from 1 May 2005 (upon the entry into force of SI 2004/1260, *The Competition Act (Land Agreements Exclusion and Revocation) Order 2004*). During the transitional period the vertical exclusion remains operative. The purpose behind the transitional period is to allow affected parties to consider relevant clauses in their vertical agreements which in the Government's view will ensure an outcome that is best for consumers whilst offering an enhanced legal certainty in the long term for firms, especially those active in the newspaper and magazine sectors.

The repeal of the verticals exclusion is an important step in supporting the efforts of UK competition authorities to ensure consistency when applying EC or UK competition law and those of the Government to eliminate or reduce any differences between EC and UK competition rules that may hinder the effective operation of UK system of competition law; though it is correct to say that under Regulation 1/2003 the Government was not required to take such a step. In light of the Government's decision to repeal the verticals exclusion and the fact that the OFT (like other national competition authorities and courts of the Member States) now has the power to apply Article 81(3), the latter has published a *Guideline on vertical agreements* (OFT419), which explains how it applies Article 81 and the Chapter I prohibition to vertical agreements. The *Guideline* states that the OFT will have regard to the European Commission's

Guidelines on vertical restraints, in relation to both Article 81 and the Chapter I prohibition. Indeed, the *Guideline* incorporates many of the key points made in the *Commission's Guidelines* such as those made in relation to the positive and negative effects of vertical restraints. The *Guideline* also acknowledges Regulation 2790/99 and refers to, and explains, the key provisions of the Regulation.

Further reading

Glynn and Howe 'Vertical restraints in UK and EU competition law' (2003) 8
    Comp. L. I. 14
Peeperkorn 'EC vertical restraints guidelines: effects based or per se policy? – a
    reply' (2002) 23 ECLR 38
Wijckmans and Tuytschaever 'Active sales restrictions revisited' (2004) 25 ECLR
    107

6
Intellectual property rights and competition law

1 Introduction

The application of competition rules in the field of intellectual property law has given rise to some of the most controversial issues in the world of competition law. Respective developments in competition law and intellectual property law over the years convey the impression that these two legal fields do not sit comfortably with one another and that there is an element of conflict in what each body of law aims to achieve. For a competition lawyer considering the relationship between competition law and intellectual property rights (IPRs), perhaps the most important question is the extent to which the existence of an IPR impacts on market power.

This chapter is concerned with the application of EC and UK competition rules in relation to transactions involving IPRs. It should be noted that competition law is also concerned with a dominant firm's refusal to enter into such transactions, but this issue is explored in chapter 9. This is a very complex area given that the extent to which competition rules can control reliance by firms on IPRs depends on the type of IPR in question. For this reason, understanding how competition law applies to a case where the existence or exercise of an IPR is in issue requires an understanding of intellectual property law itself – a highly complex and technical area in its own right. Furthermore – and this is a point relevant to the application of EC competition law – IPRs give rise to issues of market integration. Since the single market objective lies at the heart of EC competition rules, understanding their application in the area of IPRs requires an understanding of the relationship between IPRs and two important freedoms under EC law, namely the free movement of goods and the free movement of services.

2 What is an intellectual property right?

It would be helpful before considering the substantive provisions of EC and UK competition law and their application to IPRs to look briefly at the content and impact of such rights. An IPR is defined as a right granted by law to protect intangible property, such as a creative work or an idea. The rationale behind some such rights is that they act as a reward (and by corollary, an incentive) for making investments in the creation or promotion of new ideas and inventions. Other such rights constitute a means of protecting investments in other intangible property, such as goodwill and brand names, from free-riders who might tarnish the reputation of an enterprise or confuse the consumer.

The nature of the legal right depends on the type of intangible property, and an IPR can range from a limited term monopoly to a more-or-less permanent exclusive right of use. In each case, the IPR gives its holder certain rights to prevent third parties from exploiting the holder's intellectual property without the latter's consent. Thus, the holder of a patent has a near absolute right to stop any third party exploiting the subject matter of the patent, whilst, in simple terms, the holder of a copyright cannot prevent the exploitation of a work created independently. To put it differently, more extensive rights are granted to the holder of a patent, but the price of this limited monopoly is a requirement to make detailed disclosure of the subject matter such that other inventors can build upon the invention. The degree of protection given therefore reflects a balance between, on the one hand, rewarding creative endeavour and limiting third party free riding, and, on the other, not stifling consequential creativity. IPRs include, but are not limited to, copyright, patent, trade mark, design right and industry-specific rights (these are rights which are specific to a particular sector or industry, such as the rights over topographies of semiconductor chips).

3 Transactions involving intellectual property rights

There are numerous forms of transactions that may feature or involve IPRs. Some transactions deal exclusively with IPRs; in others, the IPRs may form one small aspect of the transaction. As far as competition law is concerned, this makes it difficult in practice to devise rules to deal with the application of the law to these transactions.

There are two main types of transaction involving IPRs. These are assignment of IPRs and the granting a licence. The former covers the situation in which the person who develops the IPRs does not wish or is unable to exploit it and therefore wishes to effect a complete transfer of the right to another person. This transfer is called an assignment, which may be either the sole purpose of the transaction or an ancillary feature of it. A licence on the other hand covers the situation in which no complete transfer of the right is effected, but rather the holder of the right allows a third party to exploit it, subject to conditions, such as the payment of royalties to the holder of the right. Like an assignment, the licence may be the sole purpose of the transaction or only one part of it.

4 EC law

(A) EC competition law and intellectual property rights

Application of EC competition rules to IPRs is highly complex. The complexity arises due to several factors, including the close links between the competition rules and the rules on free movement of goods. Two important points should be noted about these links. First, both sets of rules have been used to further the single market objective. In the case of the competition rules, this is achieved by preventing private firms from re-erecting national barriers to trade through anti-competitive agreements and behaviour; and in the case of the rules on free movement of goods, this is done via Article 28, a provision addressed to Member States which provides:

Quantitative restrictions on imports and all measures having equivalent effect shall be prohibited between Member States.

However, it is important to note that this is subject to an exception provided in Article 30:

The provisions of Articles 28 and 29 shall not preclude prohibitions or restrictions on imports, exports or goods in transit justified on grounds of pubic morality, public policy or public security; the protection of health and life of humans, animals or plants; the protection of national treasures possessing artistic, historic or archaeological value; or the protection of industrial and commercial property. Such prohibitions or restrictions shall not, however, constitute a means of arbitrary discrimination or a disguised restriction on trade between Member States.

It is the reference to 'protection of industrial and commercial property' which is of importance here and which should be read alongside Article 295 EC:

The Treaty shall in no way prejudice the rules in Member States governing the system of property ownership.

Secondly, looking at the jurisprudence developed by the ECJ under Articles 81 and 28, one can identify an active two-way flow of concepts and ideas established under one provision borrowed into the case law of the other. Examples of this are, first the distinction between the 'existence' and the 'exercise' of IPRs developed by the ECJ under Article 81, and, secondly, the concept of 'the specific subject-matter of an intellectual property right' developed under Article 28. Both of these ideas are explained below.

(B) Protection offered by intellectual property rights: the doctrine of exhaustion

I General

It is clear from Articles 30 and 295 that the Treaty recognises IPRs and thus that there is respect for them within the framework of the EC Treaty. However this does not mean that an IPR holder possesses absolute power by virtue of that right. Indeed, the protection given to such a right is limited under certain circumstances. One example that has emerged is contained in the doctrine of exhaustion.

To understand the doctrine of exhaustion and its application, it is essential to clarify two concepts mentioned above, namely the issue of 'existence' and 'exercise' and that of 'the specific subject-matter of an IPR'.

The first of these concepts was first enunciated by the ECJ in the case of *Consten and Grundig* (see pp. 166–173 above), where the ECJ stated that Community law does not undermine the existence of an IPR, though it could limit the exercise of that right.

The concept of specific subject-matter of an IPR, on the other hand, was referred to in the case of *Deutsche Grammophon GmbH v. Metro-SB-Grossmarkte GmBH & Co KG,* a case decided under Article 28, in which the ECJ stated at paragraph 11 that:

Amongst the prohibitions or restrictions on the free movement of goods which it concedes Article [30] refers to industrial and commercial property. On the assumption that those provisions may be relevant to a right related to copyright, it is nevertheless clear from that Article that, although the Treaty does not affect the existence of rights recognized by the legislation of a Member State with regard to industrial and commercial property, the exercise of such rights may nevertheless fall within the prohibitions laid down by the Treaty. Although it permits prohibitions or restrictions on the free movement of products, which are justified for the purpose of protecting industrial and commercial property, Article [30] only admits derogations from that freedom to the extent to which they are justified for the purpose of safeguarding rights which constitute the *specific subject-matter* of such property. [Emphasis added]

What amounts to the specific subject-matter depends of course on the right at hand. Thus in the case of a patent, the ECJ in *Deutsche Grammophon* described it as 'the exclusive right to use an invention with a view to manufacturing industrial products and putting them into circulation for the first time, either directly or by the grant of licences to third parties, as well as the right to oppose infringements'.

In the case of a trade mark, the ECJ stated in *Centrafarm v. Winthrop BV* that the subject-matter was 'the guarantee that that owner of the trade mark has the exclusive right to use that trade mark for the purposes of putting products protected by the mark into circulation for the first time'.

It was from these seeds that the doctrine of exhaustion grew into a well-recognised and well-established doctrine in EC competition law, not only in the case law of the ECJ but also in legislative instruments, such as the Trade Mark Directive, Directive 89/104, which provides in Article 7(1) that:

The trade mark shall not entitle the proprietor to prohibit its use in relation to goods which have been put on the market in the Community under that trade mark by the proprietor or with his consent.

However an exception is given under Article 7(2): that it is possible 'where there exist legitimate reasons for the proprietor to oppose further commercialisation of the goods, especially where the conditions of the goods is changed or impaired after they have been put on the market'.

Thus, it is clear that the doctrine is based essentially on whether the owner of an IPR gave his consent to the 'further commercialisation' in the EC of the products which incorporate that right. This usually takes the form of sale of the product in the EC with the consent of the owner of the IPR. If such consent was given, the right will be taken to have been exhausted.

The doctrine of exhaustion has been applied in several cases including: *Deutsche Grammophon, Centrafarm BV v. Sterling Drug, Centrafram BV v. Winthrop BV* and *Musik-Vertrieb Membran GmbH v. GEMA.*

II Does the doctrine have international application?

The cases and the points made in the previous section deal with the application of the doctrine of exhaustion within the Community. However, it was inevitable that the question would arise at some point whether the doctrine applies in a situation where the owner of the IPR consented to the sale of the products which incorporate that right outside the EC, i.e., whether the right could be said to have been exhausted in this case.

This question came before the ECJ in two interesting Article 234 references, namely the cases of *Silhouette* and *Zino Davidoff*.

Silhouette International Schmied GmbH v. Hartlauer Handelgesellschaft mbH [1998] ECR I-4799

The Austrian claimant produced fashion spectacles under the trade mark 'Silhouette' and refused to supply the defendant (Hartlauer), believing that the latter's marketing techniques (low cost pricing) would be harmful to the high quality image of its products. Some out-dated models sold to a third party for sale only in Bulgaria or the former Soviet Union were subsequently acquired by the defendant who sold them in Austria. Silhouette applied for an interim injunction on the basis of the trade mark violation. When its application was refused Silhouette appealed to the Supreme Court *('Oberster Gerichtshof')* arguing that under Article 7(1) of Directive 89/104, a trade mark owner was entitled to prohibit the parallel re-importing of branded goods put on the market outside the European Economic Area (EEA). An Article 234 reference was made to the ECJ.

ECJ

15   By its first question the Oberster Gerichtshof is in substance asking whether national rules providing for exhaustion of trade mark rights in respect of products put on the

market outside the EEA under that mark by the proprietor or with his consent are contrary to Article 7(1) of the Directive.

16   It is to be noted at the outset that Article 5 of the Directive defines the 'rights conferred by a trade mark' and Article 7 contains the rule concerning 'exhaustion of the rights conferred by a trade mark'.

17   According to Article 5(1) of the Directive, the registered trade mark confers on the proprietor exclusive rights therein. In addition, Article 5(1)(a) provides that those exclusive rights entitle the proprietor to prevent all third parties not having his consent from use in the course of trade of, *inter alia*, any sign identical with the trade mark in relation to goods or services which are identical to those for which the trade mark is registered. Article 5(3) sets out a non-exhaustive list of the kinds of practice which the proprietor is entitled to prohibit under paragraph 1, including, in particular, importing or exporting goods under the trade mark concerned.

18   Like the rules laid down in Article 6 of the Directive, which set certain limits to the effects of a trade mark, Article 7 states that, in the circumstances which it specifies, the exclusive rights conferred by the trade mark are exhausted, with the result that the proprietor is no longer entitled to prohibit use of the mark. Exhaustion is subject first of all to the condition that the goods have been put on the market by the proprietor or with his consent. According to the text of the Directive itself, exhaustion occurs only where the products have been put on the market in the Community (in the EEA since the EEA Agreement entered into force).

19   No argument has been presented to the Court that the Directive could be interpreted as providing for the exhaustion of the rights conferred by a trade mark in respect of goods put on the market by the proprietor or with his consent irrespective of where they were put on the market.

20   On the contrary, Hartlauer and the Swedish Government have maintained that the Directive left the Member States free to provide in their national law for exhaustion, not only in respect of products put on the market in the EEA but also of those put on the market in non-member countries.

21   The interpretation of the Directive proposed by Hartlauer and the Swedish Government assumes, having regard to the wording of Article 7, that the Directive, like the Court's case law concerning Articles [28] and [30] of the E.C. Treaty, is limited to requiring the Member States to provide for exhaustion within the Community, but that Article 7 does not comprehensively resolve the question of exhaustion of rights conferred by the trade mark, thus leaving it open to the Member States to adopt rules on exhaustion going further than those explicitly laid down in Article 7 of the Directive.

22   As Silhouette, the Austrian, French, German, Italian and United Kingdom Governments and the Commission have all argued, such an interpretation is contrary to the

wording of Article 7 and to the scheme and purpose of the rules of the Directive concerning the rights which a trade mark confers on its proprietor.

23   In that respect, although the third recital in the preamble to the Directive states that 'it does not appear to be necessary at present to undertake full-scale approximation of the trade mark laws of the Member States', the Directive nonetheless provides for harmonisation in relation to substantive rules of central importance in this sphere, that is to say, according to that same recital, the rules concerning those provisions of national law which most directly affect the functioning of the internal market, and that that recital does not preclude the harmonisation relating to those rules from being complete.

24   The first recital in the preamble to the Directive notes that the trade mark laws applicable in the Member States contain disparities which may impede the free movement of goods and freedom to provide services and may distort competition within the common market, so that it is necessary, in view of the establishment and functioning of the internal market, to approximate the laws of Member States. The ninth recital emphasises that it is fundamental, in order to facilitate the free movement of goods and services, to ensure that registered trade marks enjoy the same protection under the legal systems of all the Member States, but that this should not prevent Member States from granting at their option extensive protection to those trade marks which have a reputation.

25   In the light of those recitals, Articles 5 to 7 of the Directive must be construed as embodying a complete harmonisation of the rules relating to the rights conferred by a trade mark. That interpretation, it may be added, is borne out by the fact that Article 5 expressly leaves it open to the Member States to maintain or introduce certain rules specifically defined by the Community legislature. Thus, in accordance with Article 5(2), to which the ninth recital refers, the Member States have the option to grant more extensive protection to trade marks with a reputation.

26   Accordingly, the Directive cannot be interpreted as leaving it open to the Member States to provide in their domestic law for exhaustion of the rights conferred by a trade mark in respect of products put on the market in non-member countries.

27   This, moreover, is the only interpretation which is fully capable of ensuring that the purpose of the Directive is achieved, namely to safeguard the functioning of the internal market. A situation in which some Member States could provide for international exhaustion while others provided for Community exhaustion only would inevitably give rise to barriers to the free movement of goods and the freedom to provide services.

28   Contrary to the arguments of the Swedish Government, it is no objection to that interpretation that since the Directive was adopted on the basis of Article [95] of the E.C. Treaty, which governs the approximation of the laws of the Member States concerning the functioning of the internal market, it cannot regulate relations between the Member States and non-member countries, with the result that Article

7 is to be interpreted as meaning that the Directive applies only to intra-Community relations.

29   Even if Article [95] of the Treaty were to be construed in the sense argued for by the Swedish Government, the fact remains that Article 7, as has been pointed out in this judgment, is not intended to regulate relations between Member States and non-member countries but to define the rights of proprietors of trade marks in the Community.

30   Finally, the Community authorities could always extend the exhaustion provided for by Article 7 to products put on the market in non-member countries by entering into international agreements in that sphere, as was done in the context of the EEA Agreement.

31   In the light of the foregoing, the answer to be given to the first question must be that national rules providing for exhaustion of trade mark rights in respect of products put on the market outside the EEA under that mark by the proprietor or with his consent are contrary to Article 7(1) of the Directive, as amended by the EEA Agreement.

Zino Davidoff SA v. A&G Imports Ltd **[2001] ECR I-8691 (a.k.a.** *Levi Strauss & Co v. Tesco Plc*)

Zino Davidoff had an exclusive distribution contract with a third party based in Singapore restricting sale of its products to a specified territory outside the EEA and prohibiting further resale outside the specified territory. The defendant, A&G, acquired a stock of products originally placed on the Singapore market and began to sell them in the UK. Proceedings were brought in the UK alleging breach of trade mark rights. Similar infringements in the joined cases were alleged by other claimants against Tesco and Costco.

The national court sought guidance on the interpretation to be given to consent in the context of Article 7 of the Trade Marks Directive 89/104 and asked (1) whether the consent of a trade mark proprietor to marketing in the EEA could be implied; (2) whether implied consent could be inferred from the mere silence of a trade mark proprietor, and (3) as to the consequence of ignorance, on the part of the trader importing the marked goods into the EEA, of the proprietor's expressed opposition to such imports.

ECJ

32   It must also be borne in mind that in Articles 5 and 7 of the Directive the Community legislature laid down the rule of Community exhaustion, that is to say, the rule that the rights conferred by a trade mark do not entitle the proprietor to prohibit use of the mark in relation to goods bearing that mark which have been placed on the market in the EEA by him or with his consent. In adopting those provisions, the Community legislature did not leave it open to the Member States to provide in their

domestic law for exhaustion of the rights conferred by a trade mark in respect of products placed on the market in non-member countries (Case C-355/96 *Silhouette International Schmied* [1998] ECR I-4799, paragraph 26).

33   The effect of the Directive is therefore to limit exhaustion of the rights conferred on the proprietor of a trade mark to cases where goods have been put on the market in the EEA and to allow the proprietor to market his products outside that area without exhausting his rights within the EEA. By making it clear that the placing of goods on the market outside the EEA does not exhaust the proprietor's right to oppose the importation of those goods without his consent, the Community legislature has allowed the proprietor of the trade mark to control the initial marketing in the EEA of goods bearing the mark (Case C-173/98 *Sebago and Maison Dubois* [1999] ECR I-4103, paragraph 21).

34   By its questions, the national court is seeking chiefly to determine the circumstances in which the proprietor of a trade mark may be regarded as having consented, directly or indirectly, to the importation and marketing within the EEA by third parties who currently own them, of products bearing that trade mark, which have been placed on the market outside the EEA by the proprietor of the mark or with his consent.

The ECJ then went on to deal with the question of whether consent to marketing must be express or may be implied.

37   The answer to that question requires that it first be established whether, with regard to situations such as those in issue in the main proceedings, the concept of consent used in Article 7(1) of the Directive must be interpreted uniformly throughout the Community legal order.

38   The Italian Government submits that where products are placed on the market outside the EEA, trade mark rights can never be exhausted as a consequence of a provision of Community law, because such exhaustion is not provided for by the Directive. Whether or not express or implied consent has been given for reimportation into the EEA is not a matter which concerns the consent to exhaustion referred to in Article 7(1) of the Directive, but rather relates to an act disposing of the trade mark rights, which is a matter for the national law in question.

39   Articles 5 to 7 of the Directive embody a complete harmonisation of the rules relating to the rights conferred by a trade mark and accordingly define the rights of proprietors of trade marks in the Community (*Silhouette*, cited above, paragraphs 25 and 29).

40   Article 5 of the Directive confers on the trade mark proprietor exclusive rights entitling him, *inter alia*, to prevent all third parties not having his consent from importing goods bearing the mark. Article 7(1) contains an exception to that rule in that it provides that the trade mark proprietor's rights are exhausted where goods have been put on the market in the EEA by the proprietor or with his consent.

41   It therefore appears that consent, which is tantamount to the proprietor's renunciation of his exclusive right under Article 5 of the Directive to prevent all third parties from importing goods bearing his trade mark, constitutes the decisive factor in the extinction of that right.

42   If the concept of consent were a matter for the national laws of the Member States, the consequence for trade mark proprietors could be that protection would vary according to the legal system concerned. The objective of the same protection under the legal systems of all the Member States set out in the ninth recital in the preamble to Directive 89/104, where it is described as fundamental, would not be attained.

43   It therefore falls to the Court to supply a uniform interpretation of the concept of consent to the placing of goods on the market within the EEA as referred to in Article 7(1) of the Directive.

44   The parties in the main proceedings, the German, Finnish and Swedish Governments and the EFTA Surveillance Authority acknowledge, explicitly or in substance, that consent to the placing on the market in the EEA of goods previously marketed outside that area may be express or implied. By contrast, the French Government maintains that consent must be express. The Commission's view is that the question is not whether consent must be express or implied, but rather whether the trade mark proprietor has had a first opportunity to benefit from the exclusive rights he holds within the EEA.

45   In view of its serious effect in extinguishing the exclusive rights of the proprietors of the trade marks in issue in the main proceedings (rights which enable them to control the initial marketing in the EEA), consent must be so expressed that an intention to renounce those rights is unequivocally demonstrated.

46   Such intention will normally be gathered from an express statement of consent. Nevertheless, it is conceivable that consent may, in some cases, be inferred from facts and circumstances prior to, simultaneous with or subsequent to the placing of the goods on the market outside the EEA which, in the view of the national court, unequivocally demonstrate that the proprietor has renounced his rights.

47   The answer to the first question referred in each of Cases C-414/99 to C-416/99 must therefore be that, on a proper construction of Article 7(1) of the Directive, the consent of a trade mark proprietor to the marketing within the EEA of products bearing that mark which have previously been placed on the market outside the EEA by that proprietor or with his consent may be implied, where it is to be inferred from facts and circumstances prior to, simultaneous with or subsequent to the placing of the goods on the market outside the EEA which, in the view of the national court, unequivocally demonstrate that the proprietor has renounced his right to oppose placing of the goods on the market within the EEA.

The next question considered by the ECJ was whether implied consent may be inferred from the mere silence of a trade mark proprietor.

49 Referring in particular to *Silhouette* and *Sebago and Maison Dubois*, cited above, A&G, Tesco and Costco argue that the defendant in an action for infringement of a trade mark must be presumed to have acted with the consent of the trade mark proprietor unless the latter proves the contrary.

50 In their opinion, if a trade mark proprietor wishes his exclusive rights to be reserved within the EEA, he must ensure that:
  • the goods bearing the trade mark carry a clear warning of the existence of such reservations, and
  • that the reservations are stipulated in the contracts for the sale and resale of those goods.

51 A&G contends that the clause in the contract concluded between Davidoff and its distributor in Singapore under which the latter undertook to oblige his sub-distributors, sub-agents and/or retailers not to resell the products outside the stipulated territory did not prevent the distributor or his sub-distributors, sub-agents and/or retailers from selling those products to third parties within the distribution territory with unlimited rights of resale. There is no evidence in the documents in the case in the main proceedings to demonstrate that the goods in question were sold by the distributor, or his sub-distributors, sub-agents or retailers outside the distribution territory. In addition, there was no notice on the goods or their packaging of any restrictions on resale and those goods were purchased and then sold to A&G without any restriction of that kind.

52 Tesco and Costco submit that where contracts for the acquisition of trade-marked goods placed on the market outside the EEA contain no restrictions on their resale, it is irrelevant that the proprietor of the mark may have made announcements or otherwise expressed the view that it did not wish those goods to be sold in the EEA by the purchaser.

53 It follows from the answer to the first question referred in the three cases C-414/99 to C-416/99 that consent must be expressed positively and that the factors taken into consideration in finding implied consent must unequivocally demonstrate that the trade mark proprietor has renounced any intention to enforce his exclusive rights.

54 It follows that it is for the trader alleging consent to prove it and not for the trade mark proprietor to demonstrate its absence.

55 Consequently, implied consent to the marketing within the EEA of goods put on the market outside that area cannot be inferred from the mere silence of the trade mark proprietor.

56 Likewise, implied consent cannot be inferred from the fact that a trade mark proprietor has not communicated his opposition to marketing within the EEA or from

the fact that the goods do not carry any warning that it is prohibited to place them on the market within the EEA.

57 Finally, such consent cannot be inferred from the fact that the trade mark proprietor transferred ownership of the goods bearing the mark without imposing contractual reservations or from the fact that, according to the law governing the contract, the property right transferred includes, in the absence of such reservations, an unlimited right of resale or, at the very least, a right to market the goods subsequently within the EEA.

58 A rule of national law which proceeded upon the mere silence of the trade mark proprietor would not recognise implied consent but rather deemed consent. This would not meet the need for consent positively expressed required by Community law.

59 In so far as it falls to the Community legislature to determine the rights of a trade mark proprietor within the Member States of the Community it would be unacceptable on the basis of the law governing the contract for marketing outside the EEA to apply rules of law that have the effect of limiting the protection afforded to the proprietor of a trade mark by Articles 5(1) and 7(1) of the Directive.

60 The answer to be given . . . must therefore be that implied consent cannot be inferred:
- from the fact that the proprietor of the trade mark has not communicated to all subsequent purchasers of the goods placed on the market outside the EEA his opposition to marketing within the EEA;
- from the fact that the goods carry no warning of a prohibition on their being placed on the market within the EEA;
- from the fact that the trade mark proprietor has transferred the ownership of the products bearing the trade mark without imposing any contractual reservations and that, according to the law governing the contract, the property right transferred includes, in the absence of such reservations, an unlimited right of resale or, at the very least, a right to market the goods subsequently within the EEA.

The final issue addressed by the Court was the consequence of ignorance on the part of a trader importing goods bearing a trade mark into the EEA that the trade mark proprietor expressed opposition to such imports.

63 Those questions raise the issue of whether a restriction of the right to dispose freely of goods, imposed on the first purchaser by the first vendor or agreed between the two parties to the sale, may be relied upon as against a third party transferee.

64 That is a different question from those concerning the effect on trade mark rights of consent to marketing within the EEA. Since such consent cannot be inferred from the proprietor's silence, preservation of his exclusive right cannot depend on there being an express prohibition of marketing within the EEA, which the proprietor is

not obliged to impose, nor, *a fortiori*, on a repetition of that prohibition in one or more of the contracts concluded in the distribution chain.

65   The national rules on the enforceability of sales restrictions against third parties are not, therefore, relevant to the resolution of a dispute between the proprietor of a trade mark and a subsequent trader in the distribution chain concerning the preservation or extinction of the rights conferred by the trade mark.

66   The answer to be given ... must therefore be that with regard to exhaustion of the trade mark proprietor's exclusive rights, it is not relevant:
- that the importer of goods bearing the trade mark is not aware that the proprietor objects to their being placed on the market in the EEA or sold there by traders other than authorised retailers, or
- that the authorised retailers and wholesalers have not imposed on their own purchasers contractual reservations setting out such opposition, even though they have been informed of it by the trade mark proprietor.

(C) Licensing intellectual property rights

I Licences and territorial restrictions

Part 3 above explained the concept of a licence. It is important to note that the key characteristic of the licence is the grant of a permission to the licensee to exploit the technology in question; without such permission, no exploitation will be possible. Hence, by virtue of an IPR, the holder can restrict exploitation and may dictate the terms on which such exploitation may be made. Quite naturally, the nature and scope of the licence depends on the level of protection enjoyed by the technology in question (and of course aspects unique to the market in question). This protection clearly affects the application of EC competition rules to the issue of licensing.

It cannot be denied that granting licences to exploit IPRs has the important economic benefit of assimilating technology and encouraging further development. Therefore, it is legitimate to ask why competition law should be concerned with this issue at all. The reason is that the power to license IPRs on restrictive terms (or indeed to refuse to license altogether) is a form of exclusivity and this may give rise to competition-related problems, in particular creating or strengthening positions of dominance, facilitating collusion, and segmenting markets geographically. In the EC context, one of the most serious concerns apparent in the Commission's decisional practice and the case law of the ECJ is that exclusivity may undermine the single market objective by hindering the sought-after integration of the national markets of Member States. For example, even in the early case of *Consten and Grundig* (see chapter 5) the ECJ held that the grant of exclusive trade mark rights was caught by Article 81(1).

In later cases, the ECJ clarified its approach. An important case to mention here is *Nungesser v. Commission*, which concerned a decision by the Commission in which it refused to grant an exemption under Article 81(3) for territorial protection given in a licence of plant breeders' rights. The firm in question, Nungesser, appealed to the ECJ. In its judgment the ECJ held that the application of Article 81 in licensing situations depends on the nature of the territorial protection granted to the licensee, and that in such cases a distinction must be made between an open exclusive licence and the grant of absolute territorial protection. In the former situation, as was the case in *Nungesser*, the owner of an IPR merely undertakes not to grant other licences in respect of the territory of the licensee and not to compete himself with the licensee in that territory. On the facts of the case the open exclusive licence was not caught by Article 81 since it was necessary to encourage the licensee to accept the risk of cultivating and marketing the new technology in his territory. According to the ECJ this should be treated differently from the second situation (where absolute territorial protection is offered), which falls within Article 81(1) by virtue of its anti-competitive object and cannot benefit from an exemption under Article 81(3). However, it is important to note that the *Nungesser* judgment cannot be taken as representative of the general approach of the ECJ. On some occasions the ECJ has adopted a very restrictive approach as can be seen from the case of *Windsurfing v. Commission*.

II Block exemption

The Commission's initial approach to licensing of IPRs was generally permissive. However, a change in its approach gradually began to appear over the years which led to the view that licences of IPRs containing exclusivity clauses required an assessment under Article 81(1) and that most of them, at least, would infringe that provision. This change in approach could explain the large number of notifications of exclusive technology licences, which the Commission received in a relatively short period of time. Indeed, this development, coupled with the fact that the Commission was building considerable experience in this area, seems to have forced the Commission to consider adopting a block exemption mechanism in the case of certain IPR licences.

The Commission adopted Regulation 2349/84 which dealt with exclusive patent licences and Regulation 556/89 which dealt with exclusive know-how licences. These two Regulations were later replaced by Regulation 240/96, widely referred to as the 'Transfer of Technology Regulation', which regulated exclusive patent licences, exclusive know-how licences and mixed patent and know-how licences.

Like many areas in EC competition law, however, the Commission's drive for further reform did not stop with the adoption of Regulation 240/96, which was destined to expire in March 2006. Indeed, five years following its adoption, the Commission took the first step towards reforming the Regulation. This happened with the publication of the Commission's Evaluation Report in December 2001. The Report contained some of the Commission's views on Regulation

240/96, its effectiveness and its workability and came to several conclusions in this regard; it also sought the views of interested parties on reform of Regulation 240/96. Among other conclusions, the Report suggests that the approach adopted in the Regulation is too prescriptive and that it fails to employ economic analysis. On the other hand, the Commission found that some agreements fell within the scope of the Regulation but should not have done so because these agreements did not satisfy the conditions for exemption under Article 81(3). The Commission also felt that the approach under the Regulation was focused more on the form of the agreement rather than on issues of market impact.

The Report contained several proposals. One proposal was to bring the Regulation in line with existing block exemption Regulations, such as Regulation 2790/99 (considered in the previous chapter). Another proposal was to expand the scope of the Regulation to cover not only bilateral but also multilateral agreements. According to the Commission, this was necessary in light of the increasing complexity of technology and the fact that multilateral technology transfer agreements may be pro-competitive and may be efficiency enhancing; though the Commission did acknowledge that such agreements may also end up acting as disguised cartels. The Commission also suggested that a more lenient approach to agreements between competitors was desirable, while ensuring a more prudent approach to agreements between non-competitors.

Following a period of consultation during which the Commission received many interesting and detailed comments, it engaged in a period of 'in-house' consideration and further consultation at the Community and Member State level. The outcome was the publication of a proposal for a new Regulation to replace Regulation 240/96 and set of draft guidelines, which deal with the application of the new Regulation. The Commission asked interested parties again for their comments on the draft Regulation and guidelines. In April 2004 the proposal became Regulation 772/2004 and the draft guidelines became the *Guidelines on the Application of Article 81 the EC Treaty to Technology Transfer Agreements* (2004). Regulation 772/2004 entered into force on 1 May 2004.

(a) Regulation 772/2004 OJ (2004) L 123/11

THE COMMISSION OF THE EUROPEAN COMMUNITIES,
Having regard to the Treaty establishing the European Community,
Having regard to Council Regulation No 19/65/EEC of 2 March 1965 on application of Article 81(3) of the Treaty to certain categories of agreements and concerted practices[1] and in particular Article 1 thereof,
Having published a draft of this Regulation,[2]

---

1 1 OJ 36, 6.3.1965, p. 533/65. Regulation as last amended by Regulation (EC)No 1/2003 (OJ L 1, 4.1.2003, p.1).
2 OJ C 235, 1.10.2003, p. 10.

After consulting the Advisory Committee on Restrictive Practices and Dominant Positions,

Whereas:

(1) Regulation No 19/65/EEC empowers the Commission to apply Article 81(3) of the Treaty by Regulation to certain categories of technology transfer agreements and corresponding concerted practices to which only two undertakings are party, which fall within Article 81(1).

(2) Pursuant to Regulation No 19/65/EEC, the Commission has, in particular, adopted Regulation (EC) No 240/96 of 31 January 1996 on the application of Article [81(3)] of the Treaty to certain categories of technology transfer agreements.[3]

(3) On 20 December 2001 the Commission published an evaluation report on the transfer of technology block exemption Regulation (EC) No 240/96.[4] This generated a public debate on the application of Regulation (EC) No 240/96 and on the application in general of Article 81(1) and Article 81(3) of the Treaty to technology transfer agreements. The response to the evaluation report from Member States and third parties has been generally in favour of reform of Community competition policy on technology transfer agreements. It is therefore appropriate to repeal Regulation (EC) No 240/96.

(4) This Regulation should meet the two requirements of ensuring effective competition and providing adequate legal security for undertakings. The pursuit of these objectives should take account of the need to simplify the regulatory framework and its application. It is appropriate to move away from the approach of listing exempted clauses and to place greater emphasis on defining the categories of agreements which are exempted up to a certain level of market power and on specifying the restrictions or clauses which are not to be contained in such agreements. This is consistent with an economics based approach which assesses the impact of agreements on the relevant market. It is also consistent with such an approach to make a distinction between agreements between competitors and agreements between non-competitors.

(5) Technology transfer agreements concern the licensing of technology. Such agreements will usually improve economic efficiency and be pro-competitive as they can reduce duplication of research and development, strengthen the incentive for the initial research and development, spur incremental innovation, facilitate diffusion and generate product market competition.

(6) The likelihood that such efficiency enhancing and pro-competitive effects will outweigh any anti-competitive effects due to restrictions contained in technology transfer agreements depends on the degree of market power of the undertakings concerned and, therefore, on the extent to which those undertakings face competition

3 OJ L 31, 9.2.1996, p. 2. Regulation as amended by the 2003 Act of Accession.
4 COM(2001) 786 final.

from undertakings owning substitute technologies or undertakings producing substitute products.

(7) This Regulation should only deal with agreements where the licensor permits the licensee to exploit the licensed technology, possibly after further research and development by the licensee, for the production of goods or services. It should not deal with licensing agreements for the purpose of sub-contracting research and development. It should also not deal with licensing agreements to set up technology pools, that is to say, agreements for the pooling of technologies with the purpose of licensing the created package of intellectual property rights to third parties.

(8) For the application of Article 81(3) by regulation, it is not necessary to define those technology transfer agreements that are capable of falling within Article 81(1). In the individual assessment of agreements under Article 81(1), account has to be taken of several factors, and in particular the structure and the dynamics of the relevant technology and product markets.

(9) The benefit of the block exemption established by this Regulation should be limited to those agreements which can be assumed with sufficient certainty to satisfy the conditions of Article 81(3). In order to attain the benefits and objectives of technology transfer the benefit of this Regulation should also apply to provisions contained in technology transfer agreements that do not constitute the primary object of such agreements, but are directly related to the application of the licensed technology.

(10) For technology transfer agreements between competitors it can be presumed that, where the combined share of the relevant markets accounted for by the parties does not exceed 20% and the agreements do not contain certain severely anti-competitive restraints, they generally lead to an improvement in production or distribution and allow consumers a fair share of the resulting benefits.

(11) For technology transfer agreements between non-competitors it can be presumed that, where the individual share of the relevant markets accounted for by each of the parties does not exceed 30% and the agreements do not contain certain severely anti-competitive restraints, they generally lead to an improvement in production or distribution and allow consumers a fair share of the resulting benefits.

(12) There can be no presumption that above these market share thresholds technology transfer agreements do fall within the scope of Article 81(1). For instance, an exclusive licensing agreement between non-competing undertakings does often not fall within the scope of Article 81(1). There can also be no presumption that, above these market share thresholds, technology transfer agreements falling within the scope of Article 81(1) will not satisfy the conditions for exemption. However, it can also not be presumed that they will usually give rise to objective advantages of such a character and size as to compensate for the disadvantages which they create for competition.

[215]

(13) This Regulation should not exempt technology transfer agreements containing restrictions which are not indispensable to the improvement of production or distribution. In particular, technology transfer agreements containing certain severely anti-competitive restraints such as the fixing of prices charged to third parties should be excluded from the benefit of the block exemption established by this Regulation irrespective of the market shares of the undertakings concerned. In the case of such hardcore restrictions the whole agreement should be excluded from the benefit of the block exemption.

(14) In order to protect incentives to innovate and the appropriate application of intellectual property rights, certain restrictions should be excluded from the block exemption. In particular exclusive grant back obligations for severable improvements should be excluded. Where such a restriction is included in a licence agreement only the restriction in question should be excluded from the benefit of the block exemption.

(15) The market share thresholds, the non-exemption of technology transfer agreements containing severely anti-competitive restraints and the excluded restrictions provided for in this Regulation will normally ensure that the agreements to which the block exemption applies do not enable the participating undertakings to eliminate competition in respect of a substantial part of the products in question.

(16) In particular cases in which the agreements falling under this Regulation nevertheless have effects incompatible with Article 81(3), the Commission should be able to withdraw the benefit of the block exemption. This may occur in particular where the incentives to innovate are reduced or where access to markets is hindered.

(17) Council Regulation (EC) No 1/2003 of 16 December 2002 on the implementation of the rules on competition laid down in Articles 81 and 82 of the Treaty[5] empowers the competent authorities of Member States to withdraw the benefit of the block exemption in respect of technology transfer agreements having effects incompatible with Article 81(3), where such effects are felt in their respective territory, or in a part thereof, and where such territory has the characteristics of a distinct geographic market. Member States must ensure that the exercise of this power of withdrawal does not prejudice the uniform application throughout the common market of the Community competition rules or the full effect of the measures adopted in implementation of those rules.

(18) In order to strengthen supervision of parallel networks of technology transfer agreements which have similar restrictive effects and which cover more than 50% of a given market, the Commission should be able to declare this Regulation inapplicable to technology transfer agreements containing specific restraints relating to the market concerned, thereby restoring the full application of Article 81 to such agreements.

5 OJ L 1, 4.1.2003, p. 1. Regulation as amended by Regulation (EC) No 411/2004 (OJ L 68, 6.3.2004, p. 1).

(19)   This Regulation should cover only technology transfer agreements between a licensor and a licensee. It should cover such agreements even if conditions are stipulated for more than one level of trade, by for instance requiring the licensee to set up a particular distribution system and specifying the obligations the licensee must or may impose on resellers of the products produced under the licence. However, such conditions and obligations should comply with the competition rules applicable to supply and distribution agreements. Supply and distribution agreements concluded between a licensee and its buyers should not be exempted by this Regulation.

(20)   This Regulation is without prejudice to the application of Article 82 of the Treaty.

HAS ADOPTED THIS REGULATION:

Article 1 Definitions

1   For the purposes of this Regulation the following definitions shall apply:
   (a) 'agreement' means an agreement, a decision of an association of undertakings or a concerted practice;
   (b) 'technology transfer agreement' means a patent licensing agreement, a know-how licensing agreement, a software copyright licensing agreement or a mixed patent, know-how or software copyright licensing agreement, including any such agreement containing provisions which relate to the sale and purchase of products or which relate to the licensing of other intellectual property rights or the assignment of intellectual property rights, provided that those provisions do not constitute the primary object of the agreement and are directly related to the production of the contract products; assignments of patents, know-how, software copyright or a combination thereof where part of the risk associated with the exploitation of the technology remains with the assignor, in particular where the sum payable in consideration of the assignment is dependent on the turnover obtained by the assignee in respect of products produced with the assigned technology, the quantity of such products produced or the number of operations carried out employing the technology, shall also be deemed to be technology transfer agreements;
   (c) 'reciprocal agreement' means a technology transfer agreement where two undertakings grant each other, in the same or separate contracts, a patent licence, a know-how licence, a software copyright licence or a mixed patent, know-how or software copyright licence and where these licences concern competing technologies or can be used for the production of competing products;
   (d) 'non-reciprocal agreement' means a technology transfer agreement where one undertaking grants another undertaking a patent licence, a know-how licence, a software copyright licence or a mixed patent, know-how or software copyright licence, or where two undertakings grant each other such a licence but where these licences do not concern competing technologies and cannot be used for the production of competing products;

[217]

(e) 'product' means a good or a service, including both intermediary goods and services and final goods and services;

(f) 'contract products' means products produced with the licensed technology;

(g) 'intellectual property rights' includes industrial property rights, know-how, copyright and neighbouring rights;

(h) 'patents' means patents, patent applications, utility models, applications for registration of utility models, designs, topographies of semiconductor products, supplementary protection certificates for medicinal products or other products for which such supplementary protection certificates may be obtained and plant breeder's certificates;

(i) 'know-how' means a package of non-patented practical information, resulting from experience and testing, which is:
(i) secret, that is to say, not generally known or easily accessible,
(ii) substantial, that is to say, significant and useful for the production of the contract products, and
(iii) identified, that is to say, described in a sufficiently comprehensive manner so as to make it possible to verify that it fulfils the criteria of secrecy and substantiality;

(j) 'competing undertakings' means undertakings which compete on the relevant technology market and/or the relevant product market, that is to say:
(i) competing undertakings on the relevant technology market, being undertakings which license out competing technologies without infringing each others' intellectual property rights (actual competitors on the technology market); the relevant technology market includes technologies which are regarded by the licensees as interchangeable with or substitutable for the licensed technology, by reason of the technologies' characteristics, their royalties and their intended use,
(ii) competing undertakings on the relevant product market, being undertakings which, in the absence of the technology transfer agreement, are both active on the relevant product and geographic market(s)on which the contract products are sold without infringing each others' intellectual property rights (actual competitors on the product market) or would, on realistic grounds, undertake the necessary additional investments or other necessary switching costs so that they could timely enter, without infringing each others' intellectual property rights, the(se) relevant product and geographic market(s) in response to a small and permanent increase in relative prices (potential competitors on the product market); the relevant product market comprises products which are regarded by the buyers as interchangeable with or substitutable for the contract products, by reason of the products' characteristics, their prices and their intended use;

(k) 'selective distribution system' means a distribution system where the licensor undertakes to license the production of the contract products only to licensees selected on the basis of specified criteria and where these licensees undertake not to sell the contract products to unauthorised distributors;

(l) 'exclusive territory' means a territory in which only one undertaking is allowed to produce the contract products with the licensed technology, without prejudice to the possibility to allow within that territory another licensee to produce the contract products only for a particular customer where this second licence was granted in order to create an alternative source of supply for that customer;

(m) 'exclusive customer group' means a group of customers to which only one undertaking is allowed to actively sell the contract products produced with the licensed technology;

(n) 'severable improvement' means an improvement that can be exploited without infringing the licensed technology.

2   The terms 'undertaking', 'licensor' and 'licensee' shall include their respective connected undertakings.

'Connected undertakings' means:

(a) undertakings in which a party to the agreement, directly or indirectly:
   (i)   has the power to exercise more than half the voting rights, or
   (ii)   has the power to appoint more than half the members of the supervisory board, board of management or bodies legally representing the undertaking, or
   (iii) has the right to manage the undertaking's affairs;

(b) undertakings which directly or indirectly have, over a party to the agreement, the rights or powers listed in (a);

(c) undertakings in which an undertaking referred to in (b) has, directly or indirectly, the rights or powers listed in (a);

(d) undertakings in which a party to the agreement together with one or more of the undertakings referred to in (a), (b) or (c), or in which two or more of the latter undertakings, jointly have the rights or powers listed in (a);

(e) undertakings in which the rights or the powers listed in (a) are jointly held by:
   (i)   parties to the agreement or their respective connected undertakings referred to in (a) to (d), or
   (ii)   one or more of the parties to the agreement or one or more of their connected undertakings referred to in (a) to (d) and one or more third parties.

Article 2 Exemption

Pursuant to Article 81(3) of the Treaty and subject to the provisions of this Regulation, it is hereby declared that Article 81(1) of the Treaty shall not apply to technology transfer agreements entered into between two undertakings permitting the production of contract products.

This exemption shall apply to the extent that such agreements contain restrictions of competition falling within the scope of Article 81(1). The exemption shall apply for as long as the intellectual property right in the licensed technology has not expired, lapsed or been declared invalid or, in the case of know-how, for as long as the know-how remains secret, except in the event where the know-how becomes publicly known as a result of action by the licensee, in which case the exemption shall apply for the duration of the agreement.

Article 3 Market share thresholds

1   Where the undertakings party to the agreement are competing undertakings, the exemption provided for in Article 2 shall apply on condition that the combined market share of the parties does not exceed 20% on the affected relevant technology and product market.

2   Where the undertakings party to the agreement are not competing undertakings, the exemption provided for in Article 2 shall apply on condition that the market share of each of the parties does not exceed 30% on the affected relevant technology and product market.

3   For the purposes of paragraphs 1 and 2 the market share of a party on the relevant technology market(s) is defined in terms of the presence of the licensed technology on the relevant product market(s). A licensor's market share on the relevant technology market shall be the combined market share on the relevant product market of the contract products produced by the licensor and its licensees.

Article 4 Hardcore restrictions

1   Where the undertakings party to the agreement are competing undertakings, the exemption provided for in Article 2 shall not apply to agreements which, directly or indirectly, in isolation or in combination with other factors under the control of the parties, have as their object:
(a) the restriction of a party's ability to determine its prices when selling products to third parties;
(b) the limitation of output, except limitations on the output of contract products imposed on the licensee in a non-reciprocal agreement or imposed on only one of the licensees in a reciprocal agreement;
(c) the allocation of markets or customers except:
   (i) the obligation on the licensee(s) to produce with the licensed technology only within one or more technical fields of use or one or more product markets,
   (ii) the obligation on the licensor and/or the licensee, in a non-reciprocal agreement, not to produce with the licensed technology within one or more technical fields of use or one or more product markets or one or more exclusive territories reserved for the other party,
   (iii) the obligation on the licensor not to license the technology to another licensee in a particular territory,
   (iv) the restriction, in a non-reciprocal agreement, of active and/or passive sales by the licensee and/or the licensor into the exclusive territory or to the exclusive customer group reserved for the other party,

(v) the restriction, in a non-reciprocal agreement, of active sales by the licensee into the exclusive territory or to the exclusive customer group allocated by the licensor to another licensee provided the latter was not a competing undertaking of the licensor at the time of the conclusion of its own licence,

(vi) the obligation on the licensee to produce the contract products only for its own use provided that the licensee is not restricted in selling the contract products actively and passively as spare parts for its own products,

(vii) the obligation on the licensee, in a non-reciprocal agreement, to produce the contract products only for a particular customer, where the licence was granted in order to create an alternative source of supply for that customer;

(d) the restriction of the licensee's ability to exploit its own technology or the restriction of the ability of any of the parties to the agreement to carry out research and development, unless such latter restriction is indispensable to prevent the disclosure of the licensed know-how to third parties.

2   Where the undertakings party to the agreement are not competing undertakings, the exemption provided for in Article 2 shall not apply to agreements which, directly or indirectly, in isolation or in combination with other factors under the control of the parties, have as their object:

(a) the restriction of a party's ability to determine its prices when selling products to third parties, without prejudice to the possibility to impose a maximum sale price or recommending a sale price, provided that it does not amount to a fixed or minimum sale price as a result of pressure from, or incentives offered by, any of the parties;

(b) the restriction of the territory into which, or of the customers to whom, the licensee may passively sell the contract products, except:

(i) the restriction of passive sales into an exclusive territory or to an exclusive customer group reserved for the licensor,

(ii) the restriction of passive sales into an exclusive territory or to an exclusive customer group allocated by the licensor to another licensee during the first two years that this other licensee is selling the contract products in that territory or to that customer group,

(iii) the obligation to produce the contract products only for its own use provided that the licensee is not restricted in selling the contract products actively and passively as spare parts for its own products,

(iv) the obligation to produce the contract products only for a particular customer, where the licence was granted in order to create an alternative source of supply for that customer,

(v) the restriction of sales to end users by a licensee operating at the wholesale level of trade,

(vi) the restriction of sales to unauthorised distributors by the members of a selective distribution system;

(c) the restriction of active or passive sales to end users by a licensee which is a member of a selective distribution system and which operates at the retail level, without prejudice to the possibility of prohibiting a member of the system from operating out of an unauthorised place of establishment.

3   Where the undertakings party to the agreement are not competing undertakings at the time of the conclusion of the agreement but become competing undertakings afterwards, paragraph 2 and not paragraph 1 shall apply for the full life of the agreement unless the agreement is subsequently amended in any material respect.

Article 5 Excluded restrictions

1   The exemption provided for in Article 2 shall not apply to any of the following obligations contained in technology transfer agreements:
(a) any direct or indirect obligation on the licensee to grant an exclusive licence to the licensor or to a third party designated by the licensor in respect of its own severable improvements to or its own new applications of the licensed technology;
(b) any direct or indirect obligation on the licensee to assign, in whole or in part, to the licensor or to a third party designated by the licensor, rights to its own severable improvements to or its own new applications of the licensed technology;
(c) any direct or indirect obligation on the licensee not to challenge the validity of intellectual property rights which the licensor holds in the common market, without prejudice to the possibility to provide for termination of the technology transfer agreement in the event that the licensee challenges the validity of one or more of the licensed intellectual property rights.

2   Where the undertakings party to the agreement are not competing undertakings, the exemption provided for in Article 2 shall not apply to any direct or indirect obligation limiting the licensee's ability to exploit its own technology or limiting the ability of any of the parties to the agreement to carry out research and development, unless such latter restriction is indispensable to prevent the disclosure of the licensed know-how to third parties.

Article 6 Withdrawal in individual cases

1   The Commission may withdraw the benefit of this Regulation, pursuant to Article 29(1) of Regulation (EC) No 1/2003, where it finds in any particular case that a technology transfer agreement to which the exemption provided for in Article 2 applies nevertheless has effects which are incompatible with Article 81(3) of the Treaty, and in particular where:
(a) access of third parties' technologies to the market is restricted, for instance by the cumulative effect of parallel networks of similar restrictive agreements prohibiting licensees from using third parties' technologies;

(b) access of potential licensees to the market is restricted, for instance by the cumulative effect of parallel networks of similar restrictive agreements prohibiting licensors from licensing to other licensees;

(c) without any objectively valid reason, the parties do not exploit the licensed technology.

2   Where, in any particular case, a technology transfer agreement to which the exemption provided for in Article 2 applies has effects which are incompatible with Article 81(3) of the Treaty in the territory of a Member State, or in a part thereof, which has all the characteristics of a distinct geographic market, the competition authority of that Member State may withdraw the benefit of this Regulation, pursuant to Article 29(2) of Regulation (EC) No 1/2003, in respect of that territory, under the same circumstances as those set out in paragraph 1 of this Article.

Article 7 Non-application of this Regulation

1   Pursuant to Article 1a of Regulation No 19/65/EEC, the Commission may by regulation declare that, where parallel networks of similar technology transfer agreements cover more than 50% of a relevant market, this Regulation is not to apply to technology transfer agreements containing specific restraints relating to that market.

2   A regulation pursuant to paragraph 1 shall not become applicable earlier than six months following its adoption.

Article 8 Application of the market share thresholds

1   For the purposes of applying the market share thresholds provided for in Article 3 the rules set out in this paragraph shall apply.

The market share shall be calculated on the basis of market sales value data. If market sales value data are not available, estimates based on other reliable market information, including market sales volumes, may be used to establish the market share of the undertaking concerned.

The market share shall be calculated on the basis of data relating to the preceding calendar year.

The market share held by the undertakings referred to in point (e) of the second subparagraph of Article 1(2) shall be apportioned equally to each undertaking having the rights or the powers listed in point (a) of the second subparagraph of Article 1(2).

2   If the market share referred to in Article 3(1) or Article 3(2) is initially not more than 20% respectively 30% but subsequently rises above those levels, the exemption provided for in Article 2 shall continue to apply for a period of two consecutive calendar years following the year in which the 20% threshold or 30% threshold was first exceeded.

[223]

Article 9 Repeal

Regulation (EC) No 240/96 is repealed. References to the repealed Regulation shall be construed as references to this Regulation.

Article 10 Transitional period

The prohibition laid down in Article 81(1) of the Treaty shall not apply during the period from 1 May 2004 to 31 March 2006 in respect of agreements already in force on 30 April 2004 which do not satisfy the conditions for exemption provided for in this Regulation but which, on 30 April 2004, satisfied the conditions for exemption provided for in Regulation (EC) No 240/96.

Article 11 Period of validity

This Regulation shall enter into force on 1 May 2004. It shall expire on 30 April 2014. This Regulation shall be binding in its entirety and directly applicable in all Member States.

A simple reading of Regulation 240/96 and 772/2004 would reveal the major differences between the two Regulations and the valuable advantages, which the latter has in comparison to the former. As widely known, Regulation 240/96 was narrow in scope and embodied a formalistic approach, which since the 1990s the Commission has been removing from the application of Article 81 to different categories of agreements. Regulation 772/2004 has a much wider scope and is in line with the Commission's new style block exemption Regulations, such as Regulation 2790/99 on vertical agreements (see previous chapter); though the Regulation does recognise the differences which exist between licensing agreements on the one hand and distribution agreements on the other. The Regulation covers, in addition to patent and know-how licensing agreements, design right and software copyright licensing agreements, which were not within the scope of Regulation 240/96. It creates a safe harbour for such agreements (see below). In light of the Commission's experience under Regulation 2790/99, this reduces bureaucracy and increases legal certainty for firms while saving many agreements from individual scrutiny. This widening of the scope of the block exemption in this area should be welcomed as a good means towards facilitating the dissemination of technology in the Community.

(b) The Commission's Guidelines

The Commission's Guidelines on technology transfer offer a useful source of information in connection with the Regulation. In addition to explaining the application of the Regulation, they also offer guidance on the application of Article 81 to agreements not covered by its safe harbour. The *Guidelines* are not extracted in full below. They are published in the Official Journal and can be viewed at and downloaded from DG Comp's website: http://europa.eu.int/comm/competition/. The following summary of the *Guidelines* is provided for the aid of the reader.

The *Guidelines* begin by discussing general principles of IPRs and Article 81, addressing the similarities in the objectives of the two regimes in promoting efficient use of resources, innovation and consumer welfare. They take the starting point that technology transfer agreements (TTAs) are generally pro-competitive. However, some provisions (such as those set out in paragraph 14 of the *Guidelines*, e.g. price fixing or absolute territorial protection) can of course infringe Article 81(1) by virtue of anti-competitive object or a tendency in the Commission's experience to have such effect. These are not covered by the Regulation and would be unlikely in any event to satisfy the criteria in Article 81(3). The *Guidelines* explain the application of the Regulation and establish a framework for assessing the actual effect of TTAs under Article 81.

(i) Market definition (paragraphs 19–25)

Like many of the Commission's other Guidelines and Notices, the *Guidelines* show the importance of market definition. The starting point is that, as a 'prod-uct' of research and development, and an 'input' to other products, technology is a market in its own right. Accordingly, besides this market, TTAs might also restrict markets upstream or downstream which may need to be taken into ac-count when conducting a competition assessment. As regards quantification of the technology market share, this may be difficult and controversial, particularly with a new technology that is only just taking hold. For this reason the *Guide-lines* refer to Article 3(3) of the Regulation which prescribes taking the market share of downstream products incorporating the technology. Paragraph 25 of the *Guidelines* notes that in certain circumstances, it may also be appropriate to define 'innovation' markets which might be constrained by restrictions in the use of the technology.

In the application of Article 81, paragraph 11 states that the assessment of whether a licensing agreement restricts competition must be conducted within the actual context in which competition *would have* occurred in the absence of the agreements within its alleged restrictions. Paragraph 12 sets out and discusses two useful questions in considering the 'counter-factual' with regard both to *inter-technology competition* (i.e. undertakings using competing tech-nologies) and *intra-technology competition* (i.e. undertakings using the same technology). These questions ask: Does the licence agreement restrict actual or potential competition that would have existed (a) without the contemplated agreement and (b) in the absence of the contractual restraint(s)?

If a licensing agreement does not have as its object the restriction of competi-tion, it is necessary to examine its effect. Obviously, any actual or potential effect on competition must be appreciable (see pp. 85–90 above for discussion of the *de minimis* Notice) and the Commission states that there must be a sufficient likelihood of potential anti-competitive effect occurring (paragraph 15). The *Guidelines* take the view that there is a greater risk to competition in licences

[225]

between actual or potential competitors than between non-competitors. This concept is discussed in paragraphs 26–33, and one should bear in mind that there are various constellations depending on whether competitors are actual or potential and whether the relevant market is the technology market or an up- or downstream product market.

(ii) Applicability and effect of the Regulation

Part III of the *Guidelines* sets out the criteria for assessing the agreement under the Regulation. The market share thresholds (Article 3), the hardcore list (Article 4) and the excluded restrictions (Article 5) aim to restrict the application of the Regulation to agreements that will fulfil the requirements of Article 81(3). If applicable, the Regulation exempts the agreement from the Article 81(1) prohibition. Hence it remains fully enforceable and legally binding, subject to future withdrawal of the exemption.

It is important to note that paragraph 1 of Article 2 of the Regulation restricts the exemption to agreements 'between two undertakings', but the principles will also be relevant to individual Article 81(3) assessments of other TTAs (paragraph 40). The *Guidelines* note in paragraph 39 that the Regulation may nonetheless apply to multiple levels of trade, such as agreements concerning production and retail. Indeed this may oftentimes be inherent, as paragraphs 41–45 explain that the exemption only applies to production of 'contract products' (a concept defined in Article 1(f) of the Regulation), which means the licensee must be permitted to exploit or incorporate the technology in the production of goods or services. In other words, the exemption does not cover 'technology pool' agreements, which have as their primary purpose the sub-licensing of technology packages.

Paragraphs 46–53 explain the concept of TTAs and associated terms, which are defined in Article 1 of the Regulation:

46 ... the concept of 'technology' covers patents and patent applications, utility models and applications for utility models, design rights, plant breeders rights, topographies of semiconductor products, supplementary protection certificates for medicinal products or other products for which such supplementary protection certificates may be obtained, software copyright, and know-how. The licensed technology should allow the licensee with or without other inputs to produce the contract products.

47 Know-how is defined in Article 1(1)(i) as a package of non-patented practical information, resulting from experience and testing, which is secret, substantial and identified. 'Secret' means that the know-how is not generally known or easily accessible. 'Substantial' means that the know-how includes information which is significant and useful for the production of the products covered by the licence agreement or the application of the process covered by the licence agreement. In other words, the information must significantly contribute to or facilitate the production of the contract products. In cases where the licensed know-how relates to a product as

opposed to a process, this condition implies that the know-how is useful for the production the contract product. This condition is not satisfied where the contract product can be produced on the basis of freely available technology. However, the condition does not require that the contract product is of higher value than products produced with freely available technology. In the case of process technologies, this condition implies that the know-how is useful in the sense that it can reasonably be expected at the date of conclusion of the agreement to be capable of significantly improving the competitive position of the licensee, for instance by reducing his production costs. 'Identified' means that it is possible to verify that the licensed know-how fulfils the criteria of secrecy and substantiality. This condition is satisfied where the licensed know-how is described in manuals or other written form. However, in some cases this may not be reasonably possible. The licensed know-how may consist of practical knowledge possessed by the licensor's employees. For instance, the licensor's employees may possess secret and substantial knowledge about a certain production process which is passed on to the licensee in the form of training of the licensee's employees. In such cases it is sufficient to describe in the agreement the general nature of the know-how and to list the employees that will be or have been involved in passing it on to the licensee.

48   The concept of 'transfer' implies that technology must flow from one undertaking to another. Such transfers normally take the form of licensing whereby the licensor grants the licensee the right to use his technology against payment of royalties. It can also take the form of sub-licensing, whereby a licensee, having been authorised to do so by the licensor, grants licenses to third parties (sub-licensees) for the exploitation of the technology.

49   The TTBER only applies to agreements that have as their primary object the transfer of technology as defined in that Regulation as opposed to the purchase of goods and services or the licensing of other types of intellectual property. Agreements containing provisions relating to the purchase and sale of products are only covered by the TTBER to the extent that those provisions do not constitute the primary object of the agreement and are directly related to the application of the licensed technology. This is likely to be the case where the tied products take the form of equipment or process input which is specifically tailored to efficiently exploit the licensed technology. If, on the other hand, the product is simply another input into the final product, it must be carefully examined whether the licensed technology constitutes the primary object of the agreement. For instance, in cases where the licensee is already manufacturing a final product on the basis of another technology, the licence must lead to a significant improvement of the licensee's production process, exceeding the value of the product purchased from the licensor. The requirement that the tied products must be related to the licensing of technology implies that the TTBER does not cover the purchase of products that have no relation with the products incorporating the licensed technology. This is for example the case where the tied product is not intended to be used with the licensed product, but relates to an activity on a separate product market.

50   The TTBER only covers the licensing of other types of intellectual property such as trademarks and copyright, other than software copyright, to the extent that they are directly related to the exploitation of the licensed technology and do not constitute the primary object of the agreement. This condition ensures that agreements covering other types of intellectual property rights are only block exempted to the extent that these other intellectual property rights serve to enable the licensee to better exploit the licensed technology. The licensor may for instance authorise the licensee to use his trademark on the products incorporating the licensed technology. The trademark licence may allow the licensee to better exploit the licensed technology by allowing consumers to make an immediate link between the product and the characteristics imputed to it by the licensed technology. An obligation on the licensee to use the licensor's trademark may also promote the dissemination of technology by allowing the licensor to identify himself as the source of the underlying technology. However, where the value of the licensed technology to the licensee is limited because he already employs an identical or very similar technology and the main object of the agreement is the trademark, the TTBER does not apply.

51   The licensing of copyright for the purpose of reproduction and distribution of the protected work, i.e. the production of copies for resale, is considered to be similar to technology licensing. Since such licence agreements relate to the production and sale of products on the basis of an intellectual property right, they are considered to be of a similar nature as technology transfer agreements and normally raise comparable issues. Although the TTBER does not cover copyright other than software copyright, the Commission will as a general rule apply the principles set out in the TTBER and these guidelines when assessing such licensing of copyright under Article 81.

52   On the other hand, the licensing of rights in performances and other rights related to copyright is considered to raise particular issues and it may not be warranted to assess such licensing on the basis of the principles developed in these guidelines. In the case of the various rights related to performances value is created not by the reproduction and sale of copies of a product but by each individual performance of the protected work. Such exploitation can take various forms including the performance, showing or the renting of protected material such as films, music or sporting events. In the application of Article 81 the specificities of the work and the way in which it is exploited must be taken into account. For instance, resale restrictions may give rise to less competition concerns whereas particular concerns may arise where licensors impose on their licensees to extend to each of the licensors more favourable conditions obtained by one of them. The Commission will therefore not apply the TTBER and the present guidelines by way of analogy to the licensing of these other rights.

53   The Commission will also not extend the principles developed in the TTBER and these guidelines to trademark licensing. Trademark licensing often occurs in the context of distribution and resale of goods and services and is generally more akin to distribution agreements than technology licensing. Where a trademark licence

is directly related to the use, sale or resale of goods and services and does not constitute the primary object of the agreement, the licence agreement is covered by Commission Regulation (EC) No 2790/1999 on the application of Article 81(3) of the Treaty to categories of vertical agreements and concerted practices.

It is apparent from these paragraphs that technology may be an aspect of a range of different agreements and that the Regulation may therefore interface with other block exemption regulations, in particular Regulation 2658/2000 (specialisation agreements), Regulation 2659/2000 (research and development agreements) and Regulation 2790/1999 (vertical agreements). Paragraphs 56–64 of the *Guidelines* detail the applicability of and disparities between these various instruments.

(iii) The 'safe harbour' of the Regulation (paragraphs 65–73)
In the absence of any hardcore restrictions (see below), Article 3 of the Regulation sets out the market share thresholds for application of the exemption. This again calls for consideration of the relevant market. The thresholds in the Regulation differ depending on whether the undertakings are competitors or non-competitors on a given market, being 20 per cent and 30 per cent respectively. The parties are competitors where both are actually active on the relevant market (e.g. marketing a given product) or have the potential realistically to enter the market given a significant non-transitory increase in prices. However, paragraph 66 of the *Guidelines* states that *potential* competition on the technology market is not taken into account for purposes of the threshold.

Where the combined market share in any given market exceeds the threshold level, paragraph 69 explains that the Regulation will not apply *with respect to that market*. Paragraph 73 of the *Guidelines* contains several practical examples of the points made in paragraphs 65–73, both for non-competitors and competitors.

(iv) Hardcore restrictions (paragraphs 74–106)
The Commission explains in section 4 of part 3 of the *Guidelines* that there are certain restraints in TTAs that are nearly always anti-competitive. These are set out in Article 4 of the Regulation. If included in a TTA, such restrictions prevent the agreement *as a whole* from being block exempted under the Regulation and are unlikely to be granted individual exemption under Article 81(3) EC. Again, the position differs depending on whether the undertakings are competitors or non-competitors.

Article 4(1) of the Regulation concerns TTAs between competitors and provides a list of terms with various anti-competitive objects, such as restricting free determination of prices, restricting output, allocating markets, and preventing the licensee from exploiting his own technology or carrying on further research and development. These are subject to a range of exceptions which are stricter in the case of 'reciprocal' agreements (i.e. cross-licensing of competing technologies or technologies that can be used to create competing products). The *Guidelines* indicate that the Commission takes a practical approach to assessment. For example, paragraph 80 describes how calculation of royalties on the basis of individual product sales directly affects marginal cost and therefore product price, creating a potential for downstream price coordination, yet the Commission will only consider this as a price fixing situation where there is no *bone fide* transaction with pro-competitive effects. Paragraphs 79–95 describe the application of the Article 4(1) hardcore restrictions and exceptions in further detail.

Article 4(2) of the Regulation establishes a somewhat different list of anti-competitive restraints that might arise in TTAs between non-competitors. It is equally concerned with price-fixing measures but differs in that such TTAs cannot affect output. Instead subparagraph (b) of the Article addresses restrictions on passive selling outside a given territory, and subparagraph (c) prohibits selling restrictions on retail members of selective distribution systems. However, in paragraphs 99–105 the Commission emphasises the pro-competitive effects that can derive from the subparagraph (b) exceptions, primarily by protecting and encouraging the licensee's investment in the technology. The *Guidelines* in this section indicate the Commission's concern to prevent indirect price fixing (e.g. through monitoring or recommended prices) and uncover measures designed to partition markets (for example, supply quantity limitations adjusted to meet only local demand or differentiated royalty rates depending on destination).

(v) *Excluded restrictions (paragraphs 107–116)*

Certain restrictions are not covered by the Regulation but will not deprive the TTA as a whole from exemption. If they infringe Article 81(1), such provisions must be assessed individually under Article 81(3). Article 5(1) of the Regulation establishes these as (a) any obligation on the licensee to grant a licence to the licensor or a third party of any severable improvements or new applications, (b) any obligation on the licensee to assign such improvements or applications, and (c) any obligation on the licensee not to challenge the validity of the IPRs. Paragraphs 109–113 of the *Guidelines* explain that these obligations give rise to competition concerns because they *may* create a disincentive for the licensee to innovate – such provisions pass the fruits of innovation to third parties and may clutter the field with invalid IPRs. Therefore such obligations must be assessed individually. Article 5(2) sets out a further excluded restriction that only applies to non-competitors, as it corresponds to the hardcore restriction in Article 4(1)(d) with respect to competitors. The Commission explains in paragraph 114 that restrictions on the licensee's ability to use his own technology or on non-competitors' research and development activities will not *always* fail to satisfy the conditions in Article 81(3), as with competing undertakings, but paragraphs 115–116 set out situations when they will (such as *de jure* non-competitors under the former restriction and markets with few competing technologies under the latter).

(vi) Disapplication and withdrawal of the Regulation (paragraphs 117–129)
Section 6 of part III of the *Guidelines* explains the situations and procedure for disapplication and withdrawal of the benefit of the Regulation. Article 6 of the Regulation provides for withdrawal of the benefit of the exemption where the 'withdrawing authority' (the Commission or national competition authorities) finds that the agreement fails to satisfy the conditions in Article 81(3). According to paragraph 119, withdrawal implies that the agreement in question falls within Article 81(1) and does not satisfy the criteria in 81(3), and so is necessarily accompanied by a negative decision under Articles 5, 7 or 9 of Regulation 1/2003 (see chapter 14). Withdrawal may be warranted where there are networks of similar agreements restricting access of third parties' technologies or access to potential licences or where parties fail, without good reason, to exploit the technology. Article 7 of the Regulation allows the Commission to disapply the exemption, by way of a Regulation, where parallel networks cover more than 50 per cent of a relevant market thereby leaving such TTAs to be assessed under Articles 81(1) and 81(3). Such actions will only have prospective effect.

(vii) Competition provisions and TTAs outside the scope of the Regulation
Part IV of the *Guidelines* establishes a framework for applying Articles 81(1) and 81(3) to agreements not within the block exemption, for example, due to market share being above the threshold set out in the Regulation. It should be noted that absent hardcore restrictions there is no presumption of illegality under the Regulation. Section 1 of part IV describes relevant factors for assessing competition on the relevant market and any distortions that may be caused by market power of the undertakings involved. It also goes on to describe in detail the negative effects of restrictive TTAs (paragraphs 141–145) but also how to assess the positive effects (paragraphs 146–152). Section 2 outlines various types of restraints and explains how Article 81 applies to each of them. These should be familiar to the reader as they are discussed in other chapters of the book, but the *Guidelines* explain them in the context of TTAs. Sections 3 and 4 consider some specialised types of licensing agreements beyond the scope of the present discussion, namely settlement and non-assertion agreements and technology pools.

5 UK law

The previous part demonstrates quite vividly that the main concern of competition law in IPR licensing stems from the exclusivity granted to the licensee. In the EC competition law context, the concern is heightened by the single market objective. This entails that the consistency between the application of EC and UK competition law required by section 60 of the Competition Act 1998 will not be relevant in all cases when applying UK competition rules to situations involving licensing of IPRs, with the result that differences can be expected to emerge between the two systems in their treatment of transactions involving IPRs.

This does not mean, however, that the differences will be so great that UK competition law will not be concerned with IPR issues. Indeed, both the Chapter I and Chapter II prohibitions of the CA1998 could apply (respectively) to horizontal and vertical agreements and abusive behaviour by dominant firms involving IPRs. In the case of the Chapter II prohibition, the case law of the Community Courts and the decisions of the European Commission under Article 82 will be relevant. Also, the market investigation provisions contained in the Enterprise Act 2002 could be relied on to address a situation where IPRs cause a feature or combination of features on a market in the UK which prevents, restricts or distorts competition (see chapter 12).

The OFT has also published an important document dealing with the application of the CA1998 to IPR: *Guideline on intellectual property rights* (OFT418). The *Guideline* is helpful in many respects and is detailed. Its publication follows the European Commission's own reform of Regulation 240/96 and it takes proper account of the implications of the new EC Regulation 772/2004 and the Commission's *Guidelines*. The *Guideline* can be viewed at and downloaded from the OFT's website: http://www.oft.gov.uk.

Further reading

Anderman *EC Competition Law and Intellectual Property Rights* (OUP, 1998)
Korah 'Draft block exemption for technology transfer' (2004) 25 ECLR 247
Stothers 'Political exhaustion: the European Commission's working paper on possible abuses of trade mark rights within the EU in the context of Community exhaustion' (2003) 25 EIPR 457

7

Horizontal agreements I: from cartels to parallel behaviour

1 Introduction

A horizontal agreement is an agreement between two or more firms operating at the same level of the market. It happens not infrequently that such firms (whether actual or potential competitors) decide to cooperate with one another in some respect. The degree of cooperation can vary from sharing laboratory space, to carrying out research and development, to establishing a new company (a joint venture) which will carry out certain commercial activities of the parent companies. There is no doubt that some degree of cooperation between firms may be highly beneficial to the competitive structure of the market and to consumers: an agreement may seek to improve the parties' competitive position on a market by, for example, pooling resources and sharing the financial risk necessary to launch a new product on that market.

Somewhere on the spectrum of horizontal agreements, however, such cooperation will have no pro-competitive object or effect at all, but is, rather, purely intended to maximise the profits of the parties to the agreement at the expense of consumers. In such cases the parties aim to maintain their respective positions on the market and to achieve price stability or an increase in prices, and they normally do this at the expense of free competition. Such horizontal collusion is considered harmful to the economy and consumers, and it has been met by a very harsh attitude on the part of competition authorities, including those of the EC and the UK. In the world of competition law, this type of collusion is generally known as a cartel.

This chapter addresses the application of the EC and UK competition rules to cartels. The following part of the chapter considers the important question of whether all restrictions of competition are caught by competition law provisions such as Article 81(1) and the Chapter I prohibition of the Competition Act 1998 (CA1998). Part 3 is concerned with general principles, focusing on, among other things, the operation and structure of cartels. Part 4 deals with the issues of parallel behaviour, oligopolies and tacit collusion.

2 Are all restrictions of competition caught?

As previous chapters made clear, the provision that deals with anti-competitive agreements in the EC chapter on competition is Article 81 EC; its equivalent in UK competition law being section 2 CA1998. Of course when considering the application of either instrument in a particular situation, it is important to ask what kind of practice or behaviour is considered to be a restriction of competition. This question was considered in previous chapters, and in this and the following chapters the question will be considered in the context of horizontal agreements. However, before dealing with this question it would be appropriate to ask whether all restrictions of competition fall within Article 81(1) or the Chapter I prohibition. In the context of Article 81(1), for example, an agreement which gives rise to, or contains, a restriction of competition will not of course be caught under the provision, if the agreement:

- does not affect trade between Member States or, if it does have/is capable of such an effect, it does not do so appreciably; or
- does not appreciably restrict competition.

And of course, even if such an agreement is caught under Article 81(1), it can still be exempted under Article 81(3).

The above points should be obvious from the discussion in previous chapters. But, leaving them aside, the question remains whether there can be objectively justifiable restrictions on competition that are not caught. An important judgment that has dealt with this question is that of the ECJ in *Wouters*.

Wouters v. Algemene Raad can de Nederlandsche Orde van Advocaten [2002] ECR I-1577

(The facts are set out at p. 69 above.)

ECJ

74   By describing the successive versions of the rules on partnerships, the appellants in the main proceedings have set out to establish that the 1993 Regulation had the object of restricting competition.

. . .

80   In the alternative, the appellants in the main proceedings claim that, irrespective of its object, the 1993 Regulation produces effects that are restrictive of competition.

81   They maintain that multi-disciplinary partnerships of members of the Bar and accountants would make it possible to respond better to the needs of clients operating in an ever more complex and international economic environment.

82   Members of the Bar, having a reputation as experts in many fields, would be best placed to offer their clients a wide range of legal services and would, as partners in a multi-disciplinary partnership, be especially attractive to other persons active on the market in legal services.

83 Conversely, accountants would be attractive partners for members of the Bar in a professional partnership. They are experts in fields such as legislation on company accounts, the tax system, the organisation and restructuring of undertakings, and management consultancy. There would be many clients interested in an integrated service, supplied by a single provider and covering the legal as well as financial, tax and accountancy aspects of a particular matter.

84 The prohibition at issue in the main proceedings prohibits all contractual arrangements between members of the Bar and accountants which provide in any way for shared decision-making, profit-sharing or for the use of a common name, and this makes any form of effective partnership difficult.

85 By contrast, the Luxembourg Government claimed at the hearing that a prohibition of multi-disciplinary partnerships such as that laid down in the 1993 Regulation had a positive effect on competition. It pointed out that, by forbidding members of the Bar to enter into partnership with accountants, the national rules in issue in the main proceedings made it possible to prevent the legal services offered by members of the Bar from being concentrated in the hands of a few large international firms and, consequently, to maintain a large number of operators on the market.

86 It appears to the Court that the national legislation in issue in the main proceedings has an adverse effect on competition and may affect trade between Member States.

87 As regards the adverse effect on competition, the areas of expertise of members of the Bar and of accountants may be complementary. Since legal services, especially in business law, more and more frequently require recourse to an accountant, a multi-disciplinary partnership of members of the Bar and accountants would make it possible to offer a wider range of services, and indeed to propose new ones. Clients would thus be able to turn to a single structure for a large part of the services necessary for the organisation, management and operation of their business (the 'one-stop shop' advantage).

88 Furthermore, a multi-disciplinary partnership of members of the Bar and accountants would be capable of satisfying the needs created by the increasing interpenetration of national markets and the consequent necessity for continuous adaptation to national and international legislation.

89 Nor, finally, is it inconceivable that the economies of scale resulting from such multi-disciplinary partnerships might have positive effects on the cost of services.

90 A prohibition of multi-disciplinary partnerships of members of the Bar and accountants, such as that laid down in the 1993 Regulation, is therefore liable to limit production and technical development within the meaning of Article [81(1)(b)] of the Treaty.

91 It is true that the accountancy market is highly concentrated, to the extent that the firms dominating it are at present known as 'the big five' and the proposed merger between two of them, Price Waterhouse and Coopers & Lybrand, gave rise

[235]

to Commission Decision [Price Waterhouse/Coopers & Lybrand], adopted pursuant to [Regulation 4064/89, the Merger Regulation].

92   On the other hand, the prohibition of conflicts of interest with which members of the Bar in all Member States are required to comply may constitute a structural limit to extensive concentration of law-firms and so reduce their opportunities of benefiting from economies of scale or of entering into structural associations with practitioners of highly concentrated professions.

93   In those circumstances, unreserved and unlimited authorisation of multi-disciplinary partnerships between the legal profession, the generally decentralised nature of which is closely linked to some of its fundamental features, and a profession as concentrated as accountancy, could lead to an overall decrease in the degree of competition prevailing on the market in legal services, as a result of the substantial reduction in the number of undertakings present on that market.

94   Nevertheless, in so far as the preservation of a sufficient degree of competition on the market in legal services could be guaranteed by less extreme measures than national rules such as the 1993 Regulation, which prohibits absolutely any form of multi-disciplinary partnership, whatever the respective sizes of the firms of lawyers and accountants concerned, those rules restrict competition.

95   As regards the question whether intra-Community trade is affected, it is sufficient to observe that an agreement, decision or concerted practice extending over the whole of the territory of a Member State has, by its very nature, the effect of reinforcing the partitioning of markets on a national basis, thereby holding up the economic interpenetration which the Treaty is designed to bring about (Case 8/72 *Vereeniging van Cementhandelaren* v *Commission* [1972] ECR 977, paragraph 29; Case 42/84 *Remia and Others* v *Commission* [1985] ECR 2545, paragraph 22; and *CNSD*, paragraph 48).

96   That effect is all the more appreciable in the present case because the 1993 Regulation applies equally to visiting lawyers who are registered members of the Bar of another Member State, because economic and commercial law more and more frequently regulates transnational transactions and, lastly, because the firms of accountants looking for lawyers as partners are generally international groups present in several Member States.

97   However, not every agreement between undertakings or every decision of an association of undertakings which restricts the freedom of action of the parties or of one of them necessarily falls within the prohibition laid down in Article [81(1)] of the Treaty. For the purposes of application of that provision to a particular case, account must first of all be taken of the overall context in which the decision of the association of undertakings was taken or produces its effects. More particularly, account must be taken of its objectives, which are here connected with the need to make rules relating to organisation, qualifications, professional ethics, supervision and liability, in order to ensure that the ultimate consumers of legal services

and the sound administration of justice are provided with the necessary guarantees in relation to integrity and experience (see, to that effect, Case C-3/95 *Reisebüro Broede* [1996] ECR I-6511, paragraph 38). It has then to be considered whether the consequential effects restrictive of competition are inherent in the pursuit of those objectives.

98   Account must be taken of the legal framework applicable in the Netherlands, on the one hand, to members of the Bar and to the Bar of the Netherlands, which comprises all the registered members of the Bar in that Member State, and on the other hand, to accountants.

99   As regards members of the Bar, it has consistently been held that, in the absence of specific Community rules in the field, each Member State is in principle free to regulate the exercise of the legal profession in its territory (Case 107/83 *Klopp* [1984] ECR 2971, paragraph 17, and *Reisebüro*, paragraph 37). For that reason, the rules applicable to that profession may differ greatly from one Member State to another.

100   The current approach of the Netherlands, where Article 28 of the Advocatenwet entrusts the Bar of the Netherlands with responsibility for adopting regulations designed to ensure the proper practice of the profession, is that the essential rules adopted for that purpose are, in particular, the duty to act for clients in complete independence and in their sole interest, the duty, mentioned above, to avoid all risk of conflict of interest and the duty to observe strict professional secrecy.

101   Those obligations of professional conduct have not inconsiderable implications for the structure of the market in legal services, and more particularly for the possibilities for the practice of law jointly with other liberal professions which are active on that market.

102   Thus, they require of members of the Bar that they should be in a situation of independence *vis-à-vis* the public authorities, other operators and third parties, by whom they must never be influenced. They must furnish, in that respect, guarantees that all steps taken in a case are taken in the sole interest of the client.

103   By contrast, the profession of accountant is not subject, in general, and more particularly, in the Netherlands, to comparable requirements of professional conduct.

104   As the Advocate General has rightly pointed out in paragraphs 185 and 186 of his Opinion, there may be a degree of incompatibility between the 'advisory' activities carried out by a member of the Bar and the 'supervisory' activities carried out by an accountant. The written observations submitted by the respondent in the main proceedings show that accountants in the Netherlands perform a task of certification of accounts. They undertake an objective examination and audit of their clients' accounts, so as to be able to impart to interested third parties their personal opinion concerning the reliability of those accounts. It follows that in the Member State

concerned accountants are not bound by a rule of professional secrecy comparable to that of members of the Bar, unlike the position under German law, for example.

105 The aim of the 1993 Regulation is therefore to ensure that, in the Member State concerned, the rules of professional conduct for members of the Bar are complied with, having regard to the prevailing perceptions of the profession in that State. The Bar of the Netherlands was entitled to consider that members of the Bar might no longer be in a position to advise and represent their clients independently and in the observance of strict professional secrecy if they belonged to an organisation which is also responsible for producing an account of the financial results of the transactions in respect of which their services were called upon and for certifying those accounts.

106 Moreover, the concurrent pursuit of the activities of statutory auditor and of adviser, in particular legal adviser, also raises questions within the accountancy profession itself . . .

107 A regulation such as the 1993 Regulation could therefore reasonably be considered to be necessary in order to ensure the proper practice of the legal profession, as it is organised in the Member State concerned.

108 Furthermore, the fact that different rules may be applicable in another Member State does not mean that the rules in force in the former State are incompatible with Community law (see, to that effect, Case C-108/96 *Mac Quen and Others* [2001] ECR I-837, paragraph 33). Even if multi-disciplinary partnerships of lawyers and accountants are allowed in some Member States, the Bar of the Netherlands is entitled to consider that the objectives pursued by the 1993 Regulation cannot, having regard in particular to the legal regimes by which members of the Bar and accountants are respectively governed in the Netherlands, be attained by less restrictive means (see, to that effect, with regard to a law reserving judicial debt-recovery activity to lawyers, *Reisebüro*, paragraph 41).

109 In light of those considerations, it does not appear that the effects restrictive of competition such as those resulting for members of the Bar practising in the Netherlands from a regulation such as the 1993 Regulation go beyond what is necessary in order to ensure the proper practice of the legal profession (see, to that effect, Case C-250/92 *DLG* [1994] ECR I-5641, paragraph 35).

110 Having regard to all the foregoing considerations, the answer to be given to the second question must be that a national regulation such as the 1993 Regulation adopted by a body such as the Bar of the Netherlands does not infringe Article [81(1)] of the Treaty, since that body could reasonably have considered that that regulation, despite the effects restrictive of competition that are inherent in it, is necessary for the proper practice of the legal profession, as organised in the Member State concerned.

The judgment in *Wouters* represents a highly interesting step taken by the ECJ. Anyone who begins to read the judgment would think that the conclusion of the Court could be predicted: that the measure in question, the 1993 Regulation of the Bar of the Netherlands, must fall within Article 81(1). Nonetheless, however, the Court reaches a different conclusion, namely that the Regulation does not infringe Article 81(1). And for this reason the judgment is quite difficult to classify.

After dealing with the question of whether the 1993 Regulation is a decision of an association of undertakings within the meaning of Article 81(1), the ECJ then turns to the main question in the reference by the Raad van State: whether the 1993 Regulation is caught by Article 81(1) because it has as its object or effect the restriction of competition and because it affects trade between Member States.

The ECJ found that the Regulation has a negative effect on competition and may affect trade between Member States. It seems to have found this to be the case primarily because it could be attractive from many clients' point of view to receive an integrated service, combining the advice of a lawyer and an accountant. However, as the ECJ very interestingly notes in paragraph 97, not every restriction of competition falls within Article 81(1). Account must first be taken, when considering the application of Article 81(1) to a decision of an association of undertakings like the one at hand, of:

- the overall context in which the decision was taken or produces its effects; and
- the objectives of the association which according to the ECJ are linked to the need to formulate rules to govern that organisation, qualifications, professional ethics, supervision and liability of the association and its members.

What paragraphs 97–109 of the judgment really show is that non-competition considerations can be relevant when assessing the application of Article 81(1); and more importantly, such considerations, as happened in the case itself, could override competition considerations.

Several explanations can be found for this, all of which are based on the nature of the sector concerned, namely the legal profession. According to the ECJ, Member States should be free to regulate the exercise of the legal profession within their national boundaries. Therefore the adoption of a measure like the 1993 Regulation is considered a legitimate act by a Member State and necessary to ensure that the rules of professional conduct are observed by members of the Bar; that their independence as providers of legal services to clients and professional secrecy and confidentiality are protected; and that the proper practice of the legal profession is safeguarded.

No doubt the judgment has implications for how Member States choose to set the boundaries of their competition rules in relation to the legal profession, in particular those Member States whose competition rules do not exclude that profession from their scope of application. The UK used to have such an exclusion in place (CA1998, schedule 4), but this schedule was repealed when the Enterprise Act 2002 (EA2002) came into force. This means that UK competition authorities and the courts will need to consider *Wouters*, not only because of section 60 of the CA1998, but also because of the Modernisation Regulation, Regulation 1/2003 (see chapter 14).

3 Cartels

(A) General

Having dealt with the question of whether every restriction of competition is caught by Article 81(1) and the novel issues raised by the *Wouters* judgment, we now turn to the issue of cartels and the application of EC and UK competition rules to more traditional situations in which this business phenomenon arises.

Globally, firms have very strong incentives to enter into cartels in light of the considerable advantages they might gain from doing so. Adam Smith in his *Wealth of Nations* remarked:

People of the same trade seldom meet together, even for merriment and diversion, but the conversation ends in a conspiracy against the public, or in some contrivance to raise prices.

The operation of cartels tends to be complex and may vary according to the number of participants and the nature of the market in question: some cartels may have five (or even fewer) members; others may include a 'family' of twenty or more. In all cases there must be a credible mechanism in place for enforcing the agreement or understanding between the cartel members and a method of detecting any cheating on the cartel provisions. It is almost always the case that each cartel member could increase its own individual profit by violating the cartel restrictions (provided that the other participants do not also violate them). This means that there will always be a huge temptation for individual participants to cheat on a cartel.

The operation of internal enforcement methods of cartels is inevitably expensive and time-consuming. The difficulty of enforcement and monitoring compliance becomes all the more burdensome with larger numbers of participants and greater differentiation in their products. Consequently, it is entirely possible that in the long run many cartels will collapse without the intervention of a competition authority. This is not to suggest, however, that some cartels do not operate successfully for many years.

Table 7.1 spells out the details of participants, products and duration of the *Vitamins* cartel, which was investigated and uncovered by the European Commission. The Commission delivered its decision on 21 November 2001 imposing a very heavy fine on the participants (see table 7.2).

Table 7.1

Vitamin	Participants	Duration	
Vitamin A	Roche, BASF, Aventis	September 1989	February 1999
Vitamin E	Roche, BASF, Aventis, Eisai	September 1989	February 1999
Vitamin B1 (Thiamine)	Roche, Takeda, BASF	January 1991	June 1994
Vitamin B2 (Riboflavin)	Roche, BASF, Takeda	January 1991	Sept. 1995
Vitamin B5 (Calpan)	Roche, BASF, Daiichi	January 1991	February 1999
Vitamin B6	Roche, Takeda, Daiichi	January 1991	June 1994
Folic Acid (B)	Roche, Takeda, Kongo, Sumika	January 1991	June 1994
Vitamin C	Roche, BASF, Takeda, Merck	January 1991	August 1995
Vitamin D3	Roche, BASF, Solvay Pharm, Aventis	January 1994	June 1998
Vitamin H (Biotin)	Roche, Merck, Lonza, Sumitomo, Tanabe, BASF	October 1991	April 1994
Beta Carotene	Roche, BASF	September 1992	December 1998
Carotinioids	Roche, BASF	May 1993	December 1998

(B) Penalties

When a competition authority detects a cartel operation, it has the power to impose a fine on each of the participants; and the fines imposed in cartel cases in some parts of the world are extremely heavy. (See Table 7.2 below for fines imposed by the European Commission in cartel cases from 1998 to 2003.) This is done not only in order to punish guilty firms but also to discourage them from repeat offending and to deter others from engaging in cartel operations. Another penalty available to some, but not all, competition authorities is imprisonment of company directors and executives of companies. Following the enactment of the EA2002, criminal penalties are available under UK competition law. They are not, however, available under EC competition law.

Of course the fine, and in some cases the criminal penalty, can be an effective method of enforcing the competition rules in the case of cartel operations. However, their effectiveness really depends on the success of the investigation conducted by a competition authority and on the kind of evidence which is available. This means that the penalties are subject to limitations, especially since firms participating in cartels tend to be careful to destroy all incriminating

Table 7.2 Fines imposed by the European Commission in cartel cases from 1998 to 2003		
Year	*Case*	*Total amount (€ million)*
2003	industrial copper tubes cartel	78.73
2003	Organic Peroxides	69.5
2003	Carbon and graphite products	101.4
2003	Sorbates	138.4
2003	Yamaha	2.56
2003	French Beef	16.7
2002	Concrete reinforcing bars	85
2002	Speciality graphites	60.6
2002	Plasterboard	478
2002	Sotheby's/Christie's	20.4
2002	Dutch industrial gases	25.72
2002	Animal feed methionine	127
2002	Austrian Banks	124.26
2001	Vitamins	855.22
2001	Carbonless Paper	313.69
2001	Citric Acid	135.22
2001	Charges/German Banks	108.0
2001	Graphite Electrodes	218.8 (reduced to 152.8 by CFI: *Tokai Carbon v. Commission*)
2000	Amino acids	109.990
1999	Seamless steel tubes	99.0
1998	TACA	272.940
1998	Preinsulated pipes	92.210
1998	TACA	272.940

evidence, and as a result the task of the competition authority goes from being mission difficult to mission almost impossible.

(C) Leniency in cartel cases

For this reason, and given the strong desire of competition authorities to unearth as many cartels as possible and eradicate them, many competition authorities have developed an additional tool in their fight against cartels by building a leniency programme within their domestic system of competition law. The purpose behind a leniency programme, different versions of which exist in the USA, the EC, the UK and several other jurisdictions, is to encourage firms who participate in cartels to approach the relevant competition authority, to confess the existence of the cartel and their participation in it, and to cooperate with the authority. In return, the firm(s) concerned can expect some leniency, which mainly comes in the form of immunity from fine or reduction in the amount. In the case of the UK, leniency is also available in the case of criminal penalty (see pp. 259–262 below).

I EC law

The Leniency programme in EC competition law is set out in a Notice, which the Commission adopted in February 2002.

Commission notice on immunity from fines and reduction of fines in cartel cases OJ (2002) C 45/03

Introduction

1   This notice concerns secret cartels between two or more competitors aimed at fixing prices, production or sales quotas, sharing markets including bid-rigging or restricting imports or exports. Such practices are among the most serious restrictions of competition encountered by the Commission and ultimately result in increased prices and reduced choice for the consumer. They also harm European industry.

2   By artificially limiting the competition that would normally prevail between them, undertakings avoid exactly those pressures that lead them to innovate, both in terms of product development and the introduction of more efficient production methods. Such practices also lead to more expensive raw materials and components for the Community companies that purchase from such producers. In the long term, they lead to a loss of competitiveness and reduced employment opportunities.

3   The Commission is aware that certain undertakings involved in this type of illegal agreement are willing to put an end to their participation and inform it of the existence of such agreements, but are dissuaded from doing so by the high fines to which they are potentially exposed . . .

4   The Commission considered that it is in the Community interest to grant favourable treatment to undertakings which cooperate with it. The interests of consumers and citizens in ensuring that secret cartels are detected and punished outweigh the interest in fining those undertakings that enable the Commission to detect and prohibit such practices.

5   . . . Whilst the validity of the principles governing the notice has been confirmed, experience has shown that its effectiveness would be improved by an increase in the transparency and certainty of the conditions on which any reduction of fines will be granted. A closer alignment between the level of reduction of fines and the value of a company's contribution to establishing the infringement could also increase this effectiveness. This notice addresses these issues.

6   The Commission considers that the collaboration of an undertaking in the detection of the existence of a cartel has an intrinsic value. A decisive contribution to the

[243]

opening of an investigation or to the finding of an infringement may justify the granting of immunity from any fine to the undertaking in question, on condition that certain additional requirements are fulfilled.

7   Moreover, cooperation by one or more undertakings may justify a reduction of a fine by the Commission. Any reduction of a fine must reflect an undertaking's actual contribution, in terms of quality and timing, to the Commission's establishment of the infringement. Reductions are to be limited to those undertakings that provide the Commission with evidence that adds significant value to that already in the Commission's possession.

A. Immunity from fines

8   The Commission will grant an undertaking immunity from any fine which would otherwise have been imposed if:
   (a) the undertaking is the first to submit evidence which in the Commission's view may enable it to adopt a decision to carry out an investigation in the sense of Article [20(4) of Regulation 1/2003] in connection with an alleged cartel affecting the Community; or
   (b) the undertaking is the first to submit evidence which in the Commission's view may enable it to find an infringement of Article 81 EC in connection with an alleged cartel affecting the Community.

9   Immunity pursuant to point 8(a) will only be granted on the condition that the Commission did not have, at the time of the submission, sufficient evidence to adopt a decision to carry out an investigation in the sense of Article [20(4) of Regulation 1/2003] in connection with the alleged cartel.

10   Immunity pursuant to point 8(b) will only be granted on the cumulative conditions that the Commission did not have, at the time of the submission, sufficient evidence to find an infringement of Article 81 EC in connection with the alleged cartel and that no undertaking had been granted conditional immunity from fines under point 8(a) in connection with the alleged cartel.

11   In addition to the conditions set out in points 8(a) and 9 or in points 8(b) and 10, as appropriate, the following cumulative conditions must be met in any case to qualify for any immunity from a fine:
   (a) the undertaking cooperates fully, on a continuous basis and expeditiously throughout the Commission's administrative procedure and provides the Commission with all evidence that comes into its possession or is available to it relating to the suspected infringement. In particular, it remains at the Commission's disposal to answer swiftly any request that may contribute to the establishment of the facts concerned;
   (b) the undertaking ends its involvement in the suspected infringement no later than the time at which it submits evidence under points 8(a) or 8(b), as appropriate;

(c) the undertaking did not take steps to coerce other undertakings to participate in the infringement.

Procedure

12   An undertaking wishing to apply for immunity from fines should contact the Commission's Directorate-General for Competition. Should it become apparent that the requirements set out in points 8 to 10, as appropriate, are not met, the undertaking will immediately be informed that immunity from fines is not available for the suspected infringement.

13   If immunity from fines is available for a suspected infringement, the undertaking may, in order to meet conditions 8(a) or 8(b), as appropriate:
(a) immediately provide the Commission with all the evidence relating to the suspected infringement available to it at the time of the submission; or
(b) initially present this evidence in hypothetical terms, in which case the undertaking must present a descriptive list of the evidence it proposes to disclose at a later agreed date. This list should accurately reflect the nature and content of the evidence, whilst safeguarding the hypothetical nature of its disclosure. Expurgated copies of documents, from which sensitive parts have been removed, may be used to illustrate the nature and content of the evidence.

14   The Directorate-General for Competition will provide a written acknowledgement of the undertaking's application for immunity from fines, confirming the date on which the undertaking either submitted evidence under 13(a) or presented to the Commission the descriptive list referred to in 13(b).

15   Once the Commission has received the evidence submitted by the undertaking under point 13(a) and has verified that it meets the conditions set out in points 8(a) or 8(b), as appropriate, it will grant the undertaking conditional immunity from fines in writing.

16   Alternatively, the Commission will verify that the nature and content of the evidence described in the list referred to in point 13(b) will meet the conditions set out in points 8(a) or 8(b), as appropriate, and inform the undertaking accordingly. Following the disclosure of the evidence no later than on the date agreed and having verified that it corresponds to the description made in the list, the Commission will grant the undertaking conditional immunity from fines in writing.

17   An undertaking which fails to meet the conditions set out in points 8(a) or 8(b), as appropriate, may withdraw the evidence disclosed for the purposes of its immunity application or request the Commission to consider it under section B of this notice. This does not prevent the Commission from using its normal powers of investigation in order to obtain the information.

18   The Commission will not consider other applications for immunity from fines before it has taken a position on an existing application in relation to the same suspected infringement.

19   If at the end of the administrative procedure, the undertaking has met the conditions set out in point 11, the Commission will grant it immunity from fines in the relevant decision.

B. Reduction of a fine

20   Undertakings that do not meet the conditions under section A above may be eligible to benefit from a reduction of any fine that would otherwise have been imposed.

21   In order to qualify, an undertaking must provide the Commission with evidence of the suspected infringement which represents significant added value with respect to the evidence already in the Commission's possession and must terminate its involvement in the suspected infringement no later than the time at which it submits the evidence.

22   The concept of "added value" refers to the extent to which the evidence provided strengthens, by its very nature and/or its level of detail, the Commission's ability to prove the facts in question. In this assessment, the Commission will generally consider written evidence originating from the period of time to which the facts pertain to have a greater value than evidence subsequently established. Similarly, evidence directly relevant to the facts in question will generally be considered to have a greater value than that with only indirect relevance.

23   The Commission will determine in any final decision adopted at the end of the administrative procedure:
      (a) whether the evidence provided by an undertaking represented significant added value with respect to the evidence in the Commission's possession at that same time;
      (b) the level of reduction an undertaking will benefit from, relative to the fine which would otherwise have been imposed, as follows. For the:
          – first undertaking to meet point 21: a reduction of 30-50 %,
          – second undertaking to meet point 21: a reduction of 20-30 %,
          – subsequent undertakings that meet point 21: a reduction of up to 20 %.
      In order to determine the level of reduction within each of these bands, the Commission will take into account the time at which the evidence fulfilling the condition in point 21 was submitted and the extent to which it represents added value. It may also take into account the extent and continuity of any cooperation provided by the undertaking following the date of its submission.
          In addition, if an undertaking provides evidence relating to facts previously unknown to the Commission which have a direct bearing on the gravity or duration of the suspected cartel, the Commission will not take these elements into account when setting any fine to be imposed on the undertaking which provided this evidence.

Procedure

24　An undertaking wishing to benefit from a reduction of a fine should provide the Commission with evidence of the cartel in question.

25　The undertaking will receive an acknowledgement of receipt from the Directorate-General for Competition recording the date on which the relevant evidence was submitted. The Commission will not consider any submissions of evidence by an applicant for a reduction of a fine before it has taken a position on any existing application for a conditional immunity from fines in relation to the same suspected infringement.

26　If the Commission comes to the preliminary conclusion that the evidence submitted by the undertaking constitutes added value within the meaning of point 22, it will inform the undertaking in writing, no later than the date on which a statement of objections is notified, of its intention to apply a reduction of a fine within a specified band as provided in point 23(b).

27　The Commission will evaluate the final position of each undertaking which filed an application for a reduction of a fine at the end of the administrative procedure in any decision adopted.

The Notice was a very positive step towards unearthing and eradicating secret cartels, replacing an earlier Notice published in 1996. Importantly, the revised Notice provides for 'total immunity', which – although not available to firms which act as 'ring-leader' – has practical significance in inducing firms to disclose information about cartel operations. Like other Notices published by the Commission, the Leniency Notice lacks the binding force of the law. However, this does not mean that the Notice lacks any real value; nor does it mean that the Commission will ignore the Notice when hearing confessions by firms. On the contrary, as the Commission makes it clear in the Notice, it intends to follow the Notice. This should offer firms contemplating making a confession adequate certainty and comfort yet assurance of business confidentiality.

Indeed, a survey of the decisional practice of the Commission would reveal that the Commission is both committed to and serious about the leniency programme. For example, in the *Vitamins* cartel mentioned above, the firm Aventis was offered total immunity from fine because it was the first firm to cooperate with the Commission and because it provided the Commission with decisive evidence. This is the first time total immunity was offered by the Commission.

In the same case, the firms Hoffmann La Roche and BASF received a reduction of their fines because they cooperated with the Commission at an early stage during its investigation and in doing so provided crucial information on all the cartels to which the two firms were party: the reduction was 50%. Full immunity was also given in another case, the *Carbonless Paper Cartel*: the Commission started to investigate in 1996 and reached its decision at the end of 2001. The immunity in that case was granted to Sappi Ltd, a South

African firm, because it was the first among the participants in the cartel to cooperate with the Commission and provided the Commission with decisive evidence.

II UK law

A major aim behind the enactment of the CA1998 and, more recently, the EA2002 was to strengthen the powers of the OFT in its fight against cartels. Like the European Commission, the OFT has developed a stance and a policy towards cartels which are not entrenched in conventional methods of enforcement only. Thus, in the same vein, the OFT has developed a leniency programme in relation to the involvement of both firms and individuals in cartels; the leniency towards the latter was introduced following the criminalisation of cartels under the EA2002.

This section will first consider leniency in relation to firms before looking at the position of individuals.

(a) The position of firms

Details of the leniency programme in the case of firms can be found in paragraphs 3.1–3.18 of the OFT's *Guidance as to the appropriate amount of a penalty* (OFT423). The following paragraphs are worth noting.

OFT423

3.1   Undertakings participating in cartel activities might wish to terminate their involvement and inform the OFT of the existence of the cartel activity, but be deterred from doing so by the risk of incurring large financial penalties. To encourage such undertakings to come forward, the OFT will offer total immunity from financial penalties for an infringement of Article 81 and/or of the Chapter I prohibition to a participant in a cartel activity who is the first to come forward and who satisfies the requirements set out in paragraph 3.8. Alternatively, the OFT may offer total immunity from financial penalties to a member of a cartel who is the first to come forward and who satisfies the requirements set out in paragraphs 3.10 and 3.11. An undertaking which is not the first to come forward, or does not satisfy these requirements may benefit from a reduction in the amount of the penalty imposed if it satisfies the requirements set out in paragraphs 3.12 and 3.13.

3.2   The OFT considers that it is in the interest of the economy of the United Kingdom, and the European Community more generally, to have a policy of granting lenient treatment to undertakings which inform it of cartels and which then co-operate with it in the circumstances set out below. It is the secret nature of cartel activities which justifies such a policy. The interests of customers and consumers in ensuring that such activities are detected and prohibited outweigh the policy objectives of imposing financial penalties on those undertakings which participate in cartel activities but and which co-operate to a significant degree with the OFT as set out below.

. . .

Total immunity from financial penalties in cartel cases

3.7 Where an undertaking participating in a cartel is the first to come forward to provide evidence of the existence and activities of the cartel activity, and it fulfils all the requirements in paragraph 3.8 below, it will benefit from total immunity from financial penalties in respect of that infringement; if it is the first to come forward to provide such evidence and it fulfils all the requirements of paragraphs 3.10 and 3.11, it may benefit from total immunity from financial penalties in respect of that infringement.

Total immunity for the first to come forward BEFORE an investigation has commenced

3.8 In order to benefit from total immunity under this paragraph, the undertaking must be the first to provide the OFT with evidence of the existence and activities of cartel activity in a market before the OFT has commenced an investigation[26] of the undertakings involved; provided that the OFT does not already have sufficient information to establish the existence of the alleged cartel activity, and conditions (a) to (d) below are satisfied.

The undertaking must:

a) provide the OFT with all the information, documents and evidence available to it regarding the existence and activities of the cartel activity

b) maintain continuous and complete co-operation throughout the investigation and until the conclusion of any action by the OFT arising as a result of the investigation

c) not have taken steps to coerce another undertaking to take part in the cartel activity, and

d) refrain from further participation in the cartel from the time of disclosure of the cartel activity to the OFT (except as may be directed by the OFT).

3.9 If an undertaking does not qualify for total immunity under paragraph 3.8 above, it may still benefit from total immunity from financial penalties if it fulfils all the requirements in paragraphs 3.10 and 3.11 below.

Total immunity for the first to come forward AFTER an investigation has commenced

3.10 In order to benefit from the possibility of total immunity under this paragraph:

26 By the exercise of powers under sections 26–28A of the Act.

- the undertaking seeking immunity under this paragraph must be the first[27] to provide the OFT with evidence of the existence and activities of cartel activity before the OFT has given written notice of its proposal to make a decision that Article 81 and/or the Chapter I prohibition has been infringed, and
- conditions (a) to (d) in paragraph 3.8 above must be satisfied.

3.11 The grant of immunity by the OFT in these circumstances is, however, discretionary. In order for the OFT to exercise this discretion it must be satisfied that the undertaking should benefit from immunity, taking into account the stage at which the undertaking comes forward , the evidence in the OFT's possession and the evidence provided by the undertaking.

Reduction in the level of financial penalties in cartel cases

3.12 Undertakings which provide evidence of the existence and activities of cartel activity before written notice of a proposed infringement decision is given, but are not the first to come forward, or do not qualify for total immunity under paragraphs 3.8 or 3.10 and 3.11 above, may be granted a reduction of up to fifty per cent in the amount of a financial penalty which would otherwise be imposed, if conditions (a) to (c) below are met.

The undertaking must:

a) provide the OFT with all the information, documents and evidence available to it regarding the existence and activities of the cartel activity

b) maintain continuous and complete co-operation throughout the investigation and until the conclusion of any action by the OFT arising as a result of the investigation, and

c) refrain from further participation in the cartel activity from the time of disclosure of the cartel activity to the OFT (except as may be directed by the OFT).

...

Procedure for requesting immunity or a reduction in the level of penalties

3.15 An undertaking which wishes to take advantage of the lenient treatment set out in this Part must contact the office of the Director of Cartel Investigations at the OFT, or his/her equivalent at the appropriate Regulator. This step has to be taken by a person who has the power to represent the undertaking for that purpose.

Additional reduction in financial penalties

3.16 An undertaking co-operating with an investigation by the OFT under the Act in relation to cartel activities in one market (the first market) may also be involved in

---

27 i.e. there must not be any undertaking which is benefiting from total immunity under paragraph 3.4 in relation to the same cartel

...

a separate cartel in another market (the second market) which also infringes Article 81 and/or the Chapter I prohibition.

3.17   If the undertaking obtains total immunity from financial penalties under either paragraph 3.8 or paragraphs 3.10 and 3.11 above in relation to its activities in the second market, it will also receive a reduction in the financial penalties imposed on it which is additional to the reduction which it would have received for its co-operation in the first market alone.[29] For example, as a result of an investigation by the OFT of producers, including ABC Ltd, in the widgets market, ABC Ltd carries out an internal investigation and discovers that, as well as having participated in cartel activities in the widgets market, one of its divisions has participated in separate cartel activities in the sprockets market. ABC Ltd has been co-operating with the OFT's widgets investigation and is interested in seeking lenient treatment by disclosing its participation in the sprockets cartel activity. Assuming ABC Ltd qualifies for total immunity in relation to the sprockets market, it can also obtain a reduction in financial penalty in relation to the widgets market in addition to the reduction it would have received for co-operation in the widgets investigation alone, i.e. an additional reduction in respect of the widgets market (the first market) as a result of its co-operation in the investigation into the sprockets market (the second market).

Confidentiality

3.18   An undertaking coming forward with evidence of a cartel may be concerned about the disclosure of its identity as an undertaking which has volunteered information. The OFT will therefore endeavour, where possible, to keep the identity of such undertakings confidential throughout the course of its investigation.

Looking at the substance of the OFT's leniency guidance, one can identify many similarities with the European Commission's leniency Notice. Furthermore, the OFT has made clear its commitment to applying the provisions of its leniency programme where appropriate. Total immunity from fine was given to First-Group in *Market sharing by Arriva plc and FirstGroup plc* (decision 30 January 2002) and to Hasbro in *Hasbro UK Ltd, Argos Ltd and Littlewoods Ltd* (decision 19 February 2003). A reduction in the amount of fine was given to Arriva in its market sharing agreement with FirstGroup and to Hasbro in *Hasbro UK Ltd* (decision 28 November 2002).

(b) The position of individuals

Before considering leniency in the case of individuals, it is important first to understand the offence in respect of which leniency may be sought and given.

---

29   For the avoidance of doubt, the undertaking does not need to be in receipt of leniency in respect of the first market to receive this reduction. It is sufficient for the undertaking to be receiving a reduction, by way of mitigation, for co-operation.

Hence the following section will deal with the cartel offence before looking at leniency.

(i) The cartel offence
The EA2002 created a new, criminal, cartel offence, which operates alongside the existing regime that imposes civil sanctions on firms that breach the Chapter I prohibition under the CA1998. The offence will be committed in circumstances described in section 188:

S. 188 Cartel offence

(1) An individual is guilty of an offence if he dishonestly agrees with one or more other persons to make or implement, or to cause to be made or implemented, arrangements of the following kind relating to at least two undertakings (A and B).

(2) The arrangements must be ones which, if operating as the parties to the agreement intend, would –
  (a) directly or indirectly fix a price for the supply by A in the United Kingdom (otherwise than to B) of a product or service,
  (b) limit or prevent supply by A in the United Kingdom of a product or service,
  (c) limit or prevent production by A in the United Kingdom of a product,
  (d) divide between A and B the supply in the United Kingdom of a product or service to a customer or customers,
  (e) divide between A and B customers for the supply in the United Kingdom of a product or service, or
  (f) be bid-rigging arrangements.

(3) Unless subsection (2)(d), (e) or (f) applies, the arrangements must also be ones which, if operating as the parties to the agreement intend, would –
  (a) directly or indirectly fix a price for the supply by B in the United Kingdom (otherwise than to A) of a product or service,
  (b) limit or prevent supply by B in the United Kingdom of a product or service, or
  (c) limit or prevent production by B in the United Kingdom of a product.

(4) In subsections (2)(a) to (d) and (3), references to supply or production are to supply or production in the appropriate circumstances (for which see section 189).

(5) "Bid-rigging arrangements" are arrangements under which, in response to a request for bids for the supply of a product or service in the United Kingdom, or for the production of a product in the United Kingdom –
  (a) A but not B may make a bid, or
  (b) A and B may each make a bid but, in one case or both, only a bid arrived at in accordance with the arrangements.

(6) But arrangements are not bid-rigging arrangements if, under them, the person requesting bids would be informed of them at or before the time when a bid is made.

(7)   "Undertaking" has the same meaning as in Part 1 of the 1998 Act.

Section 190 of the Act deals with the issues of penalty and prosecution.

S. 190 Cartel offence: penalty and prosecution

(1)   A person guilty of an offence under section 188 is liable –
    (a) on conviction on indictment, to imprisonment for a term not exceeding five years or to a fine, or to both;
    (b) on summary conviction, to imprisonment for a term not exceeding six months or to a fine not exceeding the statutory maximum, or to both.

(2)   In England and Wales and Northern Ireland, proceedings for an offence under section 188 may be instituted only –
    (a) by the Director of the Serious Fraud Office, or
    (b) by or with the consent of the OFT.

(3)   No proceedings may be brought for an offence under section 188 in respect of an agreement outside the United Kingdom, unless it has been implemented in whole or in part in the United Kingdom.

(4)   Where, for the purpose of the investigation or prosecution of offences under section 188, the OFT gives a person written notice under this subsection, no proceedings for an offence under section 188 that falls within a description specified in the notice may be brought against that person in England and Wales or Northern Ireland except in circumstances specified in the notice.

Also, it is important to note section 191 which provides for possible extradition of individuals who commit or conspire to commit or attempt to commit the cartel offence.
    The circumstances in which the OFT may investigate individuals suspected of having committed the criminal cartel offence under section 188 and the powers it possesses when conducting its investigations are described in sections 192–195 EA2002.

S. 192 Investigation of offences under section 188

(1)   The OFT may conduct an investigation if there are reasonable grounds for suspecting that an offence under section 188 has been committed.

(2)   The powers of the OFT under sections 193 and 194 are exercisable, but only for the purposes of an investigation under subsection (1), in any case where it appears to the OFT that there is good reason to exercise them for the purpose of investigating the affairs, or any aspect of the affairs, of any person ("the person under investigation").

[253]

S. 193 Powers when conducting an investigation

(1)   The OFT may by notice in writing require the person under investigation, or any other person who it has reason to believe has relevant information, to answer questions, or otherwise provide information, with respect to any matter relevant to the investigation at a specified place and either at a specified time or forthwith.

(2)   The OFT may by notice in writing require the person under investigation, or any other person, to produce, at a specified place and either at a specified time or forthwith, specified documents, or documents of a specified description, which appear to the OFT to relate to any matter relevant to the investigation.

(3)   If any such documents are produced, the OFT may –
(a) take copies or extracts from them;
(b) require the person producing them to provide an explanation of any of them.

(4)   If any such documents are not produced, the OFT may require the person who was required to produce them to state, to the best of his knowledge and belief, where they are.

(5)   A notice under subsection (1) or (2) must indicate –
(a) the subject matter and purpose of the investigation; and
(b) the nature of the offences created by section 201.

S. 194 Power to enter premises under a warrant

(1)   On an application made by the OFT to the High Court, or, in Scotland, by the procurator fiscal to the sheriff, in accordance with rules of court, a judge or the sheriff may issue a warrant if he is satisfied that there are reasonable grounds for believing –
(a) that there are on any premises documents which the OFT has power under section 193 to require to be produced for the purposes of an investigation; and
(b) that –
   (i) a person has failed to comply with a requirement under that section to produce the documents;
   (ii) it is not practicable to serve a notice under that section in relation to them; or
   (iii) the service of such a notice in relation to them might seriously prejudice the investigation.

(2)   A warrant under this section shall authorise a named officer of the OFT, and any other officers of the OFT whom the OFT has authorised in writing to accompany the named officer –
(a) to enter the premises, using such force as is reasonably necessary for the purpose;
(b) to search the premises and –
   (i) take possession of any documents appearing to be of the relevant kind, or

        (ii) take, in relation to any documents appearing to be of the relevant kind, any other steps which may appear to be necessary for preserving them or preventing interference with them;

    (c) to require any person to provide an explanation of any document appearing to be of the relevant kind or to state, to the best of his knowledge and belief, where it may be found;

    (d) to require any information which is stored in any electronic form and is accessible from the premises and which the named officer considers relates to any matter relevant to the investigation, to be produced in a form –

        (i) in which it can be taken away, and

        (ii) in which it is visible and legible or from which it can readily be produced in a visible and legible form.

(3) Documents are of the relevant kind if they are of a kind in respect of which the application under subsection (1) was granted.

(4) A warrant under this section may authorise persons specified in the warrant to accompany the named officer who is executing it.

(5) ...

S. 195 Exercise of powers by authorised person

(1) The OFT may authorise any competent person who is not an officer of the OFT to exercise on its behalf all or any of the powers conferred by section 193 or 194.

(2) No such authority may be granted except for the purpose of investigating the affairs, or any aspect of the affairs, of a person specified in the authority.

(3) No person is bound to comply with any requirement imposed by a person exercising powers by virtue of any authority granted under this section unless he has, if required to do so, produced evidence of his authority.

The above sections demonstrate the enhanced powers which the OFT has come to enjoy when conducting an investigation related to a cartel offence. In particular, it is important to note section 193 which states that the OFT may compel a person under investigation to answer questions or provide information with respect to any matter relevant to the investigation. This is not an absolute power, however, and section 193 should be read in light of section 196 which provides that such a person may refuse to disclose information or produce any document on grounds of legal professional privilege.

S. 196 Privileged information etc.

(1) A person may not under section 193 or 194 be required to disclose any information or produce any document which he would be entitled to refuse to disclose or produce

on grounds of legal professional privilege in proceedings in the High Court, except that a lawyer may be required to provide the name and address of his client.

(2)   A person may not under section 193 or 194 be required to disclose any information or produce any document in respect of which he owes an obligation of confidence by virtue of carrying on any banking business unless –
(a) the person to whom the obligation of confidence is owed consents to the disclosure or production; or
(b) the OFT has authorised the making of the requirement.

(3)   In the application of this section to Scotland, the reference in subsection (1) –
(a) to proceedings in the High Court is to be read as a reference to legal proceedings generally; and
(b) to an entitlement on grounds of legal professional privilege is to be read as a reference to an entitlement by virtue of any rule of law whereby –
(i) communications between a professional legal adviser and his client, or
(ii) communications made in connection with or in contemplation of legal proceedings and for the purposes of those proceedings,
are in such proceedings protected from disclosure on the ground of confidentiality.

It is also important to note that there are safeguards provided in section 197 of the Act in relation to the use of statements made by a person in response to a requirement imposed by the OFT using its powers of investigation under the Act.

S. 197 Restriction on use of statements in court

(1)   A statement by a person in response to a requirement imposed by virtue of section 193 or 194 may only be used in evidence against him –
(a) on a prosecution for an offence under section 201(2); or
(b) on a prosecution for some other offence where in giving evidence he makes a statement inconsistent with it.

(2)   However, the statement may not be used against that person by virtue of paragraph (b) of subsection (1) unless evidence relating to it is adduced, or a question relating to it is asked, by or on behalf of that person in the proceedings arising out of the prosecution.

(ii) Offences which may be committed: failure to cooperate
Section 201 provides that an offence may be committed under sections 188 or 189 where a person fails to co-operate when the OFT exercises its investigation powers under the Act. The OFT has published a helpful table in its Guideline *Powers for investigating criminal cartels* (OFT505) detailing the sanctions that may be imposed by the courts on a person found guilty of a criminal offence

Table 7.3		
Offence	*Sanction on summary conviction*	*Sanction on conviction on indictment*
Fail to comply with a requirement imposed under the investigation powers	Fine of up to level five on the standard scale and/or up to six months imprisonment	This offence will not be tried in this way
Intentionally or recklessly make a false or misleading statement	Fine of up to the statutory maximum and/or up to six months imprisonment	Unlimited fine and/or up to two years imprisonment
Intentionally destroy, dispose of, falsify or conceal documents	Fine of up to the statutory maximum and/or up to six months imprisonment	Unlimited fine and/or up to five years' imprisonment
Intentionally obstruct a person carrying out an investigation with a warrant	Fine of up to the statutory maximum	Unlimited fine and/or up to two years' imprisonment

committed where a person fails to co-operate with an investigation under the EA2002.

In addition to the above-mentioned powers of the OFT, the EA2002 (which amends section 32 of the Regulation of Investigatory Powers Act 2000 ('RIPA') and section 93 of the Police Act 1997) also gives the OFT the power of intrusive surveillance along with the related power to interfere with property when conducting an investigation in the case of a cartel offence (s. 199 EA2002). These powers are expected to enhance the effectiveness of investigations by the OFT since they would allow intrusive spying on individuals who participate in cartel activities. Some guidance on the use of these powers can be found in the *OFT505*.

OFT505

5.2   Intrusive Surveillance is defined as covert surveillance carried out in relation to anything taking place on any residential premises (including hotel accommodation) or in any private vehicle[34] and involves the presence of an individual on the premises or in a vehicle or by means of a surveillance device(s) to either hear or see what is happening within the premises or vehicle. Property Interference allows for the covert installation of such a device(s) in property which would otherwise involve some element of trespass.

---

34 Subject to RIPA sections 26(4) and (6).

5.3   These forms of surveillance, which will only be used by the OFT in its investigations under the Enterprise Act, require the personal authority of the Chairman of the OFT and the prior approval of the Office of Surveillance Commissioners before deployment can take place. In cases of urgency, which are likely to be rare, if prior approval from a Surveillance Commissioner cannot be sought and granted in time, the Chairman of the OFT (or a designated officer of the OFT) will authorise the deployment of intrusive surveillance and give notice to a Surveillance Commissioner as soon as is reasonably practicable, explaining why it was necessary to use the urgency provisions. If the Surveillance Commissioner is at any time satisfied that there were no reasonable grounds for believing the case was urgent, he may quash the authorisation and the surveillance must cease immediately. The use of intrusive surveillance must be necessary to prevent or detect the cartel offence and must be proportionate to what is sought to be achieved by carrying it out.

Role of the Director of the Serious Fraud Office in criminal investigations

3.18   The OFT will exercise its powers under the Enterprise Act to investigate individuals suspected of having committed the criminal cartel offence in close co-operation with the Director of the Serious Fraud Office ('the SFO'). The SFO is the intended prosecutor for this criminal offence[21] in England, Wales and Northern Ireland. The OFT has agreed a Memorandum of Understanding with the SFO which records the basis on which they will co-operate to investigate and/or prosecute individuals in respect of the cartel offence where serious or complex fraud is suspected. The factors that the SFO take into account in defining a serious or complex fraud include cases where the sum at risk is estimated to be at least $1 million, cases that are likely to give rise to national publicity and widespread public concern (for example, those involving public bodies) and cases where legal, accountancy and investigative skills need to be brought together.

3.19   Where a case is identified by the OFT as one that may involve a criminal offence and which is likely to fall within the SFO's definition of a serious or complex fraud, the OFT will inform the SFO who will decide whether the case may be one that is suitable for criminal prosecution. Where further enquiries need to be carried out to determine the extent of a suspected criminal offence, the OFT and SFO will agree the scope of and responsibilities for the further enquiries. The enquiries made at this time are likely to involve the use by the OFT of the powers of investigation in the Enterprise Act. Once these enquiries have been completed, the SFO will decide, following consultation with the OFT, whether the case is one that should be taken forward for criminal prosecution.

3.20   ... [T]he SFO may decide at a later stage of any investigation of a suspected criminal offence to carry out additional enquiries using its powers under section 2 of the

21 Enterprise Act section 190.

Criminal Justice Act 1987 (the 'CJA 1987'). These powers are broadly the same as the OFT's powers of investigation under the Enterprise Act.

3.21   Under section 2 of the CJA 1987, the SFO has powers to require a person to answer questions, provide information or produce documents for the purposes of an investigation. Written notice is given when the SFO exercises these powers. In urgent cases the SFO may require immediate compliance with a notice. The majority of section 2 notices are issued to third parties that may, in the ordinary course of their business, have information or hold documents relevant to a suspected offence. Anyone issued with a section 2 notice is obliged to provide the information and documents required except that there is no obligation to disclose documents subject to legal professional privilege. There is also no obligation to disclose documents protected by a banking obligation of confidence subject to certain exceptions.[23] The Enterprise Act contains similar provisions to the CJA 1987 in respect of the disclosure of documents subject to legal professional privilege and confidential banking information (paragraphs 6.1 and 6.2). A person who refuses to answer questions or provide information or documents in response to a section 2 notice without a reasonable excuse commits an offence.

3.22   Section 2 of the CJA 1987 also permits the SFO, on specified grounds, to obtain search warrants from a justice of the peace in respect of an investigation which the SFO is conducting. However, search warrants sought during the course of an investigation into a suspected criminal cartel offence will normally be obtained and exercised by the OFT using its powers under the Enterprise Act. The SFO would not seek a search warrant from a justice of the peace if the OFT had already been refused a search warrant by the High Court in respect of the same premises unless new evidence had come to light during the course of the investigation that would justify the application for such a warrant.

3.23   Where the SFO and the OFT are exercising their formal powers of investigation under either the CJA 1987 or the Enterprise Act to compel documents and/or information, the SFO or the OFT will make it clear in writing to the persons concerned the specific power that is being used.

(iii) No-action letter

Leniency in the case of individuals takes the form of a 'no-action letter' sent by the OFT to individual(s) who supply the OFT with information about cartels. (See section 190(4) EA 2002.) Essentially the 'no-action letter' is an undertaking by the OFT that the individual(s) concerned will be granted immunity from prosecution. According to the OFT it is in the interest of the economic well-being of the UK to issue such an undertaking given the secret nature of cartel operations and their damaging effects. A guideline entitled *The Cartel Offence: Guidance on the issue of no-action letters for individuals* (OFT513) has been

---

23 CJA 1987 section 2(10)(a) & (b).

published by the OFT which describes the circumstances in which this immunity will be given and offers information on points of practice and procedure; a draft 'no-action letter' is annexed to the *Guideline* for information.

OFT513

No-action letters

3.2 ... A no-action letter will prevent a prosecution being brought against an individual in England and Wales or Northern Ireland for the cartel offence except in circumstances specified in the letter. Whilst guarantees of immunity from prosecution cannot be given in relation to Scotland, co-operation by an individual will be reported to the Lord Advocate who will take such co-operation into account. In suitable cases this may include an early decision as to whether or not a particular individual remains liable to be prosecuted ...

Conditions for the issue of a no-action letter

3.3 In order to benefit from a no-action letter, and subject to paragraph 3.4 and 3.9 below, an individual must:
- admit participation in the criminal offence
- provide the OFT with all information available to them regarding the existence and activities of the cartel
- maintain continuous and complete co-operation throughout the investigation and until the conclusion of any criminal proceedings arising as a result of the investigation
- not have taken steps to coerce another undertaking to take part in the cartel, and
- refrain from further participation in the cartel from the time of its disclosure to the OFT (except as may be directed by the investigating authority).

3.4 However, the fact that these conditions are satisfied in any particular case is not in itself sufficient for the issue of a no-action letter. Where the OFT believes that it already has, or is in the course of gathering, sufficient information to bring a successful prosecution of an individual, it will not issue a no-action letter to that individual.

Procedure

3.5 When an individual believes that they may require a no-action letter, or an early determination as to whether they are liable to be prosecuted in Scotland, an approach should be made to the Director of Cartel Investigations at the OFT. The approach may be made:
- directly by the individual
- by a lawyer representing the individual, or

- on behalf of named employees, directors, ex-employees or ex-directors, by an undertaking (or by a lawyer representing such undertaking) seeking leniency from the OFT in accordance with the OFT's 'Guidance as to the Appropriate Amount of a Penalty' (the OFT's Guidance) or in conjunction with an application for leniency from the European Commission in accordance with the Commission Notice on immunity from fines or reduction of fines in cartel cases (the Commission Notice on Immunity).

Initially, approaches by lawyers may be made on an anonymous basis.

3.6   When an approach is made, the Director of Cartel Investigations will give an initial indication as to whether the OFT may be prepared to issue a no-action letter. In cases where an undertaking has been granted 100 per cent leniency in accordance with the OFT's Guidance or the Commission Notice on Immunity, the OFT will normally be prepared to issue no-action letters to those named employees, directors, ex-employees or ex-directors on whose behalf an approach is made, subject to the conditions set out at paragraph 3.3 above being met and subject to paragraph 3.9.

3.7   If the OFT is prepared to issue a no-action letter the individual applying for immunity from prosecution will be interviewed. Any information they provide in such interviews will not be used against them in criminal proceedings except in the following circumstances:
- where a no-action letter is not issued, if the individual applying for immunity from prosecution has knowingly or recklessly provided information that is false or misleading in a material particular, or
- where a no-action letter is issued, if it is subsequently revoked ...

3.8   On completion of the interview (which may extend over several sessions), the OFT will advise the applicant in writing whether it is prepared to issue a no-action letter.

3.9   In cases where the OFT concludes that, on the basis of the information that has been given, the applicant is not at risk of criminal prosecution for the cartel offence, it will not issue a no-action letter for this reason and will confirm this in writing.

3.10   If, following discussions:
- the OFT considers that, without a no-action letter, there is a likelihood of prosecution, and
- the applicant confirms that they will meet the conditions for the issue of a no-action letter

a no-action letter will be issued. Alternatively, in a case where prosecution would be brought in Scotland, the cooperation given by the applicant will be reported to the Lord Advocate with a request for an early decision as to whether the individual remains liable to prosecution.

[261]

Revocation

3.11 A no-action letter may be revoked if:
- the recipient of a letter ceases to satisfy in whole or in part any of the relevant conditions (set out at paragraph 3.3 above), or
- the recipient of a letter has knowingly or recklessly provided information that is false or misleading in a material particular.

3.12 On revocation any immunity granted by the no-action letter will cease to exist as if it had never been granted and the OFT may rely on any information given by the applicant in a prosecution against them for the cartel offence.

3.13 If a no-action letter is to be revoked the recipient of the letter will be notified in writing and given a reasonable opportunity to make representations.

(iv) Disqualification of company directors

By virtue of section 204 of EA2002 the OFT and other sectoral regulators have the power to ask the court to make a Competition Disqualification Order (CDO) under the Company Directors Disqualification Act 1986 (CDDA). This is an order disqualifying a director of a company which commits a breach of competition law, prohibiting the person concerned from acting in company management or promotion or as an insolvency practitioner for a period ranging from 2 to 15 years. In lieu, the OFT can agree to accept a voluntary 'Competition Disqualification Undertaking' (CDU) from the person concerned not to act in such capacity for a similar period as a CDO. Breaching either a CDO or a CDU can result in criminal penalties or personal liability for loss and debts incurred by the company.

Before making a CDO, the court must be satisfied of two conditions: first, that there has been a breach of competition law; and secondly, that the individual concerned is unfit to act as a director. A breach of competition law in this case includes an infringement of the Chapter I or Chapter II prohibition or Article 81 or Article 82 EC. In considering the second condition the court must be satisfied that the conduct of the person was unbefitting that of a director in the running of the affairs of a company. Determining unfitness is based on the director's degree of blame (whether or not he knew of the breach) and/or constructive knowledge about the breach of competition law.

The OFT has explained the nature of the order in its guidance on *Competition disqualification orders* (OFT500).

OFT500

Factors for consideration

4.2 The OFT or Regulator will follow a five-step process when deciding to apply for a CDO. It will:

(1) consider whether an undertaking which is a company of which the person is a director has committed a breach of competition law

(2) consider whether a financial penalty has been imposed for the breach

(3) consider whether the company in question benefited from leniency (see paragraph 4.11 below for the definition of 'leniency' in this context)

(4) consider the extent of the director's responsibility for the breach of competition law, either through action or omission

(5) have regard to any aggravating and mitigating factors.

. . .

Step 1   Breach of competition law

4.6   The first question the OFT or Regulator will consider is whether a company which is an undertaking of which the person is a director has committed a breach of competition law. The OFT or Regulator only intends to apply for CDOs in respect of breaches of competition law that have been proven in decisions or judgements (as the case may be) of the:

• OFT or a Regulator
• European Commission
• Competition Appeal Tribunal, or
• European Court.[32]

4.7   In respect of breaches proven in a European Commission decision or a judgement of the European Court, it is not the intention of the OFT or Regulator to apply for CDOs where the breach to which the decision or judgement relates does or did not have an actual or potential effect on trade in the United Kingdom.

4.8   The OFT or Regulator will not apply for CDOs in respect of breaches of competition law which ended before the commencement of sections 9A to 9E CDDA. Breaches which started before the commencement of sections 9A to 9E CDDA, but which continued onto or after the date for commencement of those sections may be susceptible to CDO applications.

Appeals

4.9   An application for a CDO will not be made where the decision or judgement relating to the breach remains subject to appeal. 'Remains subject to appeal' for these purposes means either that the deadline for appeal against the decision or judgement has not yet passed, or that an appeal has been made, but not yet determined.

---

32 'European Court' means the Court of Justice of the European Communities and includes the Court of First Instance.

. . .

Step 2   Whether a financial penalty has been imposed for the breach

4.10   The next matter which the OFT or Regulator will take into account is whether a financial penalty has been imposed for the breach of competition law. The OFT or Regulator will not consider CDO applications to be appropriate in cases other than those in which a financial penalty has been imposed and, in the event of an appeal, upheld in whole or part.

Step 3   Leniency

4.11   The next question which the OFT or Regulator will consider is whether the company of which a person is a director benefited from leniency. 'Leniency' for these purposes means the immunity from, or any reduction in, financial penalty in the manner described in the *Director General of Fair Trading's Guidance as to the Appropriate Amount of a Penalty*' (the penalties guidance), or that described in the European Commission *Notice on Immunity from Fines and Reduction of Fines in Cartel Cases*'[34] (the fining notice) or any publication replacing them. 'Reduction' for these purposes does not mean any reduction in the amount of financial penalty imposed for a breach owing to the application of any mitigating factors discussed in the penalties guidance or the fining notice. (See also paragraph 4.27 below with respect to no-action letters in cartel cases.)

4.12   The OFT or Regulator will not apply for a CDO against any current director of a company whose company benefited from leniency in respect of the activities to which the grant of leniency relates.[35] Companies benefiting from leniency will receive confirmation of this policy.

4.13   However, where a director has at any time been removed as a director of a company owing to his or her role in the breach of competition law in question and/or for opposing the relevant application for leniency, then the OFT or Regulator may still consider applying for a CDO against that person, irrespective of whether his or her former company has been granted leniency by the OFT or Regulator or European Commission.

4.14   In order to minimise the risk of a CDO application being made against them, company directors whose companies have been involved in cartel activity should therefore ensure that their companies approach the OFT or Regulator or the European Commission for leniency.

---

34 OJ 2002 C45/3.

35 A CDO application may still be made against a director in respect of any breach of competition law to which the grant of leniency does not relate, provided that there has been a determination of breach. Company directors should therefore ensure that a request for leniency is made in respect of all cartel activity in which their company is, or has been, involved.

Step 4   Extent of the director's responsibility for the breach

4.15   The next step in the OFT or Regulator's assessment will be for the OFT or Regulator to consider the extent of the director's responsibility for or involvement in the breach, whether by action or omission.

4.16   The greater the degree of the director's responsibility for or involvement in a breach, the greater the likelihood that the OFT or Regulator will consider that person to be unfit to be concerned in the management of a company and hence, of a CDO application being made against that person. The OFT or Regulator:
- is likely to apply for a CDO against a director who has been directly involved in the breach
- does not rule out applying for a CDO against a director whom it considers, taking into account that director's role and responsibilities, to have failed to keep himself or herself sufficiently informed of the company's activities which constituted the breach of competition law – whether an application is made in these circumstances will depend upon the OFT or regulator's priorities.

Direct involvement – likely to apply for CDO

4.17   The OFT or Regulator will consider whether there is evidence indicating that a director was involved in the breach. The OFT or Regulators are of the view that this is evidence of the director, either alone or with other persons, having:
- actively taken steps to carry out the infringement (e.g. by drawing up a list of the company's prices and sending them to a competitor so as to enable them to align their prices)
- planned, devised, approved or encouraged the activity of the undertaking which caused the breach
- ordered or pressured those identified as having a direct or indirect role in the breach to engage in the activity causing the breach
- attended meetings (internal or external) in which the activity constituting the breach either occurred or was discussed, or both
- directed, ordered or pressured staff of the undertaking to attend meetings (internal or external) for the purpose of participating in or discussing the activity constituting the breach, or
- ordered, encouraged or advocated retaliation against other undertakings who were reluctant to or refused to participate in the activity constituting the breach of competition law.

4.18   The key consideration is whether the director had an active role in causing his or her company to carry out or agree to carry out the activity constituting the breach.

[265]

Failure to take corrective action – quite likely to apply for CDO

4.19 Where there is no evidence of direct involvement by the director in a breach, the OFT or Regulator may consider whether there is evidence that:
- knowing or having reasonable ground to suspect that persons within the company were directly or indirectly involved in the conduct which constituted a breach, he or she failed to take reasonable steps to halt the activity in question
- he or she authorised or approved expenditure of funds used to finance any activity relating to the breach, knowing or having reasonable grounds to suspect that those funds would be used for the activity and that the activity related to a breach.

Failure to keep sufficiently informed – CDO application not ruled out

4.20 When considering whether a director ought to have known that his or her company was involved in the breach, the OFT or Regulator is likely, among other things, to consider the following factors:
- the director's role in the company
- the relationship of the director's role to those responsible for the breach
- the general knowledge, skill and experience actually possessed by the director in question and that which should have been possessed by a person in his or her position
- the information relating to the breach which was available to the director prior to the breach.

4.21 While the OFT and Regulators do not expect that directors must have specific expertise in competition law, they do expect that all company directors should appreciate that competition law compliance is a crucial matter for their companies. Furthermore, the OFT and Regulators expect that every director of every company ought to know that price-fixing, market sharing and bid-rigging agreements are likely to breach competition law.

Step 5   Aggravating and mitigating factors

4.22 The final step which the OFT or a Regulator will consider when deciding whether to apply for a CDO against a director is whether any aggravating or mitigating factors (or both) apply. Aggravating factors increase the likelihood that the OFT or Regulator will apply for a CDO. Conversely, the presence of mitigating factors may reduce the likelihood that an application for a CDO will be made.

Aggravating factors

4.23 Aggravating factors include evidence that the director:
- has been directly or indirectly involved in breaches of competition law in the past
- destroyed or advised others to destroy any records relating to any breach of competition law with the objective of concealing the breach

- obstructed or impeded any investigation by the OFT or Regulator or European Commission into any breach of competition law or attempted to do so or advised others to do so
- during any investigation of a breach of competition law, unlawfully refused or advised refusing to grant access to investigators from the OFT or Regulator or European Commission to any part of the company's premises
- ordered, encouraged or advocated continued participation in the breach following commencement of an investigation into the breach by the OFT or Regulator or European Commission.

Mitigating factors

4.24   Mitigating factors include evidence indicating that:
- the undertaking committed the breach as a result of a coercion by another undertaking (for example, where the breach was committed as the only perceived way to avoid threatened retaliation by a dominant undertaking)
- there was genuine uncertainty prior to the breach as to whether the infringing activity constituted a breach
- the director contributed to the company taking quick remedial steps when the breach was brought to his or her attention, including the implementation or revision of a competition law compliance programme
- the director took disciplinary action against the employees responsible for the breach
- the director was himself or herself under severe internal pressure (such as from controlling shareholders of the company or directors of a parent company, for example) either to be involved in the breach or to allow it to occur.[36]

Cartel offence: conviction/no-action letters

4.25   Any court[37] by or before which an individual is convicted of an indictable offence (whether tried on indictment or summarily) committed in connection with the management of a company may make a disqualification order against that individual.[38]

4.26   Where an individual company director has been convicted of the cartel offence under section 188 Enterprise Act 2002, and that offence has been committed in connection with the management of a company, the convicting court has the power to make a disqualification order against that individual director.[39] The OFT and Regulators take the view that the court by or before which the individual director is convicted of the cartel offence is the most appropriate venue for consideration of

---

36 Pressure to meet sales of profitability targets will not however be a mitigating factor for these purposes.
37 Including a magistrate's court.
38 See sections 2(1) and 2(2)(b) CDDA.
39 This is because the cartel offence is an indictable offence (section 190 Enterprise Act 2002).

a disqualification order, so they would not expect to have to use their powers under section 9A CDDA in these circumstances.

4.27   The OFT or Regulator will not apply for a CDO against any beneficiary of a no-action letter in respect of that letter.[40] Recipients of no-action letters will receive individual confirmation of this policy.

4 Parallel behaviour and oligopolies

Part 3 above looked at the cartel situation, where firms collude in one way or another by way of an agreement. Of course it would be wrong to assume that such overt collusion exists in relation to every market in respect of which competition is reduced. In some markets firms do not actually meet or communicate with one another, yet those firms may, due to certain market forces or circumstances, behave in a way that makes it look like some collusion exists between them. This situation is commonly known in the world of competition law and policy as 'parallel behaviour' or 'parallelism'.

One of the theories that considers such a situation and whether it should be controlled under competition law is the theory of oligopolistic interdependence. This refers to a market situation characterised by oligopoly and interdependence between firms operating in the market. The idea behind the theory is simple: in such oligopolistic markets – i.e. those having few players, high barriers to entry and significant sunk costs (costs that a firm incurs when entering the market but cannot recover if it decides to exit from it) and homogenous products – firms are bound to be particularly aware of one another's presence and so recognise their interdependence. In other words, it is inevitable that firms operating on such a market will monitor the behaviour of competitors, because should those competitors decide, for example, to reduce prices, the firm may end up losing its customers to competitors. Of course if a firm decides to match the price cuts of its competitors, a price war may develop and as a result prices will be driven down to perhaps a lower level than that charged in a competitive market.

This is hardly good news for the firm and its competitors. Hence, the theory claims that in such a situation the firms may realise, without the need to communicate, that their interest will be best served by adopting a course of conduct that would lead to setting their prices at a profit-maximising level.

This situation presents a difficult problem for a competition authority which can be summarised in the following questions: how should the authority deal with such a situation and can such a parallel course of conduct on the part of the firms be caught within the net of the competition rules?

---

40 A no-action letter is a letter sent by the OFT to a person stating that they will not face criminal prosecution for cartel activities specified in the letter. See the OFT guidance *The cartel offence: Guidance on the Issue of No-Action Letters for Individuals* (OFT513).

This part will deal with how the competition authorities and courts in the EC and the UK have handled such a situation.

(A) EC law

Under EC law it is important to know whether the situation described above is prohibited under Article 81 or 82 EC. This part deals with the application of Article 81; the application of Article 82 is discussed in chapter 13, which deals with the issue of collective dominance. The first case that should be mentioned in the context of Article 81 is the *Dyestuffs* case.

Imperial Chemical Industries Ltd v. Commission [1972] ECR 619

The case concerned simultaneous uniform increases in the price of dyes and pigments effected in at a national level by several manufacturers, including the applicant ('ICI') which the Commission found represented a concerted practice in breach of Article 81. ICI argued that parallel behaviour due to an oligopolistic market could not constitute a concerted practice without proof of wilful collaboration. The ECJ held, however, that the nature of the market contradicted the idea that the increases were 'spontaneous' and that any conduct which replaced the hazards of competition in favour of collaboration constituted a concerted practice.

ECJ

Arguments of the parties

52   [The Commission decision] states that *prima facie* evidence that the increase of 1964, 1965 and 1967 took place as the result of concerted action is to be found in the facts that the rates introduced for each increase by the different producers in each country were the same, that with very rare exceptions the same dyestuffs were involved, and that the increases were put into effect over only a very short period, if not actually on the same date.

53   It is contended that these increases cannot be explained simply by the oligopolistic character of the structure of the market.

54   It is said to be unrealistic to suppose that without previous concertation the principal producers supplying the common market could have increased their prices on several occasions by identical percentages at practically the same moment for one and the same important range of products including speciality products for which there are few, if any, substitutes, and that they should have done so in a number of countries where conditions on the dyestuffs market are different.

[269]

55   The Commission has argued before the court that the interested parties need not necessarily have drawn up a common plan with a view to adopting a certain course of behaviour for it to be said that there has been concertation.

56   It is argued that it is enough that they should previously have informed each other of the attitude which they intended to adopt so that each could regulate his conduct safe in the knowledge that his competitors would act in the same way.

57   The applicant argues that the contested Decision is based on an inadequate analysis of the market in the products in question and on an erroneous understanding of the concept of a concerted practice, which is wrongly identified by the Decision with the conscious parallelism of members of an oligopoly, whereas such conduct is due to independent Decisions adopted by each undertaking, determined by objective business needs, and in particular by the need to increase the unsatisfactorily low rate of profit on the production of dyestuffs.

58   It is argued that in fact the prices of the products in question displayed a constant tendency to fall because of lively competition between producers which is typical of the market in those products, not only as regards the quality of the products and technical assistance to customers, but also as regards prices, particularly the large reductions granted individually to the principal purchasers.

59   The fact that the rates of increase were identical was the result, it is said, of the existence of the 'price-leadership' of one undertaking.

60   It is also argued that the large number of dyestuffs produced by each undertaking makes it impossible in practice to raise prices product by product.

61   A further argument is that different price increases for interchangeable products either could not produce economically significant results because of the limited level of stocks and of the time necessary for adapting plant to appreciably increased demand, or would lead to a ruinous price war.

62   Finally, it is said that dyestuffs for which there are no substitutes form only a small part of the producers' turnover.

63   Taking these market characteristics into account and in view of the widespread and continuous erosion of prices, each member of the oligopoly who decided to increase his prices could, it is argued, reasonably expect to be followed by his competitors, who had the same problems regarding profits.

The concept of a concerted practice

64   Article [81] draws a distinction between the concept of 'concerted practices' and that of 'agreements between undertakings' or of 'Decisions by associations of undertakings'; the object is to bring within the prohibition of that Article a form of

coordination between undertakings which, without having reached the stage where an agreement properly so-called has been concluded, knowingly substitutes practical cooperation between them for the risks of competition.

65   By its very nature, then, a concerted practice does not have all the elements of a contract but may *inter alia* arise out of coordination which becomes apparent from the behaviour of the participants.

66   Although parallel behaviour may not by itself be identified with a concerted practice, it may however amount to strong evidence of such a practice if it leads to conditions of competition which do not correspond to the normal conditions of the market, having regard to the nature of the products, the size and number of the undertakings, and the volume of the said market.

67   This is especially the case if the parallel conduct is such as to enable those concerned to attempt to stabilize prices at a level different from that to which competition would have led, and to consolidate established positions to the detriment of effective freedom of movement of the products in the common market and of the freedom of consumers to choose their suppliers.

68   Therefore the question whether there was a concerted action in this case can only be correctly determined if the evidence upon which the contested Decision is based is considered, not in isolation, but as a whole, account being taken of the specific features of the market in the products in question.

The characteristic features of the market in dyestuffs
69   The market in dyestuffs is characterized by the fact that 80 per cent of the market is supplied by about ten producers, very large ones in the main, which often manufacture these products together with other chemical products or pharmaceutical specialities.

70   The production patterns and therefore the cost structures of these manufacturers are very different and this makes it difficult to ascertain competing manufacturers' costs.

71   The total number of dyestuffs is very high, each undertaking producing more than a thousand.

72   The average extent to which these products can be replaced by others is considered relatively good for standard dyes, but it can be very low or even non-existent for speciality dyes.

73   As regards speciality products, the market tends in certain cases towards an oligopolistic situation.

74   Since the price of dyestuffs forms a relatively small part of the price of the final product of the user undertaking, there is little elasticity of demand for dyestuffs on the market as a whole and this encourages price increases in the short term.

75   Another factor is that the total demand for dyestuffs is constantly increasing, and this tends to induce producers to adopt a policy enabling them to take advantage of this increase.

76   In the territory of the Community, the market in dyestuffs in fact consists of five separate national markets with different price levels which cannot be explained by differences in costs and charges affecting producers in those countries.

77   Thus the establishment of the common market would not appear to have had any effect on this situation, since the differences between national price levels have scarcely decreased.

78   On the contrary, it is clear that each of the national markets has the characteristics of an oligopoly and that in most of them price levels are established under the influence of a 'priceleader', who in some cases is the largest producer in the country concerned, and in other cases is a producer in another Member State or a third state, acting through a subsidiary.

79   According to the experts this dividing-up of the market is due to the need to supply local technical assistance to users and to ensure immediate delivery, generally in small quantities, since, apart from exceptional cases, producers supply their sub-sidiaries established in the different Member States and maintain a network of agents and depots to ensure that user undertakings receive specific assistance and supplies.

80   It appears from the data produced during the course of the proceedings that even in cases where a producer establishes direct contact with an important user in another Member State, prices are usually fixed in relation to the place where the user is established and tend to follow the level of prices on the national market.

81   Although the foremost reason why producers have acted in this way is in order to adapt themselves to the special features of the market in dyestuffs and to the needs of their customers, the fact remains that the dividing-up of the market which results tends, by fragmenting the effects of competition, to isolate users in their national market, and to prevent a general confrontation between producers throughout the common market.

82   It is in this context, which is peculiar to the way in which the dyestuffs market works, that the facts of the case should be considered.

The ECJ turned to consider the specific price rises in issue, noting coincidence across unrelated markets and different products and the evidence of meetings attended by all the producers, such as BASF and Geigy.

99   Viewed as a whole, the three consecutive increases reveal progressive cooperation between the undertakings concerned.

100   In fact, after the experience of 1964, when the announcement of the increases and their application coincided, although with minor differences as regards the range of products affected, the increases of 1965 and 1967 indicate a different mode of operation.

Here, the undertakings taking the initiative, BASF and Geigy respectively, announced their intentions of making an increase some time in advance, which allowed the undertakings to observe each other's reactions on the different markets, and to adapt themselves accordingly.

101   By means of these advance announcements the various undertakings eliminated all uncertainty between them as to their future conduct and, in doing so, also eliminated a large part of the risk usually inherent in any independent change of conduct on one or several markets.

102   This was all the more the case since these announcements, which led to the fixing of general and equal increases in prices for the markets in dyestuffs, rendered the market transparent as regard the percentage rates of increase.

103   Therefore, by the way in which they acted, the undertakings in question temporarily eliminated with respect to prices some of the preconditions for competition on the market which stood in the way of the achievement of parallel uniformity of conduct.

104   The fact that this conduct was not spontaneous is corroborated by an examination of other aspects of the market.

105   In fact, from the number of producers concerned it is not possible to say that the European market in dyestuffs is, in the strict sense, an oligopoly in which price competition could no longer play a substantial role.

106   These producers are sufficiently powerful and numerous to create a considerable risk that in times of rising prices some of them might not follow the general movement but might instead try to increase their share of the market by behaving in an individual way.

107   Furthermore, the dividing-up of the common market into five national markets with different price levels and structures makes it improbable that a spontaneous and equal price increase would occur on all the national markets.

108   Although a general, spontaneous increase on each of the national markets is just conceivable, these increases might be expected to differ according to the particular characteristics of the different national markets.

[273]

109   Therefore, although parallel conduct in respect of prices may well have been an attractive and risk-free objective for the undertakings concerned, it is hardly conceivable that the same action could be taken spontaneously at the same time, on the same national markets and for the same range of products.

110   Nor is it any more plausible that the increases of January 1964, introduced on the Italian market and copied on the Netherlands and Belgo-Luxembourg markets which have little in common with each other either as regards the level of prices or the pattern of competition, could have been brought into effect within a period of two or three days without prior concertation.

111   As regards the increases of 1965 and 1967 concertation took place openly, since all the announcements of the intention to increase prices with effect from a certain date and for a certain range of products made it possible for producers to decide on their conduct regarding the special cases of France and Italy.

112   In proceeding in this way, the undertakings mutually eliminated in advance any uncertainties concerning their reciprocal behaviour on the different markets and thereby also eliminated a large part of the risk inherent in any independent change of conduct on those markets.

113   The general and uniform increase on those different markets can only be explained by a common intention on the part of those undertakings, first, to adjust the level of prices and the situation resulting from competition in the form of discounts, and secondly, to avoid the risk, which is inherent in any price increase, of changing the conditions of competition.

114   The fact that the price increases announced were not introduced in Italy and that ACNA only partially adopted the 1967 increase in other markets, far from undermining this conclusion, tends to confirm it.

115   The function of price competition is to keep prices down to the lowest possible level and to encourage the movement of goods between the Member States, thereby permitting the most efficient possible distribution of activities in the matter of productivity and the capacity of undertakings to adapt themselves to change.

116   Differences in rates encourage the pursuit of one of the basic objectives of the Treaty, namely the interpenetration of national markets and, as a result, direct access by consumers to the sources of production of the whole Community.

117   By reason of the limited elasticity of the market in dyestuffs, resulting from factors such as the lack of transparency with regard to prices, the interdependence of the different dyestuffs of each producer for the purpose of building up the range of products used by each consumer, the relatively low proportion of the cost of the final product of the user undertaking represented by the prices of these products, the fact that it is useful for users to have a local supplier and the influence of transport costs, the need to avoid any action which might artificially reduce the opportunities

for interpenetration of the various national markets at the consumer level becomes particularly important on the market in the products in question.

118   Although every producer is free to change his prices, taking into account in so doing the present or foreseeable conduct of his competitors, nevertheless it is contrary to the rules on competition contained in the Treaty for a producer to cooperate with his competitors, in any way whatsoever, in order to determine a coordinated course of action relating to a price increase and to ensure its success by prior elimination of all uncertainty as to each other's conduct regarding the essential elements of that action, such as the amount, subject-matter, date and place of the increases.

119   In these circumstances and taking into account the nature of the market in the products in question, the conduct of the applicant, in conjunction with other undertakings against which proceedings have been taken, was designed to replace the risks of competition and the hazards of competitors' spontaneous reactions by cooperation constituting a concerted practice prohibited by Article [81(1)] of the Treaty.

Dyestuffs was a key victory for the Commission; though one could say that the kind and amount of evidence which the Commission was able to uncover in the case played a crucial role in securing such a victory. It is arguable that the ECJ's interpretation of the concept of concerted practice is overly broad and that the ECJ does not seem to have conducted a thorough analysis of the conditions of the market in question. Nevertheless, *Dyestuffs* provides a very clear statement on the application of Article 81(1) in situations of parallel behaviour. The case shows that the Commission and the ECJ will inevitably be sensitive to exchanges of information between firms and advance price announcements without legitimate justification and to attempts to make the market artificially transparent.

One of the key points is in paragraph 118, where the ECJ says that while a firm has freedom to set its own prices, taking into account the present and foreseeable conduct of its competitors, it is prohibited from embarking on a course of conduct which could lead to collusion with its competitors. This is a point that the ECJ repeated three years later in *Sugar Cartel* (see in particular paragraph 174 of the judgment extracted at p. 72) and nine years later in *Züchner v. Bayerische Vereinsbank*.

Perhaps anyone who had read the above-mentioned judgments and the accompanying Commission decisions could have predicted that they would not be the final word from the ECJ and the Commission. In 1993, an extremely clear judgment was delivered in which the Court emphasised that conscious parallelism on the part of firms operating in an oligopolistic market was not identical to a concerted practice. This was in the case of *A. Ahlström Osakeyhtio v. Commission* ('Woodpulp'). The Commission found that the Applicants (forty Finnish, American and Canadian pulp producers and three trade associations) had breached Article 81 during the whole or part of the period from 1975

[275]

to 1981 through concerted practices involving a system of pre-publication of price information ('quarterly price announcements'). The Commission used two hypotheses to prove its case: first, that the system itself constituted a breach of Article 81. It argued that pre-publication of price information in one quarter was intentionally introduced by pulp producers in order to enable them to ascertain the prices that would be charged by their competitors in the following quarters which according to the Commission had the effect of making the market artificially transparent. In its second hypothesis, the Commission viewed the system as furnishing evidence of past concertation, which the Commission alleged was apparent from the parallel conduct of pulp producers during the six year period after 1975.

The ECJ was called upon to consider whether and when parallel conduct can constitute proof of concertation. The operation of the market was investigated by *amicus curiae* 'experts'. The ECJ held that the nature of the market, which not only featured oligopoly characteristics but also concentrated buyer power ('oligopsony'), offered an alternate explanation for the practices alleged to constitute concertation.

ECJ

2. *The other evidence adduced by the Commission*

70   Since the Commission has no documents which directly establish the existence of concertation between the producers concerned, it is necessary to ascertain whether the system of quarterly price announcements, the simultaneity or near-simultaneity of the price announcements and the parallelism of price announcements as found during the period from 1975 to 1981 constitute a firm, precise and consistent body of evidence of prior concertation.

71   In determining the probative value of those different factors, it must be noted that parallel conduct cannot be regarded as furnishing proof of concertation unless concertation constitutes the only plausible explanation for such conduct. It is necessary to bear in mind that, although Article [81] of the Treaty prohibits any form of collusion which distorts competition, it does not deprive economic operators of the right to adapt themselves intelligently to the existing and anticipated conduct of their competitors (see the judgment in *Suiker Unie*, paragraph 174).

72   Accordingly, it is necessary in this case to ascertain whether the parallel conduct alleged by the Commission cannot, taking account of the nature of the products, the size and the number of the undertakings and the volume of the market in question, be explained otherwise than by concertation.

(a) *The system of price announcements*

73   As stated above, the Commission regards the system of quarterly price announcements as evidence of concertation at an earlier stage.

74   In their pleadings, on the other hand, the applicants maintain that the system is ascribable to the particular commercial requirements of the pulp market.

75   By orders of 25 October 1990 and 14 March 1991, the Court requested two experts to examine the characteristics of the market for bleached sulphate pulp during the period covered by the contested decision. Their report sets out the following considerations.

76   The experts observe first that the system of announcements at issue must be viewed in the context of the long-term relationships which existed between producers and their customers and which were a result both of the method of manufacturing the pulp and of the cyclical nature of the market. In view of the fact that each type of paper was the result of a particular mixture of pulps having their own characteristics and that the mixture was difficult to change, a relationship based on close cooperation was established between the pulp producers and the paper manufacturers. Such relations were all the closer since they also had the advantage of protecting both sides against the uncertainties inherent in the cyclical nature of the market: they guaranteed security of supply to buyers and at the same time security of demand to producers.

77   The experts point out that it is in the context of those long-term relationships that, after the Second World War, purchasers demanded the introduction of that system of announcements. Since pulp accounts for between 50% and 75% of the cost of paper, those purchasers wished to ascertain as soon as possible the prices which they might be charged in order to estimate their costs and to fix the prices of their own products. However, as those purchasers did not wish to be bound by a high fixed price in the event of the market weakening, the announced price was regarded as a ceiling price below which the transaction price could always be renegotiated.

78   The explanation given for the use of a quarterly cycle is that it is the result of a compromise between the paper manufacturers' desire for a degree of foreseeability as regards the price of pulp and the producers' desire not to miss any opportunities to make a profit in the event of a strengthening of the market.

79   The US dollar was, according to the experts, introduced on the market by the North American producers during the 1960s. That development was generally welcomed by purchasers who regarded it as a means of ensuring that they did not pay a higher price than their competitors.

(b) The simultaneity or near-simultaneity of announcements

80   In paragraph 107 of its decision, the Commission claims that the close succession or even simultaneity of price announcements would not have been possible without a constant flow of information between the undertakings concerned.

81   According to the applicants, the simultaneity or near-simultaneity of the announcements - even if it were established - must instead be regarded as a direct result of the very high degree of transparency of the market. Such transparency, far from being artificial, can be explained by the extremely well-developed network of relations which, in view of the nature and the structure of the market, have been established between the various traders.

82   The experts have confirmed that analysis in their report and at the hearing which followed.

83   First, they pointed out, a buyer was always in contact with several pulp producers. One reason for that was connected with the paper-making process, but another was that, in order to avoid becoming overdependent on one producer, pulp buyers took the precaution of diversifying their sources of supply. With a view to obtaining the lowest possible prices, they were in the habit, especially in times of falling prices, of disclosing to their suppliers the prices announced by their competitors.

84   Secondly, it should be noted that most of the pulp was sold to a relatively small number of large paper manufacturers. Those few buyers maintained very close links with each other and exchanged information on changes in prices of which they were aware.

85   Thirdly, several producers who made paper themselves purchased pulp from other producers and were thus informed, in times of both rising prices and falling prices, of the prices charged by their competitors. That information was also accessible to producers who did not themselves manufacture paper but were linked to groups that did.

86   Fourthly, that high degree of transparency in the pulp market resulting from the links between traders or groups of traders was further reinforced by the existence of agents established in the Community who worked for several producers and by the existence of a very dynamic trade press.

87   In connection with the latter point, it should be noted that most of the applicants deny having communicated to the trade press any information on their prices and that the few producers who acknowledged having done so point out that such communications were sporadic and were made at the request of the press itself.

88   Finally, it is necessary to add that the use of rapid means of communication, such as the telephone and telex, and the very frequent recourse by the paper manufacturers to very well-informed trade buyers meant that, notwithstanding the number of stages involved – producer, agent, buyer, agent, producer – information on the level of the announced prices spreads within a matter of days, if not within a matter of hours on the pulp market.

(c) Parallelism of announced prices

89   The parallelism of announced prices on which the Commission relies as evidence of concertation is described in paragraph 22 of its decision. In that paragraph, the Commission . . finds that the prices announced by the Canadian and United States producers were the same from the first quarter of 1975 to the third quarter of 1977 and from the first quarter of 1978 to the third quarter of 1981, that the prices announced by the Swedish and Finnish producers were the same from the first quarter of 1975 to the second quarter of 1977 and from the third quarter of 1978 to the third quarter of 1981 and, finally, that the prices of all the producers were the same from the first quarter of 1976 to the second quarter of 1977 and from the third quarter of 1979 to the third quarter of 1981.

90   According to the Commission, the only explanation for such parallelism of prices is concertation between the producers. That contention is essentially based on the considerations that follow.

91   In the first place, the single price charged by the producers during the period at issue cannot be regarded as an equilibrium price, that is to say a price resulting from the natural operation of the law of supply and demand. The Commission emphasizes that there was no testing of the market 'by trial and error', as evidenced by the stability of prices established between the first quarter of 1975 and the fourth quarter of 1976, and the fact that, generally in the case of softwood from the third quarter of 1979 to the second quarter of 1980, the first higher price demanded was always followed by the other producers.

92   Nor can the argument concerning 'price leadership' be accepted: the similarity of announced prices, and that of transaction prices moreover, cannot be explained by the existence of a market leader whose prices were adopted by its competitors. The order in which the announcements were made continued to change from quarter to quarter and no one producer held a strong enough position to act as leader.

93   Secondly, the Commission considers that, since economic conditions varied from one producer to another or from one group of producers to another, they should have charged different prices. Pulp manufacturers with low costs should have lowered their prices in order to increase their market shares to the detriment of their least efficient competitors. According to the Commission, the divergences in question related to production and transport costs, the relationship between those costs (determined in the national currencies: Canadian dollar, Swedish krona or Finnish mark) and selling prices (fixed in US dollars), size of orders, variations in demand for pulp in the various importing countries, the relative importance of the European market, which was greater for Scandinavian producers than for United States and Canadian producers, and the production capacity utilization ratios which, generally speaking, were higher in the United States and Canada than in Sweden and Finland.

94   So far as the size of orders is concerned, the Commission considers that since the sale of large quantities enabled producers to cut their costs substantially, the price records should have shown significant price differences between purchasers of large quantities and purchasers of small quantities. In practice, those differences rarely amounted to more than 3%.

95   Thirdly, the Commission claims that, at any rate for a time in 1976, 1977 and 1981, announced prices for pulp stood at an artificially high level which differed widely from that which might have been expected under normal competitive conditions ... The contention that prices stood at an abnormally high level is borne out by the fact that in 1977 and 1982 the fall in prices was particularly abrupt.

96   Finally, the Commission relies on the grant of secret rebates and on changes in market shares.

97   So far as concerns the grant of secret rebates, it should be noted that there is a contradiction between the decision and what has been said subsequently. In paragraph 112 of its decision, the Commission refers to the exclusion of secret competition but then states in its pleadings that, if the rebates were secret, it was because they undermined concertation and therefore had to remain concealed from the other producers.

98   So far as concerns the shifts in market shares established between 1975 and 1981, the Commission considers that they do not justify the finding that there was no concertation. Those shifts were much less marked between 1975 and 1976 and between 1980 and 1981 than the shifts between 1978 and 1979 and between 1979 and 1980.

99   The applicants disputed the view that parallelism of prices was attributable to concertation.

100   In commissioning the second expert's report, the Court requested the experts to specify whether, in their opinion, the natural operation of the wood pulp market should lead to a differential price structure or to a uniform price structure.

101   It is apparent from the expert's report, together with the ensuing discussion, that the experts regard the normal operation of the market as a more plausible explanation for the uniformity of prices than concertation. The main thrust of their analysis may be summarized as follows:

(i) Description of the market

102   The experts describe the market as a group of oligopolies–oligopsonies consisting of certain producers and of certain buyers and each corresponding to a given kind of pulp. That market structure results largely from the method of manufacturing paper pulp: since paper is the result of a characteristic mixture of pulps, each paper manufacturer can deal only with a limited number of pulp producers and, conversely, each pulp producer can supply only a limited number of customers. Within the

groupings so constituted, cooperation was further consolidated by the finding that it offered both buyers and sellers of pulp security against the uncertainties of the market.

103   That organization of the market, in conjunction with its very high degree of transparency, leads in the short-term to a situation where prices are slow to react. The producers know that, if they were to increase their prices, their competitors would no doubt refrain from following suit and thus lure their customers away. Similarly, they would be reluctant to reduce their prices in the knowledge that, if they did so, the other producers would follow suit, assuming that they had spare production capacity. Such a fall in prices would be all the less desirable in that it would be detrimental to the sector as a whole: since overall demand for pulp is inelastic, the loss of revenue resulting from the reduction in prices could not be offset by the profits made as a result of the increased sales and there would be a decline in the producers' overall profits.

104   In the long-term, the possibility for buyers to turn, at the price of some investment, to other types of pulp and the existence of substitute products, such as Brazilian pulp or pulp from recycled paper, have the effect of mitigating oligopolistic trends on the market. That explains why, over a period of several years, fluctuations in prices have been relatively contained.

105   Finally, the transparency of the market could be responsible for certain overall price increases recorded in the short-term: when demand exceeds supply, producers who are aware - as was the case on the pulp market - that the level of their competitors' stocks is low and that their production capacity utilization rate is high would not be afraid to increase their prices. There would then be a serious likelihood of their being followed by their competitors.

(ii) Market trends from 1975 to 1981

106   The various mechanisms described above offer explanations for some of the stages in the sequence of price changes regarded by the Commission as 'abnormal', particularly the stability of prices observed during the period from 1975 to 1976, the collapse of the market in 1977 and the fresh fall in prices at the end of 1981.

. . .

(iii) Several factors established on the market are incompatible with the explanation that there was concertation

115   The experts analyse the structures of the market and price trends over the period at issue and maintain that several factors or mechanisms specific to that market are incompatible with an explanation based on concertation. Those factors are the existence of actual and potential outsiders not belonging to the group of undertakings alleged to have colluded, changing market shares and the absence of production

quotas and the finding that producers did not take advantage of the differences between the various importing countries as regards elasticity of demand.

116 So far as concerns the first point, it should be noted that in paragraph 137 of its decision, the Commission assesses production by outsiders at 40% of total consumption of pulp in the Community. In view of the size of that market share, it would have been difficult for a cartel to operate only as between the undertakings found to have committed an infringement by engaging in concertation.

117 The Commission's counterargument is that it refrained from initiating a proceeding against those other producers because, in its view, they had acted as followers during the period at issue.

118 That argument cannot be accepted. It is wholly inconsistent with the reasoning adopted by the Commission . . in identifying the producers taking part in the concertation. If, in that regard . . the mere fact of announcing the same price as another producer for the same period does indeed constitute sufficient evidence of concertation, the infringement procedure under Article [81] should clearly have been extended to those outsiders which, as the Commission acknowledges by its use of the term 'follower', announced the same price as the producers penalized in the context of Article 1(1) of the operative part of the decision.

119 With regard to the second factor, the experts find that . . there were shifts in market shares between 1975 and 1981. Such changes reveal the existence of competition between the producers and the absence of quotas.

120 Finally, so far as concerns the absence of differences in price between the various Member States, the experts consider that it is wrong to contend, as the Commission does in paragraphs 136 to 140 of the decision, that the pulp producers should have exploited the differences in price-elasticity in the different Member States. According to the experts, in order to do so, the undertakings would have had to be in a position to divide up the market, which would have been possible only if there had been an effective cartel embracing all existing and potential suppliers and capable of ensuring compliance with barriers to resale and to transfer between Member States. In those circumstances, price uniformity constitutes on the contrary an argument militating in favour of the explanation based on the normal operation of the market.

(iv) Specific criticisms of the Commission's explanation made by the experts

121 A number of specific criticisms are directed by the experts against the Commission's explanation. Those criticisms concern the impact on prices of transport costs, the size of orders and, in general, differences in costs and the grant of secret rebates.

122   In the first place, in response to the Commission's contention that prices should have varied according to the destination, the experts state that the destination of the pulp - whether Atlantic ports or Baltic ports - had only a minor influence on transport costs . . .

123   Secondly, the experts explain why, in their view, very large orders for pulp did not lead to sharp price cuts. Such orders do not enable significant cost savings to be made for various reasons: first, wood pulp is normally a standard product delivered from anonymous stock; secondly, producers are in the habit of installing storage capacity at the great receiving ports; finally, because they use a wide range of pulps, the paper manufacturers prefer, when placing orders for large quantities, to have the pulp delivered in several consignments. Ultimately, the economies of scale associated with very large orders are confined to overheads and administrative costs.

124   Thirdly, the experts consider that, even if there were real economies of scale, the differences in costs to which they led between the producers did not affect prices but the undertakings' profits.

125   Finally, if the rebates granted were secret, that was for various reasons outside the pulp producers' control: to begin with, in some countries, such as France, rebates not justified by cost-savings are illegal; next, as rebates generally relate to annual tonnage, they cannot be calculated until the end of the financial year. Lastly, it is the buyers who ask for rebates to be kept confidential, partly in order to secure an advantage over their competitors by obtaining better prices, and partly in order to prevent paper buyers from seeking a reduction in price themselves.

3. Conclusions

126   Following that analysis, it must be stated that, in this case, concertation is not the only plausible explanation for the parallel conduct. To begin with, the system of price announcements may be regarded as constituting a rational response to the fact that the pulp market constituted a long-term market and to the need felt by both buyers and sellers to limit commercial risks. Further, the similarity in the dates of price announcements may be regarded as a direct result of the high degree of market transparency, which does not have to be described as artificial. Finally, the parallelism of prices and the price trends may be satisfactorily explained by the oligopolistic tendencies of the market and by the specific circumstances prevailing in certain periods. Accordingly, the parallel conduct established by the Commission does not constitute evidence of concertation.

127   In the absence of a firm, precise and consistent body of evidence, it must be held that concertation regarding announced prices has not been established by the Commission. Article 1(1) of the contested decision must therefore be annulled.

The facts in *Woodpulp* were strong enough to show that the system of quarterly price announcement was not, in itself, evidence of concertation. The ECJ repeated its earlier statement in *Dyestuffs* that every firm was free to react intelligently to market forces taking into account present and foreseeable conduct of its competitors. Furthermore, the ECJ seems to have placed heavy emphasis on the findings reached in the reports commissioned from economic experts. Those reports analysed the wood pulp sector and the evidence in the case, and they seriously undermined the Commission's case. Paragraphs 107–114 show that the ECJ received the experts' view of market factors besides transparency prevailing in the period between 1975 and 1981, such as serious market fluctuation, and accepted that other economic factors interfered with the balance of supply and demand in this period. This included high inflation and low interest rates, a tax rebate programme instituted by the Swedish Government encouraging producer stock-building, and optimism on the US market, culminating in an industry wide over-supply relative to demand. In that way, the ECJ made clear its willingness to embark on economic analysis and to scrutinise the evidence used by the Commission to prove its case.

According to the ECJ parallel behaviour could not be used to establish the existence of a concerted practice *unless*, taking into account the size and number of undertakings, the nature of the market and the nature of the products, *it could not be explained otherwise than by concertation*. On the facts of the case, there was an alternative plausible explanation other than concertation:

- the system of price announcement in advance was explicable as a rational response to the fact that the pulp market was a mature market and the system met a legitimate business concern of customers;
- the market was inherently transparent and had oligopolistic tendencies at both the levels of suppliers (oligopolies) and buyers (oligopsonies);
- there was an active trade press; and
- paper manufacturers were in constant contact with pulp suppliers and exchanged price information amongst themselves.

(B) UK law

Chapter 1 made it clear that the Chapters I and II prohibitions of the CA1998 are modelled on Articles 81 and 82 of the Treaty. Furthermore, by virtue of section 60 of the Act, UK competition authorities and courts are required to have regard to the jurisprudence of the Community Courts and the decisional practice of the Commission. This means that the case law developed in relation to the application of Article 81(1) to situations of parallel behaviour and oligopolies – which was discussed above – is relevant for the purposes of applying the Chapter I prohibition. In addition, the UK system of competition law includes a special mechanism, which can be employed in relation to such situations, namely the market investigation references under the EA2002. This issue is discussed in chapter 12.

Further reading

Harding and Joshua 'Breaking up the hard core: prospects for the new cartel offence' (2002) 39 CMLRev. 933

Lawrence and Moffat 'A dangerous new world – practical implications of the Enterprise Act 2002' (2004) 25 ECLR 1

Monti 'Article 81 EC and public policy' (2002) 39 CMLRev. 1057

Nazzini 'Criminalisation of cartels and concurrent proceedings' (2003) 24 ECLR 483

Frignani and Rossi 'Exchanges of information between competitors: a comparative survey' (2003) 1 Bus. L. I. 54

8
Horizontal agreements II: specialisation and research and development

1 Introduction

The previous chapter revealed that horizontal cooperation can take a variety of forms depending on the situation at hand ranging from economically beneficial to competitively harmful. One of the categories which was the focus of that chapter was the cartel situation, which competition law seeks to eliminate. Another category mentioned briefly was the joint venture situation, ranging from the 'full-function' joint venture to 'partial-function' joint venture; the former type is dealt with in chapter 10.

This chapter is concerned with horizontal cooperation agreements between firms not automatically considered to be restrictive of competition and the application of EC and UK competition rules to these types of agreements. This is an important area for competition authorities as they must not be seen to inhibit legitimate competitive business activities. Although there is a variety of agreements included within this category, stretching from specialisation to research and development, commercialisation, standards and environmental control agreements, this chapter will focus on the first of these.

2 EC law

(A) The Guidelines on horizontal agreements

Horizontal cooperation agreements have received particular attention from the Commission, which endeavoured, in the formative years of the EC system of competition law, to provide guidance on how it viewed such agreements and how Article 81 should be applied in relation to them. Notable guidance here includes the 1968 and 1993 Notices. These Notices, however, have now been replaced by a document which should be characterised as the Commission's most authoritative source of guidance on its approach to such agreements, namely the *Guidelines on the applicability of Article 81 to horizontal cooperation* (2000). It is important to note that the *Guidelines* apply to a variety of agreements such as purchasing and commercialisation, and not only specialisation and research and development agreements.

Guidelines on the applicability of Article 81 of the EC Treaty to horizontal cooperation agreements OJ (2001) C 3/2

2   Horizontal cooperation may lead to competition problems. This is for example the case if the parties to a cooperation agree to fix prices or output, to share markets, or if the cooperation enables the parties to maintain, gain or increase market power and thereby causes negative market effects with respect to prices, output, innovation or the variety and quality of products.

3   On the other hand, horizontal cooperation can lead to substantial economic benefits. Companies need to respond to increasing competitive pressure and a changing market place driven by globalisation, the speed of technological progress and the generally more dynamic nature of markets. Cooperation can be a means to share risk, save costs, pool know-how and launch innovation faster. In particular for small and medium-sized enterprises cooperation is an important means to adapt to the changing market place.

4   The Commission, while recognising the economic benefits that can be generated by cooperation, has to ensure that effective competition is maintained. Article 81 provides the legal framework for a balanced assessment taking into account both anti-competitive effects as well as economic benefits.

. . .

7   The purpose of these guidelines is to provide an analytical framework for the most common types of horizontal cooperation. This framework is primarily based on criteria that help to analyse the economic context of a cooperation agreement. Economic criteria such as the market power of the parties and other factors relating to the market structure, form a key element of the assessment of the market impact likely to be caused by a cooperation and therefore for the assessment under Article 81. Given the enormous variety in types and combinations of horizontal cooperation and market circumstances in which they operate, it is impossible to provide specific answers for every possible scenario. The present analytical framework based on economic criteria will nevertheless assist businesses in assessing the compatibility of an individual cooperation agreement with Article 81.

. . .

Scope of the guidelines

9   These guidelines cover agreements or concerted practices (hereinafter referred to as 'agreements') entered into between two or more companies operating at the same level(s) in the market, e.g. at the same level of production or distribution. Within this

context the focus is on cooperation between competitors. The term 'competitors' as used in these guidelines includes both actual[8] and potential.[9]

10   The present guidelines do not, however, address all possible horizontal agreements. They are only concerned with those types of cooperation which potentially generate efficiency gains, namely agreements on R&D, production, purchasing, commercialisation, standardisation, and environmental agreements. Other types of horizontal agreements between competitors, for example on the exchange of information or on minority shareholdings, are to be addressed separately.

11   Agreements that are entered into between companies operating at a different level of the production or distribution chain, that is to say vertical agreements, are in principle excluded from these guidelines and dealt with in Commission Regulation (EC) No 2790/1999[10] (the 'Block Exemption Regulation on Vertical Restraints') and the Guidelines on vertical restraints.[11] However, to the extent that vertical agreements, e.g. distribution agreements, are concluded between competitors, the effects of the agreement on the market and the possible competition problems can be similar to horizontal agreements. Therefore, these agreements have to be assessed according to the principles described in the present guidelines. This does not exclude the

8 A firm is treated as an actual competitor if it is either active on the same relevant market or if, in the absence of the agreement, it is able to switch production to the relevant products and market them in the short term without incurring significant additional costs or risks in response to a small and permanent increase in relative prices (immediate supply-side substitutability). The same reasoning may lead to the grouping of different geographic areas. However, when supply-side substitutability would entail the need to adjust significantly existing tangible and intangible assets, to make additional investments, to take strategic decisions or to incur time delays, a company will not be treated as a competitor but as a potential competitor (see below). See Commission Notice on the definition of the relevant market for the purposes of Community competition law (OJ C372, 9.12.1997, p. 5, paragraphs 20-23).

9 A firm is treated as a potential competitor if there is evidence that, absent the agreement, this firm could and would be likely to undertake the necessary additional investments or other necessary switching costs so that it could enter the relevant market in response to a small and permanent increase in relative prices. This assessment has to be based on realistic grounds, the mere theoretical possibility to enter a market is not sufficient (see Commission Notice on the definition of the relevant market for the purposes of Community competition law (paragraph 24); see also the Commission's Thirteenth Report on Competition Policy, point 55 and Commission Decision 90/410/EEC in case *Elopak/Metal Box-Odin* (OJ L 209, 8.8.1990, p. 15). Market entry needs to take place sufficiently fast so that the threat of potential entry is a constraint on the market participants' behaviour. Normally, this means that entry has to occur within a short period. The *Guidelines on Vertical Restraints* (OJ C 291, 13.10.2000, p. 1, paragraph 26, consider a period of maximum 1 year for the purposes of application of the Block Exemption Regulation on Vertical Restraints (see footnote 11). However, in individual cases longer time periods can be taken into account. The time period needed by companies already active on the market to adjust their capacities can be used as a yardstick to determine this period.

10 OJ L 336, 29.12.1999, p. 21.

11 OJ C 291, 13.10.2000, p. 1.

[289]

additional application of the Guidelines on Vertical Restraints to these agreements to assess the vertical restraints included in such agreements.[12]

12   Agreements may combine different stages of cooperation, for example R&D and the production of its results. Unless they fall under . . . the Merger Regulation, these agreements are covered by the guidelines. The centre of gravity of the cooperation determines which section of the present guidelines applies to the agreement in question. In the determination of the centre of gravity, account is taken in particular of two factors: firstly, the starting point of the cooperation, and, secondly, the degree of integration of the different functions which are being combined. A cooperation involving both joint R&D and joint production of the results would thus normally be covered in the section on 'Agreements on Research and Development', as the joint production will only take place if the joint R&D is successful. This implies that the results of the joint R&D are decisive for production. The R&D agreement can thus be regarded as the starting point of the cooperation. This assessment would change if the agreement foresaw a full integration in the area of production and only a partial integration of some R&D activities. In this case, the possible anti-competitive effects and economic benefits of the cooperation would largely relate to the joint production, and the agreement would therefore be examined according to the principles set out in the section on 'Production Agreements'. More complex arrangements such as strategic alliances that combine a number of different areas and instruments of cooperation in varying ways are not covered by the guidelines. The assessment of each individual area of cooperation within an alliance may be carried out with the help of the corresponding chapter in the guidelines. However, complex arrangements must also be analysed in their totality. Due to the variety of areas an alliance may combine, it is impossible to give general guidance for such an overall assessment. Alliances or other forms of cooperation that primarily declare intentions are impossible to assess under the competition rules as long as they lack a precise scope.

An obvious and important feature of the *Guidelines* is the great emphasis they place on economic analysis. This reflects not only the jurisprudence of the Community courts but also the changes in the Commission's own approach in this area of law.

The *Guidelines* provide an analytical framework to assist firms and their legal advisors in making their own informed assessment of their individual circumstances, including taking into consideration economic criteria such as market power.

Circumstances must be considered on a case-by-case basis, and this is where the economic criteria take a central role. The starting point should be the position of the parties to the agreement, since this will indicate whether they are

12 The delineation between horizontal and vertical agreements will be further developed in the chapters on joint purchasing (Chapter 4) and joint commercialisation (Chapter 5). See also the Guidelines on Vertical Restraints, paragraph 26 and 29.

likely to increase their market power through cooperation. A definition of the relevant market will be required and the Commission will use the methodology developed under its Notice on market definition (see chapter 2) to assess, among other things, the market shares of the firms concerned, the relative strength of their competitors and the nature of the product affected.

A key concern is the likelihood of coordination of the competitive conduct of the parties. In some cases, this likelihood is small, such as where the agreement is entered into between competitors who cannot independently carry out the relevant project. In other cases, the likelihood may be great, especially where the cooperation is likely to lead to price fixing, market sharing or some other restriction of competition.

The *Guidelines* apply to both goods and services, although sectors in which special sectoral regulations exist, such as the transport and insurance sectors, are excluded from the scope of the *Guidelines*.

In relation to the application of Article 81(1), it should be noted that the *Guidelines* of course only apply in so far as horizontal cooperation agreements are subject to Article 81(1), that they are capable of affecting trade between Member States and appreciably restricting competition (whether by object or effect). Indeed, this should be clear from previous chapters especially the discussion in chapter 3; this however does not affect the application of Article 82 to such agreements provided of course that an abuse of a dominant position is established (the following chapter deals with Article 82).

In the following paragraphs of the *Guidelines*, the Commission deals with the basic principles for the assessment under Article 81, focusing first on Article 81(1) and then on 81(3). Only the relevant paragraphs dealing with the application of Article 81(1) are extracted below; paragraphs 31–37 which deal with the application of Article 81(3) are not reproduced since the issue of exemption under the paragraph was exhaustively covered in chapter 4 to which the reader is referred (see pp. 109–127 above). Also, the application of the provision is considered below in relation to R&D and specialisation agreements (see pp. 306–307 and 324–325 below).

The *Guidelines* make it clear that Article 81(1) applies to agreements with *either* an object *or* an effect that is restrictive of competition. They recognise however that horizontal cooperation agreements aim rarely to restrict competition, though they may have such an effect.

Guidelines on horizontal cooperation OJ (2001) C 3/2

20   Whether the agreement is able to cause such negative market effects [for the purposes of an Article 81(1) assessment] depends on the economic context taking into account both the nature of the agreement and the parties' combined market power which determines – together with other structural factors – the capability of the cooperation to affect overall competition to such a significant extent.

Nature of the agreement

21 The nature of an agreement relates to factors such as the area and objective of the cooperation, the competitive relationship between the parties and the extent to which they combine their activities. These factors indicate the likelihood of the parties coordinating their behaviour in the market.

22 Certain types of agreement, for instance most R&D agreements or cooperation to set standards or improve environmental conditions, are less likely to include restrictions with respect to prices and output. If these types of agreements have negative effects at all these are likely to be on innovation or the variety of products. They may also give rise to foreclosure problems.

23 Other types of cooperation such as agreements on production or purchasing typically cause a certain degree of commonality in (total) costs. If this degree is significant, the parties may more easily coordinate market prices and output. A significant degree of commonality in costs can only be achieved under certain conditions: First, the area of cooperation, e.g. production and purchasing, has to account for a high proportion of the total costs in a given market. Secondly, the parties need to combine their activities in the area of cooperation to a significant extent. This is, for instance, the case, where they jointly manufacture or purchase an important intermediate product or a high proportion of their total output of a final product.

Agreements that do not fall under Article 81(1)

24 Some categories of agreements do not fall under Article 81(1) because of their very nature. This is normally true for cooperation that does not imply a coordination of the parties' competitive behaviour in the market such as
   – cooperation between non-competitors,
   – cooperation between competing companies that cannot independently carry out the project or activity covered by the cooperation,
   – cooperation concerning an activity which does not influence the relevant parameters of competition.
   These categories of cooperation could only come under Article 81(1) if they involve firms with significant market power[17] and are likely to cause foreclosure problems *vis-à-vis* third parties.

Agreements that almost always fall under Article 81(1)

25 Another category of agreements can be assessed from the outset as normally falling under Article 81(1). This concerns cooperation agreements that have the object to restrict competition by means of price fixing, output limitation or sharing of

---

17 Companies may have significant market power below the level of market dominance, which is the threshold for the application of Article 82.

markets or customers. These restrictions are considered to be the most harmful, because they directly interfere with the outcome of the competitive process. Price fixing and output limitation directly lead to customers paying higher prices or not receiving the desired quantities. The sharing of markets or customers reduces the choice available to customers and therefore also leads to higher prices or reduced output. It can therefore be presumed that these restrictions have negative market effects. They are therefore almost always prohibited.[18]

Agreements that may fall under Article 81(1)

26   Agreements that do not belong to the above-mentioned categories need further analysis in order to decide whether they fall under Article 81(1). The analysis has to include market-related criteria such as the market position of the parties and other structural factors.

Market power and market structure

27   The starting point for the analysis is the position of the parties in the markets affected by the cooperation. This determines whether or not they are likely to maintain, gain or increase market power through the cooperation, i.e. have the ability to cause negative market effects as to prices, output, innovation or the variety or quality of goods and services. To carry out this analysis the relevant market(s) have to be defined by using the methodology of the Commission's market definition notice.[19] Where specific types of markets are concerned such as purchasing or technology markets, these guidelines will provide additional guidance.

28   If the parties together have a low combined market share,[20] a restrictive effect of the cooperation is unlikely and no further analysis normally is required. If one of just two parties has only an insignificant market share and if it does not possess important resources, even a high combined market share normally cannot be seen

---

18 This does, however, exceptionally not apply to a production joint venture. It is inherent to the functioning of such a joint venture that decisions on output are taken jointly by the parties. If the joint venture also markets the jointly manufactured goods, then decisions on prices need to be taken jointly by the parties to such an agreement. In this case, the inclusion of provisions on prices or output does not automatically cause the agreement to fall under Article 81(1). The provisions on prices or output will have to be assessed together with the other effects of the joint venture on the market to determine the applicability of Article 81(1) (see paragraph 90).

19 See Commission Notice on the definition of the relevant market for the purposes of Community competition law (OJ C 372, 9.12.1997, p. 5).

20 Market shares should normally be calculated on the basis of the market sales value (see Article 6 of the R&D Block Exemption Regulation and Article 6 of the Specialisation Block Exemption Regulation). In determining the market share of a party in a given market, account must be taken of the undertakings which are connected to the parties (see point 2 of Article 2 of the R&D Block Exemption Regulation and point 2 of Article 2 of the Specialisation Block Exemption Regulation).

as indicating a restrictive effect on competition in the market.[21] Given the variety of cooperation types and the different effects they may cause in different market situations, it is impossible to give a general market share threshold above which sufficient market power for causing restrictive effects can be assumed.

29 In addition to the market position of the parties and the addition of market shares, the market concentration, i.e. the position and number of competitors, may have to be taken into account as an additional factor to assess the impact of the cooperation on market competition. As an indicator the Herfindahl-Hirshman Index ('HHI'), which sums up the squares of the individual market shares of all competitors,[22] can be used: With an HHI below 1000 the market concentration can be characterised as low, between 1000 and 1800 as moderate and above 1800 as high. Another possible indicator would be the leading firm concentration ratio, which sums up the individual market shares of the leading competitors.[23]

30 Depending on the market position of the parties and the concentration in the market, other factors such as the stability of market shares over time, entry barriers and the likelihood of market entry, the countervailing power of buyers/suppliers or the nature of the products (e.g. homogeneity, maturity) have to be considered as well. Where an impact on competition in innovation is likely and cannot be assessed adequately on the basis of existing markets, specific factors to analyse these impacts may have to be taken into account (see Chapter 2, R&D agreements).

(B) Treatment of specialisation and R&D agreements

The Commission has afforded special treatment to two categories of horizontal cooperation agreements, specialisation and R&D agreements. The Commission's approach to these agreements is based on the experience that the Commission has gained over the years - that these types of agreement do not present a serious threat to competition. The Commission has adopted block exemption Regulations in relation to these agreements: Regulation 2658/00 in relation to specialisation agreements and Regulation 2659/00 in relation to R&D. Both of these Regulations replace earlier block exemption Regulations, and are wider in scope than their predecessors, representing the economic approach the Commission now takes in relation to these types of agreement. However, notable differences between Regulation 2658/00 and 2659/00 do exist and these can be identified from reading their respective texts.

21 If there are more than two parties, then the collective share of all cooperating competitors has to be significantly greater than the share of the largest single participating competitor.
22 A market consisting of four firms with shares of 30%, 25%, 25% and 20%, has a HHI of 2550 (900+625+625+400) pre-cooperation. If the first two market leaders would cooperate, the HHI would change to 4050 (3025+625+400) post-cooperation. The HHI post-cooperation is relevant for the assessment of the possible market effects of a cooperation.
23 E.g. the three-firm concentration ratio CR3 is the sum of the market shares of the leading three competitors in a market.

In the following two sections, the block exemption Regulations are reproduced along with the relevant paragraphs from the *Guidelines* which deal with the Commission's treatment of R&D and specialisation agreements.

I Specialisation agreements

Regulation 2658/00 on the application of Article 81(3) of the Treaty to categories of specialisation agreements

THE COMMISSION OF THE EUROPEAN COMMUNITIES,

Having regard to the Treaty establishing the European Community,

Having regard to Council Regulation (EEC) No 2821/71 of 20 December 1971 on the application of Article 85(3) of the Treaty to categories of agreements, decisions and concerted practices,[1] as last amended by the Act of Accession of Austria, Finland and Sweden, and in particular Article 1(1)(c) thereof,

Having published a draft of this Regulation,[2]

Having consulted the Advisory Committee on Restrictive Practices and Dominant Positions,

Whereas:

(1)   Regulation (EEC) No 2821/71 empowers the Commission to apply Article 81(3) (formerly Article 85(3)) of the Treaty by regulation to certain categories of agreements, decisions and concerted practices falling within the scope of Article 81(1) which have as their object specialisation, including agreements necessary for achieving it.

(2)   Pursuant to Regulation (EEC) No 2821/71, in particular, the Commission has adopted Regulation (EEC) No 417/85 of 19 December 1984 on the application of Article 85(3) of the Treaty to categories of specialisation agreements,[3] as last amended by Regulation (EC) No 2236/97.[4] Regulation (EEC) No 417/85 expires on 31 December 2000.

(3)   A new regulation should meet the two requirements of ensuring effective protection of competition and providing adequate legal security for undertakings. The pursuit of these objectives should take account of the need to simplify administrative supervision and the legislative framework to as great an extent as possible. Below a certain level of market power it can, for the application of Article 81(3), in general be presumed that the positive effects of specialisation agreements will outweigh any negative effects on competition.

(4)   Regulation (EEC) No 2821/71 requires the exempting regulation of the Commission to define the categories of agreements, decisions and concerted practices to which

---

1   OJ L 285, 29.12.1971, p. 46.
2   OJ C 118, 27.4.2000, p. 3.
3   OJ L 53, 22.2.1985, p. 1.
4   OJ L 306, 11.11.1997, p. 12.

it applies, to specify the restrictions or clauses which may, or may not, appear in the agreements, decisions and concerted practices, and to specify the clauses which must be contained in the agreements, decisions and concerted practices or the other conditions which must be satisfied.

(5) It is appropriate to move away from the approach of listing exempted clauses and to place greater emphasis on defining the categories of agreements which are exempted up to a certain level of market power and on specifying the restrictions or clauses which are not to be contained in such agreements. This is consistent with an economics-based approach which assesses the impact of agreements on the relevant market.

(6) For the application of Article 81(3) by regulation, it is not necessary to define those agreements which are capable of falling within Article 81(1). In the individual assessment of agreements under Article 81(1), account has to be taken of several factors, and in particular the market structure on the relevant market.

(7) The benefit of the block exemption should be limited to those agreements for which it can be assumed with sufficient certainty that they satisfy the conditions of Article 81(3).

(8) Agreements on specialisation in production generally contribute to improving the production or distribution of goods, because the undertakings concerned can concentrate on the manufacture of certain products and thus operate more efficiently and supply the products more cheaply. Agreements on specialisation in the provision of services can also be said to generally give rise to similar improvements. It is likely that, given effective competition, consumers will receive a fair share of the resulting benefit.

(9) Such advantages can arise equally from agreements whereby one participant gives up the manufacture of certain products or provision of certain services in favour of another participant ('unilateral specialisation'), from agreements whereby each participant gives up the manufacture of certain products or provision of certain services in favour of another participant ('reciprocal specialisation') and from agreements whereby the participants undertake to jointly manufacture certain products or provide certain services ('joint production').

(10) As unilateral specialisation agreements between non-competitors may benefit from the block exemption provided by Commission Regulation (EC) No 2790/1999 of 22 December 1999 on the application of Article 81(3) of the Treaty to categories of vertical agreements and concerted practices,[1] the application of the present Regulation to unilateral specialisation agreements should be limited to agreements between competitors.

(11) All other agreements entered into between undertakings relating to the conditions under which they specialise in the production of goods and/or services should

1 OJ L 336, 29.12.1999, p. 21.

fall within the scope of this Regulation. The block exemption should also apply to provisions contained in specialisation agreements which do not constitute the primary object of such agreements, but are directly related to and necessary for their implementation, and to certain related purchasing and marketing arrangements.

(12)   To ensure that the benefits of specialisation will materialise without one party leaving the market downstream of production, unilateral and reciprocal specialisation agreements should only be covered by this Regulation where they provide for supply and purchase obligations. These obligations may, but do not have to, be of an exclusive nature.

(13)   It can be presumed that, where the participating undertakings' share of the relevant market does not exceed 20%, specialisation agreements as defined in this Regulation will, as a general rule, give rise to economic benefits in the form of economies of scale or scope or better production technologies, while allowing consumers a fair share of the resulting benefits.

(14)   This Regulation should not exempt agreements containing restrictions which are not indispensable to attain the positive effects mentioned above. In principle certain severe anti-competitive restraints relating to the fixing of prices charged to third parties, limitation of output or sales, and allocation of markets or customers should be excluded from the benefit of the block exemption established by this Regulation irrespective of the market share of the undertakings concerned.

(15)   The market share limitation, the non-exemption of certain agreements and the conditions provided for in this Regulation normally ensure that the agreements to which the block exemption applies do not enable the participating undertakings to eliminate competition in respect of a substantial part of the products or services in question.

(16)   In particular cases in which the agreements falling under this Regulation nevertheless have effects incompatible with Article 81(3) of the Treaty, the Commission may withdraw the benefit of the block exemption.

(17)   In order to facilitate the conclusion of specialisation agreements, which can have a bearing on the structure of the participating undertakings, the period of validity of this Regulation should be fixed at 10 years.

(18)   This Regulation is without prejudice to the application of Article 82 of the Treaty.

(19)   In accordance with the principle of the primacy of Community law, no measure taken pursuant to national laws on competition should prejudice the uniform application throughout the common market of the Community competition rules or the full effect of any measures adopted in implementation of those rules, including this Regulation.

[297]

HAS ADOPTED THIS REGULATION:

Article 1 Exemption

1   Pursuant to Article 81(3) of the Treaty and subject to the provisions of this Regulation, it is hereby declared that Article 81(1) shall not apply to the following agreements entered into between two or more undertakings (hereinafter referred to as 'the parties') which relate to the conditions under which those undertakings specialise in the production of products (hereinafter referred to as 'specialisation agreements'):

(a) unilateral specialisation agreements, by virtue of which one party agrees to cease production of certain products or to refrain from producing those products and to purchase them from a competing undertaking, while the competing undertaking agrees to produce and supply those products; or

(b) reciprocal specialisation agreements, by virtue of which two or more parties on a reciprocal basis agree to cease or refrain from producing certain but different products and to purchase these products from the other parties, who agree to supply them; or

(c) joint production agreements, by virtue of which two or more parties agree to produce certain products jointly.

This exemption shall apply to the extent that such specialisation agreements contain restrictions of competition falling within the scope of Article 81(1) of the Treaty.

2   The exemption provided for in paragraph 1 shall also apply to provisions contained in specialisation agreements, which do not constitute the primary object of such agreements, but are directly related to and necessary for their implementation, such as those concerning the assignment or use of intellectual property rights.

The first subparagraph does, however, not apply to provisions which have the same object as the restrictions of competition enumerated in Article 5(1).

Article 2 Definitions

For the purposes of this Regulation:

1   'Agreement' means an agreement, a decision of an association of undertakings or a concerted practice.

2   'Participating undertakings' means undertakings party to the agreement and their respective connected undertakings.

3   'Connected undertakings' means:

(a) undertakings in which a party to the agreement, directly or indirectly:

    (i) has the power to exercise more than half the voting rights, or

    (ii) has the power to appoint more than half the members of the supervisory board, board of management or bodies legally representing the undertaking, or

    (iii) has the right to manage the undertaking's affairs;

(b) undertakings which directly or indirectly have, over a party to the agreement, the rights or powers listed in (a);

(c) undertakings in which an undertaking referred to in (b) has, directly or indirectly, the rights or powers listed in (a);

(d) undertakings in which a party to the agreement together with one or more of the undertakings referred to in (a), (b) or (c), or in which two or more of the latter undertakings, jointly have the rights or powers listed in (a);

(e) undertakings in which the rights or the powers listed in (a) are jointly held by:

    (i) parties to the agreement or their respective connected undertakings referred to in (a) to (d), or

    (ii) one or more of the parties to the agreement or one or more of their connected undertakings referred to in (a) to (d) and one or more third parties.

4   'Product' means a good and/or a service, including both intermediary goods and/or services and final goods and/or services, with the exception of distribution and rental services.

5   'Production' means the manufacture of goods or the provision of services and includes production by way of subcontracting.

6   'Relevant market' means the relevant product and geographic market(s) to which the products, which are the subject matter of a specialisation agreement, belong.

7   'Competing undertaking' means an undertaking that is active on the relevant market (an actual competitor) or an undertaking that would, on realistic grounds, undertake the necessary additional investments or other necessary switching costs so that it could enter the relevant market in response to a small and permanent increase in relative prices (a potential competitor).

8   'Exclusive supply obligation' means an obligation not to supply a competing undertaking other than a party to the agreement with the product to which the specialisation agreement relates.

9   'Exclusive purchase obligation' means an obligation to purchase the product to which the specialisation agreement relates only from the party which agrees to supply it.

Article 3 Purchasing and marketing arrangements

The exemption provided for in Article 1 shall also apply where:

(a) the parties accept an exclusive purchase and/or exclusive supply obligation in the context of a unilateral or reciprocal specialisation agreement or a joint production agreement, or

(b) the parties do not sell the products which are the object of the specialisation agreement independently but provide for joint distribution or agree to appoint a third party distributor on an exclusive or non-exclusive basis in the context of a joint production agreement provided that the third party is not a competing undertaking.

Article 4 Market share threshold

The exemption provided for in Article 1 shall apply on condition that the combined market share of the participating undertakings does not exceed 20% of the relevant market.

Article 5 Agreements not covered by the exemption

1   The exemption provided for in Article 1 shall not apply to agreements which, directly or indirectly, in isolation or in combination with other factors under the control of the parties, have as their object:
(a) the fixing of prices when selling the products to third parties;
(b) the limitation of output or sales; or
(c) the allocation of markets or customers.

2   Paragraph 1 shall not apply to:
(a) provisions on the agreed amount of products in the context of unilateral or reciprocal specialisation agreements or the setting of the capacity and production volume of a production joint venture in the context of a joint production agreement;
(b) the setting of sales targets and the fixing of prices that a production joint venture charges to its immediate customers in the context of point (b) of Article 3.

Article 6 Application of the market share threshold

1   For the purposes of applying the market share threshold provided for in Article 4 the following rules shall apply:
(a) the market share shall be calculated on the basis of the market sales value; if market sales value data are not available, estimates based on other reliable market information, including market sales volumes, may be used to establish the market share of the undertaking concerned;
(b) the market share shall be calculated on the basis of data relating to the preceding calendar year;
(c) the market share held by the undertakings referred to in point 3(e) of Article 2 shall be apportioned equally to each undertaking having the rights or the powers listed in point 3(a) of Article 2.

2   If the market share referred to in Article 4 is initially not more than 20% but subsequently rises above this level without exceeding 25%, the exemption provided for in Article 1 shall continue to apply for a period of two consecutive calendar years following the year in which the 20% threshold was first exceeded.

3   If the market share referred to in Article 4 is initially not more than 20% but subsequently rises above 25%, the exemption provided for in Article 1 shall continue to apply for one calendar year following the year in which the level of 25% was first exceeded.

4   The benefit of paragraphs 2 and 3 may not be combined so as to exceed a period of two calendar years.

Article 7 Withdrawal

The Commission may withdraw the benefit of this Regulation, pursuant to Article 7 of Regulation (EEC) No 2821/71, where, either on its own initiative or at the request of a Member State or of a natural or legal person claiming a legitimate interest, it finds in a particular case that an agreement to which the exemption provided for in Article 1 applies nevertheless has effects which are incompatible with the conditions laid down in Article 81(3) of the Treaty, and in particular where:

(a) the agreement is not yielding significant results in terms of rationalisation or consumers are not receiving a fair share of the resulting benefit, or

(b) the products which are the subject of the specialisation are not subject in the common market or a substantial part thereof to effective competition from identical products or products considered by users to be equivalent in view of their characteristics, price and intended use.

Article 8 Transitional period

The prohibition laid down in Article 81(1) of the Treaty shall not apply during the period from 1 January 2001 to 30 June 2002 in respect of agreements already in force on 31 December 2000 which do not satisfy the conditions for exemption provided for in this Regulation but which satisfy the conditions for exemption provided for in Regulation (EEC) No 417/85.

Article 9 Period of validity

This Regulation shall enter into force on 1 January 2001.
It shall expire on 31 December 2010.

Guidelines on horizontal cooperation OJ (2001) C 3/2

Definition

78   Production agreements may vary in form and scope. They may take the form of joint production through a joint venture, i.e. a jointly controlled company that runs one or several production facilities, or can be carried out by means of specialisation or subcontracting agreements whereby one party agrees to carry out the production of a certain product.

79   Generally, one can distinguish three categories of production agreements: joint pro-
      duction agreements, whereby the parties agree to produce certain products jointly,
      (unilateral or reciprocal) specialisation agreements, whereby the parties agree uni-
      laterally or reciprocally to cease production of a product and to purchase it from
      the other party, and subcontracting agreements whereby one party (the 'contractor')
      entrusts to another party (the 'subcontractor') the production of a product.

...

Relevant markets

82   In order to assess the competitive relationship between the cooperating parties, the
      relevant product and geographic market(s) directly concerned by the cooperation
      (i.e. the market(s) to which products subject to the agreement belong) must first be
      defined. Secondly, a production agreement in one market may also affect the com-
      petitive behaviour of the parties in a market which is downstream or upstream or a
      neighbouring market closely related to the market directly concerned by the coop-
      eration[39] (so-called 'spill-over markets'). However, spill-over effects only occur if
      the cooperation in one market necessarily results in the coordination of competitive
      behaviour in another market, i.e. if the markets are linked by interdependencies,
      and if the parties are in a strong position on the spill-over market.

Assessment under Article 81(1)

Nature of the agreement
83   The main source of competition problems that may arise from production agree-
      ments is the coordination of the parties' competitive behaviour as suppliers. This
      type of competition problem arises where the cooperating parties are actual or po-
      tential competitors on at least one of these relevant market(s), i.e. on the markets
      directly concerned by the cooperation and/or on possible spill-over markets.

84   The fact that the parties are competitors does not automatically cause the coordi-
      nation of their behaviour. In addition, the parties normally need to cooperate with
      regard to a significant part of their activities in order to achieve a substantial de-
      gree of commonality of costs. The higher the degree of commonality of costs, the
      greater the potential for a limitation of price competition, especially in the case of
      homogenous products.

85   In addition to coordination concerns, production agreements may also create fore-
      closure problems and other negative effects towards third parties. They are not
      caused by a competitive relationship between the parties, but by a strong market
      position of at least one of the parties (e.g. on an upstream market for a key com-
      ponent, which enables the parties to raise the costs of their rivals in a downstream

39 As also referred to in Article 2(4) [and 2(5)] of the Merger Regulation.

market) in the context of a more vertical or complementary relationship between the cooperating parties. Therefore, the possibility of foreclosure mainly needs to be examined in the case of joint production of an important component and of subcontracting agreements (see below).

Agreements that do not fall under Article 81(1)

86 Unless foreclosure problems arise, production agreements between non-competitors are not normally caught by Article 81(1). This is also true for agreements whereby inputs or components which have so far been manufactured for own consumption (captive production) are purchased from a third party by way of subcontracting or unilateral specialisation, unless there are indications that the company which so far has only produced for own consumption could have entered the merchant market for sales to third parties without incurring significant additional costs or risks in response to small, permanent changes in relative market prices.

87 Even production agreements between competitors do not necessarily come under Article 81(1). First, cooperation between firms which compete on markets closely related to the market directly concerned by the cooperation, cannot be defined as restricting competition, if the cooperation is the only commercially justifiable possible way to enter a new market, to launch a new product or service or to carry out a specific project.

88 Secondly, an effect on the parties' competitive behaviour as market suppliers is highly unlikely if the parties have a small proportion of their total costs in common. For instance, a low degree of commonality in total costs can be assumed where two or more companies agree on specialisation/joint production of an intermediate product which only accounts for a small proportion of the production costs of the final product and, consequently, the total costs. The same applies to a subcontracting agreement between competitors where the input which one competitor purchases from another only accounts for a small proportion of the production costs of the final product. A low degree of commonality of total costs can also be assumed where the parties jointly manufacture a final product, but only a small proportion as compared to their total output of the final product. Even if a significant proportion is jointly manufactured, the degree of commonality of total costs may nevertheless be low or moderate, if the cooperation concerns heterogeneous products which require costly marketing.

. . .

Agreements that almost always fall under Article 81(1)

90 Agreements which fix the prices for market supplies of the parties, limit output or share markets or customer groups have the object of restricting competition and

almost always fall under Article 81(1). This does, however, not apply to cases

- where the parties agree on the output directly concerned by the production agreement (e.g. the capacity and production volume of a joint venture or the agreed amount of outsourced products), or
- where a production joint venture that also carries out the distribution of the manufactured products sets the sales prices for these products, provided that the price fixing by the joint venture is the effect of integrating the various functions.[41]

In both scenarios the agreement on output or prices will not be assessed separately, but in light of the overall effects of the joint venture on the market in order to determine the applicability of Article 81(1).

Agreements that may fall under Article 81(1)

91   Production agreements that cannot be characterised as clearly restrictive or non-restrictive on the basis of the above factors may fall under Article 81(1) and have to be analysed in their economic context. This applies to cooperation agreements between competitors which create a significant degree of commonality of costs, but do not involve hard core restrictions as described above.

Market power and market structures

92   The starting point for the analysis is the position of the parties in the market(s) concerned. This is due to the fact that without market power the parties to a production agreement do not have an incentive to coordinate their competitive behaviour as suppliers. Secondly, there is no effect on competition in the market without market power of the parties, even if the parties would coordinate their behaviour.

93   There is no absolute market share threshold which indicates that a production agreement creates some degree of market power and thus falls under Article 81(1). However, agreements concerning unilateral or reciprocal specialisation as well as joint production are block exempted provided that they are concluded between parties with a combined market share not exceeding 20% in the relevant market(s) and that the other conditions for the application of the Specialisation block exemption Regulation are fulfilled. Therefore, for agreements covered by the block exemption, restrictive effects only have to be analysed if the parties combined market share exceeds 20%.

94   Agreements which are not covered by the block exemption Regulation require a more detailed analysis. The starting point is the market position of the parties. This

---

41 A production joint venture which also carries out joint distribution is, however, in most of the cases a full-function joint venture.

will normally be followed by the concentration ratio and the number of players as well as by other factors as described in Chapter 1.

95   Usually the analysis will only involve the relevant market(s) with which the cooperation is directly concerned. Under certain circumstances, e.g. if the parties have a very strong combined position on up- or downstream markets or on markets otherwise closely related to the markets with which the cooperation is directly concerned, these spill-over markets may however have to be analysed as well. This applies in particular to cooperation in upstream markets by firms which also enjoy a strong combined market position further downstream. Similarly, problems of foreclosure may need to be examined if the parties individually have a strong position as either suppliers or buyers of an input.

Market position of the parties, concentration ratio, number of players and other structural factors

96   If the parties' combined market share is larger than 20%, the likely impact of the production agreement on the market must be assessed. In this respect market concentration as well as market shares will be a significant factor. The higher the combined market share of the parties, the higher the concentration in the market concerned. However, a moderately higher market share than allowed for in the block exemption does not necessarily imply a high concentration ratio. Far instance, a combined market share of the parties of slightly more than 20% may occur in a market with a moderate concentration (HHI below 1800). In such a scenario a restrictive effect is unlikely. In a more concentrated market, however, a market share of more than 20% may, alongside other elements, lead to a restriction of competition. The picture may nevertheless change, if the market is very dynamic with new participants entering the market and market positions changing frequently.

97   For joint production, network effects, i.e. links between a significant number of competitors, can also play an important role. In a concentrated market the creation of an additional link may tip the balance and make collusion in this market likely, even if the parties have a significant, but still moderate, combined market share.

98   Under specific circumstances a cooperation between potential competitors may also raise competition concerns. This is, however, limited to cases where a strong player in one market cooperates with a realistic potential entrant, for instance, with a strong supplier of the same product or service in a neighbouring geographic market. The reduction of potential competition creates particular problems if actual competition is already weak and threat of entry is a major source of competition.

[305]

Learning Resources
Centre

Cooperation in upstream markets

99 Joint production of an important component or other input to the parties' final product can cause negative market effects under certain circumstances:

 – Foreclosure problems ... provided that the parties have a strong position on the relevant input market (non-captive use) and that switching between captive and non-captive use would not occur in the presence of a small but permanent relative price increase for the product in question.

 – Spill-over effects ... provided that the input is an important component of costs and that the parties have a strong position in the downstream market for the final product.

...

Specialisation agreements

101 Reciprocal specialisation agreements with market shares beyond the threshold of the block exemption will almost always fall under Article 81(1) and have to be examined carefully because of the risk of market partitioning.

Assessment under Article 81(3)

Economic benefits

102 Most common types of production agreements can be assumed to cause some economic benefits in the form of economies of scale or scope or better production technologies unless they are an instrument for price fixing, output restriction or market and customer allocation. Under these conditions it appears reasonable to provide for the exemption of such agreements which result in a restriction of competition up to a market share threshold below which it can, for the application of Article 81(3), in general, be presumed that the positive effects of production agreements will outweigh any negative effects on competition. Therefore, agreements concerning unilateral or reciprocal specialisation as well as joint production are block exempted (Specialisation block exemption Regulation) provided that they do not contain hard core restrictions (see Article 5) and that they are concluded between parties with a combined market share not exceeding 20% in the relevant market(s).

103 For those agreements not covered by the block exemption the parties have to demonstrate improvements of production or other efficiencies. Efficiencies that only benefit the parties or cost savings that are caused by output reduction or market allocation cannot be taken into account.

Indispensability

104 Restrictions that go beyond what is necessary to achieve the economic benefits described above will not be accepted. For instance, parties should not be restricted in their competitive behaviour on output outside the cooperation.

No elimination of competition

105 No exemption will be possible, if the parties are afforded the possibility of eliminating competition in respect of a substantial part of the products in question. Where as a consequence of a production agreement an undertaking is dominant or becoming dominant, such an agreement which produces anti-competitive effects in the meaning of Article 81 can in principle not be exempted. This has to be analysed on the relevant market to which the products subject to the cooperation belong and on possible spill-over markets.

II Research and development agreements

Regulation 2659/00 on the application of Article 81(3) of the Treaty to categories of research and development agreements

THE COMMISSION OF THE EUROPEAN COMMUNITIES,
Having regard to the Treaty establishing the European Community,
Having regard to Council Regulation (EEC) No 2821/71 of 20 December 1971 on application of Article 85(3) of the Treaty to categories of agreements, decisions and concerted practices,[1] as last amended by the Act of Accession of Austria, Finland and Sweden, and in particular Article 1(1)(b) thereof,
Having published a draft of this Regulation,[2]
Having consulted the Advisory Committee on Restrictive Practices and Dominant Positions,

Whereas:
(1) Regulation (EEC) No 2821/71 empowers the Commission to apply Article 81(3) (formerly Article 85(3)) of the Treaty by regulation to certain categories of agreements, decisions and concerted practices falling within the scope of Article 81(1) which have as their object the research and development of products or processes up to the stage of industrial application, and exploitation of the results, including provisions regarding intellectual property rights.

(2) Article 163(2) of the Treaty calls upon the Community to encourage undertakings, including small and medium-sized undertakings, in their research and technological development activities of high quality, and to support their efforts to cooperate with one another. Pursuant to Council Decision 1999/65/EC of 22 December 1998 concerning the rules for the participation of undertakings, research centres and universities and for the dissemination of research results for the implementation of the fifth framework programme of the European Community (1998-2002)[3] and Commission Regulation (EC) No 996/1999[4] on the implementation of Decision

1 OJ L 285, 29.12.1971, p. 46.
2 OJ C 118, 27.4.2000, p. 3.
3 OJ L 26, 1.2.1999, p. 46.
4 OJ L 53, 22.2.1985, p. 5.

1999/65/EC, indirect research and technological development (RTD) actions supported under the fifth framework programme of the Community are required to be carried out cooperatively.

(3)   Agreements on the joint execution of research work or the joint development of the results of the research, up to but not including the stage of industrial application, generally do not fall within the scope of Article 81(1) of the Treaty. In certain circumstances, however, such as where the parties agree not to carry out other research and development in the same field, thereby forgoing the opportunity of gaining competitive advantages over the other parties, such agreements may fall within Article 81(1) and should therefore be included within the scope of this Regulation.

(4)   Pursuant to Regulation (EEC) No 2821/71, the Commission has, in particular, adopted Regulation (EEC) No 418/85 of 19 December 1984 on the application of Article 85(3) of the Treaty to categories of research and development agreements,[5] as last amended by Regulation (EC) No 2236/97.[6] Regulation (EEC) No 418/85 expires on 31 December 2000.

(5)   A new regulation should meet the two requirements of ensuring effective protection of competition and providing adequate legal security for undertakings. The pursuit of these objectives should take account of the need to simplify administrative supervision and the legislative framework to as great an extent possible. Below a certain level of market power it can, for the application of Article 81(3), in general be presumed that the positive effects of research and development agreements will outweigh any negative effects on competition.

(6)   Regulation (EEC) No 2821/71 requires the exempting regulation of the Commission to define the categories of agreements, decisions and concerted practices to which it applies, to specify the restrictions or clauses which may, or may not, appear in the agreements, decisions and concerted practices, and to specify the clauses which must be contained in the agreements, decisions and concerted practices or the other conditions which must be satisfied.

(7)   It is appropriate to move away from the approach of listing exempted clauses and to place greater emphasis on defining the categories of agreements which are exempted up to a certain level of market power and on specifying the restrictions or clauses which are not to be contained in such agreements. This is consistent with an economics based approach which assesses the impact of agreements on the relevant market.

(8)   For the application of Article 81(3) by regulation, it is not necessary to define those agreements which are capable of falling within Article 81(1). In the individual

5 OJ L 122, 12.5.1999, p. 9.
6 OJ L 306, 11.11.1997, p. 12.

assessment of agreements under Article 81(1), account has to be taken of several factors, and in particular the market structure on the relevant market.

(9) The benefit of the block exemption should be limited to those agreements for which it can be assumed with sufficient certainty that they satisfy the conditions of Article 81(3).

(10) Cooperation in research and development and in the exploitation of the results generally promotes technical and economic progress by increasing the dissemination of know-how between the parties and avoiding duplication of research and development work, by stimulating new advances through the exchange of complementary know-how, and by rationalising the manufacture of the products or application of the processes arising out of the research and development.

(11) The joint exploitation of results can be considered as the natural consequence of joint research and development. It can take different forms such as manufacture, the exploitation of intellectual property rights that substantially contribute to technical or economic progress, or the marketing of new products.

(12) Consumers can generally be expected to benefit from the increased volume and effectiveness of research and development through the introduction of new or improved products or services or the reduction of prices brought about by new or improved processes.

(13) In order to attain the benefits and objectives of joint research and development the benefit of this Regulation should also apply to provisions contained in research and development agreements which do not constitute the primary object of such agreements, but are directly related to and necessary for their implementation.

(14) In order to justify the exemption, the joint exploitation should relate to products or processes for which the use of the results of the research and development is decisive, and each of the parties is given the opportunity of exploiting any results that interest it. However, where academic bodies, research institutes or undertakings which supply research and development as a commercial service without normally being active in the exploitation of results participate in research and development, they may agree to use the results of research and development solely for the purpose of further research. Similarly, non-competitors may agree to limit their right to exploitation to one or more technical fields of application to facilitate cooperation between parties with complementary skills.

(15) The exemption granted under this Regulation should be limited to research and development agreements which do not afford the undertakings the possibility of eliminating competition in respect of a substantial part of the products or services in question. It is necessary to exclude from the block exemption agreements between competitors whose combined share of the market for products or services capable of being improved or replaced by the results of the research and development exceeds a certain level at the time the agreement is entered into.

(16)   In order to guarantee the maintenance of effective competition during joint exploitation of the results, provision should be made for the block exemption to cease to apply if the parties' combined share of the market for the products arising out of the joint research and development becomes too great. The exemption should continue to apply, irrespective of the parties' market shares, for a certain period after the commencement of joint exploitation, so as to await stabilisation of their market shares, particularly after the introduction of an entirely new product, and to guarantee a minimum period of return on the investments involved.

(17)   This Regulation should not exempt agreements containing restrictions which are not indispensable to attain the positive effects mentioned above. In principle certain severe anti-competitive restraints such as limitations on the freedom of parties to carry out research and development in a field unconnected to the agreement, the fixing of prices charged to third parties, limitations on output or sales, allocation of markets or customers, and limitations on effecting passive sales for the contract products in territories reserved for other parties should be excluded from the benefit of the block exemption established by this Regulation irrespective of the market share of the undertakings concerned.

(18)   The market share limitation, the non-exemption of certain agreements, and the conditions provided for in this Regulation normally ensure that the agreements to which the block exemption applies do not enable the participating undertakings to eliminate competition in respect of a substantial part of the products or services in question.

(19)   In particular cases in which the agreements falling under this Regulation nevertheless have effects incompatible with Article 81(3) of the Treaty, the Commission may withdraw the benefit of the block exemption.

(20)   Agreements between undertakings which are not competing manufacturers of products capable of being improved or replaced by the results of the research and development will only eliminate effective competition in research and development in exceptional circumstances. It is therefore appropriate to enable such agreements to benefit from the block exemption irrespective of market share and to address such exceptional cases by way of withdrawal of its benefit.

(21)   As research and development agreements are often of a long-term nature, especially where the cooperation extends to the exploitation of the results, the period of validity of this Regulation should be fixed at 10 years.

(22)   This Regulation is without prejudice to the application of Article 82 of the Treaty.

(23)   In accordance with the principle of the primacy of Community law, no measure taken pursuant to national laws on competition should prejudice the uniform application throughout the common market of the Community competition rules or the full effect of any measures adopted in implementation of those rules, including this Regulation.

HAS ADOPTED THIS REGULATION:

Article 1 Exemption

1   Pursuant to Article 81(3) of the Treaty and subject to the provisions of this Regulation, it is hereby declared that Article 81(1) shall not apply to agreements entered into between two or more undertakings (hereinafter referred to as 'the parties') which relate to the conditions under which those undertakings pursue:
(a) joint research and development of products or processes and joint exploitation of the results of that research and development;
(b) joint exploitation of the results of research and development of products or processes jointly carried out pursuant to a prior agreement between the same parties; or
(c) joint research and development of products or processes excluding joint exploitation of the results.
This exemption shall apply to the extent that such agreements (hereinafter referred to as 'research and development agreements') contain restrictions of competition falling within the scope of Article 81(1).

2   The exemption provided for in paragraph 1 shall also apply to provisions contained in research and development agreements which do not constitute the primary object of such agreements, but are directly related to and necessary for their implementation, such as an obligation not to carry out, independently or together with third parties, research and development in the field to which the agreement relates or in a closely connected field during the execution of the agreement.
The first subparagraph does, however, not apply to provisions which have the same object as the restrictions of competition enumerated in Article 5(1).

Article 2 Definitions

For the purposes of this Regulation:

1   'agreement' means an agreement, a decision of an association of undertakings or a concerted practice;

2   'participating undertakings' means undertakings party to the research and development agreement and their respective connected undertakings;

3   'connected undertakings' means:
(a) undertakings in which a party to the research and development agreement, directly or indirectly:
    (i)   has the power to exercise more than half the voting rights,
    (ii) has the power to appoint more than half the members of the supervisory board, board of management or bodies legally representing the undertaking, or
    (iii) has the right to manage the undertaking's affairs;

[311]

(b) undertakings which directly or indirectly have, over a party to the research and development agreement, the rights or powers listed in (a);

(c) undertakings in which an undertaking referred to in (b) has, directly or indirectly, the rights or powers listed in (a);

(d) undertakings in which a party to the research and development agreement together with one or more of the undertakings referred to in (a), (b) or (c), or in which two or more of the latter undertakings, jointly have the rights or powers listed in (a);

(e) undertakings in which the rights or the powers listed in (a) are jointly held by:

    (i) parties to the research and development agreement or their respective connected undertakings referred to in (a) to (d), or

    (ii) one or more of the parties to the research and development agreement or one or more of their connected undertakings referred to in (a) to (d) and one or more third parties;

4   'research and development' means the acquisition of know-how relating to products or processes and the carrying out of theoretical analysis, systematic study or experimentation, including experimental production, technical testing of products or processes, the establishment of the necessary facilities and the obtaining of intellectual property rights for the results;

5   'product' means a good and/or a service, including both intermediary goods and/or services and final goods and/or services;

6   'contract process' means a technology or process arising out of the joint research and development;

7   'contract product' means a product arising out of the joint research and development or manufactured or provided applying the contract processes;

8   'exploitation of the results' means the production or distribution of the contract products or the application of the contract processes or the assignment or licensing of intellectual property rights or the communication of know-how required for such manufacture or application;

9   'intellectual property rights' includes industrial property-rights, copyright and neighbouring rights;

10   'know-how' means a package of non-patented practical information, resulting from experience and testing, which is secret, substantial and identified: in this context, 'secret' means that the know-how is not generally known or easily accessible; 'substantial' means that the know-how includes information which is indispensable for the manufacture of the contract products or the application of the contract processes; 'identified' means that the know-how is described in a sufficiently comprehensive manner so as to make it possible to verify that it fulfils the criteria of secrecy and substantiality;

11   research and development, or exploitation of the results, are carried out 'jointly' where the work involved is:
      (a) carried out by a joint team, organisation or undertaking,
      (b) jointly entrusted to a third party, or
      (c) allocated between the parties by way of specialisation in research, development, production or distribution;

12   'competing undertaking' means an undertaking that is supplying a product capable of being improved or replaced by the contract product (an actual competitor) or an undertaking that would, on realistic grounds, undertake the necessary additional investments or other necessary switching costs so that it could supply such a product in response to a small and permanent increase in relative prices (a potential competitor);

13   'relevant market for the contract products' means the relevant product and geographic market(s) to which the contract products belong.

Article 3 Conditions for exemption

1   The exemption provided for in Article 1 shall apply subject to the conditions set out in paragraphs 2 to 5.

2   All the parties must have access to the results of the joint research and development for the purposes of further research or exploitation. However, research institutes, academic bodies, or undertakings which supply research and development as a commercial service without normally being active in the exploitation of results may agree to confine their use of the results for the purposes of further research.

3   Without prejudice to paragraph 2, where the research and development agreement provides only for joint research and development, each party must be free independently to exploit the results of the joint research and development and any pre-existing know-how necessary for the purposes of such exploitation. Such right to exploitation may be limited to one or more technical fields of application, where the parties are not competing undertakings at the time the research and development agreement is entered into.

4   Any joint exploitation must relate to results which are protected by intellectual property rights or constitute know-how, which substantially contribute to technical or economic progress and the results must be decisive for the manufacture of the contract products or the application of the contract processes.

5   Undertakings charged with manufacture by way of specialisation in production must be required to fulfil orders for supplies from all the parties, except where the research and development agreement also provides for joint distribution.

Article 4 Market share threshold and duration of exemption

1   Where the participating undertakings are not competing undertakings, the exemption provided for in Article 1 shall apply for the duration of the research and development. Where the results are jointly exploited, the exemption shall continue to apply for seven years from the time the contract products are first put on the market within the common market.

2   Where two or more of the participating undertakings are competing undertakings, the exemption provided for in Article 1 shall apply for the period referred to in paragraph 1 only if, at the time the research and development agreement is entered into, the combined market share of the participating undertakings does not exceed 25% of the relevant market for the products capable of being improved or replaced by the contract products.

3   After the end of the period referred to in paragraph 1, the exemption shall continue to apply as long as the combined market share of the participating undertakings does not exceed 25% of the relevant market for the contract products.

Article 5 Agreements not covered by the exemption

1   The exemption provided for in Article 1 shall not apply to research and development agreements which, directly or indirectly, in isolation or in combination with other factors under the control of the parties, have as their object:
   (a) the restriction of the freedom of the participating undertakings to carry out research and development independently or in cooperation with third parties in a field unconnected with that to which the research and development relates or, after its completion, in the field to which it relates or in a connected field;
   (b) the prohibition to challenge after completion of the research and development the validity of intellectual property rights which the parties hold in the common market and which are relevant to the research and development or, after the expiry of the research and development agreement, the validity of intellectual property rights which the parties hold in the common market and which protect the results of the research and development, without prejudice to the possibility to provide for termination of the research and development agreement in the event of one of the parties challenging the validity of such intellectual property rights;
   (c) the limitation of output or sales;
   (d) the fixing of prices when selling the contract product to third parties;
   (e) the restriction of the customers that the participating undertakings may serve, after the end of seven years from the time the contract products are first put on the market within the common market;
   (f) the prohibition to make passive sales of the contract products in territories reserved for other parties;

(g) the prohibition to put the contract products on the market or to pursue an active sales policy for them in territories within the common market that are reserved for other parties after the end of seven years from the time the contract products are first put on the market within the common market;

(h) the requirement not to grant licences to third parties to manufacture the contract products or to apply the contract processes where the exploitation by at least one of the parties of the results of the joint research and development is not provided for or does not take place;

(i) the requirement to refuse to meet demand from users or resellers in their respective territories who would market the contract products in other territories within the common market; or

(j) the requirement to make it difficult for users or resellers to obtain the contract products from other resellers within the common market, and in particular to exercise intellectual property rights or take measures so as to prevent users or resellers from obtaining, or from putting on the market within the common market, products which have been lawfully put on the market within the Community by another party or with its consent.

2   Paragraph 1 shall not apply to:

(a) the setting of production targets where the exploitation of the results includes the joint production of the contract products;

(b) the setting of sales targets and the fixing of prices charged to immediate customers where the exploitation of the results includes the joint distribution of the contract products.

Article 6 Application of the market share threshold

1   For the purposes of applying the market share threshold provided for in Article 4 the following rules shall apply:

(a) the market share shall be calculated on the basis of the market sales value; if market sales value data are not available, estimates based on other reliable market information, including market sales volumes, may be used to establish the market share of the undertaking concerned;

(b) the market share shall be calculated on the basis of data relating to the preceding calendar year;

(c) the market share held by the undertakings referred to in point 3(e) of Article 2 shall be apportioned equally to each undertaking having the rights or the powers listed in point 3(a) of Article 2.

2   If the market share referred to in Article 4(3) is initially not more than 25% but subsequently rises above this level without exceeding 30%, the exemption provided for in Article 1 shall continue to apply for a period of two consecutive calendar years following the year in which the 25% threshold was first exceeded.

[315]

3   If the market share referred to in Article 4(3) is initially not more than 25% but subsequently rises above 30%, the exemption provided for in Article 1 shall continue to apply for one calendar year following the year in which the level of 30% was first exceeded.

4   The benefit of paragraphs 2 and 3 may not be combined so as to exceed a period of two calendar years.

Article 7 Withdrawal

The Commission may withdraw the benefit of this Regulation, pursuant to Article 7 of Regulation (EEC) No 2821/71, where, either on its own initiative or at the request of a Member State or of a natural or legal person claiming a legitimate interest, it finds in a particular case that a research and development agreement to which the exemption provided for in Article 1 applies nevertheless has effects which are incompatible with the conditions laid down in Article 81(3) of the Treaty, and in particular where:

(a) the existence of the research and development agreement substantially restricts the scope for third parties to carry-out research and development in the relevant field because of the limited research capacity available elsewhere;

(b) because of the particular structure of supply, the existence of the research and development agreement substantially restricts the access of third parties to the market for the contract products;

(c) without any objectively valid reason, the parties do not exploit the results of the joint research and development;

(d) the contract products are not subject in the whole or a substantial part of the common market to effective competition from identical products or products considered by users as equivalent in view of their characteristics, price and intended use;

(e) the existence of the research and development agreement would eliminate effective competition in research and development on a particular market.

Article 8 Transitional period

The prohibition laid down in Article 81(1) of the Treaty shall not apply during the period from 1 January 2001 to 30 June 2002 in respect of agreements already in force on 31 December 2000 which do not satisfy the conditions for exemption provided for in this Regulation but which satisfy the conditions for exemption provided for in Regulation (EEC) No 418/85.

Article 9 Period of validity

This Regulation shall enter into force on 1 January 2001.
It shall expire on 31 December 2010.

Guidelines on horizontal cooperation OJ (2001) C 3/2

39   R&D agreements may vary in form and scope. They range from outsourcing certain R&D activities to the joint improvement of existing technologies or to a cooperation concerning the research, development and marketing of completely new products. They may take the form of a cooperation agreement or of a jointly controlled company. This chapter applies to all forms of R&D agreements including related agreements concerning the production or commercialisation of the R&D results provided that the cooperation's centre of gravity lies in R&D, with the exception of mergers and joint ventures falling under the Merger Regulation.

40   Cooperation in R&D may reduce duplicative, unnecessary costs, lead to significant cross fertilisation of ideas and experience and thus result in products and technologies being developed more rapidly than would otherwise be the case. As a general rule, R&D cooperation tends to increase overall R&D activities.

41   Small and medium-sized enterprises (SMEs) form a dynamic and heterogeneous community which is confronted by many challenges, including the growing demands of larger companies for which they often work as sub-contractors. In R&D intensive sectors, fast growing SMEs, more often called 'start-up companies', also aim at becoming a leader in fast-developing market segments. To meet those challenges and to remain competitive, SMEs need constantly to innovate. Through R&D cooperation there is a likelihood that overall R&D by SMEs will increase and that they will be able to compete more vigorously with stronger market players.

42   Under certain circumstances, however, R&D agreements may cause competition problems such as restrictive effects on prices, output, innovation, or variety or quality of products.

Relevant markets

43   The key to defining the relevant market when assessing the effects of an R&D agreement is to identify those products, technologies or R&D efforts, that will act as a competitive constraint on the parties. At one end of the spectrum of possible situations, the innovation may result in a product (or technology) which competes in an existing product (or technology) market. This is the case with R&D directed towards slight improvements or variations, such as new models of certain products. Here, possible effects concern the market for existing products. At the other end, innovation may result in an entirely new product which creates its own new market (e.g. of the spectrum of a new vaccine for a previously incurable disease). In such a case, existing markets are only relevant if they are somehow related to the innovation in question. Consequently, and if possible, the effects of the cooperation on innovation have to be assessed. However, most of the cases probably concern situations in between these two extremes, i.e. situations in which innovation efforts may create products (or technology) which, over time, replace existing ones (e.g. CDs

which have replaced records). A careful analysis of those situations may have to cover both existing markets and the impact of the agreement on innovation.

Existing markets

Product markets

44   When the cooperation concerns R&D for the improvement of existing products, these existing products including its close substitutes form the relevant market concerned by the cooperation.[24]

45   If the R&D efforts aim at a significant change of an existing product or even at a new product replacing existing ones, substitution with the existing products may be imperfect or long-term. Consequently, the old and the potentially emerging new products are not likely to belong to the same relevant market. The market for existing products may nevertheless be concerned, if the pooling of R&D efforts is likely to result in the coordination of the parties' behaviour as suppliers of existing products. An exploitation of power in the existing market, however, is only possible if the parties together have a strong position with respect to both the existing product market and R&D efforts.

46   If the R&D concerns an important component of a final product, not only the market for this component may be relevant for the assessment, but the existing market for the final product as well. For instance, if car manufacturers cooperate in R&D related to a new type of engine, the car market may be affected by this R&D cooperation. The market for final products, however, is only relevant for the assessment, if the component at which the R&D is aimed, is technically or economically a key element of these final products and if the parties to the R&D agreement are important competitors with respect to the final products.

Technology markets

47   R&D cooperation may not only concern products but also technology. When rights to intellectual property are marketed separately from the products concerned to which they relate, the relevant technology market has to be defined as well. Technology markets consist of the intellectual property that is licensed and its close substitutes, i.e. other technologies which customers could use as a substitute.

48   The methodology for defining technology markets follows the same principles as product market definition.[25] Starting from the technology which is marketed by the parties, one needs to identify those other technologies to which customers could switch in response to a small but permanent increase in relative prices. Once these

24 For market definition see the Commission Notice on the definition of the relevant market.
25 See Commission Notice on the definition of the relevant market; see also, for example, Commission Decision 94/811/EC of 8 June 1994 in Case No IV/M269 – *Shell/Montecatini* (OJ L 332, 22.12.1994, p. 48).

technologies are identified, one can calculate market shares by dividing the licensing income generated by the parties with the total licensing income of all sellers of substitutable technologies.

49   The parties' position in the market for existing technology is a relevant assessment criterion where the R&D cooperation concerns the significant improvement of existing technology or a new technology that is likely to replace the existing technology. The parties' market share can however only be taken as a starting point for this analysis. In technology markets, particular emphasis must be put on potential competition. If companies, who do not currently license their technology, are potential entrants on the technology market they could constrain the ability of the parties to raise the price for their technology.

Competition in innovation (R&D efforts)

50   R&D cooperation may not – or not only – affect competition in existing markets, but competition in innovation. This is the case where cooperation concerns the development of new products/technology which either may – if emerging – one day replace existing ones or which are being developed for a new intended use and will therefore not replace existing products but create a completely new demand. The effects on competition in innovation are important in these situations, but can in some cases not be sufficiently assessed by analysing actual or potential competition in existing product/technology markets. In this respect, two scenarios can be distinguished, depending on the nature of the innovative process in a given industry.

51   In the first scenario, which is for instance present in the pharmaceutical industry, the process of innovation is structured in such a way that it is possible at an early stage to identify R&D poles. R&D poles are R&D efforts directed towards a certain new product or technology, and the substitutes for that R&D, i.e. R&D aimed at developing substitutable products or technology for those developed by the cooperation and having comparable access to resources as well as a similar timing. In this case, it can be analysed if after the agreement there will be a sufficient number of R&D poles left. The starting point of the analysis is the R&D of the parties. Then credible competing R&D poles have to be identified. In order to assess the credibility of competing poles, the following aspects have to be taken into account: the nature, scope and size of possible other R&D efforts, their access to financial and human resources, know-how/patents, or other specialised assets as well as their timing and their capability to exploit possible results. An R&D pole is not a credible competitor if it can not be regarded as a close substitute for the parties' R&D effort from the viewpoint of, for instance, access to resources or timing.

52   In the second scenario, the innovative efforts in an industry are not clearly structured so as to allow the identification of R&D poles. In this situation, the Commission would, absent exceptional circumstances, not try to assess the impact of a given

[319]

R&D cooperation on innovation, but would limit its assessment to product and/or technology markets which are related to the R&D cooperation in question.

Calculation of market shares

53   The calculation of market shares, both for the purposes of the R&D block exemption Regulation and of these guidelines, has to reflect the distinction between existing markets and competition in innovation. At the beginning of a cooperation the reference point is the market for products capable of being improved or replaced by the products under development. If the R&D agreement only aims at improving or refining existing products, this market includes the products directly concerned by the R&D. Market shares can thus be calculated on the basis of the sales value of the existing products. If the R&D aims at replacing an existing product, the new product will, if successful, become a substitute to the existing products. To assess the competitive position of the parties, it is again possible to calculate market shares on the basis of the sales value of the existing products. Consequently, the R&D block exemption Regulation bases its exemption of these situations on the market share in 'the relevant market for the products capable of being improved or replaced by the contract products'. For an automatic exemption, this market share may not exceed 25%.[26]

54   If the R&D aims at developing a product which will create a complete new demand, market shares based on sales cannot be calculated. Only an analysis of the effects of the agreement on competition in innovation is possible. Consequently, the R&D block exemption Regulation exempts these agreements irrespective of market share for a period of seven years after the product is first put on the market.[27] However, the benefit of the block exemption may be withdrawn if the agreement would eliminate effective competition in innovation.[28] After the seven year period, market shares based on sales value can be calculated, and the market share threshold of 25% applies.[29]

Assessment under Article 81(1)

Nature of the agreement

Agreements that do not fall under Article 81(1)
55   Most R&D agreements do not fall under Article 81(1). First, this can be said for agreements relating to cooperation in R&D at a rather theoretical stage, far removed from the exploitation of possible results.

---

26 Article 4(2) of the R&D Block Exemption Regulation.
27 Article 4(1) of the R&D Block Exemption Regulation.
28 Article 7(e) of the R&D Block Exemption Regulation.
29 Article 4(3) of the R&D Block Exemption Regulation.

56   Moreover, R&D cooperation between non-competitors does generally not restrict competition.[30] The competitive relationship between the parties has to be analysed in the context of affected existing markets and/or innovation. If the parties are not able to carry out the necessary R&D independently, there is no competition to be restricted. This can apply, for example, to firms bringing together complementary skills, technologies and other resources. The issue of potential competition has to be assessed on a realistic basis. For instance, parties cannot be defined as potential competitors simply because the cooperation enables them to carry out the R&D activities. The decisive question is whether each party independently has the necessary means as to assets, know-how and other resources.

57   R&D cooperation by means of outsourcing of previously captive R&D is often carried out by specialised companies, research institutes or academic bodies which are not active in the exploitation of the results. Typically such agreements are combined with a transfer of know-how and/or an exclusive supply clause concerning possible results. Due to the complementary nature of the cooperating parties in these scenarios, Article 81(1) does not apply.

58   R&D cooperation which does not include the joint exploitation of possible results by means of licensing, production and/or marketing rarely falls under Article 81(1). Those 'pure' R&D agreements can only cause a competition problem, if effective competition with respect to innovation is significantly reduced.

Agreements that almost always fall under Article 81(1)
59   If the true object of an agreement is not R&D but the creation of a disguised cartel, i.e. otherwise prohibited price fixing, output limitation or market allocation, it falls under Article 81(1). However, an R&D agreement which includes the joint exploitation of possible future results is not necessarily restrictive of competition.

Agreements that may fall under Article 81(1)
60   R&D agreements that cannot be assessed from the outset as clearly non-restrictive may fall under Article 81(1) and have to be analysed in their economic context. This applies to R&D cooperation which is set up at a stage rather close to the market launch and which is agreed between companies that are competitors on either existing product/technology markets or on innovation markets.

Market power and market structures
61   R&D cooperation can cause negative market effects in three respects: First, it may restrict innovation, secondly it may cause the coordination of the parties' behaviour

---

30 An R&D cooperation between non-competitors can however produce foreclosure effects under Article 81(1) if it relates to an exclusive exploitation of results and if it is concluded between firms, one of which has significant market power with respect to key technology.
...

in existing markets and thirdly, foreclosure problems may occur at the level of the exploitation of possible results. These types of negative market effects, however, are only likely to emerge when the parties to the cooperation have significant power on the existing markets and/or competition with respect to innovation is significantly reduced. Without market power there is no incentive to coordinate behaviour on existing markets or to reduce or slow down innovation. A foreclosure problem may only arise in the context of cooperation involving at least one player with significant market power for a key technology and the exclusive exploitation of results.

62   There is no absolute market share threshold which indicates that an R&D agreement creates some degree of market power and thus falls under Article 81(1). However, R&D agreements are exempted provided that they are concluded between parties with a combined market share not exceeding 25% and that the other conditions for the application of the R&D Block Exemption Regulation are fulfilled. Therefore, for most R&D agreements, restrictive effects only have to be analysed if the parties' combined market share exceeds 25%.

63   Agreements falling outside the R&D Block Exemption Regulation due to a stronger market position of the parties do not necessarily restrict competition. However, the stronger the combined position of the parties on existing markets and/or the more competition in innovation is restricted, the more likely is the application of Article 81(1) and the assessment requires a more detailed analysis.

64   If the R&D is directed at the improvement or refinement of existing products/technology possible effects concern the relevant market(s) for these existing products/technology. Effects on prices, output and/or innovation in existing markets are, however, only likely if the parties together have a strong position, entry is difficult and few other innovation activities are identifiable. Furthermore, if the R&D only concerns a relatively minor input of a final product, effects as to competition in these final products are, if invariably, very limited. In general, a distinction has to be made between pure R&D agreements and more comprehensive cooperation involving different stages of the exploitation of results (i.e. licensing, production, marketing). As said above, pure R&D agreements rarely come under Article 81(1). This is in particular true for R&D directed towards a limited improvement of existing products/technology. If, in such a scenario, the R&D cooperation includes joint exploitation only by means of licensing, restrictive effects such as foreclosure problems are unlikely. If, however, joint production and/or marketing of the slightly improved products/technology are included, the cooperation has to be examined more closely. First, negative effects as to prices and output in existing markets are more likely if strong competitors are involved in such a situation. Secondly, the cooperation may come closer to a production agreement because the R&D activities may de facto not form the centre of gravity of such a collaboration.

65   If the R&D is directed at an entirely new product (or technology) which creates its own new market, price and output effects on existing markets are rather unlikely. The analysis has to focus on possible restrictions of innovation concerning, for

instance, the quality and variety of possible future products/technology or the speed of innovation. Those restrictive effects can arise where two or more of the few firms engaged in the development of such a new product, start to cooperate at a stage where they are each independently rather near to the launch of the product. In such a case, innovation may be restricted even by a pure R&D agreement. In general, however, R&D cooperation concerning entirely new products is pro-competitive. This principle does not change significantly if the joint exploitation of the results, even joint marketing, is involved. Indeed, the issue of joint exploitation in these situations is only relevant where foreclosure from key technologies plays a role. Those problems would, however, not arise where the parties grant licences to third parties.

66 Most R&D agreements will lie somewhere in between the two situations described above. They may therefore have effects on innovation as well as repercussions on existing markets. Consequently, both the existing market and the effect on innovation may be of relevance for the assessment with respect to the parties' combined positions, concentration ratios, number of players/ innovators and entry conditions. In some cases there can be restrictive price/output effects on existing markets and a negative impact on innovation by means of slowing down the speed of development. For instance, if significant competitors on an existing technology market cooperate to develop a new technology which may one day replace existing products, this cooperation is likely to have restrictive effects if the parties have significant market power on the existing market (which would give an incentive to exploit it), and if they also have a strong position with respect to R&D. A similar effect can occur, if the major player in an existing market cooperates with a much smaller or even potential competitor who is just about to emerge with a new product/technology which may endanger the incumbent's position.

67 Agreements may also fall outside the block exemption irrespective of the market power of the parties. This applies for instance to agreements which restrict access of a party to the results of the work because they do not, as a general rule, promote technical and economic progress by increasing the dissemination of technical knowledge between the parties.[32] The Block exemption provides for a specific exception to this general rule in the case of academic bodies, research Regulation institutes or specialised companies which provide R&D as a service and which are not active in the industrial exploitation of the results of research and development.[33] Nevertheless, it should be noted that agreements containing exclusive access rights may, where they fall under Article 81(1), meet the criteria for exemption under Article 81(3), particularly where exclusive access rights are economically indispensable in view of the market, risks and scale of the investment required to exploit the results of the research and development.

---

32 See Art. 3(2) of the R&D Block Exemption Regulation.
33 See Art. 3(2) of the R&D Block Exemption Regulation.

Assessment under Article 81(3)

Economic benefits

68   Most R&D agreements – with or without joint exploitation of possible results – bring about economic benefits by means of cost savings and cross fertilisation of ideas and experience, thus resulting in improved or new products and technologies being developed more rapidly than would otherwise be the case. Under these conditions it appears reasonable to provide for the exemption of such agreements which result in a restriction of competition up to a market share threshold below which it can, for the application of Article 81(3), in general, be presumed that the positive effects of research and development agreements will outweigh any negative effects on competition. Therefore, the R&D Block Exemption Regulation exempts those R&D agreements which fulfil certain conditions (see Article 3) and which do not include hardcore restrictions (see Article 5), provided that the combined market share of the parties in the affected existing market(s) does not exceed 25%.

69   If considerable market power is created or increased by the cooperation, the parties have to demonstrate significant benefits in carrying out R&D, a quicker launch of new products/technology or other efficiencies.

Indispensability

70   An R&D agreement cannot be exempted if it imposes restrictions that are not indispensable to the attainment of the above-mentioned benefits. The individual clauses listed in Article 5 of the R&D block exemption Regulation will in most cases render an exemption impossible following an individual assessment too, and can therefore be regarded as a good indication of restrictions that are not indispensable to the cooperation.

No elimination of competition

71   No exemption will be possible, if the parties are afforded the possibility of eliminating competition in respect of a substantial part of the products (or technologies) in question. Where as a consequence of an R&D agreement an undertaking is dominant or becoming dominant either on an existing markets or with respect to innovation, such an agreement which produces anti-competitive effects in the meaning of Article 81 can in principle not be exempted. For innovation this is the case, for example, if the agreement combines the only two existing poles of research.

Time of the assessment and duration of the exemption

72   R&D agreements extending to the joint production and marketing of new products/technology require particular attention as to the time of the assessment.

73   At the beginning of an R&D cooperation, its success and factors such as the parties' future market position as well as the development of future product or technology

markets are often not known. Consequently, the assessment at the point in time when the cooperation is formed is limited to the (then) existing product or technology markets and/or innovation markets as described in this chapter. If, on the basis of this analysis, competition is not likely to be eliminated, the R&D agreement can benefit from an exemption. This will normally cover the duration of the R&D phase plus, in as far as the joint production and marketing of the possible results is concerned, an additional phase for a possible launch and market introduction. The reason for this additional exemption phase is that the first companies to reach the market with a new product/technology will often enjoy very high initial market shares and successful R&D is also often rewarded by intellectual property protection. A strong market position due to this 'first mover advantage' cannot normally be interpreted as elimination of competition. Therefore, the block exemption covers R&D agreements for an additional period of seven years (i.e. beyond the R&D phase) irrespective of whether or not the parties obtain with their new products/technology a high share within this period. This also applies to the individual assessment of cases falling outside the block exemption provided that the criteria of Article 81(3) as to the other aspects of the agreement are fulfilled. This does not exclude the possibility that a period of more than 7 years also meets the criteria of Article 81(3) if it can be shown to be the minimum period of time necessary to guarantee an adequate return on the investment involved.

74 If a new assessment of an R&D cooperation is made after that period – for instance, following a complaint – the analysis has to be based on the (then) existing market situation. The block exemption still continues to apply if the parties' share on the (then) relevant market does not exceed 25%. Similarly, Article 81(3) continues to apply to R&D agreements falling outside the block exemption provided that the criteria for an exemption are fulfilled.

3 UK law

Horizontal cooperation agreements in general and those dealing with specialisation and R&D in particular have not received a treatment under UK competition law which can rival that afforded to such categories of agreements by the European Commission under EC law. As a business phenomenon, these agreements are subject to the Chapter I prohibition of the CA1998; though they have not been perceived with suspicion like the case of cartels. When handling the application of the prohibition, the OFT of course has the benefit of the *Commission's Guidelines on horizontal cooperation*, which by virtue of section 60(3) CA1998 UK competition authorities (including the OFT) must have regard to. As was noted in chapters 1 and 3, the purpose behind section 60 is to ensure that UK competition authorities deal with cases under the CA1998 consistently with EC law; however only to the extent that this is possible, having regard to any relevant differences between the two laws.

Two additional key points should be noted. The first, which was made repeatedly in previous chapters and will be revisited in chapter 14, is that UK competition authorities, like other national competition authorities in Member States, now have the power to apply Article 81(3), a provision which has played an important role in the treatment of specialisation and R&D agreements. The second point, which directly arises from the fact that these two categories of agreements both enjoy block exemption, is that (in light of the discussion in chapter 4) the CA1998 confers 'parallel exemption' to an agreement which is covered by an EC block exemption Regulation or would be so covered if the agreement had an effect on trade between Member States. The same is true where under Article 10 of EC Regulation 1/2003 the European Commission declares Article 81 inapplicable to the agreement either because it is not caught by Article 81(1) or because it satisfies the exemption criteria under 81(3). The application of a parallel exemption means that the agreement will not be prohibited under the Chapter I prohibition.

9
Abuse of dominance

1 Introduction

The competition rules of the EC and the UK would have been deprived of their full effectiveness if they did not contain provisions dealing with the competition problems that may arise from the unilateral behaviour of firms possessing economic power. For this reason, both the EC and UK systems of competition law, like other systems around the world, contain provisions dealing with this business phenomenon, which is widely known as 'abuse of dominance'. The relevant provision that deals with this in the EC is Article 82, and in the UK it is the Chapter II prohibition of the Competition Act 1998; the latter is modelled on the former.

As competition theory reveals, firms cannot take unilateral action on the market to affect prices, because they are constrained by actual and potential competitors, that is unless they have the power to stem such competition before or as it emerges. Worldwide, the case law that has developed under competition law provisions dealing with abuse of dominance has not been as extensive as that dealing with anti-competitive bilateral or multilateral behaviour of firms. However, this does not mean that the issue of abuse of dominance possesses merely minor importance. On the contrary, the topic has great significance in practice as demonstrated in the case law.

The aim of this chapter is to deal with the application of Article 82 EC and the Chapter II prohibition to the unilateral behaviour of dominant firms, which engage in abusive behaviour.

2 The structure of Article 82 and the Chapter II prohibition

Article 82 states:

Any abuse by one or more undertakings of a dominant position within the common market or in a substantial part of it shall be prohibited as incompatible with the common market in so far as it may affect trade between Member States. Such abuse may, in particular, consist in:
(a) directly or indirectly imposing unfair purchase or selling prices or other unfair trading conditions;
(b) limiting production, markets or technical development to the prejudice of consumers;

(c) applying dissimilar conditions to equivalent transactions with other trading parties, thereby placing them at a competitive disadvantage;

(d) making the conclusion of contracts subject to acceptance by the other parties of supplementary obligations which, by their nature or according to commercial usage, have no connection with the subject of such contracts.

In a similar manner, section 18 of the CA1998 (the Chapter II prohibition) provides as follows:

(1) Subject to section 19, any conduct on the part of one or more undertakings which amounts to the abuse of a dominant position in a market is prohibited if it may affect trade within the United Kingdom.

(2) Conduct may, in particular, constitute such an abuse if it consists in –
   (a) directly, or indirectly imposing unfair purchase or selling prices or other unfair trading conditions;
   (b) limiting production, markets or technical development to the prejudice of consumers;
   (c) applying dissimilar conditions to equivalent transactions with other trading parties, thereby placing them at a competitive disadvantage;
   (d) making the conclusion of contracts subject to acceptance by the other parties of supplementary obligations which, by their nature or according to commercial usage, have no connection with the subject of the contracts.

(3) In this section –
   'dominant position' means a dominant position within the United Kingdom; and
   'the United Kingdom' means the United Kingdom or any part of it.

(4) The prohibition imposed by subsection (1) is referred to in this Act as 'the Chapter II prohibition'.

3 The requirements of Article 82 and the Chapter II prohibition

Looking at Article 82 and section 18 of the CA1998, it is clear that the following questions need to be asked (and answered):
- Is there a *dominant position*?
- Is this dominant position *held in the Common Market or substantial part of it* (in the case of section 18 CA1998, in a market in the United Kingdom (or a part thereof))?
- Is there an *abuse* of that dominant position?
- Is there an *effect on trade* between Member States (in the case of s. 18, effect on trade within the UK)?

However, these are not the only requirements of either provision. Early in its jurisprudence, the ECJ took the view that an additional requirement existed when considering the application of Article 82, though this is not expressed in its wording, namely whether there was any objective justification for the abuse of a dominant position and whether it satisfied the doctrine of proportionality. This requirement is now well-established within Article 82; and given that section 60 CA1998 calls for consistency between the application of EC and UK competition rules, it is also part of the assessment of the application of the Chapter II prohibition.

4 EC law

(A) Dominance

I Defining dominance

The ECJ defined 'dominance' in the case of *United Brands v. Commission* stating in paragraph 65 of the judgment that the dominant position referred to in Article 82 'relates to a position of economic strength enjoyed by an undertaking which enables it to prevent effective competition being maintained on the relevant market by giving it the power to behave to an appreciable extent independently of its competitors, customers and ultimately of its consumers'.

This definition of dominance has become authoritative through application in several other cases under Article 82; and the Commission also used the definition in its publication *Glossary of terms used in competition related matters 2003*, which is directed at non-competition law specialists and has no legal force (see http://www.europa.eu.int/comm/competition/general_info/glossary_en.html).

It is apparent from paragraph 65 of *United Brands* (above) that dominance is about market power. However, market power does not exist in the abstract but rather only in relation to a market (in the case of competition law, the 'relevant market'). This means that establishing dominance requires a definition of the relevant market – an issue which was dealt with in chapter 2. The importance of defining the relevant market was emphasised by the ECJ in the case of *Continental Can* (see pp. 18–20 above).

II Measuring dominance

While there is nothing controversial about the ECJ's definition of a dominant position, in practice establishing that such a position exists is quite a controversial and difficult issue. For example, the Commission and the firm concerned will often disagree on how the relevant market should be defined: the Commission's tendency has been to define the relevant market narrowly, making it more likely to find a dominant position. The firm concerned on the other hand wishes, of course, to convince the Commission that the relevant market is much wider, with the result that the firm would not appear to be dominant or would appear less likely to be so. Furthermore, the parties often disagree in practice over the validity, admissibility and interpretation of the data, which the Commission may wish to rely on in order to prove that a firm holds a dominant position.

[329]

(a) Market shares

In practice the existence of a dominant position is proved using several factors, none of which will be decisive on its own. The main factor used to establish dominance is the market share of the undertaking concerned. The ECJ explained the significance of market shares in the case of *Hoffmann-La Roche v. Commission*, stating at paragraph 41 of the judgment that 'although the importance of the market shares may vary from one market to another the view may legitimately be taken that very large shares are in themselves, and save in exceptional circumstances, evidence of the existence of a dominant position'. Thus, it seems that a high market share held by a firm can be sufficient in itself to show that it enjoys a dominant position in the relevant market. However, the ECJ qualified this important statement in two ways: first, by recognising that in some cases the high market share held by the firm concerned may not in itself be sufficient, and secondly, by recognising that a market share needs to be held for some time.

Whilst helpful, the judgment in *Hoffmann-La Roche* raised an obvious question: what amounts to a high market share? This question was answered by the ECJ in the subsequent case of *AKZO v. Commission* where at paragraph 61 of the judgment it stated that a market share of 50 per cent (such as that found to exist in the case itself) would lead to a presumption of a high market share and a presumption of dominance.

Of course, this is a rebuttable presumption, but the burden shifts to the firm concerned to rebut the presumption. It is important to note that the likelihood of finding dominance increases the greater the market share of the firm is.

Having said that, one must remember that *AKZO* did not create a presumption of 'non-dominance' below 50 per cent, which means that a firm with a market share of less than 50 per cent can still be found to be dominant (see e.g. *United Brands v. Commission, Hoffmann-La Roche*). Indeed, a brief look at the decisional practice of the Commission and its statements shows that the possibility of finding dominance in the case of firms possessing significantly lower market shares than 50 per cent suggests it is a rarity (see the Commission's decision in *British Airways/VirginAtlantic* where it found BA to be in a dominant position with a market share of 39.7 per cent; upheld by the CFI in *British Airways v. Commission*: see below at pp. 368–369). However, it is worth noting that where a firm's market share is less than 50 per cent it becomes particularly important to consider additional factors that may indicate a dominant position. Moreover, as the ECJ makes clear in *United Brands v. Commission*, a firm does not have to eliminate competition in order to be labelled dominant (see paragraphs 110–121).

(b) Additional indicators of dominance

The case law of the Community Courts and the decisional practice of the Commission show that several factors have been used in addition to the market share of a firm as indicators that the firm concerned holds a dominant position. It is worth noting that these factors are often referred to as 'barriers to entry', an economics term coined to deal with the question of whether a firm faces, or is likely to face, competition from firms which may qualify as 'new entrants' to the relevant market i.e. potential competitors. The application of the concept in practice has proved to be highly controversial because it is a matter of pure speculation whether other firms would enter a market even if they could, but it has nonetheless been relied on by the Community Courts and the Commission. (The OFT provides a very clear explanation of the concept of barriers to entry in its Guideline on *Assessment of Market power* (OFT415), which the reader might find useful to consult (see pp. 380–386 below); also the European Commission's *Guideline on horizontal mergers* (see pp. 481–483 below).)

Additional indicators of dominance include (but are not limited to):
- superior technology (*United Brands*, paragraphs 82–84);
- investment and financial resources capabilities (*United Brands*, paragraphs 122–124);
- ownership of intellectual property rights (*Hilti v. Commission*, paragraph 93; *Magill v. Commission*, paragraphs 46–47);
- the relationship between the market shares of the firm concerned and its competitors (*Hofmann-La Roche*, paragraph 42; *AKZO*, paragraph 56);
- brand image and advertising campaigns (*United Brands*, paragraphs 91–94);
- economies of scale (*BPB Industries plc*, paragraph 116);
- vertical integration and distribution systems (*United Brands*, paragraphs 69–81 and 85–90).

This list of indicators of dominance is by no means closed, and the way in which the Commission has handled the application of the concept under Article 82 makes it clear that the list will expand as the Commission's decisional practice grows and develops. The cases below provide an insight into how these factors, and others, have been relied on by the Commission and the Community Courts in practice.

United Brands v. Commission [1978] ECR 207

United Brands ('UBC') was a vertically integrated plantation owner, banana grower, and distributor with a well-established brand name ('Chiquita') and a 40–45 per cent market share. UBC exercised control over ripeners and wholesalers by means of three policies: a) prohibiting resale of green bananas, thereby preventing ripeners from re-exporting in competition with UBC; b) setting higher prices in certain markets, particularly Ireland; and c) discontinuing supplies to a certain ripener, the Danish firm Olesen, which had participated in an advertising campaign for a competitor.

The ECJ was asked to consider whether the market had been properly defined, what factors were relevant in determining dominance, and whether UBC's behaviour constituted abuse of a dominant position contrary to Article 82.

[331]

ECJ

58   The Commission bases its view that UBC has a dominant position on the relevant market on a series of factors which, when taken together, give UBC unchallengeable ascendancy over all its competitors: its market share compared with that of its competitors, the diversity of its sources of supply, the homogeneous nature of its product, the organization of its production and transport, its marketing system and publicity campaigns, the diversified nature of its operations and finally its vertical integration.

. . .

63   Article [82] is an application of the general objective of the activities of the Community laid down by Article [3(g)] of the Treaty: the institution of a system ensuring that competition in the common market is not distorted.

. . .

66   In general a dominant position derives from a combination of several factors which, taken separately, are not necessarily determinative.

67   In order to find out whether UBC is an undertaking in a dominant position on the relevant market it is necessary first of all to examine its structure and then the situation on the said market as far as competition is concerned.

68   In doing so it may be advisable to take account if need be of the facts put forward as acts amounting to abuses without necessarily having to acknowledge that they are abuses.

69   It is advisable to examine in turn UBC's resources for and methods of producing, packaging, transporting, selling and displaying its product.

70   UBC is an undertaking vertically integrated to a high degree.

71   This integration is evident at each of the stages from the plantation to the loading on wagons or lorries in the ports of delivery and after those stages, as far as ripening and sale prices are concerned, UBC even extends its control to ripener/distributors and wholesalers by setting up a complete network of agents.

72   At the production stage UBC owns large plantations in central and South America.

73   In so far as UBC's own production does not meet its requirements it can obtain supplies without any difficulty from independent planters since it is an established fact that unless circumstances are exceptional there is a production surplus.

74   Furthermore several independent producers have links with UBC through contracts for the growing of bananas which have caused them to grow the varieties of bananas which UBC has advised them to adopt.

75   The effects of natural disasters which could jeopardize supplies are greatly reduced by the fact that the plantations are spread over a wide geographic area and by the selection of varieties not very susceptible to diseases.

76   This situation was born out by the way in which UBC was able to react to the consequences of hurricane 'Fifi' in 1974.

77   At the production stage UBC therefore knows that it can comply with all the requests which it receives.

78   At the stage of packaging and presentation on its premises UBC has at its disposal factories, manpower, plant and material which enable it to handle the goods independently.

79   The bananas are carried from the place of production to the port of shipment by its own means of transport including railways.

80   At the carriage by sea stage it has been acknowledged that UBC is the only undertaking of its kind which is capable of carrying two thirds of its exports by means of its own banana fleet.

81   Thus UBC knows that it is able to transport regularly, without running the risk of its own ships not being used and whatever the market situation may be, two thirds of its average volume of sales and is alone able to ensure that three regular consignments reach Europe each week, and all this guarantees it commercial stability and well being.

82   In the field of technical knowledge and as a result of continual research UBC keeps on improving the productivity and yield of its plantations by improving the draining system, making good soil deficiencies and combating effectively plant disease.

83   It has perfected new ripening methods in which its technicians instruct the distributor/ripeners of the Chiquita banana.

84   That is another factor to be borne in mind when considering UBC's position since competing firms cannot develop research at a comparable level and are in this respect at a disadvantage compared with the applicant.

85   It is acknowledged that at the stage where the goods are given the final finish and undergo quality control UBC not only controls the distributor/ripeners which are direct customers but also those who work for the account of its important customers such as the Scipio group.

86   Even if the object of the clause prohibiting the sale of green bananas was only strict quality control, it in fact gives UBC absolute control of all trade in its goods so long as they are marketable wholesale, that is to say before the ripening process begins which makes an immediate sale unavoidable.

87   This general quality control of a homogeneous product makes the advertising of the brand name effective.

[333]

88   Since 1967 UBC has based its general policy in the relevant market on the quality of its Chiquita brand banana.

89   There is no doubt that this policy gives UBC control over the transformation of the product into bananas for consumption even though most of this product no longer belongs to it.

90   This policy has been based on a thorough reorganization of the arrangements for production, packaging, carriage, ripening (new plant with ventilation and a cooling system) and sale (a network of agents).

91   UBC has made this product distinctive by large-scale repeated advertising and promotion campaigns which have induced the consumer to show a preference for it in spite of the difference between the price of labelled and unlabelled bananas (in the region of 30 to 40%) and also of Chiquita bananas and those which have been labelled with another brand name (in the region of 7 to 10%).

92   It was the first to take full advantage of the opportunities presented by labelling in the tropics for the purpose of large-scale advertising and this, to use UBC's own words, has 'revolutionized the commercial exploitation of the banana'. . .

93   It has thus attained a privileged position by making Chiquita the premier banana brand name on the relevant market with the result that the distributor cannot afford not to offer it to the consumer.

94   At the selling stage this distinguishing factor – justified by the unchanging quality of the banana bearing this label – ensures that it has regular customers and consolidates its economic strength.

95   The effect of its sales networks only covering a limited number of customers, large groups or distributor/ripeners, is a simplification of its supply policy and economies of scale.

96   Since UBC's supply policy consists – in spite of the production surplus – in only meeting the requests for Chiquita bananas parsimoniously and sometimes incompletely UBC is in a position of strength at the selling stage.

In its judgment, the ECJ gave a summary of the barriers to entry facing competitors in paragraph 122.

122   The particular barriers to competitors entering the market are the exceptionally large capital investments required for the creation and running of banana plantations, the need to increase sources of supply in order to avoid the effects of fruit diseases and bad weather (hurricanes, floods), the introduction of an essential system of logistics which the distribution of a very perishable product makes necessary, economies of scale from which newcomers to the market cannot derive any immediate benefit and the actual cost of entry made up *inter alia* of all the general expenses incurred in

penetrating the market such as the setting up of an adequate commercial network, the mounting of very large-scale advertising campaigns, all those financial risks, the costs of which are irrecoverable if the attempt fails.

Hoffmann-La Roche & Co AG v. Commission [1979] ECR 461

Roche, a Swiss pharmaceutical manufacturer, sought to challenge a Commission Decision concerning an alleged breach of Article 82. The Commission had found that Roche was dominant within the European market for various groups of vitamins and had abused its dominance by requiring or inducing customers to buy their requirements of certain vitamins exclusively or preferentially from Roche.

ECJ

42   The contested decision has mentioned besides the market shares a number of other factors which together with Roche's market shares would secure for it in certain circumstances, a dominant position.

These factors which the decision classifies as additional criteria are as follows:

(a) Roche's market shares are not only large but there is also a big disparity between its shares and those of its next largest competitors (recitals 5 and 21 to the decision);

(b) Roche produces a far wider range of vitamins than its competitors (recital 21 to the decision);

(c) Roche is the world's largest vitamin manufacturer whose turnover exceeds that of all the other producers and is at the head of a multinational group which in terms of sales is the world's leading pharmaceuticals producer (recitals 5, 6 and 21 to the decision);

(d) although Roche's patents for the manufacture of vitamins have expired Roche, since it has played a leading role in this field, still enjoys technological advantages over its competitors of which the highly developed customer information and assistance service which it has is evidence (recitals 7 and 8 to the decision);

(e) Roche has a very extensive and highly specialized sales network (recital 21 to the [decision]);

(f) there is no potential competition (recital 21 to the decision).

Furthermore during the proceedings before the court the Commission adduced as a factor establishing Roche's dominant position the latter's ability, notwithstanding lively competition, to maintain its market shares substantially intact.

43   Before considering whether the factors taken into account by the Commission can in fact be confirmed in Roche's case it is necessary to ascertain, since the applicant challenges their relevance, whether these factors, in the light of the special features of the relevant markets and of the market shares, are of such a kind as to disclose the existence of a dominant position.

44   In this connexion it is necessary to reject the criterion based on retention of market shares, since this may just as well result from effective competitive behaviour as from a position which ensures that Roche can behave independently of competitors, and the Commission, while admitting that there is competition, has not mentioned the factors which may account for the stability of market shares where it has been found to exist.

However if there is a dominant position then retention of the market shares may be a factor disclosing that this position is being maintained, and, on the other hand, the methods adopted to maintain a dominant position may be an abuse within the meaning of Article [82] of the treaty.

45   The fact that Roche produces a far wider range of vitamins than its competitors must similarly be rejected as being immaterial.

The Commission regards this as a factor establishing a dominant position and asserts that 'since the requirements of many users extend to several groups of vitamins, Roche is able to employ a sales and pricing strategy which is far less dependent than that of the other manufacturers on the conditions of competition in each market'.

46   However the Commission has itself found that each group of vitamins constitutes a specific market and is not, or at least not to any significant extent, interchangeable with any other group or with any other products (recital 20 to the decision) so that the vitamins belonging to the various groups are as between themselves products just as different as the vitamins compared with other products of the pharmaceutical and food sector.

Moreover it is not disputed that Roche's competitors, in particular those in the chemical industry, market besides the vitamins which they manufacture themselves, other products which purchasers of vitamins also want, so that the fact that Roche is in a position to offer several groups of vitamins does not in itself give it any advantage over its competitors, who can offer, in addition a less or much less wide range of vitamins, other products which are also required by the purchasers of these vitamins.

47   Similar considerations lead also to the rejection as a relevant factor of the circumstance that Roche is the world's largest vitamin manufacturer, that its turnover exceeds that of all the other manufacturers and that it is at the head of the largest pharmaceuticals group in the world.

In the view of the Commission these three considerations together are a factor showing that there is a dominant position, because 'it follows that the applicant occupies a preponderant position not only within the common market but also on the world market; it therefore enjoys very considerable freedom of action, since its position enables it to adapt itself easily to the developments of the different regional markets. An undertaking operating throughout the markets of the world and having a market share which leaves all its competitors far behind it does not have to concern itself unduly about any competitors within the common market'.

Such reasoning based on the benefits reaped from economics of scale and on the possibility of adopting a strategy which varies according to the different regional markets is not conclusive, seeing that it is accepted that each group of vitamins constitutes a group of separate products which require their own particular plant and form a separate market, in that the volume of the overall production of products which are different as between themselves does not give Roche a competitive advantage over its competitors, especially over those in the chemical industry, who manufacture on a world scale other products as well as vitamins and have in principle the same opportunities to set off one market against the other as are offered by a large overall production of products which differ from each other as much as the various groups of vitamins do.

48   On the other hand the relationship between the market shares of the undertaking concerned and of its competitors, especially those of the next largest, the technological lead of an undertaking over its competitors, the existence of a highly developed sales network and the absence of potential competition are relevant factors, the first because it enables the competitive strength of the undertaking in question to be assessed, the second and third because they represent in themselves technical and commercial advantages and the fourth because it is the consequence of the existence of obstacles preventing new competitors from having access to the market.

As far as the existence or non-existence of potential competition is concerned it must however be observed that, although it is true - and this applies to all the groups of vitamins in question - that because of the amount of capital investment required the capacity of the factories is determined according to the anticipated growth over a long period so that access to the market by new producers is not easy, account must also be taken of the fact that the existence of considerable unused manufacturing capacity creates potential competition between established manufacturers. Nevertheless Roche is in this respect in a privileged position because, as it admits itself, its own manufacturing capacity was, during the period covered by the contested decision, in itself sufficient to meet world demand without this surplus manufacturing capacity placing it in a difficult economic or financial situation.

The ECJ then went on to deal with the application of the relevant criteria to the different groups of vitamins and came to the conclusion that Roche was dominant in the markets for vitamins A (paragraphs 50–52), B (paragraphs 53–56), B6 (paragraphs 59–60), C (paragraphs 61–63), E (paragraphs 64–66) and H (paragraph 67). However, dominance was not established in relation to the market for vitamin B3 (paragraphs 57–58).

AKZO Chemie BV v. Commission [1991] ECR I-3359

The Applicants, the Dutch parent company and its UK subsidiary (collectively 'AKZO'), were found by the Commission to have pursued a course of conduct intending to damage a competitor ('ECS') and/or to force it out of the market for flour bleaching peroxides in breach of Article 82. This particular market was of secondary importance to the applicants, whose focus lay in plastics manufacturing, where such peroxides are also used, but where they are exposed to competition from other chemicals.

The ECJ was called upon to consider whether the Commission applied Article 82 correctly.

ECJ

55   The Commission considers that AKZO has a dominant position within the organic peroxides market. It bases its view on AKZO's market share and on the existence of a number of factors which, combined with that market share, is said to give it a marked predominance.

56   The Commission describes these factors at point 69 of the decision as follows:
- (i) AKZO's market share is not only large in itself but is equivalent to all the remaining producers put together
- (ii) apart from Interox and Luperox the remaining producers have a limited product range and/or are of local significance only
- (iii) AKZO's market share (as well as that of the second and third placed producers Interox and Luperox) has remained steady over the period under consideration and AKZO has always successfully repulsed any attacks on its position by smaller producers
- (iv) AKZO was able even during periods of economic downturn to maintain its overall margin by regular price increases and/or increases in sales volume
- (v) AKZO offers a far broader range of products than any rival, has the most highly developed commercial and technical marketing organization, and possesses the leading knowledge in safety and toxicology
- (vi) AKZO has on its own account been able effectively to eliminate 'troublesome' competitors (besides ECS) from the market or weaken them substantially: the example of Scado for one shows that AKZO is in a position, if it so wishes, to exclude a less powerful producer
- (vii) once such small but potentially dangerous competitors are neutralized, AKZO has been able to raise the price for the particular product in respect of which their competition was felt.

57   AKZO disputes the assessment of its market share and also the existence or relevance of the other factors mentioned in the decision. In particular, it claims that its market share was evaluated wrongly because the Commission should not have regarded the organic peroxides market as a single market. It maintains, moreover, that the fact that it offers a wider range of products than its competitors cannot constitute evidence of a dominant position.

58   Those arguments cannot be accepted. Since the organic peroxides market was rightly regarded as the relevant market, it follows that AKZO's market share had to be

calculated by taking organic peroxides as a whole. In that light, it is obvious that the fact that AKZO offered a range of products wider than that of its main rivals was one of the factors that assured for AKZO a dominant position in that market.

59   It should be further observed that according to its own internal documents AKZO had a stable market share of about 50% from 1979 to 1982 (Annexes 2 and 4 to the statement of objections and Table A annexed to that statement). Furthermore, AKZO has not adduced any evidence to show that its share decreased during subsequent years.

Nederlandsche Banden Industrie Michelin NV v. Commission **[1983] ECR 3461**

Michelin NV, the Dutch subsidiary of a global group, was a major manufacturer and supplier of tyres for vans and lorries, but it held less sway in the car tyre market. Michelin had a system of granting selective individual discounts conditional on meeting annual sales targets and an extra annual bonus conditional on meeting a car tyre purchase target. The Commission held that Michelin was dominant in the Dutch market for new replacement van and lorry tyres and that its policy constituted abuse – effectively a fidelity rebate and a leveraging of dominance from one market into another – of its dominant position contrary to Article 82.

ECJ

31   The various criteria and evidence relied upon by the parties regarding the existence of a dominant position must be examined in [light of the aim of the Treaty to ensure competition is not distorted]. They concern first Michelin NV's share of the relevant product market and secondly the other factors which must be taken into consideration in the assessment of Michelin NV's position in relation to its competitors, customers and consumers.

. . .

33   In its Decision the Commission relied upon the fact that from 1975 to 1980 Michelin NV's share of the market in new replacement tyres for lorries, buses and similar vehicles in the Netherlands was 57 to 65% whereas the market shares of its main competitors were only 4 to 8%.

. . .

55   . . . [I]n order to assess the relative economic strength of Michelin NV and its competitors on the Netherlands market the advantages which those undertakings may derive from belonging to groups of undertakings operating throughout Europe or even the world must be taken into consideration. Amongst those advantages, the lead which the Michelin Group has over its competitors in the matters of investment and research and the special extent of its range of products, to which the Commission referred in its Decision, have not been denied. In fact in the case of certain

types of tyre the Michelin Group is the only supplier on the market to offer them in its range.

56   That situation ensures that on the Netherlands market a large number of users of heavy-vehicle tyres have a strong preference for Michelin tyres. As the purchase of tyres represents a considerable investment for a transport undertaking and since much time is required in order to ascertain in practice the cost-effectiveness of a type or brand of tyre, Michelin NV therefore enjoys a position which renders it largely immune to competition. As a result, a dealer established in the Netherlands normally cannot afford not to sell Michelin tyres.

57   It is not possible to uphold the objections made against those arguments by Michelin NV, supported on this point by the French government, that Michelin NV is thus penalized for the quality of its products and services. A finding that an undertaking has a dominant position is not in itself a recrimination but simply means that, irrespective of the reasons for which it has such a dominant position, the undertaking concerned has a special responsibility not to allow its conduct to impair genuine undistorted competition on the common market.

58   Due weight must also be attached to the importance of Michelin NV's network of commercial representatives, which gives it direct access to tyre users at all times. Michelin NV has not disputed the fact that in absolute terms its network is considerably larger than those of its competitors or challenged the description, in the Decision at issue, of the services performed by its network whose efficiency and quality of service are unquestioned. The direct access to users and the standard of service which the network can give them enables Michelin NV to maintain and strengthen its position on the market and to protect itself more effectively against competition.

59   As regards the additional criteria and evidence to which Michelin NV refers in order to disprove the existence of a dominant position, it must be observed that temporary unprofitability or even losses are not inconsistent with the existence of a dominant position. By the same token, the fact that the prices charged by Michelin NV do not constitute an abuse and are not even particularly high does not justify the conclusion that a dominant position does not exist. Finally, neither the size, financial strength and degree of diversification of Michelin NV's competitors at the world level nor the counterpoise arising from the fact that buyers of heavy-vehicle tyres are experienced trade users are such as to deprive Michelin NV of its privileged position on the Netherlands market.

60   It must therefore be concluded that the other criteria and evidence relevant in this case in determining whether a dominant position exists confirm that Michelin NV has such a position.

As was previously noted, the above cases serve as examples of the application of some of the indicators of dominance in practice. Of course, there are other

cases which could be mentioned. One such case is *Hugin v. Commission* which concerned an action by a Swedish cash register manufacturer and its British subsidiary ('Hugin') to annul a Commission Decision that found infringement of Article 82. Sweden was not at that time part of the EC. The alleged abuse comprised a prohibition on sales of spare parts outside Hugin's distribution network and a refusal to supply a third party, 'Liptons', a London-based firm specialising in reconditioning of used machines. The Commission took the view that the facts of the case showed that while Hugin had only a relatively small share of the cash register market – which is very competitive – it had a monopoly in spare parts for machines made by it and that consequently it occupied a dominant position for the maintenance and repair of Hugin cash registers in relation to independent companies which need a supply of Hugin spare parts. A decisive factor in reaching this view was the protection afforded to Hugin under the UK Design Copyright Act 1968. The Commission's finding of dominance was upheld by the ECJ in its judgment.

(B) Common Market and substantial part of the Common Market

Once dominance has been established under Article 82, one needs to enquire whether it is held in the Common Market or in a substantial part of it. The requirement can be regarded as a question of 'appreciability' or 'de minimis' (like in the case of Article 81(1): see chapter 3). It is important to note however, that the issue of substantiality is not related to the definition of the relevant geographic market. The case law has established that each Member State is regarded as a substantial part of the Common Market, likewise even parts of a Member State including facilities such as ports and airports. An explanation of the requirement was given by the ECJ in the case of *Sugar Cartel* (for facts see p. 72 above):

7   For the purpose of determining whether a specific territory is large enough to amount to 'a substantial part of the common market' within the meaning of Article [82] of the Treaty the pattern and volume of the production and consumption of the said product as well as the habits and economic opportunities of vendors and purchasers must be considered.

Article [82] of the Treaty refers in each case to the position occupied by the undertaking concerned on the common market as the time when the latter acted in a way which is alleged to amount to an abuse.

In order to determine in the case of a complaint made against an undertaking under this Article whether a specific area is a substantial part of the common market it is therefore only necessary to compare the statistical data relating to this area with the corresponding data relating to the common market as it was when the facts giving rise to these proceedings existed; any subsequent enlargement of the common market cannot be taken into consideration.

[341]

(C) Abuse

A finding that a dominant position is held by an undertaking in the Common Market or in a substantial part of it does not mean that the unilateral behaviour of an undertaking will be within the mischief of Article 82: the Article prohibits an *abuse* of a dominant position and not the mere holding of that position. However the ECJ stated in paragraph 57 in *Michelin NV v. Commission* (1983) (cited above, see p. 339) that regardless of the reasons for which a firm holds a dominant position, it 'has a special responsibility not to allow its conduct to impair genuine undistorted competition on the common market'. This statement has caused a significant degree of confusion among competition lawyers: to whom is a dominant firm responsible? Logic would dictate that the existence of a 'special responsibility' should connote the existence of a 'special market relationship', or at least some form of 'market relationship', such as the relationship between the dominant firm and its customer. The Community Courts and the Commission however have used this concept, though without clarifying its ambit (see e.g. *Michelin [France] v Commission* (2003), pp. 362–363 below and the Commission's recent decision in *Microsoft*, pp. 346–347 below). It seems, although it is not absolutely certain, the judgment in *Michelin [France]* and the decision in *Microsoft* would convey the impression that the responsibility is perhaps *vis-à-vis* the market and consumers.

Once a dominant position has been established, the next step is to consider whether that position has been abused.

I Defining abuse

The starting point when considering abuse in the context of Article 82 must be the wording of the Article itself. Paragraphs (a)–(d) of the Article make up a non-comprehensive list of examples of what amounts to an abuse of a dominant position. A look at the case law of the Community Courts and the decisional practice of the Commission reveals several additions to the list over the years.

A vital instrument in extending the list of potential abuses has been the special reasoning method used by the ECJ. Widely referred to as 'teleological reasoning' the ECJ does not confine itself to the specific wording of Treaty Articles but rather looks at the broader underlying objective, namely the single market objective. Also important in expanding the list has been the Commission's enthusiasm to extend the scope of Article 82 to adapt it to modern business and commercial practice, in which firms operate with rapidly changing and highly sophisticated commercial behaviour, which may have anti-competitive aims or effects. A notable example in this regard is the Commission's decision in *Microsoft* (see pp. 346–347 below), which, among other things, sets a strong precedent something that the Commission viewed as vital to establish clear principles for the future conduct of firms with a very 'strong' dominant position such as Microsoft.

Abuse has not really been defined by the ECJ, but it has said the following in paragraph 91 of *Hoffmann-La Roche v. Commission*:

The concept of abuse is an objective concept relating to the behaviour of an undertaking in a dominant position which is such as to influence the structure of a market where, as a result of the very presence of the undertaking in question, the degree of competition is weakened and which, through recourse to methods different from those which condition normal competition in products or services on the basis of the transactions of commercial operators, has the effect of hindering the maintenance of the degree of competition still existing in the market or the growth of that competition.

The ECJ has repeated this statement throughout its case law. Characterising abuse as an objective concept means that the intention of the firm whose behaviour is under scrutiny is irrelevant. Of course the absence of a definition of the concept of abuse is not fatal to understanding its application. However, it does mean that one must turn to the case law of the Community courts and decisional practice of the Commission to discover and assess the examples of abuse that have emerged over the years in order to see what kind of behaviour has been held to be an abuse of a dominant position.

Quite interestingly, the Commission in its glossary of terms (mentioned at p. 329 above) defined abuse as:

Anti-competitive business practices (including improper exploitation of customers or exclusion of competitors) in which a dominant firm may engage in order to maintain or increase its position on the market. Competition law prohibits such behaviour, as it damages true competition between firms, exploits consumers, and makes it unnecessary for the dominant undertaking to compete with other firms on the merits.

As noted above, the glossary is directed at non-competition law specialists. For a competition lawyer, the end result of the Commission's effort can be seen as a description rather than a definition of the concept.

II Examples of abuse

The following include some of the examples of abuse which have emerged in the case law over the years. One comment which applies to most, if not all, of these examples is that they, like many judgments and decisions under Article 82, are very controversial. When studying these judgments and decisions one gets the impression that the scope of the prohibition in the Article has been over-stretched and some business practices have been condemned as abusive merely because the firm in question was dominant and without undertaking sufficient analysis of the situation at hand (notable examples here include tying practices, rebates, predatory pricing and selective price-cutting). It would aid the reader when considering these examples to refer to section 5(B) below on UK competition law which contains helpful guidance published by the OFT in which it explains in clear language some of the basis and important concepts used in the examples below.

(a) Requirements contracts

In this situation, the dominant firm may impose an obligation on one or more of its customers to purchase their requirements from it. The objection to this kind of practice is that it creates exclusivity and has the effect of foreclosing the market to the firm's competitors and potentially forcing the customer to accept terms and conditions which it may not particularly desire but nonetheless have no choice but to accept. In *Hofmann-La Roche* the ECJ stated in paragraph 89 that:

> An undertaking which is in a dominant position on a market and ties purchasers – even if it does so at their request – by an obligation [or] promise on their part to obtain all or most of their requirements exclusively from the said undertaking abuses its dominant position within the meaning of Article [82] of the Treaty, whether the obligation in question is stipulated without further qualification or whether it is undertaken in consideration of the grant or a rebate.

This is an interesting statement by the ECJ. The Court refers to an obligation on customers to purchase 'all' or 'most' of their requirement. While it is clear what amounts to 'all', using the word 'most' does not aid in the quest for certainty in such a difficult and controversial area of EC competition law.

As we saw in chapter 5, Regulation 2790/99 and the Commission's *Guidelines on Vertical Restraints* (2000) refer to the situation in question as a 'non-compete obligation', which is defined in Article 1(b) of the Regulation as 'any direct or indirect obligation on the buyer to purchase from the supplier or from another undertaking designated by the supplier more than 80% of the buyer's total purchases of the contract goods or services and all their substitutes on the relevant market'. In paragraph 141 of the *Guidelines*, the Commission states clearly that a dominant firm may not impose a non-compete obligation on its customers unless it can objectively justify such practice within the context of Article 82. This is an important and sensible point because it dispels the view that there may be a *per se* approach when considering requirements contracts and exclusivity under Article 82.

As part (E) below shows however, the burden is on the firm concerned to show that there is objective justification; and obviously the duration of the contract and the extent of its clauses are key in this context. In other words, an exclusivity contract lasting for a relatively short period of time is less likely to fall within the mischief of Article 82 than another with long duration. No doubt, the precise limits on duration and scope can only be decided on the facts of each particular case.

(b) Tying

(i) General

The tying, or bundling, situation is expressly mentioned in paragraph (d) of Article 82 and occurs where, for example, the dominant firm informs a dependent customer that it will supply it with one product (X: the tying product) only if the latter agrees also to buy another product (Y: the tied product) from it. Tying may take different forms and may be employed by a dominant firm for a variety of reasons, which may include the desire of such a firm to strengthen its position on the tied product market (sometimes referred to as 'leveraging' because of the use of dominance in one market to gain access to another). Indeed, it is not hard to understand the rationale for condemning such a commercial practice as an abuse of a dominant position. The case law under Article 82 includes several examples of the tying situation (See e.g. *Hilti AG v. Commission, Napier Brown-British Sugar, Centre Belge d'Etudes des Marché-Télémarketing v. CLT* and *Tetra Pak International SA v. Commission (Tetra Pak II)*).

(ii) Tetra Pak International SA v. Commission ('Tetra Pak II')

Tetra Pak held a virtual monopoly in the market for aseptic carton packaging and about a 50 per cent share in the non-aseptic market. The Commission found that it has abused its dominant position by tying non-aseptic filling machines to carton sales and by predatory pricing, a decision upheld by the CFI. On appeal to the ECJ, Tetra Pak argued that it was an improper application of Article 82 to consider conduct in a non-dominated market not intended to reinforce the position on the dominated market and that there was a natural link between the tied sales in accordance with commercial usage. It also disputed the charge of predatory pricing without it being established that it had a reasonable prospect of recouping its losses (see pp. 371–372 below).

ECJ

34 In its third plea, Tetra Pak submits that the Court of First Instance erred in law in holding that the tied sales of cartons and filling machines were contrary to Article [82] in circumstances where there was a natural link between the two and tied sales were in accordance with commercial usage.

35 Tetra Pak interprets Article [82(d)] of the Treaty as prohibiting only the practice of making the conclusion of contracts dependent on acceptance of additional services which, by nature or according to commercial usage, have no link with the subject-matter of the contracts.

36 It must be noted, first, that the Court of First Instance explicitly rejected the argument put forward by Tetra Pak to show the existence of a natural link between the machines and the cartons. In paragraph 82 of the judgment under appeal, it found: 'consideration of commercial usage does not support the conclusion that

the machinery for packaging a product is indivisible from the cartons. For a considerable time there have been independent manufacturers who specialize in the manufacture of non-aseptic cartons designed for use in machines manufactured by other concerns and who do not manufacture machinery themselves'. That assessment, itself based on commercial usage, rules out the existence of the natural link claimed by Tetra Pak by stating that other manufacturers can produce cartons for use in Tetra Pak's machines. With regard to aseptic cartons, the Court of First Instance found, at paragraph 83 of its judgment, that 'any independent producer is quite free, as far as Community competition law is concerned, to manufacture consumables intended for use in equipment manufactured by others, unless in doing so it infringes a competitor's intellectual property right'. It also noted, at paragraph 138, rejecting the argument based on the alleged natural link, that it was not for Tetra Pak to impose certain measures on its own initiative on the basis of technical considerations or considerations relating to product liability, protection of public health and protection of its reputation. Those factors, taken as a whole, show that the Court of First Instance considered that Tetra Pak was not alone in being able to manufacture cartons for use in its machines.

37   ... [E]ven where tied sales of two products are in accordance with commercial usage or there is a natural link between the two products in question, such sales may still constitute abuse within the meaning of Article [82] unless they are objectively justified. The reasoning of the Court of First Instance in paragraph 137 of its judgment is not therefore in any way defective.

(iii) *Commission's decision in* Microsoft

In March 2004, the Commission reached its decision in *Microsoft* following one of the most important Article 82 investigations which lasted for five years. The Commission's investigation was commenced following a complaint by Sun Microsystems, another US firm that Microsoft has refused to supply it with interface information, which is vital to develop products that would 'talk' properly with the Windows PC. According to the complaint this refusal prevented Sun Microsystems from competing effectively in the market for work group server operating systems. In the course of its investigation, which after two years was expanded to cover Microsoft's 'tying' of Windows Media Player with Windows 2000 PC operating systems, the Commission discovered a wider coverage for Microsoft's practices which affected other firms and which was part of a Microsoft strategy to keep competitors out of the market.

The Commission found that as a result of Microsoft's tying practices, consumers were harmed since competing products were placed at a disadvantage which is not related to their price or quality. In a landmark decision, the Commission imposed a fine of €497.2 m on Microsoft which, according to the Commission, came to reflect the seriousness of the abuse of dominance by the firm and its duration. The Commission also ordered Microsoft to restore conditions of effective competition by disclosing, within 120 days of the decision, complete and accurate interface documentation which would allow non-Microsoft work group servers to achieve full inter-operability with windows PCs and servers. The Commission felt that such action would enable competitors to develop products that can compete on equal footing in the work group server operating systems market. Microsoft was also ordered to offer PC manufacturers a version of its Windows Client PC operating system without Windows Media player. The purpose behind this is to facilitate configuration of 'bundles' by PC manufacturers which reflects what consumers desire as opposed to what Microsoft imposes.

The Commission's decision has attracted a high level of publicity and interest. Furthermore, it has led to very severe and harsh criticism by the USA of the practices of the Commission. Microsoft has decided to contest the decision before the CFI (judgment pending).

(c) Cabinet exclusivity

The cabinet or freezer exclusivity doctrine developed by the Commission concerns a dominant firm offering a cabinet, for example a freezer, free of charge to a customer on condition that the customer will stock in that cabinet only products made by the dominant firm and not those made by its competitors. The doctrine is an interesting extension to the list of abuses under Article 82. It is directly related to the tying situation described above and the objection to it is grounded in the fact that it carries a strong form of inducement, to certain customers at least, and excludes new entrants to the market.

Van den Bergh Foods Ltd (formerly HB Ice Cream Ltd) v. Commission [2004] 4 CMLR 1

The Applicant ('HB'), a major manufacturer of ice cream in Ireland, was investigated by the Commission as a result of a complaint by a third party competitor that HB's freezer display exclusivity clauses effectively excluded third parties from a major part of the market because many small retailers had no space for more than one freezer.

CFI

159   The Court finds, as a preliminary point, that HB rightly submits that the provision of freezer cabinets on a condition of exclusivity constitutes a standard practice on the relevant market. In the normal situation of a competitive market, those agreements are concluded in the interests of the two parties and cannot be prohibited as a matter of principle. However, those considerations, which are applicable in the normal situation of a competitive market, cannot be accepted without reservation in the case of a market on which, precisely because of the dominant position held by one of the traders, competition is already restricted. Business conduct which contributes

to an improvement in production or distribution of goods and which has a beneficial effect on competition in a balanced market may restrict such competition where it is engaged in by an undertaking which has a dominant position on the relevant market. With regard to the nature of the exclusivity clause, the Court finds that the Commission rightly held in the contested decision that HB was abusing its dominant position on the relevant market by inducing retailers who, for the purpose of stocking impulse ice-cream, did not have their own freezer cabinet, or a cabinet made available by an ice-cream supplier other than HB, to accept agreements for the provision of cabinets subject to a condition of exclusivity. That infringement of Article [82] takes the form, in this case, of an offer to supply freezer cabinets to the retailers and to maintain the cabinets free of any direct charge to the retailers.

160   The fact that an undertaking in a dominant position on a market ties *de facto* – even at their own request – 40% of outlets in the relevant market by an exclusivity clause which in reality creates outlet exclusivity constitutes an abuse of a dominant position within the meaning of Article [82] of the Treaty. The exclusivity clause has the effect of preventing the retailers concerned from selling other brands of ice cream (or of reducing the opportunity for them to do so), even though there is a demand for such brands, and of preventing competing manufacturers from gaining access to the relevant market. It follows that HB's contention, set out in paragraph 149 above, that the percentage of outlets potentially likely to be inaccessible owing to the provision of freezer cabinets does not exceed 6%, is incorrect and must be rejected.

(d) Refusal to supply

Chapter 1 explained that competition law respects the freedom to compete, in the interest of economic well-being of society generally. This is of course directly linked to general notions of freedom in society and freedom to work, operate a business and deal with or supply to customers of one's choice. Hence it would not seem wholly illogical to suggest that a firm should not be condemned for deciding to halt its supplies to an existing customer or to refuse to make such supplies to a new customer.

Having said that, however, there may be circumstances where such a refusal to supply or to deal needs to or should be condemned, for example, where as a result of such a practice the process of competition as a whole may be harmed to the detriment of consumers or society generally or where irreparable (and disproportionate or unjustifiable) harm may be caused to a particular customer. Article 82 refusal to supply case law seems to be based on this sensible view. A good example is furnished by *Commercial Solvents v. Commission*. The facts of the case were as follows. Between 1966 and 1970, an Italian chemical supplier ('Instituto'), had provided large quantities of Chemical A to Zoja, a medical supplies manufacturer, which used it to make Chemical E, a tuberculosis drug. The Second Applicant ('CSC'), which was the majority owner of Instituto and a major manufacturer of Chemical A, decided that it would no longer supply Chemical A in the EC except to Instituto, which had begun producing Chemical

E and other related chemicals. The Commission held that CSC was dominant in the European market for Chemical A and that refusal to supply Zoja was an abuse of this dominant position contrary to Article 82. The ECJ stated the following in paragraph 25 of the judgment:

25   However, an undertaking being in a dominant position as regards the production of raw material and therefore able to control the supply to manufacturers of derivatives, cannot, just because it decides to start manufacturing these derivatives (in competition with its former customers) act in such a way as to eliminate their competition which in the case in question, would amount to eliminating one of the principal manufacturers of ethambutol in the common market. Since such conduct is contrary to the objectives expressed in Article [3(g)] of the Treaty and set out in greater detail in Articles [81] and [82], it follows that an undertaking which has a dominant position in the market in raw materials and which, with the object of reserving such raw material for manufacturing its own derivatives, refuses to supply a customer, which is itself a manufacturer of these derivatives, and therefore risks eliminating all competition on the part of this customer, is abusing its dominant position within the meaning of Article [82]. In this context it does not matter that the undertaking ceased to supply in the spring of 1970 because of the cancellation of the purchases by Zoja, because it appears from the applicants' own statement that, when the supplies provided for in the contract had been completed, the sale of aminobutanol would have stopped in any case.

Another example of the refusal to supply situation can be found in the case of *RTE and ITP v. Commission (Magill)*. The case actually represents a meeting point between the 'refusal to supply situation' and the 'essential facilities doctrine'.

Radio Telefis Eireann (RTE) and Independent Television Publications Ltd (ITP) v. Commission ('Magill') [1995] ECR I-743

This case was an appeal against a ruling by the CFI concerning rights to publish TV programming schedules in Ireland and Northern Ireland. At the material time, the applicants (a TV broadcaster and a publishing company) published their own separate weekly schedules and only allowed reproduction by other publishers one weekday in advance. This prevented the complainant, Magill, from compiling a comprehensive weekly guide.

The ECJ upheld the CFI ruling that the Appellants held a monopoly in the subsidiary market of weekly listings and held that national copyright provisions had to be restricted in order to reconcile their exercise with free movement of goods and effective competition. In particular, the manner of exercise of such rights must be 'legitimate' and not a manifest attempt to frustrate competition. Accordingly, the applicants were ordered to grant the rights at a reasonable price.

ECJ

48   With regard to the issue of abuse, the arguments of the appellants and IPO wrongly presuppose that where the conduct of an undertaking in a dominant position consists of the exercise of a right classified by national law as 'copyright', such conduct can never be reviewed in relation to Article [82] of the Treaty.

49   Admittedly, in the absence of Community standardization or harmonization of laws, determination of the conditions and procedures for granting protection of an intellectual property right is a matter for national rules. Further, the exclusive right of reproduction forms part of the author's rights, so that refusal to grant a licence, even if it is the act of an undertaking holding a dominant position, cannot in itself constitute abuse of a dominant position. [*Volvo v. Veng*]

50   However, it is also clear from that judgment (paragraph 9) that the exercise of an exclusive right by the proprietor may, in exceptional circumstances, involve abusive conduct.

51   In the present case, the conduct objected to is the appellants' reliance on copyright conferred by national legislation so as to prevent Magill - or any other undertaking having the same intention - from publishing on a weekly basis information (channel, day, time and title of programmes) together with commentaries and pictures obtained independently of the appellants.

52   Among the circumstances taken into account by the Court of First Instance in concluding that such conduct was abusive was, first, the fact that there was, according to the findings of the Court of First Instance, no actual or potential substitute for a weekly television guide offering information on the programmes for the week ahead. On this point, the Court of First Instance confirmed the Commission's finding that the complete lists of programmes for a 24-hour period - and for a 48-hour period at weekends and before public holidays - published in certain daily and Sunday newspapers, and the television sections of certain magazines covering, in addition, 'highlights' of the week's programmes, were only to a limited extent substitutable for advance information to viewers on all the week's programmes. Only weekly television guides containing comprehensive listings for the week ahead would enable users to decide in advance which programmes they wished to follow and arrange their leisure activities for the week accordingly. The Court of First Instance also established that there was a specific, constant and regular potential demand on the part of consumers.

53   Thus the appellants - who were, by force of circumstance, the only sources of the basic information on programme scheduling which is the indispensable raw material for compiling a weekly television guide - gave viewers wishing to obtain information on the choice of programmes for the week ahead no choice but to buy the weekly guides for each station and draw from each of them the information they needed to make comparisons.

54   The appellants' refusal to provide basic information by relying on national copyright provisions thus prevented the appearance of a new product, a comprehensive weekly guide to television programmes, which the appellants did not offer and for which there was a potential consumer demand. Such refusal constitutes an abuse under heading (b) of the second paragraph of Article [82] of the Treaty.

55   Second, there was no justification for such refusal either in the activity of television broadcasting or in that of publishing television magazines . . .

56   Third, and finally, as the Court of First Instance also held, the appellants, by their conduct, reserved to themselves the secondary market of weekly television guides by excluding all competition on that market (see the judgment in *Commercial Solvents v Commission*, paragraph 25) since they denied access to the basic information which is the raw material indispensable for the compilation of such a guide.

57   In the light of all those circumstances, the Court of First Instance did not err in law in holding that the appellants' conduct was an abuse of a dominant position within the meaning of Article [82] of the Treaty.

(e) Essential facilities

Few doctrines have caused the kind of controversy to which the essential facilities doctrine under Article 82 has given rise. The doctrine is closely linked to the refusal to supply situation, though it should be distinguished as a special type of that situation. Essentially the term 'essential facility' refers to something with the characteristics of a piece of infrastructure or an important raw material etc. Described in simple terms, the doctrine concerns the following situation: a dominant firm owns or controls a facility (such as a port, a gas or petrol pipe, an electricity cable or a distribution network) to which one of its competitors would like to gain access to so that it can sell its goods or provide its services. The highly challenging question which has faced the Commission and the Community Courts is whether a refusal to grant such access could trigger the Article 82 prohibition on the basis that such a refusal amounts to an abuse of dominance.

An important case in which this question was addressed is *Oscar Bronner v. Mediaprint*.

Oscar Bronner GmbH & Co KG v. Mediaprint Zeitungs-und Zeitschriftenverlag GmbH & Co KG [1998] ECR I-7791

The Applicant was publisher of *Der Standard* newspaper, which had 3.6 per cent of circulation and 6 per cent of advertising revenues in Austria. The defendant publisher had 46.8 per cent and 42 per cent respectively and reached 71 per cent of all newspaper readers through its control of the only nationwide early-morning home delivery service. The applicant alleged that, because its small circulation would not permit it profitably to set up such a service, it was

[351]

an 'essential facility' and defendant's refusal to allow it to use the service was an abuse of a dominant position contrary to Article 82. An Article 234 reference was made to the ECJ by the Austrian court. The ECJ's answer (following the Opinion of Advocate General Jacobs) was that there was no such abuse in the circumstances.

ECJ

37 Finally, it would need to be determined whether the refusal by the owner of the only nationwide home-delivery scheme in the territory of a Member State, which uses that scheme to distribute its own daily newspapers, to allow the publisher of a rival daily newspaper access to it constitutes an abuse of a dominant position within the meaning of Article [82] of the Treaty, on the ground that such refusal deprives that competitor of a means of distribution judged essential for the sale of its newspaper.

38 Although in *Commercial Solvents v Commission* and *CBEM* the Court of Justice held the refusal by an undertaking holding a dominant position in a given market to supply an undertaking with which it was in competition in a neighbouring market with raw materials (*Commercial Solvents v Commission*, paragraph 25) and services (*CBEM*, paragraph 26) respectively, which were indispensable to carrying on the rival's business, to constitute an abuse, it should be noted, first, that the Court did so to the extent that the conduct in question was likely to eliminate all competition on the part of that undertaking.

39 Secondly, in *Magill*, at paragraphs 49 and 50, the Court held that refusal by the owner of an intellectual property right to grant a licence, even if it is the act of an undertaking holding a dominant position, cannot in itself constitute abuse of a dominant position, but that the exercise of an exclusive right by the proprietor may, in exceptional circumstances, involve an abuse.

40 In *Magill*, the Court found such exceptional circumstances . . . [see paragraphs 53-56 of the judgment]

41 Therefore, even if that case-law on the exercise of an intellectual property right were applicable to the exercise of any property right whatever, it would still be necessary, for the *Magill* judgment to be effectively relied upon in order to plead the existence of an abuse within the meaning of Article [82] of the Treaty in a situation such as that which forms the subject-matter of the first question, not only that the refusal of the service comprised in home delivery be likely to eliminate all competition in the daily newspaper market on the part of the person requesting the service and that such refusal be incapable of being objectively justified, but also that the service in itself be indispensable to carrying on that person's business, inasmuch as there is no actual or potential substitute in existence for that home-delivery scheme.

42 That is certainly not the case even if, as in the case which is the subject of the main proceedings, there is only one nationwide home-delivery scheme in the territory of

a Member State and, moreover, the owner of that scheme holds a dominant position in the market for services constituted by that scheme or of which it forms part.

43   In the first place, it is undisputed that other methods of distributing daily newspapers, such as by post and through sale in shops and at kiosks, even though they may be less advantageous for the distribution of certain newspapers, exist and are used by the publishers of those daily newspapers.

44   Moreover, it does not appear that there are any technical, legal or even economic obstacles capable of making it impossible, or even unreasonably difficult, for any other publisher of daily newspapers to establish, alone or in cooperation with other publishers, its own nationwide home-delivery scheme and use it to distribute its own daily newspapers.

45   It should be emphasised in that respect that, in order to demonstrate that the creation of such a system is not a realistic potential alternative and that access to the existing system is therefore indispensable, it is not enough to argue that it is not economically viable by reason of the small circulation of the daily newspaper or newspapers to be distributed.

46   For such access to be capable of being regarded as indispensable, it would be necessary at the very least to establish, as the Advocate General has pointed out at point 68 of his Opinion, that it is not economically viable to create a second home-delivery scheme for the distribution of daily newspapers with a circulation comparable to that of the daily newspapers distributed by the existing scheme.

Although *Oscar Bronner* seems to narrow the scope for any finding of abuse through refusal to allow use of a given facility, the tension created by the *Magill* ruling remains, particularly with respect to intellectual property rights, where an owner refuses to grant a licence to a third party who is otherwise completely excluded from the market.

As the discussion in chapter 6 reveals, a patent or copyright is a limited monopoly granted as a reward and incentive for creativity. To punish its exercise would defeat the purpose. But such rights, particularly patents, also function to encourage publication of what might otherwise remain secret, thereby facilitating further research within the same field and leading to consequential inventions building upon the initial invention. The resolution to the tension, therefore, lies in the *use* to which the potential grantee wishes to put the licence, as can be seen from the following extracts from the case of *IMS Health v. NDC Health*.

IMS Health GmbH & Co. OHG v. NDC Health GmbH & Co. KG [2004] ECR I-0000

The parties to the dispute were competitors engaged in the collection, processing and interpretation of data concerning regional sales of pharmaceutical products in Germany. IMS had established a copyrighted system for dividing the country into research segments, a system which had become an industry standard essential for any competing company. IMS refused to grant a licence to competitors to enable them to have access to its systems. In a decision (*NDC Health/IMS Health IMS*) the Commission, applying *Magill*, ordered interim measures against IMS, ordering the firm to license the use of its system so that competitors can have access to the market. In the CFI and later the ECJ, the Presidents of the Courts suspended the decision of the Commission until final determination of the matter by the Courts. In a separate (domestic) action, IMS sought to enforce its copyright against NDC. An Article 234 reference was made to the ECJ.

Advocate General Tizzano

61   ... The judgments of the Court on the refusal to grant a licence over an intellectual property right lead me to believe that, in order for an unjustified refusal to be deemed abusive, it is not sufficient that the intangible asset forming the subject-matter of the intellectual property right be essential for operating on a market and that therefore, by virtue of that refusal, the owner of the copyright may eliminate all competition on the secondary market.

62   Even where those circumstances obtain, in weighing the balance between the interest in protection of the intellectual property right and the economic freedom of its owner, on the one hand, and the interest in protection of free competition, on the other, the balance may in my view come down in favour of the latter interest only if the refusal to grant the licence prevents the development of the secondary market to the detriment of consumers. More specifically, I consider that the refusal to grant a licence may be deemed abusive only if the requesting undertaking does not wish to limit itself essentially to duplicating the goods or services already offered on the secondary market by the owner of the intellectual property right but intends to produce goods or services of a different nature which, although in competition with those of the owner of the right, answer specific consumer requirements not satisfied by existing goods or services.

63   That was in my view clearly held in the *Magill* judgment in which, as has been seen, the Court held an unjustified refusal to grant a licence [in the circumstances of the case] to be abusive ...

...

65   Yet it is perhaps possible also to construe the [*Volvo v. Veng*] judgment in this way. In that case the Court stated that a refusal to grant ... a licence cannot in itself constitute an abuse of a dominant position. Even though in that case a registered design in respect of car body panels could be regarded as an essential input for operating on the (presumptive) market for original spare parts, it may be considered that the Court did not deem the refusal to grant a licence abusive owing to the fact

that the undertaking seeking the licence wished to do no more than duplicate the products of the owner of the registered design, and thus produce original Volvo spare parts.

66 In light of all the foregoing considerations I therefore consider that the reply to the first question should be that Article 82 EC must be interpreted as meaning that the refusal to grant a licence for the use of an intangible asset protected by copyright entails an abuse of a dominant position within the meaning of that provision where (a) there are no objective justifications for such refusal; (b) use of the intangible asset is essential for operating on a secondary market with the consequence that by way of such refusal the owner of the right would ultimately eliminate all competition on that market. However, that is subject to the condition that the undertaking seeking the licence does not wish to limit itself essentially to duplicating the goods or services already offered on the secondary market by the owner of the intellectual property right but intends to produce goods or services of a different nature which, although in competition with those of the owner of the right, answer specific consumer requirements not satisfied by existing goods or services.

Although this is only an opinion and so lacks the binding force of the law, Advocate General Tizzano seems to have struck a sensible balance as was done by the ECJ and Advocate General Jacobs in *Oscar Bronner*.

ECJ

28 It is clear from paragraphs 43 and 44 of *Bronner* that, in order to determine whether a product or service is indispensable for enabling an undertaking to carry on business in a particular market, it must be determined whether there are products or services which constitute alternative solutions, even if they are less advantageous, and whether there are technical, legal or economic obstacles capable of making it impossible or at least unreasonably difficult for any undertaking seeking to operate in the market to create, possibly in cooperation with other operators, the alternative products or services. According to paragraph 46 of *Bronner*, in order to accept the existence of economic obstacles, it must be established, at the very least, that the creation of those products or services is not economically viable for production on a scale comparable to that of the undertaking which controls the existing product or service.

29 It is for the national court to determine, in the light of the evidence submitted to it, whether such is the case in the dispute in the main proceedings. In that regard, as the Advocate General stated in points 83 and 84 of his Opinion, account must be taken of the fact that a high level of participation by the pharmaceutical laboratories in the improvement of the 1860 brick structure protected by copyright, on the supposition that it is proven, has created a dependency by users in regard to that structure, particularly at a technical level. In such circumstances, it is likely that those laboratories would have to make exceptional organisational and financial efforts in order to acquire the studies on regional sales of pharmaceutical products

presented on the basis of a structure other than that protected by copyright. The supplier of that alternative structure might therefore be obliged to offer terms which are such as to rule out any economic viability of business on a scale comparable to that of the undertaking which controls the protected structure.

30   The answer to the second and third questions must, therefore, be that, for the purposes of determining the potentially abusive character of the refusal of an undertaking in a dominant position to grant a licence to use a brick structure protected by a copyright owned by it, the degree of participation by the users in the development of that structure and the outlay, particularly in terms of cost, on the part of potential users in order to purchase regional sales studies for pharmaceutical products presented on the basis of an alternative structure, are factors which must be taken into consideration in determining whether the protected structure is indispensable for the marketing of studies of that kind.

. . .

34   According to settled case-law, the exclusive right of reproduction forms part of the owner's rights, so that refusal to grant a licence, even if it is the act of an undertaking holding a dominant position, cannot in itself constitute abuse of a dominant position (judgment in [*Volvo v. Veng*], . . . , paragraph 8, and *Magill*, paragraph 49).

35   Nevertheless, as is clear from that case-law, exercise of an exclusive right by the owner may, in exceptional circumstances, involve abusive conduct (*Volvo*, paragraph 9, and *Magill*, paragraph 50).

36   The Court held that such exceptional circumstances were present in the case giving rise to the judgment in *Magill*, in which the conduct complained of by the television channels in a dominant position involved invoking the copyright conferred by national legislation on the weekly listings of their programmes in order to prevent another undertaking from publishing information on those programmes together with commentaries, on a weekly basis.

37   According to the summary of the *Magill* judgment made by the Court at paragraph 40 of the judgment in *Bronner*, the exceptional circumstances were constituted by the fact that the refusal in question concerned a product (information on the weekly schedules of certain television channels), the supply of which was indispensable for carrying on the business in question, (the publishing of a general television guide), in that, without that information, the person wishing to produce such a guide would find it impossible to publish it and offer it for sale (paragraph 53), the fact that such refusal prevented the emergence of a new product for which there was a potential consumer demand (paragraph 54), the fact that it was not justified by objective considerations (paragraph 55), and was likely to exclude all competition in the secondary market (paragraph 56).

38   It is clear from that case-law that, in order for the refusal by an undertaking which owns a copyright to give access to a product or service indispensable for carrying

on a particular business to be treated as abusive, it is sufficient that three cumulative conditions be satisfied, namely, that that refusal is preventing the emergence of a new product for which there is a potential consumers demand, that it is unjustified and such as to exclude any competition on a secondary market.

39 In light of the order for reference and the observations submitted to the Court, which reveal a major dispute as regards the interpretation of the third condition, it is appropriate to consider that question first.

The third condition, relating to the likelihood of excluding all competition on a secondary market

40 In that regard, it is appropriate to recall the approach followed by the Court in the *Bronner* judgment, in which it was asked whether the fact that a press undertaking with a very large share of the daily newspaper market in a Member State which operates the only nationwide newspaper home-delivery scheme in that Member State refuses paid access to that scheme by the publisher of a rival newspaper, which by reason of its small circulation is unable either alone or in cooperation with other publishers to set up and operate its own home-delivery scheme under economically reasonable conditions, constitutes the abuse of a dominant position.

41 The Court, first of all, invited the national court to determine whether the home delivery schemes constituted a separate market (*Bronner*, paragraph 34), on which, in light of the circumstances of the case, the press undertaking held a *de facto* monopoly position and, thus, a dominant position (paragraph 35). It then invited the national court to determine whether the refusal by the owner of the only nationwide home-delivery scheme in a Member State, which used that scheme to distribute its own daily newspapers, to allow the publisher of a rival daily newspaper access to it deprived that competitor of a means of distribution judged essential for the sale of its newspaper (paragraph 37).

42 Therefore, the Court held that it was relevant, in order to assess whether the refusal to grant access to a product or a service indispensable for carrying on a particular business activity was an abuse, to distinguish an upstream market, constituted by the product or service, in that case the market for home delivery of daily newspapers, and a (secondary) downstream market, on which the product or service in question is used for the production of another product or the supply of another service, in that case the market for daily newspapers themselves.

43 The fact that the delivery service was not marketed separately was not regarded as precluding, from the outset, the possibility of identifying a separate market.

44 It appears, therefore, as the Advocate General set out in points 56 to 59 of his Opinion, that, for the purposes of the application of the earlier case-law, it is sufficient that a potential market or even hypothetical market can be identified. Such is the case where the products or services are indispensable in order to carry on

a particular business and where there is an actual demand for them on the part of undertakings which seek to carry on the business for which they are indispensable.

45   Accordingly, it is determinative that two different stages of production may be identified and that they are interconnected, the upstream product is indispensable in as much as for supply of the downstream product.

46   Transposed to the facts of the case in the main proceedings, that approach prompts consideration as to whether the 1860 brick structure constitutes, upstream, an indispensable factor in the downstream supply of German regional sales data for pharmaceutical products.

47   It is for the national court to establish whether that is in fact the position, and, if so be the case, to examine whether the refusal by IMS to grant a licence to use the structure at issue is capable of excluding all competition on the market for the supply of German regional sales data on pharmaceutical products.

The first condition, relating to the emergence of a new product

48   As the Advocate General stated in point 62 of his Opinion, that condition relates to the consideration that, in the balancing of the interest in protection of copyright and the economic freedom of its owner, against the interest in protection of free competition the latter can prevail only where refusal to grant a licence prevents the development of the secondary market to the detriment of consumers.

49   Therefore, the refusal by an undertaking in a dominant position to allow access to a product protected by copyright, where that product is indispensable for operating on a secondary market, may be regarded as abusive only where the undertaking which requested the licence does not intend to limit itself essentially to duplicating the goods or services already offered on the secondary market by the owner of the copyright, but intends to produce new goods or services not offered by the owner of the right and for which there is a potential consumer demand.

50   It is for the national court to determine whether such is the case in the dispute in the main proceedings.

The second condition, relating to whether the refusal was unjustified

51   As to that condition, on whose interpretation no specific observations have been made, it is for the national court to examine, if appropriate, in light of the facts before it, whether the refusal of the request for a licence is justified by objective considerations.

52   Accordingly, the answer to the first question must be that the refusal by an undertaking which holds a dominant position and is the owner of an intellectual property right over a brick structure which is indispensable for the presentation of data on regional sales of pharmaceutical products in a Member State, to grant a licence to use that structure to another undertaking which also wishes to supply such data

in the same Member State, constitutes an abuse of a dominant position within the meaning of Article 82 EC where the following conditions are fulfilled:
- the undertaking which requested the licence intends to offer, on the market for the supply of the data in question, new products or services not offered by the copyright owner and for which there is a potential consumer demand;
- the refusal is not justified by objective considerations;
- the refusal is such as to reserve to the copyright owner the market for the supply of data on sales of pharmaceutical products in the Member State concerned by eliminating all competition on that market.

(f) Excessive pricing

Every firm has a strong 'natural desire' to maximise its profits. Obviously one way in which a firm can achieve this is by charging high or excessive prices. Article 82 stipulates in paragraph (a) that 'directly or indirectly imposing unfair purchase or selling prices' can amount to an abuse of a dominant position. The Commission has not shown any hesitation in considering the excessive pricing situation within the mischief of Article 82. Linguistically speaking, there is a journey to be made between 'excessive' pricing which is the common term used in practice and 'unfair' prices, the term used in Article 82 itself. The ECJ took a positive step in *United Brands* towards mapping out the route of this journey.

United Brands v. Commission

(The case is cited above with facts at p. 331 above.)

ECJ

248   The imposition by an undertaking in a dominant position directly or indirectly of unfair purchase or selling prices is an abuse to which exception can be taken under Article [82] of the Treaty.

249   It is advisable therefore to ascertain whether the dominant undertaking has made use of the opportunities arising out of its dominant position in such a way as to reap trading benefits which it would not have reaped if there had been normal and sufficiently effective competition.

250   In this case charging a price which is excessive because it has no reasonable relation to the economic value of the product supplied would be such an abuse.

251   This excess could, *inter alia*, be determined objectively if it were possible for it to be calculated by making a comparison between the selling price of the product in question and its cost of production, which would disclose the amount of the profit margin; however the Commission has not done this since it has not analysed UBC's costs structure.

252   The questions therefore to be determined are whether the difference between the costs actually incurred and the price actually charged is excessive, and, if the answer to this question is in the affirmative, whether a price has been imposed which is either unfair in itself or when compared to competing products.

253   Other ways may be devised - and economic theorists have not failed to think up several - of selecting the rules for determining whether the price of a product is unfair.

254   While appreciating the considerable and at times very great difficulties in working out production costs which may sometimes include a discretionary apportionment of indirect costs and general expenditure and which may vary significantly according to the size of the undertaking, its object, the complex nature of its set up, its territorial area of operations, whether it manufactures one or several products, the number of its subsidiaries and their relationship with each other, the production costs of the banana do not seem to present any insuperable problems.

The approach suggested by the ECJ is highly interesting, though not free from difficulty in practice. On a narrow interpretation of the judgment, it would be correct to suggest that the ECJ seems to have established that not every form of excessive pricing is objectionable: only that which is unfair.

(g) Discounts and rebates

One of the economic objectives of protecting the process of competition identified in chapter 1 concerns achieving lower prices for customers and consumers. At the risk of stating the obvious, a rebate (or a discount) amounts to a 'lower' price, meaning lower than the 'normal' or 'previously charged' price. Thus it may seem at first odd to suggest that this type of behaviour might be within the mischief of Article 82. Nevertheless, this suggestion has been upheld in several Article 82 cases, which shows that offering various kinds of rebates may be objectionable where it acts as an incentive to customers to become tied to the dominant firm in terms of obtaining their requirements exclusively from the latter. The following are the main types of rebates which are worth mentioning.

(i) Loyalty or fidelity rebate

In *Hoffmann-La Roche* (cited above; see facts at p. 335 above), the ECJ stated at paragraph 89 of the judgment that a dominant undertaking abuses its position if without tying the purchasers by a formal obligation it 'applies, either under the terms of agreements concluded with these purchasers or unilaterally, a system of fidelity rebates, that is to say discounts conditional on the customer's obtaining all or most of its requirements – whether the quantity of its purchases be large or small – from the undertaking in a dominant position'. In paragraph 90 the ECJ explained the rationale for this attitude as follows:

90   Obligations of this kind to obtain supplies exclusively from a particular undertaking, whether or not they are in consideration of rebates or of the granting of fidelity rebates intended to give the purchaser an incentive to obtain his supplies exclusively from the undertaking in a dominant position, are incompatible with the objective of undistorted competition within the common market, because - unless there are exceptional circumstances which may make an agreement between undertakings in the context of Article [81] and in particular of paragraph (3) of that Article, permissible - they are not based on an economic transaction which justifies this burden or benefit but are designed to deprive the purchaser of or restrict his possible choices of sources of supply and to deny other producers access to the market.

The fidelity rebate, unlike quantity rebates exclusively linked with the volume of purchases from the producer concerned, is designed through the grant of a financial advantage to prevent customers from obtaining their supplies from competing producers.

Furthermore the effect of fidelity rebates is to apply dissimilar conditions to equivalent transactions with other trading parties in that two purchasers pay a different price for the same quantity of the same product depending on whether they obtain their supplies exclusively from the undertaking in a dominant position or have several sources of supply.

Finally these practices by an undertaking in a dominant position and especially on an expanding market tend to consolidate this position by means of a form of competition which is not based on the transactions effected and is therefore distorted.

(ii) Target rebates

Michelin NV v. Commission (**1983**)

(The case is cited above with facts at p. 339 above.)

ECJ

70   As regards the application of Article [82] to a system of discounts conditional upon the attainment of sales targets ... Article [82] covers practices which are likely to affect the structure of a market where, as a direct result of the presence of the undertaking in question, competition has already been weakened and which, through recourse to methods different from those governing normal competition in products or services based on traders' performance, have the effect of hindering the maintenance or development of the level of competition still existing on the market.

71   In the case more particularly of the grant by an undertaking in a dominant position of discounts to its customers the court has held in its judgments [in *Sugar Cartel* and *Hofmann-La Roche*] that in contrast to a quantity discount, which is linked solely to the volume of purchases from the manufacturer concerned, a loyalty rebate, which by offering customers financial advantages tends to prevent them from obtaining their

supplies from competing manufacturers, amounts to an abuse within the meaning of Article [82] of the Treaty.

72   As regards the system at issue in this case, which is characterized by the use of sales targets, it must be observed that this system does not amount to a mere quantity discount linked solely to the volume of goods purchased since the progressive scale of the previous year's turnover indicates only the limits within which the system applies. Michelin NV has moreover itself pointed out that the majority of dealers who bought more than 3000 tyres a year were in any case in the group receiving the highest rebates. On the other hand the system in question did not require dealers to enter into any exclusive dealing agreements or to obtain a specific proportion of their supplies from Michelin NV, and that this point distinguishes it from loyalty rebates of the type which the Court had to consider in its judgment of 13 February 1979 in *Hoffmann-La Roche*.

73   In deciding whether Michelin NV abused its dominant position in applying its discount system it is therefore necessary to consider all the circumstances, particularly the criteria and rules for the grant of the discount, and to investigate whether, in providing an advantage not based on any economic service justifying it, the discount tends to remove or restrict the buyer's freedom to choose his sources of supply, to bar competitors from access to the market, to apply dissimilar conditions to equivalent transactions with other trading parties or to strengthen the dominant position by distorting competition.

(iii) Across-the-board rebates

Across-the-board rebates refer to the situation where a dominant firm producing a range of products offers a rebate to its customers when they acquire the whole range. Obviously, this situation is directly linked to the tying situation discussed above, though it is not identical to it in the sense that, in the latter situation, the dominant firm makes the supplying of one product conditional upon the customer purchasing another product. Thus, when offering such rebates the dominant firm creates a tie-in within the meaning of paragraph (d) of Article 82. Such practice was condemned by the ECJ in *Hoffmann-La Roche* (paragraphs 109–111 of the judgment). In the case, the ECJ labelled such practice 'a conduct restricting competition'. It held that the practice created a particularly attractive incentive for customers to allow the dominant firm to supply their requirements because if the customer wanted to approach a competitor of the dominant firm for a particular product he will be prevented from doing so because he would thereby lose the benefit of the rebate.

The CFI has recently confirmed many of the statements made above, explaining in economic terms when rebates will be found to be abusive, in the case of *Manufacture française des pneumatiques Michelin [France] v. Commission* (2003). The case concerned a complex graduated system of rebates on Michelin products with a reference period of one year which was operated by Michelin France, manufacturer of new and retreaded tyres. In paragraphs

58–60 of the judgment, the CFI dealt with the issue of a quantity rebate linked solely to the volume of purchases made from a dominant firm. According to the CFI such a rebate is generally considered not to be within the mischief of Article 82. It stated that the rebate is deemed to reflect gains of efficiencies and economies of scale made by the dominant firm. Thus, a rebate in which the rate of the discount increases according to the volume purchased will not fall within Article 82 unless the system for granting rebate reveals that it is not based on an economically justified countervailing benefit but tends to prevent customers from obtaining their requirements from competing sources. According to the CFI determining this requires an examination of the circumstances in question, in particular the criteria and rules governing the grant of the rebate.

In the case, specifically, the objectionable qualities of the terms in question were that Michelin France calculated the discounts not by tranche but on the basis of turnover in Michelin products overall and with a reference period of one year (see paragraphs 81–111). In dismissing the application by Michelin France, the CFI made several important findings in these paragraphs. Some of these findings are worth mentioning:

- Michelin's quantity rebate system was intended to tie customers (truck tyre dealers in France) to it by granting advantages which were not based on any economic justification;
- Michelin failed to establish that its rebates were based on actual cost savings;
- The system was loyalty inducing and because of this the system tended to restrict customers from choosing freely among suppliers;
- The system made access to the market more difficult for competitors;
- A system such as Michelin's is within the mischief of Article 82, regardless of whether it is transparent or not;
- The Commission was wrong to say that the ECJ had held that for a system of rebates to fall outside Article 82 the reference period in the system could not exceed three months: the ECJ did not expressly hold this;
- The loyalty inducing nature of a system of rebates calculated on total turnover achieved increased in proportion to the length of the reference period;
- If a rebate is granted for purchases made during a reference period, the loyalty-inducing effect is less significant where the additional rebate applies only to the quantities exceeding a certain threshold than where the rebate applies to total turnover achieved during the reference period.

A similar example of loyalty-inducing rebates was found in bonuses granted to travel agents on sales of tickets on British Airways calculated on the overall volume for each target level met. (See *British Airways plc v. Commission*; extracted with facts at pp. 368–369 below concerning discriminatory pricing.)

(h) English clause

The term 'English clause' may sound foreign even to many English lawyers. The clause refers to the situation where a dominant firm requires a customer to report a 'better' offer which the customer may receive from a competitor and allows the customer only to accept such an offer when the dominant firm cannot match it. The Commission explains in its *Guidelines on Vertical Restraints* that such a clause can have the same effect as a non-compete obligation. It has explained that the rationale for condemning such clauses was that 'by increasing the transparency of the market, [such a clause] may facilitate collusion between the suppliers. An English clause may also work as quantity forcing. Quantity-forcing on the buyer is a weaker form of non-compete, where incentives or obligations agreed between the supplier and the buyer make the latter concentrate his purchases to a large extent with one supplier.' (paragraph 152) The ECJ condemned the English clause in *Hoffmann-La Roche* using a similar rationale (paragraphs 106–108).

(i) Price discrimination

Discrimination is declared unlawful in Article 82(2)(c) which refers to 'applying dissimilar conditions to equivalent transactions with other trading parties, thereby placing them at a competitive disadvantage'. Obviously the prohibition in that paragraph also includes the situation of price discrimination. However it is important to note that this prohibition should not be regarded as absolute. In the commercial world, firms may sometimes charge different prices to different customers purchasing the same product (an example close to home would be student discounts), and competition law should not use a *per se* approach in such situations. Indeed Article 82(2)(c) itself refers to 'equivalent transactions' and placing other trading parties at a 'competitive disadvantage'.

Whilst the ECJ has not always insisted that the Commission should prove that the latter point be established (*Corsica Ferries*), logic and sense dictate that it is essential that the former is established: it would be questionable, indeed wrong, to suggest that one can establish discrimination by a dominant firm between two customers in the context of Article 82 without showing first that the two customers are on equal footing.

Price discrimination has been condemned in several Article 82 cases. An interesting example to cite is *United Brands v. Commission* in which the price discrimination operated by United Brands had a 'geographic' dimension.

United Brands v. Commission

(The case is cited above with facts at p. 331 above.)

ECJ

204 All the bananas marketed by UBC under the brand name 'Chiquita' on the relevant market have the same geographic origin, belong to the same variety (Cavendish Valery) and are of almost the same quality.

205　　They are unloaded in two ports, Rotterdam and Bremerhaven, where unloading costs only differ by a few cents in the dollar per box of 20 kilogrammes, and are resold, except to Scipio and in Ireland, subject to the same conditions of sale and terms of payment after they have been loaded on the buyers' wagons or lorries, the price of a box amounting on average to between 3 and 4 dollars and going up to 5 dollars in 1974.

206　　The costs of carriage from the unloading ports to the ripening installations and the amount of any duty payable under the common customs tariff are borne by the purchaser except in Ireland.

207　　This being so all those customers going to Rotterdam and Bremerhaven to obtain their supplies might be expected to find that UBC offers them all the same selling price for 'Chiquita' bananas.

208　　The Commission blames the applicant for charging each week for the sale of its branded bananas – without objective justification – a selling price which differs appreciably according to the Member State where its customers are established.

209　　This policy of charging differing prices according to the Member States for which the bananas are intended has been applied at least since 1971 in the case of customers of the Federal Republic of Germany, the Netherlands and the Bleu and was extended in January 1973 to customers in Denmark and in November 1973 to customers in Ireland.

210　　The maximum weekly differences recorded between two destinations were on average during the whole of 1971, 17.6% - in 1972, 11.3% - in 1973, 14.5% - in 1974, 13.5%.

211　　The highest weekly differences (per box) were respectively between customers in Germany on the one hand and Belgo-Luxembourg and Netherlands customers on the other hand ... And between customers in Denmark on the one hand and Belgo-Luxembourg and Netherlands customers on the other hand ...

212　　The price customers in Belgium are asked to pay is on average 80% higher than that paid by customers in Ireland.

213　　The greatest difference in price is 138% between the delivered Rotterdam price charged by UBC to its customers in Ireland and the f.o.r. Bremerhaven price charged by UBC to its customers in Denmark, that is to say the price paid by Danish customers is 2.38 times the price paid by Irish customers.

214　　The Commission treats these facts as an abuse of a dominant position in that UBC has applied dissimilar conditions to equivalent transactions with the other trading parties, thereby placing them at a competitive disadvantage.

215　　The applicant states that its prices are determined by market forces and cannot therefore be discriminatory.

216   Further the average difference in the price of 'Chiquita' bananas between the national markets in question was only 5% in 1975.

217   The price in any given week is calculated so as to reflect as much as possible the anticipated yellow market price in the following week for each national market.

218   This price is fixed by the Rotterdam management after discussions and negotiations between the applicant's local representatives and the ripeners/distributors must perforce take into account the different competitive context in which ripeners/distributors in the different countries are operating.

219   It finds its objective justification in the average anticipated market price.

220   These price differences are in fact due to fluctuating market factors such as the weather, different availability of seasonal competing fruit, holidays, strikes, government measures, currency denominations.

221   In short the applicant has been asked by the Commission to take appropriate steps to establish a single banana market at a time when it has in fact been unable to do so.

222   According to the applicant as long as the Community institutions have not set up the machinery for a single banana market and the various markets remain national and respond to their individual supply/demand situations differences in prices between them cannot be prevented.

223   UBC's answers to the Commission's requests for particulars (the letters of 14 May, 13 September, 10 and 11 December 1974 and 13 February 1975) show that UBC charges its customers each week for its bananas sold under the Chiquita brand name a different selling price depending on the Member State where the latter carry on their business as ripeners/distributors according to the ratios to which the Commission has drawn attention.

224   These price differences can reach 30 to 50% in some weeks, even though products supplied under the transactions are equivalent (with the exception of the Scipio group, subject to this observation that the bananas from Scipio's ripening installations are sold at the same price as those sold by independent ripeners).

225   In fact the bananas sold by UBC are all freighted in the same ships, are unloaded at the same cost in Rotterdam or Bremerhaven and the price differences relate to substantially similar quantities of bananas of the same variety, which have been brought to the same degree of ripening, are of similar quality and sold under the same 'Chiquita' brand name under the same conditions of sale and payment for loading on to the purchaser's own means of transport and the latter have to pay customs duties, taxes and transport costs from these ports.

226   This policy of discriminatory prices has been applied by UBC since 1971 to customers of Germany, the Netherlands and the Bleu and was extended at the beginning of 1973 to customers in Denmark and in November 1973 to customers in Ireland.

227   Although the responsibility for establishing the single banana market does not lie with the applicant, it can only endeavour to take 'what the market can bear' provided that it complies with the rules for the Regulation and coordination of the market laid down by the Treaty.

228   Once it can be grasped that differences in transport costs, taxation, customs duties, the wages of the labour force, the conditions of marketing, the differences in the parity of currencies, the density of competition may eventually culminate in different retail selling price levels according to the Member States, then it follows those differences are factors which UBC only has to take into account to a limited extent since it sells a product which is always the same and at the same place to ripener/distributors who – alone – bear the risks of the consumers' market.

229   The interplay of supply and demand should, owing to its nature, only be applied to each stage where it is really manifest.

230   The mechanisms of the market are adversely affected if the price is calculated by leaving out one stage of the market and taking into account the law of supply and demand as between the vendor and the ultimate consumer and not as between the vendor (UBC) and the purchaser (the ripener/distributors).

231   Thus, by reason of its dominant position UBC, fed with information by its local reprensentatives, was in fact able to impose its selling price on the intermediate purchaser. This price and also the 'weekly quota allocated' is only fixed and notified to the customer four days before the vessel carrying the bananas berths.

232   These discriminatory prices, which varied according to the circumstances of the Member States, were just so many obstacles to the free movement of goods and their effect was intensified by the clause forbidding the resale of bananas while still green and by reducing the deliveries of the quantities ordered.

233   A rigid partitioning of national markets was thus created at price levels, which were artificially different, placing certain distributor/ripeners at a competitive disadvantage, since compared with what it should have been competition had thereby been distorted.

The judgment of the ECJ furnishes an example of the single market objective dictating competition policy. It is useful to compare this approach with that taken by many courts and competition authorities in other jurisdictions, including that of the OFT in the UK which shows that price discrimination is only abusive if it aims to exclude competitors (on the OFT's views, see pp. 393–395 below).

A further example of discriminatory pricing in the Article 82 case law is found in *British Airways plc v. Commission*.

***British Airways plc v Commission (Virgin Atlantic Airways Ltd intervening)*
[2003] ECR 1**

'BA', the largest British airline, was found to hold a dominant position in the purchasing of travel agency services, with a market share of about 40 per cent compared to the five nearest competitors holding shares ranging from about 3–7 per cent. The Commission alleged, *inter alia*, that BA abused this position contrary to Article 82 with commission bonus agreements which unfairly discriminated between agents because they were based on meeting or improving upon certain sales targets rather than overall quantities or level of service.

CFI

234   It is undisputed that, as the Commission points out in recital 29 of the contested decision, attainment by United Kingdom travel agents of their BA tickets sales growth targets led to an increase in the rate of commission paid to them by BA not only on BA tickets sold after the target was reached but also on all BA tickets handled by the agents during the reference period in question.

235   To that extent, the performance reward schemes at issue could result in different rates of commission being applied to an identical amount of revenue generated by the sale of BA tickets by two travel agents, since their respective sales figures, and hence their rates of growth, would have been different during the previous reference period.

236   By remunerating at different levels services that were nevertheless identical and supplied during the same reference period, those performance reward schemes distorted the level of remuneration which the parties concerned received in the form of commissions paid by BA.

237   As BA has stated itself, United Kingdom travel agents compete intensely with each other, and this ability to compete depends on their ability to provide seats on flights suited to travellers' wishes, at a reasonable cost.

238   Being dependent on the financial resources of each agent, that ability of agents to compete in supplying air travel agency services to travellers and to stimulate the demand of airlines for such services was naturally affected by the discriminatory conditions of remuneration inherent in BA's performance reward schemes.

239   BA's arguments based on the importance of the size of the travel agents established in the United Kingdom are irrelevant. The performance reward schemes in dispute were, in themselves, based on a parameter unrelated to the criterion of the size of the undertakings, since they were based on the extent to which travel agents increased their sales of BA tickets in relation to the threshold constituted by the number of BA tickets sold during the previous reference period.

240   In those circumstances, the Commission was right to hold that BA's performance reward schemes constituted an abuse of BA's dominant position on the United Kingdom market for air travel agency services, in that they produced discriminatory effects within the network of travel agents established in the United Kingdom, thereby inflicting on some of them a competitive disadvantage within the meaning of subparagraph (c) of the second paragraph of Article 82 EC.

(j) Predatory pricing

The concept of predatory pricing is based on facts and presumptions. In simple terms, it refers to the situation where a dominant firm (Alpha) reduces its price to below cost level for a period of time during which it will be able to eliminate or contain a competitive force. Following that, and once Alpha deems it safe enough, it will raise its price to a level above the competitive price level in order to recoup the losses it made during the reduction period. The concept, however, is extremely hard to apply in practice, mainly because the only way of separating desirable competitive price cutting from anti-competitive predation is through detailed analysis in order to determine the 'right' price on the basis of average variable costs (something the forces of competition are supposed to do automatically). Consequently, its application in the context of Article 82 has given rise to some controversy. In the UK, the OFT has in its Guideline on *Assessment of Conduct* (OFT414), set out some of the economic factors that might be used in various circumstances to estimate such costs and it may aid the reader to refer to the Guideline (see pp. 398–404 below). Some guidance on the use of the concept under Article 82 is provided in some of the key cases.

AKZO Chemie BV v. Commission

(The case is cited above with facts at pp. 337–338 above.)

ECJ

70   ... Article [82] prohibits a dominant undertaking from eliminating a competitor and thereby strengthening its position by using methods other than those which come within the scope of competition on the basis of quality. From that point of view, however, not all competition by means of price can be regarded as legitimate.

71   Prices below average variable costs (that is to say, those which vary depending on the quantities produced) by means of which a dominant undertaking seeks to eliminate a competitor must be regarded as abusive. A dominant undertaking has no interest in applying such prices except that of eliminating competitors so as to enable it subsequently to raise its prices by taking advantage of its monopolistic position, since each sale generates a loss, namely the total amount of the fixed costs (that is to say, those which remain constant regardless of the quantities produced) and, at least, part of the variable costs relating to the unit produced.

[369]

72   Moreover, prices below average total costs, that is to say, fixed costs plus variable costs, but above average variable costs, must be regarded as abusive if they are determined as part of a plan for eliminating a competitor. Such prices can drive from the market undertakings which are perhaps as efficient as the dominant undertaking but which, because of their smaller financial resources, are incapable of withstanding the competition waged against them.

...

76   The Commission found that AKZO had made direct threats to ECS during meetings held in late 1979 with managers of ECS, with the aim of securing ECS's withdrawal from the market for the organic peroxides for the 'plastics' application (Article 1(i) of the decision).

77   AKZO denies that it threatened ECS. It states that it merely informed ECS that it could not rely on the continuation of AKZO's collaboration in the flour additives sector if ECS persisted in making offers at very low prices in the plastics sector. Before the dispute ECS and AKZO used to supply one another with certain flour additives at reduced prices in order to supplement inadequate output or to meet the needs of the party which did not itself manufacture one of those products. Thus AKZO satisfied some of ECS's benzoyl-peroxide requirements while ECS supplied AKZO with vitamin mixes.

78   In order to decide whether this allegation is well founded it is necessary to determine the content of the meetings which took place on 16 November and 3 December 1979. In this respect the Court has records of these meetings prepared by officers of ECS, a statement made by a manager of AKZO and a note made by another officer of AKZO.

79   The information contained in the various documents prepared by the managers of ECS is substantially consistent. It shows in particular that during the first meeting AKZO made known its intention to make a general price reduction in the flour additives sector if ECS continued to sell benzoyl peroxide in the plastics sector, and its determination to sell at prices below its production cost, if necessary, even if this entailed incurring a loss ... During the second meeting AKZO confirmed that it was prepared to sell at below its production cost, if need be.

80   Those meetings prompted ECS to apply to the High Court in London for an order prohibiting AKZO from carrying its threats on the ground that they constituted an infringement of Article [82] of the Treaty. It was in the course of those proceedings that one of AKZO's officers described in an affidavit the content of the meetings. That affidavit also shows that AKZO was prepared to sell at below its cost prices and, if necessary, to incur a loss, if ECS did not withdraw from the plastics market.

81   The content of these meetings is further confirmed by a note of 7 December 1979 prepared by a manager of AKZO. That note makes it clear that AKZO would take aggressive measures in the milling products sector if ECS did not cease to supply its

products to the plastics industry. It contains, in addition, a detailed plan, with figures, describing the measures that would be put into effect if ECS did not refrain from supplying its products. The plan shows, in particular, that AKZO would endeavour to win all of ECS's customers by offering them the complete range of flour additives at loss-making prices.

82   In view of this concordant evidence it must be concluded that in late 1979 AKZO threatened ECS in order to secure its withdrawal from the market for organic peroxides for the 'plastics' application.

As can be seen from the *AKZO* judgment, recouping the loss by the dominant firm occupies an important place in the whole idea of predatory pricing, though the ECJ did not indicate that it was necessary to show that it was possible for the dominant firm to recoup the loss to prove the existence of predatory pricing. The subsequent case of *Tetra Pak SA v. Commission* sheds some valuable light on the issue of recoupment and very sensibly establishes that the Commission does not need to prove this; otherwise the Commission's task would be made extremely and unreasonably difficult.

Tetra Pak International SA v. Commission

(The case is cited above with facts at p. 345 above.)

ECJ

39   ... Tetra Pak submits that the Court of First Instance erred in law when, at paragraph 150 of the judgment under appeal, it characterized Tetra Pak's prices in the non-aseptic sector as predatory without accepting that it was necessary for that purpose to establish that it had a reasonable prospect of recouping the losses so incurred.

40   Tetra Pak considers that the possibility of recouping the losses incurred as a result of predatory sales is a constitutive element in the notion of predatory pricing. That is clear, it claims, from paragraph 71 of the *AKZO* judgment. Since, however, both the Commission and the Court of First Instance accept that sales below cost took place only on the non-aseptic markets, on which Tetra Pak was not found to hold a dominant position, it had no realistic chance of recouping its losses later.

41   In *AKZO* this Court did indeed sanction the existence of two different methods of analysis for determining whether an undertaking has practised predatory pricing. First, prices below average variable costs must always be considered abusive. In such a case, there is no conceivable economic purpose other than the elimination of a competitor, since each item produced and sold entails a loss for the undertaking. Secondly, prices below average total costs but above average variable costs are only to be considered abusive if an intention to eliminate can be shown.

42   At paragraph 150 of the judgment under appeal, the Court of First Instance carried out the same examination as did this Court in *AKZO*. For sales of non-aseptic cartons in Italy between 1976 and 1981, it found that prices were considerably lower than average variable costs. Proof of intention to eliminate competitors was therefore not necessary. In 1982, prices for those cartons lay between average variable costs and average total costs. For that reason, in paragraph 151 of its judgment, the Court of First Instance was at pains to establish - and the appellant has not criticized it in that regard - that Tetra Pak intended to eliminate a competitor.

43   The Court of First Instance was also right, at paragraphs 189 to 191 of the judgment under appeal, to apply exactly the same reasoning to sales of non- aseptic machines in the United Kingdom between 1981 and 1984.

44   Furthermore, it would not be appropriate, in the circumstances of the present case, to require in addition proof that Tetra Pak had a realistic chance of recouping its losses. It must be possible to penalize predatory pricing whenever there is a risk that competitors will be eliminated. The Court of First Instance found, at paragraphs 151 and 191 of its judgment, that there was such a risk in this case. The aim pursued, which is to maintain undistorted competition, rules out waiting until such a strategy leads to the actual elimination of competitors.

(k) Selective price-cutting

The final example of abusive practice to mention is selective price-cutting, a situation which is conceptually similar to that of predatory pricing but different in the sense that there is no selling below cost. Furthermore, selective price-cutting may include an aspect of discrimination within the meaning of Article 82(2)(c). However, in so far as selective price-cutting does not involve 'applying dissimilar conditions to equivalent transactions', it will not be possible to argue that discrimination exists. This raises the question of how this particular type of pricing practice and policy can amount to an abuse of a dominant position.

Like the idea of predatory pricing, selective price-cutting can be explained in simple terms: it involves a dominant firm 'selecting' a particular customer and making a favourable price discount to that customer without the price falling below cost level, whether average total cost or average variable cost.

Compagnie Maritime Belge v. Commission [2000] ECR I-1356

(The case is cited with facts at p. 590 below.)

ECJ

113   It is ... established that, in certain circumstances, abuse may occur if an undertaking in a dominant position strengthens that position in such a way that the degree of dominance reached substantially fetters competition (*Europemballage and Continental Can*, paragraph 26).

114   Furthermore, the actual scope of the special responsibility imposed on a dominant undertaking must be considered in the light of the specific circumstances of each case which show that competition has been weakened (Case C-333/94 *P. Tetra Pak v. Commission* [1996] ECR I-5951, paragraph 24).

115   The maritime transport market is a very specialised sector. It is because of the specificity of that market that the Council established, in Regulation No 4056/86, a set of competition rules different from that which applies to other economic sectors. The authorisation granted for an unlimited period to liner conferences to cooperate in fixing rates for maritime transport is exceptional in light of the relevant regulations and competition policy.

116   It is clear from the eighth recital in the preamble to Regulation No 4056/86 that the authorisation to fix rates was granted to liner conferences because of their stabilising effect and their contribution to providing adequate efficient scheduled maritime transport services. The result may be that, where a single liner conference has a dominant position on a particular market, the user of those services would have little interest in resorting to an independent competitor, unless the competitor were able to offer prices lower than those of the liner conference.

117   It follows that, where a liner conference in a dominant position selectively cuts its prices in order deliberately to match those of a competitor, it derives a dual benefit. First, it eliminates the principal, and possibly the only, means of competition open to the competing undertaking. Second, it can continue to require its users to pay higher prices for the services which are not threatened by that competition.

118   It is not necessary, in the present case, to rule generally on the circumstances in which a liner conference may legitimately, on a case by case basis, adopt lower prices than those of its advertised tariff in order to compete with a competitor who quotes lower prices, or to decide on the exact scope of the expression uniform or common freight rates in Article 1(3)(b) of Regulation No 4056/86.

119   It is sufficient to recall that the conduct at issue here is that of a conference having a share of over 90% of the market in question and only one competitor. The appellants have, moreover, never seriously disputed, and indeed admitted at the hearing, that the purpose of the conduct complained of was to eliminate G&C from the market.

120   The Court of First Instance did not, therefore, err in law, in holding that the Commission's objections to the effect that the practice known as fighting ships, as applied against G&C, constituted an abuse of a dominant position were justified. It should also be noted that there is no question at all in this case of there having been a new definition of an abusive practice.

The factors relied on by the ECJ in the case to establish that the practice of selective price-cutting amounted to an abuse of dominance can be said to be very unusual: a highly specialised sector, a very strong dominant position with 90 per cent market share, one competitor and evidence of threats against the only

competitor. In light of the judgment, it seems that selective price-cutting will not frequently be condemned as an abuse, and this means that in a situation where the special factors present in the case are absent and the firm concerned is merely 'meeting competition' as opposed to 'defeating' it such a practice will not necessarily be condemned as an abuse. To put the point differently, selective price-cutting should be looked at in light of the particular circumstances of the case and of course it is recommended that one considers whether there is objective justification for the practice and whether it is proportionate (see section (E) below).

(D) Effect on trade between Member States

The requirement of effect on trade between Member States is interpreted in the same way as that under Article 81(1). However there is an important difference to be noted in relation to Article 82 which emerged from *Commercial Solvents*, namely that an effect on the structure of the market as a result of an abuse of a dominant position will trigger the requirement.

Commercial Solvents v. Commission [1974] ECR 223

(For facts of the case see pp. 348–349 above.)

ECJ

31 This expression ['effect on trade'] is intended to define the sphere of application of Community rules in relation to national laws. It cannot therefore be interpreted as limiting the field of application of the prohibition which it contains to industrial and commercial activities supplying the Member States.

32 The prohibitions of Articles [81] and [82] must in fact be interpreted and applied in the light of Article [3(g)] of the Treaty, which provides that the activities of the Community shall include the institution of a system ensuring that competition in the common market is not distorted, and Article 2 of the Treaty, which gives the Community the task of promoting 'throughout the Community harmonious development of economic activities'. By prohibiting the abuse of a dominant position within the market in so far as it may affect trade between Member States, Article [82] therefore covers abuse which may directly prejudice consumers as well as abuse which indirectly prejudices them by impairing the effective competitive structure as envisaged by Article [3(g)] of the Treaty.

33 The Community authorities must therefore consider all the consequences of the conduct complained of for the competitive structure in the common market without distinguishing between production intended for sale within the market and that intended for export. When an undertaking in a dominant position with the common market abuses its position in such a way that a competitor in the common market is

likely to be eliminated, it does not matter whether the conduct relates to the latter's exports or its trade within the common market, once it has been established that this elimination will have repercussions on the competitive structure within the common market.

As was mentioned in chapter 3, the Commission published, as part of its modernisation package, a Notice explaining the concept of effect on trade between Member States. Chapter 3 covered the section of the Notice dealing with the general principles surrounding the requirement under Articles 81 and 82 and the application of the requirement in relation to the former Article. It would be helpful for the reader to refer to pp. 80–85 and 90–94 above for the general principles part. Paragraphs 73–76 and 93–99 of the *Notice* deal with examples of abuses covering several Member States, a single Member State and part of a Member State.

(E) Objective justification and proportionality

The inclusion of doctrines of objective justification and proportionality can be seen as vital for balancing the various ingredients of a provision like Article 82. In the absence of a specific 'exempting' paragraph (like the case of Article 81) within the Article it is important to institute appropriate tools in order to be able to distinguish between behaviour that should be caught by Article 82 and that which should not. Thus, by considering whether there is objective justification for given behaviour and whether this behaviour is proportionate, legitimate business practices of dominant firms will not be caught by the Article.

The requirements have been considered on several occasions by the Commission and the Community Courts; though it seems that the requirements have proved to be quite difficult for firms to invoke successfully in Article 82 proceedings. Examples of the type of objective justifications firms have sought to rely on when defending their behaviour include protection of health (*Tetra Pak International SA v. Commission*), and concerns for safety (*Hilti v. Commission*).

5 UK law

As noted above, section 18 CA1998 is modelled on Article 82, and clearly the EC cases referred to above will be directly in point when assessing the application of the section, not least because of the existence of section 60 CA1998. Indeed, many similarities exist with regard to the interpretation and manner of application of section 18 and Article 82. These similarities are reflected in the general views and statements of the OFT.

The OFT has published helpful and fairly comprehensive guidance on the application of section 18. Publications worth mentioning include the *Guidelines on Article 82 and the Chapter II Prohibition* (OFT402), *Assessment of Conduct*

(OFT414) and *Assessment of Market Power* (OFT415). These documents have recently been fully revised in light of EC Regulation 1/2003, the Modernisation Regulation (see chapter 14).

(A) Dominance

Naturally, the OFT's approach to assessing dominance derives from the European approach and there is some sense of reiteration in its guidance on the matter. However, it can also be argued that the OFT couches its analysis more explicitly in economics. A good example is set out in part 3 of *OFT415* which looks broadly at market factors that could allow an undertaking to maintain super-competitive prices. Moreover, there is an extensive list of entry barriers set out in part 5 of the *Guideline* which look to the economic structure of the market as a basis for a finding of dominance. It is suggested that this is a modern and desirable approach that should be adopted more widely in the world of competition law.

OFT415

2.8 The European Court ... defined a dominant market position [in *United Brands v. Commission*] ...

2.9 The OFT considers that an undertaking will not be dominant unless it has substantial market power.

2.10 Market power is not an absolute term but a matter of degree, and the degree of market power will depend on the circumstances of each case. In assessing whether an undertaking has substantial market power, it is helpful to consider whether and the extent to which an undertaking faces competitive constraints. Those constraints might be existing competitors, potential competitors and other factors such as strong buyer power from the undertaking's customers. These constraints are discussed further in Parts 3 to 6 of this guideline.

Market shares

2.11 There are no market share thresholds for defining dominance under Article 82 or the Chapter II prohibition. An undertaking's market share is an important factor in assessing dominance but does not determine on its own whether an undertaking is dominant. For example, it is also necessary to consider the position of other undertakings operating in the same market and how market shares have changed over time. An undertaking is more likely to be dominant if its competitors enjoy relatively weak positions or if it has enjoyed a high and stable market share.

2.12 The European Court has stated that dominance can be presumed in the absence of evidence to the contrary if an undertaking has a market share persistently above 50 per cent.[9] The OFT considers it unlikely that an undertaking will be individually

9 Case C62/86 *AKZO Chemie BV v Commission* [1993] 5 CMLR 215.

dominant if its market share is below 40 per cent, although dominance could be established below that figure if other relevant factors (such as the weak position of competitors in that market) provided strong evidence of dominance.

(3) A FRAMEWORK FOR ASSESSING MARKET POWER

3.1 Market power can be thought of as the ability profitably to sustain prices above competitive levels or restrict output or quality below competitive levels. An undertaking with market power might also have the ability and incentive to harm the process of competition in other ways, for example by weakening existing competition, raising entry barriers or slowing innovation. However, although market power is not solely concerned with the ability of a supplier to raise prices, this guideline often refers to market power for convenience as the ability profitably to sustain prices above competitive levels.[15]

3.2 When assessing whether and to what extent market power exists, it is helpful to consider the strength of any competitive constraints, i.e. market factors that prevent an undertaking from profitably sustaining prices above competitive levels.

3.3 Competitive Constraints include:
- *existing competitors* – 'Existing competitors' are undertakings already in the relevant market.[16] If an undertaking (or group of undertakings) attempts to sustain prices above competitive levels, this might not be profitable because customers would switch their purchases to existing competitors. The market shares of competitors in the relevant market are one measure of the competitive constraint from existing competitors. It can also be important to consider how the market shares of undertakings in the market have moved over time. Market shares are discussed further in Part 4 of this guideline
- *potential competition* – This refers to the scope for new entry. Where entry barriers are low, it might not be profitable for one or more undertakings in a market to sustain prices above competitive levels because this would attract new entry which would then drive the price down – if not immediately, then in the long term. Entry barriers are the subject of Part 5 of this guideline
- *buyer power* – Buyer power exists where buyers have a strong negotiating position with their suppliers, which weakens the potential market power of a seller. This is discussed further in Part 6 of this guideline.

3.4 Economic regulation is a further relevant factor when assessing market power in industry sectors where, for example, prices and/or service levels are subject to controls by the government or an industry sector regulator. While economic regulation

---

15 Where market power is exercised with the effect that quality, service or innovation is reduced, customers can be thought of as paying higher prices for a given level of quality, service or innovation, thus deriving poorer value for money than competition would deliver.

16 Where supply side substitution is likely, existing competitors include undertakings that would move very quickly into the market without incurring substantial sunk costs. See the competition law guideline *Market definition* (OFT403).

is not a competitive constraint in itself, it can limit the extent to which undertakings can exploit their market power.[17] This is also discussed further in Part 6 of this guideline.

3.5   Evidence about the behaviour and financial performance of undertakings is also relevant. Where there is direct evidence that, over the long term, prices substantially exceed relevant costs or profits substantially exceed competitive levels, this may point to market power. Behaviour and performance are dealt with further in Part 6.

3.6   For analytical clarity, this approach sets out the various indicators of market power as if they were separate. In practice, however, the factors are often related. Available evidence from all indicators will be considered in the round before coming to an assessment on market power.

4. MARKET SHARES

4.1   As part of the framework for assessing market power, the OFT will usually define the market and assess how market shares have developed over time.[18] This part considers the extent to which market shares indicate whether an undertaking possesses market power, how market shares may be measured, the sort of evidence likely to be relevant, and some potential problems. These issues are important when considering the intensity of existing competition.

Market shares and market power

4.2   In general, market power is more likely to exist if an undertaking (or group of undertakings) has a persistently high market share.[19] Likewise, market power is less likely to exist if an undertaking has a persistently low market share. Relative market shares can also be important. For example, a high market share might be more indicative of market power when all other competitors have very low market shares.

4.3   The history of the market shares of all undertakings within the relevant market is often more informative than considering market shares at a single point in time, partly because such a snapshot might not reveal the dynamic nature of a market. For example, volatile market shares might indicate that undertakings constantly innovate to get ahead of each other, which is consistent with effective competition. Evidence that undertakings with low market shares have grown rapidly to attain relatively large market shares might suggest that barriers to expansion are low, particularly when such growth is observed for recent entrants.

---

17 Note however that the existence of regulation does not necessarily preclude a finding that, for example, the conduct of a dominant undertaking constitutes an abuse of a dominant position – see for example the judgment of the Competition Commission Appeal Tribunal in *Napp Pharmaceutical Holdings Limited and Subsidiaries v. Director General of Fair Trading* [2002] CAT 1 (*Napp*) at paragraph 411 *et seq.*

18 The OFT's approach to market definition is set out in the competition law guideline *Market Definition* (OFT403).

19 See, for example, *Aberdeen Journals Limited v. Director General of Fair Trading* [2003] CAT 11 at paragraphs 309 to 310 (*Aberdeen Journals*).

4.4   Nevertheless, market shares alone might not be a reliable guide to market power, both as a result of potential shortcomings with the data (discussed in the next section) and for the following reasons:

- *Low entry barriers* – An undertaking with a persistently high market share may not necessarily have market power where there is a strong threat of potential competition. If entry into the market is easy, the incumbent undertaking might be constrained to act competitively so as to avoid attracting entry over time by potential competitors (see Part 5).
- *Bidding markets* – Sometimes buyers choose their suppliers through procurement auctions or tenders. In these circumstances, even if there are only a few suppliers, competition might be intense. This is more likely to be the case where tenders are large and infrequent (so that suppliers are more likely to bid), where suppliers are not subject to capacity constraints (so that all suppliers are likely to place competitive bids), and where suppliers are not differentiated (so that for any particular bid, all suppliers are equally placed to win the contract). In these types of markets, an undertaking might have a high market share at a single point in time. However, if competition at the bidding stage is effective, this currently high market share would not necessarily reflect market power.
- *Successful innovation* – In a market where undertakings compete to improve the quality of their products, a persistently high market share might indicate persistently successful innovation and so would not necessarily mean that competition is not effective.[20]
- *Product differentiation* – Sometimes the relevant market will contain products that are differentiated. In this case undertakings with relatively low market shares might have a degree of market power because other products in the market are not very close substitutes.
- *Responsiveness of customers* – Where undertakings have similar market shares, this does not necessarily mean that they have similar degrees of market power. This may be because their customers differ in their ability or willingness to switch to alternative suppliers (see also the discussion of buyer power in Part 6).
- *Price responsiveness of competitors* – Sometimes an undertaking's competitors will not be in a position to increase output in response to higher prices in the market. For example, suppose an undertaking operates in a market where all undertakings have limited capacity (e.g. are at, or close to, full capacity and so are unable to increase output substantially). In this case, the undertaking would be in a stronger position to increase prices above competitive levels than an otherwise identical undertaking with a similar market share operating in a market where its competitors were not close to full capacity.

---

20 For example, effective competition in innovation might mean that, in order to stay ahead of its rivals, the market leader must improve its products and processes on a regular basis. Innovation as a way to overcome entry barriers is discussed in Part 5.

5. ENTRY BARRIERS

. . .

5.2   Entry barriers are important in the assessment of potential competition. The lower [the] entry barriers, the more likely it is that potential competition will prevent undertakings already within a market from profitably sustaining prices above competitive levels.

5.3   Entry barriers are factors that allow an undertaking profitably to sustain supra-competitive prices in the long term, without being more efficient than its potential rivals. Even if it currently faced no existing competitors, an undertaking could not sustain supra-competitive prices in the long term in the absence of entry barriers.

5.4   An undertaking even with a large market share in a market with very low entry barriers would be unlikely to have market power. However, an undertaking with a large market share in a market protected by significant entry barriers is likely to have market power.

5.5   Entry barriers arise when an undertaking has an advantage (not solely based on superior efficiency) over potential entrants from having already entered the market and/or from special rights (e.g. to production or distribution) or privileged access to key inputs. Entry barriers may make new entry[23] less likely or less rapid by affecting the expected sunk costs of entry and/or the expected profits for new entrants once they are in the market, or by establishing physical, geographic or legal obstacles to entry.[24]

5.6   There are many ways in which different types of entry barrier can be classified, but it is useful to distinguish between the following factors which, depending on the circumstances, can contribute to barriers to entry:
- sunk costs
- poor access to key inputs and distribution outlets
- regulation
- economies of scale
- network effects, and
- exclusionary behaviour.[25]

5.7   Most of the following examples refer for simplicity to a situation where there is one incumbent already in the market[26] and one potential entrant or 'rival'. Although

---

23 New entry into a market requires that both a new undertaking is established in the industry and that new productive capacity is set up in that industry.

24 For the purposes of this guideline, entry barriers include not only those factors that prevent new entry entirely but also those that impede (without necessarily preventing) new entry.

25 Exclusionary behaviour does not refer only to behaviour that raises entry barriers. Exclusionary behaviour also refers to practices that make it harder for existing competitors to become more forceful competitors, including practices which lead to the elimination of an existing competitor.

26 This gives the incumbent a 'first-mover advantage': an advantage from being in the market before its rival.

in reality the existence of several incumbents and several potential entrants may complicate the analysis, the principles outlined remain valid.

Sunk costs

5.8   Entry will occur only if the expected profit from being in the market exceeds any sunk costs of entry.[27]

5.9   Sunk costs of entry are those costs which must be incurred to compete in a market, but which are not recoverable on exiting the market.[28] When a new entrant incurs sunk costs when entering a market, it is as if that entrant has paid a non-refundable deposit to enable it to enter.[29]

5.10   Sunk costs might give an incumbent a strategic advantage over potential entrants. Suppose an incumbent has already made sunk investments necessary to produce in a market while an otherwise identical new entrant has not. In this case, even if the incumbent charges a price at which entry would be profitable (if the price remained the same following entry), entry may not occur. This would be the case if the entrant does not expect the post-entry price to be high enough to justify incurring the sunk costs of entry.[30]

5.11   It is useful to consider the extent to which sunk costs give an incumbent undertaking an advantage over potential new entrants and to what extent sunk costs might affect entry barriers.[31] The mere existence of sunk costs in any particular industry, however, does not necessarily mean that entry barriers are high or that competition within the market is not effective.

---

27 Note that the expected profit from being in a market would also account for the possibility that exit occurs and that any associated 'exit costs' are incurred.

28 For example, suppose an entrant to a hypothetical market for long distance coach services in the North of England purchases a fleet of vehicles. On exiting that market it might be able to sell its coaches to another undertaking (e.g. one offering coach services in the South of England) and so some of the initial costs are recoverable and not sunk. However, not all of the expenditure will be recoverable. For example, any expenditure on the undertaking's livery is unlikely to be of use to another company. This latter expenditure is therefore sunk.

29 Where undertakings can determine their own sunk costs, these are sometimes called 'endogenous' sunk costs. For example, the non-recoverable components of spending on advertising and on research and development (R&D) are endogenous sunk costs. These might be used to differentiate products by brand image and/or by quality (see below).

30 Provided entry would not drive prices below average avoidable cost, the incumbent would find it profitable to remain in the market following entry. Knowing this, the potential entrant decides to stay out of the market.

31 In the economics literature there are many models which describe how an incumbent might use sunk costs strategically to deter entry or, if entry is accommodated, reduce the share of the market available to the new entrant. Some examples are given below in the discussion of exclusionary behaviour.

Poor access to key inputs and distribution outlets

5.12   Entry barriers may arise where inputs or distribution outlets are scarce, and where an incumbent obtains an advantage over a potential entrant due to privileged access (or special rights) to those inputs or outlets.

Essential facilities

5.13   At one extreme, an incumbent might own or have privileged access to an essential facility, which its rival does not. Although the assessment of whether a particular facility is essential must be on a case-by-case basis, essential facilities are rare in practice. A facility will only be viewed as essential where it can be demonstrated that access to it is indispensable in order to compete in a related market and where duplication is impossible or extremely difficult owing to physical, geographic or legal constraints (or is highly undesirable for reasons of public policy).[32] Generally if a rival does not have access to an essential facility, it cannot enter the market.

5.14   There will be circumstances in which difficulties accessing inputs or resources constitute an entry barrier without those assets or resources meeting the strict criteria required to be defined as 'essential facilities'.

Intellectual property rights

5.15   In some, but by no means all, circumstances intellectual property rights (IPRs) can be entry barriers. When assessing whether an IPR is a barrier to entry, it is important to consider whether the IPR reflects an undertaking's superior efficiency (e.g. where an incumbent successfully develops and patents a state-of-the-art production process). In this case, even though the IPR may make it harder for entrants to take on the incumbent, the IPR itself will not necessarily be an entry barrier.

Regulation

5.16   Regulation may affect barriers to entry. For example, regulation may limit the number of undertakings which can operate in a market through the granting of licences. For example, licences may be restricted so that there is an absolute limit to the number of undertakings that can operate in the market. In this case a licence can be thought of as a necessary input before production can take place and so regulation will act as an entry barrier.[33]

5.17   Sometimes regulation sets objective standards. Where these apply equally to all undertakings, such as health and safety regulations, they might not affect the cost for

---

32 See the competition law guideline *Assessment of conduct* (OFT414).

33 If licences were tradeable in a competitive market, a potential entrant could purchase a licence and enter the market if a profitable opportunity arose. However, entry by one undertaking would require exit by another and so overall output might not rise. Therefore, the fact that the licences are limited might allow those undertakings in the market to sustain prices above competitive levels even though licences were tradeable.

new entrants any more than they affect the cost for incumbents. However, regulation can lead to entry barriers when it does not apply equally to all undertakings. For example, incumbents might lobby for standards that are relatively easy for them to meet, but harder for a new entrant to achieve.

Economies of scale

5.18   Economies of scale exist where average costs fall as output rises.[34] In the presence of large economies of scale, a potential entrant may need to enter the market on a large scale (in relation to the size of the market) in order to compete effectively. Large scale entry might require relatively large sunk costs and might be more likely to attract an aggressive response from incumbents.[35] These factors may in some circumstances constitute barriers to entry.

5.19   Attaining a viable scale of production may take time and so require the new entrant to operate in the market for some time at a loss. For example, a new entrant at the manufacturing level might need to secure many distribution outlets to achieve a viable scale. If, perhaps due to long term contracts, many input suppliers or distributors are locked-in to dealing with the incumbent, the new entrant might not be able to achieve an efficient scale of production over the medium term. This could deter entry.

5.20   Even when entry is not completely deterred, entrants may take time to achieve efficient levels of production, obtain the relevant information, raise capital and build the necessary plant and machinery. In this case, even if entry occurs, the incumbent could nevertheless retain market power for a substantial period of time.

Network effects

5.21   Network effects occur where users' valuations of the network increase as more users join the network. For example, as new customers enter a telephone network, this might add value to existing customers because they would be connected to more people on the same network. If customers benefit from being on the same network (e.g. due to incompatibility with other networks), an incumbent with a well established network might have an advantage over a potential entrant that is denied access to the established network and so has to establish its own rival network.

5.22   Network effects, just like economies of scale, may make new entry harder where the minimum viable scale (e.g. in terms of users of the network) is large in relation to the size of the market.

34 Economies of *scope* mean that it costs less to produce two types of products together than to produce them separately. Economies of scope may have similar implications to economies of scale, as a potential entrant would prefer to enter the market with many as opposed to few products.
35 See paragraph 5.25.

Exclusionary behaviour

5.23   The term 'exclusionary behaviour' refers to anti-competitive behaviour which harms existing or potential competition: for example, by eliminating efficient competitors or raising barriers to entry and expansion. The following paragraphs set out some examples of how exclusionary behaviour can create barriers to entry.

Predatory response to entry

5.24   An undertaking contemplating entering a market weighs up its expected profit from being in the market with the expected sunk costs of entering. Expected profits from being in the market may depend on how the entrant expects the incumbent to react when it enters the market: the potential entrant might believe that the incumbent would, for example, reduce prices substantially if it entered and so reduce the prospective profits available.

5.25   While low prices are generally to be encouraged, if a new entrant expected an incumbent to respond to entry with predatory prices, this could deter entry. For example, if an incumbent has successfully predated in the past, it may have secured a reputation for its willingness to set predatory prices.[36] Any future potential entrants to this market (or to any other market where the incumbent operates) might then be deterred from entering due to the likelihood of facing an aggressive response.[37]

Vertical restraints

5.26   In general, vertical restraints are provisions made between undertakings operating at different levels of the supply chain which restrict the commercial freedom of one or more parties to the agreement. Many vertical restraints may be beneficial or benign, especially if there is effective competition at both the upstream and downstream levels. However, vertical restraints may also affect entry barriers.[38]

5.27   For example, a manufacturer might have a series of exclusive purchasing agreements with most retailers in a particular geographic market. This might limit the ability of a new manufacturer to operate on a viable scale in that market and therefore deter entry.

36 In *Aberdeen Journals*, the CAT accepted that Aberdeen Journals' predatory reaction to the launch of a rival newspaper would have been likely to deter others from seeking to enter the market. Predation is discussed in the competition law guideline *Assessment of conduct* (OFT414).
37 Another example might be where an incumbent sinks costs in a way that sends a credible signal as to how it would behave if another undertaking decided to enter a market: it might 'over-invest' in sunk assets so that when it operated as the only undertaking in the market, it had significant spare capacity. From the potential entrant's point of view, the mere existence of that capacity might imply that the incumbent would 'flood' the market in response to entry. The entrant might then decide not to enter if it believed that the incumbent was likely to respond to entry by lowering the price to a low level where the entrant would earn insufficient revenue to cover its sunk costs.
38 For a further discussion see the competition law guidelines *Vertical agreements* (OFT419) and *Assessment of conduct* (OFT414).

Other exclusionary practices

5.28   Discounts designed to foreclose markets, margin squeezes, and refusals to supply might also be used in a way that raises entry barriers. These practices are discussed in detail in the competition law guideline *Assessment of conduct* (OFT414).

Assessing entry barriers

5.29   Assessing the effects of entry barriers and the advantages they give to incumbents can be complex. A variety of steps may be involved. For example, incumbents and potential entrants might be asked for their views on: the sunk costs associated with a commitment to entry; the relative ease of obtaining the necessary inputs and distribution outlets; how regulation affects the prospect of entry; the cost of operating at the minimum viable scale; and any other factors that may impede entry or expansion in the market.

5.30   Claims that potential competition is waiting in the wings are more persuasive if there is fully documented evidence of plans to enter a market or where hard evidence of successful entry in the recent history of the market is provided. In the latter case, such evidence might include a historical record of entry into the market (or closely related markets), including evidence that new entrants had attained in a relatively short period of time a sufficient market share to become effective existing competitors.

5.31   It is important, but not necessarily straightforward, to assess the time that may elapse before successful entry would occur. Some producers, most likely those in neighbouring markets, may be able to enter speedily (e.g. in less than a year) and without substantial sunk costs by switching the use of existing facilities. Where this is possible, it will sometimes be taken into account in defining the market (as supply-side substitutability: see the competition law guideline *Market definition* (OFT403)).[39] New entry from scratch tends to be slower than entry from a neighbouring market, for a variety of reasons which depend on the market concerned – obtaining planning permission, recruiting and training staff, ordering equipment, appointing distributors and so on. The nature of the market may also limit the times at which entry may occur. For example, where customers award long-term contracts, a potential entrant may have to wait until these contracts are renewed before it has an opportunity to enter the market. It may also be important to assess whether enough contracts would come up for renewal to allow the entrant to attain a viable scale.

5.32   Sometimes the relevant geographic market will be international. Where this is not the case, foreign suppliers may nevertheless exert a constraint on domestic undertakings, in the absence of entry barriers, as potential competitors. However, trade

---

39 Some rivals will be able to enter the market more quickly and with a smaller sunk investment than others. Whether this is classified as supply side substitution or new entry should not make a difference to the assessment of market power. Ultimately what matters are the competitive constraints, not the way in which they are classified.

barriers – whether tariff or non-tariff – are an example of a barrier to entry that could impede international competition and shield market power.

5.33 Growth, or prospective growth, of a market will usually have a bearing on the likelihood of entry: entry will usually be more likely in a growing market than in a static or declining one because it will be easier for an entrant to achieve a viable scale, for example by selling to new customers.

5.34 In markets where products are differentiated, undertakings compete not only on price but also on features such as quality, service, convenience and innovation. Where there is scope for differentiation, this may facilitate entry, for example where a new entrant targets untapped demand by differentiating itself from incumbents (provided that incumbents have not already pre-empted all possible niches in the market).

5.35 In markets where brand image is important, a new entrant may have to invest heavily in advertising before it can attain a viable scale. However, even where advertising expenditure is a sunk cost, this does not necessarily mean that entry barriers are high. For example, incumbents may have had to establish their brands and may also have to advertise heavily to maintain them, and so will not necessarily have a cost advantage over potential entrants.

5.36 The rate of innovation is also important: in markets where high rates of innovation occur, or are expected, innovation may overcome product market barriers to entry relatively quickly (provided that there are no barriers to entry into innovative activity). Indeed, any profits that result from an entry barrier created by successful innovation (e.g. from intellectual property rights) may be an important incentive to innovate.

Barriers to expansion

5.37 New entry is not simply about introducing a new product to the market. To be an effective competitive constraint, a new entrant must be able to attain a large enough scale to have a competitive impact on undertakings already in the market. This may entail entry on a small scale, followed by growth. Barriers to entry are closely related to barriers to expansion and can be analysed in a similar way. Many of the factors discussed above that may make entry harder might also make it harder for undertakings that have recently entered the market to expand their market shares and hence their competitive impact.

6. OTHER FACTORS IN THE ASSESSMENT OF MARKET POWER

Buyer Power

6.1 The strength of buyers and the structure of the buyers' side of the market may constrain the market power of a seller. Size is not sufficient for buyer power. Buyer power requires the buyer to have choice.

6.2   The analysis of buyer power requires an understanding of the way that buyers interact with suppliers. Buyer power is most commonly found in industries where buyers and suppliers negotiate, in which case buyer power can be thought of as the degree of bargaining strength in negotiations.[40] A buyer's bargaining strength might be enhanced if the following conditions hold:

- the buyer is well informed about alternative sources of supply and could readily, and at little cost to itself, switch substantial purchases from one supplier to another while continuing to meet its needs[41]
- the buyer could commence production of the item itself or 'sponsor' new entry by another supplier (e.g. through a long-term contract) relatively quickly and without incurring substantial sunk costs
- the buyer is an important outlet for the seller (i.e. the seller would be willing to cede better terms to the buyer in order to retain the opportunity to sell to that buyer)
- the buyer can intensify competition among suppliers through establishing a procurement auction or purchasing through a competitive tender (see Part 4).

6.3   In general, buyer power is beneficial in two circumstances:

- when there are large efficiency gains that result from the factors (e.g. size) that give the buyer its power and these are passed on to the final consumer (e.g. through downstream competition), and
- when it exerts downward pressure on a supplier's prices and the lower prices are passed on to the final consumer.

6.4   However, buyer power does not always benefit the final consumer. First, where only some buyers are powerful, for example, a supplier with market power might harm downstream competition through actions which lead to weaker buyers facing higher input prices. Second, buyer power might be weakened as a result of the agreement or behaviour under investigation. Third, where the buyer also has market power as a seller in the downstream market, it may not pass on lower prices to the final consumer. Fourth, conduct by a dominant buyer may harm competition. A careful analysis of vertical relationships in the market, on a case-by-case basis, is therefore often required to assess buyer power.[42]

40 Another form of buyer occurs where, under certain conditions, a dominant purchaser from a competitive industry would have an incentive to withhold purchases in order to buy at a lower price. Where behaviour by a dominant purchaser harms competition this may be found to be abusive.

41 This need not mean that the buyer stops buying the product entirely, just that it reduces purchases by a substantial amount. This may include ceasing to promote the product in question and promoting the products of rival suppliers instead. Reducing purchases of a must-have product might not be profitable for a buyer. However, where suppliers produce must-have products and other, less important, products the buyer might exercise power by threatening to de-list a weaker product unless it obtains better terms on the must-have product.

42 Article 82 and the Chapter II prohibition prohibit abuses of buyer power by dominant undertakings. An agreement between customers to suppress prices would be likely to fall within Article 81 and/or the Chapter I prohibition.

Evidence on behaviour and performance

6.5   An undertaking's conduct in a market or its financial performance may provide evidence that it possesses market power. Depending on other available evidence, it might, for example, be reasonable to infer that an undertaking possesses market power from evidence that it has:

- set prices consistently above an appropriate measure of costs, or
- persistently earned an excessive rate of profit.

6.6   High prices or profits alone are not sufficient proof that an undertaking has market power: high profits may represent a return on previous innovation, or result from changing demand conditions. As such, they may be consistent with a competitive market, where undertakings are able to take advantage of profitable opportunities when they exist. However, persistent significantly high returns, relative to those which would prevail in a competitive market of similar risk and rate of innovation, may suggest that market power does exist. This would be especially so if those high returns did not stimulate new entry or innovation.

6.7   The assessment of excess prices or profits is discussed further in the competition law guideline *Assessment of conduct* (OFT414).

Economic regulation

6.8   In some sectors the economic behaviour of undertakings (such as the prices they set or the level of services they provide) is regulated by the government or an industry sector regulator, and an assessment of market power may need to take that into account. Although an undertaking might not face effective constraints from existing competitors, potential competitors or the nature of buyers in the market, it may still be constrained from profitably sustaining prices above competitive levels by an industry sector regulator. However, that is not to say that market power cannot exist when there is economic regulation. It is feasible, for example, that regulation of the average price or profit level across several markets supplied by an undertaking may still allow for the undertaking profitably to sustain prices above competitive levels in one (or more) of these markets and/or to engage in exclusionary behaviour of various kinds.[43]

(B) Abuse

I General

It was previously noted that section 60 CA1998 obliges the OFT to handle cases in such a way as to ensure consistency with EC competition rules. No doubt the case law of the Community Courts and decisional practice of the Commission concerning abuse and its application will be largely relevant when it comes to applying that concept in the context of the Chapter II prohibition. The OFT has

---

43 See, for example, *Napp* at paragraph 411 *et seq.*

published two important Guidelines (which were mentioned above) on how it will assess certain actions which might amount to an abuse of dominance: *Article 82 and the Chapter II Prohibition* (OFT402) and *Assessment of conduct* (OFT414); the latter guideline contains very valuable details.

OFT414 is extremely rich in its explanation of important economic concepts, which are central to understanding key types of abuse such as predatory pricing. The *Guideline* follows the case law developed under Article 82; though the *Guideline* is more helpful than the latter in many respects, especially in relation to the explanation it offers of the different examples of abuse.

II Examples of abuse

Assessment of conduct (OFT414) identifies and discusses several examples of abuse considered above in the context of Article 82, but it should be remembered that the list of abuse is by no means closed. As noted above, it can be suggested that the OFT's approach is more economically focussed. For instance, one might consider the lengthy discussion of excessive prices, which indicates an aspiration to distinguish, e.g., temporarily high prices resulting from natural competitive processes (which should not be interrupted) from abuse of a dominant position allowing the maintenance of super-competitive prices (see paragraphs 2.16–2.20 of the *Guideline*). The key is to return to economic assessments of efficiency gains and risk of market foreclosure and reduction of output (see e.g. paragraphs 3.4–3.8 with regard to price discrimination). The OFT also provides a thorough theoretical analysis of one of the more controversial topics, predation in part 4. In light of the crafty and quickly-evolving business environments to which the OFT must respond, it is submitted that such an approach will deal effectively with new business practices that might constitute abuse of a dominant position.

(a) Excessive prices

OFT414

2.1   The charging of excessive selling prices by a dominant undertaking may be an infringement of Article 82 and/or the Chapter II prohibition.[6] The European Court has held that:

'charging a price which is excessive because it has no reasonable relation to the economic value of the product supplied... would be... an abuse'.[7]

---

6 Article 82 and the Chapter II prohibition prohibit dominant undertakings from directly or indirectly imposing unfair purchase or selling prices.

7 Case 27/76 *United Brands v Commission* [1978] ECR 207, [1978] 1 CMLR 429 at paragraph 250 (*United Brands*). See also the decision of the European Commission in *Deutsche Post AG – Interception of cross-border mail* OJ [2001] L331/40, where the European Commission found the price charged by a monopolist excessive where it had 'no sufficient or reasonable relationship to real costs or to the real value of the service provided'.

2.2   In *United Brands* the European Court went on to declare that a detailed analysis of costs would be required before any judgement of excessive prices could be reached and added that the question to be asked was:

'... whether the difference between the costs actually incurred and the price actually charged is excessive, and, if the answer to this question is in the affirmative, whether a price has been imposed which is either unfair in itself or when compared to other competing products'.[8]

2.3   Not only might excessively high prices be exploitative but they may also harm competition.[9] For example, an undertaking dominant in the supply of an important input might well be in a position to set excessive prices which make it more difficult for undertakings that require the input to enter or to compete in related markets.[10]

2.4   Excessive prices may also be a sign that the process of competition is not working effectively. This would be the case, in particular, where a dominant undertaking combines excessive prices with exclusionary behaviour designed to protect its ability to maintain those excessive prices. In this case, both practices could be found abusive.

2.5   It is important, however, to distinguish excessive prices from seemingly high prices that are an integral part of the competitive process. For example, high prices may reflect short term shifts in demand or supply, provide a fair return on earlier investments, or act as a signal for existing and potential competitors, respectively, to expand output and to enter a market.

Evidence on excessive prices

2.6   In assessing questions about excessive pricing, the OFT would usually look for evidence that prices are substantially higher than would be expected in a competitive market, and that there is no effective competitive pressure to bring them down to competitive levels, nor is there likely to be.

Cost and price benchmarks

2.7   In order to address whether an undertaking's prices are higher than would be expected in a competitive market, the following benchmarks might be considered:

• *comparisons with prices of the same products[11] in other markets.* These might be useful where identical comparator products are sold in more competitive markets (e.g. markets characterised by lower concentration, lower entry barriers and no collusive behaviour), provided that these markets are subject to similar cost conditions as the market in question

8 *United Brands* at paragraph 252
9 This part discusses the analysis of selling prices. However, it is conceivable that the extraction of unfair or excessively low buying prices by a dominant buyer could also be an abuse.
10 In the extreme, the price may be so high that it amounts to 'constructive' refusal to supply. Refusal to supply is discussed in Part 8.
11 The term product is used for convenience and should be interpreted throughout this guideline to mean good, service or property right.

- *comparisons with underlying costs.* Where it is possible to derive an economically meaningful measure of an undertaking's own costs, then evidence that prices were persistently and significantly in excess of these costs could be evidence of excessive pricing (see excessive profits below), and
- *comparison with prices in another time period.* Evidence that prices were substantially higher than those of a period when competition was more effective might provide evidence of excessive pricing, provided that there were no other good explanations for the price rise (e.g. a substantial increase in cost).

2.8   The above list of indicators is not exhaustive and the analysis of excessive prices will depend on the case in hand. To demonstrate that excessive prices had been set, several indicators would usually be considered[12] as well as the possibility that seemingly high prices are an integral part of the process of competition in the market concerned (see paragraph 2.16 et seq).

Excessive profits

2.9   In a competitive market, an undertaking would be expected to earn 'normal profits' on any particular activity. These refer to the level of profits that an undertaking requires to provide a sufficient return to the lenders and shareholders that provide the undertaking with finance. His rate of return is referred to as the undertaking's 'cost of capital'. When the undertaking's profitability persistently exceeds its cost of capital profits are said to be 'supra-normal'.

2.10   Evidence of supra-normal profits may indicate that competitive pressure was not strong enough to keep prices at competitive levels and bolster other evidence that excessive prices were being charged.[13] However, supra-normal profits will not always indicate competition problems (see paragraph 2.16 *et seq*).

2.11   When considering whether supra-normal profits have been earned, a variety of measures may be considered:
- Economic measures of profitability include the internal rate of return (IRR) and net present value (NPV). When an undertaking's IRR exceeds its cost of capital or when its NPV is greater than zero, this implies that its profitability exceeds its cost of capital.

12 In *Napp Pharmaceutical Holdings Ltd v Director General of Fair Trading* [2002] CAT 1 (*Napp*) the Competition Appeal Tribunal (CAT) considered that comparisons of (i) Napp's prices with Napp's costs, (ii) Napp's prices with the costs of its next most profitable competitor, (iii) Napp's prices with those of its competitors and (iv) Napp's prices with prices charged by Napp in other markets were among the approaches that could reasonably be used to establish excessive prices in that case (paragraph 392). The CAT also noted that there are other methods that may reasonably be used to establish excessive prices.

13 Although excessive prices would normally result in high profits, this will not always be the case: an undertaking protected from competition might be under less pressure to control its costs. Information on appropriate cost comparators might help to indicate whether costs have been incurred efficiently.

- Given that the period over which prices are alleged to be excessive may be less than the economic lifetime of an activity, it may be more appropriate to employ measures such as return on sales, gross margins, 'truncated IRR',[14] return on capital employed,[15] and market valuations.
- Evidence on how an undertaking's profitability compares with that of similar undertakings operating in a competitive market may also be considered.

2.12   Undertakings often supply several markets. Often it is not the overall profitability of an undertaking which is at issue but rather the profits the undertaking earns from an individual line of business in a particular market where it enjoys a dominant position. Where a dominant undertaking does not generate supra-normal profits overall, this does not rule out the possibility that it charges excessive prices on a particular line of business.

2.13   Where an undertaking produces several products, certain costs may be 'common' to more than one product. To assess the profitability of a line of business it may be necessary to allocate common costs to the particular activities identified. Whether and how this should be carried out will depend on the circumstances of the case.[16]

2.14   A profitability assessment can require an element of judgement about the relevant rates of return, the valuation of assets, the appropriate cost of capital, and the appropriate cost and revenue allocation methods. No presumption should be made about what measure of profitability will be used, as the appropriateness of different measures will vary with each case and all the relevant evidence will be considered as a whole.

2.15   It is unlikely that a dominant undertaking would be found to have charged excessive prices solely on the evidence of supra-normal profitability. The analysis would usually consider other indicators, such as the cost and price comparators described above, as well as whether supra-normal profits could be justified as a fair return on an earlier investment.

When apparently high prices or profits are not excessive
2.16   Prices and profits of a dominant undertaking which, at first sight, might appear to be excessive will not always amount to an abuse. First, high prices will often occur for short periods within competitive markets. For example, an increase in demand

---

14 The truncated IRR facilitates assessment of profitability over a defined period by imputing appropriate asset valuations at the beginning and end of the relevant period. It requires reliable information on, for example, cashflow and asset valuations.

15 An undertaking's return on capital employed will, when certain conditions apply, give similar results to a truncated IRR, and it too can also be compared to the cost of capital.

16 In some circumstances the stand alone cost of the line of business may also be relevant. The stand alone costs of a line of business include those costs that would be incurred if the company undertook only the line of business in question. Where an activity generates revenues that persistently and significantly exceed its stand alone cost (including the cost of capital), this would be good evidence of excessive profits being earned on that activity.

that could not be met by current capacity or a supply shock that reduced production capacity would lead to higher prices. Where high prices are temporary and/or likely to encourage substantial new investment or new entry, they are unlikely to cause concern.

2.17   Second, an undertaking might be able to sustain supra-normal profits for a period if it was more efficient than its competitors. In this case, the efficient undertaking might simply be reaping the rewards of having developed lower-cost techniques of production, supplied higher quality products or been more effective at identifying market opportunities. This might be shown by the fact that the other (less efficient) undertakings in the market were not earning high profits relative to their cost of capital.

2.18   Third, prices and profits may be high in markets where there is innovation. Successful innovation may allow a firm to earn profits significantly higher than those of its competitors. However, a high return in one period could provide a fair return on the investment in an earlier period required to bring about the innovation. These costs include investment in research and development and should take into account the risk at the time of the investment that the innovation might have failed.[17]

2.19   In markets where undertakings innovate regularly, high profits may be temporary, for example because they act as a spur to competitors to innovate further and to the incumbent to innovate to maintain its position. Persistently high prices and profits are unlikely to be of concern if they result from a series of successful innovations, as distinct from exclusionary or collusive behaviour.

2.20   It is important not to interfere in natural market mechanisms where high prices and profits will lead to timely new entry or innovation and thereby increase competition. In particular, competition law should not undermine appropriate incentives for undertakings to innovate. Concern about excessive prices will be more likely in markets where price levels are persistently high without stimulating new entry or innovation.

(b) Price discrimination

3.1   An undertaking can be said to be discriminating when it applies dissimilar conditions to equivalent transactions with other trading parties. The most direct way is through the prices charged to different sets of customers. It can take two basic forms:
   • an undertaking might charge different prices to different customers, or categories of customers, for the same product - where the differences in prices do not reflect any differences in relative cost, quantity, quality or any other characteristics of the products supplied
   • an undertaking might charge different customers, or categories of customers, the same price even though the costs of supplying the product are in fact very different.

17 This risk might be reflected in the cost of capital.

A policy of uniform delivered prices throughout the country, for example, could be discriminatory if differences in transport costs were significant.

3.2   For price discrimination to be feasible an undertaking not only has to be able to segment the market in some way, but must also be able to enforce the segmentation, so that trading between the different categories of customer who are charged different prices is not possible.

3.3   Price discrimination occurs frequently and in a wide range of industries, including industries where competition is effective. It is a generic term that covers many specific types of pricing behaviour that can be either good for consumers or anticompetitive. Therefore, it is not necessarily the case that price discrimination by a dominant undertaking is an abuse.

Price discrimination as an abuse

3.4   Price discrimination, and discrimination more generally, by a dominant undertaking may be an abuse under Article 82 and/or the Chapter II prohibition. Price discrimination raises two potential issues. First, it may be exclusionary. For example, a dominant undertaking may use a discriminatory pricing structure to set predatory prices (see Part 4) and/or to set discounts which have the effect (or likely effect) of foreclosing all, or a substantial part, of a market (see Part 5). Where a vertically integrated undertaking is dominant in an upstream market and a competitor in a related downstream market, it may use discriminatory pricing to apply a margin squeeze that distorts competition in the downstream market (see Part 6).

3.5   Second, price discrimination may allow an undertaking to exploit market power by charging excessively high prices to certain customers (see Part 2).

3.6   When considering whether price discrimination is an abuse, it is often relevant to consider whether the pricing structure in question allows the efficient recovery of fixed costs and expands demand substantially or opens up new market segments.

3.7   For example, undertakings often have fixed costs of production (costs which do not vary directly with output, at least in the short run). This means that they will usually need to set at least some prices above their average variable costs to generate sufficient revenues to break even (i.e. earn normal profit). In this case, price discrimination can be beneficial if it leads to a sufficiently large increase in output in relation to the output level that would have pertained if there was no price discrimination. Indeed, in some cases price discrimination may allow a new market segment to emerge. This might occur, for example, in industries characterised by relatively high fixed costs, where customers can be split up into groups according to their willingness to pay, and where groups with low willingness to pay would not buy in the absence of price discrimination.[18]

3.8   Just because price discrimination can be beneficial does not mean that the chosen form of price discrimination adopted by a dominant undertaking in that industry is presumed beneficial. Price discrimination will be assessed on a case-by-case basis.

Non-price issues

3.9   Discrimination should be regarded as applying dissimilar conditions to equivalent transactions or similar conditions to different transactions; it is not concerned solely with price. Discrimination on terms other than price can also have anti-competitive effects. For example, an undertaking which controlled the supply of a key input might supply a downstream undertaking with a poorer quality of service than it provides to its own business competing in the same downstream market (delivery taking longer, for example). If the difference in service quality were not reflected in the pricing by the upstream undertaking, the undertaking could be regarded as acting in a discriminatory way.

3.10   The analysis of non-price discrimination, e.g. quality of service discrimination, would be similar to that for price discrimination. This is because raising the price for a product of a given quality is effectively the same as lowering the quality of a product sold at a given price. As with price discrimination, the non-price discrimination will not necessarily be abusive. It would be abusive only where it was exploitative or reduced (or could be expected to reduce) existing or potential competition.

(c) Discounts

5.1   The offering of discounts to customers is an important form of price competition and is therefore generally to be encouraged. Competition law should not deter beneficial price competition, so evidence that a discount scheme harms (or is likely to harm) competition is needed before that discount scheme will be found to be abusive.[39]

---

18 For example, consider a hypothetical dominant train operator that sets different prices for peak and off-peak rail travel. Charging commuters (who have a higher willingness to pay than leisure travellers) a higher price so as to recover a bigger proportion of fixed costs may allow a train operating company to reduce the share of these costs recovered from off-peak travellers. This may increase output overall since if both categories of customers were charged the same price, off-peak travellers might switch to another mode of transport or not travel at all, leaving peak travellers to bear more of the fixed costs. In the extreme, this might lead to both peak and off-peak travellers switching to other modes of travel or not travelling at all.

39 Discounts, when employed by an undertaking in a dominant position, can impair genuine undistorted competition and thereby be abusive. See Case 322/81 *Michelin v Commission* [1983] ECR 3461 (*Michelin*).

5.2   When assessing the effect of a dominant undertaking's discount scheme on competition, it is often important to consider whether the scheme is commercially rational
only because it has the effect (or likely effect) of foreclosing all, or a substantial
part, of the market that is open to competition.[40]

5.3   It must also be considered that a dominant undertaking's discount scheme may
reflect competition to secure orders from valued customers or have beneficial effects.
For example, it may:
- expand demand and thereby help cover fixed costs efficiently;
- lower input costs for downstream undertakings and thereby encourage them to
compete more effectively on price;
- reflect efficiency savings resulting from supplying particular customers; or
- provide an appropriate reward for the efforts of downstream undertakings to promote a dominant undertaking's product.

5.4   The following sections consider the following types of discount scheme: volume
discounts, fidelity rebates and loyalty discounts, and multiproduct rebates. The
various schemes are described according to their forms, but it is important to bear
in mind that it is the effect on competition of any particular scheme, rather than its
form, which will determine whether or not it is abusive.

Volume discounts

5.5   Volume discounts mean that customers obtain bigger discounts as the size of their
order increases. Volume discounts may often be benign. They may reflect efficiencies associated with supplying large orders to customers or, for example where a
distributor sells to a retailer, may be a legitimate way to provide incentives for the
retailer to promote the distributor's product. However, volume discounts may also
harm competition where they have exclusionary effects.

Fidelity rebates and loyalty discounts

5.6   Fidelity rebates and loyalty discounts (which are used interchangeably here) arise
where a supplier (e.g. a manufacturer) effectively offers a customer (e.g. a wholesaler
or a retailer) a discount that is conditional not on the size of the customer's order, but
on the share of the customer's needs purchased from the supplier.[41] Thus, provided
a small customer purchases most of its requirements from a supplier, it may obtain

---

40 As part of this analysis, it may be relevant to consider whether there were alternative discount
schemes that would achieve similar commercial benefits but without harming (or being as likely
to harm) competition.
41 For example, suppose a large customer typically purchases 1000 units, while a small customer
typically purchases 100 units. If a discount is offered to customers only when they purchase 80
per cent of their needs from a dominant undertaking, the large customer must purchase at least
800 units to obtain the discount while the small customer must purchase only 80 units.

the same discount as a very large customer, even though the amounts purchased may vary significantly.[42]

5.7   Various discount schemes could have a 'loyalty inducing effect'. For example, consider a growth rebate whereby the customer obtains a substantial discount only if it increases the amount purchased from a supplier by 10 per cent on purchases made the previous year. If the natural growth in the customer's market is insufficient to require such an increased volume, this sort of discount may provide an incentive for the customer to increase its purchases from (or its 'loyalty' for) this supplier at the expense of others. The same applies for target rebates, where a customer does not qualify for a rebate unless it sells at least the targeted amount of the supplier's product. If the rebate is substantial and the target is set close to the customer's total input requirement, it has a 'loyalty inducing effect' as the customer would be encouraged to increase purchases from the supplier at the expense of others.[43]

5.8   Fidelity rebates may be abusive where they lead to foreclosure effects. It is the 'loyalty inducing effect' of a fidelity rebate that generally raises potential competition concerns.[44] However, even where a discount scheme adopted by a dominant undertaking has a loyalty inducing effect, the scheme would not be found abusive if it did not (or was not likely to) harm competition.

Multi-product discounts
5.9   Multi-product discounts occur where a discount on one product is obtained when a customer purchases sufficient quantities of another. For example, if an undertaking is dominant in the market for product A, it might offer customers discounts on their purchases of another product, B, based on their purchases of product A.

(d) Refusal to supply

8.1   Undertakings are generally free to supply, or not to supply, to whomever they choose. Therefore, refusal to supply by a dominant undertaking is not normally abusive. In some circumstances, a refusal to supply may be considered to be abusive and a dominant undertaking's freedom to contract with whomever it chooses may be circumscribed. This would occur only if there is evidence of (likely) substantial harm to competition and if the behaviour cannot be objectively justified.

---

42 A commonly cited definition of a fidelity rebate is taken from the European Court's judgement in Case 85/76 *Hoffman-La Roche v Commission* [1979] ECR 461 (*Hoffmann-La Roche*) at paragraph 89: '... discounts conditional on the customer's obtaining all or most of its requirements – whether the quantity of its purchases be large or small – from the undertaking in a dominant position'. A dominant undertaking pricing according to a system of fidelity rebates may also be engaging in price discrimination. Price discrimination is discussed in Part 3 of this guideline.

43 This is not to suggest that growth and target rebates always have loyalty inducing effects, only that in some circumstances they can have a similar effect to fidelity rebates. Setting discounts dependent on dealers meeting sales targets based on their previous year's sales can be abusive, as the European Court found in *Michelin*.

44 In the extreme, a fidelity rebate scheme might provide a strong incentive for a customer to deal exclusively with a dominant supplier. Exclusive purchasing is discussed in Part 7.

8.2　A refusal to supply occurs where an undertaking stops supplying an existing customer[59] or withholds supplies from a new customer. A refusal to supply by a dominant undertaking is more likely to be considered an abuse where it results in the elimination of competition[60] or stifles the emergence of a new product.[61] A refusal to supply could result from a refusal to allow access to an essential facility (discussed below), although in practice essential facilities are rare.

8.3　Behaviour which has the same effect as a refusal to supply could also constitute an abuse (sometimes called 'constructive' refusal to supply). For example, a dominant undertaking might supply at such a high price,[62] or at such an inferior level of quality, that customers would effectively be prohibited from purchasing.

8.4　Refusal to supply might on occasion result from a vertical restraint. A manufacturer imposing a selective distribution system, for example, would, by definition, be refusing to supply outlets which were not within the system. Such cases would be considered as set out in Part 7, above, on vertical restraints and/or the competition law guideline *Vertical agreements* (OFT419).

(e) Predation

4.1　Predation is strategic behaviour whereby an undertaking deliberately incurs losses in order to eliminate a competitor so as to be able to charge excessive prices in the future. It occurs where prices are so low[19] that they could force one or more undertakings out of the market, threatening the competitive process itself.[20] Predation practised by an undertaking holding a dominant position will be an abuse.

4.2　Although consumers may benefit in the short term from such lower prices, in the longer term consumers will be worse off due to weakened competition which leads to higher prices, reduced quality and less choice. A number of issues may be relevant to an assessment of whether predation is taking (or has taken) place. This part addresses the following issues:
- pricing below cost
- intention to eliminate a competitor, and
- the feasibility of recouping losses.

---

59 *United Brands* and Case 311/84 *CBEM v CLT and IPB* [1985] ECR 3261.
60 Cases 6 & 7/73 *Instituto Chemioterapico Italiano SpA & Commercial Solvents Corp v Commission* [1974] ECR 223, [1974] 1 CMLR 309.
61 Cases C-241 & 242/91 *RTE and ITP v Commission* [1995] I ECR 743, [1995] 4 CMLR 718, which involved the refusal to license copyright. In general refusal to license an intellectual property right is not an abuse. Examples of the exceptional circumstances where it will be are described in the competition law guideline Intellectual property rights (expected 2004).
62 Excessive prices are discussed in Part 2.
19 This part focuses on predatory prices. However, the analysis could apply equally to predatory behaviour that involves increases in output.
20 A predatory strategy may harm competition without necessarily eliminating a competitor.

Pricing below cost

4.3   Usually, when assessing predation, the first question is whether the dominant undertaking is pricing below cost. This involves an assessment of:
- the relevant time period over which to measure revenues and costs
- the relevant revenues generated over that time period, and hence the relevant price,
and
- the relevant cost benchmark to use during that time period.

Relevant time period

4.4   The relevant period over which to measure revenues and costs depends on the case
in hand. The relevant time period is usually that over which the alleged predatory
price(s) prevailed or could reasonably be expected to prevail. However, this does
not rule out the use of other time periods in appropriate circumstances. For example,
suppose that the period of alleged predation covered two years and that in some
months prices were much lower than others. In this case, it may be relevant to
consider not only whether predation occurred during the whole period of alleged
predation but also whether it occurred during the shorter periods of particularly
aggressive pricing.

Relevant price

4.5   The relevant price depends on the case in hand. In some cases, the price may be
stable and easy to observe. In other cases, for example where the price varies over
the relevant time period or between customers, it may be appropriate to consider
the relevant price to be average revenues from the particular sales that are alleged
to have been made at a predatory price.

Cost benchmarks

4.6   This section considers three cost benchmarks: variable costs, avoidable costs, and
incremental costs.

Variable costs

4.7   Variable costs are those costs that vary directly with output. The variability of a cost,
and hence the level of variable costs, will depend on the time frame under consideration. The longer the time frame under consideration, the greater the opportunities
for undertakings to respond to changes in output by changing their production processes and capacity. Given sufficient time, all costs are variable to a certain degree.

Avoidable costs

4.8   Avoidable costs are those costs which could be avoided if the undertaking were to
cease the activity in question over the relevant time period. The 'activity' referred
to here is the production of the product (or group of products) that is the subject of
the investigation. Variable costs are avoidable since these costs will not be incurred
if the activity in question is ceased. Where a cost is deliberately sunk as part of a

[399]

predatory activity such a cost is also avoidable (even though, once sunk, the cost does not vary with output).[21]

4.9   When measured over the same period, variable costs and avoidable costs may often be similar. In *Aberdeen Journals (No. 2)* the CAT noted that measuring avoidable costs over the period of the alleged predation, or an intermediate period of one year, would, in practice, have given very similar results to measuring what costs were variable over the same period.[22] In cases where avoidable costs and variable costs are not very similar, it may be useful to consider whether an undertaking is covering its avoidable costs. Evidence that an undertaking prices below its average avoidable costs (AAC) may be relevant evidence when assessing an undertaking's intention (see below).

Incremental costs

4.10   Incremental cost refers to the additional cost of increasing output beyond a benchmark level of output by some pre-specified amount (the 'increment'). Incremental costs differ according to the time period over which they are measured. In certain sectors (for example telecommunications), long run incremental cost (LRIC)[23] may be a preferable cost benchmark to variable cost.[24]

Pricing below average variable cost

4.11   In *AKZO*,[25] the European Court held that where prices are below the average variable cost (AVC) of production, predation should be presumed. However, as noted in *Aberdeen Journals (No. 2)*, this presumption can be rebutted.[26]

4.12   Some possible legitimate commercial reasons for pricing below AVC are set out below:
  • *loss leading*:   loss leading occurs where a retailer cuts the price of a single product in order to increase sales of other products. Loss leading would not normally be considered predatory unless it was clear that the intention was to eliminate a competitor
  • *short run promotions*:   these often involve selling below AVC for a limited period and are widely used in many markets, especially where a new product is introduced

---

21 For example, if a dominant undertaking made a sunk investment in new capacity for the purpose of its predatory campaign, this investment would be treated as an avoidable cost.
22 See *Aberdeen Journals Limited v The Office of Fair Trading* [2003] CAT 11 (*Aberdeen Journals (No. 2)*) at paragraph 385.
23 LRIC takes into account the total long run cost, both of capital and operating, of supplying a specified additional unit of output such as a new service.
24 See the European Commission's *Notice on the Application of Competition Rules to Access Agreements*, OJ [1998] C 265/2, [1998] 5 CMLR 821 and the competition law guideline *The application of competition law in the telecommunications sector* (OFT417). See also the European Commission's decision in *Deutsche Post AG* OJ [2001] L125/27.
25 Case C 62/86 *AKZO Chemie BV v Commission* [1991] ECR I-3359 (*AKZO*).
26 Aberdeen Journals (No. 2), paragraph 357.

to a market. A dominant undertaking which adopts a one-off short term promotion of this type is unlikely to be found to have engaged in predation. However, a series of short term promotions could, taken together, amount to a predatory strategy. The time period which may be regarded as short term will inevitably vary from case to case, and it is not possible to provide general guidance as to what may and may not be abusive

- *network effects*: there are some services where the addition of more customers to the network adds to the value of the service sold to existing customers.[27] In these circumstances, it can be beneficial for the undertaking to sell part of the service to customers at below AVC. This will encourage expansion of the network, which benefits all network customers who then have access to a larger number of subscribers. The undertaking may then recoup the loss by charging higher prices for other, related services
- *economies of scale and new products*: in some cases an undertaking may introduce a new product to the market at a loss-making price in order to build up a large enough customer base to allow it to achieve and benefit from economies of scale, at which point the price would become profitable
- *unanticipated shocks*: in some markets demand and/or costs can be volatile and difficult to anticipate. For example, in some cases an undertaking may temporarily fail to cover its AVC because of unanticipated increases in input costs, or unanticipated reductions in demand, and
- *option value*: in some cases, for example in response to an unexpected fall in demand, an undertaking may wish to maintain a presence in the market (although it incurs short run losses in doing so) in case demand returns to profitable levels. This would be more likely to occur in a market which, once exited, would involve substantial sunk costs to re-enter.

4.13   Where a dominant undertaking prices below AVC in the market in which it holds dominance, defences which rely on the need to obtain an efficient scale of production may not be persuasive since the undertaking would already be large in relation to the market. However, such defences may still apply where an undertaking dominant in one market is alleged to have predated in a related market, in which it is not dominant.

Predation and pricing between AVC and average total cost

4.14   Predatory conduct is possible where an undertaking prices above its AVC and below its average total cost (ATC).[28] In *AKZO*, the European Court held that if prices are above AVC but below ATC, conduct is to be regarded as predatory where it can be established that the purpose of the conduct was to eliminate a competitor.[29] The question of intention is considered below.

---

27 Network effects may also be relevant for goods as well as services.
28 Total costs are the sum of variable costs and fixed costs, fixed costs being those costs that do not vary with output over the relevant period.
29 See also Case C-333/94P *Tetra Pak v Commission* [1996] ECR I-5951 (*Tetra Pak II*).

Intention to eliminate a competitor

4.15   This section describes the factors often considered when assessing whether an undertaking's intention is to eliminate a competitor.

Direct evidence of intentions

4.16   Documentary evidence may be used to determine whether an undertaking intended to predate. For example, in *Aberdeen Journals (No. 2)*, the CAT found that internal documents clearly demonstrated that the dominant undertaking used low prices in an attempt to force a competitor out of the market.[30] Evidence from a credible witness may also prove that an undertaking intended to eliminate a competitor.

4.17   If a dominant undertaking adopts a predatory pricing policy with the intention of eliminating a competitor (e.g. as evidenced by its own internal documents), it will be presumed to have that intention for as long as the pricing policy continues.[31]

Conduct makes no commercial sense apart from harm to competition

4.18   It may be relevant to consider whether the undertaking's strategy makes commercial sense only because it eliminates a competitor.[32] For example, there might be other strategies open to the dominant undertaking that would have met its other commercial objectives just as well while being less likely to harm competition.

4.19   As noted above, pricing below AVC leads to the presumption of an abuse. Even where prices are above AVC, when a dominant undertaking intentionally prices below AAC, it deliberately incurs a loss, since it would make a greater profit from not producing at all. Therefore pricing below AAC may be evidence of an intention to eliminate a competitor in the absence of legitimate commercial reasons for that pricing strategy.

4.20   A dominant undertaking would not be able to justify deliberately incurring losses on one product by higher profits earned on another product where the latter profits resulted from eliminating a competitor. For example, in *Napp*, the fact that losses made from below cost prices in the hospital segment of the market were outweighed by profits earned on excessive prices in the community segment was not a legitimate reason for the low prices in the hospital segment. This was because the low prices in the hospital segment were part of an exclusionary strategy designed to protect Napp's ability to charge high prices in the community segment.

---

30 See paragraphs 425 to 432.

31 *Aberdeen Journals (No. 2)* at paragraph 431.

32 A dominant undertaking might present revenue forecasts which demonstrate that, while it expects to incur losses in the short term, its pricing strategy would be profitable in the long term. In this case, when assessing whether the undertaking's strategy makes commercial sense apart from exclusion, it would be necessary to strip out any of the revenues that are expected as a result of the elimination of a competitor.

Other behavioural evidence of intention

4.21   Other forms of behaviour by the dominant undertaking may also indicate an intention to engage in predation against a rival. For example, the targeting of price cuts against a competitor, while higher prices were maintained elsewhere, might indicate predatory intent.[33]

4.22   Further evidence might include the frequency of the behaviour. For example, if the behaviour is part of a pattern of aggressive pricing or other conduct that impedes competition, it is more likely to provide evidence of predatory intent than if it had been isolated.

4.23   It may also be relevant to consider whether the alleged predatory behaviour would be likely to eliminate a competitor. A number of factors would be relevant in this context. First, whether the scale of the pricing strategy is sufficient to raise a reasonable possibility that it would eliminate a competitor. Second, whether the financial resources of the alleged predator give it sufficiently 'deep pockets' (i.e. sufficient access to finance) to sustain loss making behaviour for a period long enough to eliminate a competitor. Third, whether the dominant undertaking has sufficient capacity to win sales from its rival.

Feasibility of recouping losses

4.24   A third issue is whether the undertaking, having successfully forced a competitor out of a market, would be able to recoup its earlier losses. If the undertaking would not be able to recoup these losses (e.g. because it would still face competition from existing or potential competitors), the predatory strategy would be unprofitable.

4.25   However, the European Court has held that, whenever there is a risk that competitors will be eliminated, there is no need to prove the possibility of recoupment.[34] This is because the weakened state of competition on the market on which the undertaking holds a dominant position will, in principle, ensure that losses are recouped.[35]

4.26   Predatory pricing may be pursued in one sector (or market) in order to protect profits or share of sales in another, perhaps through establishing a reputation likely to deter other would-be entrants. This too can be seen as a form of recoupment.[36]

---

33 Where an undertaking is in a position of 'super-dominance' (that is, it has a very high degree of market power, which may be inferred, typically, from a market share in the order of 90 per cent), and it selectively cuts prices with the intent of eliminating a competitor, it may be abusing its dominant position even if the discounted prices charged are not loss making. (See Cases C-395 and 396/96P *Compagnie Maritime Belge v Commission* [2000] ECR I-1365, including the opinion of Advocate General Fennelly; Case T-228/97 *Irish Sugar v Commission* [1999] ECR II 2969; and Napp at paragraphs 337 to 339.)

34 *Tetra Pak II*, endorsed by the CAT in *Aberdeen Journals (No. 2)* at paragraphs 441 to 446.

35 Where the competitor at risk of elimination is a competitor in a market other than that in which the dominant position is held (that is to say, an associated market) then the OFT may, depending on the circumstances of the case, specifically consider the feasibility of recouping losses.

36 See *Aberdeen Journals (No. 2)* at paragraph 445.

The OFT sought to apply the Chapter II prohibition against predatory pricing in the case of *Aberdeen Journals Ltd v. Director General of Fair Trading*, where the applicant publisher allegedly sold newspaper advertising at predatory prices in an effort to exclude a new competitor. It was found that the OFT had failed sufficiently to define the relevant market in order to apply the Chapter II prohibition.

An example of proceedings against predatory pricing where the OFT was more successful is *Napp Pharmaceutical v. D-G FT*, an appeal to the CCAT (as it was then). As there was clear evidence of pricing below cost, the tribunal was concerned in the following segment of the ruling with resolving the issue of intention or objective justification in pricing policy.

Napp Pharmaceutical Holdings Limited v. Director General of Fair Trading [2002] CAT 1

Napp had a market share in a morphine-based analgesic consistently above 90 per cent, which it offered to hospitals at a fraction of the price it sold it to the 'community' market segment (through GPs), allegedly with the intention of eliminating competitors. Napp argued 'that there is a follow on effect between hospital and community sales' and accordingly that price cutting in the former segment *intended* to lead to sales in the latter, attempting to rebut the inference that Napp *intended to eliminate competition*. Relying on *Michelin* (1983) (see above at p. 339), the tribunal upheld the DGFT's ruling, finding that Napp had a special responsibility and that, given the nature of the hospital segment as a key entry point, the infringement could be inferred to have been intentional. Accordingly, it merited a severe penalty fine.

CCAT

228   ... Napp has abused its dominant position in offering prices below average variable costs to hospitals contrary to the Chapter II prohibition ... without it being necessary to find that Napp had a specific intention to eliminate competition. In view of the fact that the *AKZO* approach was laid down in a case where the dominant undertaking had only 50 per cent of the market, it seems to us that it is only in the most exceptional of circumstances that a similar approach should not be applied in cases of "super dominance" where the undertaking concerned has around 95 per cent of the market.

229   It is true, however, that in paragraph 127 of his opinion in *Compagnie Maritime Belge*, Advocate General Fennelly stated that while sales below average variable costs (for which in this case direct costs are considered to be a proxy) are "in effect presumed to be abusive", he went on to say that "a dominant firm, would be permitted to rebut this presumption by showing that such pricing was not part of a plan to eliminate its competitor". In view of the remarks at paragraphs 132 and 137 of his opinion, we doubt whether Mr Fennelly would necessarily have taken the

same approach on this point had he been considering a case, such as the present, of a virtual monopolist selling well below direct costs. Nonetheless, as a precaution we consider in this judgment whether it is shown that Napp had no plan or intention to eliminate competition, so as to bring itself within the exception to the *AKZO* test envisaged by Mr Fennelly.

230   In that connection we begin by considering Napp's fundamental argument that the *AKZO* and *Tetra Pak II* approach is not the right starting point in this case because, properly understood, Napp's hospital sales did not "generate loss" because of the "follow-on effects". That issue has to be considered also in the light of *Compagnie Maritime Belge* and *Irish Sugar*, which show that even if the prices of a dominant firm remain above costs, and simply match the price of a competitor, there may still be an abuse, at least where a super dominant firm is concerned, if the reduced prices in question are made on a selective basis and have no economic rationale other than the elimination of competition.

. . .

251   When a dominant undertaking selling below cost contends that its policy is not motivated by an intention to eliminate competition but is based on some other, legitimate, commercial rationale, the best way for that undertaking to defend itself by producing contemporary internal documents showing that such a rationale did in fact form the basis of the company's policy at the material time. In the present case, Napp did not choose to do so, either in answer to the allegations made by the Director, or in the notice of appeal.

252   Even in reply to the Tribunal's request dated 31 August 2001, Napp has been unable to produce any document referring to or explaining the rationale for its hospital pricing policy for the period of four years from 1997 to the date of the decision in March 2001. That period includes the period when, according to Napp, its prices to hospitals first went below direct costs, as well as the whole period of the infringement. Napp does not strike us as a naive or badly managed company. If its pricing policy had in fact been seen by Napp in the way that its economic consultants suggest, we would have expected the company's internal documents to demonstrate that.

253   As regards the documents which Napp did produce in reply to the Tribunal's request, relating to the period prior to 1997, those documents do not show that Napp ever took into account during that period the narrow follow-on effect which Napp now alleges.

254   While experts' reports are often relevant and helpful to understanding the issues with which this Tribunal has to deal, we find in this case that the idea of a "follow-on" effect in the narrow or mechanistic sense relied on by Napp flows not from any internal documents from Napp but from the work done by Napp's economic advisers for the purposes of the present case. In our view such work does not carry

[405]

matters any further forward in the absence of any evidence that Napp in fact took the theory upon which it is based into account in setting its prices.

255   In our view, what Napp was well aware of was not any follow-on effect in the narrow sense, but the strategic importance of hospital business, and the hospital influence thereby acquired, as the gateway to the community segment. Thus when Mr Brogden told us that Napp believed its hospital sales were profitable as a result of unquantifiable "follow-on business", what in our view he really meant was that the loss-making hospital business was still worthwhile for Napp if one took into account all the possible ways, notably referral letters, in which the influence of the hospital could lead on to sales in the community. In our judgment, for Mr Brogden, the "follow-on effect" was really the general and unquantified advantage to Napp of retaining for itself such "hospital influence", notably as a means of protecting its market share in the community segment.

256   In our judgment, that is confirmed by the documents disclosed in answer to the Tribunal's request of 31 August 2001, which we discuss at paragraphs 31 et seq. below, and by the references to links between the hospital and community segments that could benefit Zomorph, to be found in the documents disclosed in answer to the Director's letter of 15 June 2001.

257   Moreover, in our judgment the "net revenue" defence advanced by Napp, whether on the basis of the "linkages" which may result from hospital influence, or on the basis of some narrow follow-on effect, is in any event conceptually and factually wholly misconceived, for the reasons we now give.

Conceptual problems with Napp's net revenue test

258   In our view, Napp's net revenue argument, whether based on the narrow "follow-on effects" alleged by Napp, or on the "linkages" resulting from hospital influence, has at least three conceptual weaknesses, taking into account the particular circumstances of the present case.

259   The first conceptual weakness is that the net revenue test, as applied simplistically by Napp, provides no yardstick for distinguishing between what is legitimate, and what is abusive, behaviour on the part of a dominant undertaking. For instance, a monopolist driving away new entrants by predatory pricing is likely to maximise his net revenue by so doing, for example by avoiding loss of market share and erosion of prices in the profitable market where he holds a monopoly. Yet plainly such behaviour does not cease to be abusive merely because it is profitable for the monopolist to engage in it. In our judgment, therefore a "net revenue approach" cannot, standing alone, constitute a defence to a charge of abuse by a dominant undertaking, unless it is accompanied by clear evidence that there was no intention or effect of foreclosing the market and impairing competition.

260   This point may be illustrated by the circumstances of the present case. In this case (i) Napp is a virtual monopolist with a market share of 93 per cent in the hospital

segment; (ii) the hospital segment is a key gateway to the community segment; and (iii) Napp is also a virtual monopolist in the community segment with a market share of 96 per cent. Let it be assumed, in Napp's favour, that there is some sense in which its loss-making hospital sales can be considered to be profitable for Napp if one takes into account the revenue from sales in the community segment which follow from hospital influence, for example, referral letters written by hospital doctors to GPs. However, if those loss-making hospital sales also have the effect of excluding competitors, the very conduct which is profitable to Napp on a net revenue basis has at the same time the effect of eliminating competition. That in turn, protects Napp's revenue in the community segment. To then argue that the below-cost pricing in the hospital segment is justified by the revenues from the community segment is the equivalent of saying that anti-competitive behaviour which protects Napp's virtual monopoly can be justified on the basis of the profits made from the monopoly which the anti-competitive behaviour is designed to protect. The argument is circular, as the Director points out at paragraphs 151 and 195 of the decision.

261 To put the point another way, in most cases of predatory pricing, the predator is willing to forgo short-term profits, in the hope of recouping its losses on subsequent, more profitable, sales. In some cases the recoupment may take the form of raising prices again once a competitor is eliminated; in other cases it may simply be that it is well worth the cost of short-term losses in order to protect the profits that flow from a large market share. As the Director submitted in the present case, the fact that Napp's below-cost pricing in the hospital sector enables it to make money from "follow-on" sales in the community sector merely signifies that the particular form of "recoupment" available to Napp is more direct and more immediate than it is in other cases of predatory pricing.

262 For these reasons it seems to us that Napp's "net revenue approach" cannot displace the *AKZO* test as the correct starting point for the analysis of the abuse here in question. At best arguments based on a "net revenue test" *may* be relevant to show that the dominant undertaking had "no plan to eliminate competition" so as to fall within the exception to the *AKZO* test recognised by Advocate General Fennelly, but not otherwise.

263 The second conceptual weakness in Napp's argument is its contention that the hospital and community prices are "system prices". In our view that argument depends on establishing that what is being sold to the buyer is indeed a "system", as might, at least theoretically, be the case of the sale of razors and razor blades, or photocopiers and toner cartridges. However, as *Canon Kabushiki Kaisha v. Green Cartridge Co. (Hong Kong)* makes clear, an essential aspect of the legitimate use of system pricing is that the buyer is in a position to evaluate the life-time, or system-wide costs, and so make a rational choice between competing possibilities. Here, that is not the case. During the period of infringement in this case, there were two separate groups of buyers, the hospital authorities, and the GPs respectively, rather than a single buyer. Neither group of buyers was motivated to any significant extent

to take account of the cost implications, for the other group, of his decisions, or had the information to do so rationally. In this case, it seems to us, what Napp has done is exploit not the connection, but the *disconnection* between purchasing decisions taken by the different component parts of the NHS, thereby maintaining widely different prices to the different purchasers concerned. That, in our view, is the exact opposite of "system pricing" as it is properly understood.

264   Even if, in the future, the activities of PCGs/PCTs may begin to alleviate the lack of any connection between the different NHS purchasing decisions with which we are concerned in the present case, it seems to us, on the evidence, that it may be some time before the prescribing decisions of individual GPs, and the purchasing decisions of hospital authorities, can sensibly be described as forming part of a "single system". They certainly did not do so during the period of infringement.

265   The third conceptual weakness in Napp's argument based on "follow-on effects" or "linkages", is that it presents only a small part of the total picture which needs to be examined. For the reasons already given, one cannot simply arrive at the conclusion that Napp's pricing to hospitals is in some sense "incrementally profitable", and stop there as if that shows conclusively that there is no abuse. First, in order to rebut the AKZO presumption, it is necessary to examine the market circumstances, in order to show that the pricing below average variable costs in question does not have the object or effect of eliminating competition. Secondly, as *Tetra Pak II, Compagnie Maritime Belge and Irish Sugar* show, the exact scope of the "special responsibility" of a dominant or super dominant undertaking has to be determined in the particular circumstances of each case. In our view, in the light of that case law, one cannot conclude that the Chapter II prohibition is not infringed merely on the basis of some kind of "incremental profitability" without examining the effect of Napp's conduct on competition, how far Napp enjoys advantages over its competitors, and the evidence as to Napp's intentions. Napp's "net revenue" approach does not address any of those matters.

266   The three conceptual weaknesses identified above lead us to the conclusion that Napp's net revenue approach in this case is wholly insufficient, in itself, to rebut the *AKZO* presumption that Napp's hospital prices below direct costs are abusive. That conclusion is reinforced by considering the specific market circumstances of this case from the point of view of the effect of Napp's hospital pricing policy on competition, the alleged "asymmetry" between Napp and its competitors, and finally, Napp's intentions.

(f) Essential facilities

Like the practice of the Commission and the Courts under Article 82, the OFT has recognised a doctrine of essential facilities in the UK context.

OFT414

8.5   Although the assessment of whether a particular facility is essential must be on a case-by-case basis, in practice essential facilities are rare. A facility will only be viewed as essential where it can be demonstrated that access to it is indispensable in order to compete in a related market and where duplication is impossible or extremely difficult owing to physical, geographic or legal constraints (or is highly undesirable for reasons of public policy). In certain cases, the cost of duplicating the facility might also be regarded as an insuperable obstacle.[63] While potential examples include ports and utility distribution networks (for example, electricity wires, and water and gas pipelines), in practice few facilities can be described as being truly essential. Intellectual property rights by themselves are unlikely to create essential facilities in normal circumstances.

8.6   Market definition is a crucial part of the determination of whether a particular facility is essential. An asset will not be regarded as an essential facility if other similar facilities compete within the same relevant market (i.e. if there are potential substitutes), or if the facility is not indispensable to the provision of the good or service in question. For example, a port will not be regarded as an essential facility if other ports compete within the same geographic market (see the competition law guideline *Market definition* (OFT403)).

Access to essential facilities

8.7   As with refusal to supply in general, refusal to allow access to an essential facility will constitute an abuse only if there is evidence of (likely) substantial harm to competition (e.g. in a related market) without an objective justification for the dominant undertaking's behaviour.[64] Objective justifications could include normal commercial reasons, such as creditworthiness, and might depend on (for example) the lack of available spare capacity within the facility.

8.8   When determining whether refusal to allow access to an essential facility constitutes an abuse and, if so, on what terms access should be granted, care must be taken not to undermine the incentives for undertakings to make future investments and innovations, especially where the essential facility is a result of a previous innovation.

A good example of application of the essential facilities doctrine appears in the following case of *Intel v. Via Technologies*.

63 See the judgment of the European Court in Case C-7/97 *Oscar Bronner v Mediaprint and others*, [1998] ECR I-7791 (*Oscar Bronner*) and in particular the opinion of AG Jacobs, at paragraphs 47 and 65 to 66.

64 In order to establish the existence of abuse, the refusal of access to the facility must be likely to eliminate all competition in the market on the part of the person requiring access, without being objectively justified: see, for example, *Oscar Bronner* at paragraph 41.

Intel Corp v. Via Technologies Inc. [2003] UKCLR 106

Intel brought patent infringement proceedings against Via after terminating a licence to manufacture and sell components incorporating Intel's technology. Following complaints concerning abuse of dominance to the European Commission (later withdrawn), Intel approached Via with a draft contract to renew the licence. However, this offer proved unsatisfactory and Via refused. Intel sought and won summary judgment against Via for patent infringement, because the court ([2002] UKCLR 576) found, *inter alia*, no merit in Via's defence that Intel had abused a dominant position by refusing to grant a licence because such refusal did not completely eliminate downstream competition (*cf. Magill*; see facts at p. 349 above).

Via appealed successfully against the summary judgement to the Court of Appeal, arguing its defence merited a hearing because there could potentially be a breach of Article 82 even without preventing a wholly new product or eliminating competition from all sources.

Vice-Chancellor

47   Counsel for Intel submits that these cases show that there can only be exceptional circumstances within the Magill test if all the conditions in either *Magill* or [*IMS Health Inc v Commission* (Case T-184/01R II) [2002] 4 C.M.L.R. 2] are satisfied. Thus, the result of the refusal [to grant a licence] must be to exclude an entirely new product from the market (*Magill*) or all competition to the patentee (*IMS*). He contends that neither condition is pleaded or satisfied in this case for chipsets, and CPUs will continue to be produced and competition to Intel from those it has licensed will continue to exist.

48   I do not accept either the premise or the conclusion. With regard to the premise *Magill* and *IMS* indicate the circumstances which the Court of Justice and the President of the Court of First Instance respectively regarded as exceptional in the cases before them. It does not follow that other circumstances in other cases will not be regarded as exceptional. In particular it is at least arguable, as the President recognised in *IMS*, that the Court of Justice will assimilate its jurisprudence under Art. 82 more closely with that of the essential facilities doctrine applied in the United States. In that event there could be a breach of Art. 82 without the exclusion of a wholly new product or all competition. This approach seems to me to be warranted by the width of the descriptions of abuse contained in Art. 82 itself.

49   I would, in any event, reject the submission of counsel for Intel that the *IMS* test requires the exclusion of all competition from all sources. This was not a requirement in *Oscar Bronner* which referred in para. [41] only to all competition from the person requesting the service. Accordingly the summary in *IMS*, to which I have referred ... above, must be read in that light. Were it otherwise liability under Art. 82 could be simply avoided by the grant of a licence to an unenergetic rival.

50   I do not accept the conclusion either because it appears to me that the pleadings of Via in both the Chipset Action and the CPU Action satisfy either the *Magill* or the *IMS* test. Thus in the Chipset Action Via pleads in paras 19 and 44 that access to the market in x86 compatible chipsets is impossible without the licence of Intel. In the CPU Action Via pleads in paras 19(a) and 24 that Intel seeks to use its rights as patentee to exclude from the market both the Socket 370 and the EGBA format.

51   Accordingly in my view it is arguable that the range of exceptional circumstances which may give rise to the abuse by the owner of an intellectual property right of his dominant position contrary to Art. 82 can extend to the facts pleaded by Via in both the Chipset Action and the CPU Action. Whether or not they do will depend on the findings of fact made at the trial. In a case such as this such findings are an essential preliminary to any reference under Art. 234 EC Treaty. In those circumstances I consider that the defence Via seeks to advance under this head has a more than fanciful prospect of success. Further it is one which, in my view, should be disposed of at a trial. Accordingly I would grant permission to appeal and allow the appeal on this ground in both the Chipset Action and the CPU Action.

(g) Vertical restraints

Paragraphs 7.1 to 7.12 of *OFT414* deal specifically with vertical restraints infringing Article 82 and/or the Chapter II prohibition, setting out a non-exhaustive list (at paragraph 7.3) of examples of vertical restraints which may infringe these provisions. The application of Article 81 and the Chapter I prohibition on vertical restraints was discussed in chapter 5. It is vital to remember, however, as paragraph 7.5 explains, that the effect of the vertical restraint is more important than the form it takes. That is to say, any vertical restraint may be found to be abusive if it has the effect of foreclosing a market to existing or potential competition or it dampens competition in the market. Of course not all vertical restraints imposed by dominant undertakings will be abusive, and paragraph 7.10 sets out some pro-competitive features, which vertical restraints may have such as promoting efficiencies, non-price competition and investment. Consequently, vertical restraints are generally assessed on a case-by-case basis.

Although part 7 of the *Guideline* provides a number of examples of vertical restraints and their effects, the OFT's Guideline on *Vertical Agreements* (OFT419) provides further detail. Paragraph 7.7 of that publication contains a further non-exhaustive list of vertical restraints, such as resale price maintenance, selective distribution provisions, tie-in sales and bundling etc. followed by further examples of competition dampening and other negative effects that vertical restraints may have on a market. Paragraphs 7.19 to 7.29 also provide a more extensive list of benefits that vertical restraints can bring to markets, including an extended discussion of free-riding. Although it appears that *OFT419* provides more detail on the subject, it is apparent that, when dealing with the issue of vertical restraints as an example of abuse, both guidelines should be considered.

[411]

Pernod-Ricard SA and Campbell Distillers Limited v. OFT is a recent case involving vertical restraints in the retail 'on-sale' (pub and club) market for rum. Bacardi was under investigation by the OFT for alleged breach of the Chapter II prohibition by attempting to obtain exclusivity for its brand and to exclude the applicants' Havana Club rum from the market by requiring retailers to serve Bacardi by default (i.e. unless otherwise specified, bartenders were obliged to pour Bacardi).

In January 2003, following assurances given by Bacardi, the OFT announced that no competition concerns persisted and that it must therefore close its investigation. The applicants sought to challenge this 'decision' before the CAT, alleging continuing breach by Bacardi and failure by the OFT to give reasons. The OFT, supported by Bacardi, argued that no 'decision' had been made and that, if it had, the OFT is nonetheless empowered to accept assurances. In a judgment handed down on 10 June 2004, the CAT ruled that the OFT's decision to close its investigation was an appealable decision. It also decided that the OFT should have (a) provided Pernod-Ricard with a non-confidential version of the Rule 14 notice and (b) given it an opportunity to submit observations before deciding to close its investigation; although the CAT did not feel it was appropriate to set aside the OFT's decision.

Further reading

Aitman and Jones 'Competition law and copyright: has the copyright owner lost the ability to control his copyright?' (2004) 26 EIPR 137

Capobianco 'The essential facility doctrine: similarities and differences between the American and European approaches' (2001) 26 ELRev 548

Dabbah 'Conduct, dominance and abuse in "market relationship": analysis of some conceptual issues under Article 82 EC' (2000) 21 ECLR 45

Doherty 'Just what are essential facilities?' (2001) 38 CMLRev 397

Jebsen and Stevens 'Assumptions, goals and dominant undertakings: the regulation of competition under Article 86 of the European Union' (1996) 64 ALJ 443

Ridyard 'Exclusionary pricing and price discrimination abuses under Article 82 – an economic analysis' (2002) 23 ECLR 286

10

EC merger control

1 Introduction

The first chapter highlighted the phenomenal increase in significance and geographical scope which competition law has come to witness during the last decade or so. Within the field of competition law, merger control has attracted special attention, despite the fact that only about 70 of the world's about 100 systems of competition law include a specific regime for dealing with mergers. The reason lies in the special nature of mergers as a business phenomenon, especially when compared with other business phenomena, such as abuses of dominance by firms or cartel activities.

The process of relentless globalisation of business which has been fast developing since the 1990s has meant that merger operations can affect the conditions of competition in more than one jurisdiction. This means that, quite inevitably, regulatory approval in more than one jurisdiction may need to be sought. Such a consequence – as is widely accepted – can often give rise to uncertainty for the firms concerned and may cause huge expense and significant delay.

Nor are those involved in advising firms in merger situations immune from the cost and uncertainty about merger operations which have to be notified in more than one jurisdiction. Often legal advisors have to answer extremely difficult questions in merger cases, such as whether notification of the merger to the competition authorities in one or more jurisdictions is necessary or mandatory; whether the rules of the jurisdiction in question will suspend the consummation of the proposed transaction until clearance; which authorities need to be notified; what is required for this purpose and how to go about notifying the authorities concerned; and how the authorities will assess the merger, including any relevant time framework within which they will operate.

The present chapter deals with merger control in the case of mergers with an EC dimension; UK merger control is covered in the following chapter. The chapter is structured as follows. It will begin by considering developments leading up to the current (new) regime instituted in May 2004. It will then go on to consider the key concepts and terminology In the EC Merger Regulation, including the various different merger situations and jurisdictional scope of the European Commission, before reviewing substantive analysis under the Regulation. It will then examine some of the procedural constraints imposed on the Commission and how this has influenced investigations and then go on to consider defences acting in favour of allowing certain mergers to proceed. The chapter will conclude with a discussion of joint ventures, which are often classified by competition lawyers as mergers.

2 Developments over the years

The EC has acquired a vast experience in the area of merger control. This is extremely remarkable in light of the fact that for many years the EC lacked any specific mechanism for dealing with mergers and that such a mechanism was not adopted until 1989, when Regulation 4064/89 was introduced.

The years before 1989 witnessed a heated, divisive debate on whether the EC should have such a specific mechanism and if so what form it should take. The need for such a mechanism was particularly felt in those 'merger situations' where the Commission was concerned about the effect of a merger on competition in the Common Market. A notable example of this concern is the case of *Continental Can*, discussed in chapters 2 and 9. In this case, the Commission suffered a defeat on the facts (ECJ overturned the Commission's decision), but it gained a victory in principle because the ECJ confirmed that Article 82 could be used to control merger situations in that an alteration to the structure of the market could constitute abuse by a dominant firm.

With the introduction of Regulation 4064/89, the EC could pride itself on the fact that its competition law 'tool kit' was fully equipped. However, what happened in the years that followed (most notably the huge number of merger notifications the Commission received per year) clearly set the bar for the enormous task the Commission was expected to fulfil. Institutionally, the Commission could be said to have prepared well with the establishment of Merger Task Force (MTF), a specialist division to deal with mergers which has now been largely disbanded. This was extremely important given that mergers had to be treated differently from Article 81 and 82 cases: prior notification for certain mergers were mandatory and the Commission itself had to reach its decisions within a strict time limit. Its practice and procedure had to evolve quickly, and more importantly it had to be as clear and transparent as possible. Moreover, of course, it was vital that the substantive law under Regulation 4064/89 were clear to merging firms and their legal advisors.

To achieve this, the Commission published a significant number of non-legislative instruments, mainly Notices, which have proved to be of huge importance in practice (many of which are reproduced below). In addition, the Commission kept the whole operation of the Regulation under close scrutiny, focusing in particular on whether its experience in applying the Regulation indicated that changes were necessary. By 1997, based on its practical experience the Commission took the positive step of reforming certain aspects of Regulation 4064/89. This happened with the adoption of Regulation 1310/97. The Commission also adopted other important legislative measures, which clarified important points of practice and procedure. Among these is implementing Regulation 447/98, which repealed Regulation 3384/94.

3 Regulation 139/2004

The Commission's drive for legislative reform in the area of merger control was not expected to come to a halt with the adoption of Regulations 1310/97 and 447/98. In December 2001, a major step was taken by the Commission to open a wide debate on how Regulation 4064/89 should be reformed, by the publication of the *Green Paper on Merger Review*. After assessing the views and comments of various interested parties, the Commission published a proposal for a new Regulation to replace Regulation 4064/89. This was accompanied with a draft set of guidelines dealing with the appraisal of horizontal mergers. On 20 January 2004, with the approval of the Council of Ministers the proposal was adopted as a new Regulation, Regulation 139/2004 and the draft guidelines became the *Guidelines on the assessment of horizontal mergers*. Regulation 139/2004 entered into force on 1 May 2004.

Regulation 139/2004 has 'recast' Regulation 4064/89, and as such does not amend the latter but completely replaces it. The corollary is that Regulation 447/98 has also had to be replaced and so the Commission also published a draft Implementing Regulation. The draft included as annexes a draft revised Form CO (the form that is used to notify merger operations to the Commission), draft new Short (notification) Form, and a draft new form for the lodging of pre-notification referral requests (so-called Form RS). Public consultation was sought on these drafts and following that the Commission published Regulation 802/2004 implementing Regulation 139/2004.

The Commission's reform package also included the adoption of non-legislative measures designed, among other things, to strengthen the underlying economic analysis the Commission conducts in mergers, to increase the internal checks and balances and to enhance the rights of defence for merging firms. Some of these measures were put in place by the end of 2003, and they include the appointment of a Chief Competition Economist and establishing an internal panel to scrutinise the conclusions reached by the investigating team with a 'pair of fresh eyes'. It is arguable that the Commission's drive for further reform had to be strengthened following the series of defeats, which the Commission suffered before the CFI, in 2002 and 2003. (See e.g. *Airtours v. Commission, Schneider Electric v. Commission, Tetra Laval v. Commission*.)

Regulation 139/2004 on the control of concentrations between undertakings (the EC Merger Regulation) [2004] OJ L24/1

THE COUNCIL OF THE EUROPEAN UNION,

Having regard to the Treaty establishing the European Community, and in particular Articles 83 and 308 thereof,

Having regard to the proposal from the Commission,[1]

Having regard to the opinion of the European Parliament,[2]

Having regard to the opinion of the European Economic and Social Committee,[3]

Whereas:

(1) Council Regulation (EEC) No 4064/89 of 21 December 1989 on the control of concentrations between undertakings[4] has been substantially amended. Since further amendments are to be made, it should be recast in the interest of clarity.

(2) For the achievement of the aims of the Treaty, Article 3(1)(g) gives the Community the objective of instituting a system ensuring that competition in the internal market is not distorted. Article 4(1) of the Treaty provides that the activities of the Member States and the Community are to be conducted in accordance with the principle of an open market economy with free competition. These principles are essential for the further development of the internal market.

(3) The completion of the internal market and of economic and monetary union, the enlargement of the European Union and the lowering of international barriers to trade and investment will continue to result in major corporate reorganisations, particularly in the form of concentrations.

(4) Such reorganisations are to be welcomed to the extent that they are in line with the requirements of dynamic competition and capable of increasing the competitiveness of European industry, improving the conditions of growth and raising the standard of living in the Community.

(5) However, it should be ensured that the process of reorganisation does not result in lasting damage to competition; Community law must therefore include provisions governing those concentrations which may significantly impede effective competition in the common market or in a substantial part of it.

(6) A specific legal instrument is therefore necessary to permit effective control of all concentrations in terms of their effect on the structure of competition in the Community and to be the only instrument applicable to such concentrations. Regulation

---

1 OJ C 20, 28.1.2003, p. 4.
2 Opinion delivered on 9.10.2003 (not yet published in the Official Journal).
3 Opinion delivered on 24.10.2003 (not yet published in the Official Journal).
4 OJ L 395, 30.12.1989, p. 1. Corrected version in OJ L 257, 21.9.1990, p. 13. Regulation as last amended by Regulation (EC) No 1310/97 (OJ L 180, 9.7.1997, p. 1). Corrigendum in OJ L 40, 13.2.1998, p. 17.

(EEC) No 4064/89 has allowed a Community policy to develop in this field. In the light of experience, however, that Regulation should now be recast into legislation designed to meet the challenges of a more integrated market and the future enlargement of the European Union. In accordance with the principles of subsidiarity and of proportionality as set out in Article 5 of the Treaty, this Regulation does not go beyond what is necessary in order to achieve the objective of ensuring that competition in the common market is not distorted, in accordance with the principle of an open market economy with free competition.

(7)   Articles 81 and 82, while applicable, according to the case-law of the Court of Justice, to certain concentrations, are not sufficient to control all operations which may prove to be incompatible with the system of undistorted competition envisaged in the Treaty. This Regulation should therefore be based not only on Article 83 but, principally, on Article 308 of the Treaty, under which the Community may give itself the additional powers of action necessary for the attainment of its objectives, and also powers of action with regard to concentrations on the markets for agricultural products listed in Annex I to the Treaty.

(8)   The provisions to be adopted in this Regulation should apply to significant structural changes, the impact of which on the market goes beyond the national borders of any one Member State. Such concentrations should, as a general rule, be reviewed exclusively at Community level, in application of a 'one-stop shop' system and in compliance with the principle of subsidiarity. Concentrations not covered by this Regulation come, in principle, within the jurisdiction of the Member States.

(9)   The scope of application of this Regulation should be defined according to the geographical area of activity of the undertakings concerned and be limited by quantitative thresholds in order to cover those concentrations which have a Community dimension. The Commission should report to the Council on the implementation of the applicable thresholds and criteria so that the Council, acting in accordance with Article 202 of the Treaty, is in a position to review them regularly, as well as the rules regarding pre-notification referral, in the light of the experience gained; this requires statistical data to be provided by the Member States to the Commission to enable it to prepare such reports and possible proposals for amendments. The Commission's reports and proposals should be based on relevant information regularly provided by the Member States.

(10)   A concentration with a Community dimension should be deemed to exist where the aggregate turnover of the undertakings concerned exceeds given thresholds; that is the case irrespective of whether or not the undertakings effecting the concentration have their seat or their principal fields of activity in the Community, provided they have substantial operations there.

(11)   The rules governing the referral of concentrations from the Commission to Member States and from Member States to the Commission should operate as an effective corrective mechanism in the light of the principle of subsidiarity; these rules protect

the competition interests of the Member States in an adequate manner and take due account of legal certainty and the 'one-stop shop' principle.

(12)   Concentrations may qualify for examination under a number of national merger control systems if they fall below the turnover thresholds referred to in this Regulation. Multiple notification of the same transaction increases legal uncertainty, effort and cost for undertakings and may lead to conflicting assessments. The system whereby concentrations may be referred to the Commission by the Member States concerned should therefore be further developed.

(13)   The Commission should act in close and constant liaison with the competent authorities of the Member States from which it obtains comments and information.

(14)   The Commission and the competent authorities of the Member States should together form a network of public authorities, applying their respective competences in close cooperation, using efficient arrangements for information- sharing and consultation, with a view to ensuring that a case is dealt with by the most appropriate authority, in the light of the principle of subsidiarity and with a view to ensuring that multiple notifications of a given concentration are avoided to the greatest extent possible. Referrals of concentrations from the Commission to Member States and from Member States to the Commission should be made in an efficient manner avoiding, to the greatest extent possible, situations where a concentration is subject to a referral both before and after its notification.

(15)   The Commission should be able to refer to a Member State notified concentrations with a Community dimension which threaten significantly to affect competition in a market within that Member State presenting all the characteristics of a distinct market. Where the concentration affects competition on such a market, which does not constitute a substantial part of the common market, the Commission should be obliged, upon request, to refer the whole or part of the case to the Member State concerned. A Member State should be able to refer to the Commission a concentration which does not have a Community dimension but which affects trade between Member States and threatens to significantly affect competition within its territory. Other Member States which are also competent to review the concentration should be able to join the request. In such a situation, in order to ensure the efficiency and predictability of the system, national time limits should be suspended until a decision has been reached as to the referral of the case. The Commission should have the power to examine and deal with a concentration on behalf of a requesting Member State or requesting Member States.

(16)   The undertakings concerned should be granted the possibility of requesting referrals to or from the Commission before a concentration is notified so as to further improve the efficiency of the system for the control of concentrations within the Community. In such situations, the Commission and national competition authorities should decide within short, clearly defined time limits whether a referral to or from the Commission ought to be made, thereby ensuring the efficiency of the

system. Upon request by the undertakings concerned, the Commission should be able to refer to a Member State a concentration with a Community dimension which may significantly affect competition in a market within that Member State presenting all the characteristics of a distinct market; the undertakings concerned should not, however, be required to demonstrate that the effects of the concentration would be detrimental to competition. A concentration should not be referred from the Commission to a Member State which has expressed its disagreement to such a referral. Before notification to national authorities, the undertakings concerned should also be able to request that a concentration without a Community dimension which is capable of being reviewed under the national competition laws of at least three Member States be referred to the Commission. Such requests for pre-notification referrals to the Commission would be particularly pertinent in situations where the concentration would affect competition beyond the territory of one Member State. Where a concentration capable of being reviewed under the competition laws of three or more Member States is referred to the Commission prior to any national notification, and no Member State competent to review the case expresses its disagreement, the Commission should acquire exclusive competence to review the concentration and such a concentration should be deemed to have a Community dimension. Such pre-notification referrals from Member States to the Commission should not, however, be made where at least one Member State competent to review the case has expressed its disagreement with such a referral.

(17)   The Commission should be given exclusive competence to apply this Regulation, subject to review by the Court of Justice.

(18)   The Member States should not be permitted to apply their national legislation on competition to concentrations with a Community dimension, unless this Regulation makes provision therefor. The relevant powers of national authorities should be limited to cases where, failing intervention by the Commission, effective competition is likely to be significantly impeded within the territory of a Member State and where the competition interests of that Member State cannot be sufficiently protected otherwise by this Regulation. The Member States concerned must act promptly in such cases; this Regulation cannot, because of the diversity of national law, fix a single time limit for the adoption of final decisions under national law.

(19)   Furthermore, the exclusive application of this Regulation to concentrations with a Community dimension is without prejudice to Article 296 of the Treaty, and does not prevent the Member States from taking appropriate measures to protect legitimate interests other than those pursued by this Regulation, provided that such measures are compatible with the general principles and other provisions of Community law.

(20)   It is expedient to define the concept of concentration in such a manner as to cover operations bringing about a lasting change in the control of the undertakings concerned and therefore in the structure of the market. It is therefore appropriate to include, within the scope of this Regulation, all joint ventures performing on a lasting basis all the functions of an autonomous economic entity. It is moreover

appropriate to treat as a single concentration transactions that are closely connected in that they are linked by condition or take the form of a series of transactions in securities taking place within a reasonably short period of time.

(21) This Regulation should also apply where the undertakings concerned accept restrictions directly related to, and necessary for, the implementation of the concentration. Commission decisions declaring concentrations compatible with the common market in application of this Regulation should automatically cover such restrictions, without the Commission having to assess such restrictions in individual cases. At the request of the undertakings concerned, however, the Commission should, in cases presenting novel or unresolved questions giving rise to genuine uncertainty, expressly assess whether or not any restriction is directly related to, and necessary for, the implementation of the concentration. A case presents a novel or unresolved question giving rise to genuine uncertainty if the question is not covered by the relevant Commission notice in force or a published Commission decision.

(22) The arrangements to be introduced for the control of concentrations should, without prejudice to Article 86(2) of the Treaty, respect the principle of non-discrimination between the public and the private sectors. In the public sector, calculation of the turnover of an undertaking concerned in a concentration needs, therefore, to take account of undertakings making up an economic unit with an independent power of decision, irrespective of the way in which their capital is held or of the rules of administrative supervision applicable to them.

(23) It is necessary to establish whether or not concentrations with a Community dimension are compatible with the common market in terms of the need to maintain and develop effective competition in the common market. In so doing, the Commission must place its appraisal within the general framework of the achievement of the fundamental objectives referred to in Article 2 of the Treaty establishing the European Community and Article 2 of the Treaty on European Union.

(24) In order to ensure a system of undistorted competition in the common market, in furtherance of a policy conducted in accordance with the principle of an open market economy with free competition, this Regulation must permit effective control of all concentrations from the point of view of their effect on competition in the Community. Accordingly, Regulation (EEC) No 4064/89 established the principle that a concentration with a Community dimension which creates or strengthens a dominant position as a result of which effective competition in the common market or in a substantial part of it would be significantly impeded should be declared incompatible with the common market.

(25) In view of the consequences that concentrations in oligopolistic market structures may have, it is all the more necessary to maintain effective competition in such markets. Many oligopolistic markets exhibit a healthy degree of competition. However, under certain circumstances, concentrations involving the elimination of important competitive constraints that the merging parties had exerted upon each other, as well

as a reduction of competitive pressure on the remaining competitors, may, even in the absence of a likelihood of coordination between the members of the oligopoly, result in a significant impediment to effective competition. The Community courts have, however, not to date expressly interpreted Regulation (EEC) No 4064/89 as requiring concentrations giving rise to such non-coordinated effects to be declared incompatible with the common market. Therefore, in the interests of legal certainty, it should be made clear that this Regulation permits effective control of all such concentrations by providing that any concentration which would significantly impede effective competition, in the common market or in a substantial part of it, should be declared incompatible with the common market. The notion of 'significant impediment to effective competition' in Article 2(2) and (3) should be interpreted as extending, beyond the concept of dominance, only to the anti-competitive effects of a concentration resulting from the non-coordinated behaviour of undertakings which would not have a dominant position on the market concerned.

(26) A significant impediment to effective competition generally results from the creation or strengthening of a dominant position. With a view to preserving the guidance that may be drawn from past judgments of the European courts and Commission decisions pursuant to Regulation (EEC) No 4064/89, while at the same time maintaining consistency with the standards of competitive harm which have been applied by the Commission and the Community courts regarding the compatibility of a concentration with the common market, this Regulation should accordingly establish the principle that a concentration with a Community dimension which would significantly impede effective competition, in the common market or in a substantial part thereof, in particular as a result of the creation or strengthening of a dominant position, is to be declared incompatible with the common market.

(27) In addition, the criteria of Article 81(1) and (3) of the Treaty should be applied to joint ventures performing, on a lasting basis, all the functions of autonomous economic entities, to the extent that their creation has as its consequence an appreciable restriction of competition between undertakings that remain independent.

(28) In order to clarify and explain the Commission's appraisal of concentrations under this Regulation, it is appropriate for the Commission to publish guidance which should provide a sound economic framework for the assessment of concentrations with a view to determining whether or not they may be declared compatible with the common market.

(29) In order to determine the impact of a concentration on competition in the common market, it is appropriate to take account of any substantiated and likely efficiencies put forward by the undertakings concerned. It is possible that the efficiencies brought about by the concentration counteract the effects on competition, and in particular the potential harm to consumers, that it might otherwise have and that, as a consequence, the concentration would not significantly impede effective competition, in the common market or in a substantial part of it, in particular as a result of the creation or strengthening of a dominant position. The Commission should

publish guidance on the conditions under which it may take efficiencies into account in the assessment of a concentration.

(30) Where the undertakings concerned modify a notified concentration, in particular by offering commitments with a view to rendering the concentration compatible with the common market, the Commission should be able to declare the concentration, as modified, compatible with the common market. Such commitments should be proportionate to the competition problem and entirely eliminate it. It is also appropriate to accept commitments before the initiation of proceedings where the competition problem is readily identifiable and can easily be remedied. It should be expressly provided that the Commission may attach to its decision conditions and obligations in order to ensure that the undertakings concerned comply with their commitments in a timely and effective manner so as to render the concentration compatible with the common market. Transparency and effective consultation of Member States as well as of interested third parties should be ensured throughout the procedure.

(31) The Commission should have at its disposal appropriate instruments to ensure the enforcement of commitments and to deal with situations where they are not fulfilled. In cases of failure to fulfil a condition attached to the decision declaring a concentration compatible with the common market, the situation rendering the concentration compatible with the common market does not materialise and the concentration, as implemented, is therefore not authorised by the Commission. As a consequence, if the concentration is implemented, it should be treated in the same way as a non-notified concentration implemented without authorisation. Furthermore, where the Commission has already found that, in the absence of the condition, the concentration would be incompatible with the common market, it should have the power to directly order the dissolution of the concentration, so as to restore the situation prevailing prior to the implementation of the concentration. Where an obligation attached to a decision declaring the concentration compatible with the common market is not fulfilled, the Commission should be able to revoke its decision. Moreover, the Commission should be able to impose appropriate financial sanctions where conditions or obligations are not fulfilled.

(32) Concentrations which, by reason of the limited market share of the undertakings concerned, are not liable to impede effective competition may be presumed to be compatible with the common market. Without prejudice to Articles 81 and 82 of the Treaty, an indication to this effect exists, in particular, where the market share of the undertakings concerned does not exceed 25 % either in the common market or in a substantial part of it.

(33) The Commission should have the task of taking all the decisions necessary to establish whether or not concentrations with a Community dimension are compatible with the common market, as well as decisions designed to restore the situation prevailing prior to the implementation of a concentration which has been declared incompatible with the common market.

(34)   To ensure effective control, undertakings should be obliged to give prior notification of concentrations with a Community dimension following the conclusion of the agreement, the announcement of the public bid or the acquisition of a controlling interest. Notification should also be possible where the undertakings concerned satisfy the Commission of their intention to enter into an agreement for a proposed concentration and demonstrate to the Commission that their plan for that proposed concentration is sufficiently concrete, for example on the basis of an agreement in principle, a memorandum of understanding, or a letter of intent signed by all undertakings concerned, or, in the case of a public bid, where they have publicly announced an intention to make such a bid, provided that the intended agreement or bid would result in a concentration with a Community dimension. The implementation of concentrations should be suspended until a final decision of the Commission has been taken. However, it should be possible to derogate from this suspension at the request of the undertakings concerned, where appropriate. In deciding whether or not to grant a derogation, the Commission should take account of all pertinent factors, such as the nature and gravity of damage to the undertakings concerned or to third parties, and the threat to competition posed by the concentration. In the interest of legal certainty, the validity of transactions must nevertheless be protected as much as necessary.

(35)   A period within which the Commission must initiate proceedings in respect of a notified concentration and a period within which it must take a final decision on the compatibility or incompatibility with the common market of that concentration should be laid down. These periods should be extended whenever the undertakings concerned offer commitments with a view to rendering the concentration compatible with the common market, in order to allow for sufficient time for the analysis and market testing of such commitment offers and for the consultation of Member States as well as interested third parties. A limited extension of the period within which the Commission must take a final decision should also be possible in order to allow sufficient time for the investigation of the case and the verification of the facts and arguments submitted to the Commission.

(36)   The Community respects the fundamental rights and observes the principles recognised in particular by the Charter of Fundamental Rights of the European Union.[5] Accordingly, this Regulation should be interpreted and applied with respect to those rights and principles.

(37)   The undertakings concerned must be afforded the right to be heard by the Commission when proceedings have been initiated; the members of the management and supervisory bodies and the recognised representatives of the employees of the undertakings concerned, and interested third parties, must also be given the opportunity to be heard.

(38)   In order properly to appraise concentrations, the Commission should have the right to request all necessary information and to conduct all necessary inspections

5 OJ C 364, 18.12.2000, p. 1.

throughout the Community. To that end, and with a view to protecting competition effectively, the Commission's powers of investigation need to be expanded. The Commission should, in particular, have the right to interview any persons who may be in possession of useful information and to record the statements made.

(39)   In the course of an inspection, officials authorised by the Commission should have the right to ask for any information relevant to the subject matter and purpose of the inspection; they should also have the right to affix seals during inspections, particularly in circumstances where there are reasonable grounds to suspect that a concentration has been implemented without being notified; that incorrect, incomplete or misleading information has been supplied to the Commission; or that the undertakings or persons concerned have failed to comply with a condition or obligation imposed by decision of the Commission. In any event, seals should only be used in exceptional circumstances, for the period of time strictly necessary for the inspection, normally not for more than 48 hours.

(40)   Without prejudice to the case-law of the Court of Justice, it is also useful to set out the scope of the control that the national judicial authority may exercise when it authorises, as provided by national law and as a precautionary measure, assistance from law enforcement authorities in order to overcome possible opposition on the part of the undertaking against an inspection, including the affixing of seals, ordered by Commission decision. It results from the case-law that the national judicial authority may in particular ask of the Commission further information which it needs to carry out its control and in the absence of which it could refuse the authorisation. The case-law also confirms the competence of the national courts to control the application of national rules governing the implementation of coercive measures. The competent authorities of the Member States should cooperate actively in the exercise of the Commission's investigative powers.

(41)   When complying with decisions of the Commission, the undertakings and persons concerned cannot be forced to admit that they have committed infringements, but they are in any event obliged to answer factual questions and to provide documents, even if this information may be used to establish against themselves or against others the existence of such infringements.

(42)   For the sake of transparency, all decisions of the Commission which are not of a merely procedural nature should be widely publicised. While ensuring preservation of the rights of defence of the undertakings concerned, in particular the right of access to the file, it is essential that business secrets be protected. The confidentiality of information exchanged in the network and with the competent authorities of third countries should likewise be safeguarded.

(43)   Compliance with this Regulation should be enforceable, as appropriate, by means of fines and periodic penalty payments. The Court of Justice should be given unlimited jurisdiction in that regard pursuant to Article 229 of the Treaty.

(44)   The conditions in which concentrations, involving undertakings having their seat or their principal fields of activity in the Community, are carried out in third countries should be observed, and provision should be made for the possibility of the Council giving the Commission an appropriate mandate for negotiation with a view to obtaining non-discriminatory treatment for such undertakings.

(45)   This Regulation in no way detracts from the collective rights of employees, as recognised in the undertakings concerned, notably with regard to any obligation to inform or consult their recognised representatives under Community and national law.

(46)   The Commission should be able to lay down detailed rules concerning the implementation of this Regulation in accordance with the procedures for the exercise of implementing powers conferred on the Commission. For the adoption of such implementing provisions, the Commission should be assisted by an Advisory Committee composed of the representatives of the Member States as specified in Article 23,

HAS ADOPTED THIS REGULATION:

Article 1 Scope

1   Without prejudice to Article 4(5) and Article 22, this Regulation shall apply to all concentrations with a Community dimension as defined in this Article.

2   A concentration has a Community dimension where:
(a) the combined aggregate worldwide turnover of all the undertakings concerned is more than EUR 5000 million; and
(b) the aggregate Community-wide turnover of each of at least two of the undertakings concerned is more than EUR 250 million,
unless each of the undertakings concerned achieves more than two-thirds of its aggregate Community-wide turnover within one and the same Member State.

3   A concentration that does not meet the thresholds laid down in paragraph 2 has a Community dimension where:
(a) the combined aggregate worldwide turnover of all the undertakings concerned is more than EUR 2500 million;
(b) in each of at least three Member States, the combined aggregate turnover of all the undertakings concerned is more than EUR 100 million;
(c) in each of at least three Member States included for the purpose of point (b), the aggregate turnover of each of at least two of the undertakings concerned is more than EUR 25 million; and
(d) the aggregate Community-wide turnover of each of at least two of the undertakings concerned is more than EUR 100 million,
unless each of the undertakings concerned achieves more than two-thirds of its aggregate Community-wide turnover within one and the same Member State.

4   On the basis of statistical data that may be regularly provided by the Member States, the Commission shall report to the Council on the operation of the thresholds and criteria set out in paragraphs 2 and 3 by 1 July 2009 and may present proposals pursuant to paragraph 5.

5   Following the report referred to in paragraph 4 and on a proposal from the Commission, the Council, acting by a qualified majority, may revise the thresholds and criteria mentioned in paragraph 3.

Article 2 Appraisal of concentrations

1   Concentrations within the scope of this Regulation shall be appraised in accordance with the objectives of this Regulation and the following provisions with a view to establishing whether or not they are compatible with the common market.
In making this appraisal, the Commission shall take into account:
(a) the need to maintain and develop effective competition within the common market in view of, among other things, the structure of all the markets concerned and the actual or potential competition from undertakings located either within or outwith the Community;
(b) the market position of the undertakings concerned and their economic and financial power, the alternatives available to suppliers and users, their access to supplies or markets, any legal or other barriers to entry, supply and demand trends for the relevant goods and services, the interests of the intermediate and ultimate consumers, and the development of technical and economic progress provided that it is to consumers' advantage and does not form an obstacle to competition.

2   A concentration which would not significantly impede effective competition in the common market or in a substantial part of it, in particular as a result of the creation or strengthening of a dominant position, shall be declared compatible with the common market.

3   A concentration which would significantly impede effective competition, in the common market or in a substantial part of it, in particular as a result of the creation or strengthening of a dominant position, shall be declared incompatible with the common market.

4   To the extent that the creation of a joint venture constituting a concentration pursuant to Article 3 has as its object or effect the coordination of the competitive behaviour of undertakings that remain independent, such coordination shall be appraised in accordance with the criteria of Article 81(1) and (3) of the Treaty, with a view to establishing whether or not the operation is compatible with the common market.

5   In making this appraisal, the Commission shall take into account in particular:
– whether two or more parent companies retain, to a significant extent, activities in the same market as the joint venture or in a market which is downstream or

upstream from that of the joint venture or in a neighbouring market closely related to this market,

- whether the coordination which is the direct consequence of the creation of the joint venture affords the undertakings concerned the possibility of eliminating competition in respect of a substantial part of the products or services in question.

Article 3 Definition of concentration

1 A concentration shall be deemed to arise where a change of control on a lasting basis results from:
   (a) the merger of two or more previously independent undertakings or parts of undertakings, or
   (b) the acquisition, by one or more persons already controlling at least one undertaking, or by one or more undertakings, whether by purchase of securities or assets, by contract or by any other means, of direct or indirect control of the whole or parts of one or more other undertakings.

2 Control shall be constituted by rights, contracts or any other means which, either separately or in combination and having regard to the considerations of fact or law involved, confer the possibility of exercising decisive influence on an undertaking, in particular by:
   (a) ownership or the right to use all or part of the assets of an undertaking;
   (b) rights or contracts which confer decisive influence on the composition, voting or decisions of the organs of an undertaking.

3 Control is acquired by persons or undertakings which:
   (a) are holders of the rights or entitled to rights under the contracts concerned; or
   (b) while not being holders of such rights or entitled to rights under such contracts, have the power to exercise the rights deriving therefrom.

4 The creation of a joint venture performing on a lasting basis all the functions of an autonomous economic entity shall constitute a concentration within the meaning of paragraph 1(b).

5 A concentration shall not be deemed to arise where:
   (a) credit institutions or other financial institutions or insurance companies, the normal activities of which include transactions and dealing in securities for their own account or for the account of others, hold on a temporary basis securities which they have acquired in an undertaking with a view to reselling them, provided that they do not exercise voting rights in respect of those securities with a view to determining the competitive behaviour of that undertaking or provided that they exercise such voting rights only with a view to preparing the disposal of all or part of that undertaking or of its assets or the disposal of those securities and that any such disposal takes place within one year of the date of acquisition; that period may be extended by the Commission on request where

such institutions or companies can show that the disposal was not reasonably possible within the period set;

(b) control is acquired by an office-holder according to the law of a Member State relating to liquidation, winding up, insolvency, cessation of payments, compositions or analogous proceedings;

(c) the operations referred to in paragraph 1(b) are carried out by the financial holding companies referred to in Article 5(3) of Fourth Council Directive 78/660/EEC of 25 July 1978 based on Article 54(3)(g) of the Treaty on the annual accounts of certain types of companies[6] provided however that the voting rights in respect of the holding are exercised, in particular in relation to the appointment of members of the management and supervisory bodies of the undertakings in which they have holdings, only to maintain the full value of those investments and not to determine directly or indirectly the competitive conduct of those undertakings.

Article 4 Prior notification of concentrations and pre-notification referral at the request of the notifying parties

1   Concentrations with a Community dimension defined in this Regulation shall be notified to the Commission prior to their implementation and following the conclusion of the agreement, the announcement of the public bid, or the acquisition of a controlling interest.

Notification may also be made where the undertakings concerned demonstrate to the Commission a good faith intention to conclude an agreement or, in the case of a public bid, where they have publicly announced an intention to make such a bid, provided that the intended agreement or bid would result in a concentration with a Community dimension.

For the purposes of this Regulation, the term 'notified concentration' shall also cover intended concentrations notified pursuant to the second subparagraph. For the purposes of paragraphs 4 and 5 of this Article, the term 'concentration' includes intended concentrations within the meaning of the second subparagraph.

2   A concentration which consists of a merger within the meaning of Article 3(1)(a) or in the acquisition of joint control within the meaning of Article 3(1)(b) shall be notified jointly by the parties to the merger or by those acquiring joint control as the case may be. In all other cases, the notification shall be effected by the person or undertaking acquiring control of the whole or parts of one or more undertakings.

3   Where the Commission finds that a notified concentration falls within the scope of this Regulation, it shall publish the fact of the notification, at the same time indicating the names of the undertakings concerned, their country of origin, the nature of the concentration and the economic sectors involved. The Commission

---

6 OJ L 222, 14. 8. 1978, p. 11. Directive as last amended by Directive 2003/51/EC of the European Parliament and of the Council (OJ L 178, 17.7.2003, p. 16).

shall take account of the legitimate interest of undertakings in the protection of their business secrets.

4   Prior to the notification of a concentration within the meaning of paragraph 1, the persons or undertakings referred to in paragraph 2 may inform the Commission, by means of a reasoned submission, that the concentration may significantly affect competition in a market within a Member State which presents all the characteristics of a distinct market and should therefore be examined, in whole or in part, by that Member State.

The Commission shall transmit this submission to all Member States without delay. The Member State referred to in the reasoned submission shall, within 15 working days of receiving the submission, express its agreement or disagreement as regards the request to refer the case. Where that Member State takes no such decision within this period, it shall be deemed to have agreed.

Unless that Member State disagrees, the Commission, where it considers that such a distinct market exists, and that competition in that market may be significantly affected by the concentration, may decide to refer the whole or part of the case to the competent authorities of that Member State with a view to the application of that State's national competition law.

The decision whether or not to refer the case in accordance with the third sub-paragraph shall be taken within 25 working days starting from the receipt of the reasoned submission by the Commission. The Commission shall inform the other Member States and the persons or undertakings concerned of its decision. If the Commission does not take a decision within this period, it shall be deemed to have adopted a decision to refer the case in accordance with the submission made by the persons or undertakings concerned.

If the Commission decides, or is deemed to have decided, pursuant to the third and fourth subparagraphs, to refer the whole of the case, no notification shall be made pursuant to paragraph 1 and national competition law shall apply. Article 9(6) to (9) shall apply *mutatis mutandis*.

5   With regard to a concentration as defined in Article 3 which does not have a Community dimension within the meaning of Article 1 and which is capable of being reviewed under the national competition laws of at least three Member States, the persons or undertakings referred to in paragraph 2 may, before any notification to the competent authorities, inform the Commission by means of a reasoned submission that the concentration should be examined by the Commission.

The Commission shall transmit this submission to all Member States without delay.

Any Member State competent to examine the concentration under its national competition law may, within 15 working days of receiving the reasoned submission, express its disagreement as regards the request to refer the case.

Where at least one such Member State has expressed its disagreement in accordance with the third subparagraph within the period of 15 working days, the case shall not be referred. The Commission shall, without delay, inform all Member

States and the persons or undertakings concerned of any such expression of disagreement.

Where no Member State has expressed its disagreement in accordance with the third subparagraph within the period of 15 working days, the concentration shall be deemed to have a Community dimension and shall be notified to the Commission in accordance with paragraphs 1 and 2. In such situations, no Member State shall apply its national competition law to the concentration.

6   The Commission shall report to the Council on the operation of paragraphs 4 and 5 by 1 July 2009. Following this report and on a proposal from the Commission, the Council, acting by a qualified majority, may revise paragraphs 4 and 5.

Article 5 Calculation of turnover

1   Aggregate turnover within the meaning of this Regulation shall comprise the amounts derived by the undertakings concerned in the preceding financial year from the sale of products and the provision of services falling within the undertakings' ordinary activities after deduction of sales rebates and of value added tax and other taxes directly related to turnover. The aggregate turnover of an undertaking concerned shall not include the sale of products or the provision of services between any of the undertakings referred to in paragraph 4.

Turnover, in the Community or in a Member State, shall comprise products sold and services provided to undertakings or consumers, in the Community or in that Member State as the case may be.

2   By way of derogation from paragraph 1, where the concentration consists of the acquisition of parts, whether or not constituted as legal entities, of one or more undertakings, only the turnover relating to the parts which are the subject of the concentration shall be taken into account with regard to the seller or sellers.

However, two or more transactions within the meaning of the first subparagraph which take place within a two-year period between the same persons or undertakings shall be treated as one and the same concentration arising on the date of the last transaction.

3   In place of turnover the following shall be used:

(a) for credit institutions and other financial institutions, the sum of the following income items as defined in Council Directive 86/635/EEC,[7] after deduction of value added tax and other taxes directly related to those items, where appropriate:

    (i)   interest income and similar income;

    (ii) income from securities:

         – income from shares and other variable yield securities,

---

7 OJ L 372, 31. 12. 1986, p. 1. Directive as last amended by Directive 2003/51/EC of the European Parliament and of the Council.

– income from participating interests,

– income from shares in affiliated undertakings;

(iii) commissions receivable;

(iv) net profit on financial operations;

(v) other operating income.

The turnover of a credit or financial institution in the Community or in a Member State shall comprise the income items, as defined above, which are received by the branch or division of that institution established in the Community or in the Member State in question, as the case may be;

(b) for insurance undertakings, the value of gross premiums written which shall comprise all amounts received and receivable in respect of insurance contracts issued by or on behalf of the insurance undertakings, including also outgoing reinsurance premiums, and after deduction of taxes and parafiscal contributions or levies charged by reference to the amounts of individual premiums or the total volume of premiums; as regards Article 1(2)(b) and (3)(b), (c) and (d) and the final part of Article 1(2) and (3), gross premiums received from Community residents and from residents of one Member State respectively shall be taken into account.

4   Without prejudice to paragraph 2, the aggregate turnover of an undertaking concerned within the meaning of this Regulation shall be calculated by adding together the respective turnovers of the following:

(a) the undertaking concerned;

(b) those undertakings in which the undertaking concerned, directly or indirectly:

(i)   owns more than half the capital or business assets, or

(ii) has the power to exercise more than half the voting rights, or

(iii) has the power to appoint more than half the members of the supervisory board, the administrative board or bodies legally representing the undertakings, or

(iv) has the right to manage the undertakings' affairs;

(c) those undertakings which have in the undertaking concerned the rights or powers listed in (b);

(d) those undertakings in which an undertaking as referred to in (c) has the rights or powers listed in (b);

(e) those undertakings in which two or more undertakings as referred to in (a) to (d) jointly have the rights or powers listed in (b).

5   Where undertakings concerned by the concentration jointly have the rights or powers listed in paragraph 4(b), in calculating the aggregate turnover of the undertakings concerned for the purposes of this Regulation:

(a) no account shall be taken of the turnover resulting from the sale of products or the provision of services between the joint undertaking and each of the undertakings concerned or any other undertaking connected with any one of them, as set out in paragraph 4(b) to (e);

(b) account shall be taken of the turnover resulting from the sale of products and the provision of services between the joint undertaking and any third undertakings. This turnover shall be apportioned equally amongst the undertakings concerned.

Article 6 Examination of the notification and initiation of proceedings

1   The Commission shall examine the notification as soon as it is received.

(a) Where it concludes that the concentration notified does not fall within the scope of this Regulation, it shall record that finding by means of a decision.

(b) Where it finds that the concentration notified, although falling within the scope of this Regulation, does not raise serious doubts as to its compatibility with the common market, it shall decide not to oppose it and shall declare that it is compatible with the common market.

A decision declaring a concentration compatible shall be deemed to cover restrictions directly related and necessary to the implementation of the concentration.

(c) Without prejudice to paragraph 2, where the Commission finds that the concentration notified falls within the scope of this Regulation and raises serious doubts as to its compatibility with the common market, it shall decide to initiate proceedings. Without prejudice to Article 9, such proceedings shall be closed by means of a decision as provided for in Article 8(1) to (4), unless the undertakings concerned have demonstrated to the satisfaction of the Commission that they have abandoned the concentration.

2   Where the Commission finds that, following modification by the undertakings concerned, a notified concentration no longer raises serious doubts within the meaning of paragraph 1(c), it shall declare the concentration compatible with the common market pursuant to paragraph 1(b).

The Commission may attach to its decision under paragraph 1(b) conditions and obligations intended to ensure that the undertakings concerned comply with the commitments they have entered into *vis-à-vis* the Commission with a view to rendering the concentration compatible with the common market.

3   The Commission may revoke the decision it took pursuant to paragraph 1(a) or (b) where:

(a) the decision is based on incorrect information for which one of the undertakings is responsible or where it has been obtained by deceit,
or

(b) the undertakings concerned commit a breach of an obligation attached to the decision.

4   In the cases referred to in paragraph 3, the Commission may take a decision under paragraph 1, without being bound by the time limits referred to in Article 10(1).

5   The Commission shall notify its decision to the undertakings concerned and the competent authorities of the Member States without delay.

Article 7 Suspension of concentrations

1   A concentration with a Community dimension as defined in Article 1, or which is to be examined by the Commission pursuant to Article 4(5), shall not be implemented either before its notification or until it has been declared compatible with the common market pursuant to a decision under Articles 6(1)(b), 8(1) or 8(2), or on the basis of a presumption according to Article 10(6).

2   Paragraph 1 shall not prevent the implementation of a public bid or of a series of transactions in securities including those convertible into other securities admitted to trading on a market such as a stock exchange, by which control within the meaning of Article 3 is acquired from various sellers, provided that:
    (a) the concentration is notified to the Commission pursuant to Article 4 without delay; and
    (b) the acquirer does not exercise the voting rights attached to the securities in question or does so only to maintain the full value of its investments based on a derogation granted by the Commission under paragraph 3.

3   The Commission may, on request, grant a derogation from the obligations imposed in paragraphs 1 or 2. The request to grant a derogation must be reasoned. In deciding on the request, the Commission shall take into account *inter alia* the effects of the suspension on one or more undertakings concerned by the concentration or on a third party and the threat to competition posed by the concentration. Such a derogation may be made subject to conditions and obligations in order to ensure conditions of effective competition. A derogation may be applied for and granted at any time, be it before notification or after the transaction.

4   The validity of any transaction carried out in contravention of paragraph 1 shall be dependent on a decision pursuant to Article 6(1)(b) or Article 8(1), (2) or (3) or on a presumption pursuant to Article 10(6).
    This Article shall, however, have no effect on the validity of transactions in securities including those convertible into other securities admitted to trading on a market such as a stock exchange, unless the buyer and seller knew or ought to have known that the transaction was carried out in contravention of paragraph 1.

Article 8 Powers of decision of the Commission

1   Where the Commission finds that a notified concentration fulfils the criterion laid down in Article 2(2) and, in the cases referred to in Article 2(4), the criteria laid down in Article 81(3) of the Treaty, it shall issue a decision declaring the concentration compatible with the common market.
    A decision declaring a concentration compatible shall be deemed to cover restrictions directly related and necessary to the implementation of the concentration.

2   Where the Commission finds that, following modification by the undertakings concerned, a notified concentration fulfils the criterion laid down in Article 2(2) and,

in the cases referred to in Article 2(4), the criteria laid down in Article 81(3) of the Treaty, it shall issue a decision declaring the concentration compatible with the common market.

The Commission may attach to its decision conditions and obligations intended to ensure that the undertakings concerned comply with the commitments they have entered into *vis-à-vis* the Commission with a view to rendering the concentration compatible with the common market.

A decision declaring a concentration compatible shall be deemed to cover restrictions directly related and necessary to the implementation of the concentration.

3 Where the Commission finds that a concentration fulfils the criterion defined in Article 2(3) or, in the cases referred to in Article 2(4), does not fulfil the criteria laid down in Article 81(3) of the Treaty, it shall issue a decision declaring that the concentration is incompatible with the common market.

4 Where the Commission finds that a concentration:
- (a) has already been implemented and that concentration has been declared incompatible with the common market, or
- (b) has been implemented in contravention of a condition attached to a decision taken under paragraph 2, which has found that, in the absence of the condition, the concentration would fulfil the criterion laid down in Article 2(3) or, in the cases referred to in Article 2(4), would not fulfil the criteria laid down in Article 81(3) of the Treaty, the Commission may:
  - – require the undertakings concerned to dissolve the concentration, in particular through the dissolution of the merger or the disposal of all the shares or assets acquired, so as to restore the situation prevailing prior to the implementation of the concentration; in circumstances where restoration of the situation prevailing before the implementation of the concentration is not possible through dissolution of the concentration, the Commission may take any other measure appropriate to achieve such restoration as far as possible,
  - – order any other appropriate measure to ensure that the undertakings concerned dissolve the concentration or take other restorative measures as required in its decision.

In cases falling within point (a) of the first subparagraph, the measures referred to in that subparagraph may be imposed either in a decision pursuant to paragraph 3 or by separate decision.

5 The Commission may take interim measures appropriate to restore or maintain conditions of effective competition where a concentration:
- (a) has been implemented in contravention of Article 7, and a decision as to the compatibility of the concentration with the common market has not yet been taken;
- (b) has been implemented in contravention of a condition attached to a decision under Article 6(1)(b) or paragraph 2 of this Article;

(c) has already been implemented and is declared incompatible with the common market.

6   The Commission may revoke the decision it has taken pursuant to paragraphs 1 or 2 where:
(a) the declaration of compatibility is based on incorrect information for which one of the undertakings is responsible or where it has been obtained by deceit; or
(b) the undertakings concerned commit a breach of an obligation attached to the decision.

7   The Commission may take a decision pursuant to paragraphs 1 to 3 without being bound by the time limits referred to in Article 10(3), in cases where:
(a) it finds that a concentration has been implemented
   (i) in contravention of a condition attached to a decision under Article 6(1)(b), or
   (ii) in contravention of a condition attached to a decision taken under paragraph 2 and in accordance with Article 10(2), which has found that, in the absence of the condition, the concentration would raise serious doubts as to its compatibility with the common market; or
(b) a decision has been revoked pursuant to paragraph 6.

8   The Commission shall notify its decision to the undertakings concerned and the competent authorities of the Member States without delay.

Article 9 Referral to the competent authorities of the Member States

1   The Commission may, by means of a decision notified without delay to the undertakings concerned and the competent authorities of the other Member States, refer a notified concentration to the competent authorities of the Member State concerned in the following circumstances.

2   Within 15 working days of the date of receipt of the copy of the notification, a Member State, on its own initiative or upon the invitation of the Commission, may inform the Commission, which shall inform the undertakings concerned, that:
(a) a concentration threatens to affect significantly competition in a market within that Member State, which presents all the characteristics of a distinct market, or
(b) a concentration affects competition in a market within that Member State, which presents all the characteristics of a distinct market and which does not constitute a substantial part of the common market.

3   If the Commission considers that, having regard to the market for the products or services in question and the geographical reference market within the meaning of paragraph 7, there is such a distinct market and that such a threat exists, either:
(a) it shall itself deal with the case in accordance with this Regulation; or

(b) it shall refer the whole or part of the case to the competent authorities of the Member State concerned with a view to the application of that State's national competition law.

If, however, the Commission considers that such a distinct market or threat does not exist, it shall adopt a decision to that effect which it shall address to the Member State concerned, and shall itself deal with the case in accordance with this Regulation.

In cases where a Member State informs the Commission pursuant to paragraph 2(b) that a concentration affects competition in a distinct market within its territory that does not form a substantial part of the common market, the Commission shall refer the whole or part of the case relating to the distinct market concerned, if it considers that such a distinct market is affected.

4   A decision to refer or not to refer pursuant to paragraph 3 shall be taken:
(a) as a general rule within the period provided for in Article 10(1), second sub-paragraph, where the Commission, pursuant to Article 6(1)(b), has not initiated proceedings; or
(b) within 65 working days at most of the notification of the concentration con-cerned where the Commission has initiated proceedings under Article 6(1)(c), without taking the preparatory steps in order to adopt the necessary measures under Article 8(2), (3) or (4) to maintain or restore effective competition on the market concerned.

5   If within the 65 working days referred to in paragraph 4(b) the Commission, despite a reminder from the Member State concerned, has not taken a decision on referral in accordance with paragraph 3 nor has taken the preparatory steps referred to in paragraph 4(b), it shall be deemed to have taken a decision to refer the case to the Member State concerned in accordance with paragraph 3(b).

6   The competent authority of the Member State concerned shall decide upon the case without undue delay.

Within 45 working days after the Commission's referral, the competent authority of the Member State concerned shall inform the undertakings concerned of the result of the preliminary competition assessment and what further action, if any, it proposes to take. The Member State concerned may exceptionally suspend this time limit where necessary information has not been provided to it by the undertakings concerned as provided for by its national competition law.

Where a notification is requested under national law, the period of 45 working days shall begin on the working day following that of the receipt of a complete notification by the competent authority of that Member State.

7   The geographical reference market shall consist of the area in which the under-takings concerned are involved in the supply and demand of products or services, in which the conditions of competition are sufficiently homogeneous and which can be distinguished from neighbouring areas because, in particular, conditions of competition are appreciably different in those areas. This assessment should take account in particular of the nature and characteristics of the products or services

concerned, of the existence of entry barriers or of consumer preferences, of appreciable differences of the undertakings' market shares between the area concerned and neighbouring areas or of substantial price differences.

8　In applying the provisions of this Article, the Member State concerned may take only the measures strictly necessary to safeguard or restore effective competition on the market concerned.

9　In accordance with the relevant provisions of the Treaty, any Member State may appeal to the Court of Justice, and in particular request the application of Article 243 of the Treaty, for the purpose of applying its national competition law.

Article 10 Time limits for initiating proceedings and for decisions

1　Without prejudice to Article 6(4), the decisions referred to in Article 6(1) shall be taken within 25 working days at most. That period shall begin on the working day following that of the receipt of a notification or, if the information to be supplied with the notification is incomplete, on the working day following that of the receipt of the complete information.

That period shall be increased to 35 working days where the Commission receives a request from a Member State in accordance with Article 9(2)or where, the undertakings concerned offer commitments pursuant to Article 6(2) with a view to rendering the concentration compatible with the common market.

2　Decisions pursuant to Article 8(1) or (2) concerning notified concentrations shall be taken as soon as it appears that the serious doubts referred to in Article 6(1)(c) have been removed, particularly as a result of modifications made by the undertakings concerned, and at the latest by the time limit laid down in paragraph 3.

3　Without prejudice to Article 8(7), decisions pursuant to Article 8(1) to (3) concerning notified concentrations shall be taken within not more than 90 working days of the date on which the proceedings are initiated. That period shall be increased to 105 working days where the undertakings concerned offer commitments pursuant to Article 8(2), second subparagraph, with a view to rendering the concentration compatible with the common market, unless these commitments have been offered less than 55 working days after the initiation of proceedings.

The periods set by the first subparagraph shall likewise be extended if the notifying parties make a request to that effect not later than 15 working days after the initiation of proceedings pursuant to Article 6(1)(c). The notifying parties may make only one such request. Likewise, at any time following the initiation of proceedings, the periods set by the first subparagraph may be extended by the Commission with the agreement of the notifying parties. The total duration of any extension or extensions effected pursuant to this subparagraph shall not exceed 20 working days.

4　The periods set by paragraphs 1 and 3 shall exceptionally be suspended where, owing to circumstances for which one of the undertakings involved in the concentration is responsible, the Commission has had to request information by decision pursuant to Article 11 or to order an inspection by decision pursuant to Article 13.

The first subparagraph shall also apply to the period referred to in Article 9(4)(b).

5   Where the Court of Justice gives a judgment which annuls the whole or part of a Commission decision which is subject to a time limit set by this Article, the concentration shall be reexamined by the Commission with a view to adopting a decision pursuant to Article 6(1).

The concentration shall be re-examined in the light of current market conditions.

The notifying parties shall submit a new notification or supplement the original notification, without delay, where the original notification becomes incomplete by reason of intervening changes in market conditions or in the information provided. Where there are no such changes, the parties shall certify this fact without delay.

The periods laid down in paragraph 1 shall start on the working day following that of the receipt of complete information in a new notification, a supplemented notification, or a certification within the meaning of the third subparagraph.

The second and third subparagraphs shall also apply in the cases referred to in Article 6(4) and Article 8(7).

6   Where the Commission has not taken a decision in accordance with Article 6(1)(b), (c), 8(1), (2) or (3) within the time limits set in paragraphs 1 and 3 respectively, the concentration shall be deemed to have been declared compatible with the common market, without prejudice to Article 9.

Article 11 Requests for information

1   In order to carry out the duties assigned to it by this Regulation, the Commission may, by simple request or by decision, require the persons referred to in Article 3(1)(b), as well as undertakings and associations of undertakings, to provide all necessary information.

2   When sending a simple request for information to a person, an undertaking or an association of undertakings, the Commission shall state the legal basis and the purpose of the request, specify what information is required and fix the time limit within which the information is to be provided, as well as the penalties provided for in Article 14 for supplying incorrect or misleading information.

3   Where the Commission requires a person, an undertaking or an association of undertakings to supply information by decision, it shall state the legal basis and the purpose of the request, specify what information is required and fix the time limit within which it is to be provided. It shall also indicate the penalties provided for in Article 14 and indicate or impose the penalties provided for in Article 15. It shall further indicate the right to have the decision reviewed by the Court of Justice.

4   The owners of the undertakings or their representatives and, in the case of legal persons, companies or firms, or associations having no legal personality, the persons authorised to represent them by law or by their constitution, shall supply the information requested on behalf of the undertaking concerned. Persons duly authorised to act may supply the information on behalf of their clients. The latter shall remain fully responsible if the information supplied is incomplete, incorrect or misleading.

5   The Commission shall without delay forward a copy of any decision taken pursuant to paragraph 3 to the competent authorities of the Member State in whose territory the residence of the person or the seat of the undertaking or association of undertakings is situated, and to the competent authority of the Member State whose territory is affected. At the specific request of the competent authority of a Member State, the Commission shall also forward to that authority copies of simple requests for information relating to a notified concentration.

6   At the request of the Commission, the governments and competent authorities of the Member States shall provide the Commission with all necessary information to carry out the duties assigned to it by this Regulation.

7   In order to carry out the duties assigned to it by this Regulation, the Commission may interview any natural or legal person who consents to be interviewed for the purpose of collecting information relating to the subject matter of an investigation. At the beginning of the interview, which may be conducted by telephone or other electronic means, the Commission shall state the legal basis and the purpose of the interview.

    Where an interview is not conducted on the premises of the Commission or by telephone or other electronic means, the Commission shall inform in advance the competent authority of the Member State in whose territory the interview takes place. If the competent authority of that Member State so requests, officials of that authority may assist the officials and other persons authorised by the Commission to conduct the interview.

Article 12 Inspections by the authorities of the Member States

1   At the request of the Commission, the competent authorities of the Member States shall undertake the inspections which the Commission considers to be necessary under Article 13(1), or which it has ordered by decision pursuant to Article 13(4). The officials of the competent authorities of the Member States who are responsible for conducting these inspections as well as those authorised or appointed by them shall exercise their powers in accordance with their national law.

2   If so requested by the Commission or by the competent authority of the Member State within whose territory the inspection is to be conducted, officials and other accompanying persons authorised by the Commission may assist the officials of the authority concerned.

Article 13 The Commission's powers of inspection

1   In order to carry out the duties assigned to it by this Regulation, the Commission may conduct all necessary inspections of undertakings and associations of undertakings.

2   The officials and other accompanying persons authorised by the Commission to conduct an inspection shall have the power:

(a) to enter any premises, land and means of transport of undertakings and associations of undertakings;

(b) to examine the books and other records related to the business, irrespective of the medium on which they are stored;

(c) to take or obtain in any form copies of or extracts from such books or records;

(d) to seal any business premises and books or records for the period and to the extent necessary for the inspection;

(e) to ask any representative or member of staff of the undertaking or association of undertakings for explanations on facts or documents relating to the subject matter and purpose of the inspection and to record the answers.

3   Officials and other accompanying persons authorised by the Commission to conduct an inspection shall exercise their powers upon production of a written authorisation specifying the subject matter and purpose of the inspection and the penalties provided for in Article 14, in the production of the required books or other records related to the business which is incomplete or where answers to questions asked under paragraph 2 of this Article are incorrect or misleading. In good time before the inspection, the Commission shall give notice of the inspection to the competent authority of the Member State in whose territory the inspection is to be conducted.

4   Undertakings and associations of undertakings are required to submit to inspections ordered by decision of the Commission. The decision shall specify the subject matter and purpose of the inspection, appoint the date on which it is to begin and indicate the penalties provided for in Articles 14 and 15 and the right to have the decision reviewed by the Court of Justice. The Commission shall take such decisions after consulting the competent authority of the Member State in whose territory the inspection is to be conducted.

5   Officials of, and those authorised or appointed by, the competent authority of the Member State in whose territory the inspection is to be conducted shall, at the request of that authority or of the Commission, actively assist the officials and other accompanying persons authorised by the Commission. To this end, they shall enjoy the powers specified in paragraph 2.

6   Where the officials and other accompanying persons authorised by the Commission find that an undertaking opposes an inspection, including the sealing of business premises, books or records, ordered pursuant to this Article, the Member State concerned shall afford them the necessary assistance, requesting where appropriate the assistance of the police or of an equivalent enforcement authority, so as to enable them to conduct their inspection.

7   If the assistance provided for in paragraph 6 requires authorisation from a judicial authority according to national rules, such authorisation shall be applied for. Such authorisation may also be applied for as a precautionary measure.

8   Where authorisation as referred to in paragraph 7 is applied for, the national judicial authority shall ensure that the Commission decision is authentic and that the coercive measures envisaged are neither arbitrary nor excessive having regard to the subject matter of the inspection. In its control of proportionality of the coercive measures, the national judicial authority may ask the Commission, directly or through the competent authority of that Member State, for detailed explanations relating to the subject matter of the inspection. However, the national judicial authority may not call into question the necessity for the inspection nor demand that it be provided with the information in the Commission's file. The lawfulness of the Commission's decision shall be subject to review only by the Court of Justice.

Article 14 Fines

1   The Commission may by decision impose on the persons referred to in Article 3(1)b, undertakings or associations of undertakings, fines not exceeding 1% of the aggregate turnover of the undertaking or association of undertakings concerned within the meaning of Article 5 where, intentionally or negligently:

(a) they supply incorrect or misleading information in a submission, certification, notification or supplement thereto, pursuant to Article 4, Article 10(5) or Article 22(3);

(b) they supply incorrect or misleading information in response to a request made pursuant to Article 11(2);

(c) in response to a request made by decision adopted pursuant to Article 11(3), they supply incorrect, incomplete or misleading information or do not supply information within the required time limit;

(d) they produce the required books or other records related to the business in incomplete form during inspections under Article 13, or refuse to submit to an inspection ordered by decision taken pursuant to Article 13(4);

(e) in response to a question asked in accordance with Article 13(2)(e),
- they give an incorrect or misleading answer,
- they fail to rectify within a time limit set by the Commission an incorrect, incomplete or misleading answer given by a member of staff, or
- they fail or refuse to provide a complete answer on facts relating to the subject matter and purpose of an inspection ordered by a decision adopted pursuant to Article 13(4);

(f) seals affixed by officials or other accompanying persons authorised by the Commission in accordance with Article 13(2)(d) have been broken.

2   The Commission may by decision impose fines not exceeding 10% of the aggregate turnover of the undertaking concerned within the meaning of Article 5 on the persons

referred to in Article 3(1)b or the undertakings concerned where, either intentionally or negligently, they:

(a) fail to notify a concentration in accordance with Articles 4 or 22(3) prior to its implementation, unless they are expressly authorised to do so by Article 7(2) or by a decision taken pursuant to Article 7(3);

(b) implement a concentration in breach of Article 7;

(c) implement a concentration declared incompatible with the common market by decision pursuant to Article 8(3) or do not comply with any measure ordered by decision pursuant to Article 8(4) or (5);

(d) fail to comply with a condition or an obligation imposed by decision pursuant to Articles 6(1)(b), Article 7(3) or Article 8(2), second subparagraph.

3   In fixing the amount of the fine, regard shall be had to the nature, gravity and duration of the infringement.

4   Decisions taken pursuant to paragraphs 1, 2 and 3 shall not be of a criminal law nature.

Article 15 Periodic penalty payments

1   The Commission may by decision impose on the persons referred to in Article 3(1)b, undertakings or associations of undertakings, periodic penalty payments not exceeding 5% of the average daily aggregate turnover of the undertaking or association of undertakings concerned within the meaning of Article 5 for each working day of delay, calculated from the date set in the decision, in order to compel them:

(a) to supply complete and correct information which it has requested by decision taken pursuant to Article 11(3);

(b) to submit to an inspection which it has ordered by decision taken pursuant to Article 13(4);

(c) to comply with an obligation imposed by decision pursuant to Article 6(1)(b), Article 7(3) or Article 8(2), second subparagraph; or

(d) to comply with any measures ordered by decision pursuant to Article 8(4) or (5).

2   Where the persons referred to in Article 3(1)(b), undertakings or associations of undertakings have satisfied the obligation which the periodic penalty payment was intended to enforce, the Commission may fix the definitive amount of the periodic penalty payments at a figure lower than that which would arise under the original decision.

Article 16 Review by the Court of Justice

The Court of Justice shall have unlimited jurisdiction within the meaning of Article 229 of the Treaty to review decisions whereby the Commission has fixed a fine or periodic penalty payments; it may cancel, reduce or increase the fine or periodic penalty payment imposed.

Article 17 Professional secrecy

1   Information acquired as a result of the application of this Regulation shall be used only for the purposes of the relevant request, investigation or hearing.

2   Without prejudice to Article 4(3), Articles 18 and 20, the Commission and the competent authorities of the Member States, their officials and other servants and other persons working under the supervision of these authorities as well as officials and civil servants of other authorities of the Member States shall not disclose information they have acquired through the application of this Regulation of the kind covered by the obligation of professional secrecy.

3   Paragraphs 1 and 2 shall not prevent publication of general information or of surveys which do not contain information relating to particular undertakings or associations of undertakings.

Article 18 Hearing of the parties and of third persons

1   Before taking any decision provided for in Article 6(3), Article 7(3), Article 8(2) to (6), and Articles 14 and 15, the Commission shall give the persons, undertakings and associations of undertakings concerned the opportunity, at every stage of the procedure up to the consultation of the Advisory Committee, of making known their views on the objections against them.

2   By way of derogation from paragraph 1, a decision pursuant to Articles 7(3) and 8(5) may be taken provisionally, without the persons, undertakings or associations of undertakings concerned being given the opportunity to make known their views beforehand, provided that the Commission gives them that opportunity as soon as possible after having taken its decision.

3   The Commission shall base its decision only on objections on which the parties have been able to submit their observations. The rights of the defence shall be fully respected in the proceedings. Access to the file shall be open at least to the parties directly involved, subject to the legitimate interest of undertakings in the protection of their business secrets.

4   In so far as the Commission or the competent authorities of the Member States deem it necessary, they may also hear other natural or legal persons. Natural or legal persons showing a sufficient interest and especially members of the administrative or management bodies of the undertakings concerned or the recognised representatives of their employees shall be entitled, upon application, to be heard.

Article 19 Liaison with the authorities of the Member States

1   The Commission shall transmit to the competent authorities of the Member States copies of notifications within three working days and, as soon as possible, copies of the most important documents lodged with or issued by the Commission pursuant to this Regulation. Such documents shall include commitments offered by the undertakings concerned *vis-à-vis* the Commission with a view to rendering the concentration compatible with the common market pursuant to Article 6(2) or Article 8(2), second subparagraph.

2   The Commission shall carry out the procedures set out in this Regulation in close and constant liaison with the competent authorities of the Member States, which may express their views upon those procedures. For the purposes of Article 9 it shall obtain information from the competent authority of the Member State as referred to in paragraph 2 of that Article and give it the opportunity to make known its views at every stage of the procedure up to the adoption of a decision pursuant to paragraph 3 of that Article; to that end it shall give it access to the file.

3   An Advisory Committee on concentrations shall be consulted before any decision is taken pursuant to Article 8(1) to (6), Articles 14 or 15 with the exception of provisional decisions taken in accordance with Article 18(2).

4   The Advisory Committee shall consist of representatives of the competent authorities of the Member States. Each Member State shall appoint one or two representatives; if unable to attend, they may be replaced by other representatives. At least one of the representatives of a Member State shall be competent in matters of restrictive practices and dominant positions.

5   Consultation shall take place at a joint meeting convened at the invitation of and chaired by the Commission. A summary of the case, together with an indication of the most important documents and a preliminary draft of the decision to be taken for each case considered, shall be sent with the invitation. The meeting shall take place not less than 10 working days after the invitation has been sent. The Commission may in exceptional cases shorten that period as appropriate in order to avoid serious harm to one or more of the undertakings concerned by a concentration.

6   The Advisory Committee shall deliver an opinion on the Commission's draft decision, if necessary by taking a vote. The Advisory Committee may deliver an opinion even if some members are absent and unrepresented. The opinion shall be delivered in writing and appended to the draft decision. The Commission shall take the utmost account of the opinion delivered by the Committee. It shall inform the Committee of the manner in which its opinion has been taken into account.

7   The Commission shall communicate the opinion of the Advisory Committee, together with the decision, to the addressees of the decision. It shall make the opinion public together with the decision, having regard to the legitimate interest of undertakings in the protection of their business secrets.

Article 20 Publication of decisions

1   The Commission shall publish the decisions which it takes pursuant to Article 8(1) to (6), Articles 14 and 15 with the exception of provisional decisions taken in accordance with Article 18(2) together with the opinion of the Advisory Committee in the *Official Journal of the European Union*.

2   The publication shall state the names of the parties and the main content of the decision; it shall have regard to the legitimate interest of undertakings in the protection of their business secrets.

Article 21 Application of the Regulation and jurisdiction

1   This Regulation alone shall apply to concentrations as defined in Article 3, and Council Regulations (EC) No 1/ 2003,[8] (EEC) No 1017/68,[9] (EEC) No 4056/86[10] and (EEC) No 3975/87[11] shall not apply, except in relation to joint ventures that do not have a Community dimension and which have as their object or effect the coordination of the competitive behaviour of undertakings that remain independent.

2   Subject to review by the Court of Justice, the Commission shall have sole jurisdiction to take the decisions provided for in this Regulation.

3   No Member State shall apply its national legislation on competition to any concentration that has a Community dimension.

     The first subparagraph shall be without prejudice to any Member State's power to carry out any enquiries necessary for the application of Articles 4(4), 9(2) or after referral, pursuant to Article 9(3), first subparagraph, indent (b), or Article 9(5), to take the measures strictly necessary for the application of Article 9(8).

4   Notwithstanding paragraphs 2 and 3, Member States may take appropriate measures to protect legitimate interests other than those taken into consideration by this Regulation and compatible with the general principles and other provisions of Community law.

     Public security, plurality of the media and prudential rules shall be regarded as legitimate interests within the meaning of the first subparagraph.

     Any other public interest must be communicated to the Commission by the Member State concerned and shall be recognised by the Commission after an assessment of its compatibility with the general principles and other provisions of Community law before the measures referred to above may be taken. The Commission shall inform the Member State concerned of its decision within 25 working days of that communication.

---

8   OJ L 1, 4.1.2003, p. 1.

9   OJ L 175, 23. 7. 1968, p. 1. Regulation as last amended by Regulation (EC) No 1/2003 (OJ L 1, 4.1.2003, p. 1).

10   OJ L 378, 31. 12. 1986, p. 4. Regulation as last amended by Regulation (EC) No 1/2003.

11   OJ L 374. 31. 12. 1987, p. 1. Regulation as last amended by Regulation (EC) No 1/2003.

Article 22 Referral to the Commission

1   One or more Member States may request the Commission to examine any concentration as defined in Article 3 that does not have a Community dimension within the meaning of Article 1 but affects trade between Member States and threatens to significantly affect competition within the territory of the Member State or States making the request.

   Such a request shall be made at most within 15 working days of the date on which the concentration was notified, or if no notification is required, otherwise made known to the Member State concerned.

2   The Commission shall inform the competent authorities of the Member States and the undertakings concerned of any request received pursuant to paragraph 1 without delay.

   Any other Member State shall have the right to join the initial request within a period of 15 working days of being informed by the Commission of the initial request.

   All national time limits relating to the concentration shall be suspended until, in accordance with the procedure set out in this Article, it has been decided where the concentration shall be examined. As soon as a Member State has informed the Commission and the undertakings concerned that it does not wish to join the request, the suspension of its national time limits shall end.

3   The Commission may, at the latest 10 working days after the expiry of the period set in paragraph 2, decide to examine, the concentration where it considers that it affects trade between Member States and threatens to significantly affect competition within the territory of the Member State or States making the request. If the Commission does not take a decision within this period, it shall be deemed to have adopted a decision to examine the concentration in accordance with the request.

   The Commission shall inform all Member States and the undertakings concerned of its decision. It may request the submission of a notification pursuant to Article.

4   The Member State or States having made the request shall no longer apply their national legislation on competition to the concentration.

5   Article 2, Article 4(2) to (3), Articles 5, 6, and 8 to 21 shall apply where the Commission examines a concentration pursuant to paragraph 3. Article 7 shall apply to the extent that the concentration has not been implemented on the date on which the Commission informs the undertakings concerned that a request has been made.

   Where a notification pursuant to Article 4 is not required, the period set in Article 10(1) within which proceedings may be initiated shall begin on the working day following that on which the Commission informs the undertakings concerned that it has decided to examine the concentration pursuant to paragraph 3.

6   The Commission may inform one or several Member States that it considers a concentration fulfils the criteria in paragraph 1. In such cases, the Commission may invite that Member State or those Member States to make a request pursuant to paragraph 1.

Article 23 Implementing provisions

1 The Commission shall have the power to lay down in accordance with the procedure referred to in paragraph 2:
 (a) implementing provisions concerning the form, content and other details of notifications and submissions pursuant to Article 4;
 (b) implementing provisions concerning time limits pursuant to Article 4(4), (5) Articles 7, 9, 10 and 22;
 (c) the procedure and time limits for the submission and implementation of commitments pursuant to Article 6(2) and Article 8(2);
 (d) implementing provisions concerning hearings pursuant to Article 18.

2 The Commission shall be assisted by an Advisory Committee, composed of representatives of the Member States.
 (a) Before publishing draft implementing provisions and before adopting such provisions, the Commission shall consult the Advisory Committee.
 (b) Consultation shall take place at a meeting convened at the invitation of and chaired by the Commission. A draft of the implementing provisions to be taken shall be sent with the invitation. The meeting shall take place not less than 10 working days after the invitation has been sent.
 (c) The Advisory Committee shall deliver an opinion on the draft implementing provisions, if necessary by taking a vote. The Commission shall take the utmost account of the opinion delivered by the Committee.

Article 24 Relations with third countries

1 The Member States shall inform the Commission of any general difficulties encountered by their undertakings with concentrations as defined in Article 3 in a third country.

2 Initially not more than one year after the entry into force of this Regulation and, thereafter periodically, the Commission shall draw up a report examining the treatment accorded to undertakings having their seat or their principal fields of activity in the Community, in the terms referred to in paragraphs 3 and 4, as regards concentrations in third countries. The Commission shall submit those reports to the Council, together with any recommendations.

3 Whenever it appears to the Commission, either on the basis of the reports referred to in paragraph 2 or on the basis of other information, that a third country does not grant undertakings having their seat or their principal fields of activity in the Community, treatment comparable to that granted by the Community to undertakings from that country, the Commission may submit proposals to the Council for an appropriate mandate for negotiation with a view to obtaining comparable treatment for undertakings having their seat or their principal fields of activity in the Community.

4   Measures taken under this Article shall comply with the obligations of the Community or of the Member States, without prejudice to Article 307 of the Treaty, under international agreements, whether bilateral or multilateral.

Article 25 Repeal

1   Without prejudice to Article 26(2), Regulations (EEC) No 4064/89 and (EC) No 1310/97 shall be repealed with effect from 1 May 2004.

2   References to the repealed Regulations shall be construed as references to this Regulation and shall be read in accordance with the correlation table in the Annex.

Article 26 Entry into force and transitional provisions

1   This Regulation shall enter into force on the 20th day following that of its publication in the *Official Journal of the European Union*.
     It shall apply from 1 May 2004

2   Regulation (EEC) No 4064/89 shall continue to apply to any concentration which was the subject of an agreement or announcement of where control was acquired within the meaning of Article 4(1) of that Regulation before the date of application of this Regulation, subject, in particular, to the provisions governing applicability set out in Article 25(2) and (3) of Regulation (EEC) No 4064/89 and Article 2 of Regulation (EEC) No 1310/97.

3   As regards concentrations to which this Regulation applies by virtue of accession, the date of accession shall be substituted for the date of application of this Regulation.
     This Regulation shall be binding in its entirety and directly applicable in all Member States.

4 Key concepts under Regulation 139/2004

Several key concepts contained in the Regulation are worth discussing. As was mentioned above, the Commission has published several Notices; some of these are relevant when interpreting and applying these concepts. It is important to note however that some of these Notices were published under Regulation 4064/89 and so where a Notice refers to 'Merger Regulation', this refers to that Regulation. However, this should not affect the substance of the extracts that follow which are relevant under Regulation 139/2004.

(A) Concentration: Article 3

Regulation 139/2004, like its predecessor Regulation 4064/89, employs the term 'concentration' to describe what other systems of competition law around the world and most business people might describe as a 'merger' or 'acquisition'.

The definition of a concentration is contained in Article 3 of the Regulation. As can be seen from the Article, the term is in fact somewhat broader in meaning than what a business person might understand as a merger or acquisition. It covers the following situations that result in a *change of control on a lasting basis*:

I Article 3(1)(a)

Where A and B (two independent undertakings) merge together (Art. 3(1)(a)):

A $\longrightarrow$ AB $\longleftarrow$ B

Commission Notice on the concept of concentration under Council Regulation (EEC) No 4064/89 on the control of concentrations between undertakings, [1998] OJ C66/5 (footnotes omitted)

6   A merger within the meaning of Article 3(1)(a) of the Merger Regulation occurs when two or more independent undertakings amalgamate into a new undertaking and cease to exist as separate legal entities. A merger may also occur when an undertaking is absorbed by another, the latter retaining its legal identity while the former ceases to exist as a legal entity.

7   A merger within the meaning of Article 3(1)(a) may also occur where, in the absence of a legal merger, the combining of the activities of previously independent undertakings results in the creation of a single economic unit. This may arise in particular where two or more undertakings, while retaining their individual legal personalities, establish contractually a common economic management. If this leads to a *de facto* amalgamation of the undertakings concerned into a genuine common economic unit, the operation is considered to be a merger. A prerequisite for the determination of a common economic unit is the existence of a permanent, single economic management. Other relevant factors may include internal profit and loss compensation as between the various undertakings within the group, and their joint liability externally. The *de facto* amalgamation may be reinforced by cross-shareholdings between the undertakings forming the economic unit.

II Article 3(1)(b)

Where A acquires direct or indirect control of the whole or part of B (Art. 3(1)(b)):

A $\longrightarrow$ B

Notice on the concept of concentration (footnotes omitted)

8   Article 3(1)(b) provides that a concentration occurs in the case of an acquisition of control. Such control may be acquired by one undertaking acting alone or by two or more undertakings acting jointly.

Control may also be acquired by a person in circumstances where that person already controls (whether solely or jointly) at least one other undertaking or, alternatively, by a combination of persons (which controls another undertaking) and/or undertakings. The term 'person' in this context extends to public bodies and private entities, as well as individuals.

As defined, a concentration within the meaning of the Merger Regulation is limited to changes in control. Internal restructuring within a group of companies, therefore, cannot constitute a concentration.

9 Whether an operation gives rise to an acquisition of control depends on a number of legal and/or factual elements. The acquisition of property rights and shareholders' agreements are important, but are not the only elements involved: purely economic relationships may also play a decisive role. Therefore, in exceptional circumstances, a situation of economic dependence may lead to control on a *de facto* basis where, for example, very important long-term supply agreements or credits provided by suppliers or customers, coupled with structural links, confer decisive influence.

There may also be acquisition of control even if it is not the declared intention of the parties. Moreover, the Merger Regulation clearly defines control as having 'the possibility of exercising decisive influence' rather than the actual exercise of such influence.

10 Control is nevertheless normally acquired by persons or undertakings which are the holders of the rights or are entitled to rights conferring control. There may be exceptional situations where the formal holder of a controlling interest differs from the person or undertaking having in fact the real power to exercise the rights resulting from this interest. This may be the case, for example, where an undertaking uses another person or undertaking for the acquisition of a controlling interest and exercises the rights through this person or undertaking, even though the latter is formally the holder of the rights. In such a situation, control is acquired by the undertaking which in reality is behind the operation and in fact enjoys the power to control the target undertaking. The evidence needed to establish this type of indirect control may include factors such as the source of financing or family links.

11 The object of control can be one or more undertakings which constitute legal entities, or the assets of such entities, or only some of these assets. The assets in question, which could be brands or licences, must constitute a business to which a market turnover can be clearly attributed.

III Article 3(4)

Or where A and B decide together to collaborate in the creation of a new undertaking which the two of them will control, i.e. a joint venture (Art. 3(4)):

A + B ⟶ NewCo

Paragraph 4 of Article 3 provides that the creation of a joint venture performing on a lasting basis all the functions of an autonomous economic entity shall constitute a concentration within the meaning of Article 3(1)(b). Joint ventures are discussed in part 6 below.

(B) Control: Article 3

A key component in the definition of a concentration is that of 'control'. The concept is dealt with in paragraphs 2 and 3 of the Article. It is defined broadly and refers to the 'possibility' of A in situation 2 above, for example, 'exercising decisive influence'.

The acquisition of control may take the form of sole or joint control. These two ideas are discussed in the Commission's *Notice on the concept of concentration* (cited above).

I Situation of sole control

Notice on the concept of concentration

13 Sole control is normally acquired on a legal basis where an undertaking acquires a majority of the voting rights of a company. It is not in itself significant that the acquired shareholding is 50% of the share capital plus one share[12] or that it is 100% of the share capital.[13] In the absence of other elements, an acquisition which does not include a majority of the voting rights does not normally confer control even if it involves the acquisition of a majority of the share capital.

14 Sole control may also be acquired in the case of a 'qualified minority'. This can be established on a legal and/or *de facto* basis.

On a legal basis it can occur where specific rights are attached to the minority shareholding. These may be preferential shares leading to a majority of the voting rights or other rights enabling the minority shareholder to determine the strategic commercial behaviour of the target company, such as the power to appoint more than half of the members of the supervisory board or the administrative board.

A minority shareholder may also be deemed to have sole control on a *de facto* basis. This is the case, for example, where the shareholder is highly likely to achieve a majority at the shareholders' meeting, given that the remaining shares are widely dispersed.[14] In such a situation it is unlikely that all the smaller shareholders will be present or represented at the shareholders' meeting. The determination of whether or not sole control exists in a particular case is based on the evidence resulting from the presence of shareholders in previous years. Where, on the basis of the number of shareholders attending the shareholders' meeting, a minority shareholder has a

12 Case IV/M.296 - *Crédit Lyonnais/BFG Bank*, of 11 January 1993.
13 Case IV/M.299 - *Sara Lee/BP Food Division*, of 8 February 1993.
14 Case IV/M.025 - *Arjomari/Wiggins Teape*, of 10 February 1990.

stable majority of the votes at this meeting, then the large minority shareholder is taken to have sole control.[15]

Sole control can also be exercised by a minority shareholder who has the right to manage the activities of the company and to determine its business policy.

15   An option to purchase or convert shares cannot in itself confer sole control unless the option will be exercised in the near future according to legally binding agreements.[16] However, the likely exercise of such an option can be taken into account as an additional element which, together with other elements, may lead to the conclusion that there is sole control.

16   A change from joint to sole control of an undertaking is deemed to be a concentration within the meaning of the Merger Regulation because decisive influence exercised alone is substantially different from decisive influence exercised jointly.[17] For the same reason, an operation involving the acquisition of joint control of one part of an undertaking and sole control of another part is in principle regarded as two separate concentrations under the Merger Regulation.[18]

II Situation of joint control

Notice on the concept of concentration

18   As in the case of sole control, the acquisition of joint control (which includes changes from sole control to joint control) can also be established on a legal or *de facto* basis. There is joint control if the shareholders (the parent companies) must reach agreement on major decisions concerning the controlled undertaking (the joint venture).

19   Joint control exists where two or more undertakings or persons have the possibility of exercising decisive influence over another undertaking. Decisive influence in this sense normally means the power to block actions which determine the strategic commercial behaviour of an undertaking. Unlike sole control, which confers the power upon a specific shareholder to determine the strategic decisions in an undertaking, joint control is characterized by the possibility of a deadlock situation resulting from the power of two or more parent companies to reject proposed strategic decisions. It follows, therefore, that these shareholders must reach a common understanding in determining the commercial policy of the joint venture.

The issue of joint control will be explained further in part 6 below which deals with joint ventures.

15 Case IV/M.343 - *Société Générale de Belgique/Générale de Banque*, of 3 August 1993.
16 Judgment in Case T 2/93, *Air France v. Commission* [1994] ECR II-323.
17 This issue is dealt with in paragraphs 30, 31 and 32 of the *Notice on the concept of undertakings concerned.*
18 Case IV/M.409 - *ABB/Renault Automation*, of 9 March 1994.

(C) Situations where a concentration will not be deemed to arise

Article 3(5) provides 3 exceptions to where a concentration would ordinarily arise under the Regulation. These are explained in the paragraph itself and the *Notice on concept of concentration* (paragraphs 42–45).

(D) Community dimension: Article 1

Article 1 of the Regulation sets out the concept of 'Community dimension' and states that the Regulation only applies to concentrations with a Community dimension. Hence, it is important to understand the concept because it is key to determining whether a proposed concentration will be assessed under the Regulation.

The Community dimension requirement creates what has come to be known as the 'one-stop-shop principle', which established a 'bright line' demarcation of jurisdiction and competence between the Commission and national competition authorities. Concentrations with a Community dimension fall within the exclusive or sole jurisdiction of the Commission, although derogations from this principle are available (see pp. 458–459 below).

Article 1 sets out the procedure to assess whether a proposed concentration has a Community dimension which is based on the turnover of the parties. However, there are two key points to note in this regard. First, turnover refers to the turnover of all 'the undertakings concerned'. This means that one should first identify the undertakings whose turnover should be taken into account. Article 5(4) of the Regulation and the Commission's *Notice on the concept of undertakings concerned* explain how this point should be handled in practice.

| Undertakings concerned

Notice on the concept of undertakings concerned under Council Regulation No 4064/89 on the control of concentrations between undertakings, OJ (1998) C 66/14

6   In the case of a merger, the undertakings concerned will be the undertakings that are merging.

7   In the remaining cases, it is the concept of 'acquiring control' that will determine which are the undertakings concerned. On the acquiring side, there can be one or more companies acquiring sole or joint control. On the acquired side, there can be one or more companies as a whole or parts thereof, when only one of their subsidiaries or some of their assets are the subject of the transaction. As a general rule, each of these companies will be an undertaking concerned within the meaning of the Merger Regulation.

8   In concentrations other than mergers or the setting-up of new joint ventures, i.e. in cases of sole or joint acquisition of pre-existing companies or parts of them,

there is an important party to the agreement that gives rise to the operation who is to be ignored when identifying the undertakings concerned: the seller. Although it is clear that the operation cannot proceed without his consent, his role ends when the transaction is completed since, by definition, from the moment the seller has relinquished all control over the company, his links with it disappear. Where the seller retains joint control with the acquiring company (or companies), it will be considered to be one of the undertakings concerned.

The *Notice* contains helpful guidance on identifying the undertakings concerned in different concentration situations:

Mergers

12   In a merger, several previously independent companies come together to create a new company or, while remaining separate legal entities, to create a single economic unit. As mentioned earlier, the undertakings concerned are each of the merging entities.

Acquisition of sole control of the whole company

13   Acquisition of sole control of the whole company is the most straightforward case of acquisition of control; the undertakings concerned will be the acquiring company and the acquired or target company.

Acquisition of sole control of part of a company

14   The first subparagraph of Article 5(2) of the Merger Regulation provides that when the operation concerns the acquisition of parts of one or more undertakings, only those parts which are the subject of the transaction shall be taken into account with regard to the seller. The concept of 'parts' is to be understood as one or more separate legal entities (such as subsidiaries), internal subdivisions within the seller (such as a division or unit), or specific assets which in themselves could constitute a business (e. g. in certain cases brands or licences) to which a market turnover can be clearly attributed. In this case, the undertakings concerned will be the acquirer and the acquired part(s) of the target company.

15   The second subparagraph of Article 5(2) includes a special provision on staggered operations or follow-up deals, whereby if several acquisitions of parts by the same purchaser from the same seller occur within a two-year period, these transactions are to be treated as one and the same operation arising on the date of the last transaction. In this case, the undertakings concerned are the acquirer and the different acquired part(s) of the target company taken as a whole.

Acquisition of sole control after reduction or enlargement of the target company

16   The undertakings concerned are the acquiring company and the target company or companies, in their configuration at the date of the operation.

17   The Commission bases itself on the configuration of the undertakings concerned at the date of the event triggering the obligation to notify under Article 4(1) of the Merger Regulation... If the target company has divested an entity or closed a business prior to the date of the event triggering notification or where such a divestment or closure is a pre-condition for the operation,[6] then sales of the divested entity or closed business are not to be included when calculating turnover. Conversely, if the target company has acquired an entity prior to the date of the event triggering notification, the sales of the latter are to be added.[7]

Acquisition of sole control through a subsidiary of a group
18   Where the target company is acquired by a group through one of its subsidiaries, the undertakings concerned for the purpose of calculating turnover are the target company and the acquiring subsidiary.

19   All the companies within a group (parent companies, subsidiaries, etc.) constitute a single economic entity, and therefore there can only be one undertaking concerned within the one group – i.e. the subsidiary and the parent company cannot each be considered as separate undertakings concerned, either for the purposes of ensuring that the threshold requirements are fulfilled (for example, if the target company does not meet the ECU 250 million Community-turnover threshold), or that they are not (for example, if a group was split into two companies each with a Community turnover below ECU 250 million).

20   However, even though there can only be one undertaking concerned within a group, Article 5(4) of the Merger Regulation provides that it is the turnover of the whole group to which the undertaking concerned belongs that shall be included in the threshold calculations.[8]

Acquisition of joint control of a newly-created company
21   In the case of acquisition of joint control of a newly-created company, the undertakings concerned are each of the companies acquiring control of the newly set-up joint venture (which, as it does not yet exist, cannot be considered to be an undertaking concerned and moreover, as yet, has no turnover of its own).

---

6 See judgment of the Court of First Instance of 24 March 1994 in Case T-3/93 - *Air France v Commission* [1994] ECR II-21.
7 The calculation of turnover in the case of acquisitions or divestments subsequent to the date of the last audited accounts is dealt with in the Commission *Notice on calculation of turnover*, paragraph 27.
8 The calculation of turnover in the case of company groups is dealt with in the Commission *Notice on calculation of turnover*, paragraphs 36 to 42.

Acquisition of joint control of a pre-existing company

22 In the case of acquisition of joint control of a pre-existing company or business,[9] the undertakings concerned are each of the companies acquiring joint control on the one hand, and the pre-existing acquired company or business on the other.

23 However, where the pre-existing company was under the sole control of one company and one or several new shareholders acquire joint control while the initial parent company remains, the undertakings concerned are each of the jointly-controlling companies (including this initial shareholder). The target company in this case is not an undertaking concerned, and its turnover is part of the turnover of the initial parent company.

Acquisition of joint control with a view to immediate partition of assets

24 Where several undertakings come together solely for the purpose of acquiring another company and agree to divide up the acquired assets according to a pre-existing plan immediately upon completion of the transaction, there is no effective concentration of economic power between the acquirers and the target company since the assets acquired are jointly held and controlled for only a 'legal instant'. This type of acquisition with a view to immediate partition of assets will in fact be considered to be several operations, whereby each of the acquiring companies acquires its relevant part of the target company. For each of these operations, the undertakings concerned will therefore be the acquiring company and that part of the target which it is acquiring (just as if there was an acquisition of sole control of part of a company).

. . .

Change from joint control to sole control

30 In the case of a change from joint control to sole control, one shareholder acquires the stake previously held by the other shareholder(s). In the case of two shareholders, each of them has joint control over the entire joint venture, and not sole control over 50% of it; hence the sale of all of his shares by one shareholder to the other does not lead the sole remaining shareholder to move from sole control over 50% to sole control over 100% of the joint venture, but rather to move from joint control to sole control of the entire company (which, subsequent to the operation, ceases to be a 'joint' venture).

31 In this situation, the undertakings concerned are the remaining (acquiring) shareholder and the joint venture. As is the case for any other seller, the 'exiting' shareholder is not an undertaking concerned.

9 i.e. two or more companies (companies A, B, etc.) acquire a pre-existing company (company X).

32   The *ICI/Tioxide* case[13] involved such a change from joint (50/50) control to sole control. The Commission considered that '... decisive influence exercised solely is substantially different to decisive influence exercised jointly, since the latter has to take into account the potentially different interests of the other party or parties concerned . . . By changing the quality of decisive influence exercised by ICI on Tioxide, the transaction will bring about a durable change of the structure of the concerned parties . . .'. In this case, the undertakings concerned were held to be ICI (as acquirer) and Tioxide as a whole (as acquiree), but not the seller Cookson.

II The thresholds

The second point to note about Article 1 is that it contains two alternative sets of thresholds according to which a Community dimension is established. The first set, which is covered under paragraph 2 of the Article, appeared in the original version of Regulation 4064/89. The second is contained in paragraph 3, as was introduced as a result of Regulation 1310/97.

    Paragraphs 2 and 3 refer to 'worldwide turnover' and 'Community-wide turnover'. The former is intended to measure the overall size of the undertakings concerned. The latter, on the other hand, aims at localising to the Community, the size of the undertakings concerned, in order to determine that the concentration in question involves at least a minimum level of activities in the EC. In addition, the Article contain the 'two-thirds rule', which aims to remove from the jurisdiction of the Commission transactions which are largely localised to one jurisdiction within the Community, and so do not impact across the Community.

Example

It might aid the reader to consider an example of the operation of the community dimension rule. The example given below will refer to the requirements of Article 1(2).

    Let us suppose that two undertakings A (UK) and B (French) wish to merge. The details of their turnovers and where these are achieved in the Community are as follows:

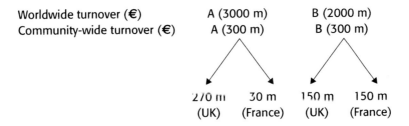

Worldwide turnover (€)	A (3000 m)	B (2000 m)
Community-wide turnover (€)	A (300 m)	B (300 m)

    270 m   30 m   150 m   150 m
    (UK)   (France)   (UK)   (France)

---

13 Case IV/M.023 - *ICI/Tioxide*, of 28 November 1990.

Clearly this concentration has a Community dimension. This is because the combined aggregate worldwide turnover of A and B (the undertakings concerned) is €5,000 m; the aggregate community-wide turnover of each of them is more than €250 m; and while A achieved more than two thirds of its Community-wide turnover in one Member State (the UK), B does not: it achieved only half of its turnover in the same Member State (the UK). So the two-thirds rule is satisfied in this case.

III Calculating the turnover of the undertakings concerned

Applying Article 1 of the Regulation requires a calculation of the turnover of the undertakings concerned. Article 5 of the Regulation deals with this important issue. More detailed information on this however can be found in the Commission's *Notice on calculation of turnover* (see paragraphs 9–48).

IV Investigating concentrations with Community dimension by national competition authorities

As we saw, a concentration which has a Community dimension falls within the sole jurisdiction of the Commission. However, it is important to note that there may be situations where although a Community dimension is established, the concentration may be assessed by a national competition authority and not the Commission. Examples of this situation can be found in Articles 4(4), 9 and 21(4) of the Regulation. Article 4(4) is a wholly new provision which did not exist under Regulation 4064/89. It provides that the undertakings concerned may, prior to notifying their proposed concentration to the Commission, inform the latter that the concentration may significantly affect competition in a market within a particular Member State which presents all the characteristics of a distinct market and that such concentration should be examined, in whole or in part, by the Member State concerned. The aim of Article 4(4) in other words is to allow certain concentrations, although they may have a Community dimension, to be investigated nonetheless by a competent national competition authority. It is also important to note Article 296(1) EC in this connection, which provides that:

> The provisions of this Treaty shall not preclude the application of the following rules:
> (a) no Member State shall be obliged to supply information the disclosure of which it considers contrary to the essential interests of its security;
> (b) any Member State may take such measures as it considers necessary for the protection of the essential interests of its security which are connected with the production of or trade in arms, munitions and war material; such measures shall not adversely affect the conditions of competition in the common market regarding products which are not intended for specifically military purposes.

The role of the provision is particularly prominent in the area of military and defence concentration, where a Member State may be particularly concerned about the sensitivity of certain information that could be disclosed through notification of a concentration to the Commission. In this case the Article could be relied on by the Member State to stop such information being disclosed which in effect means that the Commission will not be able to handle at least that particular aspect of the concentration; the Commission may be able to handle other aspects if for example they are concerned with civilian matters.

V Investigating concentrations without Community dimension by the Commission

On the other hand, a concentration which lacks Community dimension may still also be assessed by the Commission. This is the reverse of the situation described in the previous section. An example of this is the Article 22 situation, under which the Commission, following a request by one or more Member States, can examine a concentration which, although it does not satisfy Article 1 of the Regulation, in the language of Article 22(1) 'affects trade between Member States and threatens to significantly affect competition within the territory of the Member State or States making the request'.

Another example of a referral situation can be found in Article 4(5). This paragraph, which did not exist under Regulation 4064/89, provides that the undertakings concerned in a concentration which lacks Community dimension but is capable of being reviewed under the national laws of at least three Member States may, before notifying the concentration to the national competent authorities, make a reasoned submission to the Commission informing it that it should examine the concentration.

VI Case allocation and referral requests

With the addition of two wholly new provisions in Regulation 139/2004, namely Article 4(4) and 4(5), it can be expected that the issue of referral request by parties and case allocation between the Commission and the national competition authorities will have particular significance in practice. Realising this, the Commission has published a helpful document, *Notice on Case allocation* (2004), which provides practical guidance regarding the mechanisms of the referral system as well as explaining the rationale underlying the system. The Notice can be viewed on the Commission's website. Furthermore, as was mentioned in part 3 above, Regulation 802/2004 contains a pre-notification referral requests form (Form RS) in Annex III. Form RS also has particular practical significance for parties wishing to make a referral request under Article 4(4) or 4(5) and gives details of the kind of information the parties should provide.

(E) Suspension of concentrations: Article 7

Article 7(1) provides that a concentration with a Community dimension, or one which is to be examined by the Commission notwithstanding, must be suspended prior to its notification to the Commission and until it has been declared compatible with the Common Market pursuant to a decision by the

Commission. Article 7(2) and (3) respectively however provide exceptions to this rule in certain cases, and a derogation must be sought from the Commission to allow this.

(F) Prior notifications of concentrations: Article 4

A major difference between Article 81 and 82 cases and the case of concentrations with a Community dimension is that the latter must be notified to the Commission. This is provided for by Article 4, which deals with, among other things, the time when a concentration should be notified and who bears the responsibility for notification.

A notification is made using Form CO. The form can be found in Annex I to Regulation 802/2004. It should be noted that in practice the preparation of a Form CO in most cases is a time consuming exercise. The amount of information which is expected, and is actually provided, is very lengthy and complex, especially the information dealing with the issue of market definition (section 6 of Form CO). The Commission has over the years published guidance, which deal with notification-related matters of concentrations such as the *Best Practices on the conduct of EC merger control proceedings Guidelines* and more recently the *Notice on simplified procedure for treatment of certain concentrations* (2004). It has consistently encouraged pre-notification contact by firms with the Commission, something that the parties often do in practice. As was noted above, Regulation 802/2004 includes a Short Form in Annex II. The Short Form is intended to be used for notification of concentrations which are unlikely to raise competition concerns.

5 Post-notification stage: the substantive appraisal stage

Once the Commission concludes, on the basis of the information provided to it, that there is a concentration with a Community dimension which should be examined, it will move to make a substantive assessment of the concentration.

There are two vital points to note here. First, it is essential to consider what test is used when conducting substantive appraisal. Second, it is important to know the timescale restrictions on the Commission and the framework within which it operates, including the different phases of its assessment.

(A) The appraisal test and criteria

I General

The test used by the Commission to appraise concentrations with a Community dimension in order to determine whether they are 'compatible with the Common Market' appears in Article 2(2) and (3); it is different from the test which existed under Regulation 4064/89 and also not identical to that used under Articles 81 and 82. The significance of the change in the language of test is explained in Chapter 13 (see pp. 624–625 below). The test asks whether or not a concentration would *significantly impede effective competition in the common market or in a substantial part of it,* in particular as a result of the *creation or strengthening of a dominant position.*

Article 2(1) contains the appraisal criteria, which refers to, among other things, the need to maintain effective competition. According to the paragraph, the Commission must appraise concentrations within the scope of the Regulation in accordance with its objectives and the appraisal criteria. It provides guidance and a reminder to the Commission that when analysing concentrations it should not overlook some important factors when conducting its overall assessment.

II Creating or strengthening a dominant position

The concept of dominance is one that appears in Article 82. This means that the jurisprudence of the Community Courts and the decisional practice of the Commission developed under that provision are largely relevant in understanding and applying the concept of dominance under Article 2 of the Regulation (see pp. 329–341 above). However, because the Regulation is concerned with future events (meaning the effect the concentration *would have,* if implemented, on the structure of competition within the relevant market), the appraisal of the Commission under the Article 2 is different from its appraisal under Article 82, where it is a retrospective analysis looking at events in the past.

III The concept of dominance

(a) Market definition

As chapter 9 explains, dominance hinges on market power and market power does not exist in the abstract but in relation to a relevant market. Therefore, the application of the test in Article 2 requires the definition of the relevant market. Chapter 2 deals with this issue and explains that the Commission already had extensive experience in relation to market definition prior to 1989, but that the adoption of a specific regime to deal with mergers forced it to develop a more methodical approach because of the large number of merger cases it handles annually and the strict time-limits within which it must reach its decisions.

(b) Types of dominance

It should be clear from chapters 9 and 13 that dominance may exist in two different forms: single firm dominance and collective dominance; and the Regulation applies to both types.

(i) Collective dominance

The issue of collective dominance is discussed exhaustively in chapter 13. Both the case law of the Community Courts and the decisional practice of the Commission have established that this type of dominance falls within the scope of Article 2 of Regulation 4064/89. Despite the fact that that Regulation has been replaced by Regulation 139/2004, that case law and decisional practice continue to be relevant, and the 2004 Regulation will also apply to situations of collective dominance.

(ii) Single firm dominance

There is an abundance of abuse of dominance and merger cases in the EC in which the issue of single firm dominance has been considered. In the *Guidelines on appraisal of horizontal mergers* (see p. 464 below), the Commission states in paragraph 4 that despite the reformulation of the test under Article 2, it is expected that the majority of cases will continue to be assessed using this concept of dominance. The Commission states that the concept provides an important indication as to the standard of harm that is applicable when determining whether a concentration is likely to significantly impede effective competition. Obviously, leading cases under Article 82, such as *United Brands* and *Hoffmann-La Roche*, are important to consider; though, as was noted above, their application should be handled with care. The essential ingredient of dominance is the ability of a firm to act independently from its competitors, customers and consumers.

The case law shows that several factors are taken into account when assessing dominance in merger cases. These include the aggregate market shares which the firms concerned will have as a result of the concentration, the relationship between the market share of the firms concerned and those of other competitors, the stability of the market, the existence of countervailing or buying power on the market and commercial strengths of various types (superior technology, ownership of intellectual property rights, vertical integration, etc.). Clearly, establishing dominance in merger cases, even with the existence of such factors, can prove a difficult task for the Commission, especially given the pressure created by the strict time limits under the Regulation. Essentially what is required is a forecast of future events from the starting point of a present situation where not necessarily all of the facts available are free from controversy or whose validity may be questionable.

The effects produced by a concentration may be of a horizontal, vertical or conglomerate nature, or indeed a mixture of all three. When assessing cases of single firm dominance, the Commission will consider such effects; though conglomerate effects may not be relevant in every case and so may not necessarily be considered. In part III of section 6 of Form CO, the parties to a concentration are asked to supply the Commission with information identifying the 'affected' markets. These are the relevant markets where:

> *In relation to horizontal relationship(s):* when the combined market share of two or more of the parties to the concentration in the same product market will be 15 per cent or more;
>
> *In relation to vertical relationship(s):* in which one or more of the parties to the concentration is engaged in business activities in a product market which is upstream or downstream of a product market in which any other party to the concentration is engaged where any of their individual or

combined market shares in the relevant market at either level is 25 per cent or more, regardless of whether or not a supplier/customer relationship exists between the parties to the concentration;

In relation to neighbouring market relationships: when one or more of the parties to the concentration is engaged in business activities in a product market, which is a neighbouring market closely related to a product market in which any other party to the concentration is engaged where any of their individual or combined market shares in either relevant market is 25 per cent or more. The Commission explains that product markets are considered to be 'closely related neighbouring markets' when the products in question complement each other or when they belong to a range of products that is generally purchased by the same set of customers for the same end use.

The above views of the Commission in relation to affected markets are provided for guidance purposes; hence a concentration which leads to market shares above the figures of 15 per cent and 25 per cent will not necessarily be prohibited by the Commission. The decisional practice of the Commission contains very good examples of cases where the horizontal, vertical or conglomerate effects of concentrations were considered (see table 10.1 below); in some of these cases the Commission's decisions were contested before the CFI. Those advising firms who are involved in a concentration will find it useful to consider these examples. The table below contains details of some of these examples:

Table 10.1

Parties	Horizontal effects	Vertical effects	Conglomerate effects	Review by CFI
Bayer/Aventis Crop Science	*	*		No
Blokker/Toys 'R' Us	*			No
Schneider Electric/Legrand	*			Yes
Guinness/Grand Metropolitan	*		*	No
GE/Honeywell	*	*	*	Pending
Tetra Laval/Sidel		*	*	Yes
Nordic Satellite Distribution		*		No
Time Warner/AOL		*		No
Skanska/Scancem	*	*		No
VodafoneAirtouch/Mannesmann	*			No
REWE/Meinl	*			No
Hutchinson/ECT/ RMPM	*			No
Carrefour/Promodes	*			No
MCIWorldCom/Sprint	*			No
MSG Media Service		*		No
Deutsche Telekom/BetaResearch		*		No
BertelsMann/Kirch/ Premiere		*		No

IV Commission's guidance on the assessment of horizontal mergers

The increasing rate of innovation in product and services coupled with remarkable advances in technology has contributed significantly to the complexity of competition analysis in merger cases. In the Community, the Commission has been conscious of this for a considerable period of time, especially in the case of horizontal mergers. In an effort to increase transparency in analysis and methodology of assessment of such mergers, the Commission has published its *Guidelines on the assessment of horizontal mergers*. The purpose of the *Guidelines*, which lack legal force and are subject to the case law of the Community Courts, is to provide guidance on the Commission's analytical approach. The *Guidelines* are not exhaustive, which means that they do not provide details of all possible applications of this approach; nor do they apply to vertical mergers. A similar guidance on the latter may be published by the Commission in the future. The Commission's *Guidelines* are welcome as they deal with a variety of important issues including market share and concentration, the possible anti-competitive effects of horizontal mergers and possible defences which may be relied on by the parties to a concentration. It may be worth noting that in relation to using market shares as evidence of dominance, the Commission in paragraph 17 of the *Guidelines* refers to the *AKZO* presumption, namely that a market share of 50 per cent or more may be an evidence of the existence of a dominant position (see p. 330 above).

Guidelines on the assessment of horizontal mergers under the Council Regulation on the control of concentrations between undertakings [2004] OJ C31/5

8   Effective competition brings benefits to consumers, such as low prices, high quality products, a wide selection of goods and services, and innovation. Through its control of mergers, the Commission prevents mergers that would be likely to deprive customers of these benefits by significantly increasing the market power of firms. By 'increased market power' is meant the ability of one or more firms to profitably increase prices, reduce output, choice or quality of goods and services, diminish innovation, or otherwise influence parameters of competition. In this notice, the expression 'increased prices' is often used as shorthand for these various ways in which a merger may result in competitive harm.[7] Both suppliers and buyers can have market power. However, for clarity, market power will usually refer here to a supplier's market power. Where a buyer's market power is the issue, the term 'buyer power' is employed.

7 The expression should be understood to also cover situations where, for instance, prices are decreased less, or are less likely to decrease, than they otherwise would have without the merger and where prices are increased more, or are more likely to increase, than they otherwise would have without the merger.

9   In assessing the competitive effects of a merger, the Commission compares the competitive conditions that would result from the notified merger with the conditions that would have prevailed without the merger.[8] In most cases the competitive conditions existing at the time of the merger constitute the relevant comparison for evaluating the effects of a merger. However, in some circumstances, the Commission may take into account future changes to the market that can reasonably be predicted.[9] It may, in particular, take account of the likely entry or exit of firms if the merger did not take place when considering what constitutes the relevant comparison.[10]

10   The Commission's assessment of mergers normally entails:
(a) definition of the relevant product and geographic markets;
(b) competitive assessment of the merger.
The main purpose of market definition is to identify in a systematic way the immediate competitive constraints facing the merged entity. Guidance on this issue can be found in the Commission's Notice on the definition of the relevant market for the purposes of Community competition law.[11] Various considerations leading to the delineation of the relevant markets may also be of importance for the competitive assessment of the merger.

11   This notice is structured around the following elements:
(a) The approach of the Commission to market shares and concentration thresholds (Section III).
(b) The likelihood that a merger would have anti-competitive effects in the relevant markets, in the absence of countervailing factors (Section IV).
(c) The likelihood that buyer power would act as a countervailing factor to an increase in market power resulting from the merger (Section V).
(d) The likelihood that entry would maintain effective competition in the relevant markets (Section VI).
(e) The likelihood that efficiencies would act as a factor counteracting the harmful effects on competition which might otherwise result from the merger (Section VII).
(f) The conditions for a failing firm defence (Section VIII).

12   In order to assess the foreseeable impact[12] of a merger on the relevant markets, the Commission analyses its possible anti-competitive effects and the relevant countervailing factors such as buyer power, the extent of entry barriers and possible

---

8 By analogy, in the case of a merger that has been implemented without having been notified, the Commission would assess the merger in the light of the competitive conditions that would have prevailed without the implemented merger.

9 See, e.g. Commission Decision 98/526/EC in Case IV/M.950 - *Hoffmann La Roche/Boehringer Mannheim*, OJ L 234, 21.8.1998, p. 14, point 13; Case IV/M.1846 - *Glaxo Wellcome/SmithKline Beecham*, points 70-72; Case COMP/M.2547 - *Bayer/Aventis Crop Science*, points 324 et seq.

10 See, e.g. Case T-102/96, *Gencor v Commission*, [1999] ECR II-753, paragraphs 247-263.

11 OJ C 372, 9.12.1997, p. 5.

12 See Case T-102/96, *Gencor v Commission*, [1999] ECR II-753, paragraph 262, and Case T-342/99, *Airtours v Commission*, [2002] ECR II-2585, paragraph 280.

efficiencies put forward by the parties. In exceptional circumstances, the Commission considers whether the conditions for a failing firm defence are met.

13   In the light of these elements, the Commission determines, pursuant to Article 2 of the Merger Regulation, whether the merger would significantly impede effective competition, in particular through the creation or the strengthening of a dominant position, and should therefore be declared incompatible with the common market. It should be stressed that these factors are not a 'checklist' to be mechanically applied in each and every case. Rather, the competitive analysis in a particular case will be based on an overall assessment of the foreseeable impact of the merger in the light of the relevant factors and conditions. Not all the elements will always be relevant to each and every horizontal merger, and it may not be necessary to analyse all the elements of a case in the same detail.

III. MARKET SHARE AND CONCENTRATION LEVELS

14   Market shares and concentration levels provide useful first indications of the market structure and of the competitive importance of both the merging parties and their competitors.

15   Normally, the Commission uses current market shares in its competitive analysis.[13] However, current market shares may be adjusted to reflect reasonably certain future changes, for instance in the light of exit, entry or expansion.[14] Post-merger market shares are calculated on the assumption that the post-merger combined market share of the merging parties is the sum of their pre-merger market shares.[15] Historic data may be used if market shares have been volatile, for instance when the market is characterised by large, lumpy orders. Changes in historic market shares may provide useful information about the competitive process and the likely future importance of the various competitors, for instance, by indicating whether firms have been gaining or losing market shares. In any event, the Commission interprets market shares in the light of likely market conditions, for instance, if the market is highly dynamic in character and if the market structure is unstable due to innovation or growth.[16]

16   The overall concentration level in a market may also provide useful information about the competitive situation. In order to measure concentration levels, the

13 As to the calculation of market shares, see also Commission Notice on the definition of the relevant market for the purposes of Community competition law, OJ C 372, 9.12.1997, p. 3, paragraphs 54-55.
14 See, e.g. Case COMP/M.1806 - *Astra Zeneca/Novartis*, points 150 and 415.
15 When relevant, market shares may be adjusted, in particular, to account for controlling interests in other firms (See, e.g. Case IV/M.1383 - *Exxon/Mobil*, points 446-458; Case COMP/M.1879 - *Boeing/Hughes*, points 60-79; Case COMP/JV 55 - *Hutchison/RCPM/ECT*, points 66-75), or for other arrangements with third parties (See, for instance, as regards sub-contractors, Commission Decision 2001/769/EC in Case COMP/M.1940 - *Framatome/Siemens/Cogema*, OJ L 289, 6.11.2001, p. 8, point 142).
16 See, e.g. Case COMP/M.2256 - *Philips/Agilent Health Care Technologies*, points 31-32, and Case COMP/M.2609 - *HP/Compaq*, point 39.

Commission often applies the Herfindahl–Hirschman Index (HHI).[17] The HHI is calculated by summing the squares of the individual market shares of all the firms in the market.[18] The HHI gives proportionately greater weight to the market shares of the larger firms. Although it is best to include all firms in the calculation, lack of information about very small firms may not be important because such firms do not affect the HHI significantly. While the absolute level of the HHI can give an initial indication of the competitive pressure in the market post-merger, the change in the HHI (known as the 'delta') is a useful proxy for the change in concentration directly brought about by the merger.[19]

Market share levels

17   According to well-established case law, very large market shares – 50% or more – may in themselves be evidence of the existence of a dominant market position.[20] However, smaller competitors may act as a sufficient constraining influence if, for example, they have the ability and incentive to increase their supplies. A merger involving a firm whose market share will remain below 50% after the merger may also raise competition concerns in view of other factors such as the strength and number of competitors, the presence of capacity constraints or the extent to which the products of the merging parties are close substitutes. The Commission has thus in several cases considered mergers resulting in firms holding market shares between 40% and 50%,[21] and in some cases below 40%,[22] to lead to the creation or the strengthening of a dominant position.

18   Concentrations which, by reason of the limited market share of the undertakings concerned, are not liable to impede effective competition may be presumed to be compatible with the common market. Without prejudice to Articles 81 and 82 of the Treaty, an indication to this effect exists, in particular, where the market share

17 See, e.g. Case IV/M.1365 - *FCC/Vivendi*, point 40; Case COMP/JV 55 - *Hutchison/RCPM/ECT*, point 50. If appropriate, the Commission may also use other concentration measures such as, for instance, concentration ratios, which measure the aggregate market share of a small number (usually three or four) of the leading firms in a market.

18 For example, a market containing five firms with market shares of 40%, 20%, 15%, 15%, and 10%, respectively, has an HHI of 2550 ($40^2 + 20^2 + 15^2 + 15^2 + 10^2 = 2550$). The HHI ranges from close to zero (in an atomistic market) to 10000 (in the case of a pure monopoly).

19 The increase in concentration as measured by the HHI can be calculated independently of the overall market concentration by doubling the product of the market shares of the merging firms. For example, a merger of two firms with market shares of 30% and 15% respectively would increase the HHI by 900 ($30 \times 15 \times 2 = 900$). The explanation for this technique is as follows: Before the merger, the market shares of the merging firms contribute to the HHI by their squares individually: $(a)2 + (b)2$. After the merger, the contribution is the square of their sum: $(a + b)2$, which equals $(a)2 + (b)2 + 2ab$. The increase in the HHI is therefore represented by $2ab$.

20 Case T-221/95, *Endemol v Commission*, [1999] ECR II-1299, paragraph 134, and Case T-102/96, *Gencor v Commission*, [1999] ECR II-753, paragraph 205. It is a distinct question whether a dominant position is created or strengthened as a result of the merger.

21 See, e.g. Case COMP/M.2337 - *Nestlé/Ralston Purina*, points 48–50.

22 See, e.g. Commission Decision 1999/674/EC in Case IV/M.1221 - *Rewe/Meinl*, OJ L 274, 23.10.1999, p. 1, points 98-114; Case COMP/M.2337 - *Nestlé/Ralston Purina*, points 44-47.

of the undertakings concerned does not exceed 25%[23] either in the common market or in a substantial part of it.[24]

HHI levels

19   The Commission is unlikely to identify horizontal competition concerns in a market with a post-merger HHI below 1000. Such markets normally do not require extensive analysis.

20   The Commission is also unlikely to identify horizontal competition concerns in a merger with a post-merger HHI between 1000 and 2000 and a delta below 250, or a merger with a post-merger HHI above 2000 and a delta below 150, except where special circumstances such as, for instance, one or more of the following factors are present:

(a) a merger involves a potential entrant or a recent entrant with a small market share;

(b) one or more merging parties are important innovators in ways not reflected in market shares;

(c) there are significant cross-shareholdings among the market participants;[25]

(d) one of the merging firms is a maverick firm with a high likelihood of disrupting coordinated conduct;

(e) indications of past or ongoing coordination, or facilitating practices, are present;

(f) one of the merging parties has a pre-merger market share of 50% of more.[26]

21   Each of these HHI levels, in combination with the relevant deltas, may be used as an initial indicator of the absence of competition concerns. However, they do not give rise to a presumption of either the existence or the absence of such concerns.

IV. POSSIBLE ANTI-COMPETITIVE EFFECTS OF HORIZONTAL MERGERS

22   There are two main ways in which horizontal mergers may significantly impede effective competition, in particular by creating or strengthening a dominant position:

23 The calculation of market shares depends critically on market definition. It must be emphasised that the Commission does not necessarily accept the parties' proposed market definition.

24 Recital 32 of the Merger Regulation. However, such an indication does not apply to cases where the proposed merger creates or strengthens a collective dominant position involving the "undertakings concerned" and other third parties (see Joined Cases C-68/94 and C-30/95, *Kali and Salz*, [1998] ECR I-1375, paragraphs 171 et seq.; and Case T-102/96, *Gencor v Commission*, [1999] ECR II-753, paragraphs 134 *et seq.*).

25 In markets with cross-shareholdings or joint ventures the Commission may use a modified HHI, which takes into account such share-holdings (see, e.g. Case IV/M.1383 - *Exxon/Mobil*, point 256).

26 See paragraph 17.

(a) by eliminating important competitive constraints on one or more firms, which consequently would have increased market power, without resorting to coordinated behaviour (non-coordinated effects);

(b) by changing the nature of competition in such a way that firms that previously were not coordinating their behaviour, are now significantly more likely to coordinate and raise prices or otherwise harm effective competition. A merger may also make coordination easier, more stable or more effective for firms which were coordinating prior to the merger (coordinated effects).

23   The Commission assesses whether the changes brought about by the merger would result in any of these effects. Both instances mentioned above may be relevant when assessing a particular transaction.

Non-coordinated effects[27]

24   A merger may significantly impede effective competition in a market by removing important competitive constraints on one or more sellers, who consequently have increased market power. The most direct effect of the merger will be the loss of competition between the merging firms. For example, if prior to the merger one of the merging firms had raised its price, it would have lost some sales to the other merging firm. The merger removes this particular constraint. Non-merging firms in the same market can also benefit from the reduction of competitive pressure that results from the merger, since the merging firms' price increase may switch some demand to the rival firms, which, in turn, may find it profitable to increase their prices.[28] The reduction in these competitive constraints could lead to significant price increases in the relevant market.

25   Generally, a merger giving rise to such non-coordinated effects would significantly impede effective competition by creating or strengthening the dominant position of a single firm, one which, typically, would have an appreciably larger market share than the next competitor post-merger. Furthermore, mergers in oligopolistic markets[29] involving the elimination of important competitive constraints that the merging parties previously exerted upon each other together with a reduction of competitive pressure on the remaining competitors may, even where there is little likelihood of coordination between the members of the oligopoly, also result in a significant impediment to competition. The Merger Regulation clarifies that all mergers giving rise to such non-coordinated effects shall also be declared incompatible with the common market.[30]

27 Also often called "unilateral" effects.
28 Such expected reactions by competitors may be a relevant factor influencing the merged entity's incentives to increase prices.
29 An oligopolistic market refers to a market structure with a limited number of sizeable firms. Because the behaviour of one firm has an appreciable impact on the overall market conditions, and thus indirectly on the situation of each of the other firms, oligopolistic firms are interdependent.
30 Recital 25 of the Merger Regulation.

26   A number of factors, which taken separately are not necessarily decisive, may influence whether significant non-coordinated effects are likely to result from a merger. Not all of these factors need to be present for such effects to be likely. Nor should this be considered an exhaustive list.

Merging firms have large market shares

27   The larger the market share, the more likely a firm is to possess market power. And the larger the addition of market share, the more likely it is that a merger will lead to a significant increase in market power. The larger the increase in the sales base on which to enjoy higher margins after a price increase, the more likely it is that the merging firms will find such a price increase profitable despite the accompanying reduction in output. Although market shares and additions of market shares only provide first indications of market power and increases in market power, they are normally important factors in the assessment.[31]

Merging firms are close competitors

28   Products may be differentiated[32] within a relevant market such that some products are closer substitutes than others.[33] The higher the degree of substitutability between the merging firms' products, the more likely it is that the merging firms will raise prices significantly.[34] For example, a merger between two producers offering products which a substantial number of customers regard as their first and second choices could generate a significant price increase. Thus, the fact that rivalry between the parties has been an important source of competition on the market may be a central factor in the analysis.[35] High pre-merger margins[36] may also make

31 See, in particular, paragraphs 17 and 18.
32 Products may be differentiated in various ways. There may, for example, be differentiation in terms of geographic location, based on branch or stores location; location matters for retail distribution, banks, travel agencies, or petrol stations. Likewise, differentiation may be based on brand image, technical specifications, quality or level of service. The level of advertising in a market may be an indicator of the firms' effort to differentiate their products. For other products, buyers may have to incur switching costs to use a competitor's product.
33 For the definition of the relevant market, see the Commission's Notice on the definition of the relevant market for the purposes of Community competition law, cited above.
34 See for example Case COMP/M.2817 - *Barilla/BPS/Kamps*, point 34; Commission Decision 2001/403/EC in Case COMP/M.1672 - *Volvo/Scania*, OJ L 143, 29.5.2001, p. 74, points 107-148.
35 See, e.g. Commission Decision 94/893/EC in Case IV/M.430 - *Procter & Gamble/VP Schickedanz* (II), OJ L 354, 21.6.1994, p. 32, Case T-290/94, *Kaysersberg v Commission*, [1997] II-2137, paragraph 153; Commission Decision 97/610/EC in Case IV/M.774 – *Saint-Gobain/Wacker-Chemie/NOM*, OJ L 247, 10.9.1997, p. 1, point 179; Commission Decision 2002/156/EC in Case COMP/M.2097 – *SCA/Metsä Tissue*, OJ L 57, 27.2.2002, p. 1, points 94-108; Case T-310/01, *Schneider v Commission*, [2002] II-4071, paragraph 418.
36 Typically, the relevant margin (m) is the difference between price (p) and the incremental cost (c) of supplying one more unit of output expressed as a percentage of price ($m = (p - c)p$)).

significant price increases more likely. The merging firms' incentive to raise prices is more likely to be constrained when rival firms produce close substitutes to the products of the merging firms than when they offer less close substitutes.[37] It is therefore less likely that a merger will significantly impede effective competition, in particular through the creation or strengthening of a dominant position, when there is a high degree of substitutability between the products of the merging firms and those supplied by rival producers.

29   When data are available, the degree of substitutability may be evaluated through customer preference surveys, analysis of purchasing patterns, estimation of the cross-price elasticities of the products involved,[38] or diversion ratios.[39] In bidding markets it may be possible to measure whether historically the submitted bids by one of the merging parties have been constrained by the presence of the other merging party.[40]

30   In some markets it may be relatively easy and not too costly for the active firms to reposition their products or extend their product portfolio. In particular, the Commission examines whether the possibility of repositioning or product line extension by competitors or the merging parties may influence the incentive of the merged entity to raise prices. However, product repositioning or product line extension often entails risks and large sunk costs[41] and may be less profitable than the current line.

Customers have limited possibilities of switching supplier

31   Customers of the merging parties may have difficulties switching to other suppliers because there are few alternative suppliers[42] or because they face substantial switching costs.[43] Such customers are particularly vulnerable to price increases. The merger may affect these customers' ability to protect themselves against price increases. In particular, this may be the case for customers that have used dual sourcing from the two merging firms as a means of obtaining competitive prices.

---

37 See, e.g. Case IV/M.1980 – *Volvo/Renault VI*, point 34; Case COMP/M.2256 – *Philips Agilent/Health Care Solutions*, points 33-35; Case COMP/M.2537 – *Philips/Marconi Medical Systems*, points 31-34.

38 The cross-price elasticity of demand measures the extent to which the quantity of a product demanded changes in response to a change in the price of some other product, all other things remaining equal. The own-price elasticity measures the extent to which demand for a product changes in response to the change in the price of the product itself.

39 The diversion ratio from product A to product B measures the proportion of the sales of product A lost due to a price increase of A that are captured by product B.

40 Commission Decision 97/816/EC in Case IV/M.877 – *Boeing/McDonnell Douglas*, OJ L 336, 8.12.1997, p. 16, points 58 et seq.; Case COMP/M.3083 - *GE/Instrumentarium*, points 125 *et seq.*

41 Sunk costs are costs which are unrecoverable upon exit from the market.

42 See e.g. Commission Decision 2002/156/EC in Case IV/M.877 – *Boeing/McDonnell Douglas*, OJ L 336, 8.12.1997, p. 16, point 70.

43 See, e.g. Case IV/M. 986 – *Agfa Gevaert/DuPont*, OJ L 211, 29.7.1998, p. 22, points 63-71.

Evidence of past customer switching patterns and reactions to price changes may provide important information in this respect.

Competitors are unlikely to increase supply if prices increase

32   When market conditions are such that the competitors of the merging parties are unlikely to increase their supply substantially if prices increase, the merging firms may have an incentive to reduce output below the combined pre-merger levels, thereby raising market prices.[44] The merger increases the incentive to reduce output by giving the merged firm a larger base of sales on which to enjoy the higher margins resulting from an increase in prices induced by the output reduction.

33   Conversely, when market conditions are such that rival firms have enough capacity and find it profitable to expand output sufficiently, the Commission is unlikely to find that the merger will create or strengthen a dominant position or otherwise significantly impede effective competition.

34   Such output expansion is, in particular, unlikely when competitors face binding capacity constraints and the expansion of capacity is costly[45] or if existing excess capacity is significantly more costly to operate than capacity currently in use.

35   Although capacity constraints are more likely to be important when goods are relatively homogeneous, they may also be important where firms offer differentiated products.

Merged entity able to hinder expansion by competitors

36   Some proposed mergers would, if allowed to proceed, significantly impede effective competition by leaving the merged firm in a position where it would have the ability and incentive to make the expansion of smaller firms and potential competitors more difficult or otherwise restrict the ability of rival firms to compete. In such a case, competitors may not, either individually or in the aggregate, be in a position to constrain the merged entity to such a degree that it would not increase prices or take other actions detrimental to competition. For instance, the merged entity may have such a degree of control, or influence, over the supply of inputs[46] or distribution possibilities[47] that expansion or entry by rival firms may be more costly. Similarly, the merged entity's control over patents[48] or other types of intellectual property

---

44 See, e.g. Case COMP/M.2187 – *CVC/Lenzing*, points 162-170.

45 When analysing the possible expansion of capacity by rivals, the Commission considers factors similar to those described in Section VI on entry. See, e.g. Case COMP/M.2187 – *CVC/Lenzing*, points.

46 See, e.g. Case T-221/95, *Endemol v Commission*, [1999] ECR II-1299, paragraph 167.

47 See, e.g. Case T-22/97, *Kesko v Commission*, [1999], ECR II-3775, paragraphs 141 *et seq.*

48 See, e.g. Commission Decision 2001/684/EC in Case M.1671 – *Dow Chemical/Union Carbide* OJ L 245, 14.9.2001, p. 1, points 107-114.

(e.g. brands[49]) may make expansion or entry by rivals more difficult. In markets where interoperability between different infrastructures or platforms is important,[50] a merger may give the merged entity the ability and incentive to raise the costs or decrease the quality of service of its rivals.[51] In making this assessment the Commission may take into account, inter alia, the financial strength of the merged entity relative to its rivals.[52]

Merger eliminates an important competitive force

37 Some firms have more of an influence on the competitive process than their market shares or similar measures would suggest. A merger involving such a firm may change the competitive dynamics in a significant, anti-competitive way, in particular when the market is already concentrated.[53] For instance, a firm may be a recent entrant that is expected to exert significant competitive pressure in the future on the other firms in the market.

38 In markets where innovation is an important competitive force, a merger may increase the firms' ability and incentive to bring new innovations to the market and, thereby, the competitive pressure on rivals to innovate in that market. Alternatively, effective competition may be significantly impeded by a merger between two important innovators, for instance between two companies with 'pipeline' products related to a specific product market. Similarly, a firm with a relatively small market share may nevertheless be an important competitive force if it has promising pipeline products.[54]

Coordinated effects

39 In some markets the structure may be such that firms would consider it possible, economically rational, and hence preferable, to adopt on a sustainable basis a course of action on the market aimed at selling at increased prices. A merger in a concentrated market may significantly impede effective competition, through the creation or the

---

49 See, e.g. Commission Decision 96/435/EC in Case IV/M.623 – *Kimberly-Clark/Scott*, OJ L 183, 23.7.1996, p. 1; Case T-114/02, *Babyliss SA v Commission* ("Seb/Moulinex"), [2003] ECR II-000, paragraphs 343 et seq.)

50 This is, for example, the case in network industries such as energy, telecommunications and other communication industries.

51 Commission Decision 99/287/EC in Case IV/M.1069 – *Worldcom/MCI*, OJ L 116, 4.5.1999, p. 1, points 117 et seq.; Case IV/M.1741 - *MCI Worldcom/Sprint*, points 145 et seq.; Case IV/M.1795 – *Vodafone Airtouch/Mannesmann*, points 44 et seq.

52 Case T-156/98 *RJB Mining v Commission* [2001] ECR II-337.

53 Commission Decision 2002/156/EC in Case IV/M.877 – *Boeing/McDonnell Douglas*, OJ L 336, 8.12.1997, p. 16, point 58; Case COMP/M.2568 – *Haniel/Ytong*, point 126.

54 For an example of pipeline products of one merging party likely to compete with the other party's pipeline or existing products, see, e.g. Case IV/M.1846 – *Glaxo Wellcome/SmithKline Beecham*, point 188.

strengthening of a collective dominant position, because it increases the likelihood that firms are able to coordinate their behaviour in this way and raise prices, even without entering into an agreement or resorting to a concerted practice within the meaning of Article 81 of the Treaty.[55] A merger may also make coordination easier, more stable or more effective for firms, that were already coordinating before the merger, either by making the coordination more robust or by permitting firms to coordinate on even higher prices.

40   Coordination may take various forms. In some markets, the most likely coordination may involve keeping prices above the competitive level. In other markets, coordination may aim at limiting production or the amount of new capacity brought to the market. Firms may also coordinate by dividing the market, for instance by geographic area[56] or other customer characteristics, or by allocating contracts in bidding markets.

41   Coordination is more likely to emerge in markets where it is relatively simple to reach a common understanding on the terms of coordination. In addition, three conditions are necessary for coordination to be sustainable. First, the coordinating firms must be able to monitor to a sufficient degree whether the terms of coordination are being adhered to. Second, discipline requires that there is some form of credible deterrent mechanism that can be activated if deviation is detected. Third, the reactions of outsiders, such as current and future competitors not participating in the coordination, as well as customers, should not be able to jeopardise the results expected from the coordination.[57]

42   The Commission examines whether it would be possible to reach terms of coordination and whether the coordination is likely to be sustainable. In this respect, the Commission considers the changes that the merger brings about. The reduction in the number of firms in a market may, in itself, be a factor that facilitates coordination. However, a merger may also increase the likelihood or significance of coordinated effects in other ways. For instance, a merger may involve a 'maverick' firm that has a history of preventing or disrupting coordination, for example by failing to follow price increases by its competitors, or has characteristics that gives it an incentive to favour different strategic choices than its coordinating competitors would prefer. If the merged firm were to adopt strategies similar to those of other competitors, the remaining firms would find it easier to coordinate, and the merger would increase the likelihood, stability or effectiveness of coordination.

43   In assessing the likelihood of coordinated effects, the Commission takes into account all available relevant information on the characteristics of the markets concerned,

---

55 Case T-102/96, *Gencor v Commission*, [1999] ECR II-753, paragraph 277; Case T-342/99, *Airtours v Commission*, [2002] ECR II-2585, paragraph 61.(58).

56 This may be the case if the oligopolists have tended to concentrate their sales in different areas for historic reasons.

57 Case T-342/99, *Airtours v Commission*, [2002] ECR II-2585, paragraph 62.

including both structural features and the past behaviour of firms.[58] Evidence of past coordination is important if the relevant market characteristics have not changed appreciably or are not likely to do so in the near future.[59] Likewise, evidence of coordination in similar markets may be useful information.

Reaching terms of coordination

44   Coordination is more likely to emerge if competitors can easily arrive at a common perception as to how the coordination should work. Coordinating firms should have similar views regarding which actions would be considered to be in accordance with the aligned behaviour and which actions would not.

45   Generally, the less complex and the more stable the economic environment, the easier it is for the firms to reach a common understanding on the terms of coordination. For instance, it is easier to coordinate among a few players than among many. It is also easier to coordinate on a price for a single, homogeneous product, than on hundreds of prices in a market with many differentiated products. Similarly, it is easier to coordinate on a price when demand and supply conditions are relatively stable than when they are continuously changing.[60] In this context volatile demand, substantial internal growth by some firms in the market or frequent entry by new firms may indicate that the current situation is not sufficiently stable to make coordination likely.[61] In markets where innovation is important, coordination may be more difficult since innovations, particularly significant ones, may allow one firm to gain a major advantage over its rivals.

46   Coordination by way of market division will be easier if customers have simple characteristics that allow the coordinating firms to readily allocate them. Such characteristics may be based on geography; on customer type or simply on the existence of customers who typically buy from one specific firm. Coordination by way of market division may be relatively straightforward if it is easy to identify each customer's supplier and the coordination device is the allocation of existing customers to their incumbent supplier.

47   Coordinating firms may, however, find other ways to overcome problems stemming from complex economic environments short of market division. They may, for instance, establish simple pricing rules that reduce the complexity of coordinating on a large number of prices. One example of such a rule is establishing a small number of pricing points, thus reducing the coordination problem. Another example is having a fixed relationship between certain base prices and a number of other prices, such

---

58 See Commission Decision 92/553/EC in Case IV/M.190 – *Nestlé/Perrier*, OJ L 356, 5.12.1992, p. 1, points 117-118.

59 See, e.g. Case IV/M.580 – *ABB/Daimler-Benz*, point 95.

60 See, e.g. Commission Decision 2002/156/EC in Case COMP/M.2097 – *SCA/Metsä Tissue*, OJ L 57, 27.2.2002, p. 1, point 148.

61 See, e.g. Case IV/M.1298 – *Kodak/Imation*, point 60.

that prices basically move in parallel. Publicly available key information, exchange of information through trade associations, or information received through cross-shareholdings or participation in joint ventures may also help firms reach terms of coordination. The more complex the market situation is, the more transparency or communication is likely to be needed to reach a common understanding on the terms of coordination.

48   Firms may find it easier to reach a common understanding on the terms of coordination if they are relatively symmetric,[62] especially in terms of cost structures, market shares, capacity levels and levels of vertical integration.[63] Structural links such as cross-shareholding or participation in joint ventures may also help in aligning incentives among the coordinating firms.[64]

Monitoring deviations

49   Coordinating firms are often tempted to increase their share of the market by deviating from the terms of coordination, for instance by lowering prices, offering secret discounts, increasing product quality or capacity or trying to win new customers. Only the credible threat of timely and sufficient retaliation keeps firms from deviating. Markets therefore need to be sufficiently transparent to allow the coordinating firms to monitor to a sufficient degree whether other firms are deviating, and thus know when to retaliate.[65]

50   Transparency in the market is often higher, the lower the number of active participants in the market. Further, the degree of transparency often depends on how market transactions take place in a particular market. For example, transparency is likely to be high in a market where transactions take place on a public exchange or in an open outcry auction.[66] Conversely, transparency may be low in a market where transactions are confidentially negotiated between buyers and sellers on a bilateral basis.[67] When evaluating the level of transparency in the market, the key element is to identify what firms can infer about the actions of other firms from the available information.[68] Coordinating firms should be able to interpret with some

---

62 Case T-102/96, *Gencor v Commission*, [1999] ECR II-753, paragraph 222; Commission Decision 92/553/EC in Case IV/M.190 – *Nestlé/Perrier*, OJ L 356, 5.12.1992, p. 1, points 63-123.

63 In assessing whether or not a merger may increase the symmetry of the various firms present on the market, efficiency gains may provide important indications (see also paragraph 82 of the notice).

64 See, e.g. Commission Decision 2001/519/EC in Case COMP/M.1673 – *VEBA/VIAG*, OJ L 188, 10.7.2001, p. 1, point 226; Case COMP/M.2567 – *Nordbanken/Postgirot*, point 54.

65 See, e.g. Case COMP/M.2389 – *Shell/DEA*, points 112 et seq.; and Case COMP/M.2533 – *BP/E.ON*, points 102 et seq.

66 See also Commission Decision 2000/42/EC in Case IV/M.1313 – *Danish Crown/Vestjyske Slagterier*, OJ L 20, 25.1.2000, p. 1, points 176-179.

67 See, e.g. Case COMP/M.2640 – *Nestlé/Schöller*, point 37; Commission Decision 1999/641/EC in Case COMP/M.1225 - *Enso/Stora*, OJ L 254, 29.9.1999, p. 9, points 67-68.

68 See, e.g. Case IV/M.1939 – *Rexam (PLM)/American National Can*, point 24.

certainty whether unexpected behaviour is the result of deviation from the terms of coordination. For instance, in unstable environments it may be difficult for a firm to know whether its lost sales are due to an overall low level of demand or due to a competitor offering particularly low prices. Similarly, when overall demand or cost conditions fluctuate, it may be difficult to interpret whether a competitor is lowering its price because it expects the coordinated prices to fall or because it is deviating.

51 In some markets where the general conditions may seem to make monitoring of deviations difficult, firms may nevertheless engage in practices which have the effect of easing the monitoring task, even when these practices are not necessarily entered into for such purposes. These practices, such as meeting-competition or most-favoured-customer clauses, voluntary publication of information, announcements, or exchange of information through trade associations, may increase transparency or help competitors interpret the choices made. Cross-directorships, participation in joint ventures and similar arrangements may also make monitoring easier.

Deterrent mechanisms

52 Coordination is not sustainable unless the consequences of deviation are sufficiently severe to convince coordinating firms that it is in their best interest to adhere to the terms of coordination. It is thus the threat of future retaliation that keeps the coordination sustainable.[69] However the threat is only credible if, where deviation by one of the firms is detected, there is sufficient certainty that some deterrent mechanism will be activated.[70]

53 Retaliation that manifests itself after some significant time lag, or is not certain to be activated, is less likely to be sufficient to offset the benefits from deviating. For example, if a market is characterised by infrequent, large-volume orders, it may be difficult to establish a sufficiently severe deterrent mechanism, since the gain from deviating at the right time may be large, certain and immediate, whereas the losses from being punished may be small and uncertain and only materialise after some time. The speed with which deterrent mechanisms can be implemented is related to the issue of transparency. If firms are only able to observe their competitors' actions after a substantial delay, then retaliation will be similarly delayed and this may influence whether it is sufficient to deter deviation.

54 The credibility of the deterrence mechanism depends on whether the other coordinating firms have an incentive to retaliate. Some deterrent mechanisms, such as punishing the deviator by temporarily engaging in a price war or increasing output

---

69 See Case COMP/M.2389 – *Shell/DEA*, point 121, and Case COMP/M.2533 - *BP/E.ON*, point 111.

70 Although deterrent mechanisms are sometimes called "punishment" mechanisms, this should not be understood in the strict sense that such a mechanism necessarily punishes individually a firm that has deviated. The expectation that coordination may break down for a certain period of time, if a deviation is identified as such, may in itself constitute a sufficient deterrent mechanism.

significantly, may entail a short-term economic loss for the firms carrying out the retaliation. This does not necessarily remove the incentive to retaliate since the short-term loss may be smaller than the long-term benefit of retaliating resulting from the return to the regime of coordination.

55 Retaliation need not necessarily take place in the same market as the deviation.[71] If the coordinating firms have commercial interaction in other markets, these may offer various methods of retaliation.[72] The retaliation could take many forms, including cancellation of joint ventures or other forms of cooperation or selling of shares in jointly owned companies.

Reactions of outsiders

56 For coordination to be successful, the actions of non-coordinating firms and potential competitors, as well as customers, should not be able to jeopardise the outcome expected from coordination. For example, if coordination aims at reducing overall capacity in the market, this will only hurt consumers if non-coordinating firms are unable or have no incentive to respond to this decrease by increasing their own capacity sufficiently to prevent a net decrease in capacity, or at least to render the coordinated capacity decrease unprofitable.[73]

57 The effects of entry and countervailing buyer power of customers are analysed in later sections. However, special consideration is given to the possible impact of these elements on the stability of coordination. For instance, by concentrating a large amount of its requirements with one supplier or by offering long-term contracts, a large buyer may make coordination unstable by successfully tempting one of the coordinating firms to deviate in order to gain substantial new business.

Merger with a potential competitor

58 Concentrations where an undertaking already active on a relevant market merges with a potential competitor in this market can have similar anti-competitive effects to mergers between two undertakings already active on the same relevant market and, thus, significantly impede effective competition, in particular through the creation or the strengthening of a dominant position.

59 A merger with a potential competitor can generate horizontal anti-competitive effects, whether coordinated or non-coordinated, if the potential competitor significantly constrains the behaviour of the firms active in the market. This is the case if the potential competitor possesses assets that could easily be used to enter the market without incurring significant sunk costs. Anti-competitive effects may also

---

71 See, e.g. Commission Decision 2000/42/EC in Case IV/M.1313 – *Danish Crown/Vestjyske Slagterier*, OJ L 20, 25.1.2000, p. 1, point 177.

72 See Case T-102/96, *Gencor v Commission*, [1999] ECR II-753, paragraph 281.

73 These elements are analysed in a similar way to non-coordinated effects.

occur where the merging partner is very likely to incur the necessary sunk costs to enter the market in a relatively short period of time after which this company would constrain the behaviour of the firms currently active in the market.[74]

60   For a merger with a potential competitor to have significant anti-competitive effects, two basic conditions must be fulfilled. First, the potential competitor must already exert a significant constraining influence or there must be a significant likelihood that it would grow into an effective competitive force. Evidence that a potential competitor has plans to enter a market in a significant way could help the Commission to reach such a conclusion.[75] Second, there must not be a sufficient number of other potential competitors, which could maintain sufficient competitive pressure after the merger.[76]

Mergers creating or strengthening buyer power in upstream markets

61   The Commission may also analyse to what extent a merged entity will increase its buyer power in upstream markets. On the one hand, a merger that creates or strengthens the market power of a buyer may significantly impede effective competition, in particular by creating or strengthening a dominant position. The merged firm may be in a position to obtain lower prices by reducing its purchase of inputs. This may, in turn, lead it also to lower its level of output in the final product market, and thus harm consumer welfare.[77] Such effects may in particular arise when upstream sellers are relatively fragmented. Competition in the downstream markets could also be adversely affected if, in particular, the merged entity were likely to use its buyer power *vis-à-vis* its suppliers to foreclose its rivals.[78]

62   On the other hand, increased buyer power may be beneficial for competition. If increased buyer power lowers input costs without restricting downstream competition or total output, then a proportion of these cost reductions are likely to be passed onto consumers in the form of lower prices.

63   In order to assess whether a merger would significantly impede effective competition by creating or strengthening buyer power, an analysis of the competitive conditions

---

74 See, e.g. Case IV/M.1630 – *Air Liquide/BOC*, points 201 et seq. For an example of a case where entry by the other merging firm was not sufficiently likely in the short to medium term (Case T-158/00, *ARD v Commission*, [2003] ECR II-000, paragraphs 115-127).

75 Commission Decision 2001/98/EC in Case IV/M.1439 – *Telia/Telenor*, OJ L 40, 9.2.2001, p. 1, points 330-331, and Case IV/M.1681 – *Akzo Nobel/Hoechst Roussel Vet*, point 64.

76 Case IV/M.1630 – *Air Liquide/BOC*, point 219; Commission Decision 2002/164/EC in Case COMP/M.1853 – *EDF/EnBW*, OJ L 59, 28.2.2002, p. 1, points 54-64.

77 See Commission Decision 1999/674/EC in Case M.1221 – *Rewe/Meinl*, OJ L 274, 23.10.1999, p. 1, points 71–74.

78 Case T-22/97, *Kesko v Commission*, [1999] ECR II-3775, paragraph 157; Commission Decision 2002/156/EC in Case M.877 - *Boeing/McDonnell Douglas*, OJ L 336, 8.12.1997, p. 16, points 105-108.

in upstream markets and an evaluation of the possible positive and negative effects described above are therefore required.

V. COUNTERVAILING BUYER POWER

64   The competitive pressure on a supplier is not only exercised by competitors but can also come from its customers. Even firms with very high market shares may not be in a position, post-merger, to significantly impede effective competition, in particular by acting to an appreciable extent independently of their customers, if the latter possess countervailing buyer power.[79] Countervailing buyer power in this context should be understood as the bargaining strength that the buyer has *vis-à-vis* the seller in commercial negotiations due to its size, its commercial significance to the seller and its ability to switch to alternative suppliers.

65   The Commission considers, when relevant, to what extent customers will be in a position to counter the increase in market power that a merger would otherwise be likely to create. One source of countervailing buyer power would be if a customer could credibly threaten to resort, within a reasonable timeframe, to alternative sources of supply should the supplier decide to increase prices[80] or to otherwise deteriorate quality or the conditions of delivery. This would be the case if the buyer could immediately switch to other suppliers,[81] credibly threaten to vertically integrate into the upstream market or to sponsor upstream expansion or entry[82] for instance by persuading a potential entrant to enter by committing to placing large orders with this company. It is more likely that large and sophisticated customers will possess this kind of countervailing buyer power than smaller firms in a fragmented industry.[83] A buyer may also exercise countervailing buying power by refusing to buy other products produced by the supplier or, particularly in the case of durable goods, delaying purchases.

66   In some cases, it may be important to pay particular attention to the incentives of buyers to utilise their buyer power.[84] For example, a downstream firm may not wish to make an investment in sponsoring new entry if the benefits of such entry in terms of lower input costs could also be reaped by its competitors.

---

79 See, e.g. Case IV/M.1882 – *Pirelli/BICC*, points 73-80.

80 See, e.g. Case IV/M.1245 – *Valeo/ITT Industries*, point 26.

81 Even a small number of customers may not have sufficient buyer power if they are to a large extent "locked in" because of high switching costs (see Case COMP/M.2187 – *CVC/Lenzing*, point 223).

82 Commission Decision 1999/641/EC in Case COMP/M.1225 – *Enso/Stora*, OJ L 254, 29.9.1999, p. 9, points 89-91.

83 It may also be appropriate to compare the concentration existing on the customer side with the concentration on the supply side (Case COMP/JV 55 – *Hutchison/RCPM/ECT*, point 119, and Commission Decision 1999/641/EC in Case COMP/M.1225 – *Enso/Stora*, OJ L 254, 29.9.1999, p. 9, point 97).

84 Case COMP/JV 55 – *Hutchison/RCPM/ECT*, points 129-130.

67   Countervailing buyer power cannot be found to sufficiently off-set potential adverse effects of a merger if it only ensures that a particular segment of customers,[85] with particular bargaining strength, is shielded from significantly higher prices or deteriorated conditions after the merger.[86] Furthermore, it is not sufficient that buyer power exists prior to the merger, it must also exist and remain effective following the merger. This is because a merger of two suppliers may reduce buyer power if it thereby removes a credible alternative.

VI. ENTRY

68   When entering a market is sufficiently easy, a merger is unlikely to pose any significant anti-competitive risk. Therefore, entry analysis constitutes an important element of the overall competitive assessment. For entry to be considered a sufficient competitive constraint on the merging parties, it must be shown to be likely, timely and sufficient to deter or defeat any potential anti-competitive effects of the merger.

Likelihood of entry

69   The Commission examines whether entry is likely or whether potential entry is likely to constrain the behaviour of incumbents post-merger. For entry to be likely, it must be sufficiently profitable taking into account the price effects of injecting additional output into the market and the potential responses of the incumbents. Entry is thus less likely if it would only be economically viable on a large scale, thereby resulting in significantly depressed price levels. And entry is likely to be more difficult if the incumbents are able to protect their market shares by offering long-term contracts or giving targeted pre-emptive price reductions to those customers that the entrant is trying to acquire. Furthermore, high risk and costs of failed entry may make entry less likely. The costs of failed entry will be higher, the higher is the level of sunk cost associated with entry.[87]

70   Potential entrants may encounter barriers to entry which determine entry risks and costs and thus have an impact on the profitability of entry. Barriers to entry are specific features of the market, which give incumbent firms advantages over potential competitors. When entry barriers are low, the merging parties are more likely to be constrained by entry. Conversely, when entry barriers are high, price increases

---

85 Commission Decision 2002/156/EC in Case COMP/M.2097 – *SCA/Metsä Tissue*, OJ L 57, 27.2.2002, point 88. Price discrimination between different categories of customers may be relevant in some cases in the context of market definition (See the Commission's notice on the definition of the relevant market, cited above, at paragraph 43).

86 Accordingly, the Commission may assess whether the various purchasers will hold countervailing buyer power, see, e.g. Commission Decision 1999/641/EC in Case COMP/M.1225 - *Enso/Stora*, OJ L 254, 29.9.1999, p. 9, points 84-97.

87 Commission Decision 97/610/EC in Case IV/M.774 – *Saint-Gobain/Wacker-Chemie/NOM*, OJ L 247, 10.9.1997, p. 1, point 184.

by the merging firms would not be significantly constrained by entry. Historical examples of entry and exit in the industry may provide useful information about the size of entry barriers.

71 Barriers to entry can take various forms:

(a) Legal advantages encompass situations where regulatory barriers limit the number of market participants by, for example, restricting the number of licences.[88] They also cover tariff and non-tariff trade barriers.[89]

(b) The incumbents may also enjoy technical advantages, such as preferential access to essential facilities, natural resources,[90] innovation and R&D,[91] or intellectual property rights,[92] which make it difficult for any firm to compete successfully. For instance, in certain industries, it might be difficult to obtain essential input materials, or patents might protect products or processes. Other factors such as economies of scale and scope, distribution and sales networks,[93] access to important technologies, may also constitute barriers to entry.

(c) Furthermore, barriers to entry may also exist because of the established position of the incumbent firms on the market. In particular, it may be difficult to enter a particular industry because experience or reputation is necessary to compete effectively, both of which may be difficult to obtain as an entrant. Factors such as consumer loyalty to a particular brand,[94] the closeness of relationships between suppliers and customers, the importance of promotion or advertising, or other advantages relating to reputation[95] will be taken into account in this context. Barriers to entry also encompass situations where the incumbents have already committed to building large excess capacity,[96] or where the costs faced by customers in switching to a new supplier may inhibit entry.

72 The expected evolution of the market should be taken into account when assessing whether or not entry would be profitable. Entry is more likely to be profitable in a

---

88 Case IV/M.1430 - *Vodafone/Airtouch*, point 27; Case IV/M.2016 – *France Télécom/Orange*, point 33.

89 Commission Decision 2002/174/EC in Case COMP/M.1693 – *Alcoa/Reynolds*, OJ L 58, 28.2.2002, point 87.

90 Commission Decision 95/335/EC in Case IV/M.754 – *Anglo American Corp./Lonrho*, OJ L 149, 20.5.1998, p. 21, points 118-119.

91 Commission Decision 97/610/EC in Case IV/M.774 – *Saint-Gobain/Wacker-Chemie/NOM*, OJ L 247, 10.9.1997, p. 1, points 184-187.

92 Commission Decision 94/811/EC in Case IV/M.269 – *Shell/Montecatini*, OJ L 332, 22.12.1994, p. 48, point 32.

93 Commission Decision 98/327/EC in Case IV/M.833 – *The Coca-Cola Company/Carlsberg A/S*, OJ L 145, 15.5.1998, p. 41, point 74.

94 Commission Decision 98/327/EC in Case IV/M.833 – *The Coca-Cola Company/Carlsberg A/S*, OJ L 145, 15.5.1998, p. 41, points 72-73.

95 Commission Decision 2002/156/EC in Case COMP/M.2097 – *SCA/Metsä Tissue*, OJ L 57, 27.2.2002, p. 1, points 83-84.

96 Commission Decision 2001/432/EC in Case IV/M.1813 – *Industri Kapital Nordkem/Dyno*, OJ L 154, 9.6.2001, p. 41, point 100.

market that is expected to experience high growth in the future[97] than in a market that is mature or expected to decline.[98] Scale economies or network effects may make entry unprofitable unless the entrant can obtain a sufficiently large market share.[99]

73   Entry is particularly likely if suppliers in other markets already possess production facilities that could be used to enter the market in question, thus reducing the sunk costs of entry. The smaller the difference in profitability between entry and non-entry prior to the merger, the more likely such a reallocation of production facilities.

Timeliness

74   The Commission examines whether entry would be sufficiently swift and sustained to deter or defeat the exercise of market power. What constitutes an appropriate time period depends on the characteristics and dynamics of the market, as well as on the specific capabilities of potential entrants.[100] However, entry is normally only considered timely if it occurs within two years.

Sufficiency

75   Entry must be of sufficient scope and magnitude to deter or defeat the anti-competitive effects of the merger.[101] Small-scale entry, for instance into some market 'niche', may not be considered sufficient.

(B) Time limits and phases of assessment

A unique feature of the regime under the Regulation is that the Commission is subject to strict time limits. The Regulation provides for two phases (Phase I and II) for the Commission to carry out its merger review; it is important to note however that the Commission is not obliged to go through both of these phases when conducting a merger investigation and that in practice the vast majority of its decisions are reached within Phase I.

I Phase I

The relevant provisions dealing with this in the Regulation are Articles 6 and 10. Article 6 deals with the possible outcome(s) of the Phase I examination, the commitments (to remedy any adverse effects that the concentration may

---

97 See, e.g. Commission Decision 98/475/EC in Case IV/M.986 – *Agfa-Gevaert/DuPont*, OJ L 211, 29.7.1998, p. 22, points 84–85.

98 Case T-102/96, *Gencor v Commission*, [1999] ECR II-753, paragraph 237.

99 See, e.g. Commission Decision 2000/718/EC in Case IV/M.1578 – *Sanitec/Sphinx*, OJ L 294, 22.11.2000, p. 1, point 114.

100 See, e.g. Commission Decision 2002/174/EC in Case COMP/M.1693 – *Alcoa/Reynolds*, L 58, 28.2.2002, points 31–32, 38.

101 Commission Decision 91/535/EEC in Case IV/M.68 – *Tetra Pak/Alfa Laval*, OJ L 290, 22.10.1991, p. 35, point 3.4.

have on competition) the parties may offer and the cancellation of the decision taken under Article 6(1)(a) and (b) by the Commission in certain circumstances. Article 10(1) and (4) on the other hand deal respectively with the time-limits in relation to Phase I and the circumstances in which the period referred to in Article 10(1) may be suspended.

II Phase II

Within the Regulation, Articles 8 and 10 are the relevant provisions dealing with this phase. Phase II proceedings are initiated in the circumstances described in Article 6(1)(c), namely where the Commission finds that the concentration which falls within the scope of the Regulation raises serious doubts as to its compatibility with the Common Market and so requires a further, more detailed, investigation.

The flowchart and table below provide details of Phase I and II investigations and the relevant time limits.

(C) Defences

This part of the chapter considers the possible defences, which parties to a concentration may invoke in the face of an objection to the concentration by the Commission. There are two main defences to be mentioned.

I Efficiencies

An efficiency defence was not recognised by the Commission under Regulation 4064/89; though in practice parties to a concentration would raise issues of efficiency where possible. However following the adoption of Regulation 139/2004 and the publication of the *Guidelines on horizontal mergers*, the Commission now takes into account substantiated efficiency claims by the parties. This is a welcome development given that some concentrations are

Table 10.2 Time limits	
Phase	*Time limit*
Phase I	☐ **25 working days**. Time start to run starting the working day following the receipt of notification ☐ the period above must be increased to **35 working days** if parties offer commitments or a Member State makes referral request
Phase II	☐ **90 working days**. Time start to run the day that follows the date on which the in-depth inquiry was started ☐ The period above may be extended by **20 working days** if a request is made by the parties or by the Commission with their agreement. ☐ An extension to the period in point 1 above of must be increased to **105 working days** if parties offered commitments after the 54th working day after the initiation of the in-depth inquiry

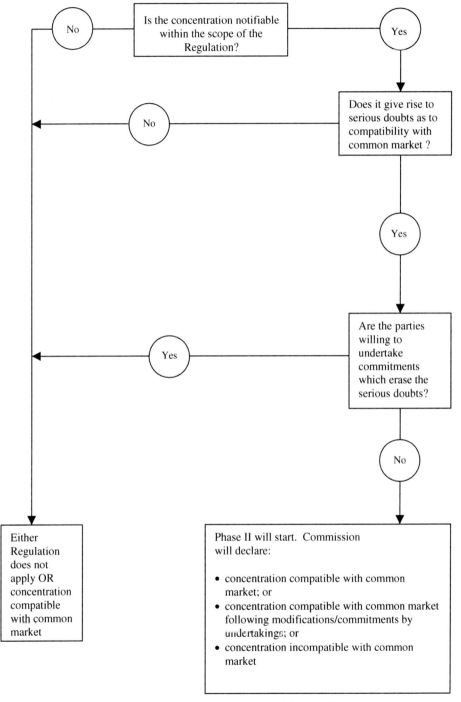

Flowchart: application of Articles 6 and 8

motivated by firms to realise efficiencies. Recitals 4 and 29 of the Regulation (which lack legal force but are persuasive guidance) provide an explanation of the Commission's views on efficiencies and why these should be taken into account when assessing the impact of a concentration on competition. Also, Article 2(1)(b) of the Regulation, which was mentioned above, refers to 'the interests of the intermediate consumers, and the development of technical and economic progress', a highly important consideration when assessing any efficiency claims. The *Guidelines* deal with the efficiencies defence in paragraphs 76–88.

Guidelines on assessment of horizontal mergers OJ 2004 C 31/5

76   Corporate reorganisations in the form of mergers may be in line with the requirements of dynamic competition and are capable of increasing the competitiveness of industry, thereby improving the conditions of growth and raising the standard of living in the Community.[102] It is possible that efficiencies brought about by a merger counteract the effects on competition and in particular the potential harm to consumers that it might otherwise have.[103] In order to assess whether a merger would significantly impede effective competition, in particular through the creation or the strengthening of a dominant position, within the meaning of Article 2(2) and (3) of the Merger Regulation, the Commission performs an overall competitive appraisal of the merger. In making this appraisal, the Commission takes into account the factors mentioned in Article 2(1), including the development of technical and economic progress provided that it is to the consumers' advantage and does not form an obstacle to competition.[104]

77   The Commission considers any substantiated efficiency claim in the overall assessment of the merger. It may decide that, as a consequence of the efficiencies that the merger brings about, there are no grounds for declaring the merger incompatible with the common market pursuant to Article 2(3) of the Merger Regulation. This will be the case when the Commission is in a position to conclude on the basis of sufficient evidence that the efficiencies generated by the merger are likely to enhance the ability and incentive of the merged entity to act pro-competitively for the benefit of consumers, thereby counteracting the adverse effects on competition which the merger might otherwise have.

78   For the Commission to take account of efficiency claims in its assessment of the merger and be in a position to reach the conclusion that as a consequence of efficiencies, there are no grounds for declaring the merger to be incompatible with the common market, the efficiencies have to benefit consumers, be merger-specific and be verifiable. These conditions are cumulative.

102 See Recital 4 of the Merger Regulation.
103 See Recital 29 of the Merger Regulation.
104 *Cf.* Article 2(1)(b) of the Merger Regulation.

Benefit to consumers

79 The relevant benchmark in assessing efficiency claims is that consumers[105] will not be worse off as a result of the merger. For that purpose, efficiencies should be substantial and timely, and should, in principle, benefit consumers in those relevant markets where it is otherwise likely that competition concerns would occur.

80 Mergers may bring about various types of efficiency gains that can lead to lower prices or other benefits to consumers. For example, cost savings in production or distribution may give the merged entity the ability and incentive to charge lower prices following the merger. In line with the need to ascertain whether efficiencies will lead to a net benefit to consumers, cost efficiencies that lead to reductions in variable or marginal costs[106] are more likely to be relevant to the assessment of efficiencies than reductions in fixed costs; the former are, in principle, more likely to result in lower prices for consumers.[107] Cost reductions, which merely result from anti-competitive reductions in output, cannot be considered as efficiencies benefiting consumers.

81 Consumers may also benefit from new or improved products or services, for instance resulting from efficiency gains in the sphere of R&D and innovation. A joint venture company set up in order to develop a new product may bring about the type of efficiencies that the Commission can take into account.

82 In the context of coordinated effects, efficiencies may increase the merged entity's incentive to increase production and reduce prices, and thereby reduce its incentive to coordinate its market behaviour with other firms in the market. Efficiencies may therefore lead to a lower risk of coordinated effects in the relevant market.

83 In general, the later the efficiencies are expected to materialise in the future, the less weight the Commission can assign to them. This implies that, in order to be considered as a counteracting factor, the efficiencies must be timely.

84 The incentive on the part of the merged entity to pass efficiency gains on to consumers is often related to the existence of competitive pressure from the remaining firms in the market and from potential entry. The greater the possible negative effects on competition, the more the Commission has to be sure that the claimed efficiencies are substantial, likely to be realised, and to be passed on, to a sufficient degree, to the consumer. It is highly unlikely that a merger leading to a market position approaching that of a monopoly, or leading to a similar level of market power,

---

105 Pursuant to Article 2(1)(b), the concept of "consumers" encompasses intermediate and ultimate consumers, i.e. users of the products covered by the merger. In other words, consumers within the meaning of this provision include the customers, potential and/or actual, of the parties to the merger.

106 Variable costs should be viewed as those costs that vary with the level of production or sales over the relevant time period. Marginal costs are those costs associated with expanding production or sales at the margin.

107 Generally, fixed cost savings are not given such weight as the relationship between fixed costs and consumer prices is normally less direct, at least in the short run.

can be declared compatible with the common market on the ground that efficiency gains would be sufficient to counteract its potential anti-competitive effects.

Merger specificity

85   Efficiencies are relevant to the competitive assessment when they are a direct consequence of the notified merger and cannot be achieved to a similar extent by less anticompetitive alternatives. In these circumstances, the efficiencies are deemed to be caused by the merger and thus, merger-specific.[108] It is for the merging parties to provide in due time all the relevant information necessary to demonstrate that there are no less anti-competitive, realistic and attainable alternatives of a non-concentrative nature (e.g. a licensing agreement, or a cooperative joint venture) or of a concentrative nature (e.g. a concentrative joint venture, or a differently structured merger) than the notified merger which preserve the claimed efficiencies. The Commission only considers alternatives that are reasonably practical in the business situation faced by the merging parties having regard to established business practices in the industry concerned.

Verifiability

86   Efficiencies have to be verifiable such that the Commission can be reasonably certain that the efficiencies are likely to materialise, and be substantial enough to counteract a merger's potential harm to consumers. The more precise and convincing the efficiency claims are, the better the Commission can evaluate the claims. Where reasonably possible, efficiencies and the resulting benefit to consumers should therefore be quantified. When the necessary data are not available to allow for a precise quantitative analysis, it must be possible to foresee a clearly identifiable positive impact on consumers, not a marginal one. In general, the longer the start of the efficiencies is projected into the future, the less probability the Commission may be able to assign to the efficiencies actually being brought about.

87   Most of the information, allowing the Commission to assess whether the merger will bring about the sort of efficiencies that would enable it to clear a merger, is solely in the possession of the merging parties. It is, therefore, incumbent upon the notifying parties to provide in due time all the relevant information necessary to demonstrate that the claimed efficiencies are merger-specific and likely to be realised. Similarly, it is for the notifying parties to show to what extent the efficiencies are likely to counteract any adverse effects on competition that might otherwise result from the merger, and therefore benefit consumers.

88   Evidence relevant to the assessment of efficiency claims includes, in particular, internal documents that were used by the management to decide on the merger, statements from the management to the owners and financial markets about the expected efficiencies, historical examples of efficiencies and consumer benefit, and

---

108 In line with the general principle set out in paragraph 9 of this notice.

pre-merger external experts' studies on the type and size of efficiency gains, and on the extent to which consumers are likely to benefit.

II Failing firm

The other possible defence which emerged under the EC system of merger control prior to the adoption of Regulation 139/2004 is the 'failing firm defence' which was recognised and clarified by the ECJ in the case of *France v. Commission* (see p. 602 below). The *Guidelines on horizontal mergers* include three short paragraphs dealing with this defence which embody the conditions set out by the ECJ that need to be satisfied in order for the defence to be successfully invoked.

Guidelines on assessment of horizontal mergers (cited above)

89   The Commission may decide that an otherwise problematic merger is nevertheless compatible with the common market if one of the merging parties is a failing firm. The basic requirement is that the deterioration of the competitive structure that follows the merger cannot be said to be caused by the merger.[109] This will arise where the competitive structure of the market would deteriorate to at least the same extent in the absence of the merger.[110]

90   The Commission considers the following three criteria to be especially relevant for the application of a 'failing firm defence'. First, the allegedly failing firm would in the near future be forced out of the market because of financial difficulties if not taken over by another undertaking. Second, there is no less anti-competitive alternative purchase than the notified merger. Third, in the absence of a merger, the assets of the failing firm would inevitably exit the market.[111]

91   It is for the notifying parties to provide in due time all the relevant information necessary to demonstrate that the deterioration of the competitive structure that follows the merger is not caused by the merger.

(D) Remedies

Part B above mentioned indirectly that certain concentrations may be cleared by the Commission subject to commitments, which the parties may offer in order

109 Joined Cases C-68/94 and C-30/95, *Kali and Salz*, paragraph 110.
110 Joined Cases C-68/94 and C-30/95, *Kali and Salz*, paragraph 114. See also Commission Decision 2002/365/EC in Case COMP/M.2314 - *BASF/Pantochim/Eurodiol*, OJ L 132, 17.5.2002, p. 45, points 157-160. This requirement is linked to the general principle set out in paragraph 9 of this notice.
111 The inevitability of the assets of the failing firm leaving the market in question may, in particular in a case of merger to monopoly, underlie a finding that the market share of the failing firm would in any event accrue to the other merging party. See Joined Cases C-68/94 and C-30/95, *Kali and Salz*, paragraphs 115-116.

to erase any concerns the Commission may have concerning the concentration. Commitments are mentioned in a few places in the Regulation: Article 6(2) and Article 8(2). These two provisions provide the legal basis for commitments. Recital 30 of the Regulation also deals with the issue of commitments.

The issue of commitments or (as it is sometimes referred to) remedies is extremely important in practice and both the Commission and business firms and their legal advisors are aware of this. Hence, the Commission has published important guidance on this issue and which explains the Commission's approach in this area (the *Notice on Remedies*). The *Notice* deals with, among other things, possible types of remedies (which are mainly structural and behavioural) and their implementation in practice.

(E) Restrictions directly related and necessary

The final issue to be considered in this part of the chapter is that of 'restrictions directly related and necessary' to the implementation of a concentration which the parties may agree to *inter se*, meaning between themselves. The concept which in the past used to be called 'ancillary restraints' can be found in four places in the Regulation: Recital 21, Article 6(1)(b) and Article 8(1) and (2), all of which make clear that a decision by the Commission declaring that a concentration is compatible with the common market must be taken to cover such restrictions. This important point did not exist originally under Regulation 4064/89 and was added into Regulation 139/2004 following the CFI's ruling in *Lagardère SCA and Canal+ SA v. Commission* requiring the Commission to consider such restrictions as part of its assessment. No doubt for business firms and their legal advisors this change of approach offers greater legal certainty. The Commission's most recent Notice dealing with such restrictions is its 2004 *Notice on restrictions directly related and necessary to concentrations* which came to replace an earlier Notice published in 2001.

6 Joint ventures

In the commercial world firms often realise that a sought after goal could be best achieved in partnership. This is the case in many industries, for example hi-tech fields such as media and telecommunications, where the investment, resources and expertise needed for the project can be considerable and the risk of project failure may be quite high or capital intensive industries such as the pharmaceutical sector. In these cases, a joint venture of two or more firms may be the best commercial solution to lessen the risks associated.

(A) Background to Regulation

Joint ventures are of particular significance in EC competition law. One must consider how joint ventures should be assessed under EC competition rules and what instrument should be used for this purpose: Article 81 or Regulation 139/2004?

As was stated earlier in the chapter, prior to the adoption of Regulation 4064/89 the EC lacked a specific mechanism to deal with mergers and so the choice this question poses could not have arisen. With the adoption of Regulation 4064/89, this question arose and is of high practical importance. The Commission's answer was to introduce a distinction between 'concentrative' and 'cooperative' joint ventures. The former were said to fall within the scope of Regulation 4064/89 and the latter had to be assessed under Article 81.

This was not an easy distinction to draw in practice and for a variety of reasons (the benefit of the strict time limits of the Regulation etc.) the tendency of lawyers was to try to classify an operation as 'concentrative' rather than 'cooperative'. In 1997 the Commission quite sensibly removed this distinction and replaced it with the concept of 'full function joint ventures'. Thus a full function joint venture fell within the scope of the Regulation and other types of joint ventures were to be assessed outside it. In 1998 the Commission in addition to publishing its helpful *Notice on the concept of concentration* also published a Notice specifically dealing with full function joint ventures (extracted below).

Article 3(4) of Regulation 139/2004, like Article 3(2) of Regulation 4064/89, states that 'the creation of a joint venture performing on a lasting basis all the functions of an autonomous economic entity shall constitute a concentration'.

The assessment of full function joint ventures under the Regulation requires an application of the appraisal test and a consideration of the appraisal criteria in Article 2. As we saw in part 5, section (A) above, this test is used in the case of other concentrations as well. However, the important point to note in the case of full function joint ventures is that Article 2 contains an additional test in paragraphs (4) and (5) which is used in situations where the creation of a full function joint venture has as its object or effect the *coordination* of the competitive behaviour of undertakings. This additional test is an application of Article 81(1) and (3) in such cases in order to establish whether or not the operation is compatible with the common market. It should be mentioned however that although this test derived from Article 81, the Commission's appraisal of this issue must be reached within the applicable time-limits of the Regulation.

(B) Joint venture within the scope of the Regulation: the requirements

It may be helpful to give a breakdown of the key requirements which should be considered and satisfied for a joint venture to amount to a concentration. Two requirements need to be satisfied:

I Joint venture must be 'full-function'

First, the joint venture must be a viable economic entity in its own right entailing a structural change in the parents rather than, for example merely being a distribution agency acting on behalf of the parents. Full function entities are characterised by dedicated management, staffing, budgeting, and access to the relevant market. The Commission has explained the requirements as follows:

Commission Notice on the concept of full-function joint ventures OJ (1998) C 66/1

11   Article [3(4)] provides that the joint venture must perform, on a lasting basis, all the functions of an autonomous economic entity. Joint ventures which satisfy this requirement bring about a lasting change in the structure of the undertakings concerned. They are referred to in this Notice as 'full-function' joint ventures.

12   Essentially this means that a joint venture must operate on a market, performing the functions normally carried out by undertakings operating on the same market. In order to do so the joint venture must have a management dedicated to its day-to-day operations and access to sufficient resources including finance, staff, and assets (tangible and intangible) in order to conduct on a lasting basis its business activities within the area provided for in the joint-venture agreement.[6]

13   A joint venture is not full-function if it only takes over one specific function within the parent companies' business activities without access to the market. This is the case, for example, for joint ventures limited to R&D or production. Such joint ventures are auxiliary to their parent companies' business activities. This is also the case where a joint venture is essentially limited to the distribution or sales of its parent companies' products and, therefore, acts principally as a sales agency. However, the fact that a joint venture makes use of the distribution network or outlet of one or more of its parent companies normally will not disqualify it as 'full-function' as long as the parent companies are acting only as agents of the joint venture.[7]

14   The strong presence of the parent companies in upstream or downstream markets is a factor to be taken into consideration in assessing the full-function character of a joint venture where this presence leads to substantial sales or purchases between the parent companies and the joint venture. The fact that the joint venture relies almost entirely on sales to its parent companies or purchases from them only for an initial start-up period does not normally affect the full-function character of the

---

6   Case IV/M.527 – *Thomson CSF/Deutsche Aerospace*, of 2 December 1994 (paragraph 10) – intellectual rights, Case IV/M.560 – *EDS/Lufthansa* of 11 May 1995 (paragraph 11) – outsourcing, Case IV/M.585 – *Voest Alpine Industrieanlagenbau GmbH/Davy International Ltd*, of 7 September 1995 (paragraph 8) – joint venture's right to demand additional expertise and staff from its parent companies, Case IV/M.686 – *Nokia/Autoliv*, of 5 February 1996 (paragraph 7), joint venture able to terminate 'service agreements' with parent company and to move from site retained by parent company, Case IV/M.791 – *British Gas Trading Ltd/Group 4 Utility Services Ltd*, of 7 October 1996, (paragraph 9) joint venture's intended assets will be transferred to leasing company and leased by joint venture.

7   Case IV/M.102 – *TNT/Canada Post etc.* of 2 December 1991 (paragraph 14).

joint venture. Such a start-up period may be necessary in order to establish the joint venture on a market. It will normally not exceed a period of three years, depending on the specific conditions of the market in question.[8]

Where sales from the joint venture to the parent companies are intended to be made on a lasting basis, the essential question is whether, regardless of these sales, the joint venture is geared to play an active role on the market. In this respect the relative proportion of these sales compared with the total production of the joint venture is an important factor. Another factor is whether sales to the parent companies are made on the basis of normal commercial conditions.[9]

In relation to purchases made by the joint venture from its parent companies, the full-function character of the joint venture is questionable in particular where little value is added to the products or services concerned at the level of the joint venture itself. In such a situation, the joint venture may be closer to a joint sales agency. However, in contrast to this situation where a joint venture is active in a trade market and performs the normal functions of a trading company in such a market, it normally will not be an auxiliary sales agency but a full-function joint venture. A trade market is characterised by the existence of companies which specialise in the selling and distribution of products without being vertically integrated in addition to those which are integrated, and where different sources of supply are available for the products in question. In addition, many trade markets may require operators to invest in specific facilities such as outlets, stockholding, warehouses, depots, transport fleets and sales personnel. In order to constitute a full-function joint venture in a trade market, an undertaking must have the necessary facilities and be likely to obtain a substantial proportion of its supplies not only from its parent companies but also from other competing sources.[10]

15 Furthermore, the joint venture must be intended to operate on a lasting basis. The fact that the parent companies commit to the joint venture the resources described above normally demonstrates that this is the case. In addition, agreements setting up a joint venture often provide for certain contingencies, for example, the failure of the joint venture or fundamental disagreement as between the parent companies.[11] This may be achieved by the incorporation of provisions for the eventual dissolution of the joint venture itself or the possibility for one or more parent companies to withdraw

---

8 Case IV/M.560 – *EDS/Lufthansa* of 11 May 1995 (paragraph 11); Case IV/M.686 *Nokia/Autoliv* of 5 February 1996 (paragraph 6); to be contrasted with Case IV/M.904 – *RSB/Tenex/Fuel Logistics* of 2 April 1997 (paragraph 15-17) and Case IV/M.979 – *Preussag/Voest-Alpine* of 1 October 1997 (paragraph 9-12). A special case exists where sales by the joint venture to its parent are caused by a legal monopoly downstream of the joint venture (Case IV/M.468 – *Siemens/Italtel* of 17 February 1995 (paragraph 12), or where the sales to a parent company consist of by-products, which are of minor importance to the joint venture (Case IV/M.550 – *Union Carbide/Enichem* of 13 March 1995 (paragraph 14).

9 Case IV/M.556 – *Zeneca/Vanderhave* of 9 April 1996 (paragraph 8); Case IV/M.751 – *Bayer/Hüls* of 3 July 1996 (paragraph 10).

10 Case IV/M.788 – *AgrEVO/Marubeni* of 3 September 1996 (paragraphs 9 and 10).

11 Case IV/M.891 – *Deutsche Bank/Commerzbank/J.M. Voith* of 23 April 1997 (paragraph 7).

from the joint venture. This kind of provision does not prevent the joint venture from being considered as operating on a lasting basis. The same is normally true where the agreement specifies a period for the duration of the joint venture where this period is sufficiently long in order to bring about a lasting change in the structure of the undertakings concerned,[12] or where the agreement provides for the possible continuation of the joint venture beyond this period. By contrast, the joint venture will not be considered to operate on a lasting basis where it is established for a short finite duration. This would be the case, for example, where a joint venture is established in order to construct a specific project such as a power plant, but it will not be involved in the operation of the plant once its construction has been completed.

II Joint control by the parents

The second criterion for assessment under the Regulation (rather than Article 81) is that the new full function joint venture must be under joint control by the parties. The issue of joint control was discussed briefly at p. 452 above. The following paragraphs are intended to complement that discussion; however they specifically concern joint ventures.

Notice on the concept of concentration (cited above)

21   Joint control may exist even where there is no equality between the two parent companies in votes or in representation in decision-making bodies or where there are more than two parent companies. This is the case where minority shareholders have additional rights which allow them to veto decisions which are essential for the strategic commercial behaviour of the joint venture.[21] These veto rights may be set out in the statute of the joint venture or conferred by agreement between its parent companies. The veto rights themselves may operate by means of a specific quorum required for decisions taken at the shareholders' meeting or by the board of directors to the extent that the parent companies are represented on this board. It is also possible that strategic decisions are subject to approval by a body, e.g. supervisory board, where the minority shareholders are represented and form part of the quorum needed for such decisions.

22   These veto rights must be related to strategic decisions on the business policy of the joint venture. They must go beyond the veto rights normally accorded to minority shareholders in order to protect their financial interests as investors in the joint venture. This normal protection of the rights of minority shareholders is related to decisions on the essence of the joint venture, such as changes in the statute, an

---

12 Case IV/M.791 – *British Gas Trading Ltd/Group* 4 Utility Services Ltd of 7 October 1996, (paragraph 10); to be contrasted with Case IV/M.722 – *Teneo/Merill Lynch/Bankers Trust* of 15 April 1996 (paragraph 15).
21 Case T 2/93 – *Air France v Commission*. Case IV/M.010 – *Conagra/Idea*, of 3 May 1991.

increase or decrease in the capital or liquidation. A veto right, for example, which prevents the sale or winding-up of the joint venture does not confer joint control on the minority shareholder concerned.[22]

23   In contrast, veto rights which confer joint control typically include decisions and issues such as the budget, the business plan, major investments or the appointment of senior management. The acquisition of joint control, however, does not require that the acquirer has the power to exercise decisive influence on the day-to-day running of an undertaking. The crucial element is that the veto rights are sufficient to enable the parent companies to exercise such influence in relation to the strategic business behaviour of the joint venture. Moreover, it is not necessary to establish that an acquirer of joint control of the joint venture will actually make use of its decisive influence. The possibility of exercising such influence and, hence, the mere existence of the veto rights, is sufficient.

24   In order to acquire joint control, it is not necessary for a minority shareholder to have all the veto rights mentioned above. It may be sufficient that only some, or even one such right, exists. Whether or not this is the case depends upon the precise content of the veto right itself and also the importance of this right in the context of the specific business of the joint venture.

Appointment of management and determination of budget

25   Normally the most important veto rights are those concerning decisions on the appointment of the management and the budget. The power to co-determine the structure of the management confers upon the holder the power to exercise decisive influence on the commercial policy of an undertaking. The same is true with respect to decisions on the budget since the budget determines the precise framework of the activities of the joint venture and, in particular, the investments it may make.

Business plan

26   The business plan normally provides details of the aims of a company together with the measures to be taken in order to achieve those aims. A veto right over this type of business plan may be sufficient to confer joint control even in the absence of any other veto right. In contrast, where the business plan contains merely general declarations concerning the business aims of the joint venture, the existence of a veto right will be only one element in the general assessment of joint control but will not, on its own, be sufficient to confer joint control.

Investments

27   In the case of a veto right on investments, the importance of this right depends, first, on the level of investments which are subject to the approval of the parent companies

---

22 Case IV/M.062 – *Eridania/ISI*, of 30 July 1991.

and, secondly, on the extent to which investments constitute an essential feature of the market in which the joint venture is active. In relation to the first criterion, where the level of investments necessitating approval of the parent companies is extremely high, this veto right may be closer to the normal protection of the interests of a minority shareholder than to a right conferring a power of co-determination over the commercial policy of the joint venture. With regard to the second, the investment policy of an undertaking is normally an important element in assessing whether or not there is joint control. However, there may be some markets where investment does not play a significant role in the market behaviour of an undertaking.

Market-specific rights

28   Apart from the typical veto rights mentioned above, there exist a number of other veto rights related to specific decisions which are important in the context of the particular market of the joint venture. One example is the decision on the technology to be used by the joint venture where technology is a key feature of the joint venture's activities. Another example relates to markets characterised by product differentiation and a significant degree of innovation. In such markets, a veto right over decisions relating to new product lines to be developed by the joint venture may also be an important element in establishing the existence of joint control.

. . .

34   In the case where a new joint venture is established, as opposed to the acquisition of minority shareholdings in a pre-existing company, there is a higher probability that the parent companies are carrying out a deliberate common policy. This is true, in particular, where each parent company provides a contribution to the joint venture which is vital for its operation (e.g. specific technologies, local know-how or supply agreements). In these circumstances, the parent companies may be able to operate the joint venture with full cooperation only with each other's agreement on the most important strategic decisions even if there is no express provision for any veto rights. The greater the number of parent companies involved in such a joint venture, however, the more remote is the likelihood of this situation occurring.

. . .

36   Joint control is not incompatible with the fact that one of the parent companies enjoys specific knowledge of and experience in the business of the joint venture. In such a case, the other parent company can play a modest or even non-existent role in the daily management of the joint venture where its presence is motivated by considerations of a financial, long-term-strategy, brand image or general policy nature. Nevertheless, it must always retain the real possibility of contesting the decisions taken by the other parent company, without which there would be sole control.

37   For joint control to exist, there should not be a casting vote for one parent company only. However, there can be joint control when this casting vote can be exercised

only after a series of stages of arbitration and attempts at reconciliation or in a very limited field.[24]

The Notices *on full function joint venture* and *the concept of concentration* include extremely valuable information. In particular, the paragraphs extracted above are worth consulting in order to assess the two important requirements which as we saw above must be met for a joint venture to amount to a concentration.

(C) Appraisal of joint ventures: case study

Paragraphs 4 and 5 of Article 2 deal with the situation where a joint venture may give rise to risk of coordination and refer to the test which is used in this case, namely that contained in Article 81(1) and (3). It is important to note that the paragraphs only apply in the case of full function joint ventures and not in the case of other types of concentration.

Although the vast majority of joint venture cases do not give rise to risk of coordination within the meaning of the paragraphs, it would be helpful to provide a case study taken from a the Commission's decision in the case of *Schibsted/Telia/Telenor*, in which the Commission considered the issue of coordination and the additional test under Article 2 (paragraphs 38–46 of the decision), as well as the other key provisions of the Regulation. The decision was adopted under Regulation 4064/89; however the decision still remains relevant.

Schibsted/Telia/Telenor OJ (1999) C 220/28

The parties planned to commence a joint venture 'NewCol' for the provision of Internet services to consumers and business customers mainly in Sweden. The Commission carried out a typical assessment identifying the operation as a concentration: assessing whether it is a full-function joint venture; performing the relevant calculations to determine that there is a Community dimension; determining the relevant product market and upstream and downstream markets; carrying out the assessment under Article 2 of the Regulation; and finally concluding that the concentration is indeed compatible with the operation of the common market.

Commission

I. PARTIES

3   The parties involved in this transaction are (1) Telia AB, wholly-owned by the Swedish state, is the main telecommunications operator in Sweden, providing a

24 Case IV/M.425 – *British Telecom/Banco Santander*, of 28 March 1994.

broad range of telecommunications services both in Sweden and abroad, including enhanced services through its shareholding in Unisource; Telia is also an Internet Service Provider (ISP); Internet services in the Swedish language are provided by Telia InfoMedia Interactive AB (2) Telenor AS is the main Norwegian telecommunications operator; its subsidiary Telenor Nextel AS offers a number of Internet related services; it is a shareholder in Telenordia (33%, the other parent companies are BT and TeleDanmark), which provides telecommunications services on the Swedish market. Telenordia's subsidiary Algonet is an ISP on the Swedish market; (3) the Norwegian Schibsted group is involved in a range of media-related activities such as newspapers, television, films and multimedia; its subsidiary Schibsted Multimedia AS has a number of Internet related activities, including the provision of content, in Sweden via Scandinavia On-Line AB, which is jointly owned by Telenor AS. Schibsted also has a stake in *Aftonbladet*, a newspaper in Sweden which also has an Internet edition.

II. THE OPERATION

4   The joint venture company will take over the assets and activities of Telia InfoMedia and Scandinavia On-Line AB (SOL). Its activities will be (1) Internet gateway services: through the gateway, consumers and businesses can have access to a range of services presently offered by SOL and InfoMedia, such as financial information, games, business and financial information, shopping, travel, ticket sales; revenues will be generated by advertising, commissions on transactions and subscriptions; related to the gateway services are the provision of Internet advertising services (2) web site production for third parties, including design of web sites and related programming. Initially, NewCoI's services will be provided in the Swedish language.

III. CONCENTRATION

Joint Control

5   Telia and Schibsted shall each own 40% of the share capital of the joint venture and Nextel shall own 20%. The Board of Directors of the joint venture will consist of seven members. . . .

6   Section 7 of the shareholders' agreement provides that certain decisions require unanimity at the board and at the general meeting. These matters include
– material changes to the business plan, and
– the fixing of the annual budget framework.

The annual budget framework includes [Deleted: business secret]. The business plan established by the parties contains inter alia [Deleted: business secret]. The unanimity requirement is reinforced by a provision in Section 7 of the shareholders' agreement stipulating that in case of doubt a matter falls under the unanimity clause.

7   The effect of this section is that NewCoI cannot act on certain critical issues except with the consent of all the parties. Consequently, NewCoI will be subject to joint control by Telia, Schibsted and Nextel.

Full function entity

8   The parties will contribute to NewCoI most of the assets and activities of InfoMedia and SOL. Both companies currently operate as independent business entities.

9   NewCoI will have its own organisation and will initially have around [Deleted: business secret] staff which will enable it to perform all its functions independently. After a start-up period NewCoI is expected to finance its activities through its own resources or financing. The sales which NewCoI will make to its parent companies are estimated by the parties to be less than 10% of its total sales. The joint venture will acquire certain services from the parents, for example [Deleted: business secret]. However, these will be acquired on an arm's length basis and will also be available from other suppliers.

10   The shareholders' agreement is valid until [Deleted: business secret] and subsequently subject to automatic renewal for [Deleted: business secret] year periods. Telia and Schibsted are prohibited from transferring their shares in NewCoI until [Deleted: business secret]. Nextel may transfer its shares from [Deleted: business secret].

     NewCoI will accordingly perform on a long-lasting basis all the functions of an autonomous economic entity.

IV. COMMUNITY DIMENSION

11   Telia has a worldwide turnover of 5,369 MECU, Nextel 3,182 MECU and Schibsted 668 MECU which taken together is more than ECU 5 billion. Telia and Nextel have an aggregate Community-wide turnover of more than ECU 250 million. Telia and Schibsted alone achieved two thirds of their aggregate Community-wide turnover within one and the same Member State, namely Sweden. Nextel did not achieve more than two thirds of its aggregate Community-wide turnover in Sweden.

     The concentration therefore has a Community dimension within the meaning of Article 1 of the Merger Regulation.

12   Telia, Nextel and Schibsted achieved more than two thirds of their annual EFTA-wide turnover in Norway. The undertakings concerned have a combined turnover in the territory of the EFTA states that equals 25% or more of their total turnover in the EEA territory. All undertakings concerned have a turnover exceeding ECU 250 million in the territory of the EFTA States. Consequently, the operation is an EFTA co-operation case pursuant to Article 58 and Protocol 24 of the EEA Agreement.

V. RELEVANT PRODUCT MARKET

13   In their notification, the parties identified three product markets: provision of 'gateway' services over the Internet; advertising on the Internet; and production of Internet web-sites and related services. These, and other possible relevant markets, are examined below.

14   Gateway services do not appear to constitute a market in themselves. As described above, gateways, such as the Passagen service currently provided by Telia InfoMedia, are essentially a kind of web-site hosting several different services or groups of services some or all of which may be provided by third parties. They are generally financed through advertising rather than subscription income and most are supplied free of charge to Internet subscribers by Internet Service Providers (ISPs) as part of the access package (see below). Gateway services can thus be taken into account in the examination of the markets defined below.

15   In Bertelsmann/Burda/HOS Lifeline [Case No. IV/M.973] the Commission found that provision of paid-for content (e.g. games, special news services) on the Internet constituted a separate market, distinct from that for Internet advertising. This was because the two activities generated revenue in different ways and from different sources (advertising from the advertiser, but paid-for content from the subscriber); moreover the two activities were frequently carried out by different undertakings and required substantially different inputs. This approach will be followed here.

16   The parties consider that the production of web sites is a separate product market as the service provided demands both design and computer skills and which implies that the service constitutes a separate market. Web site production may be sufficiently technical and specialised to justify a separate market definition.

17   The provision of access to the Internet to end users is a separate activity from those identified above. A physical connection between the final user and the ISP is usually made either by means of a connection over a public switched telephone circuit, known as "dial up" access, or by means of a dedicated private line (dedicated access). Dial up Internet access is usually the choice for lower usage customers – such as the residential or small business customers at whom the joint venture's services are mainly aimed. Such access consists essentially of the supply to subscribers of an Internet address, provision of the relevant software to enable messages to be sent and received in the correct electronic format used for Internet traffic; and 'connectivity' – access to all other networks which together make up the Internet. Other features may also be supplied as part of an access package, such as 'search engines', or gateway or content services. The joint venture company itself is not present on this dial up Internet access market, but two of its parents (Telia and Telenor) are, and it is clearly closely related to the joint venture's markets. It is accordingly not a relevant market for the assessment of dominance, but is considered further from the viewpoint of co-ordination (Article 2(4) of the Merger Regulation) below.

18   In any event, as the operation does not create or strengthen a dominant position on any of those markets, all the above market definitions can be left open.

VI. RELEVANT GEOGRAPHIC MARKET

19   According to the notifying parties, the market for advertising should normally be regarded as national, considering the adaptations to which publicity campaigns are subject when used on different national markets. Although the parties also submit that issues of language etc. are less relevant considerations when advertising on the Internet, the HOS Lifeline decision appears to confirm that this can be considered on a national basis. It appears clear that the geographic market is at least national in scope, possibly on a linguistic basis.

20   The parties did not submit that Internet subscription content was an affected market. The SOL service being proposed by the parties is Swedish language in scope and some services, such as the Stockholm city guide service will be local in scope. However, other subscription content could be demanded across borders. In the light of this operation, the likely scope for the content to be offered by the joint venture is national, especially as there are separate SOL companies offering similar services in Norway and Denmark.

21   According to the parties, the geographic scope for the market for web site production and related services is also national. This is based on the parties' experience in the market and is illustrated by the fact that the main web production undertaking in Sweden has different subsidiaries in the other Nordic countries. However, the market is unlikely to be less than national in scope and may well be wider.

22   As the market for dial up Internet access is not a relevant product market for the analysis of dominance, the relevant geographic market will be examined as part of the analysis of co-ordination effects below.

23   In any event, as the operation does not create or strengthen a dominant position on any of the above markets, all the above definitions of geographic markets can be left open.

VII. COMPETITIVE ASSESSMENT

Dominance

24   For Internet advertising, according to the notifying parties, all three parent companies are on the market. Telia, through InfoMedia, has a market share of [Business secret: between 10% and 20%] which will be contributed to the joint venture, Schibsted (through its 49% controlling stake in Aftonbladet Hierta AB) has [Business secret: less than 10%]% and Telenor a market share of [Business secret: less than 5%]%. This appears to be a rapidly growing market with many market actors. The

investigation of the Commission resulted in the conclusion that the market shares listed above will not create or strengthen a dominant position.

25   For paid for content provision, the notifying parties have not provided any data as they have not identified it as a separate market. The joint venture will offer games, financial information, business services, automotive, shopping, travel and ticketing. Most of these services will be supplied free of charge and therefore they will fall into the Internet advertising market as defined above.

26   For web site production, Telia will contribute part of its activities to the joint venture and Telenor will remain on the market. According to the parties, Telia's market share is [Business secret: less than 5%]%, Telenor is less than [Business secret: less than 5%]% and the joint venture [Business secret: less than 5%]%. This does not create or strengthen a dominant position.

27   In the light of the above information, and even based on the most unfavourable market definition, the operation does not create or strengthen a dominant position on any market.

Co-ordination of Competitive Behaviour
28   Pursuant to Article 2 (4) Merger Regulation, a joint venture having as its object or effect the co-ordination of the competitive behaviour of (at least two of) its parent companies has to be appraised in accordance with the criteria of Article [81(1)] and [81(3)] EC-Treaty. In order to establish a restriction of competition in the sense of Article [81(1)] EC-Treaty, it is necessary that the co-ordination of the parent companies' competitive behaviour is likely and appreciable and that it results from the creation of the joint venture, be it as its object or its effect.

1. Definition of candidate markets for co-ordination
29   Candidate markets for co-ordination are those on which the joint venture and at least two parent companies are active, or closely related neighbouring markets where at least two parent companies remain active.

(a) Relevant product markets (services and access markets)
30   The joint venture will be active in the provision of various services linked to the use of Internet, which are described above (Section V). As far as these markets are concerned, at least two of the parent companies are active on the market for web site production. However, beside these joint venture markets, another market could be identified on which at least two of the parent companies are active. This market, which concerns the provision of dial-up access to the Internet, constitutes a market which is closely related to that of the joint venture, in the sense of Article 2(4) of the Merger Regulation.

(i) Advertising over the Internet

31 Concerning the market for the provision of advertising over the Internet, it can be stated that only Schibsted Multimedia AS remains active on it after the creation of the joint venture. Therefore, this market can not be considered as a candidate market for co-ordination.

(ii) Paid for content provision

32 Concerning the market for the provision of subscriber content over the Internet, none of the three parent companies will remain active on the same product market as the joint venture following the operation. Telenor Nextel AS and Schibsted Multimedia AS were, prior to the creation of the joint venture, active on it through their jointly owned subsidiary Scandinavia OnLine AB. This subsidiary being entirely transferred to the joint venture as Telenor Nextel's and Schibsted's joint contribution to it, these two parent companies are not active on this market as a result of the creation of the joint venture. Telia has contributed its activities on this market to the joint venture. Schibsted provides content through the on-line version of the newspaper it owns (Aftonbladet), but this service is offered for free and therefore is on the Internet advertising market. Therefore, this market cannot be considered as a candidate market for co-ordination.

(iii) Web site production and related services

33 According to the indications submitted by the parties in the notification, two of the parent companies remain active on the market for the production of web sites. These companies are Telia, through its subsidiary Telia Promotor AB, and Telenor Nextel, through Bonnier Telenor Företagsinfo AB. InfoMedia, which also provides these services, will be contributed to the joint venture. The production of web sites therefore constitutes a candidate market for co-ordination between the parent companies of the joint venture.

(iv) Dial up Internet access

34 Generally speaking, dial up Internet access provided by Internet Service Providers (ISPs) who charge subscriptions to customers constitutes a discrete market, according to the market definitions as set out above.

35 All three parent companies are active on different markets from the above mentioned joint venture markets. Both Telia and Telenor (through Telenordia which has entered into a joint venture with BT and TeleDanmark) provide a full range of telecommunication services, whereas Schibsted is active in the field of multimedia services.

36 Telia and Telenordia (Algonet) provide dial up Internet access to users. Access to the Internet is a necessary prerequisite for the use of any Internet service. The dial up Internet access market must therefore be considered as a market upstream to

the joint venture's markets. This upstream market is to be considered as closely related to the joint venture's markets and therefore constitutes a candidate market for co-ordination in the sense of Article 2(4) of the Merger Regulation.

Given that the creation of the joint venture does not raise concerns under Article 2 of the Merger Regulation, all of the above market definitions can be left open.

(b) Relevant geographical market

37   For web site production, as it is likely to be generally done in Swedish, the relevant geographic market is at least as wide as Sweden or Sweden plus the Swedish language communities in other Nordic countries. However, there is no technical barrier to these services being provided outside Sweden and the Nordic countries. The Internet services of the joint venture will be offered in Swedish language for private and business users in Sweden. Although access to Internet content in Sweden is available from outside Sweden, this does not widen the market definition as the content offered is aimed specifically at consumers in Sweden. Therefore, the relevant geographical market for dial up Internet access is Sweden.

2. Assessment under Article 2(4)

38   The parties submitted that co-ordination of the competitive behaviour between the parent companies is not the object of the creation of the joint venture. In the absence of clear indications to prove that such an object is pursued, an intended co-ordination of the parent companies' behaviour can not be established.

39   However, it might be the effect of the operation to give way to co-ordination of competitive behaviour. This question has to be examined separately for the web site production market and for the dial up Internet access market.

Web site production and related services

40   On the web site production market, which is one of the joint venture markets, two parent companies will remain active. According to the parties' indications, the combined market share of the parent companies does not exceed [Business secret: less than 5%]% on this market and the joint venture will have a market share of [Business secret: less than 5%]%. This total market share of [Business secret: less than 10%]% on the Swedish market, which is the narrowest and most unfavourable to the parties, in any event would not allow the conclusion that any restriction of competition is appreciable.

41   Therefore, in the light of the above, even if the parent companies were to co-ordinate their activities on the web site production market this co-ordination could not lead to an appreciable restriction of competition and it is therefore not necessary to establish a causal link between the creation of the joint venture and the behaviour of the parent companies outside the joint venture on this closely related market.

Dial up Internet access

42   The dial up Internet access market is characterised by high growth [According to information obtained during the Commission's investigation, the growth rate in Sweden in the next three years will be around 30%] and relatively low barriers to entry. The costs of starting a small ISP providing a dial up service are low and small companies can and do provide dial up Internet access. According to information supplied by the parties, there are around 100 such ISPs in Sweden. Entry is also possible from both local start-up ISPs and global ISPs entering the Swedish market. In addition, as the market is very price sensitive, in particular given the low switching costs, this would prevent higher prices through co-ordination from being sustained. Any increase in prices would result in the parties quickly losing market share to rival companies as new subscribers opted for lower price offerings.

43   Telia is present on this market. Telenor, through Telenordia (33%, the other parent companies are BT and TeleDanmark), is also present. Telia and Telenordia hold substantial market shares [Telia has a [25-40%] market share and Telenordia has [10-25%] of the market defined above. The largest service provider offering dial up Internet access in Sweden is Tele2 (a telecommunications company which is a member of the Kinnevik Group, a leading Nordic media company), which has a [40-50%] market share. However, on the basis of other information received, it appears that if the market share of Telenordia were to be attributed to Telenor, their total market share would be [35-65%]. Figures in square brackets are business secrets. This data is on the basis of information obtained from the notifying parties and other third parties during the investigation. Other third party estimates have put the leading three companies market shares as being lower than these figures (Tele2: 36%; Telia: 25%; Telenordia (Algonet): 13%)]. However, market shares are of limited significance on this growing market. In any case, the combined market share of Telia and Telenordia has fallen by between 15% and 20% of the total market over the last nine months.

44   Given the characteristics identified above, the market structure is not conducive to co-ordination of competitive behaviour.

45   The relative size of the markets for Internet advertising, content and web site pro-duction (the markets of the joint venture) compared with that of dial up Internet access is relevant to the likelihood of co-ordination., The dial up Internet access market is substantially larger than the other markets mentioned above [According to information obtained by the Commission during its investigation, the proportion of revenues derived from access is 93% in Sweden compared with 7% from all other Internet revenue sources] and therefore given the relative sizes of the markets concerned, the likelihood of co-ordination is reduced further.

46   Therefore, in the light of the above and on the basis that the narrowest market definition has been chosen, there is no likelihood that the parent companies would co-ordinate on the dial up Internet access market and it is therefore not necessary to

establish a causal link between the creation of the joint venture and the behaviour of the parent companies outside the joint venture on this related market.

VIII. ANCILLARY RESTRICTIONS

47 The obligations which the parties have requested to be treated as an integral part of or ancillary to the proposed concentration include a non competition clause which states that none of the parties may provide within Sweden any service which is in direct competition with such services as the parties decide that NewCoI will provide without competition from its parents; at present only gateway services are subject to this prohibition. The non-compete obligation is applicable during the time a party holds shares in the company and for [Deleted: business secret] thereafter. This clause can be considered as directly related and necessary to the implementation of the concentration as long as the shareholder retains a controlling shareholding in the joint venture.

IX. CONCLUSION

48 In the light of the above information, the proposed concentration does not raise serious doubts as to its compatibility with the common market and with the functioning of the EEA agreement.

The Commission therefore has decided not to oppose the notified operation and to declare it compatible with the common market and with the functioning of the EEA agreement. This decision is adopted in application of Article 6 (1) b of Council Regulation No 4064/89.

7 Enforcement functions of the Commission

As chapter 14 will reveal, the Commission enjoys wide powers of investigation under Regulation 1/2003. These powers however concern the application of Articles 81 and 82. The Commission's powers of investigation under Regulation 139/2004 are not as extensive as those found in Regulation 1/2003: for example Article 21 of the latter which allows the Commission to carry out inspections in the homes of company directors has no equivalent under the Regulation.

This does not mean however that the Commission does not enjoy sufficient powers to carry out effective investigations in merger cases. Indeed, the provisions of the Regulation show that its powers of investigation under the Regulation are broadly the same as those it enjoys under Regulation 1/2003. These provisions include: Article 11 (the power to request information), Article 13 (the powers to carry out inspections), Article 14 (the power to impose fines) and Article 15 (the power to impose periodic penalties). An important

Table 10.3

Situation	Regulation 4064/89	Regulation 139/2004
Supplying incorrect or misleading information	Fines between €1,000-€5,000	Fines not exceeding 1% of the aggregate turnover of the undertakings concerned
Production of books or records required by the Commission in incomplete form during inspection by the Commission	As above	As above
Refusal to submit to an inspection ordered by decision taken by Commission	As above	As above
Periodic penalty to compel persons/undertakings concerned to supply complete and correct information requested or submit to an inspection ordered by decision taken by the Commission	Fines not exceeding €25,000 for each day of delay	Fine not exceeding 5% of the average daily turnover of the undertakings concerned for each working day of delay
Periodic penalty to compel persons/undertakings concerned to comply with an obligation imposed by the Commission in relation to a derogation granted under Article 7 or commitment accepted under Article 8	Fines not exceeding €100,000 for each day of delay	As above
Periodic penalty to compel persons/undertakings concerned to comply with orders made in relation to dissolving a concentration implemented in contravention of the provisions of the Regulation or restoring the situation prevailing before the implementation of the concentration	As above	As above

point to note about the last two provisions of the Regulation which becomes immediately obvious following a simple comparison between them and their equivalents under the old Regulation 4064/89, is that the fines and periodic penalties which the Commission can now impose in the circumstances detailed in the table above are considerably higher than those which could have been imposed under Regulation 4064/89.

Further reading

Camasasca 'The explicit efficiency defence in merger control: does it make the difference?' (1999) 20 ECLR 14

Lindsay 'The new SIEC test in the EC Merger Regulation' (2004) 7 G. C. Rev. 29

Monti and Rousseva 'Failing firm in the framework of the EC Merger Regulation' (1999) 24 ELRev 38

Navarro, Font, Floguera and Briones *Merger Control in the EU* (OUP, 2002)

Wilson *Globalisation and the Limits of National Merger Control Laws* (Kluwer Law International, 2003)

11
UK merger control

1 Introduction

The UK system of merger control underwent a fundamental and radical reform with the enactment of the Enterprise Act 2002 (EA2002). The merger control regime under the Fair Trading Act 1973 (the old regime) suffered from many shortcomings: the insufficient legal certainty, the discretion given to the Secretary of State, and the public interest test. In the new regime created under the EA2002, the role of the UK competition authorities has been considerably strengthened by reducing the scope for intervention by the Secretary of State and adopting a competition-based test for substantive analysis. The Office of Fair Trading (OFT) is run as an independent body and has a statutory duty (and in some cases a discretion) to refer mergers to a specialist investigatory panel, the Competition Commission (CC). The EA2002 also created the Competition Appeal Tribunal (CAT) giving merging parties and third parities an appeal possibility. For these reasons and others, the new system deserves a warm welcome.

2 Concepts and definitions

(A) Relevant merger situation

Section 23 of the EA2002 uses the term 'relevant merger situation' as opposed to 'merger' or 'concentration' (as in the EC) as the circumstances in which the Act applies to mergers. The first issue to consider, therefore, is the meaning of the term.

S. 23 Relevant merger situations

(1) For the purposes of this Part, a relevant merger situation has been created if–
 (a) two or more enterprises have ceased to be distinct enterprises at a time or in circumstances falling within section 24; and
 (b) the value of the turnover in the United Kingdom of the enterprise being taken over exceeds £70 million.

(2) For the purposes of this Part, a relevant merger situation has also been created if–
 (a) two or more enterprises have ceased to be distinct enterprises at a time or in circumstances falling within section 24; and

(b) as a result, one or both of the conditions mentioned in subsections (3) and (4) below prevails or prevails to a greater extent.

(3) The condition mentioned in this subsection is that, in relation to the supply of goods of any description, at least one-quarter of all the goods of that description which are supplied in the United Kingdom, or in a substantial part of the United Kingdom–
(a) are supplied by one and the same person or are supplied to one and the same person; or
(b) are supplied by the persons by whom the enterprises concerned are carried on, or are supplied to those persons.

(4) The condition mentioned in this subsection is that, in relation to the supply of services of any description, the supply of services of that description in the United Kingdom, or in a substantial part of the United Kingdom, is to the extent of at least one-quarter –
(a) supply by one and the same person, or supply for one and the same person; or
(b) supply by the persons by whom the enterprises concerned are carried on, or supply for those persons.

(5) For the purpose of deciding whether the proportion of one-quarter mentioned in subsection (3) or (4) is fulfilled with respect to goods or (as the case may be) services of any description, the decision-making authority shall apply such criterion (whether value, cost, price, quantity, capacity, number of workers employed or some other criterion, of whatever nature), or such combination of criteria, as the decision-making authority considers appropriate.

(6) References in subsections (3) and (4) to the supply of goods or (as the case may be) services shall, in relation to goods or services of any description which are the subject of different forms of supply, be construed in whichever of the following ways the decision-making authority considers appropriate –
(a) as references to any of those forms of supply taken separately;
(b) as references to all those forms of supply taken together; or
(c) as references to any of those forms of supply taken in groups.

(7) For the purposes of subsection (6) the decision-making authority may treat goods or services as being the subject of different forms of supply whenever –
(a) the transactions concerned differ as to their nature, their parties, their terms or their surrounding circumstances; and
(b) the difference is one which, in the opinion of the decision-making authority, ought for the purposes of that subsection to be treated as a material difference.

(8) The criteria for deciding when goods or services can be treated, for the purposes of this section, as goods or services of a separate description shall be such as in any particular case the decision-making authority considers appropriate in the circumstances of that case.

[510]

(9)   For the purposes of this Chapter, the question whether a relevant merger situation has been created shall be determined as at –

(a) in the case of a reference which is treated as having been made under section 22 by virtue of section 37(2), such time as the Commission may determine; and

(b) in any other case, immediately before the time when the reference has been, or is to be, made.

The OFT has further explained the term 'relevant merger situation' in its Guideline on *Mergers: Substantive assessment guidance (OFT516)*.

2.1   The Act's definition of a 'relevant merger situation' covers several different kinds of transaction and arrangement. A company that buys or proposes to buy a majority shareholding or a significant minority shareholding in another company is the most obvious example, but the transfer or pooling of assets or the creation of a joint venture may also give rise to merger situations. The Act's provisions apply both to mergers that have already taken place and to those that are proposed or in contemplation.

. . .

2.3   A merger must meet all three of the following criteria to constitute a relevant merger situation for purpose of the Act:

• two or more enterprises (broadly speaking, business activities of any kind) must cease to be distinct, or there must be arrangements in progress or in contemplation which will lead to enterprises ceasing to be distinct

• either the merger must not yet have taken place or have taken place not more than four months before the reference is made, unless the merger took place without having been made public and without the OFT being informed of it (in which case the four month period starts from the announcement or the time the OFT is told), and

• either:

    – the UK turnover associated with the enterprise which is being acquired exceeds £70 million (known as 'the turnover test'), or

    – the enterprises which cease to be distinct supply or acquire goods or services of any description and, as a result of the merger, together supply or acquire at least 25 per cent of all those particular goods or services of that kind supplied in the UK or in a substantial part of it. To qualify, the merger must result in an increment to the share of supply or consumption and the resulting share must be at least 25 per cent. In practice therefore, the share of supply test can only be met where the enterprises concerned supply or acquire goods or services of a similar kind. (This test is hereafter referred to as 'the share of supply test'.)

2.4   It is implicit in these criteria that at least one of the enterprises must be active within the UK. Where the turnover test is met, this will by definition be because the target generates turnover from sales to UK customers. For the share of supply test, both of the enterprises ceasing to be distinct must be active in supplying or acquiring goods or services within the UK or a substantial part of the UK. These principles apply equally to non-UK companies that sell to (or acquire from) UK customers or suppliers. In assessing whether a firm is active in the UK, the OFT will have regard to whether its sales are made directly or indirectly (via agents or traders) and the extent to which a firm is active at each level of trade.

Two important aspects of the definition given in section 23 should be noted: the first is the phrase 'two or more enterprises have ceased to be distinct' and the second is the 'turnover' or 'supply' test which must be satisfied.

I Enterprises ceasing to be distinct

This state of affairs is defined in section 26 as follows:

S. 26 Enterprises ceasing to be distinct enterprises

(1)   For the purposes of this Part any two enterprises cease to be distinct enterprises if they are brought under common ownership or common control (whether or not the business to which either of them formerly belonged continues to be carried on under the same or different ownership or control).

(2)   Enterprises shall, in particular, be treated as being under common control if they are –
(a) enterprises of interconnected bodies corporate;
(b) enterprises carried on by two or more bodies corporate of which one and the same person or group of persons has control; or
(c) an enterprise carried on by a body corporate and an enterprise carried on by a person or group of persons having control of that body corporate.

(3)   A person or group of persons able, directly or indirectly, to control or materially to influence the policy of a body corporate, or the policy of any person in carrying on an enterprise but without having a controlling interest in that body corporate or in that enterprise, may, for the purposes of subsections (1) and (2), be treated as having control of it.

(4)   For the purposes of subsection (1), in so far as it relates to bringing two or more enterprises under common control, a person or group of persons may be treated as bringing an enterprise under his or their control if –
(a) being already able to control or materially to influence the policy of the person carrying on the enterprise, that person or group of persons acquires a controlling interest in the enterprise or, in the case of an enterprise carried on by a body corporate, acquires a controlling interest in that body corporate; or
(b) being already able materially to influence the policy of the person carrying on the enterprise, that person or group of persons becomes able to control that policy.

The term 'enterprise' may not be one that is readily understood by all competition lawyers and so it is important to understand its exact meaning.

OFT516

2.7 The term 'enterprise' is defined in the Act as the activities, or part of the activities, of a business. This does not mean that the enterprise in question need be a separate legal entity: it simply means that the activities in question should be carried out for gain or reward. However, there is no requirement that the transferred activities generate a profit or dividend for shareholders: indeed, the transferred activities may be loss making or conducted on a not for profit basis.

2.8 An 'enterprise' may comprise any number of components, most commonly including the assets and records needed to carry on the business, together with the benefit of existing contracts and/or goodwill. The transfer of 'customer records' is likely to be important in assessing whether an enterprise has been transferred. In some cases, the transfer of physical assets alone may be sufficient to constitute an enterprise: for example, where the facilities or site transferred enables a particular business activity to be continued. Intangible assets such as intellectual property rights are unlikely, on their own, to constitute an 'enterprise' unless it is possible to identify turnover directly related to the transferred intangible assets that will also transfer to the buyer.

A further key concept in section 26 is that of 'control', which has been explained by the OFT as follows:

OFT516

2.9 'Control' is not limited to the acquisition of outright voting control but includes situations falling short of outright control. The Act distinguishes three levels of control (in ascending order):
- Company A may acquire the ability materially to influence the policy of Company B (known as 'material influence')
- Company A may acquire the ability to control the policy of Company B (known as 'de facto' control), and
- Company A may acquire a controlling interest in Company B (known as 'de jure', or 'legal' control).

2.10 Assessment of material influence requires a case-by-case analysis of the entire relationship between the acquiring entity and the target In making this assessment, the OFT will have regard to all the circumstances of the case. The variety of commercial arrangements entered into by firms makes it difficult to state categorically what will (or will not) constitute material influence. However, the following matters are of particular relevance, although this list is by no means exhaustive.

- A shareholding conferring on the holder 25 per cent or more of the voting rights in a company generally enables the holder to block special resolutions; consequently, a 25 per cent share of voting rights is likely to be seen as presumptively conferring the ability materially to influence policy – even when all the remaining shares are held by only one person. The OFT may examine any case where there is a shareholding of 15 per cent or more in order to see whether the holder might be able materially to influence the company's policy. Occasionally, a holding of less than 15 per cent might attract scrutiny where other factors indicating the ability to exercise influence over policy are present.
- Other factors relevant to an assessment of a particular shareholding may include: the distribution and holders of the remaining shares; patterns of attendance and voting at recent shareholders' meetings; the existence of any special voting or veto rights attached to the shareholding under consideration; and any other special provisions in the constitution of the company conferring an ability materially to influence policy.
- An important factor in the OFT's assessment of material influence is whether the acquiring entity has or will have board representation. In this connection, the OFT will review the proportion of board directors appointed by the acquiring entity and the corporate/industry expertise exercised by members of the board appointed by the acquirer. This in turn requires assessment of the identities, relative experience and incentives of other board members.
- The OFT may also consider whether any additional agreements with the company enable the holder to influence policy. These might include the provision of consultancy services to the target or might, in certain circumstances, include agreements between firms that one will cease production and source all its requirements from the other. Financial arrangements may confer material influence where the conditions are such that one party becomes so dependent on the other that it gains material influence over the company's commercial policy (for example, where a lender could threaten to withdraw loan facilities if a particular policy is not pursued, or where the loan conditions confer on the lender an ability to exercise rights over and above those necessary to protect its investment, say, by options to take control of the company or veto rights over certain strategic decisions).

2.11 There are no precise criteria for determining when an acquirer gains '*de facto*' control of a company's policy; a view has to be taken case by case in the light of the particular circumstances. In general terms, the OFT is likely to reach a belief that merger arrangements give rise to a position of 'de facto' control when an entity is clearly the controller of a company, notwithstanding that it holds less than a 50.1 per cent voting stake in the target company. This might arise for example when an investor's industry expertise leads to its advice being followed in nearly all cases. 'De facto' control might also arise from an ability to veto any shareholder resolution requiring a supramajority for adoption.

2.12 A 'controlling interest' generally means a shareholding of more than 50 per cent of the voting rights in a company. Only one shareholder can have a controlling interest, but it is not uncommon for a company to be subject to the control (in the wider sense) of two or more major shareholders at the same time – in a joint venture, for instance. Thus, as explained in the preceding paragraph, a significant minority shareholder may be seen as being able materially to influence a company's policy even though someone else owns a controlling interest.

The *Guideline* then goes on to explain the situation where control is acquired by stages – an issue which is dealt with under section 29.

2.13   Should a shareholding that confers the ability materially to influence a company's policy increase subsequently to a level which amounts to 'de facto' control or a controlling interest, that further acquisition will produce another merger situation potentially liable to reference to the CC. The same applies to a move from 'de facto' control to a controlling interest.

2.14   In principle, therefore, if Company A acquires Company B in stages, this could give rise to three separate mergers: first, as Company A moves to material influence; then to 'de facto' control; and, finally, to a controlling interest. But further acquisitions of a company's shares by a person who already owns a controlling interest do not give rise to a new merger situation.

2.15   For the purposes of a merger reference, where a person acquires control of an enterprise (in any of the three senses described above) during a series of transactions within a single two-year period, the Act allows them to be considered as having occurred or occurring simultaneously on the date of the last transaction. In giving effect to this provision, the OFT may take into account transactions in contemplation (i.e. where the last of the events within the two-year period has not yet occurred).

(B) Turnover and share of supply test

In addition to showing that two or more enterprises have ceased to be distinct, section 23 provides that a turnover or share of supply test must be satisfied.

| Turnover test

OFT516

2.18   The 'turnover test' is satisfied where the annual value of the UK turnover of the enterprise being taken over exceeds £70 million.

2.19   Generally, it will be straightforward to identify the acquired enterprise whose turnover should be taken into account. Where none of the enterprises remains under the same ownership and control, in a partnership merger or certain joint ventures for example, the value of the turnover of the enterprise being acquired will be calculated as the sum of the turnovers of the two enterprises ceasing to be distinct, less the turnover of the enterprise with the highest turnover.[3] In these cases, in practice, this means that the turnover of both of the enterprises ceasing to be distinct should exceed £70 million.

2.20   In principle, the turnover test applies to the turnover of the acquired enterprise that was generated by customers within the UK in the business year preceding the date of completion of the merger or, if the merger has not yet taken place, the date of the reference to the CC. The figures in the enterprise's latest published accounts will normally be sufficient to measure whether the turnover test is met, unless there have been significant changes since the accounts were prepared. In this circumstance, more recent accounts would provide a better guide to the actual turnover of the enterprises concerned. Where company accounts do not provide a relevant figure, for example because only part of a business is being acquired, OFT will consider evidence presented by the parties and other interested parties to form its own view as to what it believes to be the value of UK turnover for jurisdictional purposes.

Section 27 deals with how the value of the turnover of the enterprise being taken over for the purposes of section 23 is determined.

II Share of supply test

The share of supply test is an alternative test which is contained in subsections 23(3) and (4).

OFT516

2.22   The 'share of supply test' is satisfied only if the merged enterprises:
• both either supply or acquire goods or services of a particular description,
• and will, after the merger takes place, supply or acquire 25 per cent or more of those goods or services, in the UK as a whole or in a substantial part of it.

2.23   Where an enterprise already supplies or acquires 25 per cent of particular goods or services, the test is satisfied so long as its share is increased as a result of the merger. It does not matter how small an increase that may be.

2.24   The Act allows wide discretion in describing the relevant goods or services, requiring only that, in relation to that description, the parties' share of supply or acquisition is 25 per cent or more. The share of supply test is not a market share test, thus the group of goods or services to which the jurisdictional test is applied need not amount to a relevant economic market. Generally, the OFT will have regard to the narrowest reasonable description of a set of goods or services to determine whether

---

3 A partnership merger occurs where a full merger of A and B as equal partners is achieved by Newco C acquiring both. In this circumstance, neither A nor B survives the merger. Both firms are brought under common control, but neither remains under the same control as it was pre merger. The turnovers to be considered are those of A and B.

the share of supply test is met. In so doing, the OFT may have regard to the value, cost, price, quantity, capacity, number of workers employed or any other criterion in determining whether the 25 per cent test is met. This practice is intended to make it easier for companies and their advisers to determine whether the Act applies to a particular merger situation.

2.25   The share of supply test may be applied to the UK as a whole or to a substantial part of it. There is no statutory definition of 'a substantial part'. The House of Lords ruled in the context of similar provisions in the Fair Trading Act 1973 (FTA) that, while there can be no fixed definition, the area or areas considered must be of such size, character and importance as to make it worth consideration for the purposes of merger control.[4] Factors which have been taken into account in cases considered under the FTA include the size, population, social, political, economic, financial and geographic significance of the specified area or areas, and whether it is (or they are) special or significant in some way. The OFT expects to take similar factors into account under the Act.

3 Referral to the Competition Commission

(A) Duty to make merger references

A special feature of UK system of merger control is that a referral mechanism exists in the system whereby the OFT has a *duty* to refer certain mergers to the CC. Sections 22 and 33 respectively deal with the duty of the OFT in relation to completed mergers and anticipated mergers. It is important to note however that this is *not* an absolute duty and that there are cases where the OFT has a discretion as opposed to a duty to refer.

The duty to refer in the case of completed and anticipated mergers will be considered first before considering the discretion of the OFT.

I Completed mergers

Completed mergers concern cases where a relevant merger situation *has been* created.

S. 22 Duty to make references in relation to completed mergers

(1)   The OFT shall, subject to subsections (2) and (3), make a reference to the Commission if the OFT believes that it is or may be the case that –
(a) a relevant merger situation has been created; and
(b) the creation of that situation has resulted, or may be expected to result, in a substantial lessening of competition within any market or markets in the United Kingdom for goods or services.

---

4 See *Regina v Monopolies and Mergers Commission and another ex parte South Yorkshire Transport Limited* [1993] 1 WLR 23.

(2)   The OFT may decide not to make a reference under this section if it believes that –
       (a) the market concerned is not, or the markets concerned are not, of sufficient importance to justify the making of a reference to the Commission; or
       (b) any relevant customer benefits in relation to the creation of the relevant merger situation concerned outweigh the substantial lessening of competition concerned and any adverse effects of the substantial lessening of competition concerned.

(3)   No reference shall be made under this section if –
       (a) the making of the reference is prevented by section 74(1) or 96(3) or paragraph 4 of Schedule 7;
       (b) the OFT is considering whether to accept undertakings under section 73 instead of making such a reference;
       (c) the relevant merger situation concerned is being, or has been, dealt with in connection with a reference made under section 33;
       (d) a notice under section 42(2) is in force in relation to the matter or the matter to which such a notice relates has been finally determined under Chapter 2 otherwise than in circumstances in which a notice is then given to the OFT under section 56(1);
       (e) the European Commission is considering a request made, in relation to the matter concerned, by the United Kingdom (whether alone or with others) under article 22(3) of the European Merger Regulations, is proceeding with the matter in pursuance of such a request or has dealt with the matter in pursuance of such a request; or
       (f) subject to subsection (3A), a reasoned submission requesting referral to the European Commission has been submitted to the European Commission under article 4(5) of the EC Merger Regulation.

(3a)   Subsection (3)(f) shall cease to apply if the OFT is informed that a Member State competent to examine the concentration under its national competition law has, within the time permitted by article 4(5) of the EC Merger Regulation, expressed its disagreement as regards the request to refer the case to the European Commission; and this subsection shall be construed in accordance with that Regulation.

(4)   A reference under this section shall, in particular, specify –
       (a) the enactment under which it is made; and
       (b) the date on which it is made.

(5)   The references in this section to the creation of a relevant merger situation shall be construed in accordance with section 23, the reference in subsection (2) of this section to relevant customer benefits shall be construed in accordance with section 30 and the reference in subsection (3) of this section to a matter to which a notice under section 42(2) relates being finally determined under Chapter 2 shall be construed in accordance with section 43(4) and (5).

[518]

(6)   In this Part "market in the United Kingdom" includes –
        (a) so far as it operates in the United Kingdom or a part of the United Kingdom, any market which operates there and in another country or territory or in a part of another country or territory; and
        (b) any market which operates only in a part of the United Kingdom; and references to a market for goods or services include references to a market for goods and services.

(7)   In this Part "the decision-making authority" means –
        (a) in the case of a reference or possible reference under this section or section 33, the OFT or (as the case may be) the Commission; and
        (b) in the case of a notice or possible notice under section 42(2) or 59(2) or a reference or possible reference under section 45 or 62, the OFT, the Commission or (as the case may be) the Secretary of State.

Section 22(1)(a) provides that it is necessary for the OFT to show that OFT believes that a relevant merger situation has been created. In Guideline OFT516, the OFT explains that it needs only have a reasonable belief that a relevant merger situation has been created. In other words, it interprets the section to mean that a reference is possible if, on the basis of the evidence available to it, there is at least *a significant prospect* that a relevant merger situation exists, and that it is for the CC to determine in the course of its investigation whether the referral amounts to a relevant merger situation. Taking the word 'believe' to refer to reasonable belief is particularly important when dealing with anticipated mergers.

With respect to the OFT's belief that the merger will lead to a substantial lessening of competition under section 22(1)(b), the reader is referred to the discussion below under *One- or two-stage test?* at pp. 544–549 which considers the case of *OFT v. IBA Health*, also extracted below.

II Anticipated mergers

Anticipated mergers concern cases where the relevant merger situation *has yet* to be created.

S. 33 Duty to make references in relation to anticipated mergers

(1)   The OFT shall, subject to subsections (2) and (3), make a reference to the Commission if the OFT believes that it is or may be the case that –
        (a) arrangements are in progress or in contemplation which, if carried into effect, will result in the creation of a relevant merger situation; and
        (b) the creation of that situation may be expected to result in a substantial lessening of competition within any market or markets in the United Kingdom for goods or services.

[519]

(2)   The OFT may decide not to make a reference under this section if it believes that –

(a) the market concerned is not, or the markets concerned are not, of sufficient importance to justify the making of a reference to the Commission;

(b) the arrangements concerned are not sufficiently far advanced, or are not sufficiently likely to proceed, to justify the making of a reference to the Commission; or

(c) any relevant customer benefits in relation to the creation of the relevant merger situation concerned outweigh the substantial lessening of competition concerned and any adverse effects of the substantial lessening of competition concerned.

(3)   No reference shall be made under this section if –

(a) the making of the reference is prevented by section 74(1) or 96(3) or paragraph 4 of Schedule 7;

(b) the OFT is considering whether to accept undertakings under section 73 instead of making such a reference;

(c) the arrangements concerned are being, or have been, dealt with in connection with a reference made under section 22;

(d) a notice under section 42(2) is in force in relation to the matter or the matter to which such a notice relates has been finally determined under Chapter 2 otherwise than in circumstances in which a notice is then given to the OFT under section 56(1);

(e) the European Commission is considering a request made, in relation to the matter concerned, by the United Kingdom (whether alone or with others) under article 22(1) of the EC Merger Regulation, is proceeding with the matter in pursuance of such a request or has dealt with the matter in pursuance of such a request; or

(f) subject to subsection (3A), a reasoned submission requesting referral to the European Commission has been submitted to the European Commission under article 4(5) of the EC Merger Regulation.

(3a)   Section 33(3)(f) shall cease to apply if the OFT is informed that a Member State competent to examine the concentration under its national competition law has, within the time permitted by article 4(5) of the EC Merger Regulation, expressed its disagreement as regards the request to refer the case to the European Commission; and this subsection shall be construed in accordance with that Regulation.

(4)   A reference under this section shall, in particular, specify –

(a) the enactment under which it is made; and

(b) the date on which it is made.

Certain differences exist between sections 22 and 33. Clearly the main difference between these two provisions lies in the retrospective and prospective views, as illustrated by sections 22(1) and 33(1) respectively. The former may consider effects already caused as well as prospective effects, while the latter, understandably, can only anticipate effects that may occur. Other differences, lie in the discretion of the OFT and these are explored below.

(B) Discretion of the OFT

Under sections 22(2) and 33(2) the OFT has discretion not to make a reference in certain cases. This includes where the market or markets concerned are not of sufficient importance; where any 'relevant customer benefits' in relation to the creation of the relevant merger situation outweigh the substantial lessening of competition concerned and any adverse effects following from it; or where, according to section 33(2)(b), in the case of anticipated mergers, the arrangements are not sufficiently far advanced or are not sufficiently likely to proceed to justify the making of a reference by the OFT.

The OFT has provided guidance on the application of these three exceptions in *OFT516*:

OFT516

Exception I: Markets of insufficient importance

7.5   The OFT may decide not to refer a merger to the CC if it believes that the market or markets in question are not of sufficient importance to justify the making of a reference. The purpose of this provision is to avoid references being made where the costs involved would be disproportionate to the size of the markets concerned. By way of guidance, at the time of writing the OFT would expect a CC inquiry to cost around £400,000. This exception is likely to apply only very rarely since in the majority of cases where a substantial lessening of competition is identified, it will be appropriate for the CC to investigate.

7.6   Particular circumstances in which mergers in very small markets might in any event be considered to warrant reference include the following:
- where the product concerned is an important input into a larger market
- where the market is growing quickly, such that current market size is not a good reflection of the actual or potential importance of the market (particularly in new technology markets)
- where the goods or services concerned are considered essential to vulnerable consumers, or
- where the market is one of many smaller or local markets (for the goods or services concerned) that are together of considerable significance.

Exception II: Customer benefits

7.7   For the OFT to exercise its discretion not to refer a merger on this basis, the claimed customer benefits must be clear and, in the case of cost savings, quantifiable.[33] In

---

33 'Customers' include those who are customers of the parties to the merger, as well as intermediate customers, end-consumers, and future customers.

other words, the parties should be able to produce detailed and verifiable evidence of any anticipated price reductions or other benefits. Moreover, the OFT must believe that the claimed benefits will materialise within a reasonable period of time and must believe that such benefits would be unlikely to arise without the merger.

7.8   It is not sufficient to demonstrate that there are merely some theoretical benefits to customers: the merging parties must also show that the parties will have the incentive to pass benefits on to customers and that these benefits will be sufficient to outweigh the competition detriments caused by the merger. Illustrations of situations where such customer benefits might be weighed against the identified loss of competition include the following.

- Lower prices. A merger may, despite leading to a substantial lessening of competition, give clear scope for large cost savings through a reduction in marginal costs of production. In these circumstances, the merged firm – even if it is a monopolist – is likely to pass on some of this reduction in the form of lower prices to its customers.[34]
- Greater innovation. A merger might, in rare cases, facilitate innovation through R&D that could only be achieved through a certain critical mass, especially where larger fixed (and) sunk costs are involved. Exceptionally, the benefits likely to be passed through to customers from such innovation might outweigh the substantial lessening of competition.
- Greater choice or higher quality. One situation in which benefits of this kind might arise is where a merger increases the size of a network, and thus its value to customers.

7.9   The claimed customer benefits must accrue to customers of the merging parties (or to customers in a chain beginning with those customers), but need not necessarily arise in the market(s) where the substantial lessening of competition concerns have arisen. It is therefore conceivable that sufficient customer benefits might accrue in one market as a result of the merger that would outweigh a finding of substantial lessening of competition in another market(s). That said, the OFT's normal expectation is that these customer benefits will arise in the market where the competition concerns have been identified. To show that benefits in one market outweigh an expected substantial lessening of competition in another will require clear and compelling evidence.

7.10   As noted in chapter 4 above, efficiency claims may fall for consideration in the substantial lessening of competition test and/or subsequently in relation to the customer benefits tests. To count as customer benefits, by definition, customers need to be better off with the merger, despite the fact that the OFT believes that the merger might lessen competition substantially. These will be rare cases since, ordinarily, the

---

34 This is because a reduction in the monopolist's marginal costs will, assuming no change in the demand curve (or marginal revenue curve), increase its profit maximising level of output, leading to a reduction in price.

OFT would expect competition to deliver lower prices, higher quality and greater customer choice.

Exception III: Merger insufficiently advanced

7.2   The intention of this provision is to avoid the unnecessary expense of reference where it is still uncertain whether the parties will proceed with the merger. In particular, this provision will ensure that the duty to refer is not triggered when the OFT is informed of transactions on a confidential basis. Hence, merging parties will not be inhibited from seeking informal advice or confidential guidance from the OFT.

7.3   The OFT would usually expect a transaction to be sufficiently advanced to justify reference where:
   • the parties to a transaction have publicly announced a completed merger or their intention to merge (in whole or in part), or
   • one of the parties to a proposed transaction has announced an intention to make an offer for the other notwithstanding that this may be subject to conditions or be a hostile bid.

7.4   In practice, and where this is justified, the OFT would take a view early in an investigation that no real competition analysis is required because of the early stage of proceedings.

It is worth noting that in relation to exception II, this reflects the criteria set out in Section 30 EA2002, which deals with what may amount to a relevant customer benefit and provides that the term includes, among other things, lower prices, better quality and more choice of products to customers.

(C) Situations where a reference cannot be made

Sections 22(3) and 33(3) provide details of situations where a reference cannot be made. These include, among other things, the situation where the OFT is considering whether to accept undertakings in lieu, a situation the OFT explains in Guideline OFT516.

OFT516

Undertakings in lieu of reference

8.2   The OFT can only accept undertakings in lieu of reference in cases where it has concluded that the merger should be referred to the CC.[35] Such a conclusion must

---

35 In other words, undertakings in lieu are only available where the OFT has concluded that a reference is required; and where the exceptions to the duty to refer are not applicable. Accordingly, the OFT will only accept undertakings in lieu to address the underlying competition concerns and not to enhance any perceived customer benefits.

be published and the reasons for reference identified. Any undertakings must be aimed at remedying or preventing the adverse competition effects identified. In considering any such undertakings, the OFT will seek to achieve undertakings in lieu that are sufficient to address clearly the identified adverse competition effects and are proportionate to them. The OFT will also seek to agree undertakings that preserve any merger-specific customer benefits. However, the OFT will not accept undertakings in lieu of reference that do not address the identified competition effects but which are designed instead to 'lock in' sufficient customer benefits to outweigh the risks of a substantial lessening of competition arising.

8.3   In order to accept undertakings in lieu of reference, the OFT must be confident that the competition concerns identified can be resolved by means of undertakings without the need for further investigation. Undertakings in lieu of reference are therefore appropriate only where the competition concerns raised by the merger and the remedies proposed to address them are clear cut, and those remedies are capable of ready implementation. It is for this reason that undertakings in lieu have typically been used in merger cases in the past where a substantial lessening of competition arises from an overlap that is relatively small in the context of the merger (e.g. a few local markets affected by a national merger).

8.4   In cases in which there is doubt over the precise identification of the substantial lessening of competition or in which the effectiveness or proportionality of the proposed undertakings in lieu may be questioned, the OFT considers it unlikely that the 'clear cut' criteria mentioned above would be met. In these circumstances, acceptance of undertakings in lieu would not be appropriate.

8.5   An acquiring company can always take the initiative to propose suitable undertakings if it thinks that they may be appropriate to meet any competition concerns that it foresees. In such cases the company may be willing to resolve the problem by divesting itself of part of its business (a structural undertaking); alternatively, in order to remove the concerns that have been raised, it may give a formal commitment about its future conduct (behavioural undertakings). Alternatively, the OFT may invite companies to consider whether they want to offer undertakings where it believes that it is or may be the case that a merger may raise competition issues potentially warranting reference and which seem amenable to remedy by undertakings in lieu.

The *Guideline* mentions and discusses two types of undertakings: structural and behavioural.

Structural undertakings

8.6   A merger involves a structural change to a market. A structural solution will therefore often be the most appropriate remedy if the OFT believes that it is or may be the case that a merger may (or may be expected to) result in a substantial lessening of competition. The OFT considers that structural undertakings are more likely to be accepted as undertakings in lieu than behavioural undertakings because they clearly address the market structure issues that give rise to the competition problems.

8.7 Typically, structural undertakings require the sale of one of the overlapping businesses that have led to the concern about competition. Ideally, this should be a self-standing business, capable of being fully separated from the merging parties, and in most cases will be part of the acquired enterprise. The sale should be completed within a stated period (usually a maximum of six months). After that an independent trustee may be appointed, at the owner's expense, to monitor the operation of the business pending disposal and/or to handle the sale if the owner has not completed the divestiture within the specified period.

8.8 Before approving the sale of any business as a remedy, the OFT will approve the buyer. This is to ensure that the proposed buyer has the necessary expertise, resources and incentives to operate the divested business as an effective competitor in the market place. If that is not the case, it is unlikely that the proposed divestiture would be an effective remedy for the anti-competitive effects identified.

8.9 In appropriate cases, the OFT will consider other structural or quasi-structural undertakings in lieu of reference. For example, divestment of the buyer's existing business (or part of it) might be appropriate, although in such cases the OFT will also need to consider the competition implications of the asset swap. Alternatively, a remedy such as an amendment to intellectual property licences might in some circumstances be appropriate.

Behavioural undertakings

8.10 Behavioural undertakings can provide a means of moderating the scope for a merged company to behave anti-competitively. The OFT will consider behavioural undertakings where it considers that divestment would be impractical, or disproportionate to the nature of the concerns identified. However, given that structural undertakings are more likely to remedy any competition concerns identified since they address structural changes in the marketplace from which the competitive effects flow, the OFT is unlikely to consider generally that behavioural undertakings have sufficiently clear effects to address the identified competition concerns. Behavioural undertakings may sometimes also be necessary to support structural divestment.

It should be noted that the OFT strongly prefers structural undertakings to be given with respect to the merger for two main reasons. First, they are considered much more effective in preventing the anticipated anti-competitive effects of the merger, as they effectively limit the scope of the merger permitted or compensate for substantial lessening of competition in other ways. Second, they avoid the difficulty and expense for the OFT of enforcement of behavioural undertakings, which can prove prohibitive and undermine the effectiveness of the solution as well as eating up any cost savings of not making an investigation.

[525]

(D) Time limits and prior notice

Section 24 sets out time limits and prior notice in the case of completed mergers and provides that no reference can be made in the case of such mergers if the enterprises ceased to be distinct more than four months prior to the making of the reference or, if later, more than four months before notice of material facts was given to the OFT or the facts are made public. Under section 25 these time limits can be extended in certain cases.

(E) Important points of practice and procedure

The final issue to be mentioned in this part (before turning to consider the determination of merger references by the CC) concerns the OFT's practice prior to making a reference, in particular the notification of mergers by the parties to the OFT.

I Notification

Helpful guidance on the issue of notification has been published by the OFT which is contained in *Mergers: Procedural guidance* (Guideline OFT526). Specific paragraphs in the *Guideline* which are worth noting are paragraphs 3.3–3.26 which explain the five ways in which parties to a merger may ask the OFT to consider their operation. These ways are: informal advice, confidential guidance, pre-notification discussions, statutory voluntary pre-notification and informal submissions/common notification form. It is important to note, however, that unlike the case of the EC, there is no specific requirement for pre-notification of mergers to the OFT.

II The content of the notification

Chapter 4 of *OFT526* provides guidance to the parties and their advisers in compiling informal submissions to the OFT and stipulates three types of information that should be supplied: general background information whether the turnover test or share of supply test are met, jurisdictional information, and information relevant to the substantive assessment. Each of these groups is discussed in the *Guideline*.

III The assessment and decision making process

Chapter 5 of *OFT526* provides important information on key issues in relation to the assessment and decision making process of the OFT. These include: the powers of the OFT to gather information (paragraphs 5.2–5.4); inviting comments on any public merger situation under review from interested third parties, and seeking consultation from competitors and customers of the merging firms and the views of sectoral regulators and other government departments (paragraphs 5.5–5.7); the penalties for notifying parties and third parties supplying false or misleading information which under section 117 EA2002 take the form of a fine, or a maximum of two years imprisonment, or both (paragraph 5.8); the handling of confidential documents and information by the OFT in its operation (paragraphs 5.9–5.11); initial undertakings and orders which the OFT may accept or impose under sections 71 and 72 EA2002 respectively (paragraphs 5.12–5.15); information on the decision making process within the OFT (paragraphs 5.16-5.21); and the amount and payment of fees in merger cases (paragraphs 6.1–6.4).

4 Determination of references and substantive assessment

(A) General

This part will begin by addressing formalities of CC investigations and then turn to substantive merger assessment. Sections 35 and 36 respectively deal with the questions to be decided by the CC in relation to completed mergers and anticipated mergers. It is sufficient here to refer just to section 35.

S. 35 Questions to be decided in relation to completed mergers

(1)   Subject to subsections (6) and (7) and section 127(3), the Commission shall, on a reference under section 22, decide the following questions –
(a) whether a relevant merger situation has been created; and
(b) if so, whether the creation of that situation has resulted, or may be expected to result, in a substantial lessening of competition within any market or markets in the United Kingdom for goods or services.

(2)   For the purposes of this Part there is an anti-competitive outcome if –
(a) a relevant merger situation has been created and the creation of that situation has resulted, or may be expected to result, in a substantial lessening of competition within any market or markets in the United Kingdom for goods or services; or
(b) arrangements are in progress or in contemplation which, if carried into effect, will result in the creation of a relevant merger situation and the creation of that situation may be expected to result in a substantial lessening of competition within any market or markets in the United Kingdom for goods or services.

(3)   The Commission shall, if it has decided on a reference under section 22 that there is an anti-competitive outcome (within the meaning given by subsection (2)(a)), decide the following additional questions –
(a) whether action should be taken by it under section 41(2) for the purpose of remedying, mitigating or preventing the substantial lessening of competition concerned or any adverse effect which has resulted from, or may be expected to result from, the substantial lessening of competition;

(b) whether it should recommend the taking of action by others for the purpose of remedying, mitigating or preventing the substantial lessening of competition concerned or any adverse effect which has resulted from, or may be expected to result from, the substantial lessening of competition; and

(c) in either case, if action should be taken, what action should be taken and what is to be remedied, mitigated or prevented.

(4)   In deciding the questions mentioned in subsection (3) the Commission shall, in particular, have regard to the need to achieve as comprehensive a solution as is reasonable and practicable to the substantial lessening of competition and any adverse effects resulting from it.

(5)   In deciding the questions mentioned in subsection (3) the Commission may, in particular, have regard to the effect of any action on any relevant customer benefits in relation to the creation of the relevant merger situation concerned.

(6)   In relation to the question whether a relevant merger situation has been created, a reference under section 22 may be framed so as to require the Commission to exclude from consideration –

(a) subsection (1) of section 23;

(b) subsection (2) of that section; or

(c) one of those subsections if the Commission finds that the other is satisfied.

(7)   In relation to the question whether any such result as is mentioned in section 23(2)(b) has arisen, a reference under section 22 may be framed so as to require the Commission to confine its investigation to the supply of goods or services in a part of the United Kingdom specified in the reference.

The 'substantial lessening of competition' test is set out in subsection (2). The substantive assessment process is detailed below.

(B) Substantive analysis: 'substantial lessening of competition'

Following the adoption of the EA2002, mergers in the UK are assessed using a substantial lessening of competition test, widely referred to as 'SLC', which also exists in other jurisdictions outside the UK, most notably the USA. Both the OFT and the CC have published extremely helpful information dealing with the meaning and application of this test. Previous parts of the present chapter have already referred to the publications of the OFT (OFT516) and the CC (*Merger References: Competition Commission Guidelines*). The substance of both of these documents in relation to their respective sections on the SLC test is almost identical. In the sections below reference will predominantly be made to the OFT's Guideline (OFT516) with some reference to the CC's Guidelines where appropriate.

I Market definition

This important tool is used when deciding whether a merger results or may result in SLC. The issue of market definition and the economic analysis involved were the subject matter of chapter 2. Both OFT516 and the CC's *Guidelines* contain sections dealing with market definition. Among the other issues which are discussed in these sections are issues related to demand-side and supply-side substitutability and the SSNIP test.

II The SLC test

(a) General

OFT516 gives a good overview of the SLC test and some of the general principles surrounding it:

3.6   Not all mergers give rise to competition issues. First, some mergers are either pro-competitive (because they positively enhance levels of rivalry) or are competitively neutral. Second, many mergers may lessen competition but not substantially, because sufficient post merger competitive constraints will remain to ensure that competition (or the process of rivalry) continues to discipline the commercial behaviour of the merged firm.

3.7   A merger may be expected to lead to a substantial lessening of competition when it is expected to weaken rivalry [between firms] to such an extent that customers would be harmed. This may come about, for example, through reduced product choice, or because prices could be raised profitably, output could be reduced and/or product quality or innovation could be reduced.[7]

3.8   The core concept of the substantial lessening of competition test is a comparison of the prospects for competition with and without the merger. There are three basic merger situations that affect competition in different ways.
  • Horizontal mergers.   Mergers between parties that operate in the same economic market can reduce competitive pressure on the merged firm to the extent that it could unilaterally impose a profitable post merger price increase or otherwise behave anti-competitively. Other firms in the market might unilaterally raise their prices in response, without any collusion among participants. Also, a merger might increase the likelihood (or stability) of coordination, either tacit or explicit, between the firms remaining in the market.[9]

---

7 This guidance uses the concept of 'market power' to describe the ability of a firm or group of firms to achieve these outcomes. It is of course possible that one party or both parties might have market power in advance of the merger.
   . . .

9 Market power can also cover the exercise of monopsony or buyer power. This may arise as a result of a merger where the merged entity attains such levels of buyer power that it can reduce the price it pays to suppliers to a level below the competitive price, leading to an anticompetitive

- Vertical mergers. Mergers between parties which operate at different levels of the supply chain of an industry, though often pro-competitive, may in some circumstances reduce the competitive constraints faced by the merged firm by foreclosing a substantial part of the market to competition (e.g. through refusals to supply, enhanced barriers to entry, facilitating price discrimination raising rivals costs) or by increasing the likelihood of post merger collusion. This risk is, however, unlikely to arise except in the presence of existing market power at one level in the supply chain at least, or in markets where there is already significant vertical integration/restraints.
- Conglomerate mergers.[11] Mergers between firms in different markets will rarely lessen competition substantially. But some such mergers might reduce competition, for example, through the exercise of portfolio power.

3.9   ...Set out below is a summary of the broad analytical elements that the OFT will review in seeking to identify mergers that may be expected to lessen competition substantially.

- The proper frame (or frames) of reference for analysing the immediate competitive constraints faced by the merged entity is identified by defining the relevant product and geographic markets affected by the merger.[12]
- The nature and extent of pre and post merger competition in the identified relevant markets may indicate concerns about a possible loss of rivalry as a result of the merger, particularly where the parties may be each other's closest competitors.[13]
- Where a merger gives rise to possible competition concerns, entry by new competitors or expansion by existing competitors may be sufficient in scope, timeliness and likelihood to deter or defeat any attempt by firms to capitalise on the loss of rivalry by exploiting customers. The rate of growth, relative maturity and dynamics of the relevant product and geographic market(s) may be factors that affect entry.
- Other factors, such as buyer power, might constrain post merger behaviour.
- Notwithstanding the loss of an independent market participant through the merger, rivalry within the market as a whole might be increased through the efficiency gains enjoyed by the merged entity.
- Where one of the merging parties is thought to be failing, judgment of whether the merger would result in a substantial lessening of competition will take account of what would otherwise happen to the assets and business of that firm without the merger.

reduction in suppliers' output. The OFT will apply an analytical framework analogous to that set out in this guidance in assessing whether a merger creates, strengthens or allows the exercise of monopsony market power.

...

11 See also chapter 6 [of OFT 516].
12 See paragraphs 3.11 to 3.22 [of OFT 516].
13 The counterfactual is discussed further in paragraphs 3.23 and 3.24 [of OFT 516].

3.10   The above principles should not be regarded as a mechanical framework for analysis. The process of identifying whether a merger might be expected to lead to a substantial lessening of competition considers the above factors in the round. Different factors may be given greater or less weight depending on the details of a given case and, in many cases, it may not be necessary to consider all of the above factors. The following sections of this guidance expand upon each of these factors.

(b) Identifying the counterfactual

Paragraph 3.8 of *OFT516* states that the core concept of the substantial lessening of competition test is a comparison of prospects for competition with and without the merger. The competitive situation with the merger is of course the factual and that without the merger is referred to by the OFT as the 'counterfactual'. According to the OFT in most cases, 'the best guide to the appropriate counterfactual will be prevailing conditions of competition. However, the OFT may need to take into account likely and imminent changes in the structure of competition in order to reflect as accurately as possible the nature of rivalry without the merger' (OFT516, para 3.24).

(c) The different merger situations

Paragraph 3.8 of OFT516 states that there are three merger situations which affect competition differently: horizontal mergers, vertical mergers and conglomerate mergers. The application of the SLC test in relation to these is considered in chapters 4, 5 and 6 of the *Guideline*.

(i) Horizontal mergers
When assessing horizontal mergers, the OFT provides that the focus of its competitive analysis lies in evaluating how the competitive incentives of the merging parties and their competitors might change as a result of the merger. The starting point for this analysis is the market structure and concentration resulting from the merger.

OFT516

Market structure and concentration

4.2   The level of concentration in a market can be an indicator of competitive pressure within that market. Broadly speaking, the more concentrated the market, the weaker the competitive constraints on merging firms are likely to be. Similarly, the greater the increment to market share resulting from a merger, the more likely it is that the merger might lessen competition.

4.3   The three principal measures used by the OFT to examine market concentration and structure are described below. The choice of which measure to use will often depend on the availability of the data needed for each measure.

- Market shares.   Shares are usually measured by sales revenue. Other measures, such as production volumes, sales volumes, capacity or reserves, may be used as appropriate (for example, where the product concerned is a traded commodity and production capacity therefore represents the best indication of competition strength). Current market shares may be adjusted to reflect expected and reasonably certain future changes, such as a firm's likely exit from the market or the introduction of additional capacity.[18] Comparison of the merged parties' market shares with those of other players in the market may give an indication of potential market power and whether the other players are able to provide a competitive constraint. Historic market shares can also provide useful insights into the competitive dynamics of a market: for example, volatile shares might suggest that there has been effective competition, equally, continuing high market shares are not always indicative of market power.
- Concentration ratios (CRs).   CRs measure the aggregate market share of a small number (usually three (C3) or four (C4)) of the leading firms in a market. They are absolute measures of concentration, taking no account of differences in the relative size of the firms that make up the leading group.
- Herfindahl-Hirschman Index (HHI) . . . [Mentioned and explained at pp. 466–468 above.]

4.4   Each of these measures may be used as an initial indicator of potential competition concerns, but will not give rise to a presumption that a merger may be expected to lessen competition substantially. In other words, further investigation is always required to determine whether a merger will substantially lessen competition.

Possible anti-competitive effects of a horizontal merger

4.5   A horizontal merger is a merger between two firms active (or potentially active) in the same market at the same level of business (e.g. between two manufacturers, two distributors, or two retailers). When horizontal mergers occur, competition may be affected in a number of ways. This loss of a competitor (actual or potential) can change the competitive incentives of the merging firms, their rivals, and their customers, leading to changes in the intensity of competition.[20] A merger can affect entry barriers and buyer power. The merging parties may themselves make efficiency gains as a result of the merger, and in some circumstances this could increase competition in the industry. To assess whether these changes will result in a substantial lessening of competition, the OFT will consider whether the merger has

18 Again, this reflects the core concept of the substantial lessening of competition test. It necessitates a comparison of the extent of rivalry in a market with and without the merger. As described above, the 'without the merger' situation does not always equate to the pre-merger world because of current and imminent market developments such as market entry, expansion, or exit. In these situations, the pre-merger world must be adjusted to represent the world without the merger.
20 It is possible that a merger can reduce the level of concentration, e.g. when a firm with a high market share sells some capacity to a firm with a considerably lower market share or a new entrant.

any of these effects and, in light of this assessment, consider whether sufficient post merger competitive pressure is expected to remain to ensure that the merged entity is not expected to be able to raise prices or reduce output profitably, or otherwise restrict choice/innovation.

4.6 There are two conceptually distinct means by which a horizontal merger might be expected to result in a substantial lessening of competition: non-coordinated effects and coordinated effects. Although they are conceptually distinct, it is possible that a single merger might raise both types of concern.

Non-coordinated effects

4.7 Non-coordinated effects, also referred to as unilateral effects,[21] may arise where, as a result of a merger, the merged firm finds it profitable to raise prices (or reduce output or quality) as a result of the loss of competition between the merged entities. This is because, pre-merger, any increase in the price of the acquiring firm's products would have led to a reduction in sales. However, post merger, any sales lost as a result of a price increase will be partially recaptured by increased sales of the acquired enterprise.[22] So sales lost will no longer be foregone. In addition, the firm may find it profitable to raise also the price of the acquired products, since it will recapture some of the lost sales through higher sales of its original products. Other firms in the market may also find it profitable to raise their prices because the higher prices of the merged firm's products will cause some customers to want to switch to rival products thereby increasing rivals' demand.

4.8 Non-coordinated effects may arise where the market (or markets) concerned have a number of the following characteristics:
- there are few firms in the affected market(s)
- the merging parties are close competitors representing for a substantial number of customers the 'next best alternative' to each other's products, so a merger between the two will prevent those customers from switching to the best rival product in the event of a post merger price increase[23]

21 The term 'unilateral effects' is sometimes misunderstood as referring to action by a single firm, in particular the merged entity. In fact it refers more generally to independent or non-coordinated action by market participants. For the sake of clarity we therefore use the term 'non-coordinated effects'. This unambiguously embraces not only the effect that a merger might have on (say) the pricing of the merging parties, but also possible effects on the pricing of other firms.
22 In assessing whether a price increase would be profitable, it may also be necessary to take into account whether any reduction in sales would adversely affect a firm's cost base and so render the price increase unprofitable (e.g. because economies of scale were no longer being achieved).
23 Closeness of substitutability between the merging firms' products may be tested through assessment of price elasticities (i.e. the relationship between the volume of product sold and its own price (own-price elasticity) or the relationship between the volume of a product sold and the price of another product (cross-price elasticity)), diversion ratios (i.e. the proportion of sales of a product that may be lost to another product in the event of a price increase), other econometric techniques (where possible), or assessment of customer preferences.

- customers have little choice of alternative suppliers, whether because of the absence of alternatives, switching costs, or the ability of suppliers to price discriminate
- it is difficult for rivals to react quickly to changes in price, output or quality, e.g. through product repositioning or supply-side substitution
- there is little spare capacity in the hands of the merged entity's competitors that would allow them to expand to supply customers in the event that the merged entity reduced output, and there is little prospect of expansion of existing capacity
- there is no strong competitive fringe capable of sustaining sufficient levels of post merger rivalry
- one of the merging firms is a 'maverick' – an important rivalrous force in the market representing a competitive constraint greater than its market share indicates, whose elimination may thus be an important change in competitive dynamics
- one of the merging firms is a recent new entrant or a strong potential new entrant that may have had a significant competitive effect on the market since its entry or which was expected to grow into an effective competitive force.

4.9 This is not a checklist of factors or characteristics that must all be present before non-coordinated anti-competitive effects are likely to arise. These factors are intended simply as a broad indication of the circumstances in which the OFT may consider the risk of such anticompetitive effects to be high.

4.10 Though the profits from non-coordinated effects are generally captured by the merging parties, rival firms can also benefit from reductions in competitive pressure as a result of a merger. Even if rival firms pursue the same competitive strategies as they did prior to the merger, this can result in their increasing prices in the wake of a merger. In such cases, the firms in the marketplace are not coordinating their competitive behaviour (tacitly or explicitly); they are simply reacting independently to expected changes in each other's commercial behaviour. Such instances of anti-competitive effects are still termed 'unilateral' or non-coordinated by merger analysts since they are based on independent actions of firms. The change in the structure of the market may mean that other firms will behave differently and may react to an increase in prices by raising their own prices.

Coordinated anti-competitive effects

4.11 A merger situation may also lessen competition substantially by increasing the probability that, post merger, firms in the same market may tacitly (or explicitly) coordinate their behaviour to raise prices, reduce quality or curtail output. This does not necessarily mean express collusion (which is generally an infringement of the Chapter I prohibition of the Competition Act 1998). Given certain market conditions, and without any express agreement, tacit collusion arises merely from an understanding that it will be in the firms' mutual interests to coordinate their decisions. Coordinated effects may arise where a merger situation reduces competitive constraints in a market, thus increasing the probability that competitors will collude or strengthening a tendency to do so.

4.12   In order for tacit coordination to be successful or to become more likely, the OFT considers that three conditions must be met or be created by a merger:[24]
  • the participants must have an ability to align their behaviour in the market
  • the firms must have incentives to maintain the coordinated behaviour, which means detection of deviation from tacit coordination and perhaps also credible 'punishment' of deviating firms through retaliatory behaviour by others, and
  • the coordinated behaviour should be sustainable in the face of other competitive constraints in the market.

4.13   In appropriate cases, the OFT will examine whether each of these three conditions favourable to tacit coordination may be expected to arise. In this assessment, the OFT will review the structure of the market, its characteristics, and any history of coordination in the market concerned.

4.14   Ability to align their behaviour in the market. In order to coordinate tacitly firms need to achieve some kind of understanding as to how to do so. This need not involve an explicit agreement on what price to charge, market share quotas, or the quality of products to be attained. Nor is it necessary for the firms concerned to coordinate prices around the monopoly price, or for the coordination to involve every single firm in the market. However, it is sometimes possible for firms to find tacitly a 'focal' point around which to coordinate behaviour. Market transparency, product homogeneity, stability and symmetry (of size and cost) of the relevant firms are key elements in giving the firms the ability to align on terms of coordination.

4.15   Incentives to maintain coordinated behaviour. Though tacit coordination is in the collective interests of the oligopoly, it is often in firms' short-term individual interests to 'cheat' on the tacit coordination by cutting price, increasing market share, or selling outside 'accepted' territories. If coordinated behaviour is to be maintained, any such 'cheating' must be observable directly or indirectly. For tacit coordination to be sustainable the market concerned should therefore be sufficiently transparent that firms can monitor pricing and other terms of competition with a view to detecting cheating in a timely way and responding to it. Firms might have credible ways of 'punishing' any deviation from the tacit coordination, for example, by rapidly cutting prices or expanding output. More generally, it may be sufficient for coordinated behaviour that participating firms have a strong incentive not to deviate from the coordinated behaviour, rather than that there is a particular punishment mechanism.

4.16   Sustainability of coordinated behaviour. Overall, the conditions of competition in the market should be conducive to tacit coordination in order to sustain the relevant behaviour. Typically, this means that the market should be sufficiently mature, stable and with such limited competition (both actual and potential) that the coordination is not likely to be disrupted. For example, a strong fringe of smaller competitors

---

24 This approach is consistent with that taken by the Court of First Instance in its judgment in *Airtours v Commission* ...

(or perhaps a single maverick firm) or a strong buyer (with buyer power) might be enough to destabilise the oligopoly and render tacit coordination impossible.

Entry and expansion

4.17   Entry by new competitors or expansion by existing competitors may be sufficient in time, scope, and likelihood to deter or defeat any attempt by the merging parties or their competitors to exploit the reduction in rivalry flowing from the merger (whether through coordinated or non-coordinated strategies).

New entry

4.18   New entry and the threat of entry can represent important competitive constraints on the behaviour of merging firms. If entry is particularly easy and likely, then the mere threat of entry may be sufficient to deter the merging parties from raising their prices since any price increase or reduction in output/quality would incentivise that new entry to take place.

4.19   Before new entry (or the threat thereof) may be considered a sufficient competitive constraint, three conditions must be satisfied.

4.20   First, the OFT will examine whether new entry may be expected to occur in the event that the merging parties seek to exercise market power. In this regard, the OFT may review:
- barriers to entry to the market (or markets) and the costs of entry to determine if new entry is in fact feasible,
- the experience of any firms that have entered or withdrawn from the relevant market or markets in recent years,
- evidence of planned entry by third parties, and
- the minimum viable scale needed for entry.

. . .

4.22   Second, any new entry should be of sufficient scope to constrain any attempt to exploit greater post merger market power. Small-scale entry, perhaps into some market niche, may be insufficient to prevent a substantial lessening of competition, even when the entry may be the basis for later expansion.

4.23   Third, the OFT would also need to be satisfied that any such prospective new entry in response to any exercise of market power by the merged firm would be sufficiently timely and sustainable to provide lasting and effective post merger competition. Entry within less than two years will generally be timely, but this must be assessed on a case by case basis.

4.24   Analysis of entry conditions includes considering whether the merged entity would face competition from imports or supply-side substitution to the extent that these have not already been taken into account in market definition. What is important is that competitive constraints posed by imports and possible supply-side substitutes are counted in the analysis (whether they are counted under the heading of market definition or that of entry).

4.25 The effect of a merger on the possibility and/or likelihood of new entry might itself contribute to a substantial lessening of competition where a merger increases barriers to entry or otherwise reduces/eliminates the competitive constraint represented by new entry. This might arise, for example, where the acquired entity was one of the most likely entrants or was genuinely perceived as such by those already in the market: in other words, the merger would substantially lessen pressure from potential competitors. In addition, in some markets, a merger might lead to 'tipping', where the parties' products (or services) would become adopted as the industry standard and competitive pressure may be significantly reduced as a result.

Expansion

4.26 The ability of rival firms in the market to expand their capacity quickly can also act as an important competitive constraint on the merging parties' behaviour. When considering the probability of such expansion as a response to price increases, the OFT will consider similar factors to those set out above for new market entry.

Countervailing buyer power

4.27 The ability of a merged entity to raise prices may be constrained by the countervailing power of buyers. There is a variety of different ways in which a powerful customer might be able to discipline supplier pricing.
- Most commonly, a buyer can simply switch, or credibly threaten to switch, its demand or a part thereof to another supplier. Whether buyers will maintain the same ability to choose among suppliers after the merger is a key issue.
- Even where a customer has (or customers have) no choice but to take the supplier's products, they may still be able to constrain prices if they are able to impose substantial costs on the supplier, e.g. by refusing to buy other products produced by the supplier or by delaying purchases, that they can use as leverage to defeat proposed price increases.
- Retailers may also be able to impose costs on the supplier through their own retail practices, e.g. by positioning the supplier's products in less favourable parts of the shop.
- Buyers might also threaten to enter the market themselves, or sell own-label products or could sponsor entry by others by covering the costs of entry . . .

. . .

Efficiencies

4.29 Efficiency gains are often claimed for mergers. The Act allows the OFT to take efficiency gains into account at two separate points in the analytical framework.

4.30 First, efficiencies may be taken into account where they increase rivalry in the market so that no substantial lessening of competition would result from a merger.

For example, this could happen where two of the smaller firms in a market gain such efficiencies through merger that they can exert greater competitive pressure on larger competitors. Efficiencies in this sense are discussed in the following paragraphs because the OFT will take them into account in assessing whether a merger gives rise to any risk of a substantial lessening of competition.

4.31   Second, efficiencies might also be taken into account where they do not avert a substantial lessening of competition, but will nonetheless be passed on after the merger in the form of customer benefits. For example, if a merger would reduce rivalry in a market but proven efficiencies would be likely to result in lower prices to customers, the OFT would not take this into account in reaching a conclusion on the substantial lessening of competition test, but it might be a consideration under the customer benefits exception to the duty to refer. Efficiencies in this latter sense are discussed in chapter 7 of this guidance.

Efficiencies that increase rivalry

4.32   Where efficiency gains are claimed to have a positive effect on rivalry, their impact can be assessed as an integral part of the substantial lessening of competition analysis. The key question is whether the claimed efficiency will enhance rivalry among the remaining players in the market: for example, where two smaller firms merge to provide more effective competition to a larger rival, or where the merger stimulates the combined firm to invest more in R&D and increase rivalry through innovation.

4.33   Efficiencies are defined broadly for purposes of this guidance. Hence possible efficiencies may include cost savings (fixed or variable), more intensive use of existing capacity, economies of scale or scope, or demand-side efficiencies such as increased network size or product quality.[27] Efficiencies might also encompass pro-competitive changes in the merged entity's incentives, for example by capturing complementarities in, e.g. R&D activity, which in turn might increase incentives to invest in product development in innovation markets.

4.34   In order for the OFT to take account of efficiencies that are claimed to enhance rivalry, they must be: (a) demonstrable; (b) merger-specific; and (c) likely to be passed on to customers.

---

27 Efficiencies are more likely to be taken into account where they impact on marginal or variable costs, as such cost savings tend to stimulate competition and are likely to be passed more directly on to customers in terms of lower prices (because of their importance in short-run price setting behaviour). Generally, savings in fixed costs will not be given such weight as they often represent private gains to companies and are not so important in short-run price formation. However, reductions in fixed costs may play an important role in longer term price formation (because they become variable in the long-run). Fixed costs may also be important in short-run price formation where, for example, competition takes place via auctions and bids reflect both the fixed and variable costs of the tendered service.

- First, demonstrable efficiencies are efficiencies that can be shown to arise clearly and are very likely to arise: prospective efficiency gains are more easily claimed than achieved.
- Second, efficiency gains must be a direct consequence of the merger, i.e. they must be merger-specific. The key issue is that the analysis is incremental analysis, so that efficiencies must be judged relative to what would have happened without the merger.
- Third, the OFT must also be satisfied that there will continue to be sufficient post merger rivalry within the market to ensure that the merged entity has an incentive not only to pursue the claimed cost savings but also to pass on to customers a reasonable share of benefits.

4.35   For the reasons set out above, where mergers raise possible competition concerns, the OFT is generally sceptical, in the absence of compelling evidence, that efficiency gains will not only arise but will also be passed on to a sufficient extent to customers, especially where there are few remaining competitive constraints on the parties. Accordingly, in these situations, the evidence presented by the parties on efficiencies and their likely impact on rivalry must indeed be compelling. This is moreover the case because of the information asymmetries between the OFT and the merging parties in respect of efficiency claims. All of the information relating to such claims is in the hands of the merging parties so it is for them to demonstrate their case on the bases of the information available to them. Such evidence might, for example, include estimates and origin of likely cost-savings as evidence in pre-merger planning and strategy documents, coupled with objective factual and accounting information needed to verify proposed cost saving claims. External consultancy reports pre-dating the merger might also be helpful in this context.

Failing firm defence

4.36   As described above, merger assessment under the substantial lessening of competition test requires that prospective post merger competition be compared with competition without the merger. Where one of the parties to a merger is genuinely failing, pre-merger conditions of competition might not prevail even if the merger were prohibited. In these circumstances, the counterfactual might need to be adjusted to reflect the likely failure of one of the parties and the resulting loss of rivalry.

4.37   In order to satisfy the failing firm defence against a finding of an expected substantial lessening of competition, the following conditions need to be met.
- First, in order to rely on a failing firm defence, the firm must be in such a parlous situation that without the merger it and its assets would exit the market and that this would occur in the near future. Firms on the verge of administration may not meet these criteria whereas firms in liquidation will usually do so. Decisions by profitable parent companies to close down loss-making subsidiaries are unlikely to meet this criteria.

- Second, there must be no serious prospect of re-organising the business. Identifying the appropriate counterfactual in these types of situation is often very difficult. For example, even companies in receivership often survive and recover.
- Third, there should be no less anti-competitive alternative to the merger. Even if a sale is inevitable, there may be other realistic buyers whose acquisition of the plant/assets would produce a better outcome for competition. These buyers may be interested in obtaining the plant/assets should the merger not proceed: that could indeed be a means by which new entry can come into the market. It may also be better for competition that the firm fails and the remaining players compete for its share and assets than that the failing firm's share and assets are transferred wholesale to a single purchaser.

4.38   However, the OFT does not exclude the possibility that the acquisition of a failing firm, which results in a substantial lessening of competition, can result in customer benefits – e.g. by ensuring that customers will continue to be supplied during the process of change or through commitments to honour existing warranties. Such benefits would need to outweigh the customer detriments which arise through the loss of competition. Customer benefits, and how they are assessed, are discussed in more detail later in this guidance.

4.39   Information that the OFT would request in order to give weight to a failing firm defence may include evidence:
- that the company is indeed about to fail imminently under current ownership (including evidence that trading conditions performance are unlikely to improve)
- that all re-financing options have been explored and exhausted
- that there are no other credible bidders in the market, and that all possible options have been explored, and
- how the acquiring firm proposes using the failing firm's assets post merger.

(ii) Vertical mergers
Vertical mergers are dealt with in paragraphs 5.1–5.6 of *OFT516*.

5.1   Vertical mergers are mergers between firms that operate at different but complementary levels in the chain of production and/or distribution. Vertical mergers are often efficiency-enhancing but, even so, they may still give rise to competition concerns. In particular: is the merger expected to foreclose market access anti-competitively (e.g. by raising rivals' costs), or increase the ability and incentive of parties to collude in a market? Each of these issues is discussed below. However, common to both issues is the underlying theme that vertical merger concerns are likely to arise only if market power exists or is created in one or more markets along the supply chain.

Market foreclosure
5.2   A vertically integrated firm may be able to foreclose rivals from either an upstream market for selling inputs or a downstream market for distribution or sales. Foreclosure does not mean simply that a vertically integrated firm is expected to exclude a

non-vertically integrated firm from a market (though this may be the case), but may include a range of behaviours including a refusal to deal, raising barriers to entry, and raising rivals' costs.

- If the merged entity is an important downstream customer for a product that it also supplies upstream, it may in certain circumstances be able to dampen competition from rival suppliers of that product by, for example, sourcing all of its future needs from its own production facility, thus jeopardising the continued existence of alternative upstream suppliers of the product.
- If a merged entity supplies a large proportion of an important input to a downstream process where it also competes, it may be able to dampen competition from its rivals in the downstream market for example by diverting all its production of the input to its own downstream process.
- If the merged entity refuses to supply a product to its downstream rivals, or by only selling the input to its rivals at a price that makes them uncompetitive, this might also foreclose competition.[28] This might be particularly relevant where firms in the downstream market need to stock a full range of products to be competitive; hence, the loss of any product could harm their competitive prospects.
- If the merged entity controls an important means of distribution to a downstream market, it might be able to reduce competition from its rivals by refusing to give them access to that means of distribution, or by granting access only at discriminatory prices that favour the merged entity's own business, thus placing rivals at a cost disadvantage.

5.3 The OFT will be concerned where, in any of the above situations, rivals lack a reasonable alternative to the vertically integrated firm. In this circumstance, rivals may either be deprived of access altogether or might be allowed to obtain the product or the facility only at unfavourable prices, thereby lessening rivalry in the market.

5.4 In assessing whether a merger could have foreclosure effects of this kind, it is important to consider the ability and incentives of the merged firm to foreclose in any market. In certain cases, the merged firm may have the ability to foreclose competition in some way, but lacks incentive to do so as such a strategy would not be profitable. The OFT is developing and will, where possible, use financial modelling and simulation techniques to assess whether foreclosure is likely to be profitable post merger.

Increased potential for collusion

5.5 In rare cases, vertical integration may facilitate collusion by increasing market transparency between firms.[29] Such concerns may arise, for example, where vertical

---

28 In particular there is the possibility that a vertical merger might alter incentives so as to make refusal to supply – or worsening the terms of supply – more credible than premerger, to the detriment of competition and ultimately of consumers.

29 See chapter 4 above for a discussion of collusion as a result of horizontal mergers. The same concepts apply here: alignment, market transparency, monitoring of adherence to the coordinated strategy, incentives not to deviate from that strategy, and competitive conditions conducive to coordination.

integration affords the merged entity better knowledge of selling prices in another market, which facilitates tacit collusion in that market.

Countervailing factors

5.6   As with horizontal mergers, a firm's ability to exercise vertical market power may be constrained if there is buyer power or if barriers to entry are low. For example, if customers might in future be forced to source all their requirements for a particular product from the upstream business of a competitor, the risk of such a situation arising might be alleviated if customers were sufficiently powerful either to resist price increases or to sponsor the emergence of a new supplier. More detail is given on buyer power and barriers to entry in chapter 4.

(iii) Conglomerate mergers

The third category of mergers is conglomerate mergers. *OFT516* contains guidance on this category. It is worth noting that competition authorities in several parts of the world are not particularly concerned about this category of mergers out of their belief that these operations are unlikely – due their nature – to raise competition concerns.

OFT516

6.1   Conglomerate mergers involve firms that operate in different product markets.[30] They may be product extension mergers (i.e. between firms that produce different but related products) or pure conglomerate mergers (i.e. between firms operating in entirely different markets). Such mergers rarely lead to a substantial lessening of competition as a result solely of their conglomerate effects. In a small number of cases, usually where the products acquired are complementary to the acquirer's own products, potentially adverse effects can be identified related to so-called 'portfolio power'.

6.2   When the market power deriving from a portfolio of brands exceeds the sum of its parts, a firm may be said to have 'portfolio power'. This may enable the firm to exercise market power in individual markets more effectively, with the result that competition is substantially lessened. Portfolio effects may have anti-competitive effects where they directly affect market structure, increase the feasibility of entry deterrence strategies and/or eliminate the competitive constraint imposed by firms in neighbouring markets. Each of these is considered in turn below.

---

30 Mergers between firms that are active in the same product market, but which sell in different geographic markets are sometimes termed conglomerate mergers. However, for the purposes of this guidance, the OFT will consider these mergers as a type of horizontal merger since the competition analysis of such mergers could well focus on whether the merger eliminates a potential entrant to each geographic market.

Effect on market structure

6.3   Suppose, for example, that a merger creates a firm with many brands under its control. Where the brands relate to products that share sufficient characteristics to be considered a discrete group, customers may have an incentive to purchase the portfolio from one supplier to reduce their transaction costs. This circumstance may substantially lessen competition if non-portfolio competitors, or those competitors that control only one or a few brands, do not impose an effective competitive constraint on the firm(s) with 'portfolio power'. The circumstances in which such a lessening of competition might arise are discussed below.

Increasing the feasibility of anti-competitive strategies

6.4   Large conglomerates may seek to require or encourage customers to purchase a range of their products, whether through tying or bundling of products or through significant discounts targeted at non-portfolio rivals' customers. A merger may give rise to a significant prospect that tying or bundling may occur if the merged firm controls complementary goods. Such conduct is likely to result in adverse effects on competition, however, only if it would be difficult for rivals or new entrants to provide competing bundles and thus be unable to constrain the behaviour of the merged entity which could then engage in profitable price increases, output reductions or other strategies.

6.5   In rare cases, a conglomerate merger may also make predatory behaviour more feasible, especially where competition is localised so that firms only face a competitive threat on a few brands or a few geographic markets at any one time. A firm may be able to provide an aggressive response to entry or to induce exit by using profits earned in one market to subsidise short-run losses in another market. This may substantially lessen competition if the likely long-run outcome is a more concentrated market. Such behaviour is likely only when the merging firms already have market power in some markets and where barriers to entry are already relatively high, so that the short-run losses can be recouped by higher prices in the long run.

Increased potential for coordination

6.6   Finally, conglomerate mergers may facilitate coordination especially if the merged firm's rivals in one market are also rivals in at least one of its other markets and if other factors facilitating collusion are also present in these markets.

Buyer power and barriers to entry

6.7   In assessing whether a conglomerate merger could have anticompetitive effects, the OFT, will of course, consider the ability of buyers to exercise countervailing power, and in particular the incentives of buyers to buy the portfolio from one supplier.[31] If it is the case that customers can and do source the portfolio products

---

31 Buyer power is discussed more fully in paragraphs 4.27 to 4.28.

from multiple suppliers, and would likely continue to do so post merger, then it is unlikely that the merger would substantially lessen competition.

6.8   As to the possibility of entry constraining the conglomerate supplier, the OFT will primarily consider whether another firm could replicate the portfolio of products offered by the merged entity. In this context, the OFT would also consider whether the creation of the portfolio of products itself represented a strategic barrier to entry and could limit the ability of competitors either to extend their portfolios or to enter new product markets.[32]

OFT516 is a helpful document the substance of which reveals many similarities between the approach of the EC (see previous chapter) and the UK even though the tests applied in the two systems are worded differently.

III One- or two-stage test?

As noted above in the consideration of sections 22 and 33 at p. 519, the OFT has adopted its own view on the concept of 'belief', both with respect to the existence of a relevant merger situation and with respect to a substantial lessening in competition. The OFT has suggested that for that belief to be justified, a 'significant prospect' must exist before it makes a referral to the CC. As a result of the OFT acting as a 'first screen' of all mergers, its belief on summary examination is decisive as to whether the CC ever gets to review the situation. Hence, the question arose as to whether the OFT need only 'believe' that there is no significant prospect that SLC will arise, or whether it also needs to 'believe' that the CC on more extensive analysis will also find that there is no significant prospect of a SLC arising.

This question was considered recently by the Court of Appeal in the case of *OFT and Others v. IBA Health Ltd* in the context of section 33(1).

IBA Health Ltd v. OFT, [2003] CAT 27

The OFT held that a 'relevant merger situation', while giving the parties a large market presence, could not be expected to result in a SLC in future bidding involving the two within the meaning of section 33(1). Accordingly the OFT did not make a reference to the CC. IBA Health Ltd, a competitor to the merging firms, sought and won a declaration from the CAT that the OFT had not applied the correct test.

CAT

190   The use of the word 'may' in the second line of section 33(1) seems to us to signify that, even if those responsible at the OFT are themselves of the view that a merger

32 Barriers to entry are discussed more fully in paragraphs 4.18 to 4.25.

may not be expected to result in a substantial lessening of competition, it still 'may be the case', within the meaning of section 33(1), that the merger may be expected to lead to a substantial lessening of competition, if there is, in fact, an alternative credible view that cannot be reasonably rejected by the OFT on the basis of a 'first screen'.

191   In other words, putting the matter less technically, if there is genuinely 'room for two views' on the question whether there is at least a significant prospect that the merger may be expected to lead to a substantial lessening of competition, then in our opinion the requirement in section 33 (1) that 'it may be the case' that . . . [the merger] may be expected to lead to a substantial lessening of competition, is satisfied.

192   In our opinion, in such circumstances, the statutory duty of the OFT under section 33(1) is not to decide, definitively, which of those two views, it, the OFT, prefers. Under the scheme of the Act, the definitive decision maker, in a case where there is room for two views, is not the OFT but the Commission. If there is room for two views, the statutory duty of the OFT is to refer the matter to the Commission, whose duty is to decide on the question whether the merger may be expected to lead to a substantial lessening of competition, as section 36(1) expressly provides.

193   When we refer to the possibility of there being 'room for two views' in a given case, we do not envisage a case in which the alternative view is merely fanciful, or far-fetched. We envisage a case in which the alternative view is credible. It must be a view which cannot be confidently dismissed on the basis of a 'first screen' investigation.

194   There is also in our view a certain asymmetry under section 33(1) between the situation which arises when the OFT makes a reference, and the situation which arises when the OFT decides not to do so. Even in a case where a substantial lessening of competition seems a likely outcome, in making a reference the OFT does not decide whether, in fact, a substantial lessening of competition may be expected. The OFT simply 'believes' that such 'may be the case', without prejudging or pre-empting the Commission's investigation.

195   Where, however, the situation is the other way round, and the OFT decides not to make a reference it is deciding that the merger does not even reach the threshold of 'it may be the case'. In other words in such circumstances the OFT decides that the merger does not even reach 'the grey area' where there may be room for more than one view. In its practical effect, a decision not to make a reference effectively decides the issue of substantial lessening of competition in the negative. It not only prejudges, but also excludes, any further investigation by the Commission.

196   In the vast majority of cases no practical consequences arise from this asymmetry. An initial search by the Tribunal showed 56 published merger cases considered by the OFT under the Act, of which 21 did not qualify and 31 were cleared in short, clear decisions. Similarly, in the decisions made to refer (such as Unum/Swiss Life

and P&O/Stena) the OFT shows shortly and clearly why the OFT felt that it was under a duty to refer.

197   What is the correct approach in cases in the 'grey area' in between? In a case where real issues as to the substantial lessening of competition potentially arise, it seems to us that the words 'it may be the case' imply a two-part test. In our view, the decision maker(s) at the OFT must satisfy themselves (i) that as far as the OFT is concerned there is no significant prospect of a substantial lessening of competition and (ii) there is no significant prospect of an alternative view being taken in the context of a fuller investigation by the Commission. These two elements may resemble two sides of the same coin, but in our view they are analytically distinct.

198   It is, as we have said, implicit that the OFT in any event must have sufficient material to support its view. It also seems to us implicit in the second limb of the test that the OFT must be able reasonably to discount the possibility of the Competition Commission coming to a different view after a more in-depth investigation. It must be borne in mind throughout that the role of the OFT under the Act is 'a first screen'.

It should be noted that under the CAT's narrow approach, it will be more difficult for the OFT to clear a merger, because there must be 'no significant prospect' of the CC considering that there could be an SLC. Sending more mergers to the CC would entail additional expense, legal uncertainty and delay for mergers with only a slight risk of the CC disagreeing with the OFT's own analysis and create unnecessary legal barriers to business transactions. The merging companies and the OFT (the 'Appellants') appealed to the Court of Appeal. Although the Court of Appeal dismissed the OFT's appeal, it ruled out the existence of a two-stage test under section 33(1). The Vice-Chancellor delivered the judgment of the Court:

OFT and Others v IBA Health Ltd, [2004] EWCA Civ 142

Court of Appeal

38   I have no hesitation in preferring the submissions of the Appellants on this issue. The statutory test, so far as relevant, imposed by s. 33(1) is
       'whether OFT believes that it is or may be the case that the [merger] may be expected to result in a substantial lessening of competition...'
       Thus the relevant belief is that the merger may be expected to result in a substantial lessening of competition, not that the Commission may in due course decide that the merger may be expected to result in a substantial lessening of competition. Further, the body which is to hold that belief is OFT not the Commission.

39   If the test as formulated by CAT is right then, for the reasons advanced by counsel for OFT, other comparable provisions in the Act become unworkable if OFT does not hold the requisite belief but considers that the Commission may. Thus, unless OFT

itself holds the relevant belief it cannot conduct the balancing exercise required by s. 33(2)(c). And if OFT does not hold the relevant belief it has no power to accept undertakings in lieu as provided for in s. 73 and so could not refuse to make a reference as permitted by s. 33(3)(b).

40 Similar problems would arise in connection with the interventions by the Secretary of State as permitted by s. 42. I have set out the relevant provisions in paragraph 25 above. Not only does s. 42 point a clear contrast between a belief and a suspicion but the jurisdiction of the Secretary of State to make a reference to the Commission under s. 45 depends on the OFT holding the relevant belief and expressing it in its report under s. 44. It would be absurd if the jurisdiction of the Secretary of State to make a reference to the Commission should depend on the belief of OFT as to what the Commission might decide.

41 In paragraph 29 I have summarised provisions relating to market investigation references. These provisions also point to the contrast between a belief and a suspicion. Whether or not the Secretary of State gives his consent under s. 150(2) must depend on his own belief, not that of others. It would be contrary to the statutory test if the Secretary of State had to consent notwithstanding that he did not himself believe the relevant fact but could not dismiss as fanciful an alternative view that others might hold.

42 For all these reasons I would reject the two part test formulated by CAT in paragraph 197 of their judgment and applied in paragraphs 228 and 232. Accordingly it is not necessary to consider, assuming it would be permissible to do so, whether the test suggested by CAT would lead to more references, nor whether it would be contrary to certain parliamentary statements. However it is necessary to go further and reach a conclusion on what is the right test in order to deal with the other grounds, summarised in paragraph 266 of the judgment of CAT quoted in paragraph 6 above, on which CAT concluded that the decision of OFT should be quashed.

The Vice Chancellor then went on to deal with the question of what test should be applied under section 33(1).

43 The short (and correct) answer to the question is that the test to be applied is that stated in s. 33(1). The words are ordinary English words; they should be applied in accordance with their ordinary meaning; the Court should not substitute other words for those used by Parliament nor paraphrase nor gloss them. Nevertheless in view of the evident importance of the test and the range of meaning the word 'may' can connote it may help to explain the statutory test by reference to a series of propositions.

44 First, it is apparent from s. 33(1) and the contrast between belief and suspicion demonstrated in ss. 42 and 131 that it is necessary for OFT to form the relevant belief. Thus some form of mental assent is required as opposed to the less positive frame of mind connoted by a suspicion. As pointed out in the Shorter Oxford

English Dictionary 3rd Edition a suspicion is but a 'slight belief'. In *R v Monopolies Commission, ex parte Argyll plc* [1986] 1 WLR 763, 769 Sir John Donaldson MR recast in what he described as simpler language the provision in s. 75 empowering the Secretary of State to make a merger reference to the Commission

'where it appears to him that it is or may be the fact that arrangements are in progress or in contemplation which, if carried into effect, will result in the creation of a merger situation qualifying for investigation'.

The test he adopted was that the Secretary of State might make a merger reference 'if he knows or suspects' that a merger qualifying for investigation has been created or is in contemplation. In my view the slightly different wording of s. 33(1) and the different context of EA, in particular the imposition of a duty rather than the conferment of a power and the distinction drawn in ss. 42 and 131, do not warrant paraphrasing 'believes it … may be the case that' as 'or suspects'.

45 Second, the belief must be reasonable and objectively justified by relevant facts. In *Education Secretary v Tameside BC* [1977] AC 1014 the question was whether the Secretary of State 'is satisfied'. At p. 1047 Lord Wilberforce pointed out that

'This form of section is quite well known, and at first sight might seem to exclude judicial review. Sections in this form may, no doubt, exclude judicial review on what is or has become a matter of pure judgment. But I do not think that they go further than that. If a judgment requires, before it can be made, the existence of some facts, then, although the evaluation of those facts is for the Secretary of State alone, the court must inquire whether those facts exist, and have been taken into account, whether the judgment has been made upon a proper self-direction as to those facts, whether the judgment has not been made upon other facts which ought not to have been taken into account.'

It was not disputed that the belief must be reasonably held as accepted in paragraph 3.2 of OFT guidance quoted in paragraph 30 above.

46 Third, by themselves, the words 'may be expected to result' in paragraph (b) of both s. 33(1) and 36(1) involve a degree of likelihood amounting to an expectation. In paragraph 182 of its judgment CAT expressed the view that these words connoted more than a possibility and adopted what they described as a crude way of expressing the idea of an expectation as a more than 50% chance. No doubt this is right when applied to the single question which the Commission is required to answer under s. 36(1)(b).

47 Fourth, however, the belief that must be held by OFT under s. 33(1)(b) is 'that it is or may be the case that'. This introduces two alternatives, the certainty posed by the word 'is' and the possibility envisaged by the words 'may be'. These alternatives are to be considered in relation to the circumstances set out in sub-paragraphs (a) and (b) combined and imported by reference to 'the case that'. If these alternatives are applied to the circumstance set out in sub-paragraph (a) and then compared with the question the Commission has to answer under s. 36(1)(a) if a reference is ordered it is apparent that the degree of likelihood required by the word 'may'

is less than that required by the answer to question (a) in s. 36(1). The answer in accordance with s. 36 will be that the anticipated merger 'will result in the creation of a relevant merger situation' or not as the case may be. The test for OFT is only whether the anticipated merger 'may result in a relevant merger situation' or not. This is consistent with the respective functions of OFT and the Commission. The former is a first screen, the latter decides the matter. Accordingly, although the word 'may' appears in the opening phrase of s. 33(1) and in paragraph (b) of both s. 33(1) and 36(1) it is clear that the opening phrase 'believes that it ... may be the case' imports a lower degree of likelihood than paragraph (b) in ss. 33(1) or 36(1) would by itself involve. That lower degree of likelihood might, for example, exist in circumstances where the work done by the OFT did not justify any positive view, but left some uncertainty, and where OFT therefore believed that a substantial lessening of competition might prove to be likely on further and fuller examination of the position (which could only be undertaken by the Competition Commission).

48   At the other end of the scale it is clear that the words 'may be the case' exclude the purely fanciful because OFT acting reasonably is not going to believe that the fanciful may be the case. In between the fanciful and a degree of likelihood less than 50% there is a wide margin in which OFT is required to exercise its judgment. I do not consider that it is possible or appropriate to attempt any more exact mathematical formulation of the degree of likelihood which OFT acting reasonably must require. As Lord Mustill observed in *R v Monopolies Commission, ex p S. Yorks Ltd* [1993] 1 WLR 23, 29

   'The courts have repeatedly warned against the dangers of taking an inherently imprecise word, and by redefining it thrusting on it a spurious degree of precision.'

49   In paragraph 3.2 of OFT's published advice the requisite likelihood is described as 'a significant prospect that a merger may be expected to lessen competition substantially'. This substitutes 'significant prospect' for 'may' and is open to criticism on that account. Further I consider that the word 'significant' tends to put the requisite likelihood too far up the scale of probability. With that qualification, I agree with the first and third sentences of that paragraph. It is not necessary to reach any conclusion as to the validity of the observation in the second sentence save to point out the danger of a too ready assumption that nothing has changed.

5 CC investigations and reports-procedure

It is possible for the OFT or the CC to cancel or vary a reference. Details of circumstances where this may be done are contained in section 37. Section 38 deals with Issues related to investigations and reports by the CC such as the content of the reports prepared by the CC. Section 39 provides time-limits for investigations and reports. The CC is required to prepare its report within a period of twenty-four weeks of the date of the reference. This period may be extended by no more than eight weeks (Section 38(3)).

6 Duty to remedy effects of completed or anticipated mergers

Section 41(2) states that where the CC has prepared and published its report and has found that there is (or would be) an anti-competitive outcome, the CC has a *duty* to take such action as it considers to be reasonable and practicable to remedy, mitigate or prevent the SLC or any adverse effects of it. Section 41(3) calls for consistency on the part of the CC in its decisions. Section 41(4) requires the CC when making a decision under section 41(2) to have regard to the need to achieve as comprehensive a solution as is reasonable and practicable to the SLC and any adverse effects resulting from it. Section 41(5) provides that when making its decision the CC may have regard to the effect of any action on any relevant customer benefits in relation to the creation of the relevant merger situation.

The CC explains how it handles, or at least how it intends to handle, the issue of remedies in part 4 of its *Merger References: Competition Commission Guidelines*. Part 4 begins by considering the questions contained in ss. 35(3) and 36(2) (see p. 527 above). Paragraphs 4.6–4.8 of the *Guidelines* deal with consideration of appropriate remedy by the CC. According to paragraph 4.6, in exceptional circumstances the CC might conclude that no remedial action is appropriate, for example where the costs of any practical remedy is disproportionate in light of, among other things, size of the relevant market or where the appropriate remedial action would fall outside the UK. Paragraphs 4.9–4.13 deal with costs of remedies and proportionality. They provide that, among other things, the CC will have regard to the reasonableness of any remedy and that the CC will abide by the principle of proportionality in determining the appropriate remedy. Paragraph 4.11 states that 'environmental costs or the social costs of unemployment will not be assessed by the Commission in its consideration of remedies unless the Commission is required to do so by the Secretary of State through a specific public interest consideration'.

Paragraphs 4.14–4.17 of the *Guidelines* deal with effectiveness of remedies. It is stated that in assessing the effectiveness of remedies certain factors may be relevant. These include: whether the remedy in question is clear to the addressee(s) and to other interested parties, such as the OFT; the prospect of the remedy being implemented and complied with; and the timescale within which the effects of any remedy will occur.

The types of remedies and their appropriateness are discussed in paragraphs 4.18–4.44 of the *Guidelines*. Paragraph 4.18 identifies several types of remedies:

- Remedies intended to restore all or part of the *status quo ante* market structure (such as blocking) a proposed merger;
- Remedies intended to increase the competition that will face the merged entity; and
- Remedies directed at excluding or limiting the possibility that the merged entity will abuse the increased market power as a result of the merger.

7 Public interest cases

The repeal of the public interest test of the FTA1973 has not meant that public interest considerations have been completely eliminated from the system. Sections 42–58 of the EA2002 deal with public interest cases, which are expected to be rare in practice. Under section 42(2) the Secretary of State DTI may give an intervention notice to the OFT if he believes that one or more public interest considerations are relevant to a relevant merger situation. An example of a public interest consideration is national security (see section 58(1)). Section 44 deals with the investigation to be carried out by the OFT and the report to be prepared, which should be sent to the Secretary of State following an intervention notice by the latter. The power of the Secretary of State to make a reference to the CC is contained in section 45 with supplementary issues related to this contained in section 46. Sections 47–53 deal with the determination of the reference by the CC including the duties of the CC (s. 47), its power of variation of references (s. 48) and time limits for its investigations and reports (s. 51). The provisions dealing with the decisions of the Secretary of State and enforcement actions by him are contained in sections 54–55.

The final three sections in Chapter II of Part III of the EA2002 deal with three issues: situations where the Secretary of State decides not to make a reference on the ground that no public interest consideration is relevant (s. 56); the duties of the OFT and CC, including the duty of both authorities to inform the Secretary of State about any representations concerning the exercise of his powers under section 58(3); and national security (s. 58).

8 Other special cases

Chapter 3 of Part III of the Act is entitled 'other special cases' and deals with issues such as special public interest cases and water mergers.

9 Enforcement

Chapter 4 of Part III of the Act contains quite detailed provisions dealing with enforcement by the OFT and the CC. Sections 71–76 deal with the powers which the OFT may exercise before making a reference. These include: accepting initial undertakings from such of the parties concerned for the purpose of preventing pre-emptive action (s. 71); making initial enforcement orders for the purpose of preventing pre-emptive action (s. 72); accepting undertakings in lieu of a reference (s. 73); making an order where the undertakings accepted under section 73 are not fulfilled or false and misleading information was submitted to the OFT before accepting the undertakings in lieu (s. 75); making a supplementary interim order while an order under section 75 is being prepared (the CC may also exercise this power). Section 74 deals with the effect of undertakings accepted by the OFT under section 73. Sections 77 and 78 concern interim restrictions which are automatically imposed on certain dealings in relation to completed and anticipated mergers following the making of a reference and the powers of the CC in these situations.

Section 80 provides that the CC has the power to accept from such of the parties concerned an undertaking for the purpose of preventing a pre-emptive action, and section 81 gives it the power to make interim orders for preventing such action. Sections 79–84 give details about the powers which the CC may exercise following the completion of its investigation and the reaching of its conclusions. These powers include the power to accept final undertakings (s. 82), the power to make orders where undertakings accepted under section 82 are not fulfilled (s. 83) and the power to make final orders (s. 84).

The final orders referred to in section 84 may contain anything permitted by Schedule 8 of the Act. Schedule 8, comprising twenty-four paragraphs, is very detailed and refers to, among other things, orders imposing restrictions on conduct, obligations on a person to perform (for example to supply goods or services) and a requirement addressed to a person asking that person to publish certain information (for example price lists).

Sections 86–91 contain general provisions in relation to undertakings and orders. Section 86 provides that an enforcement order may extend in certain cases to a UK national's conduct outside the UK. Section 87 deals with the possibility of delegating the power to carry an order or to ensure it is complied with to a particular person. Section 88 gives details about the contents of certain enforcement orders, and section 89 deals with the subject matter of the undertakings. It states that the provision which may be included in an enforcement undertaking is not limited to the provisions permitted under Schedule 8 of the Act. Section 90 refers to Schedule 10 of the Act which deals with procedural requirements for certain enforcement undertakings and enforcement orders. Under section 91 the OFT is required to complete and maintain a register of undertakings and orders, the content of which must be available to the public during certain hours (10 am–4 pm).

The last four sections of the Chapter deal with: (a) the enforcement functions of the OFT in relation to monitoring undertakings and orders (s. 92) and consulting with such persons as may be required by the CC or (as the case may be) the Secretary of State with a view to discovering whether they will offer undertakings which either would be willing to accept (s. 93), and (b) the rights of a person who may be affected by a contravention of an undertaking, order or statutory restriction to bring an action for loss or damage sustained as a result of a contravention of such an undertaking and order (s. 94) and statutory restriction (s. 95).

10 Supplementary provisions

Chapter 5 of Part III consists of thirty-three sections. Sections 96–102 deal with various issues in relation to merger notices. Sections 103 and 104 deal with general duties in relation to references, such as the duty of the expedition imposed on the OFT and the Secretary of State. Provisions in relation to information and publicity requirements are contained in sections 105–108.

The investigation powers of the CC and the penalties which may be imposed are dealt with in sections 109–117. Section 109 provides for the CC's powers in relation to attendance of witnesses, production of documents and giving evidence. Section 110 gives the CC the power to impose a penalty in a situation where a person, without reasonable excuse, failed to comply with a requirement under section 109. It also provides that an offence may be committed by a person if he intentionally alters, suppresses or destroys any documents which he has been required to produce under section 109. Section 111 deals with the amount and level of the penalty.

SI 2003/1371 *The Competition Commission (Penalties) Order 2003* gives details on the maximum amount of the penalty, which the CC may impose under subsections 110(1) and (3). Sections 112–116 deal with various procedural matters in relation to imposition of a penalty by the CC.

11 Appeals

Finally, it is important to mention section 120 which provides for review of a decision taken by the OFT, the CC or the Secretary of State by the CAT. A decision reached by the CAT is subject to appeal to the Court of Appeal on any point of law arising from that decision.

S. 120 Review of decisions under Part 3

(1)   Any person aggrieved by a decision of the OFT, OFCOM, the Secretary of State or the Commission under this Part in connection with a reference or possible reference in relation to a relevant merger situation or a special merger situation may apply to the Competition Appeal Tribunal for a review of that decision.

(2)   For this purpose 'decision' –
    (a) does not include a decision to impose a penalty under section 110(1) or (3); but
    (b) includes a failure to take a decision permitted or required by this Part in connection with a reference or possible reference.

(3)   Except in so far as a direction to the contrary is given by the Competition Appeal Tribunal, the effect of the decision is not suspended by reason of the making of the application.

(4)   In determining such an application the Competition Appeal Tribunal shall apply the same principles as would be applied by a court on an application for judicial review.

(5)   The Competition Appeal Tribunal may –

    (a) dismiss the application or quash the whole or part of the decision to which it relates; and

    (b) where it quashes the whole or part of that decision, refer the matter back to the original decision maker with a direction to reconsider and make a new decision in accordance with the ruling of the Competition Appeal Tribunal.

(6)   An appeal lies on any point of law arising from a decision of the Competition Appeal Tribunal under this section to the appropriate court.

(7)   An appeal under subsection (6) requires the permission of the Tribunal or the appropriate court.

(8)   In this section –

    'the appropriate court' means the Court of Appeal or, in the case of Tribunal proceedings in Scotland, the Court of Session; and

    'Tribunal rules' has the meaning given by section 15(1).

Clearly, section 120 is a valuable tool in the system to ensure that there is a check not only on the powers of the OFT and the CC and the way they go about performing their duties but also on how the OFT chooses to exercise its discretion. Furthermore, the fact that a decision of the CAT may be appealed to the Court of Appeal provides a vital additional safety valve in the whole system. Indeed, this was demonstrated by the judgment of the Court of Appeal in *OFT and Others v. IBA Health Ltd* (see pp. 546–549 above).

12

Market investigation references

1 Introduction

'Market investigation references' are a new feature of the UK system of competition law brought into place by the Enterprise Act 2002 (EA2002). It is a procedure which does not exist in every system of competition law. It exists under UK competition law, but not under EC competition law and for this reason, this chapter is concerned solely with the former.

The procedure for market investigation references replaces the old 'monopoly' references mechanism, which existed under the Fair Trading Act 1973. The purpose of the procedure is to allow a reference to be made to the Competition Commission (CC) where there is reasonable suspicion that any market 'feature' is causing an adverse effect on competition. Like the merger control regime (discussed in the previous chapter), there are two 'inter-linked' levels within the procedure: the first is concerned with making the reference and the second with the determination of the reference. The CC determines whether an adverse effect on competition exists and decides what remedial actions should be taken.

2 Making of references

A market investigation reference can be made by one of the following: the Office of Fair Trading (OFT), sectoral regulators (listed at p. 15 above) and (in exceptional cases) the 'appropriate minister'.

(A) References by OFT

S. 131 Power of the OFT to make references

(1) The OFT may, subject to subsection (4), make a reference to the Commission if the OFT has reasonable grounds for suspecting that any feature, or combination of features, of a market in the United Kingdom for goods or services prevents, restricts or distorts competition in connection with the supply or acquisition of any goods or services in the United Kingdom or a part of the United Kingdom.

(2)   For the purposes of this Part any reference to a feature of a market in the United Kingdom for goods or services shall be construed as a reference to –
   (a) the structure of the market concerned or any aspect of that structure;
   (b) any conduct (whether or not in the market concerned) of one or more than one person who supplies or acquires goods or services in the market concerned; or
   (c) any conduct relating to the market concerned of customers of any person who supplies or acquires goods or services.

(3)   In subsection (2) 'conduct' includes any failure to act (whether or not intentional) and any other unintentional conduct.

(4)   No reference shall be made under this section if –
   (a) the making of the reference is prevented by section 156(1); or
   (b) a reference has been made under section 132 in relation to the same matter but has not been finally determined.

(5)   References in this Part to a market investigation reference being finally determined shall be construed in accordance with section 183(3) to (6).

(6)   In this Part –
   'market in the United Kingdom' includes –
   (a) so far as it operates in the United Kingdom or a part of the United Kingdom, any market which operates there and in another country or territory or in a part of another country or territory; and
   (b) any market which operates only in a part of the United Kingdom; 'market investigation reference' means a reference under this section or section 132; and references to a market for goods or services include references to a market for goods and services.

In March 2004, the OFT made its first market investigation reference to the CC. The reference was in relation to the supply of store card services. The OFT decided to make the reference following its conclusion that there were features of the sector that appeared to prevent, restrict or distort competition. The OFT was concerned about the lack of transparency in the sector in terms of the way store cards are offered and used.

(B) References by the 'appropriate Minister'

S. 132 Ministerial power to make references

(1)   Subsection (3) applies where, in relation to any goods or services, the appropriate Minister is not satisfied with a decision of the OFT not to make a reference under section 131.

(2) Subsection (3) also applies where, in relation to any goods or services, the appropriate Minister –

   (a) has brought to the attention of the OFT information which the appropriate Minister considers to be relevant to the question of whether the OFT should make a reference under section 131; but

   (b) is not satisfied that the OFT will decide, within such period as the appropriate Minister considers to be reasonable, whether to make such a reference.

(3) The appropriate Minister may, subject to subsection (4), make a reference to the Commission if he has reasonable grounds for suspecting that any feature, or combination of features, of a market in the United Kingdom for goods or services prevents, restricts or distorts competition in connection with the supply or acquisition of any goods or services in the United Kingdom or a part of the United Kingdom.

(4) No reference shall be made under this section if the making of the reference is prevented by section 156(1).

(5) In this Part 'the appropriate Minister' means –

   (a) the Secretary of State; or

   (b) the Secretary of State and one or more than one other Minister of the Crown acting jointly.

The test used in deciding whether to make a reference, as can be seen from the two provisions set out above, is that the person making the reference must have reasonable grounds for suspecting that any feature, or combination of features, of a market in the UK for goods or services *prevents, restricts or distorts competition* in connection with the supply or acquisition of any goods or services in the UK or a part of the UK. The test itself is a competition-based test and anyone familiar with the old provisions of the FTA1973 will appreciate that one great advantages this test has over the old public interest test which existed under the FTA1973 is that a great deal of discretion is no longer left to the Secretary of State.

The OFT has published guidance on this test and how it intends to apply the relevant provisions of the EA2002. This guidance is contained in OFT Guideline on *Market investigation references: Guidance about the making of references under Part 4 of the Enterprise Act* (OFT511).

(C) References by OFT: discretion or duty?

OFT511

1.10 The OFT has the discretion rather than a duty to make a market investigation reference where the statutory criteria appear to be met. Before making a reference,

it must therefore consider:
- whether it has reasonable grounds to suspect that competition is prevented, restricted or distorted in some market in the UK or in a part of the UK
- whether it is a feature, or combination of features, of a market that gives rise to this adverse effect on competition, and
- whether a market investigation reference to the CC would be the most appropriate way of proceeding.

(D) Making the reference in certain circumstances

The OFT has stated in paragraph 2.1 of Guideline *OFT511* that it will only make a reference when the test contained in section 131 and, in its opinion, each of the following conditions have been met:
- it would not be more appropriate to deal with the situation by applying the Competition Act 1998 or using other powers available to it or, where appropriate, to sectoral regulators;
- it would not be more appropriate to address the problem identified by means of undertakings in lieu of a reference;
- the scale of the suspected problem, in terms of its adverse effect on competition, is such that making a reference would be appropriate;
- there is a reasonable chance that appropriate remedies will be available.

Each of these key points is explained in detail in the *Guideline*.

I Applying the provisions of the Competition Act 1998 (CA1998) instead

OFT511 (footnotes omitted)

2.2   CA98 prohibits agreements, which have the object or effect of preventing, restricting or distorting competition, and abuses of a dominant position ... Market investigations are concerned with something different from particular anti-competitive agreements or abuses of dominance. Their purpose is to determine whether the process of competition is working effectively in markets as a whole. They will provide a framework for identifying, analysing and, where appropriate, remedying industry-wide or market-wide competition problems which there is no adequate basis for addressing under CA98.

2.3   When dealing with a suspected competition problem it is the OFT's policy always to consider first whether it may involve an infringement of one or both of the CA98 prohibitions and to investigate accordingly. It will only go on to consider a reference to the CC in one of two circumstances:
- when it has reasonable grounds to suspect that there are market features, which prevent, restrict or distort competition, but not to establish a breach of the CA98 prohibitions

- when action under CA98 has been or is likely to be ineffective for dealing with the adverse effect on competition identified.

2.4   Adverse effects on competition that do not involve either agreements between undertakings or abuses of dominance are beyond the reach of CA98. Market investigation references are therefore likely to focus on competition problems arising from uncoordinated parallel conduct by several firms or industry-wide features of a market in cases where the OFT does not have reasonable grounds to suspect the existence of anti-competitive agreements or dominance. Such problems may have a variety of sources such as competition-dampening common practices whose origins have long been forgotten, customers who are poorly informed relative to suppliers (information asymmetries), and sheer inertia on the part of ostensible competitors.

2.5   Oligopolistic markets in which firms engage in apparently parallel behaviour while falling short of actually concerting their actions (often referred to as tacit collusion) present a more complicated issue. The OFT recognises that EC case law has confirmed that the concept of collective dominance may be applicable in these circumstances, which would bring the conduct involved within the ambit of CA98. But this case law does not at present cover all types of coordinated parallel behaviour that may have an adverse effect on competition. Indeed, the judgement of the Court in the *Airtours* case appears to limit the applicability of the concept of collective dominance. Market features that can lead to adverse effects on competition in an oligopolistic market can be wider than the conditions that the case law has found to be necessary for collective dominance, that is, for oligopolists successfully to engage in tacit collusion. Furthermore, what qualifies as an abuse of collective dominance is underdeveloped in the case law. For these reasons a market investigation reference will be able to address wider competition concerns than could be addressed by a CA98 case and might, therefore, be a better way of proceeding.

2.6   Market investigation references may, in certain circumstances, also be relevant for dealing with possible competition problems arising from vertical agreements ... A market investigation reference may be the most appropriate way to proceed where vertical agreements are prevalent in a market and have the effect of preventing the entry of new competitors, but there is no evidence of collusion between the firms involved that might have caused this situation to arise.

2.7   The problems referred to in the previous three paragraphs involve industry-wide market features or multi-firm conduct. It is likely that the great majority of references the OFT makes will be of that type. Generally speaking single-firm conduct will, where necessary and possible, be dealt with under CA98 or appropriate sectoral legislation or rules. It is not the present intention of the OFT to make market references based on the conduct of a single firm, whether dominant or not, where there are no other features of a market that adversely affect competition.

2.8   This general principle is subject to the following comments and qualifications:
- In many cases anti-competitive conduct by a single firm may be associated with structural features of the market, for example barriers to entry or regulation and government policies, or conduct by customers which have adverse effects on competition. These other market features are discussed in sections 5 and 7 of this guidance. Where they are present a market investigation reference may be more appropriate than action under CA98 even though only a single firm appears to be conducting itself anti-competitively.
- The principle will be reviewed should the development of case law relating to the CA98 Chapter II prohibition give good grounds for believing that the prohibition is inadequate to deal with conduct by a single firm which has an adverse effect on competition.
- The OFT might decide to make a market investigation reference when there has been an abuse of a dominant position and it is clear that nothing short of a structural remedy going beyond what is appropriate under CA98 would be effective in dealing with the consequential adverse effect on competition.

II Accepting undertakings in lieu of a reference

Section 154 EA2002 empowers the OFT to accept undertakings in lieu of a reference. The OFT has explained the particulars of this power as follows.

OFT511 (footnotes omitted)

2.20   . . . In exercising this power the OFT must have regard to the need to achieve as comprehensive a solution, as is reasonable and practicable, to any adverse effects on competition identified (and any detrimental effects on customers so far as they result or may be expected to result from such adverse effects). It may also have regard, as appropriate, to the effect of the possible undertakings on any relevant customer benefits arising from a feature or features of the markets concerned.

2.21   Undertakings in lieu of a reference are unlikely to be common. In many cases the OFT will not have done a sufficiently detailed investigation of a competition problem, prior to making a reference to the CC, to be able to judge with any certainty whether particular undertakings will achieve as comprehensive a solution as is reasonable and practicable. This is particularly likely to be the case when the adverse effects on competition arise from market features involving several firms or industry-wide practices. Moreover, trying to negotiate undertakings with several parties, in circumstances in which possible adverse effects on competition have not been comprehensively analysed, is likely to pose serious practical difficulties. By contrast, where an adverse effect on competition arises from the conduct of a very few firms there may be more scope for accepting undertakings in lieu, provided that the OFT is confident that they will achieve a comprehensive solution.

2.22   In assessing customer benefits the OFT will take into account the same factors as the CC discusses in its guidance. Such benefits comprise lower prices, higher quality or greater choice of goods or services in any UK market, or greater innovation in relation to such goods or services.

2.23   Before accepting any undertaking in lieu the OFT must publish the proposed undertaking in a notice which, among other things, states the purpose and effect of the undertaking and identifies the adverse effect on competition and any resulting detrimental effect on customers identified by the OFT that the proposed undertaking is intended to remedy (the list of all the points to be included in such notices is given in section 155(2) of the Act). The OFT must consider any representations arising from the publication of the notice. There is a power for the Secretary of State to intervene at this stage if he believes that wider public interest matters are relevant to the case. The Secretary of State is able to block the acceptance of undertakings in lieu when he believes that a public interest consideration specified in the legislation (currently only national security) is relevant. In such a case, the outcome may be other undertakings in lieu or a reference.

As the OFT acknowledges in paragraph 2.21 above, undertakings in lieu are unlikely to be common. However, under section 155 the OFT is under an obligation to publish a notice of the proposed undertaking and to consider representations received following the notice. Furthermore, section 156 provides that if an undertaking in lieu has been accepted, neither the OFT nor the appropriate minister will be able to make a reference to the CC within the following twelve months, unless the person responsible for giving any undertaking concerned supplied false or misleading information to the OFT; or the OFT considers that any undertaking concerned has been breached. Under section 162, the OFT is required to monitor the enforcement of undertakings and to consider from time to time whether they are being complied with. The OFT is also required to consider whether an undertaking should be dissolved, varied or suppressed by a new undertaking (s. 162(4)).

III The scale of the suspected problem

OFT511 (footnotes omitted)

2.27   The OFT will only make a reference when it has reasonable grounds to suspect that the adverse effects on competition of features of a market are significant. In making this assessment it will consider whether these suspected adverse effects are likely to have a significant detrimental effect on customers through higher prices, lower quality, less choice or less innovation. Where it seems likely that this effect is not significant the OFT will normally take the view that the burden on business, particularly in terms of management time, and the public expenditure costs of an investigation by the CC are likely to be disproportionate in relation to any benefits that may be obtained from remedying the adverse effects.

2.28   It is not possible to make a definitive statement about the circumstances in which adverse effects on competition, or the customer detriments arising from them, will be regarded as not significant. However, the following factors are relevant and will be taken into account by the OFT:

- The size of the market. Generally speaking, the cost of a CC investigation into a very small market would not be justified. However, problems in some relatively small specialised or local markets could have a significant detrimental impact on customers affected by them, in which case a reference may be justified.
- The proportion of the market affected by the feature giving rise to adverse effects on competition. When this proportion is small the adverse effects will be unlikely to lead to significant customer detriment. The OFT does not think that it would be appropriate to specify a figure for the proportion of the market affected below which it would not make a reference, not least because the precise definition of the market (or markets) concerned and the extent of the market features having an adverse affect on competition may not be clearly established until after the CC has conducted its investigation. However, where possible the OFT will act in a way that is broadly consistent with its practice when applying its powers under CA98.
- The persistence of the feature giving rise to adverse effects on competition. If the feature concerned seems likely to be short-lived (for example, because of an expected change in regulations) or clearly relates to a one-off incident, and there are no other market features giving cause for concern, then a reference to the CC is not likely to be justified.

2.29   In some cases the market features that adversely affect competition may also produce offsetting customer benefits. Such benefits might arise, for example, where customers gain when more of them use the same good or service (network effects) or where there are substantial economies of scale. Where the OFT is confident that offsetting customer benefits exceed the likely detriment from the adverse effect on competition it will not make a reference. However, where there is uncertainty the OFT will normally wish to leave the weighing of benefits and detriments to the CC.

IV Availability of appropriate remedies

OFT511

2.30   The OFT will also take into account the likely availability of appropriate remedies in the event that the suspected adverse effects on competition were found by the CC to exist. Where the OFT has not investigated a market in sufficient depth to be confident that it is in a position to identify the possible remedies it will not give this factor much weight. However, where the OFT has a reasonably good understanding of a market, perhaps because it has investigated it using its own market investigation powers or because a reference is being considered following an investigation under CA98, it will not normally make a reference when it believes that no appropriate remedies (including recommendations for action by the European Commission or other bodies) are likely to be available. For example, it may have established that a particular market is global in scope, or at least goes much wider than the UK, and that any remedy for the UK (which would be all that was available under the Act) would have no discernible impact on the way the market operated even in the UK.

2.31   Similarly, where the OFT is satisfied that adverse effects on competition arise primarily from laws, regulations, or government policies it will not normally make a reference when it considers that the CC will not be able directly to remedy such adverse effects. Instead, the OFT will submit a report to the government in accordance with its own market investigation role with recommendations for changes to the relevant laws and so forth as appropriate. However, where regulatory or related problems are only one market feature among others adversely affecting competition, and it is reasonable to expect that remedies that mitigate the adverse effects arising from the other features are feasible, the OFT will consider a reference.

2.32   Although the availability of remedies will be the most important practical issue taken into account by the OFT when considering a reference, it will also consider others where relevant. In particular, it may take into account whether the evidence that would enable the CC to reach a conclusion is likely to be available.

3 The application of the reference test in section 131 EA2002

As was noted above, the test that is used to determine whether to make a reference is a competition-based test, namely the prevention, restriction or distortion of competition, a phrase which appears in both Article 81(1) and section 2 CA1998. The phrase was considered in chapter 3 and the discussion in that chapter on the meaning and application of the phrase is relevant when considering it in the context of market investigation references.

(A) 'Prevention, restriction or distortion of competition'

OFT511

4.2   . . . Conduct that adversely affects the opportunity for others to compete is not the only thing that could prevent, restrict or distort competition. Where other features of a market create a situation in which suppliers do not need to compete to the extent that they would in a competitive market, those features may be found to restrict competition.

4.3   The OFT's enquiries into a possible market investigation reference may embrace several levels of a supply chain. It might be, for example, that competition appeared to be prevented, restricted and distorted in some way by the structure of the market or the conduct of firms at the manufacturing stage, yet further examination of the situation suggested that practices at the downstream level could also have an adverse effect on competition. A market investigation reference could require that the effectiveness of competition at various levels of a supply chain should be assessed.

4.4   Although section 131 of the Act sets out the three types of market feature that could have an adverse effect on competition, in practice there may not be a clear divide between structural features and those relating to conduct. For example, exclusionary conduct by firms in the market will affect structure to the extent that it raises entry barriers. In most cases, the OFT's assessment that a reference would be appropriate is likely to be based on a combination of features and will include evidence about both structure and conduct. It may also include evidence about the performance of firms in the market.

4.5   Information on prices and profitability, in particular, can sometimes be a useful supplement to the OFT's evidence on structural features of a market and on firms' market conduct. Indeed, evidence on prices and profitability might be the beginning of the OFT's interest in a particular market. This is because complaints of anti-competitive conduct will often focus on excessive prices and high levels of profitability, perhaps making comparisons with prices or the profitability of firms in other similar markets or in other countries. Other performance indicators such as the level of costs or efficiency measures may, on occasions, also be a useful supplement to analyses of market features.

4.6   The OFT is well aware of the limitations of such information for its purpose. Performance indicators in isolation yield little useful information about the state of competition in a market. At best they should be used as an indirect indicator that a competition problem may exist. For example, profits in dynamic markets, where technological advances are important, can be lumpy so a snapshot of profitability will not give a good indication of a firm's performance. Furthermore, identifying the concept of excessive prices and profits and the 'normal' rate of return is extremely difficult. There is a need for care before any inferences about competition are drawn. Nevertheless, the OFT will consider any available and reliable information on the dynamics of prices, profitability and other performance indicators in its assessment of the case for a market investigation reference.

4.7   In short, in any competition assessment, the OFT will usually wish to consider a combination of features and their inter-relationships and will look at various types of information and sources of evidence. However, it is not required to reach firm conclusions before making references and it would be inappropriate for it to engage in extensive research. Provided it has reasonable grounds for suspecting that there are market features that adversely affect competition, the reference test has been met and further investigation can be left to the CC.

(B) Types of features in section 131

Section 131(2) refers to three types of features. Each of these features is explained in Guideline *OFT511*.

I Structural features of the market

OFT511 (footnotes omitted)

5.1   Structure describes the environment within which firms operate in a particular market. The OFT interprets it broadly to include such matters as government regulations and any information asymmetries that are inherent in the nature of the market. Any assessment of the working of competition in a market will begin with an analysis of market structure and the implications of this structure for the conduct of the firms engaged in the market. A wider range of structural features can give rise to concern under the market investigation reference provisions of the Act than would normally arise in considering whether a firm or firms had infringed one of the CA98 prohibitions.

. . .

Concentration

5.3   Market concentration is about the number and size distribution of firms in a particular market. It is generally accepted that, other things being equal, the larger the market share of a firm, the greater its market power is likely to be, particularly if its high market share has persisted over a period of time and is relatively stable. This applies to both sellers and buyers. Market shares are not conclusive indicators of a firm's market power of course. Other factors can be relevant. Notable among these are entry barriers. Markets in which firms have high market shares are often, though not necessarily, markets with high entry barriers. In assessing the degree of concentration it is important for the market to be correctly defined as too narrow a definition will overstate concentration (and vice versa).

5.4   A firm may have market power, and the capacity to act in ways that may prevent, restrict or distort competition, with a market share below that usually regarded as necessary to suggest dominance for the purposes of CA98. Much will depend upon the effectiveness of the constraints exerted by its competitors or its customers. Generally speaking, a firm with a stable market share will be more likely to have market power than one whose share fluctuates from year to year.

5.5   In markets comprising a small number of firms (oligopolies) each firm might find it relatively easy to predict the reaction of its competitors to any action it might take. This could provide an opportunity for firms to coordinate their behaviour for mutual advantage or it could simply dull the incentive to compete, leading to a situation in which rivalry to attract new customers becomes muted. By no means all oligopolistic market structures produce these results. Among the more important of the market features that may assist the coordination of behaviour are:

- the existence of substantial barriers to entry
- the homogeneity of the firms' products
- the similarity (symmetry) of the firms with respect to their market shares, their cost structures, the time horizons of their decisions and their strategies
- the stability of market conditions on both the demand and the cost side
- the degree of excess capacity
- the extent to which prices, outputs and market shares are transparent so that competitors can be well-informed about each other's behaviour
- the awareness by firms that their competitors have the ability to respond quickly and effectively to any price reductions they make
- the structure of the buying side of the market (if the issue is possible co-ordination among sellers), and
- the extent of any multi-market contacts.

5.6   This list is not exhaustive nor are any of the items on it necessary conditions for competition dampening to take place. It also is quite possible for a market displaying many of these factors to be competitive. Nevertheless, the more symmetrical the firms in the oligopoly, the more homogeneous their products, and the more stable the market conditions, the more likely it is that an understanding on, say, a particular price can be reached and sustained. It can be difficult to sustain a coordinated price where buyers are large and may encourage sellers to offer special and secret deals.

5.7   A view on the likelihood of coordination or the existence of muted rivalry can only be reached after a close study of the market concerned, not least because the influence of some of the features listed in paragraph 5.5 can be ambiguous. Therefore, product homogeneity makes it easier for oligopolists to reach a tacit understanding, but it also makes it easier for customers to compare the offerings of different firms, possibly encouraging greater keenness on price. However, research suggests as a generalisation that firm symmetries, market transparency and relatively stable demand and cost conditions appear to be the combination of market characteristics most conducive to coordination.

Vertical integration

5.8   A structural market feature that can have a bearing on market conduct and the effectiveness of competition is the degree (if any) of vertical integration of firms engaged in the market. Although vertical integration may often be efficient or pro-competitive, a vertically integrated firm can have adverse effects on competition if it can foreclose non-integrated competitors from a significant part of their market either by refusing to supply or to deal with them or by discriminating against them in its pricing. Vertical integration may also add to entry barriers if a potential competitor would have to enter at both stages in order to be able to compete effectively with incumbent firms, and if the riskiness of the necessary investment is thereby increased.

5.9   For vertical integration to have any of these effects, the vertically integrated firm(s) will need to have a sizeable share of either of the vertically linked markets. Where only a single firm is vertically integrated adverse effects on competition will usually arise only if it is dominant in terms of CA98. A market investigation reference might be appropriate, however, if a number of firms in a market are vertically integrated and they engage in some common form of anticompetitive conduct, for example, discrimination against any non-integrated competitors.

Conditions of entry, exit and expansion

5.10   Entry conditions are always a crucial part of any competition assessment. If there are no significant barriers or impediments to entry into the market under consideration, so that there is a realistic possibility that a new entrant could establish itself in the market on a viable basis within a reasonably short period of time, the established suppliers will have no lasting market power. However, while there can be such contestable markets, more often than not, in markets in which the OFT is interested there will be some significant entry barriers facing any potential entrant.

. . .

5.15   Barriers to expansion determine how easy it is for an entrant to grow once they have entered a market, thereby gaining customers and market share from the incumbents. This could be closely related to the degree of switching by consumers and the information asymmetry inherent in the market: the sunk costs for entry may be small but if customers are unwilling to switch (due to brand loyalty for example) then price competition may not provide a basis for expansion.

5.16   Barriers to exit relate to the cost of exit from the market if the business does not go according to plan. This is closely related to the degree of sunk costs incurred on entry and the extent to which investment can be recovered on exit. Where the barriers to exit are high, the firms in the market have burnt their bridges which provides them with a credible threat that they will not consider exiting the market easily. This could lead to situations where tacit collusion becomes the optimal strategy rather than intense price competition.

Regulations and government policies

5.17   Government regulations can have a direct effect upon competition when they limit the number of firms that can operate in a market. This might be achieved by a licensing system or by specified entry criteria, for example a minimum capital funds requirement as in much of the financial sector. However, It does not follow that such entry barriers will necessarily have significantly adverse effects upon competition. That will depend upon how seriously the regulations limit the number of firms in

[567]

the market, for example, whether the restrictions are quantitative or qualitative, and how active the competition is between those that are in the market.

5.18   Regulations can also affect firms' conduct. Often they will be innocuous in competition terms, such as regulations on product labelling, emissions of pollutants and hiring and firing of employees, although they will raise firms' costs and can bear more heavily on small firms than on their larger competitors. Sometimes the effects on competition will be more significant, for example the imposition of demanding product standards, restrictions on trading hours or the restrictions on advertising tobacco products or marketing drugs. The circumstances in which markets affected by regulation might be suitable for a reference to the CC were mentioned in paragraph 2.31.

5.19   Government policies can affect markets in other ways, for example by influencing the way in which public sector bodies act as providers or purchasers of services. Where such policies have a significant effect on competition they will be among the market features that OFT takes into account when considering a reference.

5.20   Competition can also be affected by the rules emanating from systems of self-regulation, for example, those applicable to financial services and to a number of occupations and professions. In many cases this can be adequately addressed using CA98 or sector-specific legislation. Where it cannot, the market affected might be suitable for a reference to the CC.

Information asymmetries

5.21   Where customers are well informed, they can make efficient choices and their purchases will provide useful information to sellers about customers' preferences. Sellers then have the incentive to provide the goods and services that customers most value. Without such information, the incentives to compete on price, quality and other terms are likely to be diminished. In short, adequate information available to customers is one of the pre-requisites for markets to work well. If customers have inadequate information, or are unwilling or unable to search for the best deal, firms may be able to exercise a degree of market power, even if there are many firms supplying the market.

5.22   In many markets, suppliers will have more information than their customers about the quality and other attributes of their products. This will not necessarily adversely affect competition, particularly if suppliers have an incentive to provide their customers with relevant information. However, where the quality of products is difficult for customers to assess, either because of their complexity or the infrequency with which they are purchased, information asymmetries can have a significant impact on the nature and degree of competition in the market for the product or service. Information asymmetries can restrict competition by adding to customers' switching costs.

Switching costs

5.23   For competition to work effectively, it is often necessary that customers are readily able to switch their patronage if a competing supplier is found to offer better value for money. Where customers face difficulties in switching between suppliers, whether because of the monetary costs, administrative hurdles or inconvenience, competition can be affected. If firms find it difficult to persuade customers to switch their incentive to compete with each other may be reduced and rivalry between them dulled.

5.24   Switching costs allow firms potentially to charge high prices to 'captive' customers. Firms face conflicting incentives. They want to offer low prices to attract new customers but to charge high prices to their existing customers. Even if the firm is unable to discriminate between the two types of customer, it is still possible that the existence of switching costs will permit firms to charge higher prices than they would set in the absence of these costs.

5.25   Firms may engage in practices that increase switching costs, for example, by not releasing information needed for a switch to be feasible or by not doing so in a timely fashion. In its report on *Banking Services to Small and Medium Sized Enterprises*, the CC identified the 'hassle in moving direct debits, standing orders etc and a fear that crucial payments could be missed whilst a switch was in progress' as a factor discouraging switching between banks. It also found that banks reduced charges selectively and in a discriminatory way to enterprises likely to switch to another bank. Marketing devices such as loyalty cards, often seen as pro-competitive, can have the effect of increasing switching costs. Negative advertising may also be used to reduce switching by creating doubts in customers' minds about the acceptability of competitors' offerings.

5.26   In some markets, the problem may be that the customer is unaware of the existence of competing products. For example a consumer may not be aware of a generic pharmaceutical product having the same medicinal properties as a more expensive branded product.

Countervailing power

5.27   The structure of the buying side of the market can also be relevant to the assessment of the effectiveness of competition between suppliers. It may suggest that any market power of suppliers would be countervailed by the bargaining power of customers, or that any attempt of suppliers not to compete on price would be eroded by the temptation to negotiate special terms with large buyers.

5.28   The effectiveness of buyer power as a constraint on suppliers will depend upon a number of factors, particularly upon the relative dependence of seller and buyer on the business of the other and the credibility of any threat by the buyer to switch its business to an alternative supplier.

[569]

II Conduct of firms

OFT511

6.1   The conduct of firms refers to their behaviour and practices in the broadest sense including what decisions they take, how they make them and the resulting action or lack of it. Section 131(3) of the Act states that conduct includes failure to act and unintentional conduct. A significant part of the evidence on which the OFT will base its case for a market investigation reference will normally concern the conduct of firms (as sellers or buyers) who, because of structural or other features of the market, are in a position to exercise a degree of market power.

6.2   The conduct of the firms in a market may affect competition in that market (horizontal effects), competition in the (upstream) market of its suppliers or in the (downstream) market of its customers (vertical effects). It is also possible for conduct adversely to affect competition in a market for some related good or service.

6.3   ... most market investigation references are likely to involve markets where the conduct of a number of firms (whether sellers or buyers) appears to have the effect of preventing, restricting or distorting competition (without an agreement or concerted practice that would be unlawful under Chapter I of CA98). This part of the guidance gives a number of examples of such conduct. However, these should not be regarded in any way as exhaustive or exclusive.

Conduct of oligopolies

6.4   Many of the markets in which the OFT is likely to be interested will be oligopolistic. These are markets comprising very few firms (or few firms of any significance) where those firms are aware of the mutual interdependence of their actions. Each firm's strategy is therefore determined at least partly by its beliefs about its rivals' likely reactions. These strategies can take various forms, ranging from competitive rivalry to conduct that is tantamount to collusion, even without an explicit agreement not to compete. With either of these extremes, the outcome can be parallel behaviour. The task will then be to determine whether the oligopolists' conduct reflects a restriction of effective competition and would be an appropriate ground for an OFT investigation.

6.5   It is a common feature of oligopolistic markets that competition takes forms other than competition in price. These include competitive advertising and promotional activity, rebates and discounts linked to purchases, and more explicit customer loyalty-inducing schemes. These forms of conduct are often pro-competitive but they may have effects that, especially when combined with other market features, blunt the competitive process, for example by adding to entry barriers.

6.6   Where firms in an oligopolistic market reach a tacit understanding to pursue their joint interests by coordinating their behaviour (tacit collusion) the adverse effects on competition are likely to be severe. The OFT will not need to establish conclusively that any observed parallel conduct reflects coordinated rather than competitive behaviour by oligopolists. However, it will need to establish that the market features that make tacit collusion a feasible strategy are present (see paragraph 5.5 for an indicative list) and will need to have a reasonable suspicion that the oligopolists are not competing effectively with consequences that are likely to be detrimental to their customers.

6.7   Among the evidence that the OFT might examine in this regard are:
- the pattern of price changes over time, with a view to establishing the degree of parallelism in the face of any changes in demand or cost conditions, and whether the pattern seems more consistent with collusive than competitive behaviour
- price inertia, such as when sustained exchange rate advantages are not exploited by importers
- any evidence that, notwithstanding evidence of parallelism in, say, published prices, the oligopolists compete in discounts or other concessions off the published price, and
- the oligopolists' rates of return compared to returns in comparable markets or to the cost of capital (since the expected outcome of tacit collusion is that the level of prices will be higher than could be sustained in a competitive market). However, where there is persistent excess capacity, excessive prices may not be reflected in high rates of return.

6.8   Even if the conditions necessary for tacit collusion are not met, other market features such as switching costs and informational inadequacies may limit the effectiveness of competition, especially price competition. Competition can be muted in oligopolistic markets without any coordination of firms' decisions. In its report on Supermarkets, for example, the CC concluded that the market was 'broadly competitive' with no suggestion of collusion, but that competition was concentrated on certain products or in certain areas and was less than fully effective elsewhere. This was held to distort the competitive process.

6.9   The OFT will therefore be concerned to consider, in contemplating a reference, whether there are any steps that could be taken to facilitate entry into an oligopolistic market and whether there is any conduct that serves to reinforce the market features that are conducive to tacit collusion and that could, if appropriate, be struck down. One such possibility is facilitating practices.

Facilitating practices
6.10   Facilitating practices are the conduct of firms that make it easier for oligopolists to arrive tacitly at a coordinated outcome and to maintain it in the face of the temptation of all the firms involved to cheat on the other participants. Examples would be a practice of announcing price increases well in advance of the date of implementation, most-favoured-customer clauses in contracts, uniform systems for

reflecting transport charges in prices, and information exchanges, for example, on costs.

6.11 There can be objective justifications for such practices and they do not necessarily have the effect of restricting competition. However, where other market features appear conducive to tacit collusion, practices of firms that appear to facilitate such conduct will be closely scrutinised by the OFT. They could even be the focus of a market investigation in their own right.

Custom and practice

6.12 Practices that may restrict competition can be adopted widely in a market as a custom of the trade and with no apparent agreement or understanding between firms. A good example is provided by the CC report on *Underwriting Fees*. Custom and practice appeared to be the reason why underwriting fees for new share issues were charged on a common basis virtually throughout the industry.

6.13 Another example could be the practice of manufacturers' recommended retail prices. While the practice can be innocuous, its widespread use in a market can have the effect of restricting competition in the downstream (retail) market by dampening price competition, should retailers generally choose to follow the recommended price; or of restricting competition in the upstream market, by making it easier for a manufacturer to monitor competitors' prices and thereby to detect, and hence to deter, competitive price cutting. Examples of anti-competitive effects of the practice are to be found in the CC's reports on *Domestic Electrical Goods*.

6.14 Any common practices in a market, that appear to reflect a restriction of competition and to have no objective justification, could be the subject of a market investigation reference.

Networks of vertical agreements

6.15 Vertical agreements of one kind or another are commonplace in industry and are frequently pro-competitive or neutral. Agreements between manufacturers and distributors (wholesalers or retailers) will often include terms that restrict the freedom of action of one or other party, as will agreements between a manufacturer and suppliers of its inputs. Such restrictions could in some circumstances adversely affect competition. Where several firms in a market have agreements with their distributors or suppliers that contain restrictions which, taken together, have an adverse effect on competition in the market of one or other party, for example, by foreclosing the market to competitors or adding to entry barriers, a market investigation reference could be justified. . . Such networks of vertical agreements can result from the independent decisions of the firms concerned, or even from long custom in a trade.

6.16 Types of vertical agreement that have been the subject of FTA monopoly references in the past and may be suitable for market investigation references in the future include exclusive purchasing (i.e. where the retailer or other downstream party is tied to a single supplier), exclusive or selective distribution (where a supplier only sells to certain downstream outlets), and tie-in sales and product bundling.

6.17 The effect on competition of vertical agreements will depend not just on the foreclosure and entry barrier-enhancing effects but also on the effectiveness of competition between suppliers and the willingness of consumers to shop around among competing suppliers' products. Where inter-brand competition is strong, the effects may not be significant. On the other hand, inter-brand competition can be weakened if consumers find that particular retailers are effectively tied to particular suppliers (or vice versa) and they are unwilling for one reason or another to shop around and switch to another retailer (brand) if it is found to offer better value for their money.

6.18 Vertical agreements are frequently efficiency enhancing so that even where the OFT suspects that they adversely affect competition it will need to consider the trade-off. A reference will only be appropriate where there are reasonable grounds to suspect that the net effect of the agreement is detrimental to the interests of customers.

III Conduct of customers

OFT511

7.1 Section 131(2)(c) of the Act identifies the conduct of customers as a market feature that could give rise to adverse effects on competition and be the subject of a market investigation reference. The customers concerned may be businesses or final consumers. It may seem rather unlikely that the conduct of consumers could affect the competitive process until it is recalled that 'conduct' includes failures to act. One feature of consumers' conduct that can then affect competition is the search process.

Search costs

7.2 Competition requires customer choice. In order to make informed choices customers need to spend at least some time and effort finding out what alternative products are available to them. Where such search costs are perceived to be high searching is likely to be curtailed. Customer sensitivity about a product may also limit the amount of search that will be contemplated. Depending on other features of the market, reduced searching may blunt sellers' incentives to compete.

7.3 Even if a proportion of customers do engage in search activity there may remain enough uninformed customers with high search costs, who purchase from the first firm they encounter, for the seller to be able to charge prices without regard to competition. In this situation, the profit foregone by losing informed consumers who buy elsewhere is more than offset by the increase in profits accruing from uninformed consumers who do not shop around. Markets serving both tourists (with high search costs) and local residents (with low search costs) may be an example.

7.4 Firms may engage in practices that increase search costs (or fail to engage in practices that would reduce search costs). For example, firms may choose not to display prices prominently. An example of price display reducing search costs is the prominent display of petrol prices at filling stations. Restrictions on advertising in the rules of many professional bodies in the past also served to increase the difficulties of search.

7.5 Firms may fail to make available all the product information needed by consumers to make an informed choice. Customers may be ignorant of all the product attributes that they should consider in choosing between competing products. This is likely to be the case with many financial products, extended warranties on electrical products, certain professional services and some consumer durables. Where one-off purchases are involved, with no repeat sales, there will be little incentive for a firm to provide consumers with the information that they need. Indeed, there may be an incentive for the firm deliberately to provide consumers with partial and potentially misleading information.

7.6 Search costs are therefore a market feature that could be a factor pointing to a market investigation reference, especially when associated with sellers' conduct that is likely to have adverse effects on competition in its own right. Structural features of the market would also be relevant, but it is noteworthy that the effect of high search costs on prices will be greater the more firms that there are in the industry.

7.7 The effects of search costs on the competitive process are likely to be compounded when they are combined with high switching costs. A good example of such a combination of market features is durable goods where the consumer needs information on the availability and costs of aftermarket services, such as spare parts and maintenance, if an informed choice is to be made between competing products. A competition problem can arise where consumers are unable to factor in to their purchase decisions all the aftermarket costs of the products or where the aftermarket is not competitive. For some durable products such as new motor cars there are adequate sources of information on lifetime aftermarket costs for any customer willing to take a little trouble. For other products such information is inherently difficult to obtain. Suppliers are well placed to take advantage of customers who are short of relevant aftermarket information with little risk of losing sales to competitors.

7.8 High search and/or switching costs will therefore be features of markets that could justify a market investigation reference. They can feed into other market features by facilitating anti-competitive or exploitative conduct by suppliers and by adding to market entry barriers. But the OFT will need to be convinced that market behaviour is affected. It is not necessary for all customers to be well informed and quick to switch suppliers in response to price differences for markets to work well.

7.9   Indicators that market behaviour may be little affected by search or switching costs with little risk of detriment to customers at large include:
- prices clustering together (in the absence of resale price maintenance or recommended retail prices)
- advertising of prices by all or most suppliers
- customary and inexpensive comparison shopping
- inability of suppliers to discriminate between informed and uninformed customers.

4 Content of references

Section 133 EA2002 sets out what references made to the CC should contain. As one would expect they should specify the statutory basis, date, and goods to which the 'feature' in question relates and should be specific enough with respect to the customer group and geographic location as to avoid wasting the CC's time on irrelevant aspects.

The OFT is empowered under section 174 EA2002 to investigate features it suspects of preventing, restricting or distorting competition, for example when it needs more information in order to frame the reference properly. The OFT has the power to require attendance of parties to give evidence and to require the production of specified documents and specified information but cannot use its special cartel investigatory powers.

5 Determination of references by the CC

S. 134 Questions to be decided on market investigation references

(1)   The Commission shall, on a market investigation reference, decide whether any feature, or combination of features, of each relevant market prevents, restricts or distorts competition in connection with the supply or acquisition of any goods or services in the United Kingdom or a part of the United Kingdom.

(2)   For the purposes of this Part, in relation to a market investigation reference, there is an adverse effect on competition if any feature, or combination of features, of a relevant market prevents, restricts or distorts competition in connection with the supply or acquisition of any goods or services in the United Kingdom or a part of the United Kingdom.

(3)   In subsections (1) and (2) "relevant market" means –
(a) in the case of subsection (2) so far as it applies in connection with a possible reference, a market in the United Kingdom-

[575]

(i) for goods or services of a description to be specified in the reference; and

(ii) which would not be excluded from investigation by virtue of section 133(2); and

(b) in any other case, a market in the United Kingdom –

(i) for goods or services of a description specified in the reference concerned; and

(ii) which is not excluded from investigation by virtue of section 133(2).

(4) The Commission shall, if it has decided on a market investigation reference that there is an adverse effect on competition, decide the following additional questions –

(a) whether action should be taken by it under section 138 for the purpose of remedying, mitigating or preventing the adverse effect on competition concerned or any detrimental effect on customers so far as it has resulted from, or may be expected to result from, the adverse effect on competition;

(b) whether it should recommend the taking of action by others for the purpose of remedying, mitigating or preventing the adverse effect on competition concerned or any detrimental effect on customers so far as it has resulted from, or may be expected to result from, the adverse effect on competition; and

(c) in either case, if action should be taken, what action should be taken and what is to be remedied, mitigated or prevented.

(5) For the purposes of this Part, in relation to a market investigation reference, there is a detrimental effect on customers if there is a detrimental effect on customers or future customers in the form of –

(a) higher prices, lower quality or less choice of goods or services in any market in the United Kingdom (whether or not the market to which the feature or features concerned relate); or

(b) less innovation in relation to such goods or services.

(6) In deciding the questions mentioned in subsection (4), the Commission shall, in particular, have regard to the need to achieve as comprehensive a solution as is reasonable and practicable to the adverse effect on competition and any detrimental effects on customers so far as resulting from the adverse effect on competition.

(7) In deciding the questions mentioned in subsection (4), the Commission may, in particular, have regard to the effect of any action on any relevant customer benefits of the feature or features of the market concerned.

(8) For the purposes of this Part a benefit is a relevant customer benefit of a feature or features of a market if –

(a) it is a benefit to customers or future customers in the form of –

(i) lower prices, higher quality or greater choice of goods or services in any market in the United Kingdom (whether or not the market to which the feature or features concerned relate); or

(ii) greater innovation in relation to such goods or services; and

(b) the Commission, the Secretary of State or (as the case may be) the OFT believes that –

   (i) the benefit has accrued as a result (whether wholly or partly) of the feature or features concerned or may be expected to accrue within a reasonable period as a result (whether wholly or partly) of that feature or those features; and

   (ii) the benefit was, or is, unlikely to accrue without the feature or features concerned.

Market Investigation References: Competition Commission Guidelines (CC3)

Adverse effects on competition

1.15   Whilst market investigation references to the Commission will be made where the OFT (or, in some circumstances, a Minister or sector regulator) has reasonable grounds for believing that competition is not working effectively, it will be for the Commission to reach its own conclusions on whether there are any adverse effects on competition.

1.16   In doing so, the Commission sees competition as a process of rivalry between firms or other suppliers (hereinafter referred to as firms) seeking to win customers' business over time . . .

1.17   Rivalry has numerous beneficial effects: prices and costs are driven down, and innovation and productivity increase, so increasing the quality and, more generally, the diversity of choice available to customers. Further, markets that are competitive generate feedback from customers to firms who, in consequence, direct their resources to customers' priorities. In addition firms are encouraged to meet the existing and future needs of customers as effectively and efficiently as possible. It is where this process is hampered, or otherwise hindered, by features of the market that competition may be adversely affected. The degree of rivalry between firms or other producers for customer business and the threat of entry faced by incumbents are the main competitive constraints on firms, although other constraints such as buyer and/or supplier power may also, in some cases, be significant.

1.18   As part of a market investigation, the Commission must consider how the competitive process in the relevant market is affected by any features of the market as described in the Act. Structural features include not only market shares, concentration, buyer power and entry barriers, but also less obvious aspects of market structure such as information asymmetries and government regulations. Conduct features include the conduct of buyers and sellers, of the firms in the market and of customers. Each of these features may have effects on competition, in both its more static sense of price, cost and profit levels and its longer term dynamic sense of experimentation with new ideas, innovation, differentiation and development of products and markets through time. In its analysis, therefore, the Commission will consider the extent to which the process of rivalry in the market will ensure that all firms in the market are open to challenge, that no firm's position or market share is insulated from competitive pressure and that none can exert market power.

1.19   In some market investigation references the Commission may find that for certain aspects of the market, or in some parts of the market, there is effective competition, but less than fully effective competition elsewhere in the market (possibly creating scope for cross-funding of some activities). In such instances the Commission will address the less competitive areas of the market, normally with the aim of securing effective competition in all areas of the market.

1.20   Inevitably a degree of judgement is involved in deciding whether there are adverse effects on competition. Where the line is to be drawn has to be judged in each individual case in the light of all the evidence that has been assembled in the course of the investigation.

The Commission approach

1.21   The Commission's approach to market investigation references will normally be framed in terms of two related issues. The first concerns the identification of the relevant market (or markets) for the goods or services concerned (hereafter referred to as products). The relevant market may not coincide with the particular goods or services that are described in the reference. The reference will have outlined the market definition that OFT believes to be relevant to the investigation, but as OFT's Guidance indicates, the OFT does not have to reach a conclusive view on market boundaries. The second concerns the Commission's assessment of competition in the market and whether any features of the market adversely affect competition.

1.22   In practice the analysis of market definition and the assessment of competition will overlap significantly, with many of the factors affecting one being relevant to the other. For instance, in contemplating the extent of supply-side substitution for the purposes of identifying the relevant market, it is likely that the potential for entry and expansion, a key issue in the assessment of competition, will also be considered. Therefore, market definition and competition assessment should not be viewed as two distinct chronological stages – rather they should be viewed as two overlapping analyses. Market definition can be thought of as a framework within which to analyse the effect of features of the market on competition.

6 Investigations and reports of the CC

S. 136 Investigations and reports on market investigation references

(1)   The Commission shall prepare and publish a report on a market investigation reference within the period permitted by section 137.

(2)   The report shall, in particular, contain –
(a) the decisions of the Commission on the questions which it is required to answer by virtue of section 134;
(b) its reasons for its decisions; and
(c) such information as the Commission considers appropriate for facilitating a proper understanding of those questions and of its reasons for its decisions.

(3)   The Commission shall carry out such investigations as it considers appropriate for the purposes of preparing a report under this section.

(4)   The Commission shall, at the same time as a report under this section is published-
(a) in the case of a reference under section 131, give it to the OFT; and
(b) in the case of a reference under section 132, give it to the appropriate Minister and give a copy of it to the OFT.

(5)   Where a reference has been made by the OFT under section 131 or by the appropriate Minister under section 132 in circumstances in which a reference could have been made by a relevant sectoral regulator under section 131 as it has effect by virtue of a relevant sectoral enactment, the Commission shall, at the same time as the report under this section is published, give a copy of it to the relevant sectoral regulator concerned.

(6)   Where a reference has been made by a relevant sectoral regulator under section 131 as it has effect by virtue of a relevant sectoral enactment, the Commission shall, at the same time as the report under this section is published, give a copy of it to the OFT.

...

7 Time limit

S. 137 Time-limits for market investigations and reports

(1)   The Commission shall prepare and publish its report under section 136 within the period of two years beginning with the date of the market investigation reference concerned.

(2)   Subsection (1) is subject to section 151(3) and (5).

(3)   The Secretary of State may by order amend subsection (1) so as to alter the period of two years mentioned in that subsection or any period for the time being mentioned in that subsection in substitution for that period.

(4)   No alteration shall be made by virtue of subsection (3) which results in the period for the time being mentioned in subsection (1) exceeding two years.

(5)   An order under subsection (3) shall not affect any period of time within which the Commission is under a duty to prepare and publish its report under section 136 in

relation to a market investigation reference if the Commission is already under that duty in relation to that reference when the order is made.

(6)   Before making an order under subsection (3) the Secretary of State shall consult the Commission and such other persons as he considers appropriate.

(7)   References in this Part to the date of a market investigation reference shall be construed as references to the date specified in the reference as the date on which it is made.

8 The Competition Commission's duty to remedy adverse effects

S. 138 Duty to remedy adverse effects

(1)   Subsection (2) applies where a report of the Commission has been prepared and published under section 136 within the period permitted by section 137 and contains the decision that there is one or more than one adverse effect on competition.

(2)   The Commission shall, in relation to each adverse effect on competition, take such action under section 159 or 161 as it considers to be reasonable and practicable –
(a) to remedy, mitigate or prevent the adverse effect on competition concerned; and
(b) to remedy, mitigate or prevent any detrimental effects on customers so far as they have resulted from, or may be expected to result from, the adverse effect on competition.

(3)   The decisions of the Commission under subsection (2) shall be consistent with its decisions as included in its report by virtue of section 134(4) unless there has been a material change of circumstances since the preparation of the report or the Commission otherwise has a special reason for deciding differently.

(4)   In making a decision under subsection (2), the Commission shall, in particular, have regard to the need to achieve as comprehensive a solution as is reasonable and practicable to the adverse effect on competition concerned and any detrimental effects on customers so far as resulting from the adverse effect on competition.

(5)   In making a decision under subsection (2), the Commission may, in particular, have regard to the effect of any action on any relevant customer benefits of the feature or features of the market concerned.

(6)   The Commission shall take no action under subsection (2) to remedy, mitigate or prevent any detrimental effect on customers so far as it may be expected to result from the adverse effect on competition concerned if –
(a) no detrimental effect on customers has resulted from the adverse effect on competition; and
(b) the adverse effect on competition is not being remedied, mitigated or prevented.

The CC offers detailed explanation of its duty to remedy adverse effect in its *Market Investigation References: Competition Commission Guidelines*. Particularly worth mentioning are paragraphs 4.2–4.41. The reader is also referred to the previous chapter for additional helpful guidance on the CC's approach.

9 Miscellaneous

(A) Variation of references

Section 135 states that it is possible for a reference to be varied at any time by the OFT or (where relevant) by the appropriate minister. Section 135(2) however provides that the CC will need to be consulted before this can happen, unless the Commission requests the variation itself.

(B) Public interest cases

Sections 139–153 deal with public interest cases and provide, among other things, details on interventions by the Secretary of State in market investigation references on public interest grounds and what happens when an intervention notice is given to the CC by the Secretary of State. It is anticipated that the application of these provisions will be rare in practice.

In its *Guidelines on market investigation references*, the CC provides some detail on the application of these provisions in paragraphs 5.1–5.10.

(C) Powers of the Competition Commission after reaching its findings

Sections 159–161 contain the final powers of the CC and respectively deal with: accepting undertakings from such persons as the CC considers appropriate; making orders in cases of non-fulfilment of undertakings; and making final orders as set out in Schedule 8.

Market Investigation References: Competition Commission Guidelines (CC3) (footnotes omitted)

Undertakings and orders

4.42　As far as its own actions are concerned, the Commission will have the choice of seeking undertakings from the persons that are to be the subject of the measures or making of an order. In general, the Commission's decision as to which form to use will be determined by issues of practicality such as the numbers of parties concerned, and their willingness to negotiate and agree undertakings in the light of the Commission's report. Another consideration will be the scope of the Commission's powers and whether the remedy that it considers appropriate falls within those powers.

4.43 The Commission's order making powers are set out in the Act. Schedule 8 sets out the types of provisions that could be included in an order and Part 1 of Schedule 9 enables the Commission to modify, by order, licence conditions in various regulated markets. While the content of any orders made by the Commission is limited by the Act, the subject matter of an undertaking is not similarly limited. The process of negotiation that is involved with undertakings and the fact that their content is not limited to the matters contained in Schedule 8 may be advantageous in terms of flexibility and suitability.

4.44 The essence of market investigations is that they are likely to be market-wide rather than focused on the conduct of one firm, and a remedy may be more effective if imposed by order than sought through undertakings. For example, because of the need to negotiate undertakings it may take longer to implement a remedy if undertakings are used instead of an order, particularly if many parties are involved. This can complicate the process of negotiation of effective undertakings. When the particular circumstances of the case point to the need for action to be taken speedily, the Commission may decide to implement the remedy by way of order to avoid delay while undertakings are negotiated. But any generalisation has to be qualified: which is the better approach must depend upon the facts of the particular case. However, in regulated sectors, if the Commission decides to modify licence conditions in connection with Part 1 of Schedule 9 to give effect to or take account of any provision of a proposed remedy, it will make an order.

(D) Review by the Competition Appeal Tribunal (CAT)

Section 174 provides for a review by the CAT of decisions of the OFT, the CC, the appropriate minister or the Secretary of State.

S. 179 Review of decisions under Part 4

(1) Any person aggrieved by a decision of the OFT, the appropriate Minister, the Secretary of State or the Commission in connection with a reference or possible reference under this Part may apply to the Competition Appeal Tribunal for a review of that decision.

(2) For this purpose "decision" –
  (a) does not include a decision to impose a penalty under section 110(1) or (3) as applied by section 176; but
  (b) includes a failure to take a decision permitted or required by this Part in connection with a reference or possible reference.

(3) Except in so far as a direction to the contrary is given by the Competition Appeal Tribunal, the effect of the decision is not suspended by reason of the making of the application.

(4)   In determining such an application the Competition Appeal Tribunal shall apply the same principles as would be applied by a court on an application for judicial review.

(5)   The Competition Appeal Tribunal may –
        (a) dismiss the application or quash the whole or part of the decision to which it relates; and
        (b) where it quashes the whole or part of that decision, refer the matter back to the original decision maker with a direction to reconsider and make a new decision in accordance with the ruling of the Competition Appeal Tribunal.

(6)   An appeal lies on any point of law arising from a decision of the Competition Appeal Tribunal under this section to the appropriate court.

(7)   An appeal under subsection (6) requires the permission of the Tribunal or the appropriate court.

(8)   In this section –
        'the appropriate court' means the Court of Appeal or, in the case of Tribunal proceedings in Scotland, the Court of Session; and
        'Tribunal rules' has the meaning given by section 15(1).

(E) Market investigation references and EC competition rules

There is one final important issue to consider, namely the relationship between the market investigation references provisions of the EA2002, and EC competition rules. This issue has received careful consideration by the OFT in its Guideline *OFT511*, which when published offered speculation on the decentralisation of enforcement of Articles 81 and 82 EC brought about by, among other things, Regulation 1/2003 (see chapter 14).

OFT511 (footnotes omitted)

2.10   The modernisation regulation gives the competition authorities and courts in Member States the responsibility, shared with the European Commission, for the application and enforcement of Articles 81 and 82. It imposes an obligation on competition authorities and courts to apply Articles 81 and 82 where they apply national competition law to agreements or practices which may affect trade between Member States. It also imposes certain limits on the use of national competition law.

2.11   [Following the coming into force of the] modernisation regulation ... , where the OFT applies national competition law such as the Enterprise Act to agreements, decisions or concerted practices within the meaning of Article 81(1) which may affect trade between Member States it must also apply Article 81. In addition, national competition law cannot prohibit agreements which may affect trade between Member States:

- that do not restrict competition within the meaning of Article 81(1)
- that fulfil the conditions of Article 81(3), or
- that are covered by an EC block exemption.

The modernisation regulation does not prevent the application of stricter national law to pursue behaviour by an undertaking not involving an agreement or concerted practice where that behaviour falls short of an abuse of dominance.

2.12 In the context of a market investigation by the CC, the obligation to apply Articles 81 or 82 in parallel with national competition law will arise only at the stage where remedies are imposed by the CC following a reference. The obligation does not affect any investigation carried out by the OFT to determine whether to make a reference, the making of a reference to the CC or the investigation by the CC.

2.13 [Following the coming into force of Regulation 1/2003], the OFT will adapt its current procedure to ensure that it applies Articles 81 and 82 in parallel with national competition law. When dealing with a suspected competition problem, the OFT will consider first both whether it might involve an infringement of CA98 and whether it might involve any infringement of Article 81 and/or 82.

2.14 For this reason it is likely to be rare that a reference to the CC will include agreements within the meaning of Article 81(1) except in the special circumstances discussed in paragraphs 2.17 to 2.18. The CC would be unable to impose remedies addressing such agreements without parallel proceedings being opened under Article 81 and the OFT would take this into account when considering whether to make a reference. If an agreement within the meaning of Article 81(1) is uncovered during the course of the CC's investigation the CC would consider whether to remit the agreement back to the OFT for consideration under Article 81.

2.15 It is possible that a reference could be made that included conduct which the CC investigation showed was in fact conduct that amounted to an abuse of a dominant position prohibited by Article 82. In such cases, the CC would complete its investigation and impose remedies under the Act. The OFT would then take these remedies into account when carrying out an Article 82 investigation.

2.16 As a general rule the OFT will avoid actually investigating a suspected infringement of Articles 81 or 82 simultaneously with a CC investigation of the same agreement, decision, concerted practice or conduct, both to reduce undue burdens on business and as a matter of administrative good practice. For the same reasons it will not normally refer a market to the CC when a significant feature of that market is being investigated by the European Commission under Articles 81 or 82.

2.17 Many vertical agreements fall within the terms of the EC block exemption regulation on vertical agreements (Regulation 2790/99/EC). Article 29 of the modernisation regulation permits the competition authorities of Member States to withdraw the benefit of any block exemption regulation from specified agreements within their own territory if both of the following conditions are met:

- the territory of the Member State, or a part of it, has all the characteristics of a distinct geographic market, and
- the agreements in question have effects incompatible with Article 81(3) in the territory of the Member State.

These provisions also apply to agreements that fall within the block exemption regulation on motor vehicles (Regulation 1400/2002/EC).

2.18   Where the OFT has reasonable grounds to suspect that these conditions apply to one or more markets in the UK, it may decide to refer the relevant markets to the CC for investigation. It will be open to the CC, if it finds that competition has been prevented, restricted or distorted by the network of similar vertical agreements and that the conditions as set out above have been met, to recommend to the OFT that it withdraw the benefit of the relevant block exemption regulation. If the OFT accepts this recommendation and the benefit of the exemption is withdrawn it may then take action against the agreements in question under Article 81 or CA98.

13
Collective dominance

1 Introduction

Chapter 9 dealt with the issues of dominance and abuse under Article 82 EC and the Chapter II prohibition of the Competition Act 1998. As may be recalled from that chapter, the ECJ has defined dominance as a position of economic strength enjoyed by *a firm* which enables it to behave independently from its competitors, customers and ultimately of its consumers. The rather interesting question that arose early in the case law of the ECJ was whether dominance can be held not only by a *single* firm but also by a group of *separate* and *autonomous* firms – a situation that has come to be known as collective (and also 'joint' or 'oligopolistic') dominance. This question has proved to be highly controversial in EC competition law.

This chapter deals with collective dominance. To facilitate a better understanding of the concept, the chapter considers its application under Article 82 EC first and then under the Merger Regulation. The concept has not been used in UK competition law and the reason for this can be traced to the OFT's view that the applicability of the concept is limited; its case law does not cover all kinds of coordinated parallel behaviour which may give rise to competition problems; and what amounts to an abuse of collective dominance is underdeveloped in the case law (see OFT's *Guideline* on *Market investigation references: Guidance about the making of references under Part 4 of the Enterprise Act* (OFT511), paragraph 2.5). Furthermore, the existence of market investigation references (dealt with in the previous chapter) and the test of substantial lessening of competition in the case of mergers (dealt with in chapter 11) under the Enterprise Act 2002 provide a means of dealing with situations where collective dominance is said to arise. For this reason, there will be no discussion of the concept under UK competition law in the remainder of this chapter.

2 Article 82

(A) General

The concept of collective dominance in EC competition law has seen a phenomenal increase in significance over the last six years or so. This is not to suggest however that the concept is a new one. Indeed its roots extend to the 1970s, though it seems that the ECJ refused to recognise it at that time. In

Hoffmann La Roche v. Commission (for the facts of the case, see p. 335 above) the ECJ stated in paragraph 39 that:

A dominant position must also be distinguished from parallel courses of conduct which are peculiar to oligopolies in that in an oligopoly the courses of conduct interact, whilst in the case of an undertaking occupying a dominant position the conduct of the undertaking which derives profits from that position is to a great extent determined unilaterally.

(B) Developments since the 1990s

A turning point in the development of the concept came in the early 1990s in the case *Italian Flat Glass*. While there was a defeat for the Commission on the facts in that case (the CFI criticising the Commission for 'recycling' facts used by the Commission when establishing a breach of Article 81 in order to prove that the three producers of flat glass abused their 'collective dominant position'), nevertheless there was victory on the question of law for the Commission: the CFI accepted collective dominance conceptually. In this way, the CFI removed any doubt that the reference in Article 82 to 'one or more undertakings' must necessarily be taken to refer not only to the situation of firms that may form a single economic unit but also where there is more than one separate and autonomous firm.

Societa Italiana Vetro SpA, Fabbrica Piasana SpA and PPG Vernante
Pennitalia SpA v. Commission ('The Italian Flat Glass case') **[1992]**
ECR II-1403

The applicants sought to contest a Commission Decision that they had infringed Articles 81 and 82. Various third parties alleged that the applicants presented a 'common front' by publishing identical product lists, adopting prescribed prices for homogenous product categories and identical sale and payment conditions, and coordinating discount scales on the basis of uniform customer classification.

CFI

357   The Court notes that the very words of the first paragraph of Article [82] provide that 'one or more undertakings' may abuse a dominant position. It has consistently been held, as indeed all the parties acknowledge, that the concept of agreement or concerted practice between undertakings does not cover agreements or concerted practices among undertakings belonging to the same group if the undertakings form an economic unit (see, for example, the judgment in Case 15/74 [*Centrafarm v. Sterling*]). It follows that when Article [81] refers to agreements or concerted practices between 'undertakings', it is referring to relations between two or more economic entities which are capable of competing with one another.

358   The Court considers that there is no legal or economic reason to suppose that the term 'undertaking' in Article [82] has a different meaning from the one given to it in the context of Article [81]. There is nothing, in principle, to prevent two or more independent economic entities from being, on a specific market, united by such economic links that, by virtue of that fact, together they hold a dominant position *vis-à-vis* the other operators on the same market. This could be the case, for example, where two or more independent undertakings jointly have, through agreements or licences, a technological lead affording them the power to behave to an appreciable extent independently of their competitors, their customers and ultimately of their consumers (judgment of the Court in *Hoffmann-La Roche*).

. . .

360   However, it should be pointed out that for the purposes of establishing an infringement of Article [82] of the Treaty, it is not sufficient, as the Commission's agent claimed at the hearing, to 'recycle' the facts constituting an infringement of Article [81], deducing from them the finding that the parties to an agreement or to an unlawful practice jointly hold a substantial share of the market, that by virtue of that fact alone they hold a collective dominant position, and that their unlawful behaviour constitutes an abuse of that collective dominant position. Amongst other considerations, a finding of a dominant position, which is in any case not in itself a matter of reproach, presupposes that the market in question has been defined (judgment of the Court of Justice in Case 6/72 [*Continental Can v. Commission*]; Case 322/81 *Michelin v Commission* [1983] ECR 3461, paragraph 57). The Court must therefore examine, firstly, the analysis of the market made in the decision and, secondly, the circumstances relied on in support of the finding of a collective dominant position.

Nothing more was said in the judgment in relation to the scope of the concept, its elements, what would be required to prove its existence etc. However, and for this reason, paragraph 358 of the judgment gave rise to what appeared at the time to be many burning questions about the concept and its role and function. Indeed, it was inevitable and important that such questions were asked, especially because the many Commission decisions and judgments of the ECJ and CFI delivered during a period of six years after 1992 shed hardly any light on the concept and the term 'links' which the CFI used in the *Italian Flat Glass* case. Hence during that period there was no meaningful advancement in the understanding of the concept as a result. The intervening decisions and judgments include *Almelo v. NV Energiebedrijf Ijsselmij, Centro Servizi Spediporto Srl v. Spedizioni Maritime del Golfo Srl, DIP Spa v. Commune di Bassano del Grappa, Sodemare SA Anni Azzurri Holding SpA and Anni Azzurri Rezzato Srl v. Regione Lombardia, Irish Sugar v. Commission, Port of Rødhy* and *Irish Sugar.*

However, some of the above-mentioned questions now seem to have been answered in some important and helpful judgments delivered by the ECJ and the CFI since 1998 which have cast a great deal of light on the concept; though it would be fair to say that these judgments have not actually fully explained and clarified the concept. A key judgment to mention in this regard is that of the ECJ in *Compagnie Maritime Belge.*

Compagnie Maritime Belge Transports SA, Compagnie MaritimeBelge SA and Dafra-Lines A/S v. Commission [2000] ECR I-1356

The applicants, shipowners and members of the Associated Central West Africa Lines (Cewal) conference, sought to appeal the CFI ruling upholding a Commission Decision that Cewal members had entered into non-competition agreements prohibiting independent operation in two other shipping conferences operating between Europe and Africa in breach of Article 82.

ECJ

29   In paragraph 64, the Court of First Instance stated that Article [82] of the Treaty could apply to the unilateral conduct of a liner conference. In paragraph 65, it stated that, in view of the evidence set out in the contested decision, the practices of which Cewal members were accused revealed an intention to adopt together the same conduct on the market in order to react unilaterally to a change, deemed to be a threat, in the competitive situation on the market on which they operate. The Court of First Instance held, consequently, in paragraph 66, that the Commission had sufficiently demonstrated that the position of Cewal members on the relevant market should be assessed collectively.

30   In paragraph 67, the Court of First Instance was responding to the argument that the Commission had recycled the facts constituting an infringement of Article [81] of the Treaty. That paragraph was not, however, intended to show links other than those already established in paragraph 65.

The ECJ then moved to consider the wording and objectives of Articles 81 and 82 and the existence of the concept of collective dominance under the latter.

33   It is clear from the very wording of Articles [81(1)(a), (b), (d) and (e)] and [82(a) to (d)] of the Treaty that the same practice may give rise to an infringement of both provisions. Simultaneous application of Articles [81] and [82] of the Treaty cannot therefore be ruled out *a priori.* However, the objectives pursued by each of those two provisions must be distinguished.

34   Article [81] of the Treaty applies to agreements, decisions and concerted practices which may appreciably affect trade between Member States, regardless of the position on the market of the undertakings concerned. Article [82] of the Treaty, on the other hand, deals with the conduct of one or more economic operators consisting in the abuse of a position of economic strength which enables the operator concerned

to hinder the maintenance of effective competition on the relevant market by allowing it to behave to an appreciable extent independently of its competitors, its customers and, ultimately, consumers (see Case 322/81 *Michelin v Commission* [1983] ECR 3461, paragraph 30).

35　In terms of Article [82] of the Treaty, a dominant position may be held by several undertakings. The Court of Justice has held, on many occasions, that the concept of undertaking in the chapter of the Treaty devoted to the rules on competition presupposes the economic independence of the entity concerned (see, in particular, Case 22/71 *Béguelin Import v G.L. Import Export* [1971] ECR 949).

36　It follows that the expression 'one or more undertakings' in Article [82] of the Treaty implies that a dominant position may be held by two or more economic entities legally independent of each other, provided that from an economic point of view they present themselves or act together on a particular market as a collective entity. That is how the expression collective dominant position, as used in the remainder of this judgment, should be understood.

37　However, a finding that an undertaking has a dominant position is not in itself a ground of criticism but simply means that, irrespective of the reasons for which it has such a dominant position, the undertaking concerned has a special responsibility not to allow its conduct to impair genuine undistorted competition on the common market (see [*Michelin v. Commission* (1983)], paragraph 57).

38　The same applies as regards undertakings which hold a collective dominant position. A finding that two or more undertakings hold a collective dominant position must, in principle, proceed upon an economic assessment of the position on the relevant market of the undertakings concerned, prior to any examination of the question whether those undertakings have abused their position on the market.

39　So, for the purposes of analysis under Article [82] of the Treaty, it is necessary to consider whether the undertakings concerned together constitute a collective entity *vis-à-vis* their competitors, their trading partners and consumers on a particular market. It is only where that question is answered in the affirmative that it is appropriate to consider whether that collective entity actually holds a dominant position and whether its conduct constitutes abuse.

A crucial paragraph in this judgment is paragraph 36 where the ECJ coin the concept of a 'collective entity' when it stated that, before one or more firms could be held to be in a collective dominant position, they must hold themselves out as a collective entity – something that the ECJ said needs to be assessed from an economic point of view. Also important is paragraph 39 in which the ECJ explained that an inquiry to establish whether a breach of Article 82 has occurred in a situation of collective dominance should proceed as follows:
1. Do the firms concerned constitute a collective entity?

2. If yes, does the collective entity hold a dominant position?
3. If yes, does the conduct of the entity constitute an abuse?
The question of course is how one can determine whether a collective entity exists. The ECJ answered this question as follows:

41   In order to establish the existence of a collective entity as defined above, it is necessary to examine the economic links or factors which give rise to a connection between the undertakings concerned (see, *inter alia*, Case C-393/92 *Almelo* [1994] ECR I-1477, paragraph 43, and Joined Cases C-68/94 and C-30/95 *France and Others v Commission* [1998] ECR I-1375, paragraph 221).

42   In particular, it must be ascertained whether economic links exist between the undertakings concerned which enable them to act together independently of their competitors, their customers and consumers (see [*Michelin v. Commission* (1983)]).

43   The mere fact that two or more undertakings are linked by an agreement, a decision of associations of undertakings or a concerted practice within the meaning of Article [81(1)] of the Treaty does not, of itself, constitute a sufficient basis for such a finding.

44   On the other hand, an agreement, decision or concerted practice (whether or not covered by an exemption under Article [81(3)] of the Treaty) may undoubtedly, where it is implemented, result in the undertakings concerned being so linked as to their conduct on a particular market that they present themselves on that market as a collective entity *vis-à-vis* their competitors, their trading partners and consumers.

45   The existence of a collective dominant position may therefore flow from the nature and terms of an agreement, from the way in which it is implemented and, consequently, from the links or factors which give rise to a connection between undertakings which result from it. Nevertheless, the existence of an agreement or of other links in law is not indispensable to a finding of a collective dominant position; such a finding may be based on other connecting factors and would depend on an economic assessment and, in particular, on an assessment of the structure of the market in question.

To determine whether a collective entity exists, according to the ECJ, one needs to examine the 'links' between the firms concerned and then ascertain whether the links enable the firms concerned to act independently of all pressures of competition. The existence of such links would follow from the nature and terms of an agreement that may exist between the firms concerned and the way such an agreement is implemented and its potential consequences. However, what the ECJ has made quite clear is that the existence of an agreement, a decision by association of undertakings or a concerted practice, which may link the firms concerned, is not in itself essential for a finding that a collective dominant position exists. Another important point related to this is made in paragraph 45 of the judgment where the ECJ states that a finding that a collective dominant position exists may be based on other connected factors and would depend on assessment in economic terms, including an assessment of the structure of the market concerned.

In paragraphs 46–58 of the judgment the ECJ turned to consider the question of whether a liner conference can be characterised as a collective entity. The ECJ stated in paragraph 48 that under Regulation 4056/86 (on the application on Articles 81 and 82 to maritime transport) and in light of a liner conference's nature and objectives, the question should be answered in the affirmative. In relation to the particular facts of the case and the implemented Cewal agreement, the ECJ stated in paragraph 57 that the CFI was right to uphold the Commission's finding that the agreement enabled the conduct of the members of the conference to be assessed collectively.

Recently, the concept of collective dominance was considered by the CFI in *Atlantic Container Line v. Commission*. The Commission had found in its decision in *Trans-Atlantic Conference Agreement* that the members of a liner conference abused their collective dominant position and imposed a fine of €273 m. The Commission's finding of a collective dominant position was upheld by the CFI in a very long and detailed judgment. Particular paragraphs to note in the judgment are paragraphs 583–636.

(C) 'Vertical' collective dominance

An interesting concept which emerged in relation to collective dominance in another Article 82 case was that of 'vertical' collective dominance.

Irish Sugar plc v. Commission [1999] ECR II-2969

The applicant, the sole processor of sugar beet in Ireland and the principal supplier of sugar both industrially and for retail, distributed its products through Sugar Distributors Ltd ('SDL'), owned by parent company Sugar Distribution (Holding) Ltd ('SDH'). In Northern Ireland, the company distributed through a subsidiary, William McKinney Ltd. The impugned Commission decision found the existence of collective dominance between the applicant and SDL.

The CFI found that economic independence did not exclude the possibility of collective dominance and accordingly that firms in vertical relationships could abuse a collective dominant position contrary to Article 82 even if the abuse is not action by all of those involved.

CFI

38   The applicant denies that it held a joint dominant position together with SDL between 1985 and February 1990.

39   In that regard, it sets out the historical background of its relations with SDH, which at that time held all the shares in SDL. It emphasises that, even though it held 51% of

the shares in SDH before acquiring all of them in February 1990, it did not control the management of that company. Since 1982, responsibilities had been allocated for practical purposes between it and its sales subsidiaries in such a way that it was responsible for technical services and marketing, including consumer promotions and rebates, while its sales subsidiaries were responsible for the operation and funding of sales, trade promotions, merchandising and distribution of the products. Contrary to what the Commission alleges in the contested decision (point 30), however, that arrangement did not deprive SDL of the right to trade in competing products. It refers in that respect to transactions by SDL which until 1991 involved, through McKinney's, the purchase and sale in Northern Ireland of sugar from a British supplier. The applicant states, moreover, that its responsibilities under that arrangement were the subject of a management services agreement pursuant to which SDL paid the applicant management charges between 1982 and 1989, the amount of which varied each year and was calculated by the financial director of SDL. It adds that, in practice, the pricing of sugar was essentially a matter for SDL. In order to confirm the autonomy of SDL's management, the applicant also cites extracts from a report drawn up by two experts appointed by the High Court in 1992 and from a report drawn up by Arthur Andersen.

40   The applicant also asserts that since its economic ties with SDH did not have the effect of uniting the two undertakings they were not capable of supporting a finding of a joint dominant position in the retail and industrial markets in granulated sugar in Ireland. It criticises the Commission for using in the contested decision (point 112) a false criterion, the parallel interests of the two companies *vis-à-vis* third parties, in order to find that they held a joint dominant position. It also claims that the reference to the judgment in Joined Cases T-68/89, T-77/89 and T-78/89 *SIV and Others v Commission* [1992] ECR II-1403, paragraph 358, is not logical.

41   The applicant maintains that its links with SDH guaranteed the independence of the board and management of the latter. The test used in the case-law to determine the existence of a joint dominant position held by linked undertakings is the adoption of the same conduct on the relevant market (Case C-393/92 *Almelo v Energiebedrijf IJsselmij* [1994] ECR I-1477, paragraph 42, and Joined Cases T-24/93, T-25/93, T-26/93 and T/28/93 *Compagnie Maritime Belge Transports and Others v Commission* [1996] ECR II-1201, paragraphs 62 to 68). Adopting the same conduct on the market represents more than mere parallel interests, which tends to be the rule in a producer-trader relationship, and the more so in a situation of structural oversupply, as in this case. The applicant also points out that in the statement of objections the Commission did not address the issue of whether the relationship between the two undertakings led them to adopt the same conduct on the market, since it merely found that there were structural ties between the applicant and SDH/SDL (statement of objections, paragraphs 102, 103 and 104 *et seq.*).

42   Similarly, the applicant points out that, whilst the absence of competition in a vertical commercial relationship between a producer and a trader may be a salient feature

of a collective dominant position, it is not sufficient to establish the existence of such a dominant position. The applicant questions the relevance of the concept of a collective dominant position in a vertical commercial relationship. Furthermore, all the collective dominant position cases decided by the Community judicature so far concerned horizontal commercial relationships. In its reply the applicant adds that a vertical commercial relationship is characterised by the absence of competition.

43 The applicant also criticises the allegedly collective nature of most of the abuses committed in the context of the joint dominance alleged. In that regard, it points out that although the Commission finds that the product swap operations were exclusively arranged by SDL (point 48 of the contested decision) and that the applicant was only informed of these on 18 July 1988 (point 52), it none the less considers that this amounted to abusive exploitation of a joint dominant position. It accuses the Commission of 'recycling' certain facts in the contested decision by using them to establish both the existence of a joint dominant position (point 112) and abusive exploitation of that joint dominant position (points 117, 127 and 128), contrary to the principle laid down in the case-law in that regard (*Compagnie Maritime Belge Transports*, paragraph 67). That 'recycling' exercise is said also to amount to an infringement of the applicant's rights of defence, and therefore of Article 4 of Regulation No 99/63, since the fact that the applicant financed the rebates allowed by SDL, as distinct from granting them, was not considered to constitute an abuse in the statement of objections.

44 It is obvious, first, that although the applicant disputes the collective nature of the dominant position which it is alleged to have held with SDH/SDL on the retail sugar market between 1985 and February 1990, it has not in any way denied in its application that it carried out more than 88% of sales registered on that market for the entire duration of the infringement period (point 159 of the contested decision). Thus, even if it formally denies having held an individual or joint dominant position on the industrial sugar market . ., it has not raised any specific arguments capable of casting doubt on the assessment that it held a dominant position on the retail sugar market.

45 Moreover, whilst the applicant castigates as inappropriate the criterion used by the Commission at point 112 of the contested decision to establish the existence of a joint dominant position, the parties nevertheless agree on a number of the conditions required by the case-law to establish the existence of a joint dominant position. They thus maintain that, according to the case-law, two independent economic entities may hold a joint dominant position on a market (*SIV*, paragraph 358, cited in point 112 of the contested decision). They also consider that there must be close links between the two entities, and that those links must be such as to be capable of leading to the adoption of the same conduct and policy on the market in question. In that respect, both parties cite the judgments in *Almelo* and *Compagnie Maritime Belge Transports*.

[595]

46   Their analysis of the state of the case-law on this question must be accepted. Following its earlier case-law and the case-law of the Court of First Instance (*Almelo*, paragraph 42; Case C-96/94 *Centro Servizi Spediporto v Spedizionia Marittima del Golfo* [1995] ECR I-2883, paragraphs 32 and 33; Joined Cases C-140/94, C-141/94 and C-142/94 *DIP and Others v Comune di Bassano del Grappa* [1995] ECR I-3257, paragraph 26; Case C-70/95 *Sodemare and Others v Regione Lombardia* [1997] ECR I-3395, paragraphs 45 and 46; *SIV*, paragraph 358; *Compagnie Maritime Belge Transports*, paragraph 62), the Court of Justice has confirmed that a joint dominant position consists in a number of undertakings being able together, in particular because of factors giving rise to a connection between them, to adopt a common policy on the market and act to a considerable extent independently of their competitors, their customers, and ultimately consumers (Joined Cases C-68/94 and C-30/95 *France and Others v Commission* [1998] ECR I-1375, paragraph 221).

47   It is therefore necessary to determine in this case whether, by reason of the factors connecting the applicant and SDL from 1985 to February 1990, they had the power to adopt a common market policy.

48   The applicant relies on the nature of its relations with SDL up to 1990 to dispute the existence of a joint dominant position. It insists that the two entities were independent, making existence of links of the type claimed by the Commission *ipso facto* impossible.

49   In the first place, the applicant's argument is based on the false premises that the economic independence of the two entities prevents them from holding a joint dominant position. In fact, the case-law relied on by the applicant and referred to in paragraph 46 above shows that the mere independence of the economic entities in question is not sufficient to remove the possibility of their holding a joint dominant position.

50   Secondly, the factors connecting the applicant and SDL identified in the contested decision show that between 1985 and February 1990 those two economic entities had the power to adopt a common market policy.

51   In the contested decision (point 112), the Commission thus identifies as connecting factors the applicant's shareholding in SDH, its representation on the boards of SDH and SDL, the policy-making structure of the companies and the communication process established to facilitate it, and the direct economic ties constituted by SDL's commitment to obtain its supplies exclusively from the applicant and the applicant's financing of all consumer promotions and rebates offered by SDL to its customers. Details thereof are set out in points 29, 30 and 111 of the contested decision.

52   The arguments whereby the applicant seeks to question the reality of those factors are both few in number and largely unfounded. It does not deny, for example, that it held 51% of the shares of SDH, which in turn held all the shares in SDL; that half the board of SDH were its representatives; that its chief executive and several of its board members sat on the board of SDL; that from July 1982 to February 1990 it was

responsible, on the basis of an allocation of tasks jointly determined in July 1982, for technical services and marketing, commercial strategy, consumer promotions and rebates; that SDL carried out the distribution of sugar produced by the applicant in Ireland; that SDL undertook, subject to the availability of supplies, to purchase its sugar requirements only from the applicant and not to become concerned or interested in the purchase, sale, resale or promotion of any products of a like or similar kind to those available from the applicant; that the applicant and SDL were required to communicate to each other certain information concerning marketing, sales, advertising, consumer promotions and financial matters; and, finally, that monthly meetings were held between representatives of SDL and of the applicant.

53   On the other hand, it claims that SDL's exclusive supply undertaking did not prevent it from trading in competing products, particularly in Northern Ireland through the intermediary of McKinney; that the management charges paid by SDL to the applicant arose from the performance of a contract, the amount varying each year and being calculated by the financial director of SDL (letter of 23 October 1991 addressed to the shareholders of Greencore); that those management charges did not constitute a financing of SDL's commercial policy; that the chairmanship of the monthly meetings between the two undertakings was assumed in turn by a representative of the applicant and a representative of SDL and not exclusively by the chief executive of the applicant's sugar division; and, finally, that the pricing of sugar was essentially a matter for SDL.

54   Those criticisms are, however, not capable of affecting the probative value of the documents used by the Commission to support its analysis of the relations between the applicant and SDL. To demonstrate that, it is sufficient to examine the extract from the minutes of the SDL board meeting of 1 July 1982 which appears in Annex 3 to the statement of objections . . .

55   Bearing in mind the contents of that document and the matters referred to in the contested decision, the applicant's claim that SDL traded competing products in Northern Ireland through the intermediary of McKinney does not in any way undermine the Commission's assessment of SDL's exclusive supply clause with the applicant. First, it is a claim not supported by any particular proof. Next, McKinney was not in principle legally bound by SDL's undertaking to the applicant. The same applies to the explanations it put forward in its reply to a written question of the Court, concerning sales of German and French sugar through the intermediary of Trilby Trading Ltd, 51% of whose shares the applicant claims to have acquired in August 1987. Contrary to the applicant's claims, the only examples which it adduces in an attempt to minimise the importance of the exclusive supply clause concluded in 1982, namely McKinney's sales in Northern Ireland and the sales by Trilby Trading Ltd after August 1984, tend rather to demonstrate that SDL remained loyal to its undertaking. The minutes of the SDL board meeting of 1 July 1982 also mention McKinney where that company is concerned. McKinney is not expressly referred to by the exclusive supply clause, as drafted in those minutes. Finally, the example of

McKinney concerns Northern Ireland, which is not part of the geographical market at issue in this case.

56   The applicant's presentation of the financing characteristics of the rebates granted by SDL to its customers is full of contradictions. For example, it acknowledges in the final subparagraph of paragraph 28 of its application that it accepted for its account all rebates granted by SDL, and advertising and promotion costs, only to deny in its reply that it financed rebates granted by SDL. In those circumstances, the Court can only find that the Commission correctly assessed the nature of the financial services organised between the applicant and SDL. The contents of the letter from the chairman of Greencore to shareholders of 23 October 1991 is of no use to the applicant in that respect, since it contains no details as to the actual allocation of roles between the applicant and SDL.

57   Similarly, the statement that the 'monthly communication meetings' between the applicant and SDL were chaired in turn by their respective representatives is not only unsupported by any probative document but is also irrelevant. Little purpose is served by stating who chaired the monthly meetings in turn, their existence alone being sufficient to demonstrate that such meetings constitute a connecting factor within the meaning of the case-law (see paragraph 46 above). The Court cannot but note, moreover, that the text of the minutes of the SDL board meeting of 1 July 1982 is quite unequivocal, since it states: 'The meetings are to be chaired by the Chief Executive of the Sugar Division'.

58   Nor do the applicant's criticisms concerning the price fixing policy, to the effect that this was essentially a matter for SDL, correspond to the minutes of the SDL board meeting of 1 July 1982, which state, in paragraph 2 of the section dealing with SDL's responsibilities: 'SDL to be responsible for sales decisions including pricing decisions for all of the three sales and distribution companies above. These decisions to be taken in accordance with policy as laid down by the Chief Executive of the Sugar Division.' Once again, moreover, these claims are not supported by any particular item of evidence. The letter from the chairman of Greencore to shareholders of 23 October 1991 makes no mention of the allocation of responsibilities in the fixing of prices.

59   The Court therefore finds that the applicant has not succeeded in demonstrating that the Commission committed an error of assessment in finding that the connecting factors mentioned in the contested decision showed that, between 1985 and February 1990, SDL and the applicant had the power to adopt a common market policy (see paragraph 46 above).

60   Furthermore, other market operators considered that the applicant and SDL formed one and the same economic entity. For example, ASI International Foods (formerly ASI International Trading Ltd), the importer of French sugar to the Irish market ('ASI'), sent a letter to the applicant on 18 July 1988 complaining about its market conduct and that of SDL. The author of that letter, which is addressed to the chief

executive of the applicant, states: 'I write to draw your attention to the unfair practices which are the direct creation of your undertaking or of SDL which is controlled by you, as regards our efforts to retail our Eurolux sugar in one kilo packets in Ireland.'

61   The fact that the applicant and SDL are in a vertical commercial relationship does not affect that finding.

62   First, documents of the applicant show that the two companies were active in the same market from 1985 to 1990, so that there could not have been an exclusively vertical commercial relationship. At paragraph 27 of its application, for example, the applicant reproduces an extract from an agreement between SDH shareholders in 1975, which stipulates that 'SDL and the Sugar Company shall continue to trade as independent and competing enterprises ...' Moreover, in its reply to a written question of the Court, the applicant insists that SDL distributed the whole of the applicant's supply on the retail sugar market only as from 1988. It also supplies information showing that on the industrial sugar market SDL and the applicant shared the market with a third undertaking, Harcourt Agency Ltd, until the beginning of the 1980s. However, although it maintains that it was no longer present in the industrial sugar market from 1985 to 1989, it does not supply any evidence in support of that allegation. In those circumstances, the applicant's argument based on the absence of competition between itself and SDL may be rejected at the outset.

63   Nor does the case-law contain anything to support the conclusion that the concept of a joint dominant position is inapplicable to two or more undertakings in a vertical commercial relationship. As the Commission points out, unless one supposes there to be a lacuna in the application of Article [82] of the Treaty, it cannot be accepted that undertakings in a vertical relationship, without however being integrated to the extent of constituting one and the same undertaking, should be able abusively to exploit a joint dominant position.

64   Moreover, since all the factual elements relied on in the contested decision to demonstrate that the applicant and SDL held a joint dominant position were mentioned in the statement of objections, the applicant cannot now accuse the Commission of not considering the relations between the two undertakings in the light of the same market conduct in the statement of objections. As the Commission emphasises in the discussion concerning the amount of the fine, the applicant was perfectly aware of the nature of its links with SDL and of the use which might be made of them in the market. A memorandum headed 'Notes on meeting dealing with S.D.L. held on 21st November 1988 in Head Office' (Annex 3 to the statement of objections) states at paragraph 6: 'Having 51% of S.D.L. should prevent any action being taken against us under Article [81]. We would have to use our influential presence in S.D.L. to prevent any breaches of Article [82] occurring.'

65   Nor can the applicant derive an argument from the alleged absence of any collective nature in the abuses of a dominant position found in the contested decision.

66   Whilst the existence of a joint dominant position may be deduced from the position which the economic entities concerned together hold on the market in question, the abuse does not necessarily have to be the action of all the undertakings in question. It only has to be capable of being identified as one of the manifestations of such a joint dominant position being held. Therefore, undertakings occupying a joint dominant position may engage in joint or individual abusive conduct. It is enough for that abusive conduct to relate to the exploitation of the joint dominant position which the undertakings hold in the market. In this case, the Commission maintains that the exploitation of that joint dominant position formed part of a continuous overall policy of maintaining and strengthening that position, and that conduct adopted by both SDL and the applicant between 1985 and February 1990 fell within that policy. Point 117 of the contested decision states: 'The actions taken by Irish Sugar before 1990 with regard to the transport restriction, by both companies with respect to border rebates, export rebates and the fidelity rebate and by SDL with respect to the product swap and selective pricing, were undertaken from a position of joint dominance.' The Commission was therefore entitled to take the view that the individual conduct of one of the undertakings together holding a joint dominant position constituted the abusive exploitation of that position.

67   Nor can the applicant complain that there has been 'recycling' of certain facts in the contested decision within the meaning that the case-law gives to that concept (*SIV*, paragraph 360; *Compagnie Maritime Belge Transports*, paragraph 67). The Commission has not used the same facts to establish both the existence of a joint dominant position and its abusive exploitation. Thus, even if the applicant's financing of rebates granted by SDL was held by the Commission to be one of the connecting factors between the two entities (see paragraph 51 above), it has not in any way been regarded as an abuse in itself. The abuse consists in having granted certain rebates in the particular circumstances of the market in question at that time. The applicant cannot therefore claim to have established infringement of its defence rights and of Article 4 of Regulation No 99/63.

In sum therefore, the scope of collective dominance under Article 82 has been clarified quite considerably in recent years and its the potential application has been expanded, which is clear in light of *Irish Sugar v. Commission* where the CFI confirmed that the concept covers not only horizontal but also vertical situations. Furthermore, it is clear that there is an obvious willingness on the part of the Commission in particular to continue to rely on the concept to establish a breach of Article 82.

3 Merger regulation

(A) General

While Article 82 refers to 'one or more undertakings', a reference which was no doubt helpful in confirming that the concept of collective dominance was included within the Article, Regulation 4064/89 did not contain such a reference; nor does its successor, Regulation 139/2004. Yet, to have ruled out the application of the concept in the case of mergers would have left a significant lacuna in EC competition law and made enforcement by the Commission all the more difficult, given the number of markets in the Community with oligopolistic tendencies which may prove fertile ground for tacit coordination between firms operating on those markets.

(B) Collective dominance in merger cases

Hence, it is not surprising that the Commission decided to invoke this concept in its early merger decisions. A notable decision of considerable importance was *Nestlé/Perrier* which was based on a set of facts which were strong enough to provide a good basis for supporting the proposition of a collective dominance doctrine under EC merger control. In the case, Nestlé SA, French subsidiary to the Swiss-based food group, sought to gain control over Source Perrier SA. They were two of the largest manufacturers in the French market for bottled 'source waters' and between them held about 60 per cent market share. The other large manufacturer was BSN with a market share of 22 per cent.

Commission

120   The reduction from three to two suppliers (duopoly) is not a mere cosmetic change in the market structure ... the reduction from three to only two national suppliers would make anti-competitive parallel behaviour leading to collective abuses much easier.

121   The mineral water suppliers in France have developed instruments of transparency facilitating a tacit co-ordination of pricing policies...

122   Their reciprocal dependency thus creates a strong common interest and incentive to maximise profits by engaging in anti-competitive parallel behaviour. This situation of common interest is further reinforced by the fact that Nestle and BSN are similar in size and nature, both active in the wider food industry and already co-operate in some sectors of that industry.

...

131   [T]he market structure resulting from the merger... would create a duopolistic dominant position on the French bottled water market which would significantly impede effective competition and would be very likely to cause considerable harm to consumers.

The Commission has applied the concept of collective dominance in the case of concentrations with a Community dimension, as have the Community Courts, despite the fact that Article 2(2) and (3) of Regulation 4064/89 (and indeed

Regulation 139/2004) refer to the creation or strengthening of *a dominant position*. Of course the wide scope of the wording of Article 2(1) of both Regulations can arguably be said to support an intervention by the Commission in cases of collective dominance. In Article 2(1)(a) there is a reference to 'the need to maintain and develop effective competition within the common market in view of, among other things, the structure of all the markets concerned ...'. It is clearly arguable that a situation of collective dominance comes within the scope of this paragraph; and indeed the wording of Article 2 was instrumental in the Community Courts' confirmation in some of the leading cases of the existence of a concept of collective dominance under the EC merger control. Nevertheless, the Commission's efforts to rely on the concept was not expected to go unchallenged by firms and even Member States, who would naturally be concerned about the increased likelihood that the concept of collective dominance gave the Commission much wider grounds to object to concentrations. A serious challenge arose as a result of the Commission's decision in *Kali and Salz/MdK/Treuhand*.

French Republic and others v. Commission [1998] ECR I-1375

Kali und Salz AG ('K+S') sought to acquire the failing Mitteldeutsche Kali AG ('MdK'), combining their respective activities in potash-salt-based products for agriculture. The Commission identified SCPA as the only potential competitor on the European market, yet it doubted the effectiveness of competition given previous behaviour of the two companies and their longstanding commercial ties. The impugned Commission decision granted clearance subject to agreement from K+S to withdraw from existing arrangements with SCPA. SCPA sought to annul this aspect of the Commission's decision.

An appeal was made to the ECJ. The ECJ agreed with the Commission that a concentration creating or strengthening a dominant oligopoly was likely to prove incompatible with the system of undistorted competition, and Regulation 4064/89 must therefore be applicable to such a situation. However, the applicants succeeded in their action because the Commission had not established that links between the firms were the cause of any anti-competitive behaviour.

ECJ

166   Second, it cannot be deduced from the wording of Article 2 of the Regulation that only concentrations which create or strengthen an individual dominant position, that is, a dominant position held by the parties to the concentration, come within the scope of the Regulation. Article 2, in referring to 'a concentration which creates or strengthens a dominant position', does not in itself exclude the possibility of applying the Regulation to cases where concentrations lead to the creation or

strengthening of a collective dominant position, that is, a dominant position held by the parties to the concentration together with an entity not a party thereto.

167 Third, with respect to the *travaux préparatoires*, it appears from the documents in the case that they cannot be regarded as expressing clearly the intention of the authors of the Regulation as to the scope of the term 'dominant position'. In those circumstances, the *travaux préparatoires* provide no assistance for the interpretation of the disputed concept ...

168 Since the textual and historical interpretations of the Regulation, and in particular Article 2 thereof, do not permit its precise scope to be assessed as regards the type of dominant position concerned, the provision in question must be interpreted by reference to its purpose and general structure (see, to that effect, Case 11/76 *Netherlands v Commission.* ... , paragraph 6).

169 As may be seen from the first and second recitals in its preamble, the Regulation is founded on the premises that the objective of instituting a system to ensure that competition in the common market is not distorted is essential for the achievement of the internal market by 1992 and for its future development.

170 It follows from the sixth, seventh, tenth and eleventh recitals in the preamble that the Regulation, unlike Articles [81] and [82] of the Treaty, is intended to apply to all concentrations with a Community dimension in so far as they are likely, because of their effect on the structure of competition within the Community, to prove incompatible with the system of undistorted competition envisaged by the Treaty.

171 A concentration which creates or strengthens a dominant position on the part of the parties concerned with an entity not involved in the concentration is liable to prove incompatible with the system of undistorted competition which the Treaty seeks to secure. Consequently, if it were accepted that only concentrations creating or strengthening a dominant position on the part of the parties to the concentration were covered by the Regulation, its purpose as indicated in particular by the abovementioned recitals would be partially frustrated. The Regulation would thus be deprived of a not insignificant aspect of its effectiveness, without that being necessary from the perspective of the general structure of the Community system of control of concentrations.

A key paragraph to note is paragraph 171 in which the ECJ made two important points that:
• Creating a collective dominant position is liable to prove incompatible with the system of undistorted competition in the Community;
• Accepting that the Regulation only applies to the creation and strengthening of a dominant position on the part of the parties to the concentration would partially frustrate the purpose of the Regulation.

These two points have laid to rest any doubt that Regulation 4064/89 (and of course now its successor, Regulation 139/2004), in particular Article 2, capture situations of collective dominance.

Having made such findings, the ECJ then turned to deal with the arguments of the parties in relation to the Commission's findings of the existence of a collective dominant position in the case (paragraphs 179–219 of the judgment). In paragraph 180 the ECJ referred to the three criteria used by the Commission to establish the existence of a collective dominant position, namely:

- the degree of concentration on the market which would follow from the concentration;
- the structural factors relating to the nature of the market and the characteristics of the product; and
- the structural links between the undertakings concerned.

The ECJ also referred in the same paragraph to the Commission's view that it does not accept that the criteria for determining the existence of a collective dominant position must be the same in the context of Article 82 as in the context of the Regulation. According to the Commission, in the case of Article 82, it is the past which must be referred to, whereas in the case of the Regulation the analysis is prospective, its purpose being to maintain an effective competitive structure in the market for the future.

Having set out the factual assessment and issues in dispute, i.e. the criteria used by the Commission for assessing collective dominance, as summarised in paragraph 180, the ECJ considered the degree of concentration resulting from the merger, the structural factors of the market, and structural links between the undertakings. On the basis of submissions by the parties the ECJ then reached the following conclusions:

221   In the case of an alleged collective dominant position, the Commission is therefore obliged to assess, using a prospective analysis of the reference market, whether the concentration which has been referred to it leads to a situation in which effective competition in the relevant market is significantly impeded by the undertakings involved in the concentration and one or more other undertakings which together, in particular because of connecting factors which exist between them, are able to adopt a common policy on the market and act to a considerable extent independently of their competitors, their customers, and also of consumers.

222   Such an approach warrants close examination in particular of the circumstances which, in each individual case, are relevant for assessing the effects of the concentration on competition in the reference market.

223   In this respect, however, the basic provisions of the Regulation, in particular Article 2 thereof, confer on the Commission a certain discretion, especially with respect to assessments of an economic nature.

224   Consequently, review by the Community judicature of the exercise of that discretion, which is essential for defining the rules on concentrations, must take account of the discretionary margin implicit in the provisions of an economic nature which form part of the rules on concentrations.

225   That being so, it must be held that the Commission's analysis of the concentration and of its effects on the market in question is flawed in certain respects which affect the economic assessment of the concentration.

226   As points 51 and 52 of the contested decision show, K+S/MdK and SCPA will hold shares of the relevant market, after the concentration, of 23% and 37% respectively, calculated on the basis of sales. A market share of approximately 60%, subdivided in that way, cannot of itself point conclusively to the existence of a collective dominant position on the part of those undertakings.

227   As to the alleged structural links between K+S and SCPA, which were the essential factor relied on by the Commission in making its own assessment, some of the applicants' criticisms playing down the significance of those links as evidence of the creation of a collective dominant position on the part of the two undertakings are well founded.

228   Thus the Commission's finding that the holding of K+S and SCPA in the Kali-Export export cartel may have an impact on their competitive behaviour in the Community would not appear to be supported by a sufficiently cogent and consistent body of evidence. The Commission merely notes, on this point, that the British producer CPL started marketing its products independently on the French market only after it had left the cartel in 1987, because it could not reconcile direct competition with SCPA on the French market with its membership of the cartel (see point 60 of the contested decision). Even if the fact were disregarded that the Commission's argument concerns the alleged effects of membership of the cartel only on part of the Community market apart from Germany, it must be observed that the Spanish producer Coposa, likewise a member of Kali-Export, markets independently in France a quantity of potash corresponding to slightly over 5% of French consumption. That quantity accounts for about 47% of Coposa's exports to the market in question as well as two-thirds of its exports to France, and was indeed also considered significant in the context of the definition of the relevant geographical market (see point 38 of the contested decision). In those circumstances, it would appear that the Commission has not established to the necessary legal standard the existence of a causal link between K+S and SCPA's membership of the export cartel and their anticompetitive behaviour on the relevant market.

229   As regards the alleged links between K+S and SCPA relating to supplies by K+S in France, the Commission required K+S to terminate its existing cooperation with SCPA as associated distributor on the French market, and accepted that K+S could conclude sales contracts with SCPA in normal market conditions (see point 63 of the contested decision). The Commission accordingly considered that there was

a partnership between K+S and SCPA for the distribution of German potash in France.

230   It appears from the documents in the case that the only specific distribution links between those two undertakings related to kieserite, that is to say, a product not forming part of the relevant product market. Apart from that, SCPA merely bought from K+S, on normal market conditions, potash used by EMC or intended for sale outside the French market.

231   It is thus apparent that K+S and SCPA did not have a privileged relationship for the distribution of potash-based products.

232   It follows from the foregoing that the cluster of structural links between K+S and SCPA, which, as the Commission itself concedes, constitutes the core of the contested decision, is not in the end as tight or as conclusive as the Commission sought to make out.

233   It should be noted, moreover, that the Commission stated in the contested decision that there was no effective competition between K+S and SCPA on the relevant market. According to point 57 of the contested decision, the main reason for assuming an absence of real competition between K+S and SCPA is the existence of exceptionally close links between the two companies extending over a long period of time.

234   It also follows from point 57 of the contested decision that the acquisition of MdK by K+S following the concentration would involve the addition of MdK's market share to K+S, an addition which the Commission described in its observations as substantial.

235   On this point, it should be noted that in addition to its market share of 7% in the Community apart from Germany, MdK, although operating its plants at only 50% of capacity, is the second largest potash producer in the Community, after K+S (see points 51, 52, 62 and 76 of the contested decision).

236   The effect of the concentration would thus be considerably to strengthen K+S's industrial capacity. K+S and MdK account for 35% and 25% respectively of total potash production in the Community, while SCPA levels off at 20% and its own potash reserves will be completely exhausted by 2004 (see points 51 and 66 of the contested decision).

237   In addition, the documents in the case show that K+S is a subsidiary of one of the leading fertiliser processors, BASF, whose economic power is much greater than that of the EMC group to which SCPA belongs.

238   Finally, it is common ground that demand for potash fell by nearly 30% in Europe from 1988 to 1993, particularly as a result of changes to the common agricultural policy. A falling market is generally considered to promote, in principle, competition between the undertakings in the sector concerned.

239   In those circumstances, and bearing in mind that the structural links between K+S and SCPA have been shown to be less substantial than alleged by the Commission, the argument underlying the finding of a collective dominant position between K+S/MdK and SCPA, namely that the substantial addition of MdK to K+S alone would preserve a common interest on the part of the German group and SCPA in not actively competing with each other, does not appear to be sufficiently well founded in the absence of other decisive factors.

240   With regard to the other evidence adduced by the Commission in support of its conclusion that the acquisition of MdK by K+S would lead to the creation of a collective dominant position, reference must be made to point 57 of the contested decision, according to which: 'The potash market is a mature commodity market characterised by a largely homogeneous product and the lack of technological innovation. The market circumstances are very transparent, information on production, demand, trade and prices being generally available in the industry. In addition, the market shares of K+S and SCPA have been stable over the last four years ... Finally, in the past there was an agreement between K+S and SCPA relating inter alia to the joint determination of the quantities and qualities of potash products exported by each party ... '

241   In the present case, those facts cannot be regarded as lending decisive support to the Commission's conclusion. In particular, the agreement between K+S and SCPA, which was declared incompatible with Article [81] of the Treaty in 1973 (OJ 1973 L 217, p. 3), constitutes, in view of the lapse of time of 20 years between the declaration of incompatibility and the notification of the proposed concentration, extremely weak, indeed insignificant evidence of the absence of competition between K+S and SCPA and *a fortiori* between K+S/MdK and SCPA. The assertion by the Commission that there is still only little cross-border trade from Germany to France that is not channelled through SCPA cannot in this case corroborate the evidential value of that agreement in the way the Commission contends. First, the alleged minor cross-border trade flow nevertheless accounts for almost half of K+S's potash sales in France. Second, the Commission's analysis, in so far as it is confined exclusively to the French market, is in any event incomplete, since the relevant market is the Community market apart from Germany.

242   As regards the Commission's analysis of the degree of competitive pressure which rivals could exert on the grouping allegedly formed by K+S/MdK and SCPA, the Commission explained in the contested decision that imports from the CIS, which in 1992 amounted to 8% of the Community market apart from Germany (including imports channelled through SCPA), appear to have declined since the anti-dumping regulation was adopted (see point 53 of the contested decision).

243   However, according to information provided by the French Government which has not been challenged by the Commission, those imports amounted in 1993 to 11% of sales within the Community.

[607]

244   In view of the fact that the German market is not easily accessible to foreign producers and that the ratio of approximately 4 to 1 between the Community market apart from Germany and the German market does not appear to have changed in the meantime, it may thus be concluded that if imports of potash from the CIS constituted 11% of sales within the Community in 1993, they must have accounted for a greater percentage of sales within the Community apart from Germany.

245   Consequently, the Commission's assertion in point 53 of the contested decision that, with reference to the Community market apart from Germany, those imports appear to have fallen, at least in part, since the anti-dumping regulation was adopted does not correspond to the true state of affairs, in that it obscures the fact that the market share of the CIS increased on the reference market.

246   Moreover, having regard to the growth in 1993 of imports from the CIS to the Community apart from Germany, the finding that the competitive pressure which those imports might exert on the K+S/MdK and SCPA grouping would be limited for reasons related to the quality of the products and the difficulty of ensuring rapid supplies delivered on time appears to be based on reasoning which is, to say the least, inconsistent. To assess with a sufficient degree of probability the effect which a concentration might have on competition on the relevant market, it is essential to rely on a rigorous analysis of the competitors' weight.

247   With regard to Coposa, which holds a market share in the Community apart from Germany of slightly under 10%, the Commission asserted that its production capacity would be considerably reduced in the following year because of the closure of one of its mines. On this point, the French Government has observed, without being challenged by the Commission, that Coposa's present level of overcapacity is about 70%. Hence the statement that Coposa's production capacity would soon fall appreciably, without further detail, does not in itself support the argument that Coposa lacks the necessary base to maintain, let alone increase, its market share and thus exert pressure on the alleged duopoly, especially as the potash market is declining, as stated in paragraph 238 above.

248   Thus the Commission has not succeeded in showing that there is no effective competitive counterweight to the grouping allegedly formed by K+S/MdK and SCPA.

249   In the light of the foregoing, and without its being necessary to decide whether the Commission's findings in the contested decision would, in the absence of the flaws described above, provide a sufficient basis for the conclusion that a collective dominant position exists, it is apparent that the Commission has not on any view established to the necessary legal standard that the concentration would give rise to a collective dominant position on the part of K+S/MdK and SCPA liable to impede significantly effective competition in the relevant market.

Paragraph 221 is very significant and merits careful attention. It states that in cases where the Commission alleges that a collective dominant position is being created or strengthened:

- The Commission is under a clear obligation to use prospective analysis of the relevant criteria;
- The Commission must assess whether effective competition in the relevant market would be significantly impeded as a result of the concentration in question, by the parties to the concentration and by one or more other firms which *together* are able to act to a considerable extent independently – in particular because of factors connecting them – from all pressures of competition.

The judgment of the ECJ in *France v. Commission* was not going to be the final word from the Community Courts on the application of the concept of collective dominance under the Merger Regulation; nor was the defeat which the Commission suffered in the case going to deter it from seeking to rely on the concept in future cases. An important case which reached the CFI and heralded a victory for the Commission was the result of an appeal against the Commission's prohibition of the merger between Gencor and Lonrho.

Gencor v. Commission [1999] [ECR] II-753

Gencor, a South African company, acted in the platinum group metals ('PGM') market through another South African company, Impals Platinum Holdings Ltd ('Implats'). Lonrho, a British company, owned 73 per cent of Eastern Platinum ('Eastplats') and Western Platinum ('Westplats'), South African PGM companies. Gencor and Lonrho arranged to acquire joint control of Implats, which in turn would be granted sole control of Eastplats and Westplats (jointly 'LPD'). After this plan was announced, Anglo American Corporation of South Africa ('AAC'), the main competitor of Gencor and Lonrho in the PGM sector through its associated company, Amplats, acquired a 6 per cent stake in Lonrho, with a right of first refusal over a further 18 per cent.

The Commission declared the concentration incompatible with Regulation 4064/89 as it could result in a restriction of output leading to upward pressure on prices through the creation of a dominant duopoly position between Amplats and Implats/LPD, potentially impeding effective competition in the common market. The Commission decision was contested before the CFI. It was held that that the Commission had jurisdiction and that the Regulation was applicable to the impugned transaction. Moreover, the CFI confirmed the application of the Regulation to collective dominance situations.

CFI

148   Since the interpretations of the Regulation, and in particular Article 2 thereof, based on their wording and the history and the scheme of the Regulation do not permit their

precise scope to be assessed as regards the type of dominant position concerned, the legislation in question must be interpreted by reference to its purpose (see, to that effect, Case 11/76 *Netherlands v Commission...*, paragraph 6, Joined Cases C-267/95 and C-268/95 *Merck and Others v Primecrown and Others and Beecham v Europharm...*, paragraphs 19 to 25, and *France and Others v Commission, ...*, paragraph 168).

149   As is apparent from the first five recitals in its preamble, the principal objective set for the Regulation, with a view to achieving the aims of the Treaty and especially of Article 3(f) thereof (Article 3(g) following the entry into force of the Treaty on European Union), is to ensure that the process of reorganising undertakings as a result in particular of the completion of the internal market does not inflict lasting damage on competition. The final part of the fifth recital accordingly states that 'Community law must therefore include provisions governing those concentrations which may significantly impede effective competition in the common market or in a substantial part of it' (see, to that effect, *France and Others v Commission*, paragraph 169).

150   Furthermore, it follows from the sixth, seventh, tenth and eleventh recitals in the preamble to the Regulation that it, unlike Articles [81] and [82] of the Treaty, is intended to apply to all concentrations with a Community dimension in so far as, because of their effect on the structure of competition within the Community, they may prove incompatible with the system of undistorted competition envisaged by the Treaty (*France and Others v Commission*, paragraph 170).

151   A concentration which creates or strengthens a dominant position on the part of the parties to the concentration with an entity not involved in the concentration is liable to prove incompatible with the system of undistorted competition laid down by the Treaty. Consequently, if it were accepted that only concentrations creating or strengthening a dominant position on the part of the parties to the concentration were covered by the Regulation, its purpose as indicated by the abovementioned recitals would be partially frustrated. The Regulation would thus be deprived of a not insignificant aspect of its effectiveness, without that being necessary from the perspective of the general structure of the Community system of control of concentrations (*France and Others v Commission*, paragraph 171).

152   The arguments regarding, first, the fact that the Regulation is capable of being applied to concentrations between undertakings whose main place of business is not in the Community and, secondly, the possibility that the Commission could control the anti-competitive behaviour of members of an oligopoly by means of Article [82] of the Treaty, are not capable of calling into question the applicability of the Regulation to cases of collective dominance resulting from a concentration.

153   As regards the first of those arguments, the applicability of the Regulation to collective dominant positions cannot depend on its territorial scope.

154　So far as concerns the possibility of applying Article [82] of the Treaty, it cannot be inferred therefrom that the Regulation does not apply to collective dominance, given that the same reasoning would hold for cases of dominance by a single undertaking, which would lead to the conclusion that the Regulation is not necessary at all.

155　Furthermore, since only the strengthening of dominant positions and not their creation can be controlled under Article [82] of the Treaty (*Europemballage and Continental Can*, . . . , paragraph 26), the effect of the Regulation not applying to concentrations creating a dominant position would be to create a gap in the Community system for the control of concentrations which would be liable to undermine the proper functioning of the common market.

156　It follows from the foregoing that collective dominant positions do not fall outside the scope of the Regulation, as the Court of Justice indeed itself held, . . . , in *France and Others v Commission* (paragraph 178).

Having confirmed the application of the Regulation to situations of collective dominance, the CFI turned to deal with the Commission's findings in the case. In paragraphs 163–165 the CFI referred to paragraphs 221, 223 and 224 of the judgment of the ECJ in *France v. Commission* which were extracted and explained above. In paragraphs 199–215 the CFI made several points which are worth extracting here.

199　The prohibition enacted in Article 2(3) of the Regulation reflects the general objective assigned by Article 3(g) of the Treaty, namely the establishment of a system ensuring that competition in the common market is not distorted (first and seventh recitals in the preamble to the Regulation). The prohibition relates to concentrations which create or strengthen a dominant position as a result of which effective competition would be significantly impeded in the common market or in a substantial part of it.

200　The dominant position referred to is concerned with a situation where one or more undertakings wield economic power which would enable them to prevent effective competition from being maintained in the relevant market by giving them the opportunity to act to a considerable extent independently of their competitors, their customers and, ultimately, of consumers.

201　The existence of a dominant position may derive from several factors which, taken separately, are not necessarily decisive. Among those factors, the existence of very large market shares is highly important. Nevertheless, a substantial market share as evidence of the existence of a dominant position is not a constant factor. Its importance varies from market to market according to the structure of those markets, especially so far as production, supply and demand are concerned (*Hoffmann-La Roche*, . . . , paragraphs 39 and 40).

202　In addition, the relationship between the market shares of the undertakings involved in the concentration and their competitors, especially those of the next largest, is relevant evidence of the existence of a dominant position. That factor enables the competitive strength of the competitors of the undertaking in question to be assessed (*Hoffmann-La Roche*, paragraph 48).

203 Accordingly, the fact that the Commission has relied in other concentration cases on higher or lower market shares in support of its assessment as to whether a collective dominant position might be created or strengthened cannot bind it in its assessment of other cases concerning, in particular, markets in which the structure of supply and demand and the conditions of competition are different.

204 Thus, since there is no reliable evidence that the mineral water market and/or the potash market examined in the Nestle-Perrier case and the Kali and Salz case, on the one hand, and the platinum and rhodium market under consideration in this case, on the other, have fundamentally similar characteristics, the applicant cannot rely on any differences in the market shares held by the members of the oligopoly which were taken into account by the Commission in one or other of those two cases in order to call into question the market-share threshold adopted as indicative of a collective dominant position in this case.

205 Furthermore, although the importance of the market shares may vary from one market to another, the view may legitimately be taken that very large market shares are in themselves, save in exceptional circumstances, evidence of the existence of a dominant position (Case C-62/86 *Akzo v Commission* ..., paragraph 60). An undertaking which has a very large market share and holds it for some time, by means of the volume of production and the scale of the supply which it stands for - without those having much smaller market shares being able rapidly to meet the demand from those who would like to break away from the undertaking which has the largest market share - is in a position of strength which makes it an unavoidable trading partner and which, already because of this, secures for it, at the very least during relatively long periods, that freedom of action which is the special feature of a dominant position (*Hoffmann-La Roche*, paragraph 41).

206 It is true that, in the context of an oligopoly, the fact that the parties to the oligopoly hold large market shares does not necessarily have the same significance, compared to the analysis of an individual dominant position, with regard to the opportunities for those parties, as a group, to act to a considerable extent independently of their competitors, their customers and, ultimately, of consumers. Nevertheless, particularly in the case of a duopoly, a large market share is, in the absence of evidence to the contrary, likewise a strong indication of the existence of a collective dominant position.

207 In the instant case, as the Commission stated in the contested decision (paragraphs 81 and 181), Implats/LPD and Amplats would, following the concentration, each have had a market share of about 30% to 35%, that is to say a combined market share of approximately 60% to 70%, in the world PGM market and approximately 89% of the world PGM reserves. Russia had a 22% market share and about 10%

of world reserves, the North American producers held a 5% market share and 1% of world reserves, and the recycling undertakings had a 6% market share. It was probable that, after Russia had disposed of its stocks, that is to say in all likelihood in the two years following the contested decision, Implats/LPD and Amplats would each have had a market share of about 40%, that is to say a combined market share of 80%, which would have constituted a very large market share.

208   Thus, having regard to the allocation of market share between the parties to the concentration and to the gap in market share which would open up following that concentration between, on the one hand, the entity arising from the merger and Amplats and, on the other, the remaining platinum producers, the Commission was entitled to conclude that the proposed concentration was liable to result in the creation of a dominant position for the South African undertakings.

209   The comparison drawn by the applicant between the market shares of the parties to the concentration and the aggregate market share of all the members of the oligopoly in the Nestle-Perrier case (82%) is incorrect. As the Commission has pointed out, it would be necessary to compare the 82% share with the aggregate market share of the parties to the concentration and Amplats after the virtual elimination of the Russian producer (Almaz) as a significant influence on the market, that is to say a total of approximately 80%. So far as concerns the Kali und Salz case, the applicant was likewise wrong in comparing the market shares of the parties to the concentration in the instant case with those of Kali und Salz and MdK (98%) in Germany, where collective dominance was not an issue. In the Kali und Salz case, the Commission found that a collective dominant position existed on the European market excluding Germany, where the undertaking resulting from the merger together with the other member of the duopoly held an aggregate market share of about 60%. The applicant thus should have made a comparison with the latter figure, which is markedly lower than the combined market share of Amplats and Implats/LPD following the concentration.

210   As regards the applicant's argument that the combined market share of Implats/LPD following the concentration would have amounted to only (...)% in the Community, it should be noted, first, that the geographical market at issue is a defined geographical area in which the conditions of competition are sufficiently homogeneous for all businesses. In that area, the undertaking or undertakings holding a dominant position would have had the potential to engage in abuses hindering effective competition (see, to that effect, Case 27/76 *United Brands v Commission* ..., paragraphs 11 and 44). Hence, the Commission was able to carry out a rational assessment of the effects of the concentration on competition in that area. Secondly, by reason of the characteristics of the PGM market set out in paragraphs 68 to 72 of the contested decision, the geographical market at issue in the instant case has a worldwide dimension, a fact which the parties do not contest.

211   It is accordingly not possible to refer to market shares' of the parties in the Community. In a world market, such as the platinum and rhodium market, the economic

[613]

power of a group of the kind which Implats/LPD and Amplats would have formed following the concentration is the power attached to its share of the world market and not to its market share in part of the world.

212   The existence of regional differences in the market-share breakdown of the members of an oligopoly dominating the market in a fungible, readily transportable product which has its price set at world level merely reflects traditional business relationships which could either easily disappear if the undertakings in a dominant position decided to engage in predatory pricing in order to eliminate their competitors, or be difficult to break in the face of abusive pricing practices if the marginal sources of supply were not in a position comfortably to satisfy demand on the part of customers of the dominant undertakings which were engaging in such abusive pricing.

213   As the applicant itself acknowledges in paragraph 4.24 of its application, there is no evidence that the undertakings operating in the platinum markets outside the duopoly identified by the Commission, any more than the members of the duopoly itself, can isolate the common market, for example in order to counter selectively a decision by the members of the dominant oligopoly to increase prices at world level.

214   Even if, in the context of a world market such as the platinum and rhodium market, it were also necessary to consider the precise level of Community sales of the relevant businesses in the instant case, the fact remains that the market share held by Implats/LPD and Amplats as a whole in the Community was not substantially different from the share held by them in the world platinum market.

215   According to the information provided by the parties to the concentration on the notification form CO, the combined market share of Implats/LPD in the Community was approximately (...)% on average during the period 1992-95 (see paragraph 6.1.10 of Form CO, Annex 6 to the application), while the market share of Amplats was estimated in 1994 at approximately 35% to 50% and that of Russia at approximately 25% to 35%. In other words, the combined Community market share of Implats/LPD and Amplats as a whole was, at the time of the concentration, approximately (...)% to 65% and was to rise, following the exhaustion of Russian stocks, to approximately (...)% to 78% since, according to information provided by the parties to the concentration themselves, Russia had, from 1994, effected roughly 50% of its sales from stocks (see paragraph 7.3.2 of Form CO, Annex 7 to the application).

Having reached its above conclusions, the CFI then turned to deal with the highly important issue of structural links first examining the arguments of the parties before making its own findings on the matter (paragraphs 273–283).

264   The applicant claims that the Commission did not take account of the case-law of the Court of First Instance (Joined Cases T-68/89, T-77/89 and T-78/89 *SIV and Others v Commission* ...; the '*Flat Glass*' case) which, in the context of Article [82]

of the Treaty, requires for findings of collective dominance that there be structural links between the two undertakings, for example through a technological lead by agreements or licences, which give them the power to behave independently of their competitors, of their customers and, ultimately, of consumers. In the instant case, the Commission has failed to demonstrate the existence of structural links or to prove that the merged entity and Amplats intended to behave as if they constituted a single dominant entity. That failure also infringes the obligation to state reasons laid down in Article [253] of the Treaty.

265   The applicant notes that, in the contested decision, the Commission refers to the following structural links between the merged entity and Amplats (paragraphs 156 and 157):
       – links in certain industries, including a joint venture in the steel industry;
       – AAC's recent purchase of 6% of Lonrho with a right of first refusal over a further 18%.

266   That analysis is inadequate in three respects.

267   First, neither of those matters directly concerned the PGM industry. The first matter specifically concerned links established with other industries, and both the first and the second were acts of AAC rather than its platinum subsidiary Amplats.

268   Second, those links were a long way from the kind of structural links envisaged in the Flat Glass judgment as sufficient to constitute joint dominance for the purposes of Article [82] of the Treaty.

269   Finally, AAC's recent investment in Lonrho was an action hostile to Gencor and to the concentration. It constituted in itself an indication that the links existing between the various companies did not stand in the way of aggressive competition between them.

270   The Commission states, first, that in its previous decision-making practice it had not always relied on the existence of economic links in order to make a finding of collective dominance, and second, that the Court of First Instance, in its judgment in the Flat Glass' case (paragraph 358), did not lay down the existence of economic links as a requirement or restrict the notion of economic links to the structural links relied on by the applicant. The Commission is therefore entitled to understand that notion as including the relationship of interdependence which exists between the members of a tight oligopoly.

271   In addition, even assuming that the Court of First Instance did lay down a require-ment of economic links in the context of Article [82] of the Treaty, that does not mean that the same requirement should exist in connection with the control of concentrations.

272   Furthermore, even if the notion of economic links were to be construed in a narrower sense, there were, despite the applicant's tendency to underestimate them, a number of such links between the parties to the proposed concentration and Amplats which

could have reinforced the common interest of the members of a tight oligopoly (paragraphs 155, 156 and 157 of the contested decision).

273 In its judgment in the *Flat Glass* case, the Court referred to links of a structural nature only by way of example and did not lay down that such links must exist in order for a finding of collective dominance to be made.

274 It merely stated (at paragraph 358 of the judgment) that there is nothing, in principle, to prevent two or more independent economic entities from being united by economic links in a specific market and, by virtue of that fact, from together holding a dominant position *vis-à-vis* the other operators on the same market. It added (in the same paragraph) that that could be the case, for example, where two or more independent undertakings jointly had, through agreements or licences, a technological lead affording them the power to behave to an appreciable extent independently of their competitors, their customers and, ultimately, of consumers.

275 Nor can it be deduced from the same judgment that the Court has restricted the notion of economic links to the notion of structural links referred to by the applicant.

276 Furthermore, there is no reason whatsoever in legal or economic terms to exclude from the notion of economic links the relationship of interdependence existing between the parties to a tight oligopoly within which, in a market with the appropriate characteristics, in particular in terms of market concentration, transparency and product homogeneity, those parties are in a position to anticipate one another's behaviour and are therefore strongly encouraged to align their conduct in the market, in particular in such a way as to maximise their joint profits by restricting production with a view to increasing prices. In such a context, each trader is aware that highly competitive action on its part designed to increase its market share (for example a price cut) would provoke identical action by the others, so that it would derive no benefit from its initiative. All the traders would thus be affected by the reduction in price levels.

277 That conclusion is all the more pertinent with regard to the control of concentrations, whose objective is to prevent anti-competitive market structures from arising or being strengthened. Those structures may result from the existence of economic links in the strict sense argued by the applicant or from market structures of an oligopolistic kind where each undertaking may become aware of common interests and, in particular, cause prices to increase without having to enter into an agreement or resort to a concerted practice.

278 In the instant case, therefore, the applicant's ground of challenge alleging that the Commission failed to establish the existence of structural links is misplaced.

279 The Commission was entitled to conclude, relying on the envisaged alteration in the structure of the market and on the similarity of the costs of Amplats and Implats/LPD, that the proposed transaction would create a collective dominant position and lead in actual fact to a duopoly constituted by those two undertakings.

[616]

280   To the same end, it was also entitled to take into account the economic links referred to in paragraphs 156 and 157 of the contested decision.

281   The applicant is not justified in challenging the relevance of those links on the ground that they did not directly concern the PGM industry and were acts of AAC rather than Amplats. Links between the principal platinum producers relating to activities outside PGM production (paragraph 156 of the contested decision) were taken into account by the Commission not as factors attesting to the existence of economic links in the strict sense given to that notion by the applicant, but as factors contributing to discipline over the members of an oligopoly by multiplying the risks of retaliation should one of its members act in a manner considered unacceptable by the others. That analysis is, moreover, confirmed by a consultant's study regarding the possible competitive responses of Implats in relation to LPD, which is one of the papers submitted to the board of Gencor and Implats dated 6 May 1994 (referred to in paragraph 158 of the contested decision): according to that consultant, one of the possible scenarios was 'disciplining attacks and signals - focused price wars, for example Rh [rhodium]'.

282   The fact that the links in question concern AAC and not Amplats directly cannot invalidate the Commission's reasoning. Since Amplats was controlled by AAC, the Commission was justified in considering that the links which existed between AAC and other undertakings, whether or not operating in the PGM markets, could have a favourable or an unfavourable impact on Amplats.

283   As for the argument that AAC's recent investment in Lonrho was an action hostile to Gencor and to the concentration, and constituted in itself an indication that the links existing between the various companies did not stand in the way of aggressive competition between them, the Court finds, first, that the applicant has not adduced the necessary proof of the hostile nature of that transaction, and secondly, that, irrespective of the reasons behind it, it tightened the links existing between the two most significant competitors in the market.

The judgment of the CFI in the case was an important victory for the Commission and it offered some clarification of the concept of collective dominance and some previous key judgments in which the concept was mentioned. Of particular interest are paragraphs 273–277 of the judgment. In paragraphs 273 and 274, when referring to *Italian Flat Glass*, the CFI offered clarity on the issue of 'links' and its place in the concept by holding that the CFI in that case did not require that such links must exist in order for a finding of collective dominance to be possible. This point was complemented by that made in paragraph 275 of the judgment where the CFI explained that the *Italian Flat Glass* case did not restrict the notion of economic links to that of structural links; something that would suggest that economic links – which should be understood as relating to or arising from the conditions of the relevant market – include structural ones.

The CFI does not say this explicitly in those paragraphs; though paragraphs 276 and 277 seem to suggest that this is actually the case.

However, the more important point to note about these two paragraphs is that the CFI seem to have made one thing abundantly clear: the question of whether the characteristics of the market will, as a result of the concentration, be rendered conducive to tacit coordination between the parties to the concentration and other players on the market rests at the centre of the application of the concept of collective dominance in the case of mergers. The point(s) made in paragraph 276 can be presented in a bullet-point format:

- A relationship of interdependence between firms in a tight oligopoly must be included in the notion of economic links;
- Those firms – because they are in a position to anticipate one another's behaviour – are strongly encouraged to align their conduct in the market;
- Where this occurs, the firms concerned will be able to maximise their joint profits by restricting production with a view to increasing prices;
- Each of the firms concerned is aware that by reducing its prices it would not derive any benefit;
- Hence, the sensible course of action from the firm's point of view is to raise prices (collectively).

On the whole, the CFI's judgment in *Gencor v. Commission* presented a highly interesting step in the advancement of the concept of collective dominance, especially the Court's statement in relation to the issue of tacit coordination.

In the following case, the CFI gave what can be regarded as the clearest account to date of the concept of collective dominance and the central place which the issue of tacit coordination occupies thereunder.

Airtours v. Commission [2002] ECR II-2585

Airtours plc, a UK tour operator and package holidays supplier, announced its intention to acquire all the shares in a UK competitor, First Choice plc. The Commission held that that the proposed merger would give rise to a collective dominant position in the UK short-haul foreign package holiday market, potentially impeding competition in the common market.

CFI

61   A collective dominant position significantly impeding effective competition in the common market or a substantial part of it may thus arise as the result of a concentration where, in view of the actual characteristics of the relevant market and of the alteration in its structure that the transaction would entail, the latter would make each member of the dominant oligopoly, as it becomes aware of common interests, consider it possible, economically rational, and hence preferable, to adopt on a lasting basis a common policy on the market with the aim of selling at above competitive prices, without having to enter into an agreement or resort to a concerted

practice within the meaning of Article 81 EC (see, to that effect, *Gencor v Commission*, paragraph 277) and without any actual or potential competitors, let alone customers or consumers, being able to react effectively.

62 As the applicant has argued and as the Commission has accepted in its pleadings, three conditions are necessary for a finding of collective dominance as defined:
  - first, each member of the dominant oligopoly must have the ability to know how the other members are behaving in order to monitor whether or not they are adopting the common policy. As the Commission specifically acknowledges, it is not enough for each member of the dominant oligopoly to be aware that interdependent market conduct is profitable for all of them but each member must also have a means of knowing whether the other operators are adopting the same strategy and whether they are maintaining it. There must, therefore, be sufficient market transparency for all members of the dominant oligopoly to be aware, sufficiently precisely and quickly, of the way in which the other members' market conduct is evolving;
  - second, the situation of tacit coordination must be sustainable over time, that is to say, there must be an incentive not to depart from the common policy on the market. As the Commission observes, it is only if all the members of the dominant oligopoly maintain the parallel conduct that all can benefit. The notion of retaliation in respect of conduct deviating from the common policy is thus inherent in this condition. In this instance, the parties concur that, for a situation of collective dominance to be viable, there must be adequate deterrents to ensure that there is a long-term incentive in not departing from the common policy, which means that each member of the dominant oligopoly must be aware that highly competitive action on its part designed to increase its market share would provoke identical action by the others, so that it would derive no benefit from its initiative (see, to that effect, *Gencor v Commission*, paragraph 276);
  - third, to prove the existence of a collective dominant position to the requisite legal standard, the Commission must also establish that the foreseeable reaction of current and future competitors, as well as of consumers, would not jeopardise the results expected from the common policy.

63 The prospective analysis which the Commission has to carry out in its review of concentrations involving collective dominance calls for close examination in particular of the circumstances which, in each individual case, are relevant for assessing the effects of the concentration on competition in the reference market (*Kali & Salz*, paragraph 222). As the Commission itself has emphasised, at paragraph 104 of its decision of 20 May 1998 *Price Waterhouse/Coopers & Lybrand* (Case IV/M.1016) (OJ 1999 L 50, p. 27), it is also apparent from the judgment in *Kali and Salz* that, where the Commission takes the view that a merger should be prohibited because it will create a situation of collective dominance, it is incumbent upon it to produce convincing evidence thereof. The evidence must concern, in particular, factors playing a significant role in the assessment of whether a situation of collective dominance exists, such as, for example, the lack of effective competition between the

operators alleged to be members of the dominant oligopoly and the weakness of any competitive pressure that might be exerted by other operators.

64   Furthermore, the basic provisions of Regulation No 4064/89, in particular Article 2 thereof, confer on the Commission a certain discretion, especially with respect to assessments of an economic nature, and, consequently, when the exercise of that discretion, which is essential for defining the rules on concentrations, is under review, the Community judicature must take account of the discretionary margin implicit in the provisions of an economic nature which form part of the rules on concentrations (*Kali & Salz*, paragraphs 223 and 224, and *Gencor v Commission*, paragraphs 164 and 165).

65   Therefore, it is in the light of the foregoing considerations that it is necessary to examine the merits of the grounds relied on by the applicant to show that the Commission made an error of assessment in finding that the conditions for, or characteristics of, collective dominance would exist were the transaction to be approved.

. . .

191   The Court notes that the Commission adopted a somewhat ambiguous approach in the Decision, since it initially stated that a 'strict retaliation mechanism' founded on coercion is not a necessary condition for collective dominance in this case (Decision, paragraph 55; see also paragraph 150), while also stating that it 'does not agree that there is no scope for retaliation in this market' and that '[r]ather there is considerable scope for retaliation, which will only increase the incentives to behave in an anti-competitive parallel way' (Decision, paragraph 55; see also paragraph 151).

192   The Court observes, *in limine*, that, as it has already pointed out (see paragraphs 61 and 62 above), the prospective analysis of the market necessary in any assessment of an alleged collective dominant position must not only view that position statically at a fixed point in time - the point when the transaction takes place and the structure of competition is altered - but must also assess it dynamically, with regard in particular to its internal equilibrium, stability, and the question as to whether any parallel anti-competitive conduct to which it might give rise is sustainable over time.

193   It is thus important to ascertain whether the individual interests of each major tour operator (maximising profits while competing with the whole range of operators) outweigh the common interests of the members of the alleged dominant oligopoly (restricting capacity in order to increase prices and make supra-competitive profits). That would be the case if the absence of deterrents induced an operator to depart from the common policy, taking advantage of the absence of competition essential to that policy, so as to take competitive initiatives and derive benefit from the advantages inherent therein (see, to that effect, *Gencor v Commission*, . . ., paragraph 227 regarding market transparency, and paragraphs 276 and 281 concerning structural links).

194   The fact that there is scope for retaliation goes some way to ensuring that the members of the oligopoly do not in the long run break ranks by deterring each of them from departing from the common course of conduct.

195   In that context, the Commission must not necessarily prove that there is a specific 'retaliation mechanism' involving a degree of severity, but it must none the less establish that deterrents exist, which are such that it is not worth the while of any member of the dominant oligopoly to depart from the common course of conduct to the detriment of the other oligopolists.

196   In this instance the following deterrents are identified in the Decision:
- the deterrent effect of the mere threat of returning to a situation of oversupply, the 1995 experience showing what could happen if a capacity war broke out (Decision, paragraph 151; see also paragraph 170);
- the scope for increasing capacity by up to 10% during the selling season, at least until February (Decision, paragraph 152);
- the scope for a tour operator to add capacity between seasons and indicate that its conduct is retaliation for a particular action so as to make clear the link between the deviation and the punishment (Decision, paragraph 152);
- the scope for de-racking or directional selling during the selling season to the detriment of an operator who has broken ranks in order to force it to sell a larger share of its holidays at discount prices (Decision, paragraph 152; see also paragraph 170).

197   It must first be observed that the characteristics of the relevant market and the way that it functions make it difficult for retaliatory measures to be implemented quickly and effectively enough for them to act as adequate deterrents.

198   Thus, in a case of deviation or, in other words, cheating, (where, for example, during the planning period one of the main tour operators attempted to turn to its advantage the overall capacity restriction resulting from parallel anti-competitive conduct), the other members of the oligopoly would find it difficult to detect the deviation because the market is not sufficiently transparent, as the Court has already held. It is difficult to detect any deviation at the planning stage, given the difficulties that a large tour operator has in anticipating the capacity decisions of its main competitors with any precision.

199   In that context, the deterrents identified by the Commission do not appear to be capable of coming into play.

200   In the first place, the Court finds that the Commission was wrong in concluding that the mere threat of reverting to a situation of oversupply acts as a deterrent. The Commission refers to the 1995 crisis to illustrate the effects of oversupply on the market. However, it should be made clear that the events of 1995 took place in a context different from that of the present case: then, all operators – regardless of whether they were large or small – boosted their capacity during the 1994 planning period in order to meet the increase in overall demand, which sectoral indicators

and the preceding two years' growth suggested would occur. However, in this case the Commission anticipates that there will be a situation in which the three major tour operators, acting appreciably more cautiously than normal, will have reduced capacity below forecast demand and in which cheating has occurred. It is against that background, which differs markedly from the 1995 capacity surplus, that the Court must examine whether a possible return to oversupply acts as a deterrent. Oversupply could occur only one season later and only if the other members of the oligopoly decided to increase capacity above estimates of demand growth, that is very significantly in comparison with the level of under-supply that would exist in the context of tacit coordination envisaged by the Commission.

201   In the second place, the scope for increasing capacity in the selling season cannot act as a deterrent for the following reasons.

202   First, as the Decision itself emphasises, the market is distinguished by an innate tendency to caution as regards capacity decisions (see paragraphs 60 to 66, 97 and 136 of the Decision), given that matching capacity to demand is critical to profitability, since package holidays are perishable goods (Decision, paragraph 60).

203   Second, in this market a decision to depart from the common policy by increasing capacity in the selling season would be taken at a stage when it would be difficult to detect it in sufficient time. Furthermore, even if the other members of the oligopoly managed to expose the deviating conduct, any reaction on their part involving a retaliatory capacity increase could not be sufficiently rapid or effective, inasmuch as it could be implemented only to a very limited extent in the same season – as is implicitly accepted in the Decision – and only subject to restrictions, which would become increasingly acute as the selling season progressed (in the best-case scenario, capacity for the forthcoming summer season could be increased by only 10% up until February) (see paragraphs 152 and 162 of the Decision).

204   Lastly, it may be assumed that, since they know that the perpetrators of any re-taliatory measures are likely to find it difficult to sell late-added package holidays because of the low quality of such products (inconvenient flight times, poor-quality accommodation), the other members of the dominant oligopoly would be cautious about increasing capacity by way of retaliation. Capacity created in that way does not appear capable of competing effectively with capacity added by the operator which has broken ranks in the planning period, since it is both late and of lower quality. The deviating operator thereby benefits from the advantages associated with having acted first.

205   In the third place, as regards the possibility of increasing capacity in the following season and the fact that capacity can be added between seasons (final part of para-graph 152 of the Decision), it is appropriate to observe that increasing capacity in that way is unlikely to be effective as a retaliatory measure, given the unpredictable way in which demand evolves from one year to the next and the time needed to implement such a measure.

206   In the fourth place, retaliatory action by the other members of the oligopoly at the distribution level (by de-racking or directional selling) would – if Airtours were targeted – affect only 16% of its sales (of which less than 10% are made through Lunn Poly (Thomson) and only 6% through Thomas Cook). As the applicant points out, responses at secondary sources of supply do not represent countervailing forces of significance. Moreover, such retaliation would entail economic loss for its perpetrators, who would have to give up the commission paid by Airtours in respect of sales made in its main competitors' networks of travel agencies. Thus, the deterrent effect of such retaliatory action is not as significant as the Decision suggests.

207   It follows from the foregoing that the Commission erred in finding that the factors mentioned in paragraphs 151 and 152 of the Decision would, in the circumstances of the present case, be a sufficient incentive for a member of the dominant oligopoly not to depart from the common policy.

The CFI's harsh criticism of the practice of the Commission and its findings in the case and its annulment of the Commission's decision delivered a severe blow to the Commission. However the judgment was helpful to all concerned, including the Commission, in highlighting the boundaries of the concept of collective dominance and where they should be placed: according to the CFI they extend to tacit coordination but no further. An important paragraph to note is paragraph 62 in which the CFI stated that three conditions were necessary for a finding of collective dominance:

- each member of the dominant oligopoly must have the ability to know how the others are behaving in order to monitor whether or not they are adopting a common policy;
- tacit collusion must be sustainable over time, which requires that retaliation against firms deviating from the common policy is feasible; and
- the foreseeable reaction of current and future competitors, and of consumers, must not jeopardise the results expected from the common policy.

The judgment in *Airtours* has many implications. An obvious one was that the Commission was forced to consider changing the way it operates internally when deciding merger cases. This issue was discussed in chapter 10. More importantly in the present context however, the *Airtours* judgment seems to have created a common ground for the concept of collective dominance and that of concerted practice in the case of oligopolies. It seems very likely that in future judgments, the ECJ and/or the CFI will need to look at this issue of common ground. One argument is that the judgment will facilitate claims by firms in future cases that the Commission has recycled the facts under Article 81 (when proving that there is a concerted practice) to establish a breach of Article 82 (an abuse of collective dominance). It will be interesting to see how the Courts will respond to such claims.

[623]

(C) The substantive test under Regulation 139/2004

As chapter 10 explains, a major reform occurred in the area of EC merger control in 2004 with the adoption of Regulation 139/2004. Article 2(2) of Regulation 4064/89 used to read:

A concentration which does not create or strengthen a dominant position as a result of which effective competition would be significantly impeded in the common market or in a substantial part of it shall be declared compatible with the common market.

Interestingly, Article 2(2) of Regulation 139/2004 now reads:

A concentration which would not significantly impede effective competition in the common market or in a substantial part of it, in particular as a result of the creation or strengthening of a dominant position, shall be declared compatible with the common market.

Under Regulation 4064/89 the substantive test was based on the concept of dominance: a concentration must be blocked if it creates or strengthens a dominant position as a result of which effective competition would be significantly impeded in the Common Market or in a substantial part of it. As the above discussion makes clear, the concept of dominance has been interpreted by the Commission and the European courts along the years as applying also to situations of 'collective dominance' or oligopolies.

This revision made to the substantive test makes clear that *all* anti-competitive mergers resulting in higher prices, less choice or innovation are covered. Dominance, in its different forms, will remain the main basis on which mergers are found incompatible with the Common Market. But the test clearly encompasses anti-competitive effects in oligopolistic markets where the merged company would not be strictly dominant in the usual sense of the word (meaning significantly *larger* than the other firms in the market). The central question is whether sufficient competition remains after the merger. To put the point differently, the reformulation of the test under Article 2 demonstrates that the Commission recognises that it is essential to make clear that the wording of the Regulation permits effective control of concentrations in oligopolistic markets which may result in a *significant impediment to effective competition* due to the elimination of important competitive constraints and a reduction of competitive pressure even in the absence of a likelihood of coordination between the members of the oligopoly. This point is specifically made in recital 25 of Regulation 139/2004 which provides:

In view of the consequences that concentrations in oligopolistic market structures may have, it is all the more necessary to maintain effective competition in such markets. Many oligopolistic markets exhibit a healthy degree of competition. However, under certain circumstances, concentrations involving the elimination of important competitive constraints that the merging parties had exerted upon each other, as well as a reduction of competitive pressure on the remaining competitors, may, even in the absence of a likelihood of coordination between the members of the oligopoly, result in a significant impediment to effective competition. The Community courts have, however, not to date expressly interpreted Regulation (EEC) No 4064/89 as requiring concentrations giving rise to such non-coordinated effects to be declared incompatible with the common market. Therefore, in the interests of legal certainty, it should be made clear that this Regulation permits effective control of all such concentrations by providing that any concentration which would significantly impede effective competition, in the common market or in a substantial part of it, should be declared incompatible with the common market. The notion of 'significant impediment to effective competition' in Article 2(2) and (3) should be interpreted as extending, beyond the concept of dominance, only to the anti-competitive effects of a concentration resulting from the non-coordinated behaviour of undertakings which would not have a dominant position on the market concerned.

No doubt such a revision to the language of Article 2 will make it much easier to control situations of collective dominance under the new Regulation, not to mention the fact that this change arguably has brought the scope of the test in line with the CFI's judgments in *Gencor* and *Airtours*.

Further reading

Etter 'The assessment of mergers in the EC under the concept of collective dominance' (2000) 23 World Competition 103

Monti 'The scope of collective dominance under Articles 82 EC' (2001) 38 CMLRev 131

Soames 'An analysis of the principles of concerted practice and collective dominance: a distinction without a difference' (1996) 17 ECLR 24

Temple Lang 'Oligopolies and joint dominance in Community antitrust law' (2002) FCLI, ch. 12

Venit 'Two steps forward and no steps back: economic analysis and oligopolisitc dominance after *Kali und Salz*' (1998) 35 CMLRev 1101

Enforcement, practice and procedure

1 Introduction

The preceding chapters of this book discussed the substantive provisions of EC and UK competition law, highlighting, among other things, the crucial practical importance of complying with the rules and the serious consequences that can result from their breach. While it is very important for firms to be aware of the existence of the competition rules, it is equally important to know how the competent authorities go about enforcing them, the details of their practice and the procedures they will use in enforcement.

This chapter is concerned with the topic of enforcement, practice and procedure in the EC and UK systems of competition law. As a result of legislative reforms within the two systems, the topic has come to possess considerable significance. This chapter is divided as follows: Part 2 considers enforcement by EC and UK competition authorities. Part 3 deals with enforcement of Articles 81 and 82 in national courts. Part 4 deals with appeals and private enforcement.

2 Enforcement

(A) EC law

As we saw in previous chapters, the European Commission is responsible for enforcing EC competition law, with judicial review of its practice and decisions available first in the CFI and on appeal to the ECJ. The Commission enjoys considerable powers to enforce the rules. Originally, its powers derived from Regulation 17/62, the first Council Regulation implementing Articles 81 and 82. Regulation 17/62 gave the Commission many of the tools it needed to uncover and punish business practices harmful to competition. However, with the expansion and growth of the EC and the Commission's desire to modernise the EC system of competition law, the Commission gradually came to believe that it was necessary to introduce important 'changes' to the system under the Regulation.

This became all the more pressing when it became clear that the Community was soon to welcome at least ten new Member States, which eventually happened on 1 May 2004. Thus towards the end of the 1990s the Commission began its 'modernisation' debate, and in 1999 it published its *White Paper on Modernisation*. Following a long consultation and debate period, the decision was made to propose a new Regulation to replace Regulation 17/62. A draft Regulation was published in 2001, which was eventually adopted in 2002 and bears the number 1/2003 and the infrequently used long title *'Council Regulation (EC) No 1/2003 of 16 December 2002 on the implementation of the Rules on Competition laid down in Articles 81 and 82 of the Treaty'* but is also referred to more commonly as the 'Modernisation Regulation'.

Regulation 1/2003 came into force on 1 May 2004. The Community's modernisation reform package also included the adoption of a Regulation numbered 773/2004 relating to the conduct of proceedings by the Commission pursuant to Articles 81 and 82 as well as important non-legislative instruments (Notices), bundled together under the title 'Modernisation Package', which the Commission first published in draft in October 2003 and finalised in April 2004. The following Notices (some of which were referred to in previous chapters) are contained in the Package: *Notice on cooperation within the Network of Competition Authorities*; *Notice on the cooperation between the Commission and the courts of the EU Member States in the application of Articles 81 and 82 EC*; *Notice on the handling of complaints by the Commission under Articles 81 and 82 of the EU Treaty*; *Notice on informal guidance relating to novel questions concerning Articles 81 and 82 of the EC Treaty that arise in individual cases (guidance letters)*; Commission Notice entitled *Guidelines on the effect on trade concept contained in Articles 81 and 82 of the Treaty*; and Commission Notice entitled *Guidelines on the application of Article 81(3) of the Treaty*.

As the long title of the Regulation implies, Regulation 1/2003 is concerned with Articles 81 and 82. It is not concerned with mergers. The powers of the Commission in relation to the latter are contained in Regulation 139/2004, the Merger Regulation, considered in chapter 10.

Regulation 1/2003 [recitals deleted]

CHAPTER I – PRINCIPLES

Article 1 Application of Articles 81 and 82 of the Treaty

1   Agreements, decisions and concerted practices caught by Article 81(1) of the Treaty which do not satisfy the conditions of Article 81(3) of the Treaty shall be prohibited, no prior decision to that effect being required.

2   Agreements, decisions and concerted practices caught by Article 81(1) of the Treaty which satisfy the conditions of Article 81(3) of the Treaty shall not be prohibited, no prior decision to that effect being required.

3   The abuse of a dominant position referred to in Article 82 of the Treaty shall be prohibited, no prior decision to that effect being required.

Article 2 Burden of proof

In any national or Community proceedings for the application of Articles 81 and 82 of the Treaty, the burden of proving an infringement of Article 81(1) or of Article 82 of the Treaty shall rest on the party or the authority alleging the infringement. The undertaking or association of undertakings claiming the benefit of Article 81(3) of the Treaty shall bear the burden of proving that the conditions of that paragraph are fulfilled.

Article 3 Relationship between Articles 81 and 82 of the Treaty and national competition laws

1   Where the competition authorities of the Member States or national courts apply national competition law to agreements, decisions by associations of undertakings or concerted practices within the meaning of Article 81(1) of the Treaty which may affect trade between Member States within the meaning of that provision, they shall also apply Article 81 of the Treaty to such agreements, decisions or concerted practices. Where the competition authorities of the Member States or national courts apply national competition law to any abuse prohibited by Article 82 of the Treaty, they shall also apply Article 82 of the Treaty.

2   The application of national competition law may not lead to the prohibition of agreements, decisions by associations of undertakings or concerted practices which may affect trade between Member States but which do not restrict competition within the meaning of Article 81(1) of the Treaty, or which fulfil the conditions of Article 81(3) of the Treaty or which are covered by a Regulation for the application of Article 81(3) of the Treaty. Member States shall not under this Regulation be precluded from adopting and applying on their territory stricter national laws which prohibit or sanction unilateral conduct engaged in by undertakings.

3   Without prejudice to general principles and other provisions of Community law, paragraphs 1 and 2 do not apply when the competition authorities and the courts of the Member States apply national merger control laws nor do they preclude the application of provisions of national law that predominantly pursue an objective different from that pursued by Articles 81 and 82 of the Treaty.

CHAPTER II – POWERS

Article 4 Powers of the Commission

For the purpose of applying Articles 81 and 82 of the Treaty, the Commission shall have the powers provided for by this Regulation.

Article 5 Powers of the competition authorities of the Member States

The competition authorities of the Member States shall have the power to apply Articles 81 and 82 of the Treaty in individual cases. For this purpose, acting on their own initiative or on a complaint, they may take the following decisions:
- requiring that an infringement be brought to an end,
- ordering interim measures,
- accepting commitments,
- imposing fines, periodic penalty payments or any other penalty provided for in their national law.

Where on the basis of the information in their possession the conditions for prohibition are not met they may likewise decide that there are no grounds for action on their part.

Article 6 Powers of the national courts

National courts shall have the power to apply Articles 81 and 82 of the Treaty.

CHAPTER III − COMMISSION DECISIONS

Article 7 Finding and termination of infringement

1   Where the Commission, acting on a complaint or on its own initiative, finds that there is an infringement of Article 81 or of Article 82 of the Treaty, it may by decision require the undertakings and associations of undertakings concerned to bring such infringement to an end. For this purpose, it may impose on them any behavioural or structural remedies which are proportionate to the infringement committed and necessary to bring the infringement effectively to an end. Structural remedies can only be imposed either where there is no equally effective behavioural remedy or where any equally effective behavioural remedy would be more burdensome for the undertaking concerned than the structural remedy. If the Commission has a legitimate interest in doing so, it may also find that an infringement has been committed in the past.

2   Those entitled to lodge a complaint for the purposes of paragraph 1 are natural or legal persons who can show a legitimate interest and Member States.

Article 8 Interim measures

1   In cases of urgency due to the risk of serious and irreparable damage to competition, the Commission, acting on its own initiative may by decision, on the basis of a prima facie finding of infringement, order interim measures.

2   A decision under paragraph 1 shall apply for a specified period of time and may be renewed in so far this is necessary and appropriate.

Article 9 Commitments

1 Where the Commission intends to adopt a decision requiring that an infringement be brought to an end and the undertakings concerned offer commitments to meet the concerns expressed to them by the Commission in its preliminary assessment, the Commission may by decision make those commitments binding on the undertakings. Such a decision may be adopted for a specified period and shall conclude that there are no longer grounds for action by the Commission.

2 The Commission may, upon request or on its own initiative, reopen the proceedings:
   (a) where there has been a material change in any of the facts on which the decision was based;
   (b) where the undertakings concerned act contrary to their commitments; or
   (c) where the decision was based on incomplete, incorrect or misleading information provided by the parties.

Article 10 Finding of inapplicability

Where the Community public interest relating to the application of Articles 81 and 82 of the Treaty so requires, the Commission, acting on its own initiative, may by decision find that Article 81 of the Treaty is not applicable to an agreement, a decision by an association of undertakings or a concerted practice, either because the conditions of Article 81(1) of the Treaty are not fulfilled, or because the conditions of Article 81(3) of the Treaty are satisfied.

The Commission may likewise make such a finding with reference to Article 82 of the Treaty.

CHAPTER IV − COOPERATION

Article 11 Cooperation between the Commission and the competition authorities of the Member States

1 The Commission and the competition authorities of the Member States shall apply the Community competition rules in close cooperation.

2 The Commission shall transmit to the competition authorities of the Member States copies of the most important documents it has collected with a view to applying Articles 7, 8, 9, 10 and Article 29(1). At the request of the competition authority of a Member State, the Commission shall provide it with a copy of other existing documents necessary for the assessment of the case.

3 The competition authorities of the Member States shall, when acting under Article 81 or Article 82 of the Treaty, inform the Commission in writing before or without delay after commencing the first formal investigative measure. This information may also be made available to the competition authorities of the other Member States.

4   No later than 30 days before the adoption of a decision requiring that an infringement be brought to an end, accepting commitments or withdrawing the benefit of a block exemption Regulation, the competition authorities of the Member States shall inform the Commission. To that effect, they shall provide the Commission with a summary of the case, the envisaged decision or, in the absence thereof, any other document indicating the proposed course of action. This information may also be made available to the competition authorities of the other Member States. At the request of the Commission, the acting competition authority shall make available to the Commission other documents it holds which are necessary for the assessment of the case. The information supplied to the Commission may be made available to the competition authorities of the other Member States. National competition authorities may also exchange between themselves information necessary for the assessment of a case that they are dealing with under Article 81 or Article 82 of the Treaty.

5   The competition authorities of the Member States may consult the Commission on any case involving the application of Community law.

6   The initiation by the Commission of proceedings for the adoption of a decision under Chapter III shall relieve the competition authorities of the Member States of their competence to apply Articles 81 and 82 of the Treaty. If a competition authority of a Member State is already acting on a case, the Commission shall only initiate proceedings after consulting with that national competition authority.

Article 12 Exchange of information

1   For the purpose of applying Articles 81 and 82 of the Treaty the Commission and the competition authorities of the Member States shall have the power to provide one another with and use in evidence any matter of fact or of law, including confidential information.

2   Information exchanged shall only be used in evidence for the purpose of applying Article 81 or Article 82 of the Treaty and in respect of the subject-matter for which it was collected by the transmitting authority. However, where national competition law is applied in the same case and in parallel to Community competition law and does not lead to a different outcome, information exchanged under this Article may also be used for the application of national competition law.

3   Information exchanged pursuant to paragraph 1 can only be used in evidence to impose sanctions on natural persons where:
– the law of the transmitting authority foresees sanctions of a similar kind in relation to an infringement of Article 81 or Article 82 of the Treaty or, in the absence thereof,
– the information has been collected in a way which respects the same level of protection of the rights of defence of natural persons as provided for under the national rules of the receiving authority. However, in this case, the information exchanged cannot be used by the receiving authority to impose custodial sanctions.

Article 13 Suspension or termination of proceedings

1   Where competition authorities of two or more Member States have received a complaint or are acting on their own initiative under Article 81 or Article 82 of the Treaty against the same agreement, decision of an association or practice, the fact that one authority is dealing with the case shall be sufficient grounds for the others to suspend the proceedings before them or to reject the complaint. The Commission may likewise reject a complaint on the ground that a competition authority of a Member State is dealing with the case.

2   Where a competition authority of a Member State or the Commission has received a complaint against an agreement, decision of an association or practice which has already been dealt with by another competition authority, it may reject it.

Article 14 Advisory Committee

1   The Commission shall consult an Advisory Committee on Restrictive Practices and Dominant Positions prior to the taking of any decision under Articles 7, 8, 9, 10, 23, Article 24(2) and Article 29(1).

2   For the discussion of individual cases, the Advisory Committee shall be composed of representatives of the competition authorities of the Member States. For meetings in which issues other than individual cases are being discussed, an additional Member State representative competent in competition matters may be appointed. Representatives may, if unable to attend, be replaced by other representatives.

3   The consultation may take place at a meeting convened and chaired by the Commission, held not earlier than 14 days after dispatch of the notice convening it, together with a summary of the case, an indication of the most important documents and a preliminary draft decision. In respect of decisions pursuant to Article 8, the meeting may be held seven days after the dispatch of the operative part of a draft decision. Where the Commission dispatches a notice convening the meeting which gives a shorter period of notice than those specified above, the meeting may take place on the proposed date in the absence of an objection by any Member State. The Advisory Committee shall deliver a written opinion on the Commission's preliminary draft decision. It may deliver an opinion even if some members are absent and are not represented. At the request of one or several members, the positions stated in the opinion shall be reasoned.

4   Consultation may also take place by written procedure. However, if any Member State so requests, the Commission shall convene a meeting. In case of written procedure, the Commission shall determine a time-limit of not less than 14 days within which the Member States are to put forward their observations for circulation to all other Member States. In case of decisions to be taken pursuant to Article 8, the time-limit of 14 days is replaced by seven days. Where the Commission determines a time-limit for the written procedure which is shorter than those specified above,

[633]

the proposed time-limit shall be applicable in the absence of an objection by any Member State.

5   The Commission shall take the utmost account of the opinion delivered by the Advisory Committee. It shall inform the Committee of the manner in which its opinion has been taken into account.

6   Where the Advisory Committee delivers a written opinion, this opinion shall be appended to the draft decision. If the Advisory Committee recommends publication of the opinion, the Commission shall carry out such publication taking into account the legitimate interest of undertakings in the protection of their business secrets.

7   At the request of a competition authority of a Member State, the Commission shall include on the agenda of the Advisory Committee cases that are being dealt with by a competition authority of a Member State under Article 81 or Article 82 of the Treaty. The Commission may also do so on its own initiative. In either case, the Commission shall inform the competition authority concerned.

    A request may in particular be made by a competition authority of a Member State in respect of a case where the Commission intends to initiate proceedings with the effect of Article 11(6).

    The Advisory Committee shall not issue opinions on cases dealt with by competition authorities of the Member States. The Advisory Committee may also discuss general issues of Community competition law.

Article 15 Cooperation with national courts

1   In proceedings for the application of Article 81 or Article 82 of the Treaty, courts of the Member States may ask the Commission to transmit to them information in its possession or its opinion on questions concerning the application of the Community competition rules.

2   Member States shall forward to the Commission a copy of any written judgment of national courts deciding on the application of Article 81 or Article 82 of the Treaty. Such copy shall be forwarded without delay after the full written judgment is notified to the parties.

3   Competition authorities of the Member States, acting on their own initiative, may submit written observations to the national courts of their Member State on issues relating to the application of Article 81 or Article 82 of the Treaty. With the permission of the court in question, they may also submit oral observations to the national courts of their Member State. Where the coherent application of Article 81 or Article 82 of the Treaty so requires, the Commission, acting on its own initiative, may submit written observations to courts of the Member States. With the permission of the court in question, it may also make oral observations.

    For the purpose of the preparation of their observations only, the competition authorities of the Member States and the Commission may request the relevant court of the Member State to transmit or ensure the transmission to them of any documents necessary for the assessment of the case.

4   This Article is without prejudice to wider powers to make observations before courts conferred on competition authorities of the Member States under the law of their Member State.

Article 16   Uniform application of Community competition law

1   When national courts rule on agreements, decisions or practices under Article 81 or Article 82 of the Treaty which are already the subject of a Commission decision, they cannot take decisions running counter to the decision adopted by the Commission. They must also avoid giving decisions which would conflict with a decision contemplated by the Commission in proceedings it has initiated. To that effect, the national court may assess whether it is necessary to stay its proceedings. This obligation is without prejudice to the rights and obligations under Article 234 of the Treaty.

2   When competition authorities of the Member States rule on agreements, decisions or practices under Article 81 or Article 82 of the Treaty which are already the subject of a Commission decision, they cannot take decisions which would run counter to the decision adopted by the Commission.

CHAPTER V – POWERS OF INVESTIGATION

Article 17   Investigations into sectors of the economy and into types of agreements

1   Where the trend of trade between Member States, the rigidity of prices or other circumstances suggest that competition may be restricted or distorted within the common market, the Commission may conduct its inquiry into a particular sector of the economy or into a particular type of agreements across various sectors. In the course of that inquiry, the Commission may request the undertakings or associations of undertakings concerned to supply the information necessary for giving effect to Articles 81 and 82 of the Treaty and may carry out any inspections necessary for that purpose.

The Commission may in particular request the undertakings or associations of undertakings concerned to communicate to it all agreements, decisions and concerted practices.

The Commission may publish a report on the results of its inquiry into particular sectors of the economy or particular types of agreements across various sectors and invite comments from interested parties.

2   Articles 14, 18, 19, 20, 22, 23 and 24 shall apply mutatis mutandis.

Article 18 Requests for information

1   In order to carry out the duties assigned to it by this Regulation, the Commission may, by simple request or by decision, require undertakings and associations of undertakings to provide all necessary information.

2   When sending a simple request for information to an undertaking or association of undertakings, the Commission shall state the legal basis and the purpose of the request, specify what information is required and fix the time-limit within which the information is to be provided, and the penalties provided for in Article 23 for supplying incorrect or misleading information.

3   Where the Commission requires undertakings and associations of undertakings to supply information by decision, it shall state the legal basis and the purpose of the request, specify what information is required and fix the time-limit within which it is to be provided. It shall also indicate the penalties provided for in Article 23 and indicate or impose the penalties provided for in Article 24. It shall further indicate the right to have the decision reviewed by the Court of Justice.

4   The owners of the undertakings or their representatives and, in the case of legal persons, companies or firms, or associations having no legal personality, the persons authorised to represent them by law or by their constitution shall supply the information requested on behalf of the undertaking or the association of undertakings concerned. Lawyers duly authorised to act may supply the information on behalf of their clients. The latter shall remain fully responsible if the information supplied is incomplete, incorrect or misleading.

5   The Commission shall without delay forward a copy of the simple request or of the decision to the competition authority of the Member State in whose territory the seat of the undertaking or association of undertakings is situated and the competition authority of the Member State whose territory is affected.

6   At the request of the Commission the governments and competition authorities of the Member States shall provide the Commission with all necessary information to carry out the duties assigned to it by this Regulation.

Article 19 Power to take statements

1   In order to carry out the duties assigned to it by this Regulation, the Commission may interview any natural or legal person who consents to be interviewed for the purpose of collecting information relating to the subject-matter of an investigation.

2   Where an interview pursuant to paragraph 1 is conducted in the premises of an undertaking, the Commission shall inform the competition authority of the Member State in whose territory the interview takes place. If so requested by the competition authority of that Member State, its officials may assist the officials and other accompanying persons authorised by the Commission to conduct the interview.

Article 20 The Commission's powers of inspection

1   In order to carry out the duties assigned to it by this Regulation, the Commission may conduct all necessary inspections of undertakings and associations of undertakings.

2   The officials and other accompanying persons authorised by the Commission to conduct an inspection are empowered:
   (a) to enter any premises, land and means of transport of undertakings and associations of undertakings;
   (b) to examine the books and other records related to the business, irrespective of the medium on which they are stored;
   (c) to take or obtain in any form copies of or extracts from such books or records;
   (d) to seal any business premises and books or records for the period and to the extent necessary for the inspection;
   (e) to ask any representative or member of staff of the undertaking or association of undertakings for explanations on facts or documents relating to the subject-matter and purpose of the inspection and to record the answers.

3   The officials and other accompanying persons authorised by the Commission to conduct an inspection shall exercise their powers upon production of a written authorisation specifying the subject matter and purpose of the inspection and the penalties provided for in Article 23 in case the production of the required books or other records related to the business is incomplete or where the answers to questions asked under paragraph 2 of the present Article are incorrect or misleading. In good time before the inspection, the Commission shall give notice of the inspection to the competition authority of the Member State in whose territory it is to be conducted.

4   Undertakings and associations of undertakings are required to submit to inspections ordered by decision of the Commission. The decision shall specify the subject matter and purpose of the inspection, appoint the date on which it is to begin and indicate the penalties provided for in Articles 23 and 24 and the right to have the decision reviewed by the Court of Justice. The Commission shall take such decisions after consulting the competition authority of the Member State in whose territory the inspection is to be conducted.

5   Officials of as well as those authorised or appointed by the competition authority of the Member State in whose territory the inspection is to be conducted shall, at the request of that authority or of the Commission, actively assist the officials and other accompanying persons authorised by the Commission. To this end, they shall enjoy the powers specified in paragraph 2.

6   Where the officials and other accompanying persons authorised by the Commission find that an undertaking opposes an inspection ordered pursuant to this Article, the Member State concerned shall afford them the necessary assistance, requesting where appropriate the assistance of the police or of an equivalent enforcement authority, so as to enable them to conduct their inspection.

7   If the assistance provided for in paragraph 6 requires authorisation from a judicial authority according to national rules, such authorisation shall be applied for. Such authorisation may also be applied for as a precautionary measure.

8   Where authorisation as referred to in paragraph 7 is applied for, the national judicial authority shall control that the Commission decision is authentic and that the coercive measures envisaged are neither arbitrary nor excessive having regard to the subject matter of the inspection. In its control of the proportionality of the coercive measures, the national judicial authority may ask the Commission, directly or through the Member State competition authority, for detailed explanations in particular on the grounds the Commission has for suspecting infringement of Articles 81 and 82 of the Treaty, as well as on the seriousness of the suspected infringement and on the nature of the involvement of the undertaking concerned. However, the national judicial authority may not call into question the necessity for the inspection nor demand that it be provided with the information in the Commission's file. The lawfulness of the Commission decision shall be subject to review only by the Court of Justice.

Article 21 Inspection of other premises

1   If a reasonable suspicion exists that books or other records related to the business and to the subject-matter of the inspection, which may be relevant to prove a serious violation of Article 81 or Article 82 of the Treaty, are being kept in any other premises, land and means of transport, including the homes of directors, managers and other members of staff of the undertakings and associations of undertakings concerned, the Commission can by decision order an inspection to be conducted in such other premises, land and means of transport.

2   The decision shall specify the subject matter and purpose of the inspection, appoint the date on which it is to begin and indicate the right to have the decision reviewed by the Court of Justice. It shall in particular state the reasons that have led the Commission to conclude that a suspicion in the sense of paragraph 1 exists. The Commission shall take such decisions after consulting the competition authority of the Member State in whose territory the inspection is to be conducted.

3   A decision adopted pursuant to paragraph 1 cannot be executed without prior authorisation from the national judicial authority of the Member State concerned. The national judicial authority shall control that the Commission decision is authentic and that the coercive measures envisaged are neither arbitrary nor excessive having regard in particular to the seriousness of the suspected infringement, to the importance of the evidence sought, to the involvement of the undertaking concerned and to the reasonable likelihood that business books and records relating to the subject matter of the inspection are kept in the premises for which the authorisation is requested. The national judicial authority may ask the Commission, directly or through the Member State competition authority, for detailed explanations on

those elements which are necessary to allow its control of the proportionality of the coercive measures envisaged.

However, the national judicial authority may not call into question the necessity for the inspection nor demand that it be provided with information in the Commission's file. The lawfulness of the Commission decision shall be subject to review only by the Court of Justice.

4   The officials and other accompanying persons authorised by the Commission to conduct an inspection ordered in accordance with paragraph 1 of this Article shall have the powers set out in Article 20(2)(a), (b) and (c). Article 20(5) and (6) shall apply mutatis mutandis.

Article 22 Investigations by competition authorities of Member States

1   The competition authority of a Member State may in its own territory carry out any inspection or other fact-finding measure under its national law on behalf and for the account of the competition authority of another Member State in order to establish whether there has been an infringement of Article 81 or Article 82 of the Treaty. Any exchange and use of the information collected shall be carried out in accordance with Article 12.

2   At the request of the Commission, the competition authorities of the Member States shall undertake the inspections which the Commission considers to be necessary under Article 20(1) or which it has ordered by decision pursuant to Article 20(4). The officials of the competition authorities of the Member States who are responsible for conducting these inspections as well as those authorised or appointed by them shall exercise their powers in accordance with their national law.

If so requested by the Commission or by the competition authority of the Member State in whose territory the inspection is to be conducted, officials and other accompanying persons authorised by the Commission may assist the officials of the authority concerned.

CHAPTER VI – PENALTIES

Article 23 Fines

1   The Commission may by decision impose on undertakings and associations of undertakings fines not exceeding 1% of the total turnover in the preceding business year where, intentionally or negligently:
(a) they supply incorrect or misleading information in response to a request made pursuant to Article 17 or Article 18(2);
(b) in response to a request made by decision adopted pursuant to Article 17 or Article 18(3), they supply incorrect, incomplete or misleading information or do not supply information within the required time-limit;

(c) they produce the required books or other records related to the business in incomplete form during inspections under Article 20 or refuse to submit to inspections ordered by a decision adopted pursuant to Article 20(4);

(d) in response to a question asked in accordance with Article 20(2)(e),
- they give an incorrect or misleading answer,
- they fail to rectify within a time-limit set by the Commission an incorrect, incomplete or misleading answer given by a member of staff, or
- they fail or refuse to provide a complete answer on facts relating to the subject-matter and purpose of an inspection ordered by a decision adopted pursuant to Article 20(4);

(e) seals affixed in accordance with Article 20(2)(d) by officials or other accompanying persons authorised by the Commission have been broken.

2   The Commission may by decision impose fines on undertakings and associations of undertakings where, either intentionally or negligently:

(a) they infringe Article 81 or Article 82 of the Treaty; or

(b) they contravene a decision ordering interim measures under Article 8; or

(c) they fail to comply with a commitment made binding by a decision pursuant to Article 9.

For each undertaking and association of undertakings participating in the infringement, the fine shall not exceed 10% of its total turnover in the preceding business year.

Where the infringement of an association relates to the activities of its members, the fine shall not exceed 10% of the sum of the total turnover of each member active on the market affected by the infringement of the association.

3   In fixing the amount of the fine, regard shall be had both to the gravity and to the duration of the infringement.

4   When a fine is imposed on an association of undertakings taking account of the turnover of its members and the association is not solvent, the association is obliged to call for contributions from its members to cover the amount of the fine.

Where such contributions have not been made to the association within a time-limit fixed by the Commission, the Commission may require payment of the fine directly by any of the undertakings whose representatives were members of the decision-making bodies concerned of the association.

After the Commission has required payment under the second subparagraph, where necessary to ensure full payment of the fine, the Commission may require payment of the balance by any of the members of the association which were active on the market on which the infringement occurred.

However, the Commission shall not require payment under the second or the third subparagraph from undertakings which show that they have not implemented the infringing decision of the association and either were not aware of its existence or have actively distanced themselves from it before the Commission started investigating the case.

The financial liability of each undertaking in respect of the payment of the fine shall not exceed 10% of its total turnover in the preceding business year.

5   Decisions taken pursuant to paragraphs 1 and 2 shall not be of a criminal law nature.

Article 24 Periodic penalty payments

1   The Commission may, by decision, impose on undertakings or associations of under-takings periodic penalty payments not exceeding 5% of the average daily turnover in the preceding business year per day and calculated from the date appointed by the decision, in order to compel them:
   (a) to put an end to an infringement of Article 81 or Article 82 of the Treaty, in accordance with a decision taken pursuant to Article 7;
   (b) to comply with a decision ordering interim measures taken pursuant to Article 8;
   (c) to comply with a commitment made binding by a decision pursuant to Article 9;
   (d) to supply complete and correct information which it has requested by decision taken pursuant to Article 17 or Article 18(3);
   (e) to submit to an inspection which it has ordered by decision taken pursuant to Article 20(4).

2   Where the undertakings or associations of undertakings have satisfied the obliga-tion which the periodic penalty payment was intended to enforce, the Commission may fix the definitive amount of the periodic penalty payment at a figure lower than that which would arise under the original decision. Article 23(4) shall apply correspondingly.

CHAPTER VII – LIMITATION PERIODS

Article 25 Limitation periods for the imposition of penalties

1   The powers conferred on the Commission by Articles 23 and 24 shall be subject to the following limitation periods:
   (a) three years in the case of infringements of provisions concerning requests for information or the conduct of inspections;
   (b) five years in the case of all other infringements.

2   Time shall begin to run on the day on which the infringement is committed. However, in the case of continuing or repeated infringements, time shall begin to run on the day on which the infringement ceases.

3   Any action taken by the Commission or by the competition authority of a Member State for the purpose of the investigation or proceedings in respect of an infringement shall interrupt the limitation period for the imposition of fines or periodic penalty payments. The limitation period shall be interrupted with effect from the date on which the action is notified to at least one undertaking or association of undertakings

[641]

which has participated in the infringement. Actions which interrupt the running of the period shall include in particular the following:

(a) written requests for information by the Commission or by the competition authority of a Member State;

(b) written authorisations to conduct inspections issued to its officials by the Commission or by the competition authority of a Member State;

(c) the initiation of proceedings by the Commission or by the competition authority of a Member State;

(d) notification of the statement of objections of the Commission or of the competition authority of a Member State.

4   The interruption of the limitation period shall apply for all the undertakings or associations of undertakings which have participated in the infringement.

5   Each interruption shall start time running afresh. However, the limitation period shall expire at the latest on the day on which a period equal to twice the limitation period has elapsed without the Commission having imposed a fine or a periodic penalty payment. That period shall be extended by the time during which limitation is suspended pursuant to paragraph 6.

6   The limitation period for the imposition of fines or periodic penalty payments shall be suspended for as long as the decision of the Commission is the subject of proceedings pending before the Court of Justice.

Article 26 Limitation period for the enforcement of penalties

1   The power of the Commission to enforce decisions taken pursuant to Articles 23 and 24 shall be subject to a limitation period of five years.

2   Time shall begin to run on the day on which the decision becomes final.

3   The limitation period for the enforcement of penalties shall be interrupted:

(a) by notification of a decision varying the original amount of the fine or periodic penalty payment or refusing an application for variation;

(b) by any action of the Commission or of a Member State, acting at the request of the Commission, designed to enforce payment of the fine or periodic penalty payment.

4   Each interruption shall start time running afresh.

5   The limitation period for the enforcement of penalties shall be suspended for so long as:

(a) time to pay is allowed;

(b) enforcement of payment is suspended pursuant to a decision of the Court of Justice.

CHAPTER VIII – HEARINGS AND PROFESSIONAL SECRECY

Article 27 Hearing of the parties, complainants and others

1 Before taking decisions as provided for in Articles 7, 8, 23 and Article 24(2), the Commission shall give the undertakings or associations of undertakings which are the subject of the proceedings conducted by the Commission the opportunity of being heard on the matters to which the Commission has taken objection. The Commission shall base its decisions only on objections on which the parties concerned have been able to comment. Complainants shall be associated closely with the proceedings.

2 The rights of defence of the parties concerned shall be fully respected in the proceedings. They shall be entitled to have access to the Commission's file, subject to the legitimate interest of undertakings in the protection of their business secrets. The right of access to the file shall not extend to confidential information and internal documents of the Commission or the competition authorities of the Member States. In particular, the right of access shall not extend to correspondence between the Commission and the competition authorities of the Member States, or between the latter, including documents drawn up pursuant to Articles 11 and 14. Nothing in this paragraph shall prevent the Commission from disclosing and using information necessary to prove an infringement.

3 If the Commission considers it necessary, it may also hear other natural or legal persons. Applications to be heard on the part of such persons shall, where they show a sufficient interest, be granted. The competition authorities of the Member States may also ask the Commission to hear other natural or legal persons.

4 Where the Commission intends to adopt a decision pursuant to Article 9 or Article 10, it shall publish a concise summary of the case and the main content of the commitments or of the proposed course of action. Interested third parties may submit their observations within a time limit which is fixed by the Commission in its publication and which may not be less than one month. Publication shall have regard to the legitimate interest of undertakings in the protection of their business secrets.

Article 28 Professional secrecy

1 Without prejudice to Articles 12 and 15, information collected pursuant to Articles 17 to 22 shall be used only for the purpose for which it was acquired.

2 Without prejudice to the exchange and to the use of information foreseen in Articles 11, 12, 14, 15 and 27, the Commission and the competition authorities of the Member States, their officials, servants and other persons working under the supervision of these authorities as well as officials and civil servants of other authorities of the Member States shall not disclose information acquired or exchanged by them pursuant to this Regulation and of the kind covered by the obligation of professional

[643]

secrecy. This obligation also applies to all representatives and experts of Member States attending meetings of the Advisory Committee pursuant to Article 14.

CHAPTER IX – EXEMPTION REGULATIONS

Article 29 Withdrawal in individual cases

1 Where the Commission, empowered by a Council Regulation, such as Regulations 19/65/EEC, (EEC) No 2821/71, (EEC) No 3976/87, (EEC) No 1534/91 or (EEC) No 479/92, to apply Article 81(3) of the Treaty by regulation, has declared Article 81(1) of the Treaty inapplicable to certain categories of agreements, decisions by associations of undertakings or concerted practices, it may, acting on its own initiative or on a complaint, withdraw the benefit of such an exemption Regulation when it finds that in any particular case an agreement, decision or concerted practice to which the exemption Regulation applies has certain effects which are incompatible with Article 81(3) of the Treaty.

2 Where, in any particular case, agreements, decisions by associations of undertakings or concerted practices to which a Commission Regulation referred to in paragraph 1 applies have effects which are incompatible with Article 81(3) of the Treaty in the territory of a Member State, or in a part thereof, which has all the characteristics of a distinct geographic market, the competition authority of that Member State may withdraw the benefit of the Regulation in question in respect of that territory.

CHAPTER X – GENERAL PROVISIONS

Article 30 Publication of decisions

1 The Commission shall publish the decisions, which it takes pursuant to Articles 7 to 10, 23 and 24.

2 The publication shall state the names of the parties and the main content of the decision, including any penalties imposed. It shall have regard to the legitimate interest of undertakings in the protection of their business secrets.

Article 31 Review by the Court of Justice

The Court of Justice shall have unlimited jurisdiction to review decisions whereby the Commission has fixed a fine or periodic penalty payment. It may cancel, reduce or increase the fine or periodic penalty payment imposed.

Article 32 Exclusions

This Regulation shall not apply to:
(a) international tramp vessel services as defined in Article 1(3)(a) of Regulation (EEC) No 4056/86;

(b) a maritime transport service that takes place exclusively between ports in one and the same Member State as foreseen in Article 1(2) of Regulation (EEC) No 4056/86;

(c) air transport between Community airports and third countries.

Article 33 Implementing provisions

1 The Commission shall be authorised to take such measures as may be appropriate in order to apply this Regulation. The measures may concern, *inter alia*:

(a) the form, content and other details of complaints lodged pursuant to Article 7 and the procedure for rejecting complaints;

(b) the practical arrangements for the exchange of information and consultations provided for in Article 11;

(c) the practical arrangements for the hearings provided for in Article 27.

2 Before the adoption of any measures pursuant to paragraph 1, the Commission shall publish a draft thereof and invite all interested parties to submit their comments within the time-limit it lays down, which may not be less than one month. Before publishing a draft measure and before adopting it, the Commission shall consult the Advisory Committee on Restrictive Practices and Dominant Positions.

CHAPTER XI – TRANSITIONAL, AMENDING AND FINAL PROVISIONS

Article 34 Transitional provisions

1 Applications made to the Commission under Article 2 of Regulation No 17, notifications made under Articles 4 and 5 of that Regulation and the corresponding applications and notifications made under Regulations (EEC) No 1017/68, (EEC) No 4056/86 and (EEC) No 3975/87 shall lapse as from the date of application of this Regulation.

2 Procedural steps taken under Regulation No 17 and Regulations (EEC) No 1017/68, (EEC) No 4056/86 and (EEC) No 3975/87 shall continue to have effect for the purposes of applying this Regulation.

Article 35 Designation of competition authorities of Member States

1 The Member States shall designate the competition authority or authorities responsible for the application of Articles 81 and 82 of the Treaty in such a way that the provisions of this regulation are effectively complied with. The measures necessary to empower those authorities to apply those Articles shall be taken before 1 May 2004. The authorities designated may include courts.

2   When enforcement of Community competition law is entrusted to national adminis-
     trative and judicial authorities, the Member States may allocate different powers and
     functions to those different national authorities, whether administrative or judicial.

3   The effects of Article 11(6) apply to the authorities designated by the Member
     States including courts that exercise functions regarding the preparation and the
     adoption of the types of decisions foreseen in Article 5. The effects of Article 11(6)
     do not extend to courts insofar as they act as review courts in respect of the types
     of decisions foreseen in Article 5.

4   Notwithstanding paragraph 3, in the Member States where, for the adoption of
     certain types of decisions foreseen in Article 5, an authority brings an action before
     a judicial authority that is separate and different from the prosecuting authority and
     provided that the terms of this paragraph are complied with, the effects of Article
     11(6) shall be limited to the authority prosecuting the case which shall withdraw its
     claim before the judicial authority when the Commission opens proceedings and
     this withdrawal shall bring the national proceedings effectively to an end.

[Articles 36-45 set out the amendments this Regulation makes to previous
statutory provisions and the commencement date etc.]

(B) Comments on the Regulation

Looking at the text of the new Regulation alongside Regulation 17/62, it is
obvious that many important changes have been introduced which are worth
noting.

I Article 81(3)

The first change to be noted is that, following the entry into force of the Modernisation Regulation, national courts and national competition authorities (NCAs)
now have the power to apply Article 81(3), previously within the exclusive competence of the Commission. The Commission, realising the significance of this
change, published a *Notice on the application of Article 81(3)* which is intended
to establish an analytical framework for the application of the provision and to
develop a methodology for its application. The *Notice*, which should prove extremely valuable to national courts and NCAs, was discussed in chapter 4.

II Self-assessment and Guidance letters

One of the key changes introduced by Regulation 1/2003 is the elimination
of the notification and authorisation system, which existed for many years and
which represented a major proportion of the Commission's workload. The Regulation has replaced that system with a 'legal exception' regime under which
agreements which fall within Article 81(1) but which meet the exemption

criteria in Article 81(3) are automatically exempt and legally enforceable at the outset. As a result of this change, firms have been made 'self-reliant' and are responsible under the system for making their own assessment of the compatibility of their business practices with Articles 81 and 82 in light of the relevant legislation and case law.

The elimination of the notification process presents a challenge to firms and their legal advisors. The Commission, aware of the need to ensure legal certainty within the system as a whole, has accepted that in certain cases firms should have the opportunity to seek informal written guidance on questions concerning the interpretation of Articles 81 and/or 82, and which the Commission *may* provide where it considers it appropriate to do so and subject to its enforcement priorities. To this end, the Modernisation Package includes a '*Notice on informal guidance relating to novel questions concerning Articles 81 and 82 of the EC Treaty that arise in individual cases (guidance letters)*' in which the Commission describes this new procedure. The *Notice* refers to the informal written guidance as 'guidance letters' and states that the questions should be novel or unresolved. In a similar approach to that of the Commission, (following the abolishing of notification under CA1998) the UK Government has decided to establish (with the OFT) a system of non-binding 'written opinions' in cases which present genuine uncertainty because they present novel or unresolved questions of law under the CA1998 or Articles 81 and 82.

III The powers of the Commission

While the new system introduced as a result of Regulation 1/2003 provides for a greater involvement (and power) for NCAs and national courts within the system, the Commission has not relinquished certain key and extensive powers. On the contrary, the Regulation strengthens and clarifies the Commission's powers, widens the range of available remedies and provides tougher penalties for procedural infringements. Several provisions deal with these powers: Article 7 (finding and termination of infringement), Article 8 (interim measures), Article 9 (commitments), Article 10 (inapplicability of Article 81 and/or Article 82), Article 17 (investigations into sectors of the economy and into types of agreements), Article 18 (requests for information), Article 19 (taking statements), Article 20 (inspection of business premises), Article 21 (inspection of other premises), Article 23 (imposition of fines) and Article 24 (imposition of periodic penalty). Of these provisions, Article 21, a wholly new provision, deserves special mention because it arms the Commission with the power to extend the scope of its investigation and carry out 'dawn raids' in certain circumstances on non-business premises, which may include private homes. As can be seen from the wording of Article 21 itself, this power is not without limitation, in particular the requirement to seek approval from a national court (for example a warrant) prior to execution of such a search.

IV European Competition Network

The Regulation creates a system of parallel competences under which Articles 81 and 82 can be applied in concert by the Commission and NCAs. The Commission and the NCAs together form a 'European Competition Network', which aims to establish cooperation between the Commission and NCAs in order to discuss issues of enforcement of EC competition rules, facilitate a process of close cooperation between Member States by exchanging information and conducting investigations on each other's behalf, protect competition and maintain a common competition culture in Europe.

It is worth noting that under the Regulation national courts and NCAs are required to apply the Article in any situation where there is an effect on trade between Member States. The domestic laws of Member States may be applied in parallel but national courts and NCAs must not reach decisions following the application of provisions domestic laws the outcome of which differs from that which would be reached under EC law.

The Commission has published, as part of its Modernisation Package, a Notice *on cooperation within the Network of Competition Authorities*. The *Notice* addresses, among other things, the division of work between the members of the Network, the mechanisms of cooperation for the purposes of case allocation and giving assistance, and the importance of consistent application and effective enforcement of EC competition rules and the rights and position of complainants or guilty undertakings, in particular those who offer their cooperation in cartel investigations in return for lenient treatment (see chapter 7).

V Complainants

Complainants have always had an important role in EC competition law enforcement, as they provide vital information about potential infringement situations which the Commission might not necessarily be able to discover through investigation. (Following the adoption of the CA1998, complainants now have a similar role in UK competition law.) In its various statements and the *White Paper on Modernisation*, the Commission has highlighted the importance of complainants. The Commission's policy has been to encourage companies and individuals to make complaints to it. (Now, following the establishment of the 'European Competition Network' under Regulation 1/2003, complainants apply to NCAs.) This is a sensible policy approach to enforcement, because many serious infringements of Articles 81 and 82 are nearly impossible to uncover unless reported by those affected.

In light of this, the Commission included in its Modernisation Package a *Notice on the handling of complaints by the Commission under Articles 81 and 82*. The Notice includes valuable details on many issues of interest for complainants, such as how to decide whether to complain to the Commission, a NCA or the national court; the complementary roles of private and public enforcement; work-sharing between the Commission and NCAs; how to make a complaint to the Commission using the complaint form; how the Commission will handle and assess complaints; and the procedures which the Commission follows, including important information dealing with matters such as the procedural rights of complainants.

(C) UK law

The UK competition enforcement authority, the OFT, is armed with extensive powers deriving from the CA1998 and EA2002 to aid it in detecting and punishing serious breaches of the competition rules. Chapter 7, in particular, outlines some of the important powers which the OFT has come to enjoy, such as the power to prosecute individuals and seek to disqualify directors of companies. That chapter also considers how the UK system of competition law enforcement has been aligned to the EC system (although differences do remain).

I OFT investigations

Sections 25-29 CA1998 deal with investigations conducted by the OFT. In light of Regulation 1/2003, the Government decided to introduce several *amendments* to these sections. The amendments have been effected by Statutory Instrument 2004/1261 *The Competition Act 1998 and Other Enactments (Amendment) Regulations 2004* ('SI 2004/1261'), which came into force in May 2004. Notable aspects of the amendments include the new requirement that entry into domestic premises must be authorised by a warrant in *all* cases. Furthermore, as a result of the amendments the OFT will have an express power to seal when inspecting business premises without a warrant and any premises under a warrant. It is understood that the OFT will in due course publish guidance on how long seals can be affixed for.

S.25 Power of OFT to investigate

(1) In any of the following cases, the OFT may conduct an investigation.

(2) The first case is where there are reasonable grounds for suspecting that there is an agreement which –
(a) may affect trade within the United Kingdom; and
(b) has as its object or effect the prevention, restriction or distortion of competition within the United Kingdom.

(3) The second case is where there are reasonable grounds for suspecting that there is an agreement which –
(a) may affect trade between Member States; and
(b) has as its object or effect the prevention, restriction or distortion of competition within the Community.

(4)   The third case is where there are reasonable grounds for suspecting that the Chapter II prohibition has been infringed.

(5)   The fourth case is where there are reasonable grounds for suspecting that the prohibition in Article 82 has been infringed.

(6)   The fifth case is where there are reasonable grounds for suspecting that, at some time in the past, there was an agreement which at that time –
(a) may have affected trade within the United Kingdom; and
(b) had as its object or effect the prevention, restriction or distortion of competition within the United Kingdom.

(7)   The sixth case is where there are reasonable grounds for suspecting that, at some time in the past, there was an agreement which at that time –
(a) may have affected trade between Member States; and
(b) had as its object or effect the prevention, restriction or distortion of competition within the Community.

(8)   Subsection (2) does not permit an investigation to be conducted in relation to an agreement if the OFT –
(a) considers that the agreement is exempt from the Chapter I prohibition as a result of a block exemption or a parallel exemption; and
(b) does not have reasonable grounds for suspecting that the circumstances may be such that it could exercise its power to cancel the exemption.

(9)   Subsection (3) does not permit an investigation to be conducted if the OFT –
(a) considers that the agreement is an agreement to which the prohibition in Article 81(1) is inapplicable by virtue of a regulation of the Commission ('the relevant regulation'); and
(b) does not have reasonable grounds for suspecting that the conditions set out in Article 29(2) of the EC Competition Regulation for the withdrawal of the benefit of the relevant regulation may be satisfied in respect of that agreement.

(10)   Subsection (6) does not permit an investigation to be conducted in relation to any agreement if the OFT considers that, at the time in question, the agreement was exempt from the Chapter I prohibition as a result of a block exemption or a parallel exemption.

(11)   Subsection (7) does not permit an investigation to be conducted in relation to any agreement if the OFT considers that, at the time in question, the agreement was an agreement to which the prohibition in Article 81(1) was inapplicable by virtue of a regulation of the Commission.

(12)   It is immaterial for the purposes of subsection (6) or (7) whether the agreement in question remains in existence.

[650]

S. 26 Powers when conducting investigations

(1) For the purposes of an investigation under section 25, the OFT may require any person to produce to it a specified document, or to provide it with specified information, which he considers relates to any matter relevant to the investigation.

(2) The power conferred by subsection (1) is to be exercised by a notice in writing.

(3) A notice under subsection (2) must indicate–
(a) the subject matter and purpose of the investigation; and
(b) the nature of the offences created by sections 42 to 44.

(4) In subsection (1) 'specified' means –
(a) specified, or described, in the notice; or
(b) falling within a category which is specified, or described, in the notice.

(5) The OFT may also specify in the notice –
(a) the time and place at which any document is to be produced or any information is to be provided;
(b) the manner and form in which it is to be produced or provided.

(6) The power under this section to require a person to produce a document includes power –
(a) if the document is produced –
(i) to take copies of it or extracts from it;
(ii) to require him, or any person who is a present or past officer of his, or is or was at any time employed by him, to provide an explanation of the document;
(b) if the document is not produced, to require him to state, to the best of his knowledge and belief, where it is.

S. 27 Power to enter premises without a warrant

(1) Any officer of the OFT who is authorised in writing by the OFT to do so ('an investigating officer') may enter any business premises in connection with an investigation.

(2) No investigating officer is to enter any premises in the exercise of his powers under this section unless he has given to the occupier of the premises a written notice which –
(a) gives at least two working days' notice of the intended entry;
(b) indicates the subject matter and purpose of the investigation; and
(c) indicates the nature of the offences created by sections 42 to 44.

(3) Subsection (2) does not apply –
(a) if the OFT has a reasonable suspicion that the premises are, or have been, occupied by–
(i) a party to an agreement which it is investigating under section 25; or
(ii) an undertaking the conduct of which it is investigating under section 25; or

[651]

(b) if the investigating officer has taken all such steps as are reasonably practicable to give notice but has not been able to do so.

(4)   In a case falling within subsection (3), the power of entry conferred by subsection (1) is to be exercised by the investigating officer on production of –

(a) evidence of his authorisation; and

(b) a document containing the information referred to in subsection (2)(b) and (c) .

(5)   An investigating officer entering any premises under this section may –

(a) take with him such equipment as appears to him to be necessary;

(b) require any person on the premises –

    (i) to produce any document which he considers relates to any matter relevant to the investigation; and

    (ii) if the document is produced, to provide an explanation of it;

(c) require any person to state, to the best of his knowledge and belief, where any such document is to be found;

(d) take copies of, or extracts from, any document which is produced;

(e) require any information which is stored in any electronic form and is accessible from the premises and which the investigating officer considers relates to any matter relevant to the investigation, to be produced in a form –

    (i) in which it can be taken away, and

    (ii) in which it is visible and legible or from which it can readily be produced in a visible and legible form;

(f) take any steps which appear to be necessary for the purpose of preserving interference with any document which he considers relates to any matter relevant to the investigation.

(6)   In this section 'business premises' means premises (or any part of premises) not used as a dwelling.

S. 28 Power to enter premises under a warrant

(1)   On an application made by the OFT to the court in accordance with rules of court, a judge may issue a warrant if he is satisfied that –

(a) there are reasonable grounds for suspecting that there are on any business premises documents –

    (i) the production of which has been required under section 26 or 27; and

    (ii) which have not been produced as required;

(b) there are reasonable grounds for suspecting that –

    (i) there are on any business premises documents which the OFT has power under section 26 to require to be produced; and

    (ii) if the documents were required to be produced, they would not be produced but would be concealed, removed, tampered with or destroyed; or

(c) an investigating officer has attempted to enter premises in the exercise of his powers under section 27 but has been unable to do so and that there are reasonable grounds for suspecting that there are on the premises documents the production of which could have been required under that section.

(2)   A warrant under this section shall authorise a named officer of the OFT, and any other of the OFT's officers whom the OFT has authorised in writing to accompany the named officer –

(a) to enter the premises specified in the warrant, using such force as is reasonably necessary for the purpose;

(b) to search the premises and take copies of, or extracts from, any document appearing to be of a kind in respect of which the application under subsection (1) was granted ('the relevant kind');

(c) to take possession of any documents appearing to be of the relevant kind if –

(i) such action appears to be necessary for preserving the documents of preventing interference with them; or

(ii) it is not reasonably practicable to take copies of the documents on the premises;

(d) to take any other steps which appear to be necessary for the purpose mentioned in paragraph (c)(i);

(e) to require any person to provide an explanation of any document appearing to be of the relevant kind or to state, to the best of his knowledge and belief, where it may be found;

(f) to require any information which is stored in any electronic form and is accessible from the premises and which the named officer considers relates to any matter relevant to the investigation, to be produced in a form –

(i) in which it can be taken away, and

(ii) in which it is visible and legible or from which it can readily be produced in a visible and legible form.

(3)   If, in the case of a warrant under subsection (1)(b), the judge is satisfied that it is reasonable to suspect that there are also on the premises other documents relating to the investigation concerned, the warrant shall also authorise action mentioned in subsection (2) to be taken in relation to any such document.

(3A)   A warrant under this section may authorise persons specified in the warrant to accompany the named officer who is executing it.

(4)   Any person entering premises by virtue of a warrant under this section may take with him such equipment as appears to him to be necessary.

(5)   On leaving any premises which he has entered by virtue of a warrant under this section, the named officer must, if the premises are unoccupied or the occupier is temporarily absent, leave them as effectively secured as he found them.

(6)   A warrant under this section continues in force until the end of the period of one month beginning with the day on which it is issued.

[653]

(7)   Any document of which possession is taken under subsection (2)(c) may be retained for a period of three months.

(8)   In this section 'business premises' has the same meaning as in section 27.

S. 28A Power to enter domestic premises under a warrant

(1)   On an application made by the OFT to the court in accordance with rules of court, a judge may issue a warrant if he is satisfied that –
(a) there are reasonable grounds for suspecting that there are on any domestic premises documents –
   (i) the production of which has been required under section 26; and
   (ii) which have not been produced as required; or
(b) there are reasonable grounds for suspecting that –
   (i) there are on any domestic premises documents which the OFT has power under section 26 to require to be produced; and
   (ii) if the documents were required to be produced, they would not be produced but would be concealed, removed, tampered with or destroyed.

(2)   A warrant under this section shall authorise a named officer of the OFT, and any other of its officers whom the OFT has authorised in writing to accompany the named officer –
(a) to enter the premises specified in the warrant, using such force as is reasonably necessary for the purpose;
(b) to search the premises and take copies of, or extracts from, any document appearing to be of a kind in respect of which the application under subsection (1) was granted ('the relevant kind');
(c) to take possession of any documents appearing to be of the relevant kind if –
   (i) such action appears to be necessary for preserving the documents or preventing interference with them; or
   (ii) it is not reasonably practicable to take copies of the documents on the premises;
(d) to take any other steps which appear to be necessary for the purpose mentioned in paragraph (c)(i);
(e) to require any person to provide an explanation of any document appearing to be of the relevant kind or to state, to the best of his knowledge and belief, where it may be found;
(f) to require any information which is stored in any electronic form and is accessible from the premises and which the named officer considers relates to any matter relevant to the investigation, to be produced in a form –
   (i) in which it can be taken away, and
   (ii) in which it is visible and legible or from which it can readily be produced in a visible and legible form.

(3)   If, in the case of a warrant under subsection (1)(b), the judge is satisfied that it is reasonable to suspect that there are also on the premises other documents relating to the investigation concerned, the warrant shall also authorise action mentioned in subsection (2) to be taken in relation to any such document.

(4)   A warrant under this section may authorise persons specified in the warrant to accompany the named officer who is executing it.

(5)   Any person entering premises by virtue of a warrant under this section may take with him such equipment as appears to him to be necessary.

(6)   On leaving any premises which he has entered by virtue of a warrant under this section, the named officer must, if the premises are unoccupied or the occupier is temporarily absent, leave them as effectively secured as he found them.

(7)   A warrant under this section continues in force until the end of the period of one month beginning with the day on which it is issued.

(8)   Any document of which possession is taken under subsection (2)(c) may be retained for a period of three months.

(9)   In this section, 'domestic premises' means premises (or any part of premises) that are used as a dwelling and are –
        (a) premises also used in connection with the affairs of an undertaking or association of undertakings; or
        (b) premises where documents relating to the affairs of an undertaking or association of undertakings are kept.

S. 29 Entry of premises under warrant: supplementary

(1)   A warrant issued under section 28 or 28A must indicate –
        (a) the subject matter and purpose of the investigation;
        (b) the nature of the offences created by sections 42 to 44.

(2)   The powers conferred by section 28 or 28A are to be exercised on production of a warrant issued under that section.

(3)   If there is no one at the premises when the named officer proposes to execute such a warrant he must, before executing it –
        (a) take such steps as are reasonable in all the circumstances to inform the occupier of the intended entry; and
        (b) if the occupier is informed, afford him or his legal or other representative a reasonable opportunity to be present when the warrant is executed.

(4)   If the named officer is unable to inform the occupier of the intended entry he must, when executing the warrant, leave a copy of it in a prominent place on the premises.

(5)   In this section –
            'named officer' means the officer named in the warrant; and
            'occupier', in relation to any premises, means a person whom the named officer reasonably believes is the occupier of those premises.

[655]

Under section 31, where the OFT, following an investigation conducted under section 25, proposes to make a decision finding an infringement of the Chapter I prohibition, II prohibition, Article 81 or Article 82, it *must* give written notice to the person(s) likely to be affected by the proposed decision and give such person(s) an opportunity to be heard. This written notice (known as 'Rule 14 Notice') is equivalent to the 'statement of objections' used by the European Commission. In cases where the OFT finds an infringement, it may give directions to such person(s) as it considers appropriate ordering them to bring the infringement of Chapter I or Article 81 (s. 32) or Chapter II or Article 82 (s. 33) to an end. Should such person(s) fail to comply, without reasonable excuse, the OFT may apply to the court for an order to enforce its direction(s) (s. 34). There is an additional power reserved to the OFT to adopt interim measures in certain circumstances, specified in section 35: where the OFT considers it necessary to act under the section as a matter of urgency to prevent a serious, irreparable damage to a particular person or category of persons or to protect the public interest. Section 35 applies if the OFT has begun an investigation (which it has the power to conduct) under section 25 and not completed it, unless either of subsections 8 or 9 applies. The subsections concern the situation where a person has produced evidence to the OFT in connection with the investigation that satisfies it (on a balance of probabilities) that, if it finds an infringement of the Chapter I prohibition, it would also conclude that the suspected agreement is exempt as a result of section 9 of the CA1998 (s. 35(8)), or where it would find that there is an agreement which is caught by Article 81(1), it would reach the conclusion that the suspected agreement is exempt under Article 81(3) (s. 35(9)). By virtue of section 35(5), a direction given under the section may if the circumstances permit be replaced by a direction under section 32 or (as appropriate) section 33, or commitments accepted under section 31A.

II Privileged communications and use of statements

Sections 30 and 30A set the limitations on investigations by the OFT in relation to privileged communications and statements made during an investigation. Privileged communication is defined in section 30(2) as communication between a professional legal advisor and his client or one made in connection with, or in contemplation of, litigation and for the purposes of that litigation which in proceedings in the High Court would be protected from disclosure on grounds of legal professional privilege. It is worth noting that the scope of privileged communications is wider in the UK legal system than in the EC system. Under EC law, communications with a lawyer not qualified in an EC Member State or with in-house counsel are not considered privileged and so admissible for the purposes of EC competition rules. Under UK law such communications are privileged.

The Court of Appeal recently delivered a significant judgment on the scope of privileged communications in the case of *Three Rivers Council v. The Governor and Company of the Bank of England*. It was held that only communications between a client and a lawyer (regardless of the involvement of an intermediary) for the purposes of seeking legal advice, and documents evidencing such communications, were considered privileged communications. According to the Court the same does not apply to other types of documents, such as those prepared by the employees of the client for the purposes of receiving legal advice but which were not themselves communicated to lawyers. The Bank of England's application for permission to appeal was rejected by the House of Lords on the grounds that the case does not raise an arguable point of law of general public importance and that it was not suitable for consideration as it was an interlocutory decision. The judgment of the Court of Appeal has obvious practical implications in cases of lawyers preparing evidence in relation to non-adversarial proceedings. What impact will these implications have will depend on the particular facts of the case; however it will, among other things, be necessary for lawyers in particular to be particularly cautious when handling evidential matters in practice.

III Penalties and fines

Chapter 7 dealt with the issue of penalties and fines that may be imposed by the OFT. Five provisions in the CA1998 addressing penalties are worth mentioning. These are set out in sections 36–40. In light of Regulation 1/2003, the Government decided to make some notable amendments to the provisions of the CA1998 dealing with penalties and fines. These amendments include:

- making section 38(9) applicable when the OFT is considering breaches of Articles 81 and 82. The Government's view is that this offers a logical extension to the provision, which aims to prevent double jeopardy.
- Bringing the UK position with regard to the amount of penalty in line with that of the EC by amending SI 2000/309, *the Competition Act 1998 (Determination of Turnover for Penalties) Order 2000*, so that the maximum penalty for infringing Article 81, 82, the Chapter I prohibition or the Chapter II prohibition will be 10 per cent of an undertaking's worldwide turnover for the previous financial year as opposed to 10 per cent of an undertaking's UK turnover.

S. 36 Penalties

(1) On making a decision that an agreement has infringed the Chapter I prohibition or that it has infringed the prohibition in Article 81, the OFT may require an undertaking which is a party to the agreement to pay the OFT a penalty in respect of the infringement.

(2) On making a decision that conduct has infringed the Chapter II prohibition or that it has infringed the prohibition in Article 82, the OFT may require the undertaking concerned to pay the OFT a penalty in respect of the infringement.

(3)   The OFT may impose a penalty on an undertaking under subsection (1) or (2) only if the OFT is satisfied that the infringement has been committed intentionally or negligently by the undertaking.

(4)   Subsection (1) is subject to section 39 and does not apply in relation to a decision that an agreement has infringed the Chapter I prohibition if the OFT is satisfied that the undertaking acted on the reasonable assumption that that section gave it immunity in respect of the agreement.

(5)   Subsection (2) is subject to section 40 and does not apply in relation to a decision that conduct has infringed the Chapter II prohibition if the OFT is satisfied that the undertaking acted on the reasonable assumption that that section gave it immunity in respect of the conduct.

(6)   Notice of a penalty under this section must –
        (a) be in writing; and
        (b) specify the date before which the penalty is required to be paid.

(7)   The date specified must not be earlier than the end of the period within which an appeal against the notice may be brought under section 46.

(8)   No penalty fixed by the OFT under this section may exceed 10% of the turnover of the undertaking (determined in accordance with such provisions as may be specified in an order made by the Secretary of State).

(9)   Any sums received by the OFT under this section are to be paid into the Consolidated Fund.

S. 37 Recovery of penalties

(1)   If the specified date in a penalty notice has passed and –
        (a) the period during which an appeal against the imposition, or amount, of the penalty may be made has expired without an appeal having been made, or
        (b) such an appeal has been made and determined,
           the OFT may recover from the undertaking, as a civil debt due to the OFT, any amount payable under the penalty notice which remains outstanding.

(2)   In this section –
        'penalty notice' means a notice given under section 36; and
        'specified date' means the date specified in the penalty notice.

S. 38 The appropriate level of a penalty

(1)   The OFT must prepare and publish guidance as to the appropriate amount of any penalty under this Part.

(1A)   The guidance must include provision about the circumstances in which, in determining a penalty under this Part, the OFT may take into account effects in another Member State of the agreement or conduct concerned

(2)   The OFT may at any time alter the guidance.

(3)   If the guidance is altered, the OFT must publish it as altered.

(4)   No guidance is to be published under this section without the approval of the Secretary of State.

(5)   The OFT may, after consulting the Secretary of State, choose how it publishes its guidance.

(6)   If the OFT is preparing or altering guidance under this section it must consult such persons as it considers appropriate.

(7)   If the proposed guidance or alteration relates to a matter in respect of which a regulator exercises concurrent jurisdiction, those consulted must include that regulator.

(8)   When setting the amount of a penalty under this Part, the OFT must have regard to the guidance for the time being in force under this section.

(9)   If a penalty or a fine has been imposed by the Commission, or by a court or other body in another Member State, in respect of an agreement or conduct, the OFT an appeal tribunal or the appropriate court must take that penalty or fine into account when setting the amount of a penalty under this Part in relation to that agreement or conduct.

(10)   In subsection (9) 'the appropriate court' means –
(a) in relation to England and Wales, the Court of Appeal;
(b) in relation to Scotland, the Court of Session;
(c) in relation to Northern Ireland, the Court of Appeal in Northern Ireland;
(d) the House of Lords.

S. 39 Limited immunity in relation to the Chapter I prohibition

(1)   In this section 'small agreement' means an agreement –
(a) which falls within a category prescribed for the purposes of this section; but
(b) is not a price fixing agreement.

(2)   The criteria by reference to which a category of agreement is prescribed may, in particular, include –
(a) the combined turnover of the parties to the agreement (determined in accordance with prescribed provisions);
(b) the share of the market affected by the agreement (determined in that way).

[659]

(3)   A party to a small agreement is immune from the effect of section 36(1) so far as that provision relates to decisions about infringement of the Chapter I prohibition; but the OFT may withdraw that immunity under subsection (4).

(4)   If the OFT has investigated a small agreement, it may make a decision withdrawing the immunity given by subsection (3) if, as a result of its investigation, it considers that the agreement is likely to infringe the Chapter I prohibition.

(5)   The OFT must give each of the parties in respect of which immunity is withdrawn written notice of its decision to withdraw the immunity.

(6)   A decision under subsection (4) takes effect on such date ('the withdrawal date') as may be specified in the decision.

(7)   The withdrawal date must be a date after the date on which the decision is made.

(8)   In determining the withdrawal date, the OFT must have regard to the amount of time which the parties are likely to require in order to secure that there is no further infringement of the Chapter I prohibition with respect to the agreement.

(9)   In subsection (1) 'price fixing agreement' means an agreement which has as its object or effect, or one of its objects or effects, restricting the freedom of a party to the agreement to determine the price to be charged (otherwise than as between that party and another party to the agreement) for the product, service or other matter to which the agreement relates.

S. 40 Limited immunity in relation to the Chapter II prohibition

(1)   In this section 'conduct of minor significance' means conduct which falls within a category prescribed for the purposes of this section.

(2)   The criteria by reference to which a category is prescribed may, in particular, include –
        (a) the turnover of the person whose conduct it is (determined in accordance with prescribed provisions);
        (b) the share of the market affected by the conduct (determined in that way).

(3)   A person is immune from the effect of section 36(2), so far as that provision relates to decisions about infringement of the Chapter II prohibition, if his conduct is conduct of minor significance; but the OFT may withdraw that immunity under subsection (4).

(4)   If the OFT has investigated conduct of minor significance, it may make a decision withdrawing the immunity given by subsection (3) if, as a result of its investigation, it considers that the conduct is likely to infringe the Chapter II prohibition.

(5)   The OFT must give the person, or persons, whose immunity has been withdrawn written notice of its decision to withdraw the immunity.

(6)   A decision under subsection (4) takes effect on such date ('the withdrawal date') as may be specified in the decision.

(7)   The withdrawal date must be a date after the date on which the decision is made.

(8)   In determining the withdrawal date, the OFT must have regard to the amount of time which the person or persons affected are likely to require in order to secure that there is no further infringement of the Chapter II prohibition.

IV Inspections and investigations

SI 2004/1261 has made extensive changes to Part 2 of the CA1998. Following these changes, Part 2, which contains (ss. 61, 62, 62A, 62B, 63, 64, 65, 65A and 65B), now deals with *inspections* ordered by a European Commission decision under Articles 20(4) or 21 of Regulation 1/2003, or requested by Commission under Article 22(2) of the Regulation. Four of the provisions in Part 2 are worth noting in particular. Under section 62 (which applies in relation to business premises), on an application by the OFT, a High Court judge *shall* issue a warrant where the Commission has ordered an inspection under Article 20 of the Regulation and that inspection is being, or is likely to be, obstructed and the measures that would be authorised by the warrant are neither arbitrary nor excessive having regard to the subject matter of the inspection. Section 62A deals with entry to non-business premises under a warrant following an inspection ordered by the Commission under Article 21 of the Regulation. Sections 62B and 63 deal with case where the Commission requests the OFT to conduct inspections under Article 22 of the Regulation. There is also an offence created for the obstruction of inspections conducted under section 62, 62A or 63 (s. 65).

SI 2004/1261 has also added a new part (Part 2A which consists of 12 sections, 65C–65N) to the CA1998 which deals with *investigations* under Article 22(1) of Regulation 1/2003, meaning investigations conducted by the OFT on behalf and for the account of a competition authority of another Member State.

V Offences

Sections 42–44 CA1998 (as amended by EA2002) deal with offences that may be committed during an investigation or enforcement proceedings by the OFT as a result of the parties' failure to comply with a requirement or order imposed by the OFT (s. 42 as further amended by SI 2004/1261), or in cases where documents are destroyed or falsified (s. 43 as amended by 2004/1261) or, false or misleading information is supplied to the OFT (s. 44).

3 Enforcement of Articles 81 and 82 in national courts

(A) National courts' duty to enforce

Since Regulation 1/2003 entered into force, Articles 81 and 82 now have full direct effect, which means that they create rights and obligations for individuals which national courts must protect. The issue of direct effect in the case of these two provisions should be considered within a broader framework, i.e. the relationship between EC competition law and national competition laws and the relationship between the Commission and the national courts. Regulation 1/2003 includes specific provisions delineating the boundaries of the relationship. Articles 1 and 6 of the Regulation deal with direct applicability of Articles 81 and 82; Article 3 deals with the relationship between Articles 81 and 82 and national competition laws; Article 15 concerns cooperation between the Commission and the national courts; and Article 16 deals with the uniform application of Articles 81 and 82 by the Commission and the national courts.

The duty of national courts to enforce the competition rules of the EC and to cooperate with Community institutions was addressed by the ECJ in the following case

Masterfoods Ltd v. HB Ice Cream Ltd [2000] ECR I-11369

Masterfoods, a producer of frozen foodstuffs, appealed against a decision by the High Court of Ireland *not* to declare null and void a so-called 'freezer exclusivity clause'. Prior to the hearing, acting on Masterfood's complaint, the Commission had ruled that the clause infringed Article 81(1) and Article 82. HB, the freezer owners, had immediately applied to the CFI for an annulment of the Commission's ruling and suspensive measures. A reference to the ECJ sought clarification on the extent of the duty of cooperation between national courts and the Community judicature and how it should proceed in these circumstances.

ECJ

48 ... [I]n order to fulfil the role assigned to it by the Treaty, the Commission cannot be bound by a decision given by a national court in application of Articles [81(1)] and [82] of the Treaty. The Commission is therefore entitled to adopt at any time individual decisions under Articles [81] and [82] of the Treaty, even where an agreement or practice has already been the subject of a decision by a national court and the decision contemplated by the Commission conflicts with that national court's decision.

49 It is also clear from the case-law of the Court that the Member States' duty under Article [10] of the EC Treaty to take all appropriate measures, whether general or particular, to ensure fulfilment of the obligations arising from Community law and to abstain from any measure which could jeopardise the attainment of the objectives of the Treaty is binding on all the authorities of Member States including, for matters within their jurisdiction, the courts ...

50   Under the fourth paragraph of Article [249] of the Treaty, a decision adopted by the Commission implementing Articles [81(1), 81(3) or 82] of the Treaty is to be binding in its entirety upon those to whom it is addressed.

51   The Court has held, in paragraph 47 of *Delimitis*, that in order not to breach the general principle of legal certainty, national courts must, when ruling on agreements or practices which may subsequently be the subject of a decision by the Commission, avoid giving decisions which would conflict with a decision contemplated by the Commission in the implementation of Articles [81(1)] and [82] and Article [81(3)] of the Treaty.

52   It is even more important that when national courts rule on agreements or practices which are already the subject of a Commission decision they cannot take decisions running counter to that of the Commission, even if the latter's decision conflicts with a decision given by a national court of first instance.

53   In that connection, the fact that the President of the Court of First Instance suspended the application of Decision 98/531 until the Court of First Instance has given judgment terminating the proceedings before it is irrelevant. Acts of the Community institutions are in principle presumed to be lawful until such time as they are annulled or withdrawn ... The decision of the judge hearing an application to order the suspension of the operation of the contested act, pursuant to Article [242] of the Treaty, has only provisional effect. It must not prejudge the points of law or fact in issue or neutralise in advance the effects of the decision subsequently to be given in the main action ...

54   Moreover, if a national court has doubts as to the validity or interpretation of an act of a Community institution it may, or must, in accordance with the second and third paragraphs of Article [234] of the Treaty, refer a question to the Court of Justice for a preliminary ruling.

55   If, as here in the main proceedings, the addressee of a Commission decision has, within the period prescribed in the fifth paragraph of Article [234] of the Treaty, brought an action for annulment of that decision pursuant to that article, it is for the national court to decide whether to stay proceedings until a definitive decision has been given in the action for annulment or in order to refer a question to the Court for a preliminary ruling.

56   It should be borne in mind in that connection that application of the Community competition rules is based on an obligation of sincere cooperation between the national courts, on the one hand, and the Commission and the Community Courts, on the other, in the context of which each acts on the basis of the role assigned to it by the Treaty.

57   When the outcome of the dispute before the national court depends on the validity of the Commission decision, it follows from the obligation of sincere cooperation that

the national court should, in order to avoid reaching a decision that runs counter to that of the Commission, stay its proceedings pending final judgment in the action for annulment by the Community Courts, unless it considers that, in the circumstances of the case, a reference to the Court of Justice for a preliminary ruling on the validity of the Commission decision is warranted.

58   If a national court stays proceedings, it is incumbent on it to examine whether it is necessary to order interim measures in order to safeguard the interests of the parties pending final judgment.

(B) Commission cooperation with national courts

The Commission has long realised the importance of forging close links with the courts of Member States and fostering further involvement and cooperation in interpreting, applying and enforcing EC competition rules. For many years, the Commission regarded that extending the jurisdiction of national courts would, among other things, alleviate some of its extensive caseload.

In 1993 the Commission published an important document which high-lighted both the Commission's efforts to encourage parties to seek remedy in legal action before national courts rather than complaining to it and to highlight the importance the Commission attaches to the issue of compliance with EC competition rules. This document bore the title *Notice Concerning Co-operation between the Commission and Courts of the Member States with Regards to the Application of Articles 85 (now Article 81) and 86 (now Article 82)*. The *Notice* has now been replaced by a new Notice dealing with the same subject-matter, published as part of the 'Modernisation Package'.

Commission Notice on the co-operation between the Commission and the courts of the EU Member States in the application of Articles 81 and 82 EC

(I) THE SCOPE OF THE NOTICE

1   The present notice addresses the co-operation between the Commission and the courts of the EU Member States, when the latter apply Articles 81 and 82 EC. For the purpose of this notice, the 'courts of the EU Member States' (hereinafter 'national courts') are those courts and tribunals within an EU Member State that can apply Articles 81 and 82 EC and that are authorised to ask a preliminary question to the Court of Justice of the European Communities pursuant to Article 234 EC.[1]

---

1 For the criteria to determine which entities can be regarded as courts or tribunals within the meaning of Article 234 EC, see e.g. case C-516/99 *Schmid* [2002] ECR 4573, 34: 'The Court takes account of a number of factors, such as whether the body is established by law, whether it is permanent, whether its jurisdiction is compulsory, whether its procedure is *inter partes*, whether it applies rules of law and whether it is independent.'

2   The national courts may be called upon to apply Articles 81 or 82 EC in lawsuits between private parties, such as actions relating to contracts or actions on damages. They may also act as public enforcer or as review court. A national court may indeed be designated as a competition authority of a Member State (hereinafter 'the national competition authority') pursuant to Article 35(1) of Regulation (EC) No 1/2003 (hereinafter 'the regulation').[2] In that case, the co-operation between the national courts and the Commission is not only covered by the present notice, but also by the notice on the co-operation within the network of competition authorities.[3]

(II) THE APPLICATION OF EC COMPETITION RULES BY NATIONAL COURTS

A. The competence of national courts to apply EC competition rules

3   To the extent that national courts have jurisdiction to deal with a case,[4] they have the power to apply Articles 81 and 82 EC.[5] Moreover, it should be remembered that Articles 81 and 82 EC are a matter of public policy and are essential to the accomplishment of the tasks entrusted to the Community, and, in particular, for the functioning of the internal market.[6] According to the Court of Justice, where, by virtue of domestic law, national courts must raise of their own motion points of law based on binding domestic rules which have not been raised by the parties, such an obligation also exists where binding Community rules, such as the EC competition rules, are concerned. The position is the same if domestic law confers on national courts a discretion to apply of their own motion binding rules of law: national courts must apply the EC competition rules, even when the party with an interest in application of those provisions has not relied on them, where domestic law allows such application by the national court. However, Community law does not require national courts to raise of their own motion an issue concerning the breach of provisions of Community law where examination of that issue would oblige them to abandon the passive role assigned to them by going beyond the ambit of the dispute defined by the parties themselves and relying on facts and

---

2 Council Regulation (EC) No 1/2003 of 16 December 2002 on the implementation of the rules on competition laid down in Articles 81 and 82 of the Treaty (OJ L 1, 4.1.2003, p. 1).

3 Notice on the co-operation within the network of competition authorities ... For the purpose of this notice, a 'national competition authority' is the authority designated by a Member State in accordance with Article 35(1) of the regulation.

4 The jurisdiction of a national court depends on national, European and international rules of jurisdiction. In this context, it may be recalled that Council Regulation 44/2001 of 22 December 2000 on jurisdiction and the recognition and enforcement of judgements in civil and commercial matters (OJ L 12, 16.1.2001, p.1) is applicable to all competition cases of a civil or commercial nature.

5 See Article 6 of the regulation.

6 See Articles 2 and 3 EC, case C-126/97 *Eco Swiss* [1999] ECR I-3055, 36; case T-34/92 *Fiatagri UK and New Holland Ford* [1994] ECR II-905, 39 and case T-128/98 *Aéroports de Paris* [2000] ECR II-3929, 241.

circumstances other than those on which the party with an interest in application of those provisions bases his claim.[7]

4   Depending on the functions attributed to them under national law, national courts may be called upon to apply Articles 81 and 82 EC in administrative, civil or criminal proceedings.[8] In particular, where a natural or legal person asks the national court to safeguard his individual rights, national courts play a specific role in the enforcement of Articles 81 and 82 EC, which is different from the enforcement in the public interest by the Commission or by national competition authorities.[9] Indeed, national courts can give effect to Articles 81 and 82 EC by finding contracts to be void or by awards of damages.

5   National courts can apply Articles 81 and 82 EC, without it being necessary to apply national competition law in parallel. However, where a national court applies national competition law to agreements, decisions by associations of undertakings or concerted practices which may affect trade between Member States within the meaning of Article 81(1) EC[10] or to any abuse prohibited by Article 82 EC, they also have to apply EC competition rules to those agreements, decisions or practices.[11]

6   The regulation does not only empower the national courts to apply EC competition law. The parallel application of national competition law to agreements, decisions of associations of undertakings and concerted practices which affect trade between Member States may not lead to a different outcome from that of EC competition law. Article 3(2) of the regulation provides that agreements, decisions or concerted practices which do not infringe Article 81(1) EC or which fulfil the conditions of Article 81(3) EC cannot be prohibited either under national competition law.[12] On the other hand, the Court of Justice has ruled that agreements, decisions or concerted practices that violate Article 81(1) and do not fulfil the conditions of Article 81(3) EC cannot be upheld under national law.[13] As to the parallel application of national competition law and Article 82 EC in the case of unilateral conduct, Article 3 of the regulation does not provide for a similar convergence obligation. However, in case of conflicting provisions, the general principle of primacy of Community law requires national courts to disapply any provision of national law which contravenes a Community rule, regardless of whether that national law provision was adopted before or after the Community rule.[14]

---

7 Joined cases C-430/93 and C-431/93 *van Schijndel* [1995] ECR I-4705, 13 to 15 and 22.

8 According to the last sentence of recital 8 of Regulation 1/2003, the regulation does not apply to national laws which impose criminal sanctions on natural persons except to the extent that such sanctions are the means whereby competition rules applying to undertakings are enforced.

9 Case T-24/90 *Automec* [1992] ECR II-2223, 85.

10 For further clarification of the effect on trade concept, see the notice on this issue ...

11 Article 3(1) of the regulation.

12 See also the notice on the application of Article 81(3) EC ...

13 Case 14/68 *Walt Wilhelm* [1969] ECR 1 and joined cases 253/78 and 1 to 3/79 *Giry and Guerlain* [1980] ECR 2327, 15 to 17.

14 Case 106/77 *Simmenthal* [1978] ECR 629, 21 and case C-198/01 *Consorzio Industrie Fiammiferi (CIF)* [2003] ECR *, 49.

7   Apart from the application of Articles 81 and 82 EC, national courts are also com-
        petent to apply acts adopted by EU institutions in accordance with the EC Treaty or
        in accordance with the measures adopted to give the Treaty effect, to the extent that
        these acts have direct effect. National courts may thus have to enforce Commission
        decisions[15] or regulations applying Article 81(3) EC to certain categories of agree-
        ments, decisions or concerted practices. When applying these EC competition rules,
        national courts act within the framework of Community law and are consequently
        bound to observe the general principles of Community law.[16]

8   The application of Articles 81 and 82 EC by national courts often depends on
        complex economic and legal assessments.[17] When applying EC competition rules,
        national courts are bound by the case law of the Community courts as well as by
        Commission regulations applying Article 81(3) EC to certain categories of agree-
        ments, decisions or concerted practices.[18] Furthermore, the application of Articles
        81 and 82 EC by the Commission in a specific case binds the national courts when
        they apply EC competition rules in the same case in parallel with or subsequent to the
        Commission.[19] Finally, and without prejudice to the ultimate interpretation of the
        EC Treaty by the Court of Justice, national courts may find guidance in Commission
        regulations and decisions which present elements of analogy with the case they are
        dealing with, as well as in Commission notices and guidelines relating to the appli-
        cation of Articles 81 and 82 EC[20] and in the annual report on competition policy.[21]

B. Procedural aspects of the application of EC competition rules by national courts

9   The procedural conditions for the enforcement of EC competition rules by national
        courts and the sanctions they can impose in case of an infringement of those rules,
        are largely covered by national law. However, to some extent, Community law
        also determines the conditions in which EC competition rules are enforced. Those
        Community law provisions may provide for the faculty of national courts to avail
        themselves of certain instruments, e.g. to ask for the Commission's opinion on

15 E.g. a national court may be asked to enforce a Commission decision taken pursuant to Articles
    7 to 10, 23 and 24 of the regulation.
16 See e.g. case 5/88 *Wachauf* [1989] ECR 2609, 19.
17 Joined cases C-215/96 and C-216/96 *Bagnasco* [1999] ECR I-135, 50.
18 Case 63/75 *Fonderies Roubaix* [1976] ECR 111, 9 to 11 and case C-234/89 *Delimitis* [1991]
    ECR I- 935, 46.
19 On the parallel or consecutive application of EC competition rules by national courts and the
    Commission, see also points 11 to 14.
20 Case 66/86 *Ahmed Saeed Flugreisen* [1989] ECR 803, 27 and case C-234/89 *Delimitis*
    [1991] ECR I 935, 50. A list of Commission guidelines, notices and regulations in the
    field of competition policy, in particular the regulations applying Article 81(3) EC to cer-
    tain categories of agreements, decisions or concerted practices, are annexed to this notice.
    For the decisions of the Commission applying Articles 81 and 82 EC (since 1964), see
    http://www.europa.eu.int/comm/competition/antitrust/cases/.
21 Joined cases C-319/93, C-40/94 and C-224/94 *Dijkstra* [1995] ECR I-4471, 32.

questions concerning the application of EC competition rules[22] or they may create rules that have an obligatory impact on proceedings before them, e.g. allowing the Commission and national competition authorities to submit written observations.[23] These Community law provisions prevail over national rules. Therefore, national courts have to set aside national rules which, if applied, would conflict with these Community law provisions. Where such Community law provisions are directly applicable, they are a direct source of rights and duties for all those affected, and must be fully and uniformly applied in all the Member States from the date of their entry into force.[24]

10   In the absence of Community law provisions on procedures and sanctions related to the enforcement of EC competition rules by national courts, the latter apply national procedural law and – to the extent that they are competent to do so – impose sanctions provided for under national law. However, the application of these national provisions must be compatible with the general principles of Community law. In this regard, it is useful to recall the case law of the Court of Justice, according to which:

(a) where there is an infringement of Community law, national law must provide for sanctions which are effective, proportionate and dissuasive;[25]

(b) where the infringement of Community law causes harm to an individual, the latter should under certain conditions be able to ask the national court for damages;[26]

(c) the rules on procedures and sanctions which national courts apply to enforce Community law

– must not make such enforcement excessively difficult or practically impossible (the principle of effectiveness)[27] and they

– must not be less favourable than the rules applicable to the enforcement of equivalent national law (the principle of equivalence).[28]

---

22 On the possibility for national courts to ask the Commission for an opinion, see further in points 27 to 30.

23 On the submission of observations, see further in points 31 to 35.

24 Case 106/77 *Simmenthal* [1978] ECR 629, 14 and 15.

25 Case 68/88 *Commission v Greece* [1989] ECR 2965, 23 to 25.

26 On damages in case of an infringement by an undertaking, see case C-453/99 *Courage and Crehan* [2001] ECR 6297, 26 and 27. On damages in case of an infringement by a Member State or by an authority which is an emanation of the State and on the conditions of such state liability, see e.g. joined cases C-6/90 and C-9/90 *Francovich* [1991] ECR I-5357, 33 to 36; case C-271/91 *Marshall v Southampton and South West Hampshire Area Health Authority* [1993] ECR I-4367, 30 and 34 to 35; joined cases C-46/93 and C-48/93 *Brasserie du Pêcheur and Factortame* [1996] ECR I-1029; case C- 392/93 *British Telecommunications* [1996] ECR I-1631, 39 to 46 and joined cases C-178/94, C-179/94 and C-188/94 to 190/94 *Dillenkofer* [1996] ECR I-4845, 22 to 26 and 72.

27 See e.g. case 33/76 *Rewe* [1976] ECR 1989, 5; case 45/76 *Comet* [1976] ECR 2043, 12 and case 79/83 *Harz* [1984] ECR 1921, 18 and 23.

28 See e.g. case 33/76 *Rewe* [1976] ECR 1989, 5; case 158/80 *Rewe* [1981] ECR 1805, 44; case 199/82 *San Giorgio* [1983] ECR 3595, 12 and case C-231/96 *Edis* [1998] ECR I-4951, 36 and 37.

On the basis of the principle of primacy of Community law, a national court may not apply national rules that are incompatible with these principles.

C. Parallel or consecutive application of EC competition rules by the Commission and by national courts

11   A national court may be applying EC competition law to an agreement, decision, concerted practice or unilateral behaviour affecting trade between Member States at the same time as the Commission or subsequent to the Commission.[29] The following points outline some of the obligations national courts have to respect in those circumstances.

12   Where a national court comes to a decision before the Commission does, it must avoid adopting a decision that would conflict with a decision contemplated by the Commission.[30] To that effect, the national court may ask the Commission whether it has initiated proceedings regarding the same agreements, decisions or practices[31] and if so, about the progress of proceedings and the likelihood of a decision in that case.[32] The national court may, for reasons of legal certainty, also consider staying its proceedings until the Commission has reached a decision.[33] The Commission, for its part, will endeavour to give priority to cases for which it has decided to initiate proceedings within the meaning of Article 2(1) of Commission Regulation (EC) No 773/2004 and that are the subject of national proceedings stayed in this way, in particular when the outcome of a civil dispute depends on them. However, where the national court cannot reasonably doubt the Commission's contemplated decision or where the Commission has already decided on a similar case, the national court may decide on the case pending before it in accordance with that contemplated or earlier decision without it being necessary to ask the Commission for the information mentioned above or to await the Commission's decision.

13   Where the Commission reaches a decision in a particular case before the national court, the latter cannot take a decision running counter to that of the Commission. The binding effect of the Commission's decision is of course without prejudice

---

29 Article 11(6), *juncto* Article 35(3) and (4) of the regulation prevents a parallel application of Articles 81 or 82 EC by the Commission and a national court only when the latter has been designated as a national competition authority.

30 Article 16(1) of the regulation.

31 The Commission makes the initiation of its proceedings with a view to adopting a decision pursuant to Article 7 to 10 of the regulation public (see Article 2(2) of Commission Regulation (EC) No 773/2004 of date relating to proceedings pursuant to Articles 81 and 82 of the EC Treaty ... According to the Court of Justice, the initiation of proceedings implies an authoritative act of the Commission, evidencing its intention of taking a decision (case 48/72 *Brasserie de Haecht* [1973] ECR 77, 16).

32 Case C-234/89 *Delimitis* [1991] ECR I-935, 53, and joined cases C-319/93, C-40/94 and C-224/94 *Dijkstra* [1995] ECR I-4471, 34. See further on this issue point 21 of this notice.

33 See Article 16(1) of the regulation and case C-234/89 *Delimitis* [1991] ECR I-935, 47 and case C-344/98 *Masterfoods* [2000] ECR I-11369, 51.

[669]

to the interpretation of Community law by the Court of Justice. Therefore, if the national court doubts the legality of the Commission's decision, it cannot avoid the binding effects of that decision without a ruling to the contrary by the Court of Justice.[34] Consequently, if a national court intends to take a decision that runs counter to that of the Commission, it must refer a question to the Court of Justice for a preliminary ruling (Article 234 EC). The latter will then decide on the compatibility of the Commission's decision with Community law. However, if the Commission's decision is challenged before the Community courts pursuant to Article 230 EC and the outcome of the dispute before the national court depends on the validity of the Commission's decision, the national court should stay its proceedings pending final judgment in the action for annulment by the Community courts unless it considers that, in the circumstances of the case, a reference to the Court of Justice for a preliminary ruling on the validity of the Commission decision is warranted.[35]

14   When a national court stays proceedings, e.g. awaiting the Commission's decision (situation described in point 12 of this notice) or pending final judgement by the Community courts in an action for annulment or in a preliminary ruling procedure (situation described in point 13), it is incumbent on it to examine whether it is necessary to order interim measures in order to safeguard the interests of the parties.[36]

(III) THE CO-OPERATION BETWEEN THE COMMISSION AND NATIONAL COURTS

15   Other than the co-operation mechanism between the national courts and the Court of Justice under Article 234 EC, the EC Treaty does not explicitly provide for co-operation between the national courts and the Commission. However, in its interpretation of Article 10 EC, which obliges the Member States to facilitate the achievement of the Community's tasks, the Community courts found that this Treaty provision imposes on the European institutions and the Member States mutual duties of loyal co-operation with a view to attaining the objectives of the EC Treaty. Article 10 EC thus implies that the Commission must assist national courts when they apply Community law.[37] Equally, national courts may be obliged to assist the Commission in the fulfilment of its tasks.[38]

16   It is also appropriate to recall the co-operation between national courts and national authorities, in particular national competition authorities, for the application of Articles 81 and 82 EC. While the co-operation between these national authorities

---

34 Case 314/85 *Foto-Frost* [1987] ECR 4199, 12 to 20.
35 See Article 16(1) of the regulation and case C-344/98 *Masterfoods* [2000] ECR I-11369, 52 to 59.
36 Case C-344/98 *Masterfoods* [2000] ECR, I-11369, 58.
37 Case C-2/88 Imm *Zwartveld* [1990] ECR I-3365, 16 to 22 and case C-234/89 *Delimitis* [1991] I-935, 53.
38 C-94/00 *Roquette Frères* [2002] ECR 9011, 31.

is primarily governed by national rules, Article 15(3) of the regulation provides for the possibility for national competition authorities to submit observations before the national courts of their Member State. Points 31 and 33 to 35 of this notice are mutatis mutandis applicable to those submissions.

A. *The Commission as amicus curiae*

17   In order to assist national courts in the application of EC competition rules, the Commission is committed to help national courts where the latter find such help necessary to be able to decide on a case. Article 15 of the regulation refers to the most frequent types of such assistance: the transmission of information (points 21 to 26) and the Commission's opinions (points 27 to 30), both at the request of a national court and the possibility for the Commission to submit observations (points 31 to 35). Since the regulation provides for these types of assistance, it cannot be limited by any Member States' rule. However, in the absence of Community procedural rules to this effect and to the extent that they are necessary to facilitate these forms of assistance, Member States must adopt the appropriate procedural rules to allow both the national courts and the Commission to make full use of the possibilities the regulation offers.[39]

18   The national court may send its request for assistance in writing to European Commission Directorate General for Competition, B-1049 Brussels, Belgium, or send it electronically to comp-amicus@cec.eu.int.

19   It should be recalled that whatever form the co-operation with national courts takes, the Commission will respect the independence of national courts. As a consequence, the assistance offered by the Commission does not bind the national court. The Commission has also to make sure that it respects its duty of professional secrecy and that it safeguards its own functioning and independence.[40] In fulfilling its duty under Article 10 EC, of assisting national courts in the application of EC competition rules, the Commission is committed to remaining neutral and objective in its assistance. Indeed, the Commission's assistance to national courts is part of its duty to defend the public interest. It has therefore no intention to serve the private interests of the parties involved in the case pending before the national court. As a consequence, the Commission will not hear any of the parties about its assistance to the national court. In case the Commission has been contacted by any of the parties in the case pending before the court on issues which are raised before the national court, it will inform the national court thereof, independent of whether these contacts took place before or after the national court's request for co-operation.

20   The Commission will publish a summary concerning its co-operation with national courts pursuant to this notice in its annual Report on Competition Policy. It may also make its opinions and observations available on its website.

---

39 On the compatibility of such national procedural rules with the general principles of Community law, see points 9 and 10 of this notice.
40 On these duties, see e.g. points 23 to 26 of this notice.

1. The Commission's duty to transmit information to national courts

21   The duty for the Commission to assist national courts in the application of EC competition law is mainly reflected in the obligation for the Commission to transmit information it holds to national courts. A national court may, e.g., ask the Commission for documents in its possession or for information of a procedural nature to enable it to discover whether a certain case is pending before the Commission, whether the Commission has initiated a procedure or whether it has already taken a position. A national court may also ask the Commission when a decision is likely to be taken, so as to be able to determine the conditions for any decision to stay proceedings or whether interim measures need to be adopted.[41]

22   In order to ensure the efficiency of the co-operation with national courts, the Commission will endeavour to provide the national court with the requested information within one month from the date it receives the request. Where the Commission has to ask the national court for further clarification of its request or where the Commission has to consult those who are directly affected by the transmission of the information, that period starts to run from the moment that it receives the required information.

23   In transmitting information to national courts, the Commission has to uphold the guarantees given to natural and legal persons by Article 287 EC.[42] Article 287 EC prevents members, officials and other servants of the Commission from disclosing information covered by the obligation of professional secrecy. The information covered by professional secrecy may be both confidential information and business secrets. Business secrets are information of which not only disclosure to the public but also mere transmission to a person other than the one that provided the information might seriously harm the latter's interests.[43]

24   The combined reading of Articles 10 and 287 EC does not lead to an absolute prohibition for the Commission to transmit information which is covered by the obligation of professional secrecy to national courts. The case law of the Community courts confirms that the duty of loyal co-operation requires the Commission to provide the national court with whatever information the latter asks for, even information covered by professional secrecy. However, in offering its co-operation to the national courts, the Commission may not in any circumstances undermine the guarantees laid down in Article 287 EC.

25   Consequently, before transmitting information covered by professional secrecy to a national court, the Commission will remind the court of its obligation under Community law to uphold the rights which Article 287 EC confers on natural and

---

41 Case C-234/89 *Delimitis* [1991] ECR I-935, 53, and joined cases C-319/93, C-40/94 and C-224/94 *Dijkstra* [1995] ECR I-4471, 34.

42 Case C-234/89 *Delimitis* [1991] I-935, 53.

43 Case T-353/94 *Postbank* [1996] ECR II-921, 86 and 87 and case 145/83 *Adams* [1985] ECR 3539, 34.

legal persons and it will ask the court whether it can and will guarantee protection of confidential information and business secrets. If the national court cannot offer such guarantee, the Commission shall not transmit the information covered by professional secrecy to the national court.[44] Only when the national court has offered a guarantee that it will protect the confidential information and business secrets, will the Commission transmit the information requested, indicating those parts which are covered by professional secrecy and which parts are not and can therefore be disclosed.

26   There are further exceptions to the disclosure of information by the Commission to national courts. Particularly, the Commission may refuse to transmit information to national courts for overriding reasons relating to the need to safeguard the interests of the Community or to avoid any interference with its functioning and independence, in particular by jeopardising the accomplishment of the tasks entrusted to it.[45] Therefore, the Commission will not transmit to national courts information voluntarily submitted by a leniency applicant without the consent of that applicant.

2. Request for an opinion on questions concerning the application of EC competition rules

27   When called upon to apply EC competition rules to a case pending before it, a national court may first seek guidance in the case law of the Community courts or in Commission regulations, decisions, notices and guidelines applying Articles 81 and 82 EC.[46] Where these tools do not offer sufficient guidance, the national court may ask the Commission for its opinion on questions concerning the application of EC competition rules. The national court may ask the Commission for its opinion on economic, factual and legal matters.[47] The latter is of course without prejudice to the possibility or the obligation for the national court to ask the Court of Justice for a preliminary ruling regarding the interpretation or the validity of Community law in accordance with Article 234 EC.

28   In order to enable the Commission to provide the national court with a useful opinion, it may request the national court for further information.[48] In order to ensure the efficiency of the co-operation with national courts, the Commission will endeavour to provide the national court with the requested opinion within four months from the date it receives the request. Where the Commission has requested

---

44 Case C-2/88 *Zwartveld* [1990] ECR I-4405, 10 and 11 and case T-353/94 *Postbank* [1996] ECR II-921, 93.

45 Case C-2/88 *Zwartveld* [1990] ECR I-4405, 10 and 11; case C-275/00 *First and Franex* [2002] ECR I- 10943, 49 and case T 353/94 *Postbank* [1996] ECR II-921, 93.

46 See point 8 of this notice.

47 Case C-234/89 *Delimitis* [1991] ECR I-935, 53, and joined cases C-319/93, C-40/94 and C-224/94 *Dijkstra* [1995] ECR I-4471, 34.

48 48 Compare with case 96/81 *Commission v the Netherlands* [1982] ECR 1791, 7 and case 272/86 *Commission v Greece* [1988] ECR 4875, 30.

the national court for further information in order to enable it to formulate its opinion, that period starts to run from the moment that it receives the additional information.

29   When giving its opinion, the Commission will limit itself to providing the national court with the factual information or the economic or legal clarification asked for, without considering the merits of the case pending before the national court. Moreover, unlike the authoritative interpretation of Community law by the Community courts, the opinion of the Commission does not legally bind the national court.

30   In line with what has been said in point 19 of this notice, the Commission will not hear the parties before formulating its opinion to the national court. The latter will have to deal with the Commission's opinion in accordance with the relevant national procedural rules, which have to respect the general principles of Community law.

3. The Commission's submission of observations to the national court

31   According to Article 15(3) of the regulation, the national competition authorities and the Commission may submit observations on issues relating to the application of Articles 81 or 82 EC to a national court which is called upon to apply those provisions. The regulation distinguishes between written observations, which the national competition authorities and the Commission may submit on their own initiative, and oral observations, which can only be submitted with the permission of the national court.[49]

32   The regulation specifies that the Commission will only submit observations when the coherent application of Articles 81 or 82 EC so requires. That being the objective of its submission, the Commission will limit its observations to an economic and legal analysis of the facts underlying the case pending before the national court.

33   In order to enable the Commission to submit useful observations, national courts may be asked to transmit or ensure the transmission to the Commission of a copy of all documents that are necessary for the assessment of the case. In line with Article 15(3), second subparagraph, of the regulation, the Commission will only use those documents for the preparation of its observations.[50]

34   Since the regulation does not provide for a procedural framework within which the observations are to be submitted, Member States' procedural rules and practices determine the relevant procedural framework. Where a Member State has not yet established the relevant procedural framework, the national court has to determine which procedural rules are appropriate for the submission of observations in the case pending before it.

49 According to Article 15(4) of the regulation, this is without prejudice to wider powers to make observations before courts conferred on national competition authorities under national law.
50 See also Article 28(2) of the regulation, which prevents the Commission from disclosing the information it has acquired and which is covered by the obligation of professional secrecy.

35   The procedural framework should respect the principles set out in point 10 of this notice. That implies amongst others that the procedural framework for the submission of observations on issues relating to the application of Articles 81 or 82 EC

    (a) has to be compatible with the general principles of Community law, in particular the fundamental rights of the parties involved in the case;

    (b) cannot make the submission of such observations excessively difficult or practically impossible (the principle of effectiveness)[51]; and

    (c) cannot make the submission of such observations more difficult than the submission of observations in court proceedings where equivalent national law is applied (the principle of equivalence).

B. The national courts facilitating the role of the Commission in the enforcement of EC competition rules

36   Since the duty of loyal co-operation also implies that Member States' authorities assist the European institutions with a view to attaining the objectives of the EC Treaty,[52] the regulation provides for three examples of such assistance: (1) the transmission of documents necessary for the assessment of a case in which the Commission would like to submit observations (see point 33), (2) the transmission of judgements applying Articles 81 or 82 EC and (3) the role of national courts in the context of a Commission inspection.

1. The transmission of judgements of national courts applying Articles 81 or 82 EC

37   According to Article 15(2) of the regulation, Member States shall send to the Commission a copy of any written judgement of national courts applying Articles 81 or 82 EC without delay after the full written judgement is notified to the parties. The transmission of national judgements on the application of Articles 81 or 82 EC and the resulting information on proceedings before national courts primarily enable the Commission to become aware in a timely fashion of cases for which it might be appropriate to submit observations where one of the parties lodges an appeal against the judgement.

2. The role of national courts in the context of a Commission inspection

38   Finally, national courts may play a role in the context of a Commission inspection of undertakings and associations of undertakings. The role of the national courts depends on whether the inspections are conducted in business premises or in non-business premises.

---

51 Joined cases 46/87 and 227/88 *Hoechst* [1989] ECR, 2859, 33. See also Article 15(3) of the regulation.

52 Case C-69/90 *Commission v Italy* [1991] ECR 6011, 15.

39   With regard to the inspection of business premises, national legislation may require authorisation from a national court to allow a national enforcement authority to assist the Commission in case of opposition of the undertaking concerned. Such authorisation may also be sought as a precautionary measure. When dealing with the request, the national court has the power to control that the Commission's inspection decision is authentic and that the coercive measures envisaged are neither arbitrary nor excessive having regard to the subject matter of the inspection. In its control of the proportionality of the coercive measures, the national court may ask the Commission, directly or through the national competition authority, for detailed explanations in particular on the grounds the Commission has for suspecting infringement of Articles 81 and 82 EC, as well as on the seriousness of the suspected infringement and on the nature of the involvement of the undertaking concerned.[53]

40   With regard to the inspection of non-business premises, the regulation requires the authorisation from a national court before a Commission decision ordering such an inspection can be executed. In that case, the national court may control that the Commission's inspection decision is authentic and that the coercive measures envisaged are neither arbitrary nor excessive having regard in particular to the seriousness of the suspected infringement, to the importance of the evidence sought, to the involvement of the undertaking concerned and to the reasonable likelihood that business books and records relating to the subject matter of the inspection are kept in the premises for which the authorisation is requested. The national court may ask the Commission, directly or through the national competition authority, for detailed explanations on those elements that are necessary to allow its control of the proportionality of the coercive measures envisaged.[54]

41   In both cases referred to in points 39 and 40, the national court may not call into question the lawfulness of the Commission's decision or the necessity for the inspection nor can it demand that it be provided with information in the Commission's file.[55] Furthermore, the duty of loyal co-operation requires the national court to take its decision within an appropriate timeframe that allows the Commission to effectively conduct its inspection.[56]

(iv) FINAL PROVISIONS

42   This notice is issued in order to assist national courts in the application of Articles 81 and 82 EC. It does not bind the national courts, nor does it affect the rights and obligations of the EU Member States and natural or legal persons under Community law.

---

53   Article 20(6) to (8) of the regulation and case C-94/00 *Roquette Frères* [2002] ECR 9011.
54   Article 21(3) of the regulation.
55   Case C-94/00 *Roquette Frères* [2002] ECR 9011, 39 and 62 to 66.
56   See also *ibidem*, 91 and 92.

43   This notice replaces the 1993 notice on co-operation between national courts and
the Commission in applying Articles 85 and 86 of the EEC Treaty.[57]

The Notice also contains an annex setting out a current list of Commission Block
Exemption Regulations, divided between 'Non-sector specific rules', such as
Regulation 2790/99, and 'Sector specific rules' for industries such as insurance,
motor vehicles, telecommunications and postal services, and transport.

4 Private enforcement and appeals

The final part in this chapter deals with private enforcement and appeals under
the EC and UK systems of competition law. In recent years this has become a
topic of huge practical and strategic significance, especially given the European
Commission's interest in encouraging private enforcement of Articles 81 and
82 in national courts.

It should also be apparent from the extracts included in the preceding chapters that firms and their legal representatives have also been eager to take
advantage of the protections afforded by competition law provisions and to exploit them for business purposes. Accordingly, many of the cases establishing
the principles of competition law came before the ECJ on Article 234 references
from national courts attempting to resolve disputes between individuals and/or
firms. Thus, for example, because Article 81(2) renders the offending term(s)
in a contract that breaches the provisions of Article 81(1) void, it may well be in
the interest of a firm 'trapped' in a contract that it finds onerous to plead breach
of competition law thereby trying to escape its obligations under the contract.
Conversely, a firm sued for breach of contract may wish to defend itself by
claiming that the contract (or the term in question) is void and unenforceable.

(A) Damages

Firms involved in or affected by anti-competitive agreements may not only wish
to escape their obligations but to reverse the losses caused to them. However,
this can give rise to policy concerns about parties to illegal contracts relying
on them for the purpose of claiming damages. Another situation where a firm
might wish to avail itself of the direct effect of competition law to right perceived
wrongs and obtain redress is where it operates in an oligopolistic market or a
market upstream or downstream from a market with a firm in a dominant
position and feels that abusive business practices of the latter have caused it
loss. Naturally, such a firm would wish to rely on provisions like Article 82 or the
Chapter II prohibition of the CA1990 to seek financial compensation. Against
this background, the following extracts address the issue of damages flowing

---

57 *OJ* C 39, 13.2.93, p. 6.

from breach of competition law provisions claimed directly in local courts, first with respect to EC law and then UK law.

I EC law

It is instructive to begin an examination of the recovery of damages under EC competition law with the judgment of the ECJ in *Courage Ltd v. Crehan*.

Courage Ltd v. Crehan [2001] ECR I-6297

Courage, a UK brewery, sought compensation for unpaid beer deliveries made to the defendant, a tenant in a tied Courage pub. Crehan argued that the tying clause in his lease, requiring him to purchase a fixed minimum quantity of beer from Courage, infringed Article 81(1) and counter-claimed for damages. The Court of Appeal made a reference to the ECJ concerning English legal rules precluding a party to an illegal agreement from claiming damages from the other party. A previous Court of Appeal judgment had ruled that Article 81(1) aimed to protect third parties and not the parties to the prohibited agreement, given that they could be considered the cause, rather than the victims, of the restriction of competition.

ECJ

17   By its first, second and third questions, which should be considered together, the referring court is asking essentially whether a party to a contract liable to restrict or distort competition within the meaning of Article [81] of the Treaty can rely on the breach of that provision before a national court to obtain relief from the other contracting party. In particular, it asks whether that party can obtain compensation for loss which he alleges to result from his being subject to a contractual clause contrary to Article [81] and whether, therefore, Community law precludes a rule of national law which denies a person the right to rely on his own illegal actions to obtain damages.

18   If Community law precludes a national rule of that sort, the national court wishes to know, by its fourth question, what factors must be taken into consideration in assessing the merits of such a claim for damages.

19   It should be borne in mind, first of all, that the Treaty has created its own legal order, which is integrated into the legal systems of the Member States and which their courts are bound to apply. The subjects of that legal order are not only the Member States but also their nationals. Just as it imposes burdens on individuals, Community law is also intended to give rise to rights which become part of their legal assets. Those rights arise not only where they are expressly granted by the Treaty but also by virtue of obligations which the Treaty imposes in a clearly defined manner both on individuals and on the Member States and the Community institutions ...

20   Secondly, according to Article [3(1)(g) EC], Article [81] of the Treaty constitutes a fundamental provision which is essential for the accomplishment of the tasks entrusted to the Community and, in particular, for the functioning of the internal market . . .

21   Indeed, the importance of such a provision led the framers of the Treaty to provide expressly, in Article [81(2)] of the Treaty, that any agreements or decisions prohibited pursuant to that article are to be automatically void . . .

22   That principle of automatic nullity can be relied on by anyone, and the courts are bound by it once the conditions for the application of Article [81(1)] are met and so long as the agreement concerned does not justify the grant of an exemption under Article [81(3)] of the Treaty . . . Since the nullity referred to in Article [81(2)] is absolute, an agreement which is null and void by virtue of this provision has no effect as between the contracting parties and cannot be set up against third parties . . . Moreover, it is capable of having a bearing on all the effects, either past or future, of the agreement or decision concerned . . .

23   Thirdly, it should be borne in mind that the Court has held that Article [81(1)] of the Treaty and Article [82] produce direct effects in relations between individuals and create rights for the individuals concerned which the national courts must safeguard . . .

24   It follows from the foregoing considerations that any individual can rely on a breach of Article [81(1)] of the Treaty before a national court even where he is a party to a contract that is liable to restrict or distort competition within the meaning of that provision.

25   As regards the possibility of seeking compensation for loss caused by a contract or by conduct liable to restrict or distort competition, it should be remembered from the outset that, in accordance with settled case-law, the national courts whose task it is to apply the provisions of Community law in areas within their jurisdiction must ensure that those rules take full effect and must protect the rights which they confer on individuals . . .

26   The full effectiveness of Article [81] of the Treaty and, in particular, the practical effect of the prohibition laid down in Article [81(1)] would be put at risk if it were not open to any individual to claim damages for loss caused to him by a contract or by conduct liable to restrict or distort competition.

27   Indeed, the existence of such a right strengthens the working of the Community competition rules and discourages agreements or practices, which are frequently covert, which are liable to restrict or distort competition. From that point of view, actions for damages before the national courts can make a significant contribution to the maintenance of effective competition in the Community.

28   There should not therefore be any absolute bar to such an action being brought by a party to a contract which would be held to violate the competition rules.

[679]

29   However, in the absence of Community rules governing the matter, it is for the domestic legal system of each Member State to designate the courts and tribunals having jurisdiction and to lay down the detailed procedural rules governing actions for safeguarding rights which individuals derive directly from Community law, provided that such rules are not less favourable than those governing similar domestic actions (principle of equivalence) and that they do not render practically impossible or excessively difficult the exercise of rights conferred by Community law (principle of effectiveness) ...

30   In that regard, the Court has held that Community law does not prevent national courts from taking steps to ensure that the protection of the rights guaranteed by Community law does not entail the unjust enrichment of those who enjoy them ...

31   Similarly, provided that the principles of equivalence and effectiveness are respected ..., Community law does not preclude national law from denying a party who is found to bear significant responsibility for the distortion of competition the right to obtain damages from the other contracting party. Under a principle which is recognised in most of the legal systems of the Member States and which the Court has applied in the past ..., a litigant should not profit from his own unlawful conduct, where this is proven.

32   In that regard, the matters to be taken into account by the competent national court include the economic and legal context in which the parties find themselves and, as the United Kingdom Government rightly points out, the respective bargaining power and conduct of the two parties to the contract.

33   In particular, it is for the national court to ascertain whether the party who claims to have suffered loss through concluding a contract that is liable to restrict or distort competition found himself in a markedly weaker position than the other party, such as seriously to compromise or even eliminate his freedom to negotiate the terms of the contract and his capacity to avoid the loss or reduce its extent, in particular by availing himself in good time of all the legal remedies available to him.

34   Referring to the judgments in ... *Brasserie de Haecht* [and] *Delimitis* ... the Commission and the United Kingdom Government also rightly point out that a contract might prove to be contrary to Article [81(1)] of the Treaty for the sole reason that it is part of a network of similar contracts which have a cumulative effect on competition. In such a case, the party contracting with the person controlling the network cannot bear significant responsibility for the breach of Article [81], particularly where in practice the terms of the contract were imposed on him by the party controlling the network.

35   Contrary to the submission of Courage, making a distinction as to the extent of the parties' liability does not conflict with the case-law of the Court to the effect that it does not matter, for the purposes of the application of Article [81] of the Treaty, whether the parties to an agreement are on an equal footing as regards their economic position and function ... That case-law concerns the conditions for application of

Article [81] of the Treaty while the questions put before the Court in the present case concern certain consequences in civil law of a breach of that provision.

It is important to note that the ECJ not only reasons out the legal basis for allowing parties to contracts infringing Article 81(1) to bring an action for damages but that it also highlights the policy benefits in allowing such claims, which are based, perhaps predictably, on furthering of general objectives of the EC Treaty (specifically Article (g) 'ensuring that competition in the internal market is not distorted'). However, the ECJ explicitly leaves it open to national courts to disallow a party any 'profit from his own unlawful conduct' by taking into account relative blame for the infringement, the strength of bargaining power and the claimant's initiative in exercising rights to bring the infringement to an end (paragraphs 30 *ff*).

II UK law

When the CA1998 was introduced, it became possible to launch a private action in national courts for breaches of UK competition rules, although perhaps indirectly, from section 58. Following amendments made to the CA1998 by the EA2002, the former Act now contains three provisions which deal with claims for damages.

S. 47A Monetary claims before Tribunal

(1) This section applies to –
(a) any claim for damages, or
(b) any other claim for a sum of money,
which a person who has suffered loss or damage as a result of the infringement of a relevant prohibition may make in civil proceedings brought in any part of the United Kingdom.

(2) In this section 'relevant prohibition' means any of the following –
(a) the Chapter I prohibition;
(b) the Chapter II prohibition;
(c) the prohibition in Article 81(1) of the Treaty;
(d) the prohibition in Article 82 of the Treaty;
(e) the prohibition in Article 65(1) of the Treaty establishing the European Coal and Steel Community;
(f) the prohibition in Article 66(7) of that Treaty.

(3) For the purpose of identifying claims which may be made in civil proceedings, any limitation rules that would apply in such proceedings are to be disregarded.

(4) A claim to which this section applies may (subject to the provisions of this Act and Tribunal rules) be made in proceedings brought before the Tribunal.

[681]

(5) But no claim may be made in such proceedings –

(a) until a decision mentioned in subsection (6) has established that the relevant prohibition in question has been infringed; and

(b) otherwise than with the permission of the Tribunal, during any period specified in subsection (7) or (8) which relates to that decision.

(6) The decisions which may be relied on for the purposes of proceedings under this section are –

(a) a decision of the OFT that the Chapter I prohibition or the Chapter II prohibition has been infringed;

(b) a decision of the OFT that the prohibition in Article 81(1) or Article 82 of the Treaty has been infringed;

(c) a decision of the Tribunal (on an appeal from a decision of the OFT) that the Chapter I prohibition, the Chapter II prohibition or the prohibition in Article 81(1) or Article 82 of the Treaty has been infringed;

(d) a decision of the European Commission that the prohibition in Article 81(1) or Article 82 of the Treaty has been infringed; or

(e) a decision of the European Commission that the prohibition in Article 65(1) of the Treaty establishing the European Coal and Steel Community has been infringed, or a finding made by the European Commission under Article 66(7) of that Treaty.

(7) The periods during which proceedings in respect of a claim made in reliance on a decision mentioned in subsection (6)(a), (b) or (c) may not be brought without permission are –

(a) in the case of a decision of the OFT, the period during which an appeal may be made to the Tribunal under section 46, section 47 or the EC Competition Law (Articles 84 and 85) Enforcement Regulations 2001 (S.I. 2001/2916);

(b) in the case of a decision of the OFT which is the subject of an appeal mentioned in paragraph (a), the period following the decision of the Tribunal on the appeal during which a further appeal may be made under section 49 or under those Regulations;

(c) in the case of a decision of the Tribunal mentioned in subsection (6)(c), the period during which a further appeal may be made under section 49 or under those Regulations;

(d) in the case of any decision which is the subject of a further appeal, the period during which an appeal may be made to the House of Lords from a decision on the further appeal;

and, where any appeal mentioned in paragraph (a), (b), (c) or (d) is made, the period specified in that paragraph includes the period before the appeal is determined.

(8) The periods during which proceedings in respect of a claim made in reliance on a decision or finding of the European Commission may not be brought without permission are –

(a) the period during which proceedings against the decision or finding may be instituted in the European Court; and

(b) if any such proceedings are instituted, the period before those proceedings are determined.

(9) In determining a claim to which this section applies the Tribunal is bound by any decision mentioned in subsection (6) which establishes that the prohibition in question has been infringed.

(10) The right to make a claim to which this section applies in proceedings before the Tribunal does not affect the right to bring any other proceedings in respect of the claim.

S. 47B Claims brought on behalf of consumers

(1) A specified body may (subject to the provisions of this Act and Tribunal rules) bring proceedings before the Tribunal which comprise consumer claims made or continued on behalf of at least two individuals.

(2) In this section 'consumer claim' means a claim to which section 47A applies which an individual has in respect of an infringement affecting (directly or indirectly) goods or services to which subsection (7) applies.

(3) A consumer claim may be included in proceedings under this section if it is –
(a) a claim made in the proceedings on behalf of the individual concerned by the specified body; or
(b) a claim made by the individual concerned under section 47A which is continued in the proceedings on his behalf by the specified body;
and such a claim may only be made or continued in the proceedings with the consent of the individual concerned.

(4) The consumer claims included in proceedings under this section must all relate to the same infringement.

(5) The provisions of section 47A(5) to (10) apply to a consumer claim included in proceedings under this section as they apply to a claim made in proceedings under that section.

(6) Any damages or other sum (not being costs or expenses) awarded in respect of a consumer claim included in proceedings under this section must be awarded to the individual concerned; but the Tribunal may, with the consent of the specified body and the individual, order that the sum awarded must be paid to the specified body (acting on behalf of the individual).

(7) This subsection applies to goods or services which –
(a) the individual received, or sought to receive, otherwise than in the course of a business carried on by him (notwithstanding that he received or sought to receive them with a view to carrying on a business); and

    (b) were, or would have been, supplied to the individual (in the case of goods whether by way of sale or otherwise) in the course of a business carried on by the person who supplied or would have supplied them.

(8)   A business includes –
    (a) a professional practice;
    (b) any other undertaking carried on for gain or reward;
    (c) any undertaking in the course of which goods or services are supplied otherwise than free of charge.

(9)   'Specified' means specified in an order made by the Secretary of State, in accordance with criteria to be published by the Secretary of State for the purposes of this section.

(10)   An application by a body to be specified in an order under this section is to be made in a form approved by the Secretary of State for the purpose.

S. 58A Findings of infringements

(1)   This section applies to proceedings before the court in which damages or any other sum of money is claimed in respect of an infringement of –
    (a) the Chapter I prohibition;
    (b) the Chapter II prohibition;
    (c) the prohibition in Article 81(1) of the Treaty;
    (d) the prohibition in Article 82 of the Treaty.

(2)   In such proceedings, the court is bound by a decision mentioned in subsection (3) once any period specified in subsection (4) which relates to the decision has elapsed.

(3)   The decisions are –
    (a) a decision of the OFT that the Chapter I prohibition or the Chapter II prohibition has been infringed;
    (b) a decision of the OFT that the prohibition in Article 81(1) or Article 82 of the Treaty has been infringed;
    (c) a decision of the Tribunal (on an appeal from a decision of the OFT) that the Chapter I prohibition or the Chapter II prohibition has been infringed, or that the prohibition in Article 81(1) or Article 82 of the Treaty has been infringed.

(4)   The periods mentioned in subsection (2) are –
    (a) in the case of a decision of the OFT, the period during which an appeal may be made to the Tribunal under section 46 or 47 or the EC Competition Law (Articles 84 and 85) Enforcement Regulations 2001 (S.I. 2001/2916);
    (b) in the case of a decision of the Tribunal mentioned in subsection (3)(c), the period during which a further appeal may be made under section 49 or under those Regulations;
    (c) in the case of any decision which is the subject of a further appeal, the period during which an appeal may be made to the House of Lords from a decision on the further appeal;

and, where any appeal mentioned in paragraph (a), (b) or (c) is made, the period specified in that paragraph includes the period before the appeal is determined.

(B) Appeals

I EC law

Chapter 1 discussed relevant aspects of the institutional structure of the EC. As noted, Commission decisions may be contested before the CFI on the basis of Article 230, which deals with applications for judicial review by persons affected by decisions 'of direct and individual concern'. Where a Member State wishes to challenge a decision of the Commission, the action will be heard by the ECJ and not the CFI (as happened in *France v. Commission*, cited at p. 602 above).

II UK law

Previous chapters outline the multi-tier appeal mechanism within the UK system of competition law. Appeals from decisions of the OFT or the Competition Commission are heard first by the Competition Appeal Tribunal (CAT). Parties can also appeal further on points of law to the Court of Appeal. The following are the three provisions in the CA1998 dealing with appeals.

S. 46 Appealable decisions

(1)   Any party to an agreement in respect of which the OFT has made a decision may appeal to the Tribunal against, or with respect to, the decision.

(2)   Any person in respect of whose conduct the OFT has made a decision may appeal to the Tribunal against, or with respect to, the decision.

(3)   In this section 'decision' means a decision of the OFT –
(a) as to whether the Chapter I prohibition has been infringed,
(b) as to whether the prohibition in Article 81(1) has been infringed,
(c) as to whether the Chapter II prohibition has been infringed,
(d) as to whether the prohibition in Article 82 has been infringed,
(e) cancelling a block or parallel exemption,
(f) withdrawing the benefit of a regulation of the Commission pursuant to Article 29(2) of the EC Competition Regulation,
(g) not releasing commitments pursuant to a request made under section 31A(4)(b)(i),
(h) releasing commitments under section 31A(4)(b)(ii),
(i) as to the imposition of any penalty under section 36 or as to the amount of any such penalty, and includes a direction under section 32, 33 or 35 and such other decisions under this Part as may be prescribed.

[685]

(4)   Except in the case of an appeal against the imposition, or the amount, of a penalty, the making of an appeal under this section does not suspend the effect of the decision to which the appeal relates.

(5)   Part I of Schedule 8 makes further provision about appeals.

S. 47 Third party appeals

(1)   A person who does not fall within section 46(1) or (2) may appeal to the Tribunal with respect to –
(a) a decision falling within paragraphs (a) to (f) of section 46(3);
(b) a decision falling within paragraph (g) of section 46(3);
(c) a decision of the OFT to accept or release commitments under section 31A, or to accept a variation of such commitments other than a variation which is not material in any respect;
(d) a decision of the OFT to make directions under section 35;
(e) a decision of the OFT not to make directions under section 35; or
(f) such other decision of the OFT under this Part as may be prescribed.

(2)   A person may make an appeal under subsection (1) only if the Tribunal considers that he has a sufficient interest in the decision with respect to which the appeal is made, or that he represents persons who have such an interest.

(3)   The making of an appeal under this section does not suspend the effect of the decision to which the appeal relates.

S. 49 Further appeals

(1)   An appeal lies to the appropriate court –
(a) from a decision of the Tribunal as to the amount of a penalty under section 36;
(b) from any decision of an appeal tribunal as to the amount of a penalty;
(c) on a point of law arising from any other decision of the Tribunal on an appeal under section 46 or 47.

(2)   An appeal under this section –
(a) may be brought by a party to the proceedings before the Tribunal or by a person who has a sufficient interest in the matter; and
(b) requires the permission of the Tribunal or the appropriate court.

(3)   In this section 'the appropriate court' means the Court of Appeal or, in the case of an appeal from Tribunal proceedings in Scotland, the Court of Session.

Further reading

Kerse EC *Antitrust Procedure* (Sweet & Maxwell, 4th edn. 1998)

Rodger 'Private enforcement and the Enterprise Act: an exemplary system of
    awarding damages?' (2003) 24 ECLR 103
Gilliams 'Modernisation: from policy to practice' (2003) 28 ELRev 451
Smith *Competition Law: Enforcement and Procedure* (Butterworths, 2001)
Wesseling *The Modernisation of EC Antitrust* (Hart Publishing, 2000)

Appendix: case studies

Case study I

US-based ACM Inc. is a firm active in the manufacturing of highly sophisticated lap-top computers. ACM sells its products throughout the world. In Canada, ACM has a wholly-owned subsidiary, ACMCanada, which is responsible for the distribution of its products there. In Spain and Italy ACM makes use of independent distributors: Alpha, which has the exclusive distribution rights for Spain, and Beta, which has the rights for Italy. Alpha and Beta are required to purchase lap-top computers only from ACM.

The prices for ACM's lap-tops are, at the moment, much higher in Italy than they are in Canada and Spain. ACM has been receiving complaints, both from Beta and from retailers of its products in Italy, about the increasing amount of parallel trade, in particular from Canada and Spain.

Within Italy, Beta operates a selective distribution system. It sells to a number of wholesalers, upon whom it imposes various restrictions:

- wholesalers may supply only retailers who have been officially appointed by Beta;
- wholesalers may not actively sell to Beta's other wholesalers in Italy, although they may react to passive orders;
- wholesalers may not sell direct to the public.

ACM has agreed with ACMCanada that ACMCanada will not export lap-tops to Europe; it also intends to reduce the number of lap-top computers it sells to Alpha in Spain. Alpha is displeased that this reduction is about to happen, but realises that there is little that it can do about.

Advise ACM whether these measures and arrangements (including Beta's selective distribution system) infringe EC competition law. What further information would you require from ACM?

Model answer I

1 Restricting exports on the part of ACM Canada to Europe

(A) Is this the result of an agreement between ACM and Beta?
    Can an agreement not to sell from a country outside the EC into the EC infringe Article 81(1)? See *Javico v. Yves St Laurent* (pp. 73–76 above): this case is not quite the same, as here the agreement would be with Beta,

the distributor in Italy, which is the territory to be protected, whereas in *Javico* the agreement was with the Russian/Ukrainian distributor, who had no interest in protecting the EC market. However, the principle of *Javico* would presumably still apply in the same way, therefore it is necessary to apply the *Javico* criteria (see paragraph 28 of the judgment).

(B) Is this the result of an agreement between ACM and ACMCanada? But that is an agreement between a parent company and its wholly owned subsidiary, which falls outside Article 81(1) under the doctrine of 'single economic entity': see *Viho v. Commission* (pp. 58–59 above).

(C) Could ACM be guilty of abusing a dominant position (Article 82)? (See chapter 9.)

(D) Could ACM or Beta (if it is authorised to do so) use the ACM Trademark to repel parallel imports? (See chapter 6: *Silhouette; Zino Davidoff* on the doctrine of exhaustion)

2 The agreements with Alpha and Beta

(A) Would the exclusive distribution terms infringe Article 81(1)? And, if so, would they be block exempted under Regulation 2790/99?

Article 81(1):
Dealing with the application of Article 81(1) requires a discussion of the following:
• *Consten and Grundig* (see pp. 166–174 above)
• *STM* (see p. 174 above)
• *De minimis* doctrine (Commission's Notice on *Agreements of Minor Importance* 2001, see pp. 85–90 above)
• Also the Commission's *Guidelines on vertical restraints* in relation to exclusive distribution (paragraphs 161–174)
• Effect on trade (Commission's Notice on *Effect on trade between Member States* 2004, see pp. 79–85 and 90–94 above)
Block exemption (Regulation 2790/99):
• Article 2 – definition of vertical agreement
• Article 3 – market share
• Article 4 – hardcore restrictions
• Article 5 – Single branding (purchasing laptops only from ACM). Note the limitation on duration in the Article. Is the period in question too long? Article 5 is a severable provision, meaning that the other clauses in the agreement (i.e. other than the exclusive purchasing clause) may benefit from block exemption. See paragraph 67 of the *Guidelines on vertical restraints*.

3 Reducing the supplies to Alpha in Spain

This depends on whether there is an agreement: *Commission v. Bayer* (see pp. 59–68 above).

4 Selective distribution in Italy

(A) Would this selective distribution system infringe Article 81(1)? This requires a discussion of the *Metro* doctrine (see pp. 177–185 above). See also paragraphs 184-198 of the *Guidelines on vertical restraints*.

(B) If there is a possibility that Article 81(1) is being infringed, it will be necessary to consider whether the system would satisfy Regulation 2790/99. In particular it is important to consider:

- Article 1(d) – definition of selective distribution system
- Article 4 – hardcore restrictions:
  - Supplying only retailers officially appointed by Beta: This is permissible under the third indent of Article 4(b).
  - Ban on active sale: This is permissible under the first indent of Article 4(b).
  - Ban on active sale: This is a hardcore restriction under Article 4(d) which means that the whole agreement cannot benefit from block exemption if such a restriction is included in the agreement.
- Article 5(c): is there a direct or indirect obligation causing the members of Beta's selective distribution system not to sell the brands of particular competing suppliers? Such an obligation cannot benefit from block exemption.

Case study II

PM, a UK company, specialises in the production of printers. PM produces two main types of printers: *PM 500*, a large-size printer, suitable for the office, with a printing capacity of 120 pages per minute; and *PM 100*, a considerably smaller printer in size, suitable for both office and home use but with a printing capacity of ten pages per minute. PM is the leading producer in the market for large-size printers market in the EC, with a market share of approximately 53 per cent. There are three other major producers in that market operating throughout the EC, Alpha, Beta and Gamma, with market shares of 19, 14 and 9 per cent respectively. There are many producers of small-size printers. The production of printers requires a considerable amount of commercial and technical know-how.

PM has recently acquired *Portables*, a Swedish company, which specialises in the production of portable printers. Portable printers are not very popular among customers in the EC, but PM is confident that, with its technology and well-established system of advertising, it can make portable printers successful in the printers market generally.

PM seeks your advice on a variety of arrangements:

(a) PM offers rebates off its list prices to customers if they purchase printers only from PM over a period of two years.

(b) A further rebate is offered to customers by PM if they exceed the number of *PM 500* printers sold in the preceding year.

(c) PM has insisted that it will supply *PM 500* printers to customers in Spain only if they also agree to purchase *PM 100* and portable printers from it as well.
(d) PM requires its UK customers to purchase most of their requirements of printers from it.
(e) PM has refused to supply *PM 500* printers to Epsilon, a customer with whom PM has been dealing for the last three years. PM claims that Epsilon has entered into an agreement to promote printers produced by one of PM's competitors and that it has not received the last two monthly payments from Epsilon.
(f) PM has introduced a policy whereby it offers very favourable discounts to certain customers whom PM believes are likely to place orders for printers with PM's competitors. PM is reluctant to make a similar offer to its other customers.
Advise PM whether any of its arrangements might infringe EC and UK competition law. What further information would you require from PM?

Model answer II

The facts reveal a unilateral behaviour on the part of PM. The relevant provisions in EC and UK competition law which deal with unilateral behaviour are Article 82 and section 18 of the Competition Act 1998 (CA1998) respectively. These provisions prohibit the abuse of a dominant position. Hence, the advice will centre around whether PM's behaviour amounts to an abuse of a dominant position. The answer will deal with the application of Article 82 first and then section 18 CA1998.

1 Article 82

The application of Article 82 requires a consideration of the following issues:
• Is there a dominant position held by PM?
• If yes, is this dominant position held in the Common Market or substantial part of it?
• Is there an abuse of dominance by PM?
• Is there an effect on trade between Member States?
• Is there any objective justification for the abuse and does it satisfy the doctrine of proportionality?
(A) Dominance
Dominance was defined by the ECJ in *United Brands v. Commission* (see p. 329 above). It is clear from that definition that dominance is about market power. As the discussion in chapters 2 and 9 revealed, market power does not exist in the abstract but rather in relation to a relevant market. Hence, establishing whether PM holds a dominant position requires a definition of the relevant market.

- Relevant market
Chapter 2 shows that there are three dimensions to market definition. Two of these need to be considered here: relevant product market and relevant geographic market.

Relevant product market
The legal test, as enunciated by the ECJ in *Continental Can v. Commission* (see p. 18 above) and adopted by the Commission in its *Notice on market definition* (see pp. 20–33 above), is that of product substitutability or interchangeability. Three factors used to measure interchangeability: physical characteristics, price (see SSNIP test) and intended use. Applying these factors in PM's case, it is very arguable that there are three relevant product markets: a market for large printers, a market for small printers and a third market for portable printers.

Relevant geographic market
Definition given by the ECJ in *United Brands*. Further information is required to reach a conclusive answer. It is possible that the relevant geographic market is EC wide, but might be narrower than this.
- PM seems to be dominant in the large printers market:
  - Importance of market shares (*Hoffmann La Roche v. Commission*, see p. 330 above). PM has 53 per cent market share: the *AKZO v. Commission* presumption applies (see p. 330 above)
  - Three major competitors with market share of 42 per cent
  - Gap of 34 per cent between PM's market share and that of Alpha
  - Ownership of know-how
  - Technology
  - Well-established system of advertising
- Further information (market share etc.) is needed to determine whether PM is dominant in the small printers market and the portable printers market. Of course if PM is the only producer of portable printers then its market share will be 100 per cent and so dominant on that market.

Note: PM does not have to be dominant in all three markets: a firm can be dominant in one market and abuse its position in another market.
(B) Dominance in the Common Market of substantial part of it: Sugar Cartel (see p. 341 above)
(C) Abuse
Objective concept so PM's intention is irrelevant

Arrangement (a)
Hoffmann La Roche states such discount is an abuse of a dominant position. Does the period make it otherwise? See *Michelin [France] v. Commission* (pp. 362–363).

Arrangement (b)
This is a target rebate which was condemned by the ECJ in *Michelin v. Commission* (see p. 361–362 above).

Arrangement (c)
This is a tie in: PM is tying PM 500 (the tying product) to PM 100 and portable printers (the tied products). ECJ condemned tying practices as an abuse of a dominant position in several cases, most notably *Tetra Pak v. Commission* (see pp. 345–346 above). Could there be discrimination (Article 82(c))?

Arrangement (d)
Clarification (indeed substitution) of the word 'most' is desirable, though the ECJ in *Hoffmann La Roche* condemned as an abuse of a dominant position a requirement contract under which the customer was obliged to purchase 'all or most' of its requirements from the dominant firm. The Commission's *Guidelines on vertical restraints* (following Regulation 2790/99) define a non-compete obligation as one where the customer is required to purchase more than 80 per cent of its requirements from the supplier (see paragraph 141 in particular: a dominant firm may not impose a non-compete obligation on its customers unless it can objectively justify such practice). Also, could there be discrimination (Article 82(c))?

Arrangement (e)
This is a refusal to supply, a practice condemned by the ECJ in *Commercial Solvents v. Commission* (see pp. 348–349 above). Can PM argue that there is objective justification for its refusal: Epsilon's failure to keep up the monthly payments? But PM needs to satisfy the doctrine of proportionality: did PM, for example, make a demand for the overdue payments before halting supplies?

Arrangement (f)
Further information is required on the extent of the discount: is the reduction below cost? If yes, there may be an issue of predatory pricing (see *Tetra Pak v. Commission*). If not, this would be a selective price-cutting situation, a practice condemned by the ECJ in *Compagnie Maritime Belge v. Commission* (see pp. 374–376 above). However, one could argue that the present case is different from *Compagnie Maritime Belge*: not very high market shares; no specialised sector; a few competitors; no threats appear to be made by PM to its competitors.
Acquisition of Portables: could this be regarded as strengthening a dominant position and so an abuse? (see *Continental Can v. Commission*) Alternatively, could it be regarded as an indicator of market power?

(D) Effect on trade
See test in *STM* (p. 79 above); *Commercial Solvents* (pp. 374–375 above); Commission Notice on *effect on trade between Member States* (pp. 80–85 above).

2 Section 18 CA1998

Obviously the points made under Article 82 above will be relevant when considering section 18 CA1998: see section 60 CA1998 (extracted at pp. 95–96 above). Two of the above-mentioned requirements under Article 82 will not be relevant however when dealing with the application of section 18 CA1998, namely that the dominant position needs to be held in the Common Market or a substantial part of it and the requirement of the effect on trade between Member States. Under section 18 the dominant position needs to be held in a market in the UK or a part thereof and the abuse needs to affect trade in the UK. On the application of the Section to the different arrangements see pp. 389–409 above.

Case study III

Alpha and Beta are both manufacturers of commercial aircraft, including jumbo jets, medium-size jets and small private jets. They are interested in developing a new jet which will be much larger than existing jumbo jets and which will meet the demands of twenty-first-century travel: for example the new jet will have luxury facilities, low fuel consumption, more passenger seats, more space and much greater flying time capability than existing jets. The investment required for this project is too great for Alpha's and Beta's own resources. They have therefore developed the following proposal:

(i) Alpha and Beta will establish a company called NewJet.

(ii) Alpha will have 80 per cent of the shares in NewJet and Beta will have 20 per cent.

(iii) NewJet will carry out research into the possibility of developing the new jet. If successful, NewJet will enter into production; it will sell the complete jet for the first year only to Alpha and Beta, but after that it will be able to market them itself.

(iv) If the proposal has not achieved success after eight years, NewJet will be dissolved.

(v) Alpha and Beta will not develop independently jets of the kind that NewJet will be developing.

Alpha and Beta seek your advice as to whether this proposal might be caught by the EC Regulation 139/2004. What further information would you require from Alpha and Beta?

Model answer III

Regulation 139/2004 applies to concentrations with Community dimension.

1 Is there a concentration?

(A) Article 3(4) of the Regulation

This depends on two conditions:

- Whether there is joint control by the parents (Alpha and Beta)

  Notice on the *concept of concentration*, in particular paragraphs 21–24, 26 and 34 (see pp. 494–497 above). A division of 80 per cent and 20 per cent is not fatal to finding joint control provided that Beta enjoys additional rights (such as veto rights), which relate to the strategic decisions on the business policy of NewJet. Further information is required from the parties on this.

- Whether NewJet is a full-function entity

  Notice on the *concept of full function joint ventures*, in particular paragraphs 11–15 (see pp. 492–494 above). Does NewJet bring about a lasting change in the structure of Alpha and Beta?

  NewJet must operate on the market carrying out functions normally performed by firms operating on the same market.

  NewJet needs to have: management dedicated to its day-to-day operations and access to sufficient resources and staff and assets. Presumably this is the case, but it is desirable to seek further information from the parties on the issue.

  NewJet must have access to the market. Sale to its parents during the first year does not disqualify NewJet from being a full-function entity.

  NewJet must be intended to operate on a lasting basis. Setting a period for the duration of NewJet is not fatal as long as the period is sufficiently long in order to bring about a lasting change in the structure of the parents. Five years was considered long enough in *TKS/ITW Signode/Titan*.

2 Community dimension

Assuming that NewJet is a concentration, the next question is whether this concentration has a Community dimension. If it does not, then it will fall outside the jurisdiction of the Commission (through a referral to the Commission might still be possible: see Articles 4(5) and Article 22 of the Regulation). If the concentration has Community dimension, then it will be within the jurisdiction of the Commission (unless a request is made for referral of the concentration to a national competition authority (see Article 4(4) and Article 9 of the Regulation).

By virtue of Article 4 of the Regulation, there is a requirement of prior notification of the concentration to the Commission.

It is clear from Article 1 of the Regulation that establishing this depends on turnover figures. No information is furnished on this and so the parties need to supply this information.

3 Substantive appraisal

Appraisal of concentrations with Community dimension is carried out in accordance with the test and criteria in Article 2 of the Regulation. The test is whether the concentration would significantly impede effective competition in the Common Market or in a substantial part of it, in particular as a result of the creation or strengthening of a dominant position.

To apply this test, the relevant market(s) need to be defined (see chapter 2 and also case study II).

In the absence of further information it is not possible to give advice on the application of the test. In particular, one needs to have information on market shares, the structure of the market and the degree of market concentration etc.

Also, one may need to consider the additional (Article 81 EC) test under Article 2(4) and (5) of the Regulation (see pp. 491 and 497 above).

4 Restrictions directly related and necessary

Clause (v) of the proposal is a non-competition clause and can be regarded as a restriction which is directly related and necessary: see paragraphs 36–40 of the Commission's *Notice on restrictions directly related and necessary to concentrations*. The Commission will not assess this clause individually as it will be covered in a decision in which the Commission finds the concentration to be compatible with the Common Market. (see Article 6(1)(b) and Article 8(2) of the Regulation).

Case study IV

Thirteen firms are active in the European production of paint in the European Community. Four of these firms are UK-based. In March, July and December of each year, the firms announce increases in price in the paint-magazine. The implementation of price increases usually takes place three weeks following the announcement. Gamma is a UK firm active in the retail business of paint. It has noticed that the increases in price by the thirteen firms are always identical and suspects that there is no explanation for the parallel behaviour of the firms other than that of collusion between them.

Advise Gamma whether the practices of the paint producers infringe EC and UK competition law?

Model answer IV

1 EC law

Do the practices of the paint producers infringe Article 81 and/or Article 82?
(A) Article 81
   Are the price increases the result of collusion to fix prices? If there is col-
   lusion, then such practices will fall within Article 81(1). However, if there
   has been no collusion, then the practices will be regarded as a pure (inno-
   cent) parallel behaviour, which falls outside the scope of the prohibition in
   Article 81(1): see *ICI v. Commission* (Dyestuffs) (pp. 269–276 above) and
   A. Ahlström Osakeyhtio v. Commission (Woodpulp) (pp. 276–284 above).

We are not being told about an 'agreement', but there may be a 'concerted practice' (see pp. 71–73 above). Obviously the European Commission bears the burden of proving that there is collusion. Can the Commission rely on the parallel behaviour in this case? *Woodpulp* establishes that this is possible only where there is no other plausible explanation for the behaviour. In light of the facts of *Woodpulp* itself, finding such an explanation is possible even where there may be a large number of producers on the market.

Is the announcement of price increase in advance illegal? According to the ECJ in *Woodpulp*, this depends on whether this meets a legitimate business interest (for example, customers need to plan their own production etc.). Thus, announcement of price increases in advance is not illegal *per se*. It is doubtful however, whether there is such 'legitimate business interest' in this case. If this is true, then the practice may be condemned as an unlawful exchange of price information.

(B) Article 82

Is there an abuse of a collective dominant position by the firms? This may be quite hard to establish for several reasons, among which the fact that the concept of abuse of collective dominance is still in its infancy.

Is there a collective dominant position?

Obviously, an economic analysis will need to be conducted, including defining the relevant market. Establishing such a position depends on: whether there is a collective entity: do the thirteen firms hold themselves out as a collective entity? And whether that entity holds a dominant position (see *Compagnie Maritime Belge v. Commission*, at pp. 590–593 above). To answer this question, one needs to examine the 'links' between the firms: for example any agreement which may exist between them or other connecting factors. This requires an assessment in economic terms, including an assessment of the structure of the paint market.

If a collective dominant position is established, this will not mean that the practices of the firms will be within the mischief of Article 82. One still needs to consider whether that position is held in the Common Market or a substantial part of it and very crucially whether there is an abuse of that position which affects trade between Member States. There is no indication in the case law that parallel price increases can be controlled under Article 82 which makes the application of the Article in this case fraught with difficulty. One possibility that may be open to the Commission is to argue that the parallel price increases amount to 'excessive price' which should be condemned as being 'unfair' within the meaning of paragraph (a) of Article 82 (see *United Brands v. Commission*, at pp. 359–360 above).

2 UK law

(A) The Competition Act 1998

The important question here is whether section 2 of the Competition Act 1998 (the Chapter I Prohibition) is infringed. Obviously the points made on collusion and announcement of price increases in advance in part 1(A) above will be relevant when considering the application of the section. However, it is important to note the main differences between section 2 and Article 81(1) EC (on which the section is modelled), such as the absence of the requirement of effect on trade between Member States from the latter.

The UK competition authorities have not made use of a concept of collective dominance when applying section 18 of the Competition Act (the Chapter II Prohibition).

(B) The Enterprise Act 2002

As chapter 12 shows, the UK system of competition law includes an important mechanism which could be used in situations such as the one at hand, namely market investigations (see section 131 of the Act).

[699]

List of websites

1. EFTA Surveillance Authority
   http://www.efta.int/structure/SURV/efta-srv.cfm
2. European Commission, the Competition Directorate
   http://europa.eu.int/comm/competition
3. European Court of Justice
   http://curia.eu.int
4. International Competition Network (ICN)
   http://www.internationalcompetitionnetwork.org
5. OECD, Competition Policy
   http://www.oecd.org/daf/clp
6. UK Competition Appeal Tribunal
   http://www.catribunal.org.uk
7. UK Competition Commission
   http://www.competition-commission.org.uk
8. UK Department of Trade and Industry
   http://www.dti.gov.uk
9. UK Office of Fair Trading
   http://www.oft.gov.uk
10. US Department of Justice, Antitrust Division
    http://www.usdoj.gov
11. US Fair Trade Commission
    http://www.ftc.gov
12. World Bank
    http://www.worldbank.org
13. World Biggest Antitrust Sites
    http://www.clubi.ie/competition
14. WTO
    http://www.wto.org

Index